MORE PRAISE FROM ... FOR THE JOB ...

"If you are looking for a job ... before you go to the newspapers and the help-wanted ads, listen to Bob Adams, publisher of *The Metropolitan New York JobBank*."
-Tom Brokaw, *NBC*

"Help on the job hunt ... Anyone who is job-hunting in the New York area can find a lot of useful ideas in a new paperback called *The Metropolitan New York JobBank* ..."
-Angela Taylor, *New York Times*

"One of the better publishers of employment almanacs is Adams Media Corporation ... publisher of *The Metropolitan New York JobBank* and similarly named directories of employers in Texas, Boston, Chicago, Northern and Southern California, and Washington DC. A good buy ..."
-*Wall Street Journal's*
National Business Employment Weekly

"For those graduates whose parents are pacing the floor, conspicuously placing circled want ads around the house and typing up resumes, [*The Carolina JobBank*] answers job-search questions."
-*Greensboro News and Record*

"A timely book for Chicago job hunters follows books from the same publisher that were well received in New York and Boston ... [*The Chicago JobBank* is] a fine tool for job hunters ..."
-Clarence Peterson, *Chicago Tribune*

"Because our listing is seen by people across the nation, it generates lots of resumes for us. We encourage unsolicited resumes. We'll always be listed [in *The Chicago JobBank*] as long as I'm in this career."
-Tom Fitzpatrick, Director of Human Resources
Merchandise Mart Properties, Inc.

"Job-hunting is never fun, but this book can ease the ordeal ... [*The Los Angeles JobBank*] will help allay fears, build confidence, and avoid wheel-spinning."
-Robert W. Ross, *Los Angeles Times*

"*The Seattle JobBank* is an essential resource for job hunters."
-Gil Lopez, Staffing Team Manager
Battelle Pacific Northwest Laboratories

"*The Florida JobBank* is an invaluable job-search reference tool. It provides the most up-to-date information and contact names available for companies in Florida. I should know – it worked for me!"
-Rhonda Cody, Human Resources Consultant
Aetna Life and Casualty

"Job hunters can't afford to waste time. *The Minneapolis-St. Paul JobBank* contains information that used to require hours of research in the library."
-Carmella Zagone
Minneapolis-based Human Resources Administrator

"*The Boston JobBank* provides a handy map of employment possibilities in greater Boston. This book can help in the initial steps of a job search by locating major employers, describing their business activities, and for most firms, by naming the contact person and listing typical professional positions. For recent college graduates, as well as experienced professionals, *The Boston JobBank* is an excellent place to begin a job search."
-Juliet F. Brudney, Career Columnist
Boston Globe

"No longer can jobseekers feel secure about finding employment just through want ads. With the tough competition in the job market, particularly in the Boston area, they need much more help. For this reason, *The Boston JobBank* will have a wide and appreciative audience of new graduates, job changers, and people relocating to Boston. It provides a good place to start a search for entry-level professional positions."
-Journal of College Placement

"*The Phoenix JobBank* is a first-class publication. The information provided is useful and current."
-Lyndon Denton
Director of Human Resources and Materials Management
Apache Nitrogen Products, Inc.

"[*The Atlanta JobBank* is] one of the best sources for finding a job in Atlanta!"
-Luann Miller, Human Resources Manager
Prudential Preferred Financial Services

"*The San Francisco Bay Area JobBank* ... is a highly useful guide, with plenty of how-to's ranging from resume tips to interview dress codes and research shortcuts."
-A.S. Ross, ***San Francisco Examiner***

What makes the JobBank series the nation's premier line of employment guides?

With vital employment information on thousands of employers across the nation, the JobBank series is the most comprehensive and authoritative set of career directories available today.

Each book in the series provides information on **dozens of different industries** in a given city or area, with the primary employer listings providing contact information, telephone and fax numbers, e-mail addresses, Websites, a summary of the firm's business, and in many cases descriptions of the firm's typical professional job categories, the principal educational backgrounds sought, internships, and the fringe benefits offered.

In addition to the **detailed primary employer listings,** JobBank books give telephone numbers and addresses for **thousands of additional employers,** as well as information about executive search firms, placement agencies, and professional associations.

All of the reference information in the JobBank series is as up-to-date and accurate as possible. Every year, the entire database is thoroughly researched and verified by mail and by telephone. Adams Media Corporation publishes **more local employment guides more often** than any other publisher of career directories.

In addition, the JobBank series features current information about the local job scene – **forecasts on which industries are the hottest** and **lists of regional professional associations,** so you can get your job hunt started off right.

The JobBank series offers **28 regional titles**, from Minneapolis to Houston, and from Boston to San Francisco. All of the information is organized geographically, because most people look for jobs in specific areas of the country.

A condensed, but thorough, review of the entire job search process is presented in the chapter **The Basics of Job Winning**, a feature which has received many compliments from career counselors. In addition, each JobBank directory includes a section on **resumes and cover letters** the *New York Times* has acclaimed as "excellent."

The JobBank series gives job hunters the most comprehensive, timely, and accurate career information, organized and indexed to facilitate your job search. An entire career reference library, JobBank books are designed to help you find optimal employment in any market.

Top career publications from Adams Media Corporation

The JobBank Series:
each JobBank book is $16.95

The Atlanta JobBank, 14th Ed.
The Austin/San Antonio JobBank, 3rd Ed.
The Boston JobBank, 18th Ed.
The Carolina JobBank, 6th Ed.
The Chicago JobBank, 17th Ed.
The Connecticut JobBank, 2nd Ed.
The Dallas-Fort Worth JobBank, 13th Ed.
The Denver JobBank, 12th Ed.
The Detroit JobBank, 9th Ed.
The Florida JobBank, 14th Ed.
The Houston JobBank, 11th Ed.
The Indiana JobBank, 3rd Ed.
The Las Vegas JobBank, 2nd Ed.
The Los Angeles JobBank, 16th Ed.
The Minneapolis-St. Paul JobBank, 11th Ed.
The Missouri JobBank, 3rd Ed.
The New Jersey JobBank, 1st Ed.
The Metropolitan New York JobBank, 17th Ed.
The Ohio JobBank, 10th Ed.
The Greater Philadelphia JobBank, 13th Ed.
The Phoenix JobBank, 8th Ed.
The Pittsburgh JobBank, 2nd Ed.
The Portland JobBank, 3rd Ed.
The San Francisco Bay Area JobBank, 16th Ed.
The Seattle JobBank, 12th Ed.
The Tennessee JobBank, 5th Ed.
The Virginia JobBank, 3rd Ed.
The Metropolitan Washington DC JobBank, 15th Ed.

The JobBank Guide to Computer & High-Tech Companies, 2nd Ed. ($17.95)
The JobBank Guide to Health Care Companies, 2nd Ed. ($17.95)

The National JobBank, 2001
  (Covers the entire U.S.: $395.00 hc)
The JobBank Guide to Employment Services, 2000 - 2001
  (Covers the entire U.S.: $230.00 hc)

Other Career Titles:

The Adams Cover Letter Almanac ($12.95)
The Adams Internet Job Search Almanac, 2001-2002, ($10.95)
The Adams Executive Recruiters Almanac, 2nd Ed. ($17.95)
The Adams Job Interview Almanac ($12.95)
The Adams Jobs Almanac, 8th Ed. ($16.95)
The Adams Resume Almanac ($10.95)
Business Etiquette in Brief ($7.95)
Campus Free College Degrees, 8th Ed. ($16.95)
Career Tests ($12.95)
Closing Techniques, 2nd Ed. ($8.95)
Cold Calling Techniques, 4th Ed. ($8.95)
College Grad Job Hunter, 4th Ed. ($14.95)
The Complete Resume & Job Search Book for College Students, 2nd Ed. ($12.95)
Cover Letters That Knock 'em Dead, 4th Ed. ($10.95)
Every Woman's Essential Job Hunting & Resume Book ($10.95)
The Everything Cover Letter Book ($12.95)
The Everything Get-A-Job Book ($12.95)
The Everything Online Business Book ($12.95)
The Everything Online Job Search Book ($12.95)
The Everything Resume Book ($12.95)
The Everything Selling Book ($12.95)
First Time Resume ($7.95)
How to Become Successfully Self-Employed, 2nd Ed. ($9.95)
How to Start and Operate a Successful Business ($9.95)
Knock 'em Dead, 2001 ($12.95)
Market Yourself and Your Career, 2nd Ed. ($12.95)
The New Professional Image ($12.95)
The 150 Most Profitable Home Businesses for Women ($9.95)
Over 40 and Looking for Work? ($7.95)
The Resume Handbook, 3rd Ed. ($7.95)
Resumes That Knock 'em Dead, 4th Ed. ($10.95)
The Road to CEO ($20.00 hc)
The 250 Job Interview Questions You'll Most Likely Be Asked ($9.95)
Your Executive Image ($10.95)

JobBank List Service: If you are interested in variations of JobBank company profiles in electronic format for job search or sales mailings, please call **800/872-5627** or e-mail us at **JobbankList@adamsmedia.com**.

If you cannot find these titles at your favorite book outlet, you may order them directly from the publisher.

BY PHONE: Call 800/872-5627 (in Massachusetts 781/767-8100). We accept Visa, Mastercard, and American Express. $4.95 will be added to your total for shipping and handling. **BY MAIL:** Write out the full titles of the books you'd like to order and send payment, including $4.95 for shipping and handling to: Adams Media Corporation, 260 Center Street, Holbrook MA 02343. 30 day money back guarantee.
BY FAX: 800/872-5628. **BY E-MAIL:** jobbank@adamsonline.com
Discounts available for standing orders.

Visit our Website at www.adamsmedia.com

13th Edition
THE Dallas-Fort Worth JobBank

Managing Editor:	Michelle Roy Kelly
Senior Editors:	Heather L. Vinhateiro
	Jennifer M. Wood
Associate Editors:	Anne M. Grignon
	Michael Paydos
Editorial Assistants:	Lesley Bolton
	Bethany L. Brown

Adams Media Corporation
HOLBROOK, MASSACHUSETTS

Published by Adams Media Corporation
260 Center Street, Holbrook, MA 02343. U.S.A.
www.adamsmedia.com

ISBN: 1-58062-413-8
ISSN: 1069-5435
Manufactured in Canada.

Copyright © 2000 by Adams Media Corporation. All rights reserved. This book, or parts thereof, may not be reproduced or used in any form or by any means, electronic or mechanical, including photocopying, recording, or by any information storage retrieval system without permission from the publisher. Exceptions are made for brief excerpts used in published reviews.

The Dallas-Fort Worth JobBank, 13th Edition and its cover design are trademarks of Adams Media Corporation.

Product or brand names used in this book are proprietary property of the applicable firm, subject to trademark protection, and registered with government offices. Any use of these names does not convey endorsement by or other affiliation with the name holder.

Because addresses and telephone numbers of smaller companies change rapidly, we recommend you call each company and verify the information before mailing to the employers listed in this book. Mass mailings are not recommended.

While the publisher has made every reasonable effort to obtain and verify accurate information, occasional errors are possible due to the magnitude of the data. Should you discover an error, or if a company is missing, please write the editors at the above address so that we may update future editions.

"This publication is designed to provide accurate and authoritative information with regard to the subject matter covered. It is sold with the understanding that the publisher is not engaged in rendering legal, accounting, or other professional advice. If legal advice or other expert assistance is required, the services of a competent professional person should be sought."
 --From a *Declaration of Principles* jointly adopted by a Committee of the American Bar Association and a Committee of Publishers and Associations

This book is available on standing order and at quantity discounts for bulk purchases.
For information, call 800/872-5627 (in Massachusetts, 781/767-8100)
or email at jobbank@adamsonline.com

Visit our job and career site at www.careercity.com

TABLE OF CONTENTS

SECTION ONE: INTRODUCTION

How to Use This Book/12
An introduction to the most effective way to use The Dallas-Fort Worth JobBank.

SECTION TWO: THE JOB SEARCH

The Basics of Job Winning/16
A review of the elements of a successful job search campaign. Includes advice on developing effective strategies, time planning, and preparing for interviews. Special sections address situations faced by jobseekers who are currently employed, those who have lost a job, and graduates conducting their first job search.

Resumes and Cover Letters/30
Advice on creating strong resumes and cover letters.

CD-ROM Job Search/48
Information on selected CD-ROM products for jobseekers.

SECTION THREE: PRIMARY EMPLOYERS

The Employers/52
The Dallas-Fort Worth JobBank is organized according to industry. Many listings include the address and phone number of each major firm listed, along with a description of the company's basic product lines and services, and, in many cases, a contact name and other relevant hiring information. Also included are hundreds of secondary listings providing addresses and phone numbers for small- and medium-sized employers.

Accounting and Management Consulting/52
Advertising, Marketing, and Public Relations/57
- Direct Mail Marketers, Market Researchers

Aerospace/61
- Aerospace Products and Services
- Aircraft Equipment and Parts

Apparel, Fashion, and Textiles/65
- Broadwoven Fabric Mills, Knitting Mills, and Yarn and Thread Mills
- Curtains and Draperies
- Footwear
- Nonwoven Fabrics
- Textile Goods and Finishing

Architecture, Construction, and Engineering/68
- Architectural and Engineering Services
- Civil and Mechanical Engineering Firms
- Construction Products, Manufacturers, and Wholesalers
- General Contractors/Specialized Trade Contractor

Arts, Entertainment, Sports, and Recreation/79
- Botanical and Zoological Gardens
- Entertainment Groups
- Motion Picture and Video Tape Production and Distribution
- Museums and Art Galleries
- Physical Fitness Facilities
- Professional Sports Clubs; Sporting and Recreational Camps

- Public Golf Courses and Racing and Track Operations
- Theatrical Producers and Services

Automotive/83
- Automotive Repair Shops
- Automotive Stampings
- Industrial Vehicles and Moving Equipment
- Motor Vehicles and Equipment
- Travel Trailers and Campers

Banking/Savings and Loans/86

Biotechnology, Pharmaceuticals, and Scientific R&D/89
- Clinical Labs
- Lab Equipment Manufacturers
- Pharmaceutical Manufacturers and Distributors

Business Services and Non-Scientific Research/91
- Adjustment and Collection Services
- Cleaning, Maintenance, and Pest Control Services
- Credit Reporting Services
- Detective, Guard, and Armored Car Services/Security Systems Services
- Miscellaneous Equipment Rental and Leasing
- Secretarial and Court Reporting Services

Charities and Social Services/95
- Job Training and Vocational Rehabilitation Services

Chemicals/Rubber and Plastics/98
- Adhesives, Detergents, Inks, Paints, Soaps, Varnishes
- Agricultural Chemicals and Fertilizers
- Carbon and Graphite Products
- Chemical Engineering Firms
- Industrial Gases

Communications: Telecommunications and Broadcasting/105
- Cable/Pay Television Services
- Communications Equipment
- Radio and Television Broadcasting Stations
- Telephone, Telegraph, and Other Message Communications

Computer Hardware, Software, and Services/112
- Computer Components and Hardware Manufacturers
- Consultants and Computer Training Companies
- Internet and Online Service Providers
- Networking and Systems Services
- Repair Services/Rental and Leasing
- Resellers, Wholesalers, and Distributors
- Software Developers/Programming Services

Educational Services/124
- Business/Secretarial/Data Processing Schools
- Colleges/Universities/Professional Schools
- Community Colleges/Technical Schools/Vocational Schools
- Elementary and Secondary Schools
- Preschool and Child Daycare Services

Electronic/Industrial Electrical Equipment/138
- Electronic Machines and Systems
- Semiconductor Manufacturers

Environmental and Waste Management Services/145
- Environmental Engineering Firms
- Sanitary Services

Fabricated/Primary Metals and Products/147
- Aluminum and Copper Foundries
- Die-Castings
- Iron and Steel Foundries/Steel Works, Blast Furnaces, and Rolling Mills

Financial Services/151
- Consumer Financing and Credit Agencies
- Investment Specialists
- Mortgage Bankers and Loan Brokers
- Security and Commodity Brokers, Dealers, and Exchanges

Food and Beverages/Agriculture/156
- Crop Services and Farm Supplies
- Dairy Farms
- Food Manufacturers/Processors and Agricultural Producers
- Tobacco Products

Government/167
- Courts
- Executive, Legislative, and General Government
- Public Agencies (Firefighters, Military, Police)
- United States Postal Service

Health Care: Services, Equipment, and Products/173
- Dental Labs and Equipment
- Home Health Care Agencies
- Hospitals and Medical Centers
- Medical Equipment Manufacturers and Wholesalers
- Offices and Clinics of Health Practitioners
- Residential Treatment Centers/Nursing Homes
- Veterinary Services

Hotels and Restaurants/195
Insurance/204
Legal Services/209
Manufacturing: Miscellaneous Consumer/212
- Art Supplies
- Batteries
- Cosmetics and Related Products
- Household Appliances and Audio/Video Equipment
- Jewelry, Silverware, and Plated Ware
- Miscellaneous Household Furniture and Fixtures
- Musical Instruments
- Tools
- Toys and Sporting Goods

Manufacturing: Miscellaneous Industrial/217
- Ball and Roller Bearings
- Commercial Furniture and Fixtures
- Fans, Blowers, and Purification Equipment
- Industrial Machinery and Equipment
- Motors and Generators/Compressors and Engine Parts
- Vending Machines

Mining/Gas/Petroleum/Energy Related/224
- Anthracite, Coal, and Ore Mining
- Mining Machinery and Equipment
- Oil and Gas Field Services
- Petroleum and Natural Gas

Paper and Wood Products/231
- Forest and Wood Products and Services
- Lumber and Wood Wholesale
- Millwork, Plywood, and Structural Members
- Paper and Wood Mills

Printing and Publishing/234
- Book, Newspaper, and Periodical Publishers
- Commercial Printing Services
- Graphic Designers

Real Estate/241
- *Land Subdividers and Developers*
- *Real Estate Agents, Managers, and Operators*
- *Real Estate Investment Trusts*

Retail/243

Stone, Clay, Glass, and Concrete Products/259
- *Cement, Tile, Sand, and Gravel*
- *Crushed and Broken Stone*
- *Glass and Glass Products*
- *Mineral Products*

Transportation/Travel/262
- *Air, Railroad, and Water Transportation Services*
- *Courier Services*
- *Local and Interurban Passenger Transit*
- *Ship Building and Repair*
- *Transportation Equipment*
- *Travel Agencies*
- *Trucking*
- *Warehousing and Storage*

Utilities: Electric/Gas/Water/271

Miscellaneous Wholesaling/273
- *Exporters and Importers*

SECTION FOUR: EMPLOYMENT SERVICES

Temporary Employment Agencies/281
Includes addresses, phone numbers, and descriptions of companies specializing in temporary placement of clients. Also includes contact names, specializations, and a list of positions commonly filled.

Permanent Employment Agencies/286
Includes addresses, phone numbers, and descriptions of companies specializing in permanent placement of clients. Also includes contact names, specializations, and a list of positions commonly filled.

Executive Search Firms/293
Includes addresses, phone numbers, and descriptions of companies specializing in permanent placement of executive-level clients. Also includes contact names, specializations, and a list of positions commonly filled.

Contract Services Firms/306
Includes addresses, phone numbers, and descriptions of companies specializing in contract services.

Resume/Career Counseling Services/308
Includes addresses, phone numbers, and descriptions of companies providing resume writing services and/or career counseling services.

SECTION FIVE: INDEX

Alphabetical Index of Primary Employers/309
Includes larger employer listings only. Does not include employers that fall under the headings "Additional Employers."

INTRODUCTION

HOW TO USE THIS BOOK

Right now, you hold in your hands one of the most effective job-hunting tools available anywhere. In *The Dallas-Fort Worth JobBank*, you will find a wide array of valuable information to help you launch or continue a rewarding career. But before you open to the book's employer listings and start calling about current job openings, take a few minutes to learn how best to use the resources presented in *The Dallas-Fort Worth JobBank*.

The Dallas-Fort Worth JobBank will help you to stand out from other jobseekers. While many people looking for a new job rely solely on newspaper help-wanted ads, this book offers you a much more effective job-search method – direct contact. The direct contact method has been proven twice as effective as scanning the help-wanted ads. Instead of waiting for employers to come looking for you, you'll be far more effective going to them. While many of your competitors will use trial and error methods in trying to set up interviews, you'll learn not only how to get interviews, but what to expect once you've got them.

In the next few pages, we'll take you through each section of the book so you'll be prepared to get a jump-start on your competition.

Basics of Job Winning

Preparation. Strategy. Time-management. These are three of the most important elements of a successful job search. *Basics of Job Winning* helps you address these and all the other elements needed to find the right job.

One of your first priorities should be to define your personal career objectives. What qualities make a job desirable to you? Creativity? High pay? Prestige? Use *Basics of Job Winning* to weigh these questions. Then use the rest of the chapter to design a strategy to find a job that matches your criteria.

In *Basics of Job Winning*, you'll learn which job-hunting techniques work, and which don't. We've reviewed the pros and cons of mass mailings, help-wanted ads, and direct contact. We'll show you how to develop and approach contacts in your field; how to research a prospective employer; and how to use that information to get an interview and the job.

Also included in *Basics of Job Winning*: interview dress code and etiquette, the "do's and don'ts" of interviewing, sample interview questions, and more. We also deal with some of the unique problems faced by those jobseekers who are currently employed, those who have lost a job, and college students conducting their first job search.

Resumes and Cover Letters

The approach you take to writing your resume and cover letter can often mean the difference between getting an interview and never being noticed. In this section, we discuss different formats, as well as what to put on (and what to leave off) your resume. We review the benefits and drawbacks of professional resume writers, and the importance of a follow-up letter. Also included in this section are sample resumes and cover letters which you can use as models.

CD-ROM Job Search

Jobseekers who are looking for an edge against the competition may want to check out these CD-ROM products.

The Employer Listings

Employers are listed alphabetically by industry, and within each industry, by company names. When a company does business under a person's name, like "John Smith & Co.," the company is usually listed by the surname's spelling (in this case "S"). Exceptions occur when a company's name is widely recognized, like "JCPenney" or "Howard Johnson Motor Lodge." In those cases, the company's first name is the key ("J" and "H" respectively).

The Dallas-Fort Worth JobBank covers a very wide range of industries. Each company profile is assigned to one of the industry chapters listed below.

Accounting and Management Consulting
Advertising, Marketing, and Public Relations
Aerospace
Apparel, Fashion, and Textiles
Architecture, Construction, and Engineering
Arts, Entertainment, Sports, and Recreation
Automotive
Banking/Savings and Loans
Biotechnology, Pharmaceuticals, and Scientific R&D
Business Services and Non-Scientific Research
Charities and Social Services
Chemicals/Rubber and Plastics
Communications: Telecommunications and Broadcasting
Computer Hardware, Software, and Services
Educational Services
Electronic/Industrial Electrical Equipment
Environmental and Waste Management Services
Fabricated/Primary Metals and Products
Financial Services
Food and Beverages/Agriculture
Government
Health Care: Services, Equipment, and Products
Hotels and Restaurants
Insurance
Legal Services
Manufacturing: Miscellaneous Consumer
Manufacturing: Miscellaneous Industrial
Mining/Gas/Petroleum/Energy Related
Paper and Wood Products
Printing and Publishing
Real Estate
Retail
Stone, Clay, Glass, and Concrete Products
Transportation/Travel
Utilities: Electric/Gas/Water
Miscellaneous Wholesaling

Many of the company listings offer detailed company profiles. In addition to company names, addresses, and phone numbers, these listings also include contact names or hiring departments, and descriptions of each company's products and/or services. Many of these listings also feature a variety of additional information including:

Common positions - A list of job titles that the company commonly fills when it is hiring, organized in alphabetical order from Accountant to X-ray Technician. Note: Keep in mind that *The Dallas-Fort Worth JobBank* is a directory of major employers in the area, not a directory of openings currently available. Many of the companies listed will be hiring, others will not. However, since most professional job openings are filled without the placement of help-wanted ads, contacting the employers in this book directly is still a more effective method than browsing the Sunday papers.

Educational backgrounds sought - A list of educational backgrounds that companies seek when hiring.

Benefits - What kind of benefits packages are available from these employers? Here you'll find a broad range of benefits, from the relatively common (medical insurance) to those that are much more rare (health club membership; child daycare assistance).

Special programs - Does the company offer training programs, internships, or apprenticeships? These programs can be important to first time jobseekers and college students looking for practical work experience. Many employer profiles will include information on these programs.

Parent company - If an employer is a subsidiary of a larger company, the name of that parent company will often be listed here. Use this information to supplement your company research before contacting the employer.

Number of employees - The number of workers a company employs.

Company listings may also include information on other U.S. locations and any stock exchanges the firm may be listed on.

Because so many job openings are with small and mid-sized employers, we've also included the addresses and phone numbers of such employers. While none of these listings include any additional hiring information, many of them do offer rewarding career opportunities. These companies are found under each industry heading. Within each industry, they are organized by the type of product or service offered.

A note on all employer listings that appear in *The Dallas-Fort Worth JobBank*: This book is intended as a starting point. It is not intended to replace any effort that you, the jobseeker, should devote to your job hunt. Keep in mind that while a great deal of effort has been put into collecting and verifying the company profiles provided in this book, addresses and contact names change regularly. Inevitably, some contact names listed herein have changed even before you read this. We recommend you contact a company before mailing your resume to ensure nothing has changed.

At the end of each industry section, we have included a directory of other industry-specific resources to help you in your job search. These include: professional and industrial associations, many of which can provide employment advice and job-search help; magazines that cover the industry; and additional directories that may supplement the employer listings in this book.

Employment Services

Immediately following the employer listings section of this book are listings of local employment services firms. Many jobseekers supplement their own efforts by contracting "temp" services, headhunters, and other employment search firms to generate potential job opportunities.

This section is a comprehensive listing of such firms, arranged alphabetically under the headings Temporary Employment Agencies, Permanent Employment Agencies, and Executive Search Firms. Each listing includes the firm's name, address, telephone number, and contact person. Most listings also include the industries the firm specializes in, the type of positions commonly filled, and the number of jobs filled annually.

Index

The Dallas-Fort Worth JobBank index is a straight alphabetical listing.

THE JOB SEARCH

THE BASICS OF JOB WINNING: A CONDENSED REVIEW

This chapter is divided into four sections. The first section explains the fundamentals that every jobseeker should know, especially first-time jobseekers. The next three sections deal with special situations faced by specific types of jobseekers: those who are currently employed, those who have lost a job, and college students.

THE BASICS:
Things Everyone Needs to Know

The first step to finding your ideal job is to clearly define your objectives. This is better known as career planning (or life planning if you wish to emphasize the importance of combining the two). Career planning has become a field of study in and of itself.

If you are thinking of choosing or switching careers, we particularly emphasize two things. First, choose a career where you will enjoy most of the day-to-day tasks. This sounds obvious, but most of us have at some point found the idea of a glamour industry or prestigious job title attractive without thinking of the key consideration: Would we enjoy performing the *everyday* tasks the position entails?

The second key consideration is that you are not merely choosing a career, but also a lifestyle. Career counselors indicate that one of the most common problems people encounter in jobseeking is that they fail to consider how well-suited they are for a particular position or career. For example, some people, attracted to management consulting by good salaries, early responsibility, and high-level corporate exposure, do not adapt well to the long hours, heavy travel demands, and constant pressure to produce. Be sure to ask yourself how you might adapt to the day-to-day duties and working environment that a specific position entails. Then ask yourself how you might adapt to the demands of that career or industry as a whole.

Assuming that you've established your career objectives, the next step of the job search is to develop a strategy. If you don't take the time to develop a plan, you may find yourself going in circles after several weeks of randomly searching for opportunities that always seem just beyond your reach.

The most common jobseeking techniques are:

- following up on help-wanted advertisements (in the newspaper or online)
- using employment services
- relying on personal contacts
- contacting employers directly (the Direct Contact method)

Each of these approaches can lead to better jobs. However, the Direct Contact method boasts twice the success rate of the others. So unless you have specific reasons to employ other strategies, Direct Contact should form the foundation of your job search.

If you choose to use other methods as well, try to expend at least half your energy on Direct Contact. Millions of other jobseekers have already proven that Direct Contact has been twice as effective in obtaining employment, so why not follow in their footsteps?

Okay, so now that you've targeted a strategy it's time to work out the details of your job search. The most important detail is setting up a schedule. Of course, since job searches aren't something most people do regularly, it may be hard to estimate how long each step will take. Nonetheless, it is important to have a plan so that you can monitor your progress.

When outlining your job search schedule, have a realistic time frame in mind. If you will be job-searching full-time, your search could take at least two months or more. If you can only devote part-time effort, it will probably take at least four months.

You probably know a few people who seem to spend their whole lives searching for a better job in their spare time. Don't be one of them. If you are presently working and don't feel like devoting a lot of energy to jobseeking right now, then wait. Focus on enjoying your present position, performing your best on the job, and storing up energy for when you are really ready to begin your job search.

> **The first step in beginning your job search is to clearly define your objectives.**

Those of you who are currently unemployed should remember that *job-hunting is tough work, both physically and emotionally*. It is also intellectually demanding work that requires you to be at your best. So don't tire yourself out by working on your job campaign around the clock. At the same time, be sure to discipline yourself. The most logical way to manage your time while looking for a job is to keep your regular working hours.

If you are searching full-time and have decided to choose several different strategies, we recommend that you divide up each week, designating some time for each method. By trying several approaches at once, you can evaluate how promising each seems and alter your schedule accordingly. Keep in mind that the *majority of openings are filled without being advertised*. Remember also that positions advertised on the Internet are just as likely to already be filled as those found in the newspaper!

If you are searching part-time and decide to try several different contact methods, we recommend that you try them sequentially. You simply won't have enough time to put a meaningful amount of effort into more than one method at once. Estimate the length of your job search, and then allocate so many weeks or months for each contact method, beginning with Direct Contact. The purpose of setting this schedule is not to rush you to your goal but to help you periodically evaluate your progress.

Once you have scheduled your time, you are ready to begin your search in earnest. Beginning with the Direct Contact method, the first step is to develop a checklist for categorizing the types of firms for which you'd like to work. You might categorize firms by product line, size, customer type (such as industrial or consumer), growth prospects, or geographical location. Keep in mind, the shorter the list the easier it will be to locate a company that is right for you.

Next you will want to use this *JobBank* book to assemble your list of potential employers. Choose firms where *you* are most likely to be able to find a job. Try matching your skills with those that a specific job demands. Consider where your skills might be in demand, the degree of competition for employment, and the employment outlook at each company.

Separate your prospect list into three groups. The first 25 percent will be your primary target group, the next 25 percent will be your secondary group, and the remaining names will be your reserve group.

After you form your prospect list, begin working on your resume. Refer to the Resumes and Cover Letters section following this chapter for more information.

Once your resume is complete, begin researching your first batch of prospective employers. You will want to determine whether you would be happy working at the firms you are researching and to get a better idea of what their employment needs might be. You also need to obtain enough information to sound highly informed about the company during phone conversations and in mail correspondence. But don't go all out on your research yet! You probably won't be able to arrange interviews with some of these firms, so save your big research effort until you start to arrange interviews. Nevertheless, you should plan to spend several hours researching each firm. Do your research in batches to save time and energy. Start with this book, and find out what you can about each of the firms in your primary target group. For answers to specific questions, contact any pertinent professional associations that may be able to help you learn more about an employer. Read industry publications looking for articles on the firm. (Addresses of associations and names of important publications are listed after each section of employer listings in this book.) Then look up the company on the Internet or try additional resources at your local library. Keep organized, and maintain a folder on each firm.

> **The more you know about a company, the more likely you are to catch an interviewer's eye. (You'll also face fewer surprises once you get the job!)**

Information to look for includes: company size; president, CEO, or owners name; when the company was established; what each division does; and benefits that are important to you. An abundance of company information can now be found electronically, through the World Wide Web or commercial online services. Researching companies online is a convenient means of obtaining information quickly and easily. If you have access to the Internet, you can search from your home at any time of day.

You may search a particular company's Website for current information that may be otherwise unavailable in print. In fact, many companies that maintain a site update their information daily. In addition, you may also search articles written about the company online. Today, most of the nation's largest newspapers, magazines, trade publications, and regional business periodicals have online versions of their publications. To find additional resources, use a search engine like Yahoo! or Alta Vista and type in the keyword "companies" or "employers."

If you discover something that really disturbs you about the firm (they are about to close their only local office), or if you discover that your chances of getting a job there are practically nil (they have just instituted a hiring freeze), then cross them off your prospect list. If possible, supplement your research efforts by contacting individuals who know the firm well. Ideally you should make an informal contact with someone at that particular firm, but often a direct competitor or a major customer will be able to supply you with just as much information. At the very least, try to obtain whatever printed information the company has available -- not just annual reports, but product brochures, company profiles, or catalogs. This information is often available on the Internet.

Now it is time to make Direct Contact with the goal of arranging interviews. If you have read any books on job-searching, you may have noticed that most of these books tell you to avoid the personnel office like the plague. It is said that the personnel office never hires people; they screen candidates. Unfortunately, this is often the case. If you can identify the appropriate manager with the authority to hire you, you should try to contact that person directly.

The obvious means of initiating Direct Contact are:

- Mail (postal or electronic)
- Phone calls

Mail contact is a good choice if you have not been in the job market for a while. You can take your time to prepare a letter, say exactly what you want, and of course include your resume. Remember that employers receive many resumes every day. Don't be surprised if you do not get a response to your inquiry, *and don't spend weeks waiting for responses that may never come.* If you do send a letter, follow it up (or precede it) with a phone call. This will increase your impact, and because of the initial research you did, will underscore both your familiarity with and your interest in the firm. Bear in mind that your goal is to make your name a familiar one with prospective employers, so that when a position becomes available, your resume will be one of the first the hiring manager seeks out.

DEVELOPING YOUR CONTACTS: NETWORKING

Some career counselors feel that the best route to a better job is through somebody you already know or through somebody to whom you can be introduced. These counselors recommend that you build your contact base beyond your current acquaintances by asking each one to introduce you, or refer you, to additional people in your field of interest.

The theory goes like this: You might start with 15 personal contacts, each of whom introduces you to three additional people, for a total of 45 additional contacts. Then each of these people introduces you to three additional people, which adds 135 additional contacts. Theoretically, you will soon know every person in the industry.

Of course, developing your personal contacts does not work quite as smoothly as the theory suggests because some people will not be able to introduce you to anyone. The further you stray from your initial contact base, the weaker your references may be. So, if you do try developing your own contacts, try to begin with as many people that you know personally as you can. Dig into your personal phone book and your holiday greeting card list and locate old classmates from school. Be particularly sure to approach people who perform your personal business such as your lawyer, accountant, banker, doctor, stockbroker, and insurance agent. These people develop a very broad contact base due to the nature of their professions.

If you send a fax, always follow with a hard copy of your resume and cover letter in the mail. Often, through no fault of your own, a fax will come through illegibly and employers do not often have time to let candidates know.

Another alternative is to make a "cover call." Your cover call should be just like your cover letter: concise. Your first statement should interest the employer in you. Then try to subtly mention your familiarity with the firm. Don't be overbearing; keep your introduction to three sentences or less. Be pleasant, self-confident, and relaxed. This will greatly increase the chances of the person at the other end of the line developing the conversation. But don't press. If you are asked to follow up with "something in the mail," this signals the conversation's natural end. Don't try to prolong the conversation once it has ended, and don't ask what they want to receive in the mail. Always send your resume and a highly personalized follow-up letter, reminding the addressee of the phone conversation. *Always* include a cover letter if you are asked to send a resume, and treat your resume and cover letter as a total package. Gear your letter toward the specific position you are applying for and prove why you would be a "good match" for the position.

> **Always include a cover letter if you are asked to send a resume.**

Unless you are in telephone sales, making smooth and relaxed cover calls will probably not come easily. Practice them on your own, and then with your friends or relatives.

DON'T BOTHER WITH MASS MAILINGS OR BARRAGES OF PHONE CALLS

Direct Contact does not mean burying every firm within a hundred miles with mail and phone calls. Mass mailings rarely work in the job hunt. This also applies to those letters that are personalized -- but dehumanized -- on an automatic typewriter or computer. Don't waste your time or money on such a project; you will fool no one but yourself.

The worst part of sending out mass mailings, or making unplanned phone calls to companies you have not researched, is that you are likely to be remembered as someone with little genuine interest in the firm, who lacks sincerity -- somebody that nobody wants to hire.

If you obtain an interview as a result of a telephone conversation, be sure to send a thank-you note reiterating the points you made during the conversation. You will appear more professional and increase your impact. However, unless specifically requested, don't mail your resume once an interview has been arranged. Take it with you to the interview instead.

You should never show up to seek a professional position without an appointment. Even if you are somehow lucky enough to obtain an interview, you will appear so unprofessional that you will not be seriously considered.

> ## HELP WANTED ADVERTISEMENTS
>
> Only a small fraction of professional job openings are advertised. Yet the majority of jobseekers -- and quite a few people not in the job market -- spend a lot of time studying the help wanted ads. As a result, the competition for advertised openings is often very severe.
>
> A moderate-sized employer told us about their experience advertising in the help wanted section of a major Sunday newspaper:
>
> *It was a disaster. We had over 500 responses from this relatively small ad in just one week. We have only two phone lines in this office and one was totally knocked out. We'll never advertise for professional help again.*
>
> If you insist on following up on help wanted ads, then research a firm before you reply to an ad. Preliminary research might help to separate you from all of the other professionals responding to that ad, many of whom will have only a passing interest in the opportunity. It will also give you insight about a particular firm, to help you determine if it is potentially a good match. That said, your chances of obtaining a job through the want ads are still much smaller than they are with the Direct Contact method.

As each interview is arranged, begin your in-depth research. You should arrive at an interview knowing the company upside-down and inside-out. You need to know the company's products, types of customers, subsidiaries, parent company, principal locations, rank in the industry, sales and profit trends, type of ownership, size, current plans, and much more. By this time you have probably narrowed your job search to one industry. Even if you haven't, you should still be familiar with common industry terms, the trends in the firm's industry, the firm's principal competitors and their relative performance, and the direction in which the industry leaders are headed.

Dig into every resource you can! Surf the Internet. Read the company literature, the trade press, the business press, and if the company is public, call your stockbroker (if you have one) and ask for additional information. If possible, speak to someone at the firm before the interview, or if not, speak to someone at a competing firm. The more time you spend, the better. Even if you feel extremely pressed for time, you should set aside several hours for pre-interview research.

> **You should arrive at an interview knowing the company upside-down and inside-out.**

If you have been out of the job market for some time, don't be surprised if you find yourself tense during your first few interviews. It will probably happen every time you re-enter the market, not just when you seek your first job after getting out of school.

Tension is natural during an interview, but knowing you have done a thorough research job should put you more at ease. Make a list of questions that you think might be asked in each interview. Think out your answers carefully and practice them with a friend. Tape record your responses to the problem questions. (*See also in this chapter: Informational Interviews.*) If you feel particularly unsure of your interviewing skills, arrange your first interviews at firms you are not as interested in. (But remember it is common courtesy to seem enthusiastic about the possibility of working for any firm at which you interview.) Practice again on your own after these first few interviews. Go over the difficult questions that you were asked.

Take some time to really think about how you will convey your work history. Present "bad experiences" as "learning experiences." Instead of saying "I hated my position as a salesperson because I had to bother people on the phone," say "I realized that cold-calling was not my strong suit. Though I love working with people, I decided my talents would be best used in a more face-to-face atmosphere." Always find some sort of lesson from previous jobs, as they all have one.

How important is the proper dress for a job interview? Buying a complete wardrobe, donning new shoes, and having your hair styled every morning are not enough to guarantee you a career position as an investment banker. But on the other hand, if you can't find a clean, conservative suit or won't take the time to wash your hair, then you are just wasting your time by interviewing at all.

Personal grooming is as important as finding appropriate clothes for a job interview. Careful grooming indicates both a sense of thoroughness and self-confidence. This is not the time to make a statement – take out the extra earrings and avoid any garish hair colors not found in nature. Women should not wear excessive makeup, and both men and women should refrain from wearing any perfume or cologne (it only takes a small spritz to leave an allergic interviewer with a fit of sneezing and a bad impression of your meeting). Men should be freshly shaven, even if the interview is late in the day, and men with long hair should have it pulled back and neat.

Men applying for any professional position should wear a suit, preferably in a conservative color such as navy or charcoal gray. It is easy to get away with wearing the same dark suit to consecutive interviews at the same company; just be sure to wear a different shirt and tie for each interview.

Women should also wear a business suit. Professionalism still dictates a suit with a skirt, rather than slacks, as proper interview garb for women. This is usually true even at companies where pants are acceptable attire for female employees. As much as you may disagree with this guideline, the more prudent time to fight this standard is after you land the job.

The final selection of candidates for a job opening won't be determined by dress, of course. However, inappropriate dress can quickly eliminate a first-round candidate. So while you shouldn't

---

SKIRT VS. PANTS:
An Interview Dilemma

For those women who are still convinced that pants are acceptable interview attire, listen to the words of one career counselor from a prestigious New England college:

I had a student who told me that since she knew women in her industry often wore pants to work, she was going to wear pants to her interviews. Almost every recruiter commented that her pants were "too casual," and even referred to her as "the one with the pants." The funny thing was that one of the recruiters who commented on her pants had been wearing jeans!

spend a fortune on a new wardrobe, you should be sure that your clothes are adequate. The key is to dress at least as formally or slightly more formally and more conservatively than the position would suggest.

Be complete. Everyone needs a watch, a pen, and a notepad. Finally, a briefcase or a leather-bound folder (containing extra, *unfolded*, copies of your resume) will help complete the look of professionalism.

Sometimes the interviewer will be running behind schedule. Don't be upset, be sympathetic. There is often pressure to interview a lot of candidates and to quickly fill a demanding position. So be sure to come to your interview with good reading material to keep yourself occupied and relaxed.

The very beginning of the interview is the most important part because it determines the tone for the rest of it. Those first few moments are especially crucial. Do you smile when you meet? Do you establish enough eye contact, but not too much? Do you walk into the office with a self-assured and confident stride? Do you shake hands firmly? Do you make small talk easily without being garrulous? It is human nature to judge people by that first impression, so make sure it is a good one. But most of all, try to be yourself.

BE PREPARED:
Some Common Interview Questions

Tell me about yourself.

Why did you leave your last job?

What excites you in your current job?

Where would you like to be in five years?

How much overtime are you willing to work?

What would your previous/present employer tell me about you?

Tell me about a difficult situation that you faced at your previous/present job.

What are your greatest strengths?

What are your weaknesses?

Describe a work situation where you took initiative and went beyond your normal responsibilities.

Why should we hire you?

Often the interviewer will begin, after the small talk, by telling you about the company, the division, the department, or perhaps, the position. Because of your detailed research, the information about the company should be repetitive for you, and the interviewer would probably like nothing better than to avoid this regurgitation of the company biography. So if you can do so tactfully, indicate to the interviewer that you are very familiar with the firm. If he or she seems intent on providing you with background information, despite your hints, then acquiesce.

But be sure to remain attentive. If you can manage to generate a brief discussion of the company or the industry at this point, without being forceful, great. It will help to further build rapport, underscore your interest, and increase your impact.

> **The interviewer's job is to find a reason to turn you down; your job is to not provide that reason.**
>
> -John L. LaFevre, author,
> *How You Really Get Hired*
>
> Reprinted from the 1989/90 *CPC Annual*, with permission of the National Association of Colleges and Employers (formerly College Placement Council, Inc.), copyright holder.

Soon (if it didn't begin that way) the interviewer will begin the questions, many of which you will have already practiced. This period of the interview usually falls into one of two categories (or somewhere in between): either a structured interview, where the interviewer has a prescribed set of questions to ask; or an unstructured interview, where the interviewer will ask only leading questions to get you to talk about yourself, your experiences, and your goals. Try to sense as quickly as possible in which direction the interviewer wishes to proceed. This will make the interviewer feel more relaxed and in control of the situation.

Remember to keep attuned to the interviewer and make the length of your answers appropriate to the situation. If you are really unsure as to how detailed a response the interviewer is seeking, then ask.

As the interview progresses, the interviewer will probably mention some of the most important responsibilities of the position. If applicable, draw parallels between your experience and the demands of the position as detailed by the interviewer. Describe your past experience in the same manner that you do on your resume: emphasizing results and achievements and not merely describing activities. But don't exaggerate. Be on the level about your abilities.

The first interview is often the toughest, where many candidates are screened out. If you are interviewing for a very competitive position, you will have to make an impression that will last. Focus on a few of your greatest strengths that are relevant to the position. Develop these points carefully, state them again in different words, and then try to summarize them briefly at the end of the interview.

Often the interviewer will pause toward the end and ask if you have any questions. Particularly in a structured interview, this might be the one chance to really show your knowledge of and interest in the firm. Have a list prepared of specific questions that are of real interest to you. Let your questions subtly show your research and your knowledge of the firm's activities. It is wise to have an extensive list of questions, as several of them may be answered during the interview.

Do not turn your opportunity to ask questions into an interrogation. Avoid reading directly from your list of questions, and ask questions that you are fairly certain the interviewer can answer (remember how you feel when you cannot answer a question during an interview).

Even if you are unable to determine the salary range beforehand, do not ask about it during the first interview. You can always ask later. Above all, don't ask about fringe benefits until you have been offered a position. (Then be sure to get all the details.)

Try not to be negative about anything during the interview, particularly any past employer or any previous job. Be cheerful. Everyone likes to work with someone who seems to be happy. Even if you detest your current/former job or manager, do not make disparaging comments. The interviewer may construe this as a sign of a potential attitude problem and not consider you a strong candidate.

Don't let a tough question throw you off base. If you don't know the answer to a question, simply say so – do not apologize. Just smile. Nobody can answer every question – particularly some of the questions that are asked in job interviews.

Before your first interview, you may be able to determine how many rounds of interviews there usually are for positions at your level. (Of course it may differ quite a bit even within the different levels of one firm.) Usually you can count on attending at least two or three interviews, although some firms are known to give a minimum of six interviews for all professional positions. While you should be more relaxed as you return for subsequent interviews, the pressure will be on. The more prepared you are, the better.

Depending on what information you are able to obtain, you might want to vary your strategy quite a bit from interview to interview. For instance, if the first interview is a screening interview, then be sure a few of your strengths really stand out. On the other hand, if later interviews are primarily with people who are in a position to veto your hiring, but not to push it forward, then you should primarily focus on building rapport as opposed to reiterating and developing your key strengths.

If it looks as though your skills and background do not match the position the interviewer was hoping to fill, ask him or her if there is another division or subsidiary that perhaps could profit from your talents.

Write a follow-up letter immediately after the interview, while it is still fresh in the interviewer's mind (see the sample follow-up letter format found in the Resumes and Cover Letters chapter). Not only is this a thank-you, but it also gives you the chance to provide the interviewer with any details you may have forgotten (as long as they can be tactfully added in). If you haven't heard back from the interviewer within a week of sending your thank-you letter, call to stress your continued interest in the firm and the position. If you lost any points during the interview for any reason, this letter can help you regain footing. Be polite and make sure to stress your continued interest and competency to fill the position. Just don't forget to proofread it thoroughly. If you are unsure of the spelling of the interviewer's name, call the receptionist and ask.

THE BALANCING ACT:
Looking for a New Job While Currently Employed

For those of you who are still employed, job-searching will be particularly tiring because it must be done in addition to your normal work responsibilities. So don't overwork yourself to the point where you show up to interviews looking exhausted or start to slip behind at your current job. On the other hand, don't be tempted to quit your present job! The long hours are worth it. Searching for a job while you have one puts you in a position of strength.

If you must be at your office during the business day, then you have additional problems to deal with. How can you work interviews into the business day? And if you work in an open office, how can you even call to set up interviews? Obviously, you should keep up the effort and the appearances on your present job. So maximize your use of the lunch hour, early mornings, and late afternoons for calling. If you keep trying, you'll be surprised how often you will be able to reach the executive you are trying to contact during your out-of-office hours. You can catch people as early as 8 a.m. and as late as 6 p.m. on frequent occasions.

Your inability to interview at any time other than lunch just might work to your advantage. If you can, try to set up as many interviews as possible for your lunch hour. This will go a long way to creating a relaxed atmosphere. But be sure the interviews don't stray too far from the agenda on hand.

Lunchtime interviews are much easier to obtain if you have substantial career experience. People with less experience will often find no alternative to taking time off for interviews. If you have to take time off, you have to take time off. But try to do this as little as possible. Try to take the whole day off in order to avoid being blatantly obvious about your job search, and try to schedule two to three interviews for the same day. (It is very difficult to maintain an optimum level of energy at more than three interviews in one day.) Explain to the interviewer why you might have to juggle your interview schedule; he/she should honor the respect you're showing your current employer by minimizing your days off and will probably appreciate the fact that another prospective employer is interested in you.

> **Try calling as early as 8 a.m. and as late as 6 p.m. You'll be surprised how often you will be able to reach the executive you want during these times of the day.**

What do you tell an interviewer who asks for references from your current employer? Just say that while you are happy to have your former employers contacted, you are trying to keep your job search confidential and would rather that your current employer not be contacted until you have been given a firm offer.

IF YOU'RE FIRED OR LAID OFF:
Picking Yourself Up and Dusting Yourself Off

If you've been fired or laid off, you are not the first and will not be the last to go through this traumatic experience. In today's changing economy, thousands of professionals lose their jobs every year. Even if you were terminated with just cause, do not lose heart. Remember, being fired is not a reflection on you as a person. It is usually a reflection of your company's staffing needs and its perception of your recent job performance and attitude. And if you were not performing up to par or enjoying your work, then you will probably be better off at another company anyway.

> **Be prepared for the question "Why were you fired?" during job interviews.**

A thorough job search could take months, so be sure to negotiate a reasonable severance package, if possible, and determine to what benefits, such as health insurance, you are still legally entitled. Also, register for unemployment compensation immediately. Don't be surprised to find other professionals collecting unemployment compensation -- it is for everyone who has lost their job.

Don't start your job search with a flurry of unplanned activity. Start by choosing a strategy and working out a plan. Now is not the time for major changes in your life. If possible, remain in the same career and in the same geographical location, at least until you have been working again for a while. On the other hand, if the only industry for which you are trained is leaving, or is severely depressed in your area, then you should give prompt consideration to moving or switching careers.

Avoid mentioning you were fired when arranging interviews, but be prepared for the question "Why were you fired?" during an interview. If you were laid off as a result of downsizing, briefly explain, being sure to reinforce that your job loss was not due to performance. If you were in fact fired, be honest, but try to detail the reason as favorably as possible and portray what you have learned from your mistakes. If you are confident one of your past managers will give you a good reference, tell the interviewer to contact that person. Do not to speak negatively of your past employer and try not to sound particularly worried about your status of being temporarily unemployed.

Finally, don't spend too much time reflecting on why you were let go or how you might have avoided it. Think positively, look to the future, and be sure to follow a careful plan during your job search.

THE COLLEGE STUDENT:
Conducting Your First Job Search

While you will be able to apply many of the basics covered earlier in this chapter to your job search, there are some situations unique to the college student's job search.

> **THE GPA QUESTION**
>
> You are interviewing for the job of your dreams. Everything is going well: You've established a good rapport, the interviewer seems impressed with your qualifications, and you're almost positive the job is yours. Then you're asked about your GPA, which is pitifully low. Do you tell the truth and watch your dream job fly out the window?
>
> *Never* lie about your GPA (they may request your transcript, and no company will hire a liar). You can, however, explain if there is a reason you don't feel your grades reflect your abilities, and mention any other impressive statistics. For example, if you have a high GPA in your major, or in the last few semesters (as opposed to your cumulative college career), you can use that fact to your advantage.

Perhaps the biggest problem college students face is lack of experience. Many schools have internship programs designed to give students exposure to the field of their choice, as well as the opportunity to make valuable contacts. Check out your school's career services department to see what internships are available. If your school does not have a formal internship program, or if there are no available internships that appeal to you, try contacting local businesses and offering your services. Often, businesses will be more than willing to have an extra pair of hands (especially if those hands are unpaid!) for a day or two each week. Or try contacting school alumni to see if you can "shadow" them for a few days, and see what their daily duties are like.

Although many jobseekers do not do this, it can be extremely helpful to arrange an informational interview with a college alumnus or someone else who works in your desired industry. You interview them about their job, their company, and their industry with questions you have prepared in advance. This can be done over the phone but is usually done in person. This will provide you with a contact in the industry who may give you more valuable information – or perhaps even a job opportunity – in the future. Always follow up with a thank you letter that includes your contact information.

The goal is to try to begin building experience and establishing contacts as early as possible in your college career.

What do you do if, for whatever reason, you weren't able to get experience directly related to your desired career? First, look at your previous jobs and see if there's anything you can highlight. Did you supervise or train other employees? Did you reorganize the accounting system, or boost productivity in some way? Accomplishments like these demonstrate leadership, responsibility, and innovation -- qualities that most companies look for in employees. And don't forget volunteer activities and school clubs, which can also showcase these traits.

Companies will often send recruiters to interview on-site at various colleges. This gives students a chance to interview with companies that may not have interviewed them otherwise. This is particularly true if a company schedules "open" interviews, in which the only screening process is who is first in line at the sign-ups. Of course, since many more applicants gain interviews in this format, this also means that many more people are rejected. The on-campus interview is generally a screening interview, to see if it is worth the company's time to invite you in for a second interview. So do everything possible to make yourself stand out from the crowd.

The first step, of course, is to check out any and all information your school's career center has on the company. If the information seems out of date, check out the company on the Internet or call the company's headquarters and ask for any printed information.

Many companies will host an informational meeting for interviewees, often the evening before interviews are scheduled to take place. DO NOT MISS THIS MEETING. The recruiter will almost certainly ask if you attended. Make an effort to stay after the meeting and talk with the company's representatives. Not only does this give you an opportunity to find out more information about both the company and the position, it also makes you stand out in the recruiter's mind. If there's a particular company that you had your heart set on, but you weren't able to get an interview with them, attend the information session anyway. You may be able to persuade the recruiter to squeeze you into the schedule. (Or you may discover that the company really isn't the right fit for you after all.)

Try to check out the interview site beforehand. Some colleges may conduct "mock" interviews that take place in one of the standard interview rooms. Or you may be able to convince a career counselor (or even a custodian) to let you sneak a peek during off-hours. Either way, having an idea of the room's setup will help you to mentally prepare.

Arrive at least 15 minutes early to the interview. The recruiter may be ahead of schedule, and might meet you early. But don't be surprised if previous interviews have run over, resulting in your 30-minute slot being reduced to 20 minutes (or less). Don't complain or appear anxious; just use the time you do have as efficiently as possible to showcase the reasons *you* are the ideal candidate. Staying calm and composed in these situations will work to your advantage.

LAST WORDS

A parting word of advice. Again and again during your job search you will face rejection. You will be rejected when you apply for interviews. You will be rejected after interviews. For every job offer you finally receive, you probably will have been rejected many times. Don't let rejections slow you down. Keep reminding yourself that the sooner you go out, start your job search, and get those rejections flowing in, the closer you will be to obtaining the job you want.

RESUMES AND COVER LETTERS

When filling a position, an employer will often have 100-plus applicants, but time to interview only a handful of the most promising ones. As a result, he or she will reject most applicants after only briefly skimming their resumes.

Unless you have phoned and talked to the employer – which you should do whenever you can – you will be chosen or rejected for an interview entirely on the basis of your resume and cover letter. *Your cover letter must catch the employer's attention, and your resume must hold it.* (But remember – a resume is no substitute for a job search campaign. *You* must seek a job. Your resume is only one tool, albeit a critical one.)

RESUME FORMAT:
Mechanics of a First Impression

Employers dislike long resumes, so unless you have an unusually strong background with many years of experience and a diversity of outstanding achievements, keep your resume length to one page. If you must squeeze in more information than would otherwise fit, try using a smaller typeface or changing the margins. Watch also for "widows" at the end of paragraphs. You can often free up some space if you can shorten the information enough to get rid of those single words taking up an entire line. Another tactic that works with some word processing programs is to decrease the font size of your paragraph returns and changing the spacing between lines.

Print your resume on standard 8 1/2" x 11" paper. Since recruiters often get resumes in batches of hundreds, a smaller-sized resume may be lost in the pile. Oversized resumes are likely to get crumpled at the edges, and won't fit easily in their files.

First impressions matter, so make sure the recruiter's first impression of your resume is a good one. Never hand-write your resume (or cover letter)! Print your resume on quality paper that has weight and texture, in a conservative color such as white, ivory, or pale gray. Good resume paper is easy to find at many stores that sell stationary or office products. It is even available at some drug stores. Use *matching paper and envelopes* for both your resume and cover letter. One hiring manager at a major magazine throws out all resumes that arrive on paper that differs in color from the envelope!

Do not buy paper with images of clouds and rainbows in the background or anything that looks like casual stationary that you would send to your favorite aunt. Do not spray perfume or cologne on your resume. Do not include your picture with your resume unless you have a specific and appropriate reason to do so.

Another tip: Do a test print of your resume (and cover letter), to make sure the watermark is on the same side as the text so that you can read it. Also make sure it is right-side up. As trivial as this may sound, some recruiters check for this! One recruiter at a law firm in New Hampshire sheepishly admitted this is the first thing he checks. *"I open each envelope and check the watermarks on the resume and cover letter. Those candidates that have it wrong go into a different pile."*

Modern photocomposition typesetting gives you the clearest, sharpest image, a wide variety of type styles, and effects such as italics, bold-facing, and book-like justified margins. It is also too expensive for many jobseekers. The quality of today's laser printers mean that a computer-generated resume can look just as impressive as one that has been professionally typeset.

A computer with a word processing or desktop publishing program is the most common way to generate your resume. This allows you the flexibility to make changes almost instantly and to store different drafts on disk. Word processing and desktop publishing programs also offer many different fonts to choose from, each taking up different amounts of space. (It is generally best to stay between 9-point and 12-point font size.) Many other options are also available, such as bold-facing or italicizing for emphasis and the ability to change and manipulate spacing. It is generally recommended to leave the right-hand margin unjustified as this keeps the spacing between the text even and therefore easier to read. It is not wrong to justify both margins of text, but if possible try it both ways before you decide if possible.

For a resume on paper, the end result will be largely determined by the quality of the printer you use. Laser printers will generally provide the best quality. Do not use a dot matrix printer.

Many companies now use scanning equipment to screen the resumes they receive, and certain paper, fonts, and other features are more compatible with this technology. White paper is preferable, as well as a standard font such as Courier or Helvetica. You should use at least a 10-point font, and avoid bolding, italics, underlining, borders, boxes, or graphics.

Household typewriters and office typewriters with nylon or other cloth ribbons are *not* good enough for typing your resume. If you don't have access to a quality word processing program, hire a professional with the resources to prepare your resume for you. Keep in mind that businesses such as Kinko's (open 24 hours) provide access to computers with quality printers.

Don't make your copies on an office photocopier. Only the personnel office may see the resume you mail. Everyone else may see only a copy of it, and copies of copies quickly become unreadable. Furthermore, sending photocopies of your resume or cover letter is completely unprofessional. Either print out each copy individually, or take your resume to a professional copy shop, which will generally offer professionally-maintained, extra-high-quality photocopiers and charge fairly reasonable prices. You want your resume to represent you with the look of polished quality.

> **The one piece of advice I give to everyone about their resume is: Show it to people, show it to people, show it to people. Before you ever send out a resume, show it to at least a dozen people.**
>
> -Cate Talbot Ashton,
> Associate Director,
> Career Services,
> Colby College

Whether you typed it or paid to have it produced professionally, mistakes on resumes are not only embarrassing, but will usually remove you from consideration (particularly if something obvious such as your name is misspelled). No matter how much you paid someone else to type, write, or typeset your resume, *you* lose if there is a mistake. So proofread it as carefully as possible. Get a friend to help you. Read your draft aloud as your friend checks the proof copy. Then have your friend read aloud while you check. Next, read it letter by letter to check spelling and punctuation.

If you are having it typed or typeset by a resume service or a printer, and you don't have time to proof it, pay for it and take it home. Proof it there and bring it back later to get it corrected and printed.

If you wrote your resume with a word processing program, use the built-in spell checker to double-check for spelling errors. Keep in mind that a spell checker will not find errors such as "to" for "two" or "wok" for "work." Many spell check programs do not recognize missing or misused punctuation, nor are they set to check the spelling of capitalized words. It's important that you still proofread your resume to check for grammatical mistakes and other problems, even <u>after</u> it has been spellchecked.

If you find mistakes, do not make edits in pen or pencil or use white-out to fix them on the final copy!

As companies rely increasingly on emerging technologies to find qualified candidates for job openings, you may opt to create an electronic resume in order to remain competitive in today's job market. Why is this important? Companies today sometimes request that resumes be submitted by e-mail, and many hiring managers regularly check online resume databases for candidates to fill unadvertised job openings. Other companies enlist the services of electronic employment database services, which charge jobseekers a nominal fee to have their resume posted to the database to be viewed by potential employers. Still other companies use their own automated applicant tracking systems, in which case your resume is fed through a scanner that sends the image to a computer which "reads" your resume, looking for keywords, and files it accordingly in its database.

Whether you're posting your resume online, e-mailing it directly to an employer, sending it to an electronic employment database, or sending it to a company you suspect uses an automated applicant tracking system, you must create some form of electronic resume to take advantage of the technology. Don't panic! An electronic resume is simply a modified version of your conventional resume. An electronic resume is one that is sparsely formatted, but filled with keywords and important facts.

In order to post your resume to the Internet – either to an online resume database or through direct e-mail to an employer – you will need to change the way your resume is formatted. Instead of a Word, WordPerfect, or other word processing document, save your resume as a plain text, DOS, or ASCII file. These three terms are basically interchangeable, and describe text at its simplest, most basic level, without the formatting such as boldface or italics that most jobseekers use to make their resumes look more interesting. If you use e-mail, you'll notice that all of your messages are written and received in this format. First, you should remove all formatting from your resume including boldface, italics, underlining, bullets, differing font sizes, and graphics. Then, convert and save your resume as a plain text file. Most word processing programs have a "save as" feature that allows you to save files in different formats. Here, you should choose "text only" or "plain text."

Another option is to create a resume in HTML (hypertext markup language), the text formatting language used to publish information on the World Wide Web. However, the real usefulness of HTML resumes is still being explored. Most of the major online databases do not accept HTML resumes, and the vast majority of companies only accept plain text resumes through their e-mail.

Finally, if you simply wish to send your resume to an electronic employment database or a company that uses an automated applicant tracking system, there is no need to convert your resume to a plain text file. The only change you need to make is to organize the information in your resume by keywords. Employers are likely to do keyword searches for information, such as degree held or knowledge of particular types of software. Therefore, using the right keywords or key phrases in your resume is critical to its ultimate success. Keywords are usually nouns or short phrases that the computer searches for which refer to experience, training, skills, and abilities. For example, let's say an employer searches an employment database for a sales representative with the following criteria:

BS/BA
exceeded quota
cold calls
high energy
willing to travel

Even if you have the right qualifications, neglecting to use these keywords would result in the computer passing over your resume. Although there is no way to know for sure which keywords employers are most likely to likely to search for, you can make educated guesses by checking the help-wanted ads or online job postings for your type of job. You should also arrange keywords in a keyword summary, a paragraph listing your qualifications that immediately follows your name and address (see sample letter in this chapter). In addition, choose a nondecorative font with clear, distinct characters, such as Helvetica or Times. It is more difficult for a scanner to accurately pick up the more unusual fonts. Boldface and all capital letters are best used only for major section headings, such as "Experience" and "Education." It is also best to avoid using italics or underlining, since this can cause the letters to bleed into one another.

For more specific information on creating and sending electronic resumes, see *The Adams Electronic Job Search Almanac*.

The most common resume formats are the functional resume, the chronological resume, and the combination resume. (Examples can be found at the end of this chapter.) A functional resume focuses on skills and de-emphasizes job titles, employers, etc. A functional resume is best if you have been out of the work force for a long time or are changing careers. It is also good if you want to highlight specific skills and strengths, especially if all of your work experience has been at one company. This format can also be a good choice if you are just out of school or have no experience in your desired field at all.

Choose a chronological format if you are currently working or were working recently, and if your most recent experiences relate to your desired field. Use reverse chronological order and include dates. To a recruiter your last job and your latest schooling are the most important, so put the last first and list the rest going back in time.

A combination resume is perhaps the most common. This resume simply combines elements of the functional and chronological resume formats. This is used by many jobseekers with a solid track record who find elements of both types useful.

Your name, phone number, e-mail address (if you have one), and a complete mailing address should be at the top of your resume. Try to make your name stand out by using a slightly larger font size or all capital letters. Be sure to spell out everything. Never abbreviate St. for Street or Rd. for Road. If you are a college student, you should also put your home address and phone number at the top. Change your message on your answering machine if necessary — RUSH blaring in the background or your sorority sisters screaming may not come across well to all recruiters. If you think you may be moving within six months then include a second address and phone number of a trusted friend or relative who can reach you no matter where you are.

Remember that employers will keep your resume on file and may contact you months later if a position opens that fits your qualifications. All too often, candidates are unreachable because they have moved and had not previously provided enough contact options on their resume.

Next, list your experience, then your education. If you are a recent graduate, list your education first, unless your experience is more important than your education. (For example, if you have just graduated from a teaching school, have some business experience, and are applying for a job in business, you would list your business experience first.)

Keep everything easy to find. Put the dates of your employment and education on the left of the page. Put the names of the companies you worked for and the schools you attended a few spaces to the right of the dates. Put the city and state, or the city and country, where you studied or worked to the right of the page.

The important thing is simply to break up the text in some logical way that makes your resume visually attractive and easy to scan, so experiment to see which layout works best for your resume. However you set it up, *stay consistent*. Inconsistencies in fonts, spacing, or tenses will make your resume look sloppy. Also, be sure to use tabs to keep your information vertically lined up, rather than the less precise space bar.

RESUME CONTENT:
Say it with Style

You are selling your skills and accomplishments in your resume, so it is important to inventory yourself and know yourself. If you have achieved something, say so. Put it in the best possible light. But avoid subjective statements, such as "I am a hard worker" or "I get along well with my coworkers." Just stick to the facts.

While you shouldn't hold back or be modest, don't exaggerate your achievements to the point of misrepresentation. <u>Be honest</u>. Many companies will immediately drop an applicant from consideration (or fire a current employee) upon discovering inaccurate or untrue information on a resume or other application material.

Write down the important (and pertinent) things you have done, but do it in as few words as possible. Your resume will be scanned, not read, and short, concise phrases are much more effective than long-winded sentences. Avoid the use of "I" when emphasizing your accomplishments. Instead, use brief phrases beginning with action verbs.

While some technical terms will be unavoidable, you should try to avoid excessive "technicalese." Keep in mind that the first person to see your resume may be a human resources person who won't necessarily know all the jargon — and how can they be impressed by something they don't understand?

Also, try to hold your paragraphs to six lines or less. If you have more than six lines of information about one job or school, put it in two or more paragraphs. A short resume will be examined more carefully. Remember: Your resume usually has between eight and 45 seconds to catch an employer's eye. So make every second count.

A functional resume may require a job objective to give it focus. One or two sentences describing the job you are seeking can clarify in what capacity your skills will be best put to use. Be sure that your stated objective is in line with the position you're applying for.

Examples:

>An entry-level editorial assistant position in the publishing industry.
>A senior management position with a telecommunications firm.

Don't include a job objective on a chronological resume unless your previous work experiences are <u>completely</u> unrelated to the position for which you're applying. The presence of an overly specific job objective might eliminate you from consideration for other positions that a recruiter feels are a better match for your qualifications. But even if you don't put an objective on paper, having a career goal in mind as you write can help give your resume a solid sense of direction.

USE ACTION VERBS

How you write your resume is just as important as *what* you write. In describing previous work experiences, the strongest resumes use short phrases beginning with action verbs. Below are a few you may want to use. (This list is not all-inclusive.)

achieved	developed	integrated	purchased
administered	devised	interpreted	reduced
advised	directed	interviewed	regulated
analyzed	discovered	invented	reorganized
arranged	distributed	launched	represented
assembled	eliminated	maintained	researched
assisted	established	managed	resolved
attained	evaluated	marketed	restored
budgeted	examined	mediated	restructured
built	executed	monitored	revised
calculated	expanded	negotiated	scheduled
collaborated	expedited	obtained	selected
collected	facilitated	operated	served
compiled	formulated	ordered	sold
completed	founded	organized	solved
computed	generated	participated	streamlined
conducted	headed	performed	studied
consolidated	identified	planned	supervised
constructed	implemented	prepared	supplied
consulted	improved	presented	supported
controlled	increased	processed	tested
coordinated	initiated	produced	trained
created	installed	proposed	updated
designed	instituted	provided	upgraded
determined	instructed	published	wrote

Some jobseekers may choose to include both "Relevant Experience" and "Additional Experience" sections. This can be useful, as it allows the jobseeker to place more emphasis on certain experiences and to de-emphasize others.

Emphasize continued experience in a particular job area or continued interest in a particular industry. De-emphasize irrelevant positions. It is okay to include one opening line providing a general description of each company you've worked at. Delete positions that you held for less than four months (unless you are a very recent college grad or still in school). Stress your <u>results</u> and your achievements, elaborating on how you contributed in your previous jobs. Did you increase sales, reduce costs, improve a product, implement a new program? Were you promoted? Use specific numbers (i.e., quantities, percentages, dollar amounts) whenever possible.

Keep it brief if you have more than two years of career experience. Elaborate more if you have less experience. If you are a recent college graduate, you may choose to include any high school activities that are directly relevant to your career. If you've been out of school for a while you don't need to list your education prior to college.

Mention degrees received and any honors or special awards. Note individual courses or projects you participated in that might be relevant for employers. For example, if you are an English major applying for a position as a business writer, be sure to mention any business or economics courses. Previous experience such as Editor-in-Chief of the school newspaper would be relevant as well.

If you are uploading your resume to an online job hunting site such as CareerCity, action verbs are still important, but the key words or key nouns that a computer would search for become more important. For example, if you're seeking an accounting position, key nouns that a computer would search for such as "Lotus 1-2-3" or "CPA" or "payroll" become very important.

Be sure to mention any computer skills you may have. You may wish to include a section entitled "Additional Skills" or "Computer Skills," in which you list any software programs you know. An additional skills section is also an ideal place to mention fluency in a foreign language.

This section is optional, but if you choose to include it, keep it brief. A one-word mention of hobbies such as fishing, chess, baseball, cooking, etc., can give the person who will interview you a good way to open up the conversation. Team sports experience is looked at favorably. It doesn't hurt to include activities that are somewhat unusual (fencing, Akido, '70s music) or that somehow relate to the position or the company you're applying. For instance, it would be worth noting if you are a member of a professional organization in your industry of interest.

> **Those things [marital status, church affiliations, etc.] have no place on a resume. Those are illegal questions, so why even put that information on your resume?**
>
> -Becky Hayes, Career Counselor
> Career Services, Rice University

Never include information about your age, alias, date of birth, health, physical characteristics, marital status, religious affiliation, or political/moral beliefs.

The most that is needed is the sentence "References available upon request" at the bottom of your resume. If you choose to leave it out, that's fine. This line is not really necessary. It is understood that references will most likely be asked for and provided by you later on in the interviewing process. Do not actually send references with your resume and cover letter unless specifically requested.

HIRING A RESUME WRITER:
Is it the Right Choice for You?

If you write reasonably well, it is to your advantage to write your own resume. Writing your resume forces you to review your experiences and figure out how to explain your accomplishments in clear, brief phrases. This will help you when you explain your work to interviewers. It is also easier to tailor your resume to each position you're applying for when you have put it together yourself.

If you write your resume, everything will be in your own words; it will sound like you. It will say what you want it to say. If you are a good writer, know yourself well, and have a good idea of which parts of your background employers are looking for, you should be able to write your own resume better than someone else. If you decide to write your resume yourself, have as many people as possible review and proofread it. Welcome objective opinions and other perspectives.

If you have difficulty writing in "resume style" (which is quite unlike normal written language), if you are unsure which parts of your background to emphasize, or if you think your resume would make your case better if it did not follow one of the standard forms outlined either here or in a book on resumes, then you should consider having it professionally written.

Even some professional resume writers we know have had their resumes written with the help of fellow professionals. They sought the help of someone who can be objective about their background, as well as provide an experienced sounding board to help focus their thoughts.

The best way to choose a writer is by reputation: the recommendation of a friend, a personnel director, your school placement officer, or someone else knowledgeable in the field.

Important questions:
- "How long have you been writing resumes?"
- "If I'm not satisfied with what you write, will you go over it with me and change it?"
- "Do you charge by the hour or a flat rate?"

There is no sure relation between price and quality, except that you are unlikely to get a good writer for less than $50 for an uncomplicated resume and you shouldn't have to pay more than $300 unless your experience is very extensive or complicated. There will be additional charges for printing. Assume nothing no matter how much you pay. It is your career at stake if there are mistakes on your resume!

Few resume services will give you a firm price over the phone, simply because some resumes are too complicated and take too long to do for a predetermined price. Some services will quote you a price that applies to almost all of their customers. Once you decide to use a specific writer, you should insist on a firm price quote *before* engaging their services. Also, find out how expensive minor changes will be.

COVER LETTERS:
Quick, Clear, and Concise

Always mail a cover letter with your resume. In a cover letter you can show an interest in the company that you can't show in a resume. You can also point out one or two of your skills or accomplishments the company can put to good use.

The more personal you can get, the better, so long as you keep it professional. If someone known to the person you are writing has recommended that you contact the company, get permission to include his/her name in the letter. If you can get the name of a person to send the letter to, address it directly to that person (after first calling the company to verify the spelling of the person's name, correct title, and mailing address). Be sure to put the person's name and title on both the letter and the envelope. This will ensure that your letter will get through to the proper person, even if a new person now occupies this position. It will not always be possible to get the name of a person. Always strive to get at least a title.

Be sure to mention something about why you have interest in the company – *so many candidates apply for jobs with no apparent knowledge of what the company does!* This conveys the message that they just want any job.

Type cover letters in full. Don't try the cheap and easy ways, like using a computer mail merge program or photocopying the body of your letter and typing in the inside address and salutation. You will give the impression that you are mailing to a host of companies and have no particular interest in any one.

Print your cover letter on the same color and same high-quality paper as your resume.

Cover letter basic format

Paragraph 1: State what the position is that you are seeking. It is not always necessary to state how you found out about the position – often you will apply without knowing that a position is open.

Paragraph 2: Include what you know about the company and why you are interested in working there. Mention any prior contact with the company or someone known to the hiring person if relevant. Briefly state your qualifications and what you can offer. (Do not talk about what you cannot do).

Paragraph 3: Close with your phone number and where/when you can be reached. Make a request for an interview. State when you will follow-up by phone (or mail or e-mail if the ad requests no phone calls). Do not wait long – generally five working days. If you say you're going to follow-up, then actually do it! This phone call can get your resume noticed when it might otherwise sit in a stack of 225 other resumes.

Cover letter do's and don'ts

- *Do* keep your cover letter brief and to the point.
- *Do* be sure it is error-free.
- *Do* accentuate what you can offer the company, not what you hope to gain from them.
- *Do* be sure your phone number and address is on your cover letter just in case it gets separated from your resume (this happens!).
- *Do* check the watermark by holding the paper up to a light – be sure it is facing forward so it is readable – on the same side as the text, and right-side up.

- *Do* sign your cover letter (or type your name if you are sending it electronically). Blue or black ink are both fine. Do not use red ink.
- *Don't* just repeat information verbatim from your resume.
- *Don't* overuse the personal pronoun "I."
- *Don't* send a generic cover letter – show your personal knowledge of and interest in that particular company.

THANK YOU LETTERS:
Another Way to Stand Out

As mentioned earlier, *always* send a thank you letter after an interview (see the sample later in this section). So few candidates do this and it is yet another way for you to stand out. Be sure to mention something specific from the interview and restate your interest in the company and the position.

It is generally acceptable to handwrite your thank you letter on a generic thank you card (but *never* a postcard). Make sure handwritten notes are neat and legible. However, if you are in doubt, typing your letter is always the safe bet. If you met with several people it is fine to send them each an individual thank you letter. Call the company if you need to check on the correct spelling of their names.

Remember to:
- Keep it short.
- Proofread it carefully.
- Send it *promptly*.

FUNCTIONAL RESUME

C.J. RAVENCLAW
129 Pennsylvania Avenue
Washington DC 20500
202/555-6652
e-mail: ravenclaw@dcpress.net

Objective
A position as a graphic designer commensurate with my acquired skills and expertise.

Summary
Extensive experience in plate making, separations, color matching, background definition, printing, mechanicals, color corrections, and personnel supervision. A highly motivated manager and effective communicator. Proven ability to:

- Create Commercial Graphics
- Produce Embossed Drawings
- Color Separate
- Control Quality
- Resolve Printing Problems
- Analyze Customer Satisfaction

Qualifications
Printing:
Knowledgeable in black and white as well as color printing. Excellent judgment in determining acceptability of color reproduction through comparison with original. Proficient at producing four- or five-color corrections on all media, as well as restyling previously reproduced four-color artwork.

Customer Relations:
Routinely work closely with customers to ensure specifications are met. Capable of striking a balance between technical printing capabilities and need for customer satisfaction through entire production process.

Specialties:
Practiced at creating silk screen overlays for a multitude of processes including velo bind, GBC bind, and perfect bind. Creative design and timely preparation of posters, flyers, and personalized stationery.

Personnel Supervision:
Skillful at fostering atmosphere that encourages highly talented artists to balance high-level creativity with maximum production. Consistently beat production deadlines. Instruct new employees, apprentices, and students in both artistry and technical operations.

Experience
Graphic Arts Professor, Ohio State University, Columbus OH (1992-1996).
Manager, Design Graphics, Washington DC (1997-present).

Education
Massachusetts Conservatory of Art, Ph.D. 1990
University of Massachusetts, B.A. 1988

CHRONOLOGICAL RESUME

HARRY SEABORN
557 Shoreline Drive
Seattle, WA 98404
(206) 555-6584
e-mail: hseaborn@centco.com

EXPERIENCE

THE CENTER COMPANY   Seattle, WA
Systems Programmer   1996-present
- Develop and maintain customer accounting and order tracking database using a Visual Basic front end and SQL server.
- Plan and implement migration of company wide transition from mainframe based dumb terminals to a true client server environment using Windows NT Workstation and Server.
- Oversee general local and wide are network administration including the development of a variety of intranet modules to improve internal company communication and planning across divisions.

INFO TECH, INC.   Seattle, WA
Technical Manager   1994-1996
- Designed and managed the implementation of a network providing the legal community with a direct line to Supreme Court cases across the Internet using SQL Server and a variety of Internet tools.
- Developed a system to make the entire library catalog available on line using PERL scripts and SQL.
- Used Visual Basic and Microsoft Access to create a registration system for university registrar.

EDUCATION

SALEM STATE UNIVERSITY   Salem, OR
    M.S. in Computer Science.   1993
    B.S. in Computer Science.   1991

COMPUTER SKILLS

- Programming Languages: Visual Basic, Java, C++, SQL, PERL
- Software: SQL Server, Internet Information Server, Oracle
- Operating Systems: Windows NT, UNIX, Linux

FUNCTIONAL RESUME

Donna Hermione Moss
703 Wizard's Way
Chicago, IL 60601
(312) 555-8841
e-mail: donna@cowfire.com

OBJECTIVE:
To contribute over five years of experience in promotion, communications, and administration to an entry-level position in advertising.

SUMMARY OF QUALIFICATIONS:
- Performed advertising duties for small business.
- Experience in business writing and communications skills.
- General knowledge of office management.
- Demonstrated ability to work well with others, in both supervisory and support staff roles.
- Type 75 words per minute.

SELECTED ACHIEVEMENTS AND RESULTS:
Promotion:
Composing, editing, and proofreading correspondence and public relations materials for own catering service. Large-scale mailings.

Communication:
Instruction; curriculum and lesson planning; student evaluation; parent-teacher conferences; development of educational materials. Training and supervising clerks.

Computer Skills:
Proficient in MS Word, Lotus 1-2-3, Excel, and Filemaker Pro.

Administration:
Record-keeping and file maintenance. Data processing and computer operations, accounts receivable, accounts payable, inventory control, and customer relations. Scheduling, office management, and telephone reception.

PROFESSIONAL HISTORY:
Teacher; Self-Employed (owner of catering service); Floor Manager; Administrative Assistant; Accounting Clerk.

EDUCATION:
Beloit College, Beloit, WI, BA in Education, 1991

CHRONOLOGICAL RESUME

PERCY ZIEGLER
16 Josiah Court
Marlborough CT 06447
203/555-9641 (h)
203/555-8176, x14 (w)

EDUCATION   Keene State College, Keene NH
Bachelor of Arts in Elementary Education, 1998
- Graduated *magna cum laude*
- English minor
- Kappa Delta Pi member, inducted 1996

EXPERIENCE
September 1998-
Present

Elmer T. Thienes Elementary School, Marlborough CT
Part-time Kindergarten Teacher
- Instruct kindergartners in reading, spelling, language arts, and music.
- Participate in the selection of textbooks and learning aids.
- Organize and supervise class field trips and coordinate in-class presentations.

Summers
1995-1997

Keene YMCA, Youth Division, Keene NH
Child-care Counselor
- Oversaw summer program for low-income youth.
- Budgeted and coordinated special events and field trips, working with Program Director to initiate variations in the program.
- Served as Youth Advocate in cooperation with social worker to address the social needs and problems of participants.

Spring 1997

Wheelock Elementary School, Keene NH
Student Teacher
- Taught third-grade class in all elementary subjects.
- Designed and implemented a two-week unit on Native Americans.
- Assisted in revision of third-grade curriculum.

Fall 1996

Child Development Center, Keene NH
Daycare Worker
- Supervised preschool children on the playground and during art activities.
- Created a "Wishbone Corner," where children could quietly look at books or take a voluntary "time-out."

ADDITIONAL INTERESTS
Martial arts, Pokemon, politics, reading, skiing, writing.

ELECTRONIC RESUME

GRIFFIN DORE
69 Dursley Drive
Cambridge, MA 02138
(617) 555-5555

KEYWORD SUMMARY

Senior financial manager with over ten years experience in Accounting and Systems Management, Budgeting, Forecasting, Cost Containment, Financial Reporting, and International Accounting. MBA in Management. Proficient in Lotus, Excel, Solomon, and Windows.

EXPERIENCE

COLWELL CORPORATION, Wellesley, MA
Director of Accounting and Budgets, 1990 to present
　Direct staff of twenty in General Ledger, Accounts Payable, Accounts Receivable, and International Accounting.
　Facilitate month-end closing process with parent company and auditors.
　Implemented team-oriented cross-training program within accounting group, resulting in timely month-end closings and increased productivity of key accounting staff.
　Developed and implemented a strategy for Sales and Use Tax Compliance in all fifty states.
　Prepare monthly financial statements and analyses.

FRANKLIN AND DELANEY COMPANY, Melrose, MA
Senior Accountant, 1987-1990
　Managed Accounts Payable, General Ledger, transaction processing, and financial reporting. Supervised staff of five.

Staff Accountant, 1985-1987
　Managed Accounts Payable, including vouchering, cash disbursements, and bank reconciliation.
　Wrote and issued policies.
　Maintained supporting schedules used during year-end audits.
　Trained new employees.

EDUCATION

MBA in Management, Northeastern University, Boston, MA, 1989
BS in Accounting, Boston College, Boston, MA, 1985

ASSOCIATIONS

National Association of Accountants

GENERAL MODEL
FOR A COVER LETTER

Your mailing address
Date

Contact's name
Contact's title
Company
Company's mailing address

Dear Mr./Ms. _____:

Immediately explain why your background makes you the best candidate for the position that you are applying for. Describe what prompted you to write (want ad, article you read about the company, networking contact, etc.). Keep the first paragraph short and hard-hitting.

Detail what you could contribute to this company. Show how your qualifications will benefit this firm. Describe your interest in the corporation. Subtly emphasizing your knowledge about this firm and your familiarity with the industry will set you apart from other candidates. Remember to keep this letter short; few recruiters will read a cover letter longer than half a page.

If possible, your closing paragraph should request specific action on the part of the reader. Include your phone number and the hours when you can be reached. Mention that if you do not hear from the reader by a specific date, you will follow up with a phone call. Lastly, thank the reader for their time, consideration, etc.

Sincerely,

(signature)

Your full name (typed)

Enclosure (use this if there are other materials, such as your resume, that are included in the same envelope)

SAMPLE COVER LETTER

16 Josiah Court
Marlborough CT 06447
January 16, 2000

Ms. Leona Malfoy
Assistant Principal
Laningham Elementary School
43 Mayflower Drive
Keene NH 03431

Dear Ms. Malfoy:

Toby Potter recently informed me of a possible opening for a third grade teacher at Laningham Elementary School. With my experience instructing third-graders, both in schools and in summer programs, I feel I would be an ideal candidate for the position. Please accept this letter and the enclosed resume as my application.

Laningham's educational philosophy that every child can learn and succeed interests me, since it mirrors my own. My current position at Elmer T. Thienes Elementary has reinforced this philosophy, heightening my awareness of the different styles and paces of learning and increasing my sensitivity toward special needs children. Furthermore, as a direct result of my student teaching experience at Wheelock Elementary School, I am comfortable, confident, and knowledgeable working with third-graders.

I look forward to discussing the position and my qualifications for it in more detail. I can be reached at 203/555-9641 evenings or 203/555-8176, x14 weekdays. If I do not hear from you before Tuesday of next week, I will call to see if we can schedule a time to meet. Thank you for your time and consideration.

Sincerely,

P. Ziegler

Percy Ziegler

Enclosure

GENERAL MODEL FOR A
THANK YOU/FOLLOW-UP LETTER

Your mailing address
Date

Contact's name
Contact's title
Company
Company's mailing address

Dear Mr./Ms._____:

Remind the interviewer of the reason (i.e., a specific opening, an informational interview, etc.) you were interviewed, as well as the date. Thank him/her for the interview, and try to personalize your thanks by mentioning some specific aspect of the interview.

Confirm your interest in the organization (and in the opening, if you were interviewing for a particular position). Use specifics to re-emphasize that you have researched the firm in detail and have considered how you would fit into the company and the position. This is a good time to say anything you wish you had said in the initial meeting. Be sure to keep this letter brief; a half-page is plenty.

If appropriate, close with a suggestion for further action, such as a desire to have an additional interview, if possible. Mention your phone number and the hours that you can be reached. Alternatively, you may prefer to mention that you will follow up with a phone call in several days. Once again, thank the person for meeting with you, and state that you would be happy to provide any additional information about your qualifications.

Sincerely,

(signature)

Your full name (typed)

CD-ROM JOB SEARCH

Jobseekers who are looking for any edge they can find may want to check out the following selected CD-ROM products. Since most of these databases cost upwards of $500, and are designed for use by other businesses or libraries, don't expect to find these at your local software store. Of course, not all libraries will have all of these resources. Depending on how technologically advanced your library is, you may find only one or two of these electronic databases. Call your library to find out what electronic resources it has available. Many of these databases can also be found in the offices of career counselors or outplacement specialists.

AMERICAN BIG BUSINESS DIRECTORY
5711 South 86th Circle
P.O. Box 27347
Omaha NE 68127
800/555-5211
Provides profiles of 189,000 privately and publicly held companies employing over 100 people. The CD-ROM contains company descriptions which include company type, industry, products, and sales information. Also included are contact names for each company, with a total of over 645,000. You can search the database by industry, SIC code, sales volume, employee size, or zip code.

AMERICAN MANUFACTURER'S DIRECTORY
5711 South 86th Circle
P.O. Box 27347
Omaha NE 68127
800/555-5211
Made by the same company that created *American Big Business Directory*, *American Manufacturer's Directory* lists over 600,000 manufacturing companies of all sizes and industries. The directory contains product and sales information, company size, and key contact information for each company. The user can search by region, SIC code, sales volume, employee size, or zip code.

BUSINESS U.S.A.
5711 South 86th Circle
P.O. Box 27347
Omaha NE 68127
800/555-5211
Also from the makers of *American Big Business Directory* and *American Manufacturer's Directory*, this CD-ROM contains information on 10 million U.S. companies. The profiles provide contact information, industry type, number of employees, and sales volume. Each listing also indicates whether the company is public or private, as well as providing information about the company's products. There are a number of different search methods available, including key words, SIC code, geographic location, and number of employees.

CORPTECH DIRECTORY
12 Alfred Street, Suite 200
Woburn MA 01801-1915
800/333-8036

The *CorpTech Directory* on CD-ROM contains detailed descriptions of over 48,000 U.S. technology companies. It also lists the names and titles of nearly 155,000 executives – CEOs, sales managers, R&D managers, and human resource professionals. World Wide Web and e-mail addresses are also available. In addition to contact information, you can find detailed information about each company's products or services and annual revenues. The *CorpTech Directory* also lists both the number of current employees, and the number of employees one year ago. Some companies also list the number of employees they project having in one year. You can search the database by type of company, geographic location, or sales revenue. This product is updated quarterly.

DUN & BRADSTREET MILLION DOLLAR DISC PLUS
3 Sylvan Way
Parsippany NJ 07054
800/526-0651
This CD-ROM provides information on over 400,000 companies in virtually every industry. About 90 percent of the companies listed are privately held, and all have at least $3 million in annual sales or at least 50 employees. Each company's listing includes the number of employees, sales volume, name of the parent company, and corporate headquarters or branch locations. The *Million Dollar Disc Plus* also provides the names and titles of top executives, as well as biographical information on those executives, including education and career background. Searches can be done by location, industry, SIC code, executive names, or key words in the executive biographies. This directory is updated quarterly.

ENCYCLOPEDIA OF ASSOCIATIONS:
NATIONAL ORGANIZATIONS OF THE U.S.
835 Penobscot Building
645 Griswald Street
Detroit MI 48226
800/877-GALE
Contains descriptions and contact information for nearly 23,000 national organizations. You can search by association name, geographic location, and key words. This CD-ROM is available in both single- and multi-user formats.

HARRIS INFOSOURCE NATIONAL
2057 East Aurora Road
Twinsburg OH 44087
800/888-5900
This directory of manufacturers profiles more than 375,000 companies. All of the companies listed are located in the United States. The listings include the number of employees, plant size, and sales revenue, as well as the names and titles of top executives. This CD-ROM is updated twice a year and can be purchased in smaller regional or state editions.

MOODY'S COMPANY DATA
99 Church Street
New York NY 10007
800/342-5647
Moody's Company Data is a CD-ROM which has detailed listings for over 10,000 publicly traded companies. In addition to information such as industry, company address, and phone and fax numbers, each listing includes the names and titles of its

top officers including the CEO, president, and vice president; company size; number of shareholders; corporate history; subsidiaries; and financial statements. Users can conduct searches by region, SIC codes, industry, or earnings. This CD-ROM is updated monthly.

STANDARD & POOR'S REGISTER
65 Broadway
8th Floor
New York NY 10004
800/221-5277
Contact: Steve Lazarus, Electronic Reference Products
The CD-ROM version of this three-volume desk reference provides the same information as its printed companion. The database lists over 85,000 companies, including more than 25,000 public companies. In addition to contact information, which includes the names and titles of over 500,000 executives, you can find out about each company's primary and secondary sources of business, annual revenues, number of employees, parent company, and subsidiaries. When available, the *Standard & Poor's Register* also lists the names of banks, accounting firms, and law firms used by each company. Also, the directory provides biographies of more than 75,000 top executives, which include information such as directorships held and schools attended. There are 60 different search modes available on the database. You can search geographically, by zip code, industry, SIC code, or stock symbol. You can also limit your search to only private or only public companies. This directory is updated quarterly.

PRIMARY EMPLOYERS

ACCOUNTING AND MANAGEMENT CONSULTING

You can expect to find the following types of companies in this chapter:
Consulting and Research Firms • Industrial Accounting Firms • Management Services • Public Accounting Firms • Tax Preparation Companies

Some helpful information: The average salary for entry-level accountants is $25,000 - $30,000 per year, with experienced accountants and supervisors earning approximately $45,000 - $75,000.

ARTHUR ANDERSEN
901 Main Street, Suite 5600, Dallas TX 75202. **Contact:** Personnel. **Description:** One of the largest certified public accounting firms in the world. Arthur Andersen's four key practice areas include Audit and Business Advisory, Tax and Business Advisory, Business Consulting, and Economic and Financial Consulting. Arthur Andersen is a segment of the Arthur Andersen Worldwide Organization, one of the leading providers of professional services in the world. With over 380 worldwide locations, the global practice of its member firms is conducted through two business units: Arthur Andersen and Andersen Consulting, which provides global management and technology consulting. **NOTE:** This firm does not accept unsolicited resumes. Please only respond to advertised openings.

BOOZ-ALLEN & HAMILTON, INC.
901 Main Street, Suite 6500, Dallas TX 75202. 214/746-6500. **Contact:** Personnel Administrator. **World Wide Web address:** http://www.bah.com. **Description:** A diversified, international management consulting organization offering services in both the commercial and public sectors. Areas of expertise include technology, strategy, and planning, as well as social research and many other technical fields. Specific services include corporate strategy and long-range planning; organization design; human resources management; financial management and control; acquisitions and divestiture; information systems and automation; manufacturing; inventory and distribution control; qualitative and quantitative market research; attitudinal and demographic trend research; marketing strategy and positioning; venture management; transportation and environmental systems; technology research; new products and process development; government programs; and regulatory compliance. Booz-Allen & Hamilton operates 15 regional offices in the United States and eight in Europe, North Africa, and Latin America, all offering a full range of services. **Common positions include:** Biomedical Engineer; Chemical Engineer; Computer Programmer; Electrical/Electronics Engineer; Financial Analyst; Industrial Engineer; Industrial Production Manager; Marketing Specialist; Petroleum Engineer; Statistician; Systems Analyst. **Educational backgrounds include:** Accounting; Business Administration; Computer Science; Economics; Engineering; Finance; Marketing; Mathematics. **Benefits:** Dental Insurance; Disability Coverage; Life Insurance; Medical Insurance; Pension Plan; Profit Sharing; Savings Plan; Tuition Assistance. **Special programs:** Internships. **Corporate headquarters location:** McLean VA. **Operations at this facility include:** Administration; Manufacturing; Research and Development. **Number of employees at this location:** 65.

CHESHIER AND FULLER, L.L.P.
14175 Proton Road, Dallas TX 75244-3604. 972/387-4300. **Toll-free phone:** 800/834-8586. **Fax:** 972/960-2810. **Contact:** Firm Administrator. **E-mail address:** cfllp@cheshier-fuller.com. **World Wide Web address:** http://www.cheshier-fuller.com. **Description:** Offers accounting, tax, audit, management advisory, business valuation, and litigation support services. Founded in 1956. **Common positions include:** Accountant; Administrative Assistant; Auditor; Secretary. **Educational backgrounds include:** Accounting; MBA; Microsoft Office; Microsoft Word; Spreadsheets. **Benefits:** 401(k); Cafeteria Plan; Casual Dress - Fridays; Disability Coverage; Life Insurance; Medical Insurance; Pension Plan; Profit Sharing; Sick Days (1 - 5); Vacation Days (6 - 10). **Special programs:** Summer Jobs; Training. **Office hours:** Monday - Friday, 8:30 a.m. - 5:30 p.m. **Corporate headquarters location:** This Location. **Listed on:** Privately held. **Annual sales/revenues:** Less than $5 million. **Number of employees at this location:** 35.

DELOITTE & TOUCHE
2200 Ross Avenue, Suite 1600, Chase Tower, Dallas TX 75201. 214/777-7000. **Contact:** Steve Gass, Human Resources Director. **World Wide Web address:** http://www.us.deloitte.com. **Description:** Deloitte & Touche is an international firm of certified public accountants, providing professional accounting, auditing, tax, and management consulting services to

widely diversified clients. Deloitte & Touche has a specialized program consisting of some 25 national industry groups and 50 functional (technical) groups that cross industry lines. Groups are involved in various disciplines including accounting, auditing, taxation management advisory services, small and growing businesses, mergers and acquisitions, and computer applications. Deloitte & Touche has more than 500 offices throughout the world. **Common positions include:** Accountant/Auditor; Actuary. **Educational backgrounds include:** Accounting. **Benefits:** Dental Insurance; Disability Coverage; Life Insurance; Medical Insurance; Savings Plan. **Special programs:** Internships. **Corporate headquarters location:** Wilton CT. **Operations at this facility include:** Regional Headquarters. **Number of employees at this location:** 450. **Number of employees nationwide:** 16,000.

DELOITTE & TOUCHE
5550 Lyndon B. Johnson Freeway, Suite 700, Dallas TX 75240. 972/776-6000. **Contact:** Office Manager. **World Wide Web address:** http://www.us.deloitte.com. **Description:** Deloitte & Touche is an international firm of certified public accountants, providing professional accounting, auditing, tax, and management consulting services to widely diversified clients. Deloitte & Touche has a specialized program consisting of some 25 national industry groups and 50 functional (technical) groups that cross industry lines. Groups are involved in various disciplines including accounting, auditing, taxation management advisory services, small and growing businesses, mergers and acquisitions, and computer applications. Deloitte & Touche has more than 500 offices throughout the world. **Corporate headquarters location:** Wilton CT. **Number of employees nationwide:** 16,000.

ERNST & YOUNG
2121 San Jacinto, Suite 1500, Dallas TX 75201. 214/969-8000. **Fax:** 214/969-8587. **Contact:** Director of Human Resources. **World Wide Web address:** http://www.ey.com. **Description:** A certified public accounting firm that also provides its clients with management consulting services. Ernst & Young operates more than 300 offices in 70 countries worldwide. The consulting staff is involved in such fields as data processing, financial modeling, financial feasibility studies, production planning and inventory management, management sciences, health care planning, human resources, and cost accounting and budgeting systems. The company provides services to numerous industries including health care, finance, insurance, manufacturing, retailing, government, utilities, and transportation. **Corporate headquarters location:** New York NY. **Other U.S. locations:** Nationwide. **Listed on:** Privately held. **Number of employees nationwide:** 25,000. **Number of employees worldwide:** 73,000.

FARROW AND FARROW CPAS
P.O. Box 180309, Dallas TX 75218. 214/328-4615. **Contact:** Human Resources. **Description:** Offers accounting, auditing, and bookkeeping services.

GRANT THORNTON LLP
1717 Main Street, Suite 500, Dallas TX 75201. 214/855-7300. **Fax:** 214/561-2370. **Contact:** Human Resources. **World Wide Web address:** http://www.grantthornton.com. **Description:** An international certified public accounting organization offering consulting and accounting services as well as strategic and tactical planning assistance to a diverse clientele. **NOTE:** Entry-level positions are offered. **Common positions include:** Accountant/Auditor; Management Analyst/Consultant; Market Research Analyst; Software Engineer; Systems Analyst; Tax Specialist; Typist/Word Processor. **Educational backgrounds include:** Accounting; Business Administration; Computer Science; Engineering; M.I.S. **Benefits:** 401(k); Dental Insurance; Disability Coverage; Employee Discounts; Leave Time; Life Insurance; Medical Insurance; Public Transit Available; Telecommuting; Tuition Assistance. **Special programs:** Internships; Training. **Corporate headquarters location:** Chicago IL. **Other U.S. locations:** Nationwide. **Operations at this facility include:** Administration; Regional Headquarters; Sales; Service. **Listed on:** Privately held. **Annual sales/revenues:** More than $100 million. **Number of employees at this location:** 125. **Number of employees nationwide:** 2,700. **Number of employees worldwide:** 23,000.

H&R BLOCK
3701 West NW Highway, Suite 210, Dallas TX 75220. 214/358-4560. **Contact:** Debbie Ruggeia, District Manager. **World Wide Web address:** http://www.hrblock.com. **Description:** Primarily engaged in consumer tax preparation, operating more than 9,500 United States offices and preparing more than 10 million tax returns each year. H&R Block has established offices in over 750 Sears stores in both the United States and Canada. The company is also engaged in a number of other tax-related activities including group tax programs, executive tax service, tax training schools, and real estate tax awareness seminars. **Corporate headquarters**

location: Kansas City MO. **Listed on:** New York Stock Exchange. **Number of employees nationwide:** 80,000.

KPMG
200 Crescent Court, Suite 300, Dallas TX 75201. 214/754-2000. **Contact:** Personnel Department. **World Wide Web address:** http://www.kpmg.com. **Description:** Delivers a wide range of value-added assurance, tax, and consulting services. **Corporate headquarters location:** Montvale NJ. **Parent company:** KPMG International is a leader among professional service firms engaged in capturing, managing, assessing, and delivering information to create knowledge that will help its clients maximize shareholder value. KPMG International has more than 85,000 employees worldwide.

MERCER MANAGEMENT CONSULTING
3500 Chase Tower, 2200 Ross Avenue, Suite 3500, Dallas TX 75201. 214/758-1880. **Contact:** Human Resources. **World Wide Web address:** http://www.mercermc.com. **Description:** One of the world's largest corporate strategy firms. Mercer Management Consulting helps companies achieve optimum success by helping in the development and implementation of customer-focused business designs. **Corporate headquarters location:** New York NY.

PRICEWATERHOUSECOOPERS
2001 Ross Avenue, Suite 1800, Dallas TX 75201-2997. 214/999-1400. **Contact:** Kelly Shipley, Human Resources Coordinator. **World Wide Web address:** http://www.pricewaterhousecoopers.com. **Description:** One of the largest certified public accounting firms in the world. **Corporate headquarters location:** New York NY. **Other U.S. locations:** Nationwide.

Note: Because addresses and telephone numbers of smaller companies can change rapidly, we recommend you call each company to verify the information below before inquiring about job opportunities. Mass mailings are not recommended.

Additional small employers:

ACCOUNTING, AUDITING, AND BOOKKEEPING SERVICES

CBS Employer Services Inc.
1215 Country Club Ln, Ste 100, Fort Worth TX 76112. 817/457-8877.

Choicepoint Inc.
101 W Renner Rd, Ste 300, Richardson TX 75082-2002. 972/234-7200.

Fritz Companies Inc.
PO Box 610008, Dallas TX 75261-0008. 972/304-6606.

Lane Gorman Trubitt LLP
2626 Howell Street, Floor 7, Dallas TX 75204-4064. 214/871-7500.

PricewaterhouseCoopers
125 John Carpenter Freeway, Irving TX 75062-2324. 972/969-5881.

PricewaterhouseCoopers
301 Commerce St, Ste 1900, Fort Worth TX 76102-4119. 817/877-2203.

Viastar Services Corp.
1349 Empire Central Drive, Dallas TX 75247-4066. 214/525-6600.

BUSINESS CONSULTING SERVICES

Action Systems Holdings Inc.
13155 Noel Rd, Ste 1700, Dallas TX 75240-5057. 972/385-0680.

Aegis Communication Group
PO Box 141863, Irving TX 75014-1863. 561/398-2018.

Ajilon Services Inc.
3625 N Hall St, Ste 800, Dallas TX 75219-5119. 972/263-8450.

BPI Corporation
2000 E Lamar Blvd, Ste 730, Arlington TX 76006-7341. 817/226-5600.

Brightstar Information Technology
1950 N Stemmons Fwy, Dallas TX 75207-3107. 214/744-4004.

Brightstar Information Technology
2515 McKinney Ave, Dallas TX 75201-1978. 214/922-9030.

CBI
2121 San Jacinto St, Dallas TX 75201-2739. 214/871-8717.

Channel Solutions Group
6051 State Highway 161, Irving TX 75038-2212. 972/870-4800.

Contract Consultants Inc.
505 Bedford Rd, Ste E, Bedford TX 76022-6542. 817/268-5600.

CPRC
500 N Central Expy, Plano TX 75074-6772. 972/424-6996.

HCL Technologies America Inc.
1700 Alma Dr, Plano TX 75075-6937. 972/509-9000.

ICS
4006 Belt Line Rd, Ste 115, Addison TX 75001-4388. 972/980-7777.

Labat-Anderson Inc.
4141 N St. Augustine, Mesquite TX 75149. 214/489-4001.

Lavinski Allan & Associates
10670 N Central Expy, Dallas TX 75231-2111. 214/739-1553.

Legacy Services LLC
2000 N Central Expy, Plano TX 75074-8801. 972/398-8000.

M/A/R/C Inc.
1700 Wilshire St, Denton TX 76201-6572. 940/566-6668.

McKinsey & Company Inc.
2200 Ross Ave, Ste 5200, Dallas TX 75201-2794. 214/665-1200.

Accounting and Management Consulting/55

Nexcare
1220 Senlac Dr, Carrollton TX 75006-7019. 972/446-4800.

Novation LLC
220 Las Colinas Blvd E, Irving TX 75039-5500. 972/581-5000.

Origin Technology In Business
5000 S Bowen Rd, Arlington TX 76017-2616. 817/264-8200.

Pace American of Texas
PO Box 317, McGregor TX 76657-0317. 254/840-4323.

Paladin Consulting Inc.
8131 LBJ Fwy, Ste 210, Dallas TX 75251-1352. 972/783-1995.

Priority Fulfillment Services
500 N Central Expy, Plano TX 75074-6772. 972/881-4700.

Regency Communications Inc.
3301 Airport Fwy, Ste 300, Bedford TX 76021-6035. 817/283-9292.

Staubach Company-West Inc.
15610 Dallas Pkwy, StE 400, Dallas TX 75248-3304. 972/385-0500.

Telecom Technologies Inc.
1701 N Collins Blvd, Richardson TX 75080-3564. 972/918-0202.

Test Masters
308 NW 2nd St, Ste 600, Grand Prairie TX 75050-5684. 972/264-3312.

Total Dealers Solutions
165 W Main St, Lewisville TX 75057-3973. 972/219-0748.

Towers Perrin Inc.
12377 Merit Dr, St 1200, Dallas TX 75251-2248. 972/701-2600.

Tucker McDowell & Co. Inc.
5228 Village Creek Dr, Plano TX 75093-5066. 972/407-9921.

VHA Inc.
PO Box 140909, Irving TX 75014-0909. 972/830-0050.

Watson Wyatt Worldwide
PO Box 58, Dallas TX 75221-0058. 214/978-3400.

West Hudson
5420 LBJ Fwy, Ste 1600, Dallas TX 75240-6222. 972/982-8700.

Wolverine Management Co.
15601 Dallas Pkwy, Ste 400, Addison TX 75001-3367. 972/960-4212.

For more information on career opportunities in accounting and management consulting:

Associations

AMERICAN ACCOUNTING ASSOCIATION
5717 Bessie Drive, Sarasota FL 34233. 941/921-7747. World Wide Web address: http://www.aaa-edu.org. An academically-oriented accounting association that offers two quarterly journals, a semi-annual journal, a newsletter, and a wide variety of continuing education programs.

AMERICAN INSTITUTE OF CERTIFIED PUBLIC ACCOUNTANTS (AICPA)
1211 Avenue of the Americas, New York NY 10036. 212/596-6200. World Wide Web address: http://www.aicpa.org. A national professional organization for all CPAs. AICPA offers a comprehensive career package to students.

AMERICAN MANAGEMENT ASSOCIATION INTERNATIONAL
1601 Broadway, 8th Floor, New York NY 10019. 212/586-8100. Fax: 212/903-8168. World Wide Web address: http://www.amanet.org. Provides a variety of publications, training videos, and courses, as well as an Information Resource Center, which provides management information, and a library service.

ASSOCIATION OF GOVERNMENT ACCOUNTANTS
2208 Mount Vernon Avenue, Alexandria VA 22301. 703/684-6931. World Wide Web address: http://www.agacgfm.org. Serves financial management professionals and offers continuing education workshops.

ASSOCIATION OF MANAGEMENT CONSULTING FIRMS
380 Lexington Avenue, Suite 1700, New York NY 10168. 212/551-7887. World Wide Web address: http://www.amcf.org.

THE INSTITUTE OF INTERNAL AUDITORS
249 Maitland Avenue, Altamonte Springs FL 32701. 407/830-7600. World Wide Web address: http://www.theiia.org. Publishes magazines and newsletters. The institute provides information on current issues, a network of more than 50,000 members in 100 countries, professional development and research services, and also offers continuing education seminars.

INSTITUTE OF MANAGEMENT ACCOUNTANTS
10 Paragon Drive, Montvale NJ 07645. 201/573-9000. World Wide Web address: http://www.imanet.org. Offers a Certified Management Accountant Program, periodicals, seminars, educational programs, a research program, a financial management network, and networking services. The association has about 80,000 members and 300 local chapters.

INSTITUTE OF MANAGEMENT CONSULTANTS
1200 19th Street NW, Suite 200, Washington DC 20036. Toll-free phone: 800/221-2557. World Wide Web address: http://www.imcusa.org. Offers certification programs, professional development, and a directory of members.

NATIONAL ASSOCIATION OF TAX PRACTITIONERS
720 Association Drive, Appleton WI 54914-1483. 920/749-1040. World Wide Web address: http://www.natptax.com. Offers seminars, research, newsletters, preparer worksheets, state chapters, insurance, and other tax-related services.

NATIONAL SOCIETY OF ACCOUNTANTS
1010 North Fairfax Street, Alexandria VA 22314. 703/549-6400. World Wide Web address: http://www.nsacct.org. Offers professional development services, government representation, a variety of publications, practice aids, low-cost group insurance, annual seminars, and updates for members on new tax laws.

Career Fairs

CAREER FAIRS INTERNATIONAL
World Wide Web address: http://www.career-fairs.com. Organizes career fairs in the fields of accounting, banking, finance, and insurance.

Magazines

CPA JOURNAL
The New York State Society, 530 Fifth Avenue, 5th Floor, New York NY 10036. 212/719-8300. World Wide Web address: http://www.nysscpa.org. Published monthly.

CPA LETTER
American Institute of Certified Public Accountants, 1211 Avenue of the Americas, New York NY 10036. 212/596-6200. World Wide Web address: http://www.aicpa.org/pubs/cpaltr/index.htm

JOURNAL OF ACCOUNTANCY
American Institute of Certified Public Accountants, 1211 Avenue of the Americas, New York NY 10036. 212/596-6200. World Wide Web address: http://www.aicpa.org.

STRATEGIC FINANCE
Institute of Management Accountants, 10 Paragon Drive, Montvale NJ 07645. 201/573-9000. World Wide Web address: http://www.strategicfinancemag.com.

Online Services

ACCOUNTANTS FORUM
Go: Aicpa. A CompuServe forum sponsored by the American Institute of Certified Public Accountants.

ACCOUNTING & FINANCE JOBS
World Wide Web address: http://www.accountingjobs.com. Provides national and international job listings and offers links to related sites.

ACCOUNTING NET
World Wide Web address: http://www.accountingnet.com. Provides national and international job listings and offers links to related sites.

ACCOUNTING.COM
World Wide Web address: http://www.accounting.com. Offers job listings, discussion groups, and resume writing tips.

FINANCIAL, ACCOUNTING, AND INSURANCE JOBS PAGE
World Wide Web address: http://www.nationjob.com/financial. This Website provides a list of financial, accounting, and insurance job openings.

JOBS IN ACCOUNTING
World Wide Web address: http://www.cob.ohio-state.edu/dept/fin/jobs/account.htm#Link7. Provides information on the accounting profession, including salaries, trends, and resources.

ADVERTISING, MARKETING, AND PUBLIC RELATIONS

You can expect to find the following types of companies in this chapter:
Advertising Agencies • Direct Mail Marketers •
Market Research Firms • Public Relations Firms

Some helpful information: The average salary for an entry-level assistant position in an advertising/marketing agency is $25,000 - $30,000 annually, and these coveted positions are very difficult to attain. Senior agents and supervisors often earn $50,000 or more, while partners and executives frequently exceed $100,000 per year in this highly competitive field. Entry-level positions in public relations firms usually earn under $25,000 per year, with higher salaries in a corporate setting. Experienced representatives earn an average of $50,000 (higher figures are usually reserved for those with 10 or more years of experience).

ACKERMAN McQUEEN, INC.
545 East John Carpenter Freeway, Suite 600, Irving TX 75062-3932. 972/444-9000. **Fax:** 972/869-4363. **Contact:** Shalla R. Bennett, Traffic Director. **World Wide Web address:** http://www.am.com. **Description:** A full-service advertising agency. Founded in 1939. **NOTE:** Entry-level positions are offered. **Common positions include:** Administrative Assistant; Advertising Executive; Computer Support Technician; Desktop Publishing Specialist; Graphic Designer; Technical Writer/Editor. **Educational backgrounds include:** Advertising; Art/Design; Business Administration; Communications; Journalism; Liberal Arts; Marketing; Microsoft Word; Public Relations; QuarkXPress; Spreadsheets. **Benefits:** 401(k); Casual Dress - Fridays; Dental Insurance; Life Insurance; Medical Insurance; Sick Days (1 - 5). **Special programs:** Internships. **Internship information:** Unpaid internships are offered every fall, spring, and summer for college credit. **Corporate headquarters location:** Oklahoma City OK. **Other U.S. locations:** Colorado Springs CO; Washington DC; Tulsa OK.

AEGIS COMMUNICATIONS GROUP
7880 Bent Branch Drive, Suite 150, Irving TX 75063. 972/830-1800. **Fax:** 972/830-1801. **Contact:** Human Resources. **World Wide Web address:** http://www.aegiscomgroup.com. **Description:** A teleservices provider that offers integrated marketing services to large corporations. **Corporate headquarters location:** This Location. **Listed on:** NASDAQ. **Stock exchange symbol:** AGIS.

BERRY BROWN ADVERTISING
3100 McKinnon Street, Suite 1100, Dallas TX 75201-1046. 214/871-1001. **Fax:** 214/871-1137. **Contact:** Ms. Virdie Horton, Personnel Manager. **Description:** An advertising agency. **Common positions include:** Accountant/Auditor; Administrative Manager; Clerical Supervisor; Commercial Artist; Computer Operator; Marketing Manager; Media Specialist; Payroll Clerk; Receptionist; Secretary; Typist/Word Processor. **Educational backgrounds include:** Accounting; Art/Design; Business Administration; Communications; Liberal Arts; Marketing. **Benefits:** Dental Insurance; Disability Coverage; Life Insurance; Medical Insurance; Pension Plan; Profit Sharing; Savings Plan; Tuition Assistance. **Special programs:** Internships. **Corporate headquarters location:** This Location. **Number of employees at this location:** 55.

BURK ADVERTISING & MARKETING, INC.
2906 McKinney Avenue, Suite 100, Dallas TX 75204. 214/953-0494. **Contact:** Personnel. **World Wide Web address:** http://www.wambam.com. **Description:** An advertising and marketing agency offering a variety of print and multimedia services.

DDB NEEDHAM
3500 Maple Avenue, Suite 1700, Dallas TX 75219. 214/599-5500. **Contact:** Human Resources Department. **World Wide Web address:** http://www.ddbn.com. **Description:** A full-service, international advertising agency. **Corporate headquarters location:** New York NY.

DECISION ANALYST, INC.
604 Avenue H East, Arlington TX 76011. 817/640-6166. **Fax:** 817/640-6567. **Contact:** Human Resources. **World Wide Web address:** http://www.decisionanalyst.com. **Description:** A market

research and consulting firm offering product testing, tracking research, and Internet surveys. **Corporate headquarters location:** This Location.

THE DOZIER COMPANY
P.O. Box 565125, Dallas TX 75356. 214/744-2800. **Fax:** 214/744-1240. **Contact:** Human Resources. **Description:** A full-service advertising and public relations agency. Founded in 1987. **Common positions include:** Administrative Assistant; Advertising Clerk; Advertising Executive; Editor; Editorial Assistant; Graphic Artist; Graphic Designer; Marketing Manager; Marketing Specialist; Media Planner; Public Relations Specialist; Typist/Word Processor; Web Advertising Specialist. **Educational backgrounds include:** Art/Design; Marketing; Microsoft Word; Public Relations; Publishing; QuarkXPress. **Benefits:** Life Insurance; Medical Insurance. **Special programs:** Internships. **Corporate headquarters location:** This Location. **Number of employees at this location:** 10.

BERNARD HODES ADVERTISING
7502 Greenville Avenue, Suite 630, Dallas TX 75231. 214/361-9986. **Contact:** Branch Manager. **World Wide Web address:** http://www.hodes.com. **Description:** An advertising agency specializing in recruitment and employee communications. **Corporate headquarters location:** New York NY. **Other U.S. locations:** Phoenix AZ; Chicago IL; Cambridge MA. **Parent company:** Omnicom.

THE M/A/R/C GROUP
7850 North Beltline Road, Irving TX 75063. 972/506-3400. **Contact:** Human Resources. **World Wide Web address:** http://www.marcgroup.com. **Description:** The M/A/R/C Group is a holding company for M/A/R/C Research and Targetbase. M/A/R/C Research (also at this location) specializes in providing strategic customer research for marketing purposes. Targetbase (also at this location) is a customer relationship management firm. **Other U.S. locations:** Los Angeles CA; Atlanta GA; Chicago IL; Greensboro NC.

PROFORMA WATSONRISE BUSINESS SYSTEMS
501 Duncan Perry Road, Arlington TX 76011-5414. 817/640-1184. **Contact:** Human Resources. **Description:** An advertising agency specializing in printing and promotional materials.

PUBLICIS
14185 North Dallas Parkway, Dallas TX 75240. 972/628-7500. **Contact:** Personnel Director. **Description:** An advertising agency. Founded in 1952. **NOTE:** In June 2000, Publicis and Saatchi & Saatchi announced that they would merge to form one of the world's largest advertising agencies. The merger is expected to be complete by late 2000. Please call this location for more information. **Number of employees nationwide:** 300.

THE RICHARDS GROUP, INC.
8750 North Central Expressway, Suite 1200, Dallas TX 75231-6437. 214/891-5700. **Contact:** Human Resources. **World Wide Web address:** http://www.richards.com. **Description:** A full-service advertising agency offering direct marketing, promotional marketing, naming, graphic design, and interactive communications services. **Listed on:** Privately held.

WITHERSPOON ADVERTISING & PUBLIC RELATIONS
1000 West Weatherford, Fort Worth TX 76102. 817/335-1373. **Contact:** Human Resources. **World Wide Web address:** http://www.witherspoon.com. **Description:** A national advertising and public relations agency. **Common positions include:** Graphic Artist. **Educational backgrounds include:** Art/Design; Business Administration; Marketing. **Benefits:** Life Insurance; Medical Insurance. **Corporate headquarters location:** This Location.

Note: Because addresses and telephone numbers of smaller companies can change rapidly, we recommend you call each company to verify the information below before inquiring about job opportunities. Mass mailings are not recommended.

Additional small employers:

DIRECT MAIL ADVERTISING SERVICES

Advo Inc.
10155 Technolog Blvd E, Dallas TX 75220-4324. 214/630-7404.

Epsilon
2410 Gateway Dr, Irving TX 75063-2727. 972/582-9600.

Harte-Hanks
905 W North Carrier Pkwy, Grand Prairie TX 75050-1102. 972/660-4242.

Lee Marketing Services
PO Box 227077, Dallas TX 75222-7077. 972/293-5000.

National Presort Services Inc.
921 W Commerce St, Dallas TX
75208-1729. 214/745-8870.

MISC. ADVERTISING SVCS.

Levenson Public Relations
PO Box 219051, Dallas TX
75221-9051. 214/880-0200.

LMS/Marc Advertising LP
2501 Cedar Springs Road,
Dallas TX 75201-1472.
214/979-5000.

Sports Promotion Network
PO Box 200548, Arlington TX
76006-0548. 972/606-1930.

Temerlin McClain Inc.
PO Box 619200, Dallas TX
75261-9200. 972/556-1100.

PUBLIC RELATIONS SERVICES

TLP Inc.
200 Crescent Cort, Dallas TX
75201. 214/969-9000.

For more information on career opportunities in advertising, marketing, and public relations:

Associations

ADVERTISING RESEARCH FOUNDATION
641 Lexington Avenue, 11th Floor, New York NY 10022. 212/751-5656. Fax: 212/319-5265. E-mail address: email@arfsite.org. World Wide Web address: http://www.arfsite.org. A nonprofit organization comprised of advertising, marketing, and media research companies. For institutions only.

AMERICAN ASSOCIATION OF ADVERTISING AGENCIES
405 Lexington Avenue, 18th Floor, New York NY 10174. 212/682-2500. World Wide Web address: http://www.aaaa.org. Offers educational and enrichment benefits such as publications, videos, and conferences.

AMERICAN MARKETING ASSOCIATION
311 South Wacker Drive, Suite 5800, Chicago IL 60606. 312/542-9000. Toll-free phone: 800/AMA-1150. World Wide Web address: http://www.ama.org. An association with nearly 45,000 members worldwide. Offers a reference center, 25 annual conferences, and eight publications for marketing professionals and students.

THE DIRECT MARKETING ASSOCIATION
1120 Avenue of the Americas, New York NY 10036-6700. 212/768-7277. World Wide Web address: http://www.the-dma.org. This association offers monthly newsletters, seminars, and an annual telephone marketing conference.

MARKETING RESEARCH ASSOCIATION
1344 Silas Deane Highway, Suite 306, Rocky Hill CT 06067. 860/257-4008. World Wide Web address: http://www.mra-net.org. Publishes several magazines and newsletters.

PUBLIC RELATIONS SOCIETY OF AMERICA
33 Irving Place, New York NY 10003-2376. 212/995-2230. World Wide Web address: http://www.prsa.org. Publishes books and magazines for public relations professionals.

Directories

AAAA ROSTER AND ORGANIZATION
American Association of Advertising Agencies, 405 Lexington Avenue, 18th Floor, New York NY 10147. 212/682-2500.

O'DWYER'S DIRECTORY OF PUBLIC RELATIONS FIRMS
J.R. O'Dwyer Company, 271 Madison Avenue, Room 600, New York NY 10016. 212/679-2471.

PUBLIC RELATIONS CONSULTANTS DIRECTORY
American Business Directories, Division of American Business Lists, 5711 South 86th Circle, Omaha NE 68137. 402/593-4500.

STANDARD DIRECTORY OF ADVERTISING AGENCIES
Reed Elsevier New Providence, 121 Chanlon Road, New Providence NJ 07974. 908/665-6775. Toll-free phone: 800/521-8110. World Wide Web address: http://www.reedref.com.

Magazines

ADVERTISING AGE
Crain Communications Inc., 220 East 42nd Street, New York NY 10017-5846. 212/210-0100. World Wide Web address: http://www.adage.com.

ADWEEK
BPI Communications, 1515 Broadway, 12th Floor, New York NY 10036-8986. 212/764-7300. World Wide Web address: http://www.adweek.com.

BUSINESS MARKETING
Crain Communications Inc., 220 East 42nd Street, New York NY 10017-5846. 212/210-0100. World Wide Web address: http://www.businessmarketing.com.

JOURNAL OF MARKETING
American Marketing Association, 250 South Wacker Drive, Suite 200, Chicago IL 60606. 312/648-0536.

THE MARKETING NEWS
American Marketing Association, 250 South Wacker Drive, Suite 200, Chicago IL 60606. 312/648-0536. A biweekly magazine offering new ideas and developments in marketing.

PR REPORTER
PR Publishing Company, P.O. Box 600, Exeter NH 03833. 603/778-0514. World Wide Web address: http://www.prpublishing.com.

PUBLIC RELATIONS NEWS
Phillips Business Information, Inc., 1201 Seven Locks Road, Suite 300, Potomac MD 20854. 301/424-3338. Fax: 301/309-3847. World Wide Web address: http://www.phillips.com.

Newsletters

PUBLIC RELATIONS CAREER OPPORTUNITIES
101 South Whiting Street, Suite 305, Alexandria VA 22304. 703/823-4094. Fax: 703/823-5352. World Wide Web address: http://www.careeropps.com/prcareer1. A newsletter listing public relations, public affairs, special events, and investor positions nationwide compensating above $35,000 annually. Available on a subscription basis, published 24 times a year. Produced by the Public Relations Society of America, which also publishes

other newsletters including *CEO Job Opportunities Update* and *ASAE Career Opportunities* (for the American Society of Association Executives).

Online Services

ADVERTISING & MEDIA JOBS PAGE
World Wide Web address: http://www.nationjob.com/media. This Website offers advertising and media job openings that can be searched by a variety of criteria including location, type of position, and salary. This site also offers a service that will perform the search for you.

DIRECT MARKETING WORLD'S JOB CENTER
World Wide Web address: http://www.dmworld.com. Posts professional job openings for the direct marketing industry. This site also provides a career reference library, a list of direct marketing professionals, and a list of events within the industry.

MARKETING CLASSIFIEDS ON THE INTERNET
World Wide Web address: http://www.marketingjobs.com. Offers job listings by state, resume posting, discussions with other marketing professionals, and links to other career sites and company home pages.

For information about the JobBank List Service visit www.adamsjobbank.com

AEROSPACE

You can expect to find the following types of companies in this chapter:
Aerospace Products and Services • Aircraft Equipment and Parts

Some helpful information: *Salaries in parts manufacturing are normally concurrent with other manufacturing jobs (running approximately $21,000 - $35,000 per year), while aeronautical and astronautical engineers with a reasonable amount of experience (5 - 10 years) can earn over $50,000 annually.*

ASSOCIATED AIRCRAFT SUPPLY CO., INC.
6020 Cedar Springs Road, Dallas TX 75235. 214/331-4381. **Fax:** 214/339-9840. **Contact:** Tommy DeRossett, Personnel. **World Wide Web address:** http://www.associated-aircraft.com. **Description:** A distributor of aircraft parts and machinery. Products include switches, relays, and circuit-breakers. **Corporate headquarters location:** This location.

BELL HELICOPTER TEXTRON
P.O. Box 482, Fort Worth TX 76101. 817/280-2011. **Contact:** Employment Department. **World Wide Web address:** http://www.bellhelicopter.textron.com. **Description:** Bell Helicopter Textron manufactures a variety of commercial and civilian helicopters and also conducts extensive research and development activities. **Corporate headquarters location:** This Location. **Parent company:** Textron Inc.

BFGOODRICH AEROSPACE
4000 South Highway 157, Euless TX 76040-7012. 817/283-4471. **Contact:** Human Resources. **World Wide Web address:** http://www.bfg-aerospace.com. **Description:** Manufactures aircraft landing gear. The company's primary customers are major airframe manufacturers and the U.S. Department of Defense. **Common positions include:** Accountant; Blue-Collar Worker Supervisor; Buyer; Computer Programmer; Department Manager; General Manager; Human Resources Manager; Machinist; Mechanical Engineer; Metallurgical Engineer; Operations/Production Manager; Quality Control Supervisor. **Educational backgrounds include:** Accounting; Business Administration; Computer Science; Engineering; Finance; Marketing. **Benefits:** Dental Insurance; Disability Coverage; Life Insurance; Medical Insurance; Pension Plan; Savings Plan; Tuition Assistance. **Corporate headquarters location:** Charlotte NC. **Operations at this facility include:** Administration; Divisional Headquarters; Manufacturing; Research and Development. **Listed on:** New York Stock Exchange.

BOEING-IRVING
P.O. Box 152707, Irving TX 75015-2707. 972/659-2600. **Contact:** Human Resources Department. **World Wide Web address:** http://www.boeing.com. **Description:** Manufactures electrical components for aircraft. **Corporate headquarters location:** Seattle WA. **Parent company:** The Boeing Company. **Number of employees at this location:** 1,150.

W. PAT CROW FORGINGS
200 Luxton Street, Fort Worth TX 76104. 817/536-2861. **Contact:** Human Resources. **World Wide Web address:** http://www.associated-aircraft.com. **Description:** Produces high-quality, high-tolerance forgings for the aerospace and various other industries. **Corporate headquarters location:** This Location.

DALFORT AVIATION
7701 Lemmon Avenue, P.O. Box 7556, Dallas TX 75209. 214/358-6019. **Contact:** Human Resources. **Description:** Repairs and modifies commercial planes. **Common positions include:** Accountant; Administrator; Aerospace Engineer; Blue-Collar Worker Supervisor; Civil Engineer; Computer Programmer; Credit Manager; Draftsperson; Financial Analyst; General Manager; Human Resources Manager; Industrial Engineer; Management Trainee; Marketing Specialist; Operations; Public Relations Specialist; Purchasing Agent; Quality Control Supervisor. **Benefits:** 401(k); Dental Insurance; Disability Coverage; Employee Discounts; Life Insurance; Medical Insurance; Savings Plan. **Number of employees at this location:** 1,200.

FOXTRONICS INC.
3448 West Mockingbird Lane, Dallas TX 75235. 214/358-2490. **Contact:** Human Resources. **World Wide Web address:** http://www.foxtronics.com. **Description:** Engaged in the sale and service of aircraft batteries.

GULFSTREAM AEROSPACE CORPORATION
P.O. Box 7145, Dallas TX 75209. 214/902-7500. **Fax:** 214/630-9107. **Contact:** Eric Pate, Personnel Director. **World Wide Web address:** http://www.gulfstream.com. **Description:** Refurbishes and performs completion work on corporate aircraft. **Parent company:** General Dynamics.

HELI-DYNE SYSTEMS, INC.
P.O. Box 966, Hurst TX 76053. 817/282-9804. **Contact:** Human Resources. **World Wide Web address:** http://www.heli-dyne.com. **Description:** A helicopter completion company with a specialty in special mission, air medical, executive transport, and multi-mission aircraft. The company is an affiliate of Corporate Jets, Inc.

INTERNATIONAL AVIATION COMPOSITES
P.O. Box 376, Haslet TX 76052-0376. 817/491-6755. **Contact:** Human Resources. **Description:** Repairs main and tail rotor blades on helicopters. **Common positions include:** Accountant/Auditor; Aerospace Engineer; Aircraft Mechanic/Engine Specialist; General Manager; Mechanical Engineer; Typist/Word Processor. **Educational backgrounds include:** Engineering. **Benefits:** Medical Insurance. **Special programs:** Apprenticeships. **Corporate headquarters location:** This Location. **Listed on:** Privately held. **Annual sales/revenues:** Less than $5 million. **Number of employees at this location:** 10.

LOCKHEED MARTIN TACTICAL AIRCRAFT SYSTEMS
P.O. Box 748, Fort Worth TX 76101-0748. 817/777-2000. **Recorded jobline:** 817/777-1000. **Contact:** Human Resources. **World Wide Web address:** http://www.lmtas.com. **Description:** Engaged in the development and production of tactical aircraft. **Common positions include:** Aerospace Engineer; Electrical/Electronics Engineer; Materials Engineer; Mechanical Engineer; Software Engineer; Systems Analyst. **Benefits:** 401(k); Dental Insurance; Disability Coverage; Life Insurance; Medical Insurance; Pension Plan; Savings Plan. **Other U.S. locations:** Nationwide. **Parent company:** Lockheed Martin Corporation operates in five major areas: Space Systems develops space technology systems such as rocket systems, Space Shuttle support technology, and other products; Missile Systems produces fleet ballistic missiles for military applications; Advanced Systems operates as the research and development organization exploring military, commercial, and scientific needs; Information Processing develops comprehensive database systems to process the specific needs of other company divisions; and the Austin Division is responsible for designing and producing military tactical support systems. **Listed on:** New York Stock Exchange. **Number of employees at this location:** 12,000. **Number of employees nationwide:** 180,000.

LOCKHEED MARTIN VOUGHT SYSTEMS
P.O. Box 650003, Mail Stop LHR-PE, Dallas TX 75265-0003. 972/603-1000. **Contact:** Personnel. **World Wide Web address:** http://www.lmco.com. **Description:** Manufactures advanced tactical missiles, rockets, and space systems. **Common positions include:** Accountant/Auditor; Administrator; Aerospace Engineer; Attorney; Buyer; Ceramics Engineer; Computer Programmer; Department Manager; Electrical/Electronics Engineer; Financial Analyst; General Manager; Human Resources Manager; Industrial Engineer; Mechanical Engineer; Metallurgical Engineer; Physicist; Purchasing Agent/Manager; Systems Analyst. **Educational backgrounds include:** Accounting; Business Administration; Computer Science; Engineering; Finance; Marketing; Physics. **Benefits:** Dental Insurance; Disability Coverage; Employee Discounts; Life Insurance; Medical Insurance; Profit Sharing; Tuition Assistance. **Corporate headquarters location:** This Location. **Parent company:** Lockheed Martin Corporation operates in five major areas: Space Systems develops space technology systems such as rocket systems, Space Shuttle support technology, and other products; Missile Systems produces fleet ballistic missiles for military applications; Advanced Systems operates as the research and development organization exploring military, commercial, and scientific needs; Information Processing develops comprehensive database systems to process the specific needs of other company divisions; and the Austin Division is responsible for designing and producing military tactical support systems. **Listed on:** New York Stock Exchange. **Number of employees at this location:** 2,800. **Number of employees nationwide:** 180,000.

LUMINATOR
1200 East Plano Parkway, Plano TX 75074. 972/424-6511. **Contact:** Denise Boyd, Human Resources Manager. **World Wide Web address:** http://www.luminatorusa.com. **Description:** Manufactures aircraft parts, bus products, and rail products. Luminator aircraft products include batteries, lamps, search lights, interiors, and crew stations. Bus products include flip-out signs and voice systems. Rail products include various types of lighting, flip dot sign systems,

electronic maps, voice systems, and air diffusers. **Corporate headquarters location:** This Location. **Parent company:** Mark IV Industries.

MARATHON POWER TECHNOLOGIES COMPANY
P.O. Box 8233, Waco TX 76714-8233. 254/776-0650. **Fax:** 254/776-1309. **Contact:** Jeff Oliver, Personnel Manager. **Description:** Manufactures nickel-cadmium aircraft batteries and electronic assemblies. **Common positions include:** Accountant/Auditor; Blue-Collar Worker Supervisor; Buyer; Chemical Engineer; Chemist; Clinical Lab Technician; Computer Programmer; Draftsperson; Electrical/Electronics Engineer; Electrician; General Manager; Human Resources Manager; Industrial Engineer; Industrial Production Manager; Mechanical Engineer; Purchasing Agent/Manager; Quality Control Supervisor; Services Sales Representative. **Educational backgrounds include:** Accounting; Business Administration; Chemistry; Engineering; Liberal Arts; Marketing. **Benefits:** 401(k); Dental Insurance; Disability Coverage; Life Insurance; Medical Insurance; Tuition Assistance. **Corporate headquarters location:** This Location. **Parent company:** Metapoint Partners. **Number of employees at this location:** 190.

PRATT & WHITNEY
1177 Great Southwest Parkway, Grand Prairie TX 75050. 972/647-7800. **Fax:** 972/647-3024. **Contact:** Human Resources Manager. **World Wide Web address:** http://www.pratt-whitney.com. **Description:** Repairs aircraft engine components, blades, vanes, and casings. **NOTE:** Entry-level positions and second and third shifts are offered. **Common positions include:** Account Manager; Account Representative; Accountant; Administrative Assistant; Administrative Manager; Blue-Collar Worker Supervisor; Budget Analyst; Buyer; Computer Programmer; Controller; Customer Service Representative; Financial Analyst; General Manager; Human Resources Manager; Industrial Engineer; Industrial Production Manager; Manufacturing Engineer; Marketing Manager; Mechanical Engineer; Metallurgical Engineer; MIS Specialist; Network/Systems Administrator; Operations Manager; Production Manager; Project Manager; Purchasing Agent/Manager; Quality Assurance Engineer; Quality Control Supervisor; Sales Manager; Sales Representative. **Educational backgrounds include:** Accounting; Business Administration; Engineering; Finance; Marketing; MBA; Microsoft Office. **Benefits:** 401(k); Casual Dress - Daily; Daycare Assistance; Dental Insurance; Disability Coverage; Employee Discounts; Life Insurance; Medical Insurance; Pension Plan; Profit Sharing; Relocation Assistance; Savings Plan; Tuition Assistance. **Special programs:** Co-ops; Internships. **Number of employees at this location:** 350. **Number of projected hires for 2000 - 2001 at this location:** 200.

PRECISION AVIATION
5240 South Collins Street, Suite 100, Arlington TX 76018. 817/465-0908. **Contact:** Personnel. **Description:** An aircraft maintenance company that works primarily on small passenger planes.

ROCKWELL COLLINS
P.O. Box 833807, Richardson TX 75083-3807. 972/705-3598. **Fax:** 972/705-1124. **Recorded jobline:** 972/705-1870. **Contact:** Human Resources. **E-mail address:** hrresume@collins.rockwell.com. **World Wide Web address:** http://www.collins.rockwell.com. **Description:** Manufactures electronic aviation systems for use in both commercial and military aircraft. **NOTE:** Entry-level positions are offered. Please call the jobline for a listing of open positions. **Common positions include:** Administrative Assistant; Electrical/Electronics Engineer; Mechanical Engineer; Secretary; Software Engineer. **Educational backgrounds include:** Engineering. **Benefits:** 401(k); Casual Dress - Daily; Dental Insurance; Disability Coverage; Employee Discounts; Flexible Schedule; Life Insurance; Medical Insurance; Pension Plan; Profit Sharing; Savings Plan; Tuition Assistance. **Special programs:** Co-ops; Internships; Summer Jobs. **Corporate headquarters location:** Costa Mesa CA. **Other U.S. locations:** Pomona CA; Melbourne FL; Cedar Rapids IA. **International locations:** Worldwide. **Listed on:** New York Stock Exchange. **Stock exchange symbol:** ROK. **Annual sales/revenues:** More than $100 million. **Number of employees at this location:** 750.

SKYLINE INDUSTRIES, INC.
P.O. Box 821, Fort Worth TX 76101. 817/551-1967. **Contact:** Personnel Department. **World Wide Web address:** http://www.skyline-usa.com. **Description:** A manufacturer of aircraft parts including armored pilot seats, floor armor, seat covers, ground handling equipment, and aerospace fasteners. **Corporate headquarters location:** This Location.

SPECTRO INC.
P.O. Box 1227, Arlington TX 76004-1227. 817/861-3357. **Contact:** Rex Havis, Owner. **Description:** Conducts oil and wear-wheel oil analysis on aircraft.

Note: Because addresses and telephone numbers of smaller companies can change rapidly, we recommend you call each company to verify the information below before inquiring about job opportunities. Mass mailings are not recommended.

Additional small employers:

AIRCRAFT

American Eurocopter Corp.
2701 Forum Dr, Grand Prairie TX 75052-7099. 972/641-0000.

Beal Aerospace Inc.
8000 Dallas Pkwy, Frisco TX 75034-8534. 972/668-2000.

Galaxy Aerospace Company LP
1 Galaxy Way, Fort Worth TX 76177. 817/837-3700.

Leading Edge Aircraft Detailing
10801 Baker St, Amarillo TX 79111-1235. 806/335-2616.

Premier Aviation Inc.
2621 Aviation Pkwy, Grand Prairie TX 75052-7608. 972/988-6181.

AIRCRAFT EQUIPMENT AND PARTS

Aerobotics Industries Inc.
1400 Westpark Way, Euless TX 76040-6734. 817/868-1707.

Aerospace Optics Inc.
3201 Sandy Ln, Fort Worth TX 76112-7203. 817/451-1141.

Bergman Forged Products
PO Box 461148, Garland TX 75046-1148. 972/276-5131.

Bombardier Aerospace
14651 Dallas Pkwy, Fl 6, Dallas TX 75240-7476. 972/720-2800.

Luminator Aircraft Parts
PO Box 278, Plano TX 75074. 972/881-5483.

Mayday Manufacturing Co. Inc.
1500 Interstate 35 W, Denton TX 76207-2402. 940/898-8301.

Nordam-Texas
5101 Blue Mound Rd, Fort Worth TX 76106-1937. 817/625-4106.

Pratt & Whitney
PO Box 2425, Wichita Falls TX 76307-2425. 940/855-8401.

Sikorsky Aircraft Corporation
PO Box 1025, Killeen TX 76540-1025. 254/532-8355.

Triangle Machine & Manufacturing Co.
PO Box 9, Hurst TX 76053-0009. 817/267-1641.

For more information on career opportunities in aerospace:

Associations

AHS INTERNATIONAL – THE VERTICAL FLIGHT SOCIETY
217 North Washington Street, Alexandria VA 22314. 703/684-6777. Fax: 703/739-9279. E-mail address: ahs703@aol.com. World Wide Web address: http://www.vtol.org. Promotes the advancement of vertical flight technology.

AMERICAN ASTRONAUTICAL SOCIETY
6352 Rolling Mill Place, Suite 102, Springfield VA 22152-2354. 703/866-0020. Fax: 703/866-3526. E-mail address: info@astronautical.org. World Wide Web address: http://www.astronautical.org. Offers conferences for members and scholarships for students.

AMERICAN INSTITUTE OF AERONAUTICS AND ASTRONAUTICS, INC.
1801 Alexander Bell Drive, Suite 500, Reston VA 20191-4344. 703/264-7500. Toll-free phone: 800/NEW-AIAA. Fax: 703/264-7551. World Wide Web address: http://www.aiaa.org. Membership required. Publishes 10 journals and books. The Website provides information on employment opportunities, resume services, aerospace news, career placement services, continuing education resources, and a mentor program.

NATIONAL AERONAUTIC ASSOCIATION
1815 North Fort Myer Drive, Suite 700, Arlington VA 22209. 703/527-0226. World Wide Web address: http://www.naa.ycg.org. Publishes a magazine. Membership required.

PROFESSIONAL AVIATION MAINTENANCE ASSOCIATION
1707 H Street NW, Suite 700, Washington DC 20006-3915.202/730-0260. World Wide Web address: http://www.pama.org. Conducts local and national seminars; publishes industry news journals; and addresses government issues. Members have access to the Worldwide Membership Directory.

Newsletters

AIR JOBS DIGEST
World Air Data, Department 700, P.O. Box 42360, Washington DC 20015. This monthly resource provides current job openings in aerospace, space, and aviation industries. Subscription rates: $96.00 annually, $69.00 for six months, and $49.00 for three months.

Online Services

AVIATION EMPLOYMENT.COM
World Wide Web address: http://www.aviationemployment.com. Offers employer profiles and job listings.

SPACE JOBS
World Wide Web address: http://www.spacejobs.com. Provides national and international job listings in the aerospace field. Includes an e-mail service that notified jobseekers of opportunities that match their criteria.

For information about the JobBank List Service visit www.adamsjobbank.com

APPAREL, FASHION, AND TEXTILES

You can expect to find the following types of companies in this chapter:
Broadwoven Fabric Mills • Knitting Mills • Curtains and Draperies • Footwear • Nonwoven Fabrics • Textile Goods and Finishing • Yarn and Thread Mills

Some helpful information: *The average salary for machine operators and other apparel and textile production workers is normally under $25,000 per year but can increase based on experience, particularly for workers who attain supervisory positions. Upholsterers earn, on average, $18,000 - $22,000 per year.*

BONHAM MANUFACTURING
2525 North Center Street, Bonham TX 75418. 903/583-9595. **Contact:** Human Resources. **Description:** Manufactures men's Western apparel.

L.D. BRINKMAN/HOLLYTEX
1655 Waters Ridge Drive, Louisville TX 75057. 972/353-3500. **Contact:** Human Resources. **Description:** A wholesale distributor of carpet and related flooring products.

COLESCE COUTURE INTERNATIONAL INC.
9004 Ambassador Row, Dallas TX 75247. 214/631-4860. **Contact:** Human Resources. **World Wide Web address:** http://www.colesce.com. **Description:** One of the world's oldest and largest manufacturers of women's lingerie and loungewear.

DE LONG SPORTSWEAR
P.O. Box 299, Crowell TX 79227. 940/684-1561. **Contact:** Human Resources. **Description:** Manufactures baseball caps.

EARL'S APPAREL INC.
P.O. Box 939, Crockett TX 75835. 936/544-5521. **Contact:** Human Resources. **Description:** Manufactures jeans for men and women.

HAGGAR CLOTHING COMPANY
6113 Lemmon Avenue, Dallas TX 75209. 214/956-4235. **Fax:** 214/956-4419. **Contact:** Human Resources. **World Wide Web address:** http://www.haggar.com. **Description:** A leading designer, manufacturer, importer, and marketer of men's dress and casual clothing. **Common positions include:** Accountant/Auditor; Blue-Collar Worker Supervisor; Computer Programmer; Industrial Engineer; Management Trainee; Operations/Production Manager; Systems Analyst. **Educational backgrounds include:** Accounting; Business Administration; Communications; Computer Science; Engineering; Marketing. **Benefits:** 401(k); Daycare Assistance; Dental Insurance; Disability Coverage; Employee Discounts; Life Insurance; Medical Insurance; Profit Sharing; Tuition Assistance. **Special programs:** Internships. **Corporate headquarters location:** This Location. **Parent company:** Haggar Corporation. **Listed on:** NASDAQ. **Number of employees at this location:** 800.

HATCO
601 Marion Drive, Garland TX 75042. 972/494-0511. **Contact:** Personnel Manager. **Description:** Manufactures a variety of men's weather-resistant hats and headgear. **Corporate headquarters location:** This Location.

JLN, INC.
205 North Main Street, Ferris TX 75125. 972/842-3200. **Contact:** Human Resources. **Description:** Manufactures leather bags and belts.

JUSTIN BOOT COMPANY
610 West Dagget Street, Fort Worth TX 76104. 817/332-4385. **Contact:** Personnel Director. **World Wide Web address:** http://www.justinboots.com. **Description:** Manufactures cowboy boots, leather belts, handbags, and billfolds. Founded in 1879.

PILLOWTEX CORPORATION
4111 Mint Way, Dallas TX 75237. 214/333-3225x114. **Fax:** 214/337-8398. **Contact:** Personnel Director. **World Wide Web address:** http://www.pillowtex.com. **Description:** A manufacturer of bed pillows, comforters, and mattress pads. **Common positions include:**

Manufacturer's/Wholesaler's Sales Rep. **Benefits:** Dental Insurance; Disability Coverage; Employee Discounts; Life Insurance; Medical Insurance; Pension Plan; Tuition Assistance. **Corporate headquarters location:** This Location. **Other U.S. locations:** Monroe NC; Lando SC. **Operations at this facility include:** Administration.

PINDLER & PINDLER INC.
1617 Hi Line Drive, Suite 250, Dallas TX 75207. 214/939-9116. **Contact:** Human Resources. **World Wide Web address:** http://www.pindler.com. **Description:** Designs and distributes upholstery and drapery fabrics.

RUSSELL-NEWMAN MANUFACTURING COMPANY
Route 4, Box 6, Cisco TX 76437. 254/442-2005. **Contact:** Human Resources. **Description:** Manufactures women's lingerie and daywear.

SCOTT GROUP
5495 Beltline Road, Suite 290, Dallas TX 75240-7658. 972/991-4919. **Contact:** Human Resources. **Description:** Manufactures hand-woven carpets.

SIDRAN INC.
2875 Merrell Road, Dallas TX 75229. 214/352-7979. **Contact:** Human Resources. **Description:** Manufactures and wholesales men's Western apparel.

TANDY BRANDS ACCESSORIES, INC.
690 East Lamar Boulevard, Suite 200, Arlington TX 76011. 817/548-0090. **Contact:** Human Resources. **World Wide Web address:** http://www.tandybrands.com. **Description:** Manufactures belts, ties, suspenders, and other leather products for men, women, and children.

UNICO CARPET COMPANY
5051 Sharp Street, Dallas TX 75247. 214/630-7875. **Contact:** Human Resources. **Description:** A manufacturer and distributor of floor coverings and carpets.

VF WORKWEAR
P.O. Box 1409, Clarksville TX 75426. 903/427-3888. **Contact:** Human Resources. **World Wide Web address:** http://www.vfworkwear.com. **Description:** This location manufactures men's jeans. Overall, VF Workwear manufactures occupational apparel. Specialties include safety and flame-resistant products including high-visibility and reflective trim garments, as well as fluid-resistant and other protective apparel. The company also produces durable press, easy-care, 100 percent cotton products. Brand names of work utility wear include Big Ben and WorkWear. **Corporate headquarters location:** Nashville TN. **Parent company:** VF Corporation.

WALLS INDUSTRIES, INC.
1905 North Main Street, Cleburne TX 76031. 817/645-4366. **Contact:** Human Resources. **World Wide Web address:** http://www.wallsoutdoors.com. **Description:** Manufactures outerwear for men, women, and children.

WALLS INDUSTRIES, INC.
P.O. Box 196, Sweetwater TX 79556-0196. 915/235-5455. **Fax:** 915/235-8512. **Contact:** Human Resources. **World Wide Web address:** http://www.wallsoutdoors.com. **Description:** Manufactures outerwear for men, women, and children.

WALLS INDUSTRIES, INC.
P.O. Box 18, Gatesville TX 76528. 254/865-7215. **Physical address:** 1501 West Main, Gatesville TX 76528. **Contact:** Human Resources. **World Wide Web address:** http://www.wallsoutdoors.com. **Description:** Manufactures outerwear for men, women, and children. **Corporate headquarters location:** This Location.

WILLIAMSON-DICKIE MANUFACTURING COMPANY
P.O. Box 1779, Fort Worth TX 76101. 817/336-7201. **Contact:** Estelle Lewis, Director of Human Resources. **World Wide Web address:** http://www.dickies.com. **Description:** Manufactures apparel for men and boys including casual slacks and work pants. **Corporate headquarters location:** This Location.

HOWARD B. WOLF INC.
3710 Rawlins, Suite 970, Dallas TX 75219. 214/252-0124. **Fax:** 214/219-7410. **Contact:** Eugene K. Friesen, Senior Vice President. **E-mail address:** gene@hbwolf.com. **World Wide**

Web address: http://www.hbwolf.com. **Description:** An apparel company specializing in the manufacture of women's fashions. **Benefits:** Employee Discounts; Life Insurance; Medical Insurance; Profit Sharing; Public Transit Available. **Annual sales/revenues:** $11 - $20 million.

Note: Because addresses and telephone numbers of smaller companies can change rapidly, we recommend you call each company to verify the information below before inquiring about job opportunities. Mass mailings are not recommended.

Additional small employers:

BROADWOVEN FABRIC MILLS

Eastlander Designs
202 North College Ave, Eastland TX 76448-1606. 254/629-2514.

Hobbs Industries
PO Box 640, Groesbeck TX 76642-0640. 254/729-3223.

CURTAINS AND DRAPERIES

CHF Industries Inc.
1072 East Highway 175, Kaufman TX 75142-3560. 972/932-2173.

FOOTWEAR

Chippewa Boot
PO Box 548, Fort Worth TX 76101-0548. 817/348-2841.

G&W Shoe Manufacturing LLC
1421 Patton Place, Carrollton TX 75007-4879. 972/323-1133.

MEN'S AND BOYS' CLOTHING

Wolf Manufacturing Company
PO Box 3100, Waco TX 76707-0100. 254/753-7301.

TEXTILE GOODS

Rose Tree
7900 Ambassador Row, Dallas TX 75247-4814. 214/637-6900.

WOMEN'S AND MISSES' CLOTHING

Jerell Inc.
1431 Regal Row, Dallas TX 75247-3617. 214/637-5300.

Watters & Watters
4320 Spring Valley Rd, Dallas TX 75244-3701. 972/991-6994.

For more information on career opportunities in the apparel, fashion, and textiles industries:

Associations

AMERICAN APPAREL MANUFACTURERS ASSOCIATION
2500 Wilson Boulevard, Suite 301, Arlington VA 22201. 703/524-1864. World Wide Web address: http://www.americanapparel.org.

AMERICAN TEXTILE MANUFACTURERS INSTITUTE
Office of the Chief Economist, 1130 Connecticut Avenue NW, Suite 1200, Washington DC 20036. 202/862-0500. Fax: 202/862-0570. World Wide Web address: http://www.atmi.org.

THE FASHION GROUP INTERNATIONAL, INC.
597 Fifth Avenue, 8th Floor, New York NY 10017. 212/593-1715. World Wide Web address: http://www.fgi.org.

INTERNATIONAL ASSOCIATION OF CLOTHING DESIGNERS
475 Park Avenue South, 9th Floor, New York NY 10016. 212/685-6602. Fax: 212/545-1709.

Directories

AAMA DIRECTORY
American Apparel Manufacturers Association, 2500 Wilson Boulevard, Suite 301, Arlington VA 22201. 703/524-1864.

APPAREL TRADES BOOK
Dun & Bradstreet Inc., One Diamond Hill Road, Murray Hill NJ 07974. 908/665-5000.

FAIRCHILD'S MARKET DIRECTORY OF WOMEN'S AND CHILDREN'S APPAREL
Fairchild Publications, 7 West 34th Street, New York NY 10001. 212/630-4000. World Wide Web address: http://www.fairchildpub.com.

Magazines

AMERICA'S TEXTILES INTERNATIONAL
Billiam Publishing, 555 North Pleasantburg Drive, Suite 132, Greenville SC 29607. 864/242-5300.

APPAREL INDUSTRY MAGAZINE
Bill Communications, 1115 Northmeadow Parkway, Roswell GA 30046. 770/569-1540. Toll-free phone: 800/241-9034. Fax: 770/569-5105. World Wide Web address: http://www.aimagazine.com.

TEXTILE HILIGHTS
American Textile Manufacturers Institute, Office of the Chief Economist, 1130 Connecticut Avenue NW, Washington DC 20036.

WOMEN'S WEAR DAILY (WWD)
Fairchild Publications, 7 West 34th Street, New York NY 10001. 212/630-4000. World Wide Web address: http://www.fairchildpub.com.

Online Services

THE INTERNET FASHION EXCHANGE
World Wide Web address: http://www.fashionexch.com.

For information about the JobBank List Service visit www.adamsjobbank.com

ARCHITECTURE, CONSTRUCTION, AND ENGINEERING

You can expect to find the following types of companies in this chapter:
Architectural and Engineering Services • Civil and Mechanical Engineering Firms • Construction Products, Manufacturers, and Wholesalers • General Contractors/Specialized Trade Contractors

Some helpful information: The average salary for an entry-level architect is $20,000 - $30,000, with licensed, experienced architects earning $33,000 - $45,000 and firm partners earning as much as $80,000 per year. Construction workers' salaries depend heavily on the season and the housing economy; on average, experienced workers earn around $25,000 annually. Engineers with strong academic backgrounds can earn as much as $40,000 initially. Salary increases are largely dependent upon performance in this field, and talented, experienced engineers frequently earn over $75,000 annually. In particular, chemical and electrical engineers are in considerable demand.

ANDERSON INDUSTRIES, INC.
12457 Montego Plaza, Dallas TX 75230. 972/233-1805. **Contact:** Personnel Department. **Description:** Produces prefabricated building materials. **Corporate headquarters location:** This Location.

APAC TEXAS, INC.
P.O. Box 224048, Dallas TX 75222-4048. 214/741-3531. **Fax:** 214/742-3540. **Contact:** Personnel. **Description:** A general contracting company specializing in concrete and asphalt paving work. **Other U.S. locations:** Beaumont TX.

AUSTIN COMMERCIAL INC.
P.O. Box 2879, Dallas TX 75221. 214/443-5700. **Contact:** Human Resources Department. **E-mail address:** jbox@austin-ind.com. **World Wide Web address:** http://www.austin-ind.com. **Description:** A commercial construction company providing general contracting, construction management, and preconstruction services including cost estimating and scheduling. **Parent company:** Austin Industries.

JOHN F. BEASLEY CONSTRUCTION
4001 Jaffee Street, Dallas TX 75216. 214/376-3000. **Contact:** Personnel Department. **Description:** A general contracting firm.

BUELL DOOR COMPANY
5200 East Grand Avenue, Dallas TX 75223. 214/827-9260. **Toll-free phone:** 800/556-0155. **Fax:** 214/826-9163. **Contact:** Personnel Department. **World Wide Web address:** http://www.buelldoor.com. **Description:** A manufacturer of architectural doors and hardware.

THOMAS S. BYRNE INC.
900 Summit Avenue, Fort Worth TX 76102. 817/335-3394. **Contact:** Personnel. **Description:** A general construction company.

CAVALIER HOMES, INC.
P.O. Box 5003, Wichita Falls TX 76307. 940/723-5523. **Physical address:** 719 Scott Street, Suite 600, Wichita Falls TX 76301. **Contact:** Human Resources. **World Wide Web address:** http://www.cavhomesinc.com. **Description:** This location houses administrative offices. Overall, Cavalier Homes, Inc. designs and manufactures a wide range of homes and markets them through approximately 500 independent dealers nationwide. **Corporate headquarters location:** Addison AL. **Subsidiaries include:** Cavalier Acceptance Corporation provides installment sale financing to qualifying retail customers of these exclusive dealers.

CENTEX CONSTRUCTION COMPANY, INC.
P.O. Box 299009, Dallas TX 75229-9009. 214/357-1891. **Fax:** 214/902-6391. **Contact:** David Preston, Vice President of Administration. **World Wide Web address:** http://www.centex-construction.com. **Description:** A commercial general contractor providing preconstruction,

construction, management, and general contracting services. **Common positions include:** Civil Engineer; Construction Contractor; Cost Estimator; Project Manager; Purchasing Agent/Manager; Quality Control Supervisor. **Educational backgrounds include:** Construction. **Benefits:** 401(k); Dental Insurance; Disability Coverage; Life Insurance; Medical Insurance; Profit Sharing. **Corporate headquarters location:** This Location. **Other U.S. locations:** Fairfax VA. **Subsidiaries include:** Centex Landis (New Orleans LA). **Parent company:** Centex Corporation (Dallas TX). **Listed on:** New York Stock Exchange. **Number of employees at this location:** 220.

CENTEX CORPORATION
P.O. Box 199000, Dallas TX 75219. 214/981-5000. **Contact:** Human Resources. **World Wide Web address:** http://www.centex.com. **Description:** Provides home building, mortgage banking, contracting, and construction products and services. **Corporate headquarters location:** This Location. **Subsidiaries include:** Centex Homes is one of America's largest home builders; CTX Mortgage Company is among the top retail originators of single-family home mortgages; Centex Construction Company, Inc. is one of the largest general building contractors in the U.S., as well as one of the largest constructors of health care facilities; Centex Construction Products, Inc., which manufactures and distributes cement, ready-mix concrete, aggregates, and gypsum wallboard, is one of the largest U.S.-owned cement producers; Centex Development Company, LP conducts real estate development activities. **Listed on:** New York Stock Exchange. **Annual sales/revenues:** More than $100 million.

CONTINENTAL CABINETS
2841 Pierce Street, Dallas TX 75233. 214/467-4444. **Contact:** Human Resources. **Description:** Manufactures kitchen cabinets and bathroom vanities.

CULLUM CONSTRUCTION COMPANY
2814 Industrial Lane, Garland TX 75041. 214/987-9191. **Contact:** Personnel. **Description:** A contractor specializing in heavy utility construction.

ELCOR CORPORATION
14643 Dallas Parkway, Suite 1000, Dallas TX 75240-8871. 972/851-0500. **Contact:** Human Resources. **World Wide Web address:** http://www.elcor.com. **Description:** Through Elk Corporation and its subsidiaries, Elcor Corporation is engaged in the manufacture and sale of laminated fiberglass asphalt. **Corporate headquarters location:** This Location. **Subsidiaries include:** Elk Corporation.

ELK CORPORATION
202 Cedar Road, Ennis TX 75119. 972/875-9611. **Fax:** 972/872-2392. **Contact:** Human Resources. **World Wide Web address:** http://www.elcor.com. **Description:** Manufactures residential roofing products and fiberglass mats. **Common positions include:** Accountant/Auditor; Blue-Collar Worker Supervisor; Chemical Engineer; Clerical Supervisor; Designer; Electrical/Electronics Engineer; Human Resources Manager; Manufacturer's/Wholesaler's Sales Rep.; Mechanical Engineer. **Educational backgrounds include:** Accounting; Engineering; Marketing. **Benefits:** 401(k); Disability Coverage; Life Insurance; Medical Insurance; Profit Sharing; Savings Plan; Tuition Assistance. **Corporate headquarters location:** Dallas TX. **Other U.S. locations:** Tuscaloosa AL; Shafter CA. **Parent company:** Elcor Corporation. **Operations at this facility include:** Administration; Manufacturing; Sales. **Listed on:** New York Stock Exchange.

FM GLOBAL
5800 Granite Parkway, Suite 600, Plano TX 75024. 972/377-4808. **Fax:** 972/731-1800. **Contact:** Human Resources. **World Wide Web address:** http://www.fmglobal.com. **Description:** A loss control services organization. FM Global helps owner company policyholders to protect their properties and occupancies from damage caused by fire, wind, flood, and explosion; boiler, pressure vessel, and machinery accidents; and many other insured hazards.

GAF MATERIALS CORPORATION
2600 Singleton Boulevard, Dallas TX 75212. 214/637-1060. **Contact:** Human Resources. **World Wide Web address:** http://www.gaf.com. **Description:** A multiproduct manufacturer with sales in both consumer and industrial markets. The company's product line includes building, roofing, and insulation materials for the construction trades; specialty chemicals and plastics; and reprographic products. **Common positions include:** Accountant/Auditor; Blue-Collar Worker Supervisor; Customer Service Representative; Electrical/Electronics Engineer; Industrial Engineer; Manufacturer's/Wholesaler's Sales Rep.; Operations/Production Manager;

Production Worker; Purchasing Agent/Manager; Quality Control Supervisor. **Educational backgrounds include:** Accounting; Business Administration; Engineering; Manufacturing Management. **Benefits:** 401(k); Dental Insurance; Disability Coverage; Life Insurance; Medical Insurance; Pension Plan; Tuition Assistance. **Corporate headquarters location:** Wayne NJ. **Other U.S. locations:** Nationwide. **Listed on:** Privately held.

GENERAL ALUMINUM CORPORATION
1001 West Crosby Road, Carrollton TX 75006. 972/242-5271. **Contact:** Personnel. **Description:** Manufactures aluminum doors and windows, partition screens, sliding glass doors, and related products.

HNTB CORPORATION
14114 Dallas Parkway, Suite 630, Dallas TX 75240. 972/661-5626. **Fax:** 972/661-5614. **Contact:** Laura Black, Manager of Administration. **World Wide Web address:** http://www.hntb.com. **Description:** Offers architectural, engineering, and planning services to public agencies and private industry. **NOTE:** Entry-level positions are offered. Interested jobseekers should check the company's employment page on the World Wide Web and fax a resume. **Common positions include:** Civil Engineer; Construction and Building Inspector; Construction Contractor; Cost Estimator; Design Engineer; Designer; Draftsperson; Environmental Engineer; Structural Engineer; Technical Writer/Editor; Transportation/Traffic Specialist; Typist/Word Processor; Urban/Regional Planner. **Educational backgrounds include:** Engineering. **Benefits:** 401(k); Dental Insurance; Disability Coverage; Life Insurance; Medical Insurance; Profit Sharing; Tuition Assistance. **Special programs:** Training. **Corporate headquarters location:** Kansas City MO. **Other U.S. locations:** Nationwide. **Subsidiaries include:** Alcyone Group, Inc.; Infrastructure Management Group; Thomas K. Dyer, Inc. **Listed on:** Privately held. **Annual sales/revenues:** $5 - $10 million. **Number of employees at this location:** 30. **Number of employees nationwide:** 1,880.

HALLIBURTON
3600 Lincoln Plaza, Dallas TX 75201. 214/978-2600. **Fax:** 214/978-2611. **Contact:** Human Resources. **World Wide Web address:** http://www.halliburton.com. **Description:** A leading diversified energy services, engineering, construction, maintenance, and energy equipment company. **Corporate headquarters location:** This Location. **Other U.S. locations:** Nationwide. **International locations:** Worldwide. **Subsidiaries include:** Brown & Root Energy Services; Brown & Root Services; Dresser Equipment Company; Halliburton Energy Services; Kellogg Brown & Root; Landmark Graphics. **Listed on:** New York Stock Exchange. **Stock exchange symbol:** HAL.

HENNINGSON, DURHAM & RICHARDSON, INC.
12700 Hillcrest Road, Suite 125, Dallas TX 75230-2096. 972/960-4000. **Fax:** 972/960-4185. **Contact:** Human Resources. **Description:** Offers architectural and engineering design services, construction consulting, and interior design services. The company's three main business sectors are health care, justice, and science and industry. Founded in 1917. **Common positions include:** Administrative Assistant; Administrative Manager; Architect; Architectural Engineer; Controller; Draftsperson; Electrical/Electronics Engineer; Marketing Specialist; Mechanical Engineer; Project Manager; Systems Analyst. **Educational backgrounds include:** Art/Design; Engineering; Health Care; Marketing. **Special programs:** Internships. **Corporate headquarters location:** Omaha NE. **Other U.S. locations:** Alexandria VA. **Listed on:** Privately held. **Number of employees at this location:** 85. **Number of employees nationwide:** 1,600.

D.R. HORTON, INC.
1901 Ascension Boulevard, Suite 210, Arlington TX 76006. 817/856-8200. **Fax:** 817/856-8238. **Contact:** Human Resources. **World Wide Web address:** http://www.drhorton.com. **Description:** D.R. Horton, Inc. and its operating subsidiaries are engaged primarily in the construction and sale of single-family homes designed principally for the entry-level and move-up market segments. Through its various financial subsidiaries, D.R. Horton also provides mortgage financing and title services. **Corporate headquarters location:** This location. **Other U.S. locations:** Nationwide. **Subsidiaries include:** Arappco; CH Mortgage; Cambridge; Century Title Agency; Continental Homes; DRH Title Company; Dobson; Mareli Construction; Metro Title; Milburn Homes; Joe Miller; RMP Properties; Regency; SGS; Torrey; Travis County Title Company; Trimark. **Number of employees nationwide:** 400.

HOWE-BAKER ENGINEERS, INC.
P.O. Box 956, Tyler TX 75710. 903/597-0311. **Physical address:** 3102 East Fifth Street, Tyler TX 75701. **Contact:** Human Resources. **Description:** Provides mechanical, civil, and electrical engineering services.

INSITUFORM TEXARK, INC.
3001 Roy Orr Boulevard, Grand Prairie TX 75050. 972/228-8888. **Contact:** Human Resources. **Description:** This location conducts pipeline rehabilitation. Overall, Insituform Texark, Inc. uses various trenchless technologies for rehabilitation, new construction, and improvements of pipeline systems including sewers; gas lines; industrial waste lines; water lines; and oil field, mining, and industrial process pipelines. **Parent company:** Insituform Mid-America, Inc. provides a wide variety of technologies including Insituform, PALTEM, Tite Liner, and tunneling.

LAUREN ENGINEERS & CONSTRUCTORS
901 South First Street, Abilene TX 79602. 915/670-9660. **Contact:** Paula Ford, Personnel. **World Wide Web address:** http://www.laurenec.com. **Description:** Designs and builds power plants, refineries, and related large-scale projects. **Corporate headquarters location:** This location.

LENNOX INTERNATIONAL, INC.
P.O. Box 799900, Dallas TX 75379-9900. 972/497-5000. **Physical address:** 2100 Lake Park Boulevard, Dallas TX. **Fax:** 972/497-5476. **Contact:** Human Resources. **Description:** Produces heating and air conditioning equipment through its subsidiaries. **Common positions include:** Accountant/Auditor; Buyer; Computer Programmer; Customer Service Representative; Manufacturing Engineer; Mechanical Engineer; Sales Representative; Systems Analyst. **Educational backgrounds include:** Accounting; Business Administration; Computer Science; Engineering; Finance; Liberal Arts; Marketing. **Benefits:** 401(k); Dental Insurance; Disability Coverage; Employee Discounts; Life Insurance; Medical Insurance; Pension Plan; Profit Sharing; Tuition Assistance. **Special programs:** Internships. **Corporate headquarters location:** This Location. **Subsidiaries include:** Armstrong Air Conditioning Inc.; Heatcraft Inc.; Lennox Global Ltd.; Lennox Industries Inc. **Operations at this facility include:** Administration. **Listed on:** Privately held. **Annual sales/revenues:** More than $100 million. **Number of employees at this location:** 1,000. **Number of employees nationwide:** 9,000. **Number of employees worldwide:** 10,000.

MORGAN
P.O. Box 660280, Dallas TX 75266-0280. 972/840-1200. **Physical address:** 2800 McCree Road, Garland TX 75041. **Fax:** 972/864-7316. **Contact:** Leslie McLoed, Personnel Coordinator. **E-mail address:** employ@morganusa.com. **World Wide Web address:** http://www.morganusa.com. **Description:** Manufactures, transports, and retails relocatable buildings of all sizes and uses, as well as spas, recreational vehicles, swimming pools, and decks to consumers, businesses, government buyers, and institutional buyers. The firm has four manufacturing facilities in the United States, 25 company-owned stores, and 40 dealer outlets. Founded in 1961. **Common positions include:** Accountant/Auditor; Advertising Clerk; Architect; Attorney; Blue-Collar Worker Supervisor; Branch Manager; Budget Analyst; Buyer; Clerical Supervisor; Computer Programmer; Cost Estimator; Draftsperson; Financial Analyst; Human Resources Manager; Management Trainee; Manufacturer's/Wholesaler's Sales Rep.; Operations/Production Manager; Paralegal; Purchasing Agent/Manager; Quality Control Supervisor; Structural Engineer; Systems Analyst; Wholesale and Retail Buyer. **Educational backgrounds include:** Accounting; Art/Design; Business Administration; Computer Science; Engineering; Mathematics. **Benefits:** Dental Insurance; Disability Coverage; Employee Discounts; Life Insurance; Medical Insurance; Tuition Assistance. **Corporate headquarters location:** This Location. **Other U.S. locations:** Nationwide. **Operations at this facility include:** Administration. **Listed on:** Privately held. **Number of employees at this location:** 120. **Number of employees nationwide:** 800.

MORRISON SUPPLY COMPANY, INC.
P.O. Box 70, Fort Worth TX 76101. 817/336-0451. **Fax:** 817/338-1612. **Contact:** Charles Allen, Personnel Manager. **World Wide Web address:** http://www.morsco.com. **Description:** A wholesaler of plumbing and heating equipment, tools, and supplies. **Corporate headquarters location:** This location.

O'HAIR SHUTTERS
P.O. Box 2764, Lubbock TX 79408. 806/765-5791. **Contact:** Hiring Manager. **World Wide Web address:** http://www.ohair.com. **Description:** Manufactures outdoor shutters for homes. **Corporate headquarters location:** This Location.

OVERHEAD DOOR CORPORATION OF TEXAS
6750 LBJ Freeway, Suite 1200, Dallas TX 75240. 972/233-6611. **Contact:** Human Resources. **Description:** Manufactures aluminum, steel, fiberglass, and wooden overhead doors; rolling

steel fire doors; grilles; and metal insulated entrance doors. Products are distributed through a network of more than 400 authorized distributors in the United States and Canada. The company also manufactures truck and trailer doors. **Corporate headquarters location:** This Location. **Other area locations:** Carrollton TX; Corpus Christi TX; Fort Worth TX; Houston TX; Mount Pleasant TX; Richardson TX. **Listed on:** New York Stock Exchange.

QUALITY CABINETS
515 Big Stone Gap Road, Duncanville TX 75137. 972/298-6101. **Fax:** 972/298-6251. **Contact:** Human Resources. **World Wide Web address:** http://www.qualitycabinets.com. **Description:** Manufactures cabinets. **Corporate headquarters location:** This Location. **Parent company:** Texwood Industries.

R.E. SWEENEY COMPANY INC.
3700 Noble Avenue, Fort Worth TX 76111. 817/834-7191. **Contact:** Ron Belota, Controller. **Description:** A wholesaler of building materials.

TD INDUSTRIES, INC.
P.O. Box 819060, Dallas TX 75381-9060. 972/888-9505. **Physical address:** 13850 Diplomat Drive, Dallas TX 75234. **Fax:** 972/888-9507. **Contact:** Ms. Jessie McCain, Vice President of Administration. **E-mail address:** jessie.mccain@tdindustries.com. **World Wide Web address:** http://www.tdindustries.com. **Description:** A national construction and service company that designs, installs, and repairs HVAC, plumbing, high-purity process piping, and energy management systems in commercial and industrial markets. Founded in 1946. **NOTE:** Entry-level positions are offered. **Common positions include:** Electrical/Electronics Engineer; Mechanical Engineer; Project Manager. **Educational backgrounds include:** Engineering. **Benefits:** Tuition Assistance; Vacation Days (10 - 20). **Special programs:** Apprenticeships; Co-ops; Internships; Summer Jobs. **Corporate headquarters location:** This Location. **Other U.S. locations:** Houston TX; San Antonio TX. **Listed on:** Privately held. **CEO:** Jack Lowe. **Annual sales/revenues:** More than $100 million. **Number of employees at this location:** 800. **Number of employees nationwide:** 1,150. **Number of projected hires for 2000 - 2001 at this location:** 100.

UNITED STATES BRASS CORPORATION
P.O. Box 3033, Abilene TX 79604-3033. 915/673-5046. **Contact:** Human Resources. **Description:** Manufactures various kinds of brass faucets. **Corporate headquarters location:** Dallas TX.

THE VISTAWALL GROUP
P.O. Box 629, 803 Airport Road, Terrell TX 75160. 972/551-6100. **Contact:** Human Resources. **World Wide Web address:** http://www.vistawall.com. **Description:** The Vistawall Group, through its subsidiaries, designs, manufactures, and distributes entrances, storefront and low-rise framing systems, skylight systems, and engineered curtain wall systems. **Corporate headquarters location:** This Location. **Subsidiaries include:** Modulino Window Systems; Naturalite Skylight Systems; Skywall Translucent Systems; Vistawall Architectural Products. **Parent company:** Butler Manufacturing Company.

WING INDUSTRIES INC.
6202 Industrial Drive, Greenville TX 75402. 903/455-1200. **Contact:** Human Resources. **Description:** Manufactures wooden doors.

H.B. ZACHRY COMPANY
P.O. Box 531558, Grand Prairie TX 75053-1558. 972/262-8898. **Contact:** Human Resources. **World Wide Web address:** http://www.zachry.com. **Description:** This location is a district field office. Overall, H.B. Zachry Company is an industrial construction management company operating through the following divisions: Process; Power; Heavy; Maintenance & Service; Commercial; International; and Pipeline. The company builds power plants, highways, and pipelines in the southern United States, as well as in foreign countries. H.B. Zachry Company does not handle residential construction contracts. Founded in 1923. **Corporate headquarters location:** San Antonio TX. **Listed on:** Privately held. **Annual sales/revenues:** More than $100 million. **Number of employees nationwide:** 10,000. **Number of employees worldwide:** 14,000.

H.B. ZACHRY COMPANY
P.O. Box 7309, Longview TX 75607-7309. 903/643-2253. **Fax:** 903/643-9103. **Contact:** Human Resources. **World Wide Web address:** http://www.zachry.com. **Description:** An industrial construction management company operating through the following divisions:

Process; Power; Heavy; Maintenance & Service; Commercial; International; and Pipeline. The company builds power plants, highways, and pipelines in the southern United States, as well as in foreign countries. H.B. Zachry Company does not handle residential construction contracts. Founded in 1923. **Corporate headquarters location:** San Antonio TX. **Listed on:** Privately held. **Annual sales/revenues:** More than $100 million. **Number of employees nationwide:** 10,000. **Number of employees worldwide:** 14,000.

Note: Because addresses and telephone numbers of smaller companies can change rapidly, we recommend you call each company to verify the information below before inquiring about job opportunities. Mass mailings are not recommended.

Additional small employers:

ARCHITECTURAL SERVICES

Aguirre Inc.
12700 Park Central Dr, Dallas TX 75251-1500. 972/788-1508.

Corgan Associates Inc.
501 Elm St, Ste 500, Dallas TX 75202-3339. 214/748-2000.

FDS International
8615 Freeport Pkwy, Ste 100, Irving TX 75063. 972/915-3004.

HKS Inc.
1919 McKinney Ave, Dallas TX 75201-1610. 214/969-5599.

RTKL Associates Inc.
2828 Routh St, Ste 200, Dallas TX 75201-1435. 214/871-8877.

CARPENTRY AND FLOOR WORK

Fixture Perfect International
8950 N Central Expy, Dallas TX 75231-6427. 214/373-4700.

CONCRETE WORK

Advanced Foundation Systems
5601 W Jefferson Blvd, Dallas TX 75211-3861. 972/263-1616.

A.H. Beck Foundation Co. Inc.
PO Box 2925, Coppell TX 75019-8925. 972/304-1593.

Cortez Group Inc.
1401 Cates St, Ste 201, Bridgeport TX 76426-3117. 940/683-3273.

Mobley-Speed Cement
PO Box 35148, Dallas TX 75235-0148. 214/637-3270.

Potter Concrete Co. Inc.
4820 Gretna St, Dallas TX 75207-5204. 214/630-2191.

Potter Concrete Co. Inc.
5601 Bridge St, Fort Worth TX 76112-2384. 817/429-7919.

Statewide Paving Inc.
4110 Cedar Lake Dr, Dallas TX 75227-4093. 214/275-4244.

Striland Construction Inc.
10860 Switzer Ave, Ste 109, Dallas TX 75238-5302. 214/340-1811.

TAS Construction Inc.
8321 Rendon Bloodworth Rd, Mansfield TX 76063-6179. 817/477-1514.

CONSTRUCTION MATERIALS WHOLESALE

ACI Distribution
PO Box 815547, Dallas TX 75381-5547. 972/484-3691.

Cameron Ashley Building Products
PO Box 551476, Dallas TX 75355-1478. 214/860-5100.

Custom Stone Supply
2624 Joe Field Rd, Dallas TX 75229-4601. 972/488-8131.

ELECTRICAL WORK

Alman Electric Inc.
7677 Hunnicut Rd, Dallas TX 75228-6947. 214/388-1800.

Cactus Service Co.
PO Box 11357, Lubbock TX 79408-7357. 806/744-4240.

Clark Electrical Construction
PO Box 2049, Fort Worth TX 76113-2049. 817/831-0678.

Datastar Computer Systems Inc.
2033 Chenault Dr, Ste 142, Carrollton TX 75006-5064. 972/661-1223.

Electra Link Inc.
17817 Davenport Rd, Dallas TX 75252-5871. 972/818-7225.

Fox Electric Ltd.
PO Box 13338, Arlington TX 76094-0338. 817/461-2571.

Gentzler Electrical Contractors
PO Box 550369, Dallas TX 75355-0369. 214/503-0302.

Hargrove Electric Company Inc.
PO Box 566077, Dallas TX 75356-6077. 214/742-8665.

Houston Stafford Electric
2500 Chandler Dr, Rowlett TX 75088-3928. 972/463-1455.

HTE Contractors
1181 Empire Central Dr, Dallas TX 75247-4301. 214/951-0001.

Humphrey & Associates Inc.
PO Box 59247, Dallas TX 75229-1247. 972/620-1075.

Imperial Contracting
228 Irby Ln, Irving TX 75061-7046. 972/254-3480.

Integrated Electrical Services
1860 Crown Dr, Ste 1408, Dallas TX 75234-9415. 972/831-1756.

JBI Electrical Systems
5705 Azle Ave, Fort Worth TX 76114-1120. 817/589-1545.

Lanehart Electrical Contractors
2411 River Hill Rd, Irving TX 75061-8909. 972/721-1004.

Mills Electrical Contractors
PO Box 59186, Dallas TX 75229-1186. 214/357-4300.

Reata Construction Corp.
1310 S Stemmons Fwy, Lewisville TX 75067-6308. 972/434-3001.

Regional Electrical Systems
13350 Euless St, Euless TX 76040-7225. 817/267-2231.

Rogers Electrical Contractors
8200 Springwood Dr, Irving TX 75063-5811. 972/869-4040.

Simpson Red Inc.
PO Drawer U, Marshall TX 75671-0470. 903/935-0968.

The Industrial Company
997 Hampshire Ln, Ste 100, Richardson TX 75080-5192. 972/699-1111.

Walker Engineering Inc.
14600 Trinity Blvd 300, Fort Worth TX 76155-2512. 817/858-8600.

Walker Engineering Inc.
10999 Petal St, Dallas TX 75238-2424. 214/349-5900.

ENGINEERING SERVICES

Atec Associates
11356 Mathis Ave, Dallas TX 75229-3157. 972/556-2204.

CHR Solutions
PO Box 65700, Lubbock TX 79464-5700. 806/791-7700.

Factory Mutual Engineering
12222 Merit Dr, Ste 1800, Dallas TX 75251-3296. 972/661-9202.

Fluor Daniel Power Service
PO Box 1109, Tatum TX 75691-1109. 903/836-2086.

Freese & Nichols Inc.
4055 International Plaza, Fort Worth TX 76109. 817/735-7300.

Huitt-Zollars Inc.
3131 McKinney Ave, Ste 600, Dallas TX 75204-2489. 214/871-3311.

Rone Engineers
8908 Ambassador Row, Dallas TX 75247-4510. 214/630-9745.

TPA Inc.
9101 LBJ Fwy, Dallas TX 75243-1921. 972/773-2156.

Turner Engineers Inc.
4849 Greenville Ave, Ste 1200, Dallas TX 75206. 214/378-5200.

GENERAL CONTRACTORS

Capitol Painting & Construction Inc.
811 S Central Expy, Richardson TX 75080-7415. 972/644-6046.

Covenant Group Holding Inc.
5601 Bridge St, Ste 504, Fort Worth TX 76112-2306. 817/446-4792.

Diamond Homes
1424 Gables Ct, Ste 101, Plano TX 75075-7649. 972/596-0301.

FF Development LP
PO Box 5407, Arlington TX 76005-5407. 817/640-1182.

Highland Homes of Dallas
12850 Hillcrest Rd, Dallas TX 75230-1529. 972/387-7905.

Nu Home Design LLC
10208 Carolina Oaks Dr, Dallas TX 75227-7107. 972/329-8260.

Richard Fuller Homes
201 Willow St, Crowley TX 76036-3519. 817/297-7674.

Sovereign Homes Corporation
8440 Walnut Hill Ln, Dallas TX 75231-3833. 214/361-9292.

TCR Galleria Construction LP
717 N Harwood St, Ste 1100, Dallas TX 75201-6503. 214/922-8588.

The Babcock & Wilcox Company
PO Box 9090, Paris TX 75461-9090. 903/784-2571.

Twin Cities Contracting Inc.
PO Box 3805, Arlington TX 76007-3805. 817/261-5622.

Watkins Engineers & Construction
PO Drawer 20, Midlothian TX 76065-0020. 972/775-2050.

GENERAL INDUSTRIAL CONTRACTORS

Architectural Utilities Inc.
PO Box 11586, Fort Worth TX 76110-0586. 817/926-4377.

Austin Industries
PO Box 1590, Dallas TX 75221-1590. 214/443-5500.

BFW Construction Co. Inc.
PO Box 628, Temple TX 76503-0628. 254/778-8941.

Clark Construction Group
13760 Noel Rd, Dallas TX 75240-7336. 972/490-9390.

Clark Contractors
5949 Sherry Ln, Ste 650, Dallas TX 75225-8055. 214/636-6063.

Dal-Mac Construction Partners
PO Box 830160, Richardson TX 75083-0160. 972/238-0401.

HC Beck Ltd.
1700 Pacific Ave, Ste 3800, Dallas TX 75201-4691. 214/965-1100.

Henderson Property Co.
1985 Forest Ln, Garland TX 75042-7952. 972/272-5466.

Horn Construction Co.
819 Penn St, Fort Worth TX 76102-3413. 817/737-6163.

JRJ Construction
PO Box 7611, Fort Worth TX 76111-0611. 817/831-2418.

Manhattan Construction Co.
3890 W Northwest Hwy, Dallas TX 75220-8108. 214/357-7400.

Matrix Interior Construction
1206 Tappan Cir, Carrollton TX 75006-6911. 972/245-1022.

Medco Construction
2625 Elm St, Ste 216, Dallas TX 75226-1497. 214/820-2492.

Omega Contracting Inc.
2818 Ruder St, Dallas TX 75212-4217. 214/689-3815.

Rogers-O'Brien Construction Co.
11145 Morrison Ln, Dallas TX 75229-5608. 972/243-1335.

RPR Construction Company
301 S Southeast Loop 323, Tyler TX 75702-8645. 903/592-7166.

Tech Data Corporation
5100 Liberty Way, Fort Worth TX 76178-4008. 817/490-4156.

Waco Construction Inc.
PO Box 3216, Waco TX 76707-0216. 254/772-3660.

Walker Building Corporation
PO Box 820217, Fort Worth TX 76182-0217. 817/595-1121.

Western Builders Amarillo Inc.
PO Box 15368, Amarillo TX 79105-5368. 806/376-4321.

HEAVY CONSTRUCTION

B&W Backhoe Service Inc.
PO Box 459, Sanger TX 76266-0459. 940/458-3125.

Driver Pipeline Company Inc.
2019 Ruder St, Dallas TX 75212-5542. 214/638-7131.

Dynamic Technical Services
720 E Park Blvd, Ste 204, Plano TX 75074-8802. 972/578-1088.

Electrical Construction Services
PO Box 1261, Amarillo TX 79170-0001. 806/378-4164.

Enerpipe Corporation
PO Box 2329, Amarillo TX 79105-2329. 806/371-8851.

Flowers Construction Co.
PO Box 1207, Hillsboro TX 76645-1207. 254/582-2501.

Haines Construction Company
PO Box 1717, Kilgore TX 75663-1717. 903/984-1964.

Architecture, Construction, and Engineering/75

John Burns Construction Co.
PO Box 1117, Lewisville TX 75067-1117. 972/434-6789.

Mastec North America Inc.
PO Box 542257, Dallas TX 75354-2257. 214/571-2521.

Murray Construction Co. Inc.
515 N Kealy St, Lewisville TX 75057-3129. 972/436-4566.

SM&P Utility Resources Inc.
2211 E Division St, Arlington TX 76011-6621. 817/633-4085.

Sulphur River Gathering LP
5949 Cherry Ln, Ste 755, Dallas TX 75225. 214/373-1091.

Tri Stone
540 Commerce St, Southlake TX 76092-9113. 817/481-2886.

MASONRY, STONEWORK, AND PLASTERING

Brazos Masonry Inc.
PO Box 23428, Waco TX 76702-3428. 254/848-5830.

Dee Brown Inc.
PO Box 28335, Dallas TX 75228-0335. 214/321-6443.

DMG Masonry Inc.
1007 Commercial Blvd N, Arlington TX 76001-7124. 817/784-0880.

Ellis Skinner Company Inc.
PO Box 35245, Dallas TX 75235-0245. 214/638-8044.

Martin Concrete
PO Box 24321, Fort Worth TX 76124-1321. 817/446-0644.

Metro Masonry Construction Inc.
3900 Split Trail Rd, Plano TX 75074-2105. 972/881-8100.

Morgan & Associates Inc.
1344 W Euless Blvd, Euless TX 76040-4968. 817/571-6874.

Quality Brick Works
1000 Beard Ave, Waco TX 76706-5058. 254/662-3680.

Texas Stone & Tile Inc.
PO Box 540755, Dallas TX 75354-0755. 214/358-4621.

Wilks Masonry Inc.
PO Box 1032, Cisco TX 76437-1032. 254/442-1800.

MISC. SPECIAL TRADE CONTRACTORS

Granite Construction Company
2400 N Interstate 35E, Carrollton TX 75006-1303. 972/446-0993.

Haley-Greer Inc.
2257C Lombardy Ln, Dallas TX 75220-2300. 972/556-1177.

Hall Excavating Co. Inc.
201 NE 29th St, Fort Worth TX 76106-5901. 817/624-7207.

Jericho Services
11163 Shady Trl, Ste 101, Dallas TX 75229-4632. 972/247-6618.

Kone Inc.
2101 Couch Dr, McKinney TX 75069-7314. 972/542-0351.

RW Cox Inc.
Rural Rte 7, Box 35, Paris TX 75462-9640. 903/739-8088.

Site Concrete Inc.
PO Box 154489, Irving TX 75015-4489. 972/313-0733.

Southland Contracting Inc.
PO Box 40664, Fort Worth TX 76140-0664. 817/293-4263.

Weir Bros. Inc.
PO Box 541793, Dallas TX 75354-1793. 972/556-9696.

OPERATIVE BUILDERS

Weekley Homes LP
3010 LBJ Fwy, Ste 1420, Dallas TX 75234-2713. 972/243-8414.

PLUMBING, HEATING, AND A/C

Axon Services
PO Box 45028, Dallas TX 75245-0028. 214/634-3500.

Beard Mechanical
PO Box 4130, Dallas TX 75208-0130. 214/941-0392.

Berger Engineering Co.
10900 Shady Trl, Dallas TX 75220-1308. 214/358-4451.

Brandt Engineering Company
PO Box 29559, Dallas TX 75229-0559. 972/241-9611.

Buckner Boulevard Plumbing
4030 Gus Thomasson Rd, Mesquite TX 75150-2224. 972/681-2425.

Ceramic Cooling Tower Company
1100 Northway Dr, Fort Worth TX 76131-1425. 817/232-4661.

Decker Mechanical
PO Box 53, Cedar Hill TX 75106-0053. 972/291-9907.

Dyna Ten Corp.
7415 Whitehall St, Fort Worth TX 76118-6427. 817/595-1391.

Dynamic Systems Inc.
PO Box 543346, Dallas TX 75354-3346. 214/358-4786.

Grinnell Fire Protection Systems
11590 Emerald St, Dallas TX 75229-2010. 972/488-1060.

Grinnell Fire Protection Systems
PO Box 2806, Lubbock TX 79408-2806. 806/765-6691.

K&N Plumbing & Mechanical
2706 W Pioneer Pkwy, Arlington TX 76013-5906. 817/261-2117.

Ski Hi Enterprises Inc.
PO Box 11618, Fort Worth TX 76110-0618. 817/923-0292.

Turner Mechanical & Insulation Co.
10930 Switzer Ave, Ste 122, Dallas TX 75238-1362. 214/349-6356.

United Mechanical
PO Box 551206, Dallas TX 75355-1206. 214/341-2042.

PLUMBING, HEATING, AND A/C EQUIPMENT WHOLESALE

Advantage Systems Inc.
PO Box 152170, Irving TX 75015-2170. 972/438-0232.

Crane Plumbing
8300 S Central Expy, Dallas TX 75241-7815. 214/371-7800.

Eljer Plumbingware
17120 Dallas Pkwy, Dallas TX 75248-1144. 972/407-2600.

Ferguson Enterprises Inc.
PO Box 698, Euless TX 76039-0698. 817/540-1888.

Mansfield Plumbing Products
PO Box 259, Kilgore TX 75663-0259. 903/984-3525.

Titus
990 Security Row, Richardson TX 75081-6101. 972/699-1030.

ROAD CONSTRUCTION

AK Gillis & Sons Inc.
PO Box 576, Sulphur Springs TX 75483-0576. 903/885-3124.

AL Helmcamp Inc.
PO Box 456, Buffalo TX 75831-0456. 903/626-5911.

Amarillo Road Company
PO Box 32075, Amarillo TX
79120-2075. 806/335-2922.

Archer Western Contractors
1170 W Corp Dr, Ste 109,
Arlington TX 76006. 817/640-3898.

Austin Bridge & Road Inc.
PO Box 1590, Dallas TX 75221-1590. 972/241-0699.

Brookshore Construction Services
2306 Penn St, Irving TX 75061-5752. 972/579-7855.

Ed Bell Construction Company
PO Box 540787, Dallas TX 75354-0787. 214/358-6581.

Edwards Construction
193 Industrial Blvd, McKinney TX 75069-7220. 972/562-6522.

Gilvin-Terrill Inc.
PO Box 9027, Amarillo TX 79105-9027. 806/374-0932.

Glenn Thurman Inc.
PO Box 850842, Mesquite TX 75185-0842. 972/286-6333.

J. Lee Milligan Inc.
PO Box 30188, Amarillo TX 79120-0188. 806/373-4386.

JD Abrams Inc.
PO Box 540425, Dallas TX 75354-0425. 214/688-0525.

JH Strain & Sons Inc.
PO Box 277, Tye TX 79563-0277. 915/692-0067.

Lipham Construction Co. Inc.
PO Box J, Aspermont TX 79502-0908. 940/989-3503.

Rodman Paving Inc.
PO Box 957, Frisco TX 75034-0957. 972/335-4510.

Rosiek Construction Co. Inc.
2000 E Lamar Blvd, Ste 410, Arlington TX 76006-7338. 817/277-4342.

Rushing Paving Company
PO Box 365, Denison TX 75021-0365. 903/465-3872.

Williams & Peters Construction Co. Inc.
PO Box 3907, Lubbock TX 79452-3907. 806/745-4171.

ROOFING, SIDING, AND SHEET METAL WORK

AC Parsons Roofing Company
PO Box 21835, Waco TX 76702-1835. 254/881-1733.

Atlas Roofing Corporation
PO Box 700, Daingerfield TX 75638-0700. 903/645-3988.

Empire Roofing Inc.
5301 Sun Valley Dr, Fort Worth TX 76119-6568. 817/572-2250.

Johnson Roofing Inc.
PO Box 11009, Waco TX 76716-1009. 254/662-5571.

Panel Constructors Inc.
2321 E Pioneer Dr, Irving TX 75061-8807. 972/721-1825.

Paragon Roofing Inc.
PO Box 225629, Dallas TX 75222-5629. 214/630-6363.

Seyforth Roofing Co. Inc.
PO Box 550576, Dallas TX 75355-0576. 972/864-8591.

Supreme Roofing
1355 N Walton Walker Blvd, Dallas TX 75211-1042. 214/330-8913.

Williams Insulation Inc.
11111 Plano Rd, Dallas TX 75238-1309. 214/341-0668.

Wind River Roofing Inc.
3200 Handley Ederville Rd, Fort Worth TX 76118-5813. 817/284-1361.

For more information on career opportunities in architecture, construction, and engineering:

Associations

AACE INTERNATIONAL: THE ASSOCIATION FOR ADVANCEMENT OF COST ENGINEERING
209 Prairie Avenue, Suite 100, Morgantown WV 26501. 304/296-8444. Toll-free phone: 800/858-2678. Fax: 304/291-5728. World Wide Web address: http://www.aacei.org. A membership organization which offers *Cost Engineering*, a monthly magazine; employment referral services; technical reference information and assistance; insurance; and a certification program accredited by the Council of Engineering Specialty Boards. Toll-free number provides information on scholarships for undergraduates.

ASM INTERNATIONAL: THE MATERIALS INFORMATION SOCIETY
9639 Kinsman Road, Materials Park OH 44073. 440/338-5151. World Wide Web address: http://www.asm-intl.org. Gathers, processes, and disseminates technical information to foster the understanding and application of engineered materials.

ACOUSTICAL SOCIETY OF AMERICA
2 Huntington Quadrangle, Suite 1NO1, Melville NY 11747. 516/576-2360. Fax: 516/576-2377. E-mail address: asa@aip.org. World Wide Web address: http://asa.aip.org.

AMERICAN ASSOCIATION OF ENGINEERING SOCIETIES
1111 19th Street NW, Suite 403, Washington DC 20036-3690. 202/296-2237. Fax: 202/296-1151. World Wide Web address: http://www.aaes.org. A multidisciplinary organization of professional engineering societies. Publishes reference works, including *Who's Who in Engineering*, *International Directory of Engineering Societies*, and the *Thesaurus of Engineering and Scientific Terms*, as well as statistical reports from studies conducted by the Engineering Workforce Commission.

AMERICAN CONGRESS ON SURVEYING AND MAPPING
5410 Grosvenor Lane, Suite 100, Bethesda MD 20814. 301/493-0200. Publishes *Cartography and Geographic Information Systems: A Career Guide*, which includes educational and government information.

AMERICAN CONSULTING ENGINEERS COUNCIL
1015 15th Street NW, Suite 802, Washington DC 20005. 202/347-7474. Fax: 202/898-0068. World Wide Web address: http://www.acec.org. A national organization of more than 5,000 member firms. Offers *Last Word*, a weekly newsletter; *American Consulting Engineer* magazine; life and health insurance programs; books, manuals, video- and audiotapes, and contract documents; conferences and seminars; and voluntary peer reviews.

AMERICAN DESIGN DRAFTING ASSOCIATION
P.O. Box 11937, Columbia SC 29211. 803/771-

0008. Fax: 803/771-4272. World Wide Web address: http://www.adda.org.

AMERICAN INSTITUTE OF ARCHITECTS
1735 New York Avenue NW, Washington DC 20006. 202/626-7300. Toll-free phone: 800/365-2724. World Wide Web address: http://www.aiaonline.org.

AMERICAN INSTITUTE OF CONSTRUCTORS
1300 North 17th Street, Suite 830, Arlington VA 22209. 703/812-2021. World Wide Web address: http://www.aicnet.org.

AMERICAN SOCIETY FOR ENGINEERING EDUCATION
1818 N Street NW, Suite 600, Washington DC 20036. 202/331-3500. World Wide Web address: http://www.asee.org. Publishes magazines and journals including the *Journal of Engineering Education*.

AMERICAN SOCIETY OF CIVIL ENGINEERS
1801 Alexander Bell Drive, Reston VA 20191-4400. 703/295-6300. World Wide Web address: http://www.asce.org. A membership organization which offers subscriptions to *Civil Engineering* magazine and *ASCE News*, discounts on various other publications, seminars, video- and audiotapes, specialty conferences, an annual convention, group insurance programs, and pension plans.

AMERICAN SOCIETY OF HEATING, REFRIGERATING AND AIR CONDITIONING ENGINEERS
1791 Tullie Circle NE, Atlanta GA 30329. 404/636-8400. Fax: 404/321-5478. World Wide Web address: http://www.ashrae.org. A society of 50,000 members which offers handbooks, a monthly journal, a monthly newspaper, discounts on other publications, group insurance, continuing education, and registration discounts for meetings, conferences, seminars, and expositions.

AMERICAN SOCIETY OF LANDSCAPE ARCHITECTS
636 Eye Street NW, Washington DC 20001. 202/898-2444. World Wide Web address: http://www.asla.org. Check out the Website's Joblink for listings of employment opportunities.

AMERICAN SOCIETY OF MECHANICAL ENGINEERS
3 Park Avenue, New York NY 10016. 212/591-7722. World Wide Web address: http://www.asme.org. Provides educational materials and scholarships for certified engineers.

AMERICAN SOCIETY OF NAVAL ENGINEERS
1452 Duke Street, Alexandria VA 22314. 703/836-6727. World Wide Web address: http://www.navalengineers.org.

AMERICAN SOCIETY OF PLUMBING ENGINEERS
3617 Thousand Oaks Boulevard, Suite 210, Westlake CA 91362. 805/495-7120. Provides technical and educational information.

AMERICAN SOCIETY OF SAFETY ENGINEERS
1800 East Oakton Street, Des Plaines IL 60018-2187. 847/699-2929. Jobline service available at ext. 243. Fax: 847/768-3434. World Wide Web address: http://www.asse.org. A membership organization offering *Professional Safety*, a monthly journal; educational seminars; an annual professional development conference and exposition; technical publications; certification preparation programs; career placement services; and group and liability insurance programs.

ASSOCIATED BUILDERS & CONTRACTORS
1300 North 17th Street, 8th Floor, Rosslyn VA 22209. 703/812-2000. World Wide Web address: http://www.abc.org. Sponsors annual career fair.

ASSOCIATED GENERAL CONTRACTORS OF AMERICA, INC.
333 John Carlyle Street, Suite 200, Alexandria VA 22314. 202/393-2040. World Wide Web address: http://www.agc.org. A full-service construction association of subcontractors, specialty contractors, suppliers, equipment manufacturers, and professional firms. Services include government relations, education and training, jobsite services, legal services, and information services.

THE ENGINEERING CENTER (TEC)
One Walnut Street, Boston MA 02108-3616. 617/227-5551. Contact: Abbie Goodman. World Wide Web address: http://www.engineers.org. An association that provides services for many engineering membership organizations.

ILLUMINATING ENGINEERING SOCIETY OF NORTH AMERICA
120 Wall Street, 17th Floor, New York NY 10005-4001. 212/248-5000. World Wide Web address: http://www.iesna.org. An organization for industry professionals involved in the manufacturing, design, specification, and maintenance of lighting systems. Conference held annually. Offers a Technical Knowledge Examination.

JUNIOR ENGINEERING TECHNICAL SOCIETY
1420 King Street, Suite 405, Alexandria VA 22314-2794. 703/548-JETS. Fax: 703/548-0769. E-mail address: jets@nae.edu. World Wide Web address: http://www.jets.org. A nonprofit, educational society promoting interest in engineering, technology, mathematics, and science. Provides information to high school students and teachers regarding careers in engineering and technology.

NATIONAL ACTION COUNCIL FOR MINORITIES IN ENGINEERING
350 Fifth Avenue, Suite 2212, New York NY 10118. 212/279-2626. World Wide Web address: http://www.nacme.org. Offers scholarship programs for students.

NATIONAL ASSOCIATION OF HOME BUILDERS
1201 15th Street NW, Washington DC 20005. 202/822-0200. World Wide Web address: http://www.nahb.com.

NATIONAL ASSOCIATION OF MINORITY ENGINEERING PROGRAM ADMINISTRATORS,
1133 West Morse Boulevard, Suite 201, Winter Park FL 32789. 407/647-8839. World Wide Web address: http://www.namepa.org.

NATIONAL ELECTRICAL CONTRACTORS ASSOCIATION
3 Bethesda Metro Center, Suite 1100, Bethesda MD 20814. 301/657-3110. World Wide Web address: http://www.necanet.org. Provides information on hiring and trade shows. The

association also publishes a magazine called *Electrical Contractor.*

NATIONAL SOCIETY OF BLACK ENGINEERS
1454 Duke Street, Alexandria VA 22314. 703/549-2207. World Wide Web address: http://www.nsbe.org. A nonprofit organization run by college students. Offers scholarships, editorials, and magazines.

NATIONAL SOCIETY OF PROFESSIONAL ENGINEERS
1420 King Street, Alexandria VA 22314-2794. 703/684-2800. Call 703/684-2830 for scholarship information for students. Fax: 703/836-4875. World Wide Web address: http://www.nspe.org. A society of over 73,000 engineers. Membership includes the monthly magazine *Engineering Times;* continuing education; scholarships and fellowships; discounts on publications; and health and life insurance programs.

SOCIETY OF AMERICAN REGISTERED ARCHITECTS (SARA)
305 East 64th Street, New York NY 10017. 212/759-2007. Toll-free phone: 888/385-7272. World Wide Web address: http://www.sara-national.org.

SOCIETY OF FIRE PROTECTION ENGINEERS
7315 Wisconsin Avenue, Suite 1225W, Bethesda MD 20814. 301/718-2910. Fax: 301/718-2242. World Wide Web address: http://www.sfpe.org. A professional society which offers members reports, newsletters, *Journal of Fire Protecting Engineering,* insurance programs, short courses, symposiums, tutorials, an annual meeting, and engineering seminars.

Directories

DIRECTORY OF ENGINEERING SOCIETIES
American Association of Engineering Societies, 1111 19th Street NW, Suite 403, Washington DC 20036. 202/296-2237. World Wide Web address: http://www.aaes.org. $185.00. Lists other engineering association members, publications, and convention exhibits.

DIRECTORY OF ENGINEERS IN PRIVATE PRACTICE
National Society of Professional Engineers, 1420 King Street, Alexandria VA 22314-2794. 703/684-2800. World Wide Web address: http://www.nspe.org. $50.00. Lists members and companies.

Magazines

THE CAREER ENGINEER
National Society of Black Engineers, 1454 Duke Street, Alexandria VA 22314. 703/549-2207. World Wide Web address: http://www.nsbe.org.

CHEMICAL & ENGINEERING NEWS
American Chemical Society, 1155 16th Street NW, Washington DC 20036. 202/872-4600. World Wide Web address: http://www.acs.org.

COMPUTER-AIDED ENGINEERING
Penton Media, 1100 Superior Avenue, Cleveland OH 44114. 216/696-7000.

EDN CAREER NEWS
Cahners Business Information, 275 Washington Street, Newton MA 02458. 617/964-3030. World Wide Web address: http://www.cahners.com.

ENGINEERING TIMES
National Society of Professional Engineers, 1420 King Street, Alexandria VA 22314. 703/684-2800. World Wide Web address: http://www.nspe.org.

NAVAL ENGINEERS JOURNAL
American Society of Naval Engineers, 1452 Duke Street, Alexandria VA 22314. 703/836-6727. World Wide Web address: http://www.navalengineers.org/services.htm#journal. Subscription: $48.00.

Online Services

ARCHITECTURE & BUILDING FORUM
Go: Arch. A CompuServe discussion group for architectural professionals.

ENGINEERJOBS.COM
World Wide Web address: http://www.engineerjobs.com. This site caters to engineering positions in the Great Lakes area. Detailed job descriptions are provided as well as links to other related sites.

HOT JOBS! - CONSTRUCTION
World Wide Web address: http://www.kbic.com/construction.htm. Provides construction employment opportunities organized by job title.

P.L.A.C.E.S. FORUM
Keyword: places. A discussion group available to America Online subscribers who are professionals in the fields of architecture, construction, and engineering.

ARTS, ENTERTAINMENT, SPORTS, AND RECREATION

You can expect to find the following types of companies in this chapter:
Botanical and Zoological Gardens • Entertainment Groups • Motion Picture and Video Tape Production and Distribution • Museums and Art Galleries • Physical Fitness Facilities • Professional Sports Clubs • Public Golf Courses • Racing and Track Operations • Sporting and Recreational Camps • Theatrical Producers

Some helpful information: Salaries in the entertainment industry vary widely. Scientists hired to work in public zoos and gardens can make $30,000 - $40,000 per year (at the upper end of the range, advanced degrees are required). Experienced museum curators make, on average, $50,000 per year. In theater, the payscale of directors depends partly upon the success of the production. A director can expect a fee, which can be as low as a $5,000 at a small theater or over $40,000 for a Broadway production, as well as a percentage of the box office profits. In sports, athletic directors at competitive universities earn $50,000 on average.

ALLIED DIGITAL TECHNOLOGIES CORPORATION
6305 North O'Connor Road, Suite 111, Building 4, Irving TX 75039. 972/869-0100. **Fax:** 972/869-2117. **Contact:** Human Resources. **World Wide Web address:** http://www.allied-digital.com. **Description:** One of the nation's leading independent multimedia manufacturing companies, offering CD-audio and CD-ROM mastering and replication, videocassette and audiocassette duplication, laser video disc recording, off-line and online video editing, motion picture film processing, film-to-tape and tape-to-film transfers and complete finishing, packaging, warehousing, and fulfillment services. **Listed on:** Privately held.

DALLAS COWBOYS
One Cowboys Parkway, Irving TX 75063-4945. 972/556-9900. **Fax:** 972/556-9304. **Contact:** Human Resources. **World Wide Web address:** http://www.dallascowboys.com. **Description:** Administrative offices for the National Football League team. **Corporate headquarters location:** This Location.

DALLAS MUSEUM OF ART
1717 North Harwood Street, Dallas TX 75201. 214/922-1200. **Contact:** Scott Gensemer, Director of Personnel. **World Wide Web address:** http://www.dm-art.org. **Description:** Offers a wide range of exhibits in all art media. **Common positions include:** Administrator; Curatorial Specialist; Financial Analyst. **Educational backgrounds include:** Art/Design; Master's; Ph.D.

DALLAS MUSEUM OF NATURAL HISTORY
P.O. Box 150349, Dallas TX 75315-0349. 214/421-3466. **Contact:** Robert B. Townsend, Executive Director. **World Wide Web address:** http://www.dallasdino.org. **Description:** Operates a natural history museum offering a full range of exhibits and presentations.

DAVE & BUSTER'S, INC.
2481 Manana Drive, Dallas TX 75220. 214/357-9588. **Contact:** Human Resources. **Description:** An operator of 12 restaurant/entertainment complexes. Each location houses eating venues and amusement facilities including billiards, video games, and virtual reality games. Founded in 1982. **Corporate headquarters location:** This Location. **Other area locations:** Houston TX. **Other U.S. locations:** Ontario CA; Denver CO; Hollywood FL; Atlanta GA; Chicago IL; North Bethesda MD; Detroit MI; Cincinnati OH; Philadelphia PA. **Listed on:** NASDAQ. **Stock exchange symbol:** DANB.

DISCTRONICS
2800 Summit Avenue, Plano TX 75074. 972/881-8800. **Contact:** Human Resources. **Description:** Manufactures CDs and CD-ROMs.

GENERAL CINEMA CORPORATION
12377 Merit Drive, Suite 1530, Dallas TX 75251. 972/934-7700. **Contact:** Human Resources. **Description:** Operates movie theaters. **Corporate headquarters location:** Boston MA. **Operations at this facility include:** Regional Headquarters.

MALIBU ENTERTAINMENT WORLDWIDE
717 North Harwood Street, Suite 1650, Dallas TX 75201. 214/210-8701. **Contact:** Human Resources. **Description:** Develops, owns, and operates entertainment centers called Mountasia Family FunCenters. FunCenters are located in suburban communities and feature miniature golf courses, state-of-the-art video and skill game rooms, go-cart raceways, bumper boats, batting cages, and roller skating arenas. Founded in 1986. **Corporate headquarters location:** This Location.

NESTFAMILY.COM, INC.
6100 Colwell Boulevard, Irving TX 75039. 972/402-7100. **Contact:** Human Resources. **World Wide Web address:** http://www.nestfamily.com. **Description:** Develops educational games, CD-ROMs, music, and videotapes for children. Founded in 1988.

PRIMEDIA WORKPLACE LEARNING
4101 International Parkway, Carrollton TX 75007. 972/309-4000. **Contact:** Human Resources. **Description:** Produces and distributes educational videos to academic, corporate, and industrial clients.

Q THE SPORTS CLUB
4600 West Park Boulevard, Plano TX 75093. 972/612-6960. **Contact:** Manager. **World Wide Web address:** http://www.qclub.com. **Description:** A sports and fitness facility.

TEXAS STADIUM
2401 East Airport Freeway, Irving TX 75062. 972/438-7676. **Contact:** Human Resources Department. **Description:** A sporting arena. Texas Stadium is the home field of the Dallas Cowboys professional football team.

Note: Because addresses and telephone numbers of smaller companies can change rapidly, we recommend you call each company to verify the information below before inquiring about job opportunities. Mass mailings are not recommended.

Additional small employers:

AMUSEMENT AND RECREATION SERVICES

Billy Bob's Texas Inc.
2520 Rodeo Plz, Fort Worth TX 76106-8208. 817/624-7117.

Caldwell Zoo
PO Box 4280, Tyler TX 75712-4280. 903/593-0121.

Colonial Tennis Club
PO Box 1320, Ennis TX 75120-1320. 972/875-5884.

Dallas Stars
211 Cowboys Pkwy, Irving TX 75063-5931. 972/831-2400.

Discovery Zone
1118 W Arbrook Blvd, Arlington TX 76015-4205. 817/472-9973.

Discovery Zone
15240 Dallas Pkwy, Dallas TX 75248-4610. 972/392-4386.

Discovery Zone
3301 W Airport Fwy, Irving TX 75062-5937. 972/256-1900.

Southfork Ranch
3000 Hogge Dr, Allen TX 75002-6734. 972/442-7800.

Surf & Swim
634 Apollo Rd, Garland TX 75040-3401. 972/205-2757.

Ticketmaster
4849 Greenville Ave, Dallas TX 75206-4130. 214/750-7400.

ENTERTAINERS AND ENTERTAINMENT GROUPS

Dallas Symphony Orchestra
2301 Flora St, Ste 300, Dallas TX 75201-2404. 214/871-4000.

East Texas Symphony Orchestra
PO Box 6323, Tyler TX 75711-6323. 903/592-1427.

Fort Worth Symphony Orchestra
330 E 4th St, Ste 200, Fort Worth TX 76102-4021. 817/665-6500.

GOLF COURSES

Arlington Municipal Golf Course
PO Box 231, Arlington TX 76004-0231. 817/275-3271.

Indian Creek Golf Course
PO Box 110535, Carrollton TX 75011-0535. 972/466-3110.

MUSEUMS AND ART GALLERIES

Fort Worth Museum of Science & History
1501 Montgomery St, Fort Worth TX 76107-3017. 817/732-1631.

The Science Place
PO Box 151469, Dallas TX 75315-1469. 214/428-7200.

PHYSICAL FITNESS FACILITIES

Cooper Fitness Center
12200 Preston Rd, Dallas TX 75230-2223. 972/233-4832.

Gold's Gym
4502 Buffalo Gap Rd, Abilene TX 79606-2704. 915/695-8900.

Greenhouse Spa
PO Box 1144, Arlington TX 76004-1144. 817/640-4000.

Q the Sports Club
1375 E Campbell Rd, Richardson TX 75081-1938. 972/644-4888.

Signature Athletic Club
PO Box 796607, Dallas TX 75379-6607. 972/490-7777.

Arts, Entertainment, Sports, and Recreation

Spa at the Crescent
400 Crescent Court, Dallas TX 75201-1888. 214/871-3232.

University Club of Dallas
13350 Dallas Parkway, Dallas TX 75240-6670. 972/239-0050.

PROFESSIONAL SPORTS CLUBS AND PROMOTERS

Streetball Partner International
4006 Belt Line Rd, Ste 230, Addison TX 75001-4373. 972/392-5700.

Texas Rangers
PO Box 90111, Arlington TX 76004-3111. 817/273-5222.

RACING AND TRACK OPERATION

Lone Star Park
1000 Lone Star Pkwy, Grand Prairie TX 75050-7941. 972/263-7223.

Texas Motor Speedway Inc.
PO Box 500, Fort Worth TX 76101-2500. 817/215-8500.

THEATRICAL PRODUCERS AND SERVICES

Lyrick Studios Inc.
2435 N Central Expy, Richardson TX 75080-2753. 972/390-6000.

Vari-Lite International Inc.
201 Regal Row, Dallas TX 75247-5201. 214/630-1963.

For more information on career opportunities in arts, entertainment, sports, and recreation:

Associations

AMERICAN ASSOCIATION OF MUSEUMS
1575 Eye Street NW, Suite 400, Washington DC 20005. 202/289-1818. Fax: 202/289-6578. World Wide Web address: http://www.aam-us.org. Publishes *Aviso*, a monthly newsletter containing employment listings for museums nationwide.

AMERICAN CAMPING ASSOCIATION
5000 State Road 67 North, Martinsville IN 46151. 765/342-8456. World Wide Web address: http://www.aca-camps.org. Provides information on job opportunities at day and overnight camps for children and adults with special needs.

AMERICAN CRAFTS COUNCIL
72 Spring Street, New York NY 10012-4019. 212/274-0630. Operates a research library. Publishes *American Crafts* magazine.

AMERICAN DANCE GUILD
P.O. Box 2006, Lenox Hill Station, New York NY 10021. World Wide Web address: http://www.americandanceguild.org. Holds an annual conference with panels, performances, and workshops. Operates a job listings service (available at a discount to members).

AMERICAN FEDERATION OF MUSICIANS
1501 Broadway, Suite 600, New York NY 10036. 212/869-1330. World Wide Web address: http://www.afm.org.

AMERICAN FILM INSTITUTE
2021 North Western Avenue, Los Angeles CA 90027. 323/856-7600. Toll-free phone: 800/774-4AFI. World Wide Web address: http://www.afionline.org. Membership is required, and includes a newsletter; and members-only discounts on events, seminars, workshops, and exhibits.

AMERICAN MUSIC CENTER
30 West 26th Street, Suite 1001, New York NY 10010-2011. 212/366-5260. Fax: 212/366-5265. World Wide Web address: http://www.amc.net. A nonprofit research and information center for contemporary music and jazz. Provides information services and grant programs.

AMERICAN SOCIETY OF COMPOSERS, AUTHORS, AND PUBLISHERS (ASCAP)
One Lincoln Plaza, New York NY 10023. 212/621-6000. World Wide Web address: http://www.ascap.com. A membership association which licenses members' work and pays members' royalties. Offers showcases and educational seminars and workshops. The society also has an events hotline: 212/621-6485.

AMERICAN SYMPHONY ORCHESTRA LEAGUE
33 West 60th Street, 5th Floor, New York NY 10023-7905. 212/262-5161. Fax: 212/262-5198. World Wide Web address: http://www.symphony.org.

AMERICAN ZOO AND AQUARIUM ASSOCIATION
8403 Colesville Road, Suite 710, Silver Spring MD 20910. 301/562-0777. World Wide Web address: http://www.aza.org. Publishes a monthly newspaper with employment opportunities for members.

AMERICANS FOR THE ARTS
One East 53rd Street, New York NY 10022. 212/223-2787. World Wide Web address: http://www.artsusa.org. A nonprofit organization for the literary, visual, and performing arts. Supports K-12 education and promotes public policy through meetings, forums, and seminars.

ASSOCIATION OF INDEPENDENT VIDEO AND FILMMAKERS
304 Hudson Street, 6th Floor, New York NY 10013. 212/807-1400. World Wide Web address: http://www.aivf.org.

THE CENTER FOR THE STUDY OF SPORT IN SOCIETY
Northeastern University, 360 Huntington Avenue, Suite 161CP, Boston MA 02120. 617/373-4025. World Wide Web address: http://www.sportinsociety.org. Develops programs and provides publications on the interaction of sports and society.

NATIONAL ARTISTS' EQUITY ASSOCIATION
P.O. Box 28068, Central Station, Washington DC 20038-8068. 202/628-9633. A national, nonprofit organization dedicated to improving economic, health, and legal conditions for visual artists.

NATIONAL ENDOWMENT FOR THE ARTS
1100 Pennsylvania Avenue NW, Washington DC 20506. 202/682-5400. World Wide Web address: http://www.arts.endow.gov.

NATIONAL RECREATION AND PARK ASSOCIATION
22377 Belmont Ridge Road, Ashburn VA 20148. 703/858-0784. Fax: 703/858-0794. World Wide

Web address: http://www.nrpa.org. A national, nonprofit service organization. Offers professional development and training opportunities in recreation, parks, and leisure services. Publishes a newsletter and magazine that offer employment opportunities for members only.

PRODUCERS GUILD OF AMERICA
400 South Beverly Drive, Suite 211, Beverly Hills CA 90212. 310/557-0807. Fax: 310/557-0436. World Wide Web address: http://www.producersguild.com. Membership is required, and includes credit union access; subscription to *P.O.V. Magazine* and the association newsletter; attendance at the organization's annual Golden Laurel Awards and other events; and special screenings of motion pictures at the time of the Academy Awards.

Directories

ARTIST'S AND GRAPHIC DESIGNER'S MARKET
Writer's Digest Books, 1507 Dana Avenue, Cincinnati OH 45207. 513/531-2222.

BLACK BOOK ILLUSTRATION
The Black Book, 10 Astor Place, 6th Floor, New York NY 10003. 212/539-9800. World Wide Web address: http://www.blackbook.com.

BLACK BOOK PHOTOGRAPHY
The Black Book, 10 Astor Place, 6th Floor, New York NY 10003. 212/539-9800. World Wide Web address: http://www.blackbook.com.

ROSS REPORTS TELEVISION AND FILM
BPI Communications, Inc., 1515 Broadway, 14th Floor, New York NY 10036-8986. 212/764-7300.

Magazines

AMERICAN CINEMATOGRAPHER
American Society of Cinematographers, 1782 North Orange Drive, Hollywood CA 90028. Toll-free phone: 800/448-0154. World Wide Web address: http://www.cinematographer.com.

ARTFORUM
65 Bleecker Street, 13th Floor, New York NY 10012. 212/475-4000. World Wide Web address: http://www.artforum.com.

AVISO
American Association of Museums, 1575 Eye Street NW, Suite 400, Washington DC 20005. 202/289-1818.

BACK STAGE
BPI Communications, Inc., 1515 Broadway, New York NY 10036-8986. 212/764-7300. World Wide Web address: http://www.backstage.com.

BILLBOARD
BPI Communications, Inc., 1515 Broadway, New York NY 10036-8986. 212/764-7300. World Wide Web address: http://www.billboard.com.

CRAFTS REPORT
300 Water Street, Box 1992, Wilmington DE 19899. 302/656-2209. World Wide Web address: http://www.craftsreport.com.

DRAMA-LOGUE
P.O. Box 38771, Los Angeles CA 90038. 213/464-5079.

HOLLYWOOD REPORTER
BPI Communications, Inc., 5055 Wilshire Boulevard, 6th Floor, Los Angeles CA 90036. 213/525-2000. World Wide Web address: http://www.hollywoodreporter.com.

VARIETY
245 West 17th Street, 5th Floor, New York NY 10011. 212/337-7001. Toll-free phone: 800/323-4345.

WOMEN ARTIST NEWS
300 Riverside Drive, New York NY 10025. 212/666-6990.

Online Services

ARTJOB
Gopher://gopher.tmn.com/11/Artswire/artjob. Provides information on jobs, internships, and conferences in theater, dance, opera, and museums. This site is only accessible through America Online.

COOLWORKS
World Wide Web address: http://www.coolworks.com. Provides links to 22,000 job openings in national parks, summer camps, ski areas, river areas, ranches, fishing areas, cruise ships, and resorts. This site also includes information on volunteer openings.

THE INTERNET MUSIC PAGES
World Wide Web address: http://www.musicpages.com. Offers job listings at well-known companies such as Dolby, Microsoft, and Fender and also provides links to music-related newsgroups.

JOBS IN SPORTS
World Wide Web address: http://careerexperience.com. Offers members direct access to full contact information for hundreds of jobs in sports and recreation. Fees are $9.95 for one day; $49.00 for one month; $399.00 for a year.

VISUAL NATION ARTS JOBS LINKS
World Wide Web address: http://www.visualarts.com. Provides links to other sites that post arts and academic job openings and information.

AUTOMOTIVE

You can expect to find the following types of companies in this chapter:
Automotive Repair Shops • Automotive Stampings • Industrial Vehicles and Moving Equipment • Motor Vehicles and Equipment • Travel Trailers and Campers

Some helpful information: *The average salary range for automotive mechanics and servicers is $25,000 - $35,000 per year. Commissioned mechanics, as well as specialist mechanics, can earn considerably more.*

DAIMLERCHRYSLER CORPORATION
P.O. Box 110370, Carrollton TX 75011. 972/418-4600. **Contact:** Human Resources. **World Wide Web address:** http://www1.daimlerchrysler.com. **Description:** Manufactures cars, trucks, minivans, and sport-utility vehicles for customers in more than 100 countries.

GNB TECHNOLOGIES INC.
P.O. Box 819023, Dallas TX 75381-9023. 972/243-1011. **Contact:** Kevin Williams, Regional Human Resources Manager. **World Wide Web address:** http://www.gnb.com. **Description:** This location manufactures batteries for automobiles, trucks, farm equipment, and industrial uses. Overall, GNB Technologies has three divisions: Automotive Battery, Industrial Battery, and Resource Recycling, with primary operations in North America. **Common positions include:** Environmental Engineer; Human Resources Manager; Industrial Engineer; Quality Control Supervisor. **Educational backgrounds include:** Business Administration; Chemistry; Engineering. **Benefits:** 401(k); Dental Insurance; Disability Coverage; Life Insurance; Medical Insurance; Pension Plan; Profit Sharing; Tuition Assistance.

HILITE INDUSTRIES, INC.
P.O. Box 814649, Dallas TX 75381. 972/242-2116. **Contact:** Personnel Department. **World Wide Web address:** http://www.hilite-ind.com. **Description:** Designs, manufactures, and sells automotive components including brake proportioning valves, electromagnetic clutches and machined components, springs, stampings, and assemblies.

PETERBILT MOTORS COMPANY
P.O. Box 550, Denton TX 76202. 940/566-7100. **Contact:** Human Resources. **World Wide Web address:** http://www.peterbilt.com. **Description:** Designs heavy-duty trucks. **Common positions include:** Accountant; Electrical Engineer; Mechanical Engineer; Systems Analyst. **Educational backgrounds include:** Accounting; Computer Science; Engineering; Marketing.

SCS/FRIGETTE CORPORATION
P.O. Box 40550, Fort Worth TX 76140. 817/293-5313. **Contact:** Human Resources. **World Wide Web address:** http://www.scsfrigette.com. **Description:** A manufacturer of automobile air conditioning and heating systems, cruise controls, security systems, and accessories. **Common positions include:** Accountant/Auditor; Buyer; Clerical Supervisor; Credit Manager; Customer Service Representative; Designer; Draftsperson; Electrical/Electronics Engineer; Manufacturer's/Wholesaler's Sales Rep.; Materials Engineer; Mechanical Engineer; Purchasing Agent/Manager; Quality Control Supervisor; Services Sales Representative. **Educational backgrounds include:** Accounting; Art/Design; Business Administration; Engineering; Finance; Marketing. **Benefits:** 401(k); Dental Insurance; Life Insurance; Medical Insurance; Savings Plan. **Corporate headquarters location:** This Location. **Listed on:** Privately held.

Note: Because addresses and telephone numbers of smaller companies can change rapidly, we recommend you call each company to verify the information below before inquiring about job opportunities. Mass mailings are not recommended.

Additional small employers:

AUTOMOTIVE REPAIR SHOPS

City Motor Supply Inc.
11670 Harry Hines Boulevard, Dallas TX 75229-2203.
972/484-2611.

DC Bumper
3044 Morrell Ave, Dallas TX 75203-4053. 214/942-8444.

Fibre Body Industries Inc.
PO Box 1058, Gatesville TX 76528-6058. 254/248-1324.

Luxury Conversions
PO Box 970, Grandview TX 76050-0970. 817/866-2901.

Pep Boys
1130 E Kearney St, Mesquite TX 75149-2604. 972/216-9977.

AUTOMOTIVE STAMPINGS

Raylock Industries
PO Box 908, Stephenville TX 76401-0908. 254/965-5075.

INDUSTRIAL VEHICLES AND MOVING EQUIPMENT

K-D Manitou Inc.
PO Box 154009, Waco TX 76715-4009. 254/799-0232.

Serco
1612 Hutton Dr, Ste 140, Carrollton TX 75006-6642. 972/466-0707.

Standard Manufacturing Company
PO Box 210300, Dallas TX 75211-0300. 214/337-8911.

Trailer Jockey
401 Capacity Dr, Longview TX 75604-5341. 903/759-0610.

MOTOR VEHICLE EQUIPMENT WHOLESALE

AC Delco
PO Box 40370, Fort Worth TX 76140-0370. 817/551-3546.

Adesa Dallas
PO Box 270159, Dallas TX 75227-0159. 972/288-7585.

Around the Clock Freightliner
PO Box 161579, Fort Worth TX 76161-1579. 817/870-9101.

Chrome Specialties Inc.
4200 Diplomacy Rd, Fort Worth TX 76155-2634. 817/868-2000.

Cosmos International Inc.
501 Industrial Dr, Ste 101, Richardson TX 75081-2811. 972/699-1683.

Dallas Parts Depot
2205 E Belt Line Rd, Carrollton TX 75006-5608. 972/418-4665.

Dealers Auto Auction of Dallas
2717 E Main St, Grand Prairie TX 75050-6214. 972/642-3900.

DSR Automotive LLC
7537 Jack Newell Blvd N, Fort Worth TX 76118-7111. 817/284-4564.

Ford Motor Company
PO Box 110037, Carrollton TX 75011-0037. 972/417-6100.

Fort Worth Auto Auction
2245 Jacksboro Hwy, Fort Worth TX 76114-2319. 817/626-5494.

Fort Worth Freightliner
PO Box 560505, Dallas TX 75356-0505. 214/631-2620.

Interstate Battery Systems
12770 Merit Dr, Ste 400, Dallas TX 75251-1200. 972/991-1444.

Nissan North America Inc.
PO Box 167728, Irving TX 75016-7728. 972/929-2600.

PBE Warehouse Sales Inc.
808 N Grove Rd, Richardson TX 75081-2747. 972/235-3127.

Regency Conversions
2800 Golden Triangle Blvd, Fort Worth TX 76177-7016. 817/847-7171.

Tiner Machine
PO Box 2685, Lubbock TX 79408-2685. 806/747-7833.

Western Auto Distribution Center
PO Box 6120, Temple TX 76503-6120. 254/771-8100.

MOTOR VEHICLES AND EQUIPMENT

AER Manufacturing Inc.
PO Box 979, Carrollton TX 75011. 972/418-6499.

Astro Air Inc.
PO Box 1988, Jacksonville TX 75766-1988. 903/586-3691.

Four Seasons
PO Box 2508, Fort Worth TX 76113-2508. 817/831-7100.

Four Seasons
1801 Waters Ridge Dr, Lewisville TX 75057-6027. 972/316-8100.

Four Seasons
PO Box 1955, Coppell TX 75019-1955. 972/471-8000.

Four Seasons
500 Industrial Park Dr, Grapevine TX 76051. 214/471-8000.

Heil Trailer International
1121 Cantrell Sansom Rd, Fort Worth TX 76131-1411. 817/232-8954.

Holland Hitch Company
1301 Martinez Ln, Wylie TX 75098-4023. 972/442-3556.

J&L Tank
PO Box 247, Rhome TX 76078-0247. 817/636-2201.

Ledwell & Son Enterprises
PO Box 1106, Texarkana TX 75504-1106. 903/838-6531.

Metro Electric Co.
PO Box 1856, Amarillo TX 79105-1856. 806/376-5603.

Prior Remanufacturing Inc.
PO Box 462167, Garland TX 75046-2167. 972/494-4254.

Sanden International
601 Sanden Blvd, Wylie TX 75098-4923. 972/442-8400.

Stemco Inc.
PO Box 1989, Longview TX 75606-1989. 903/758-9981.

Supreme Corporation of Texas
PO Box 2828, Cleburne TX 76033-2828. 817/641-6282.

Tymco Inc.
PO Box 2368, Waco TX 76703-2368. 254/799-5546.

US Liberty Trailer
PO Box 759, Mansfield TX 76063-0759. 817/477-1734.

Watson & Chalin Manufacturing Inc.
2060 Couch Dr, McKinney TX 75069-7313. 972/547-6020.

Wells Cargo
PO Box 7128, Waco TX 76714-7128. 254/772-1740.

For more information on career opportunities in the automotive industry:

Associations

ALLIANCE OF AUTOMOBILE MANUFACTURERS
1401 H Street NW, Suite 900, Washington DC 20005. 202/326-5500. Fax: 202/326-5567. World Wide Web address: http://www.autoalliance.org. A trade association. Reviews social and public policies pertaining to the motor vehicle industry and its customers.

AUTOMOTIVE AFTERMARKET INDUSTRY ASSOCIATION
25 Northwest Point Boulevard, Suite 425, Elk Grove Village IL 60007-1035. 847/228-1310. World Wide Web address: http://www.aftermarket.org. Members are manufacturers and distributors of automobile replacement parts. Sponsors a trade show. Publishes educational guidebooks and training manuals.

AUTOMOTIVE SERVICE ASSOCIATION
P.O. Box 929, Bedford TX 76095. 817/283-6205. World Wide Web address: http://www.asashop.org. Works with shops to find workers.

Directories

AUTOMOTIVE NEWS MARKET DATA BOOK
Crain Communications, Automotive News, 1400 Woodbridge Avenue, Detroit MI 48207-3187. 313/446-6000.

WARD'S AUTOMOTIVE YEARBOOK
Ward's Communications, Inc., 3000 Town Center, Suite 2750, Southville MI 48075. 248/357-0800. World Wide Web address: http://www.wardsauto.com.

Magazines

AUTOMOBILE MAGAZINE
PRIMEDIA, Inc., 120 East Liberty Street, Ann Arbor MI 48104. 734/994-3500. World Wide Web address: http://www.automobilemag.com.

AUTOMOTIVE NEWS
Crain Communications, 1400 Woodbridge Avenue, Detroit MI 48207-3187. 313/446-6000.

WARD'S AUTO WORLD
WARD'S AUTOMOTIVE REPORTS
Ward's Communications, Inc., 3000 Town Center, Suite 2750, Southville MI 48075. 248/357-0800. World Wide Web address: http://www.wardsauto.com.

For information about the JobBank List Service visit www.adamsjobbank.com

BANKING/SAVINGS AND LOANS

You can expect to find the following types of companies in this chapter:
Banks • Bank Holding Companies and Associations •
Lending Firms/Financial Services Institutions

Some helpful information: *The average salary range for entry-level bank and loan officers is $30,000 - $40,000 annually. Senior officers and directors can earn over $50,000, and executives often top $100,000. Tellers' and clerks' salaries are usually under $20,000. Loan officers generally earn between $30,000 and $70,000, depending upon their specialty (in particular, commercial real estate mortgage loan officers earn salaries at the upper end of the range).*

AMARILLO NATIONAL BANK
P.O. Box 1, Amarillo TX 79105. 806/378-8000. **Fax:** 806/378-8066. **Contact:** Human Resources. **World Wide Web address:** http://www.anb.com. **Description:** A full-service bank with 12 locations. Services include intra-bank funds transfers, mortgages, and online banking.

BANK ONE TEXAS
500 Throckmorton Street, Fort Worth TX 76102. 817/884-4000. **Contact:** Human Resources. **World Wide Web address:** http://www.bankone.com. **Description:** A full-service, commercial bank. **Common positions include:** Accountant/Auditor; Bank Officer/Manager. **Educational backgrounds include:** Accounting; Finance. **Benefits:** Dental Insurance; Disability Coverage; Employee Discounts; Life Insurance; Medical Insurance; Pension Plan; Profit Sharing; Savings Plan; Tuition Assistance. **Corporate headquarters location:** Chicago IL. **Other U.S. locations:** AZ; CO; IL; IN; KY; MI; OH; OK; UT; WI; WV. **Parent company:** Banc One Corporation. **Listed on:** New York Stock Exchange. **Number of employees nationwide:** 89,000.

CHASE BANK OF TEXAS
2200 Ross Avenue, Suite 720, Dallas TX 75201. 214/922-2421. **Contact:** Human Resources. **World Wide Web address:** http://www.chase.com. **Description:** Operates through a network of 40 member banks in Texas. Operations include energy, commercial, real estate, and international banking. **Corporate headquarters location:** Houston TX. **Other U.S. locations:** Denver CO; New York NY. **International locations:** Worldwide.

CHASE BANK OF TEXAS
P.O. Box 250, Arlington TX 76004-0250. 817/856-3277. **Contact:** Human Resources. **World Wide Web address:** http://www.chase.com. **Description:** A banking organization operating through a network of 40 member banks in Texas. Operations include energy, commercial, real estate, and international banking. **Corporate headquarters location:** Houston TX. **Other U.S. locations:** Denver CO; New York NY. **International locations:** Worldwide.

FEDERAL RESERVE BANK OF DALLAS
P.O. Box 655906, Dallas TX 75265-5906. 214/922-6000. **Physical address:** 2200 North Pearl Street, Dallas TX 75201. **Recorded jobline:** 214/922-6166. **Contact:** Employment. **World Wide Web address:** http://www.dallasfed.org. **Description:** One of 12 regional Federal Reserve banks that, along with the Federal Reserve Board of Governors in Washington DC and the Federal Open Market Committee, comprise the Federal Reserve System. As the nation's central bank, the Federal Reserve is charged with three major responsibilities: monetary policy, banking supervision and regulation, and processing payments. **Common positions include:** Accountant/Auditor; Attorney; Computer Programmer; Economist; Financial Analyst. **Educational backgrounds include:** Accounting; Business Administration; Computer Science; Economics; Finance. **Benefits:** 401(k); Dental Insurance; Medical Insurance; Public Transit Available. **Special programs:** Internships.

FIRST NATIONAL BANK OF ABILENE
P.O. Box 701, Abilene TX 79604. 915/627-7000. **Contact:** Pam Mann, Director of Human Resources. **World Wide Web address:** http://www.fnbabilene.com. **Description:** A full-service bank that offers online banking, loan, and investment services.

INDEPENDENT BANKSHARES, INC.
P.O. Box 3296, Abilene TX 79604. 915/677-5550. **Fax:** 915/677-5943. **Contact:** Human Resources. **Description:** A bank holding company. Founded in 1981. **Common positions**

Banking/Savings and Loans/87

include: Accountant/Auditor; Administrative Assistant; Bank Officer/Manager; Chief Financial Officer; Controller; Operations/Production Manager; Secretary. **Educational backgrounds include:** Accounting; Business Administration; Finance. **Benefits:** 401(k); Dental Insurance; Disability Coverage; Employee Discounts; ESOP; Life Insurance; Medical Insurance. **Corporate headquarters location:** This Location. **Subsidiaries include:** Independent Financial Corporation (Abilene TX) owns First State Bank, N.A. **Listed on:** American Stock Exchange. **Stock exchange symbol:** IBK. **Annual sales/revenues:** $11 - $20 million. **Number of employees at this location:** 20. **Number of employees nationwide:** 125.

NORWEST BANK
P.O. Box 1241, Lubbock TX 79408-1241. 806/765-8611. **Contact:** Human Resources. **World Wide Web address:** http://www.norwest.com. **Description:** A full-service bank. Norwest Bank has over 580 branches in 15 states in the northwestern U.S. The bank offers corporate and community banking services, credit card products, trust and investment services, and insurance. **Parent company:** Wells Fargo (San Francisco CA).

Note: Because addresses and telephone numbers of smaller companies can change rapidly, we recommend you call each company to verify the information below before inquiring about job opportunities. Mass mailings are not recommended.

Additional small employers:

COMMERCIAL BANKS

Alliance Bank Inc.
PO Box 500, Sulphur Springs TX 75483-0500. 903/885-2187.

American Bank of Texas
PO Box 1234, Sherman TX 75091-1234. 903/893-7555.

American National Bank of Texas
PO Box 40, Terrell TX 75160-9003. 972/563-2611.

Bank of America
1401 Elm St, Dallas TX 75202-2958. 214/508-6552.

Bank of America
PO Box 831000, Dallas TX 75283-1000. 214/508-6262.

Bank of America
500 West 7th Street, Fort Worth TX 76102-4700. 817/390-6161.

Bank One Texas
PO Box 655415, Dallas TX 75265-5415. 214/290-2000.

Bank One Texas
PO Box 540, Wichita Falls TX 76307-0540. 940/689-6505.

Chase Bank of Texas
PO Box 660197, Dallas TX 75266-0197. 214/922-2674.

Compass Bank
PO Box 650561, Dallas TX 75265-0561. 972/705-4200.

First Community Bank Shares
PO Drawer 937, Killeen TX 76540. 254/634-2161.

First State Bank
PO Box 100, Rio Vista TX 76093-0100. 817/373-2944.

First State Bank
PO Box 100, Denton TX 76202-0100. 940/382-5421.

First Texas Bank
PO Box 609, Killeen TX 76540-0609. 254/634-2132.

Longview Bank & Trust Company
PO Box 3188, Longview TX 75606-3188. 903/237-5500.

Nationsbank
PO Box 1331, Amarillo TX 79180-0001. 806/378-1400.

North Dallas Bank & Trust Co.
PO Box 679001, Dallas TX 75367-9001. 972/387-1300.

Norwest Bank
PO Box 1480, Fort Worth TX 76101-1480. 817/347-8422.

Norwest Bank
811 Washington Ave, Waco TX 76701-1252. 254/754-5431.

Plains National Bank
PO Box 271, Lubbock TX 79408-0271. 806/795-7131.

Southside Bank
PO Box 1079, Tyler TX 75710-1079. 903/531-7236.

Texas Independent Bank
PO Box 560528, Dallas TX 75356-0528. 972/650-6000.

Town North National Bank
PO Box 814810, Dallas TX 75381-4810. 972/391-6800.

CREDIT UNIONS

American Airlines Employees Federal Credit Union
PO Box 619001, Dallas TX 75261-9001. 817/963-6000.

Community Credit Union
PO Box 867119, Plano TX 75086-7119. 972/578-5000.

Dallas Teachers Credit Union
PO Box 517028, Dallas TX 75251-7028. 972/301-1800.

Educational Employees Credit Union
PO Box 1777, Fort Worth TX 76101-1777. 817/882-0000.

OmniAmerican Federal Credit Union
PO Box 150099, Fort Worth TX 76108-0099. 817/246-0111.

Southwest Corporation Federal Credit Union
7920 Belt Line Rd, Dallas TX 75240-8145. 972/861-3000.

OFFICES OF BANK HOLDING COMPANIES

Norwest Bank
PO Box 4377, Wichita Falls TX 76308-0377. 940/767-8321.

SAVINGS INSTITUTIONS

Bank One Texas
PO Box 12000, Dallas TX 75225. 214/360-4330.

Guaranty Federal Bank
8333 Douglas Ave, Ste 200, Dallas TX 75225-5800. 214/360-3360.

For more information on career opportunities in the banking/savings and loans industry:

Associations

AMERICA'S COMMUNITY BANKERS
900 19th Street NW, Suite 400, Washington DC 20006. 202/857-3100. World Wide Web address: http://www.acbankers.org. A trade association representing the expanded thrift industry. Membership is limited to institutions.

AMERICAN BANKERS ASSOCIATION
1120 Connecticut Avenue NW, Washington DC 20036. 202/663-5221. World Wide Web address: http://www.aba.com. Provides banking education and training services, sponsors industry programs and conventions, and publishes articles, newsletters, and the *ABA Service Member Directory*.

Career Fairs

CAREER FAIRS INTERNATIONAL
World Wide Web address: http://www.career-fairs.com. Organizes career fairs in the fields of accounting, banking, finance, and insurance.

Directories

AMERICAN FINANCIAL DIRECTORY
Thomson Financial Publications, 4709 West Golf Road, Skokie IL 60076. Toll-free phone: 800/321-3373.

AMERICAN SAVINGS DIRECTORY
Thomson Financial Publications, 4709 West Golf Road, Skokie IL 60076. Toll-free phone: 800/321-3373.

MOODY'S BANK AND FINANCE MANUAL
Moody's Investors Service, Inc., 99 Church Street, 1st Floor, New York NY 10007-2701. 212/553-0300. World Wide Web address: http://www.moodys.com.

RANKING THE BANKS
American Banker, Inc., One State Street Plaza, New York NY 10004. 212/803-6700. World Wide Web address: http://www.americanbanker.com.

Magazines

ABA BANKING JOURNAL
American Bankers Association, 1120 Connecticut Avenue NW, Washington DC 20036. 202/663-5221. World Wide Web address: http://www.aba.com.

BANKERS MAGAZINE
Faulkner & Gray, 11 Penn Plaza, New York NY 10001. Toll-free phone: 800/200-8963.

BANKING STRATEGIES
Bank Administrators Institute, One North Franklin, Suite 1000, Chicago IL 60606. Toll-free phone: 800/224-9889. World Wide Web address: http://www.bai.org.

JOURNAL OF LENDING AND CREDIT RISK MANAGEMENT
Robert Morris Associates, 1650 Market Street, Suite 2300, Philadelphia PA 19103. 215/446-4000.

Online Services

AMERICAN BANKER ONLINE'S CAREERZONE
World Wide Web address: http://www.americanbanker.com. Provides listings of financial job openings, updated daily.

JOBS FOR BANKERS
World Wide Web address: http://www.bankjobs.com. This site provides access to a database of over 15,000 banking-related job openings. Jobs for Bankers is run by Careers, Inc. This Website also includes a resume database.

JOBS IN COMMERCIAL BANKING
World Wide Web address: http://www.cob.ohio-state.edu/dept/fin/jobs/commbank.htm. Provides information and resources for jobseekers looking to work in the field of commercial banking.

NATIONAL BANKING NETWORK: RECRUITING FOR BANKING AND FINANCE
World Wide Web address: http://www.banking-financejobs.com.

For information about the JobBank List Service visit www.adamsjobbank.com

BIOTECHNOLOGY, PHARMACEUTICALS, AND SCIENTIFIC R&D

You can expect to find the following types of companies in this chapter:
Clinical Labs • Lab Equipment Manufacturers
Pharmaceutical Manufacturers and Distributors

Some helpful information: The average annual salary for entry-level biological scientists with bachelor's degrees depends largely on the industry in which they work, but on average they earn approximately $25,000 - $30,000 (scientists with advanced degrees can earn more). Laboratory technicians earn between $20,000 and $40,000 per year. Experienced scientists, such as pharmacologists, may earn more, particularly if they work for a larger company. Research scientists generally earn less than those in the private sector.

ABBOTT DIAGNOSTICS
1921 Hurd Street, Irving TX 75038. 972/518-6000. **Contact:** Personnel Department. **World Wide Web address:** http://www.abbott.com. **Description:** Designs, develops, and manufactures automated laboratory instruments, primarily used in the fields of clinical chemistry, microbiology, and therapeutic drug monitoring. **Corporate headquarters location:** Abbott Park IL. **Parent company:** Abbott Laboratories is an international manufacturer of a wide range of health care products including pharmaceuticals, hospital products, diagnostic products, chemical products, and nutritional products.

ALLERGAN, INC.
8301 Mars Drive, Waco TX 76712. 254/666-3331. **Contact:** Human Resources. **World Wide Web address:** http://www.allergan.com. **Description:** Develops, manufactures, and distributes prescription and non-prescription pharmaceutical products in the specialty fields of ophthalmology and dermatology.

CARRINGTON LABORATORIES
2001 Walnut Hill Lane, Irving TX 75038. 972/518-1300. **Contact:** Human Resources. **World Wide Web address:** http://www.carringtonlabs.com. **Description:** Develops, manufactures, and markets a number of wound care products, pharmaceutical products, and veterinary products, all of which are based on complex carbohydrates derived from aloe vera. Products include Carrasyn Hydrogel Wound Dressing; CarraSorb H Calcium Alginate Wound Dressing; CarraFilm Transparent Film Dressing; CarraSorb M Freeze-Dried Gel; DiaB, a line of wound care products for diabetics; and RadiaCare, a line of products to treat radiation dermatitis. **Corporate headquarters location:** This Location. **Subsidiaries include:** Caraloe, Inc. manufactures and markets nutritional aloe drinks.

LTC MEDICAL LABORATORIES, INC.
4747 Irving Boulevard, Suite 245, Dallas TX 75247. 214/630-5227. **Contact:** Human Resources. **Description:** A full-service medical laboratory that provides comprehensive clinical laboratory services, such as tests and blood work, for long-term care facilities and home health care patients. **Parent company:** Horizon/CMS Healthcare Corporation acquires and operates long-term care facilities throughout the United States; provides health care services, such as nursing care, rehabilitation, and other therapies; provides institutional pharmacy services; provides specialty care to Alzheimer's patients; and offers subacute care.

LABORATORY CORPORATION OF AMERICA (LABCORP)
7777 Forest Lane, Building C, Suite 350, Dallas TX 75230. 972/566-3353. **Toll-free phone:** 800/788-9892. **Fax:** 972/991-0381. **Recorded jobline:** 800/645-5680. **Contact:** Human Resources. **E-mail address:** employment@labcorp.com. **World Wide Web address:** http://www.labcorp.com. **Description:** One of the nation's leading clinical laboratory companies, providing services to physicians, hospitals, clinics, nursing homes, and other clinical labs nationwide. LabCorp performs tests on blood, urine, and other body fluids and tissues, aiding the diagnosis of disease. **Common positions include:** Account Representative; Customer Service Representative; Data Entry Clerk; Medical Technologist. **Educational backgrounds include:** Biology; Chemistry. **Benefits:** 401(k); Credit Union; Dental Insurance; Disability Coverage; Life Insurance; Medical Insurance; Pension Plan; Profit Sharing; Public Transit Available; Savings Plan; Tuition Assistance. **Office hours:** Monday - Friday, 7:30 a.m. -

5:30 p.m. **Corporate headquarters location:** Burlington NC. **Other U.S. locations:** Nationwide. **Listed on:** American Stock Exchange; NASDAQ; New York Stock Exchange. **Stock exchange symbol:** LH. **Co-CEO:** Dr. Larry Leonard. **Number of employees at this location:** 2,000. **Number of employees nationwide:** 18,000.

QUEST DIAGNOSTICS INCORPORATED
SMITHKLINE BEECHAM CLINICAL LABORATORIES
8000 Sovereign Row, Dallas TX 75247. 214/638-1301. **Contact:** Human Resources. **World Wide Web address:** http://www.questdiagnostics.com. **Description:** One of the largest clinical laboratories in North America, providing a broad range of clinical laboratory services to health care clients which include physicians, hospitals, clinics, dialysis centers, pharmaceutical companies, and corporations. The company offers and performs tests on blood, urine, and other bodily fluids and tissues to provide information on health and well-being.

TEXAS VETERINARY MEDICAL DIAGNOSTIC LABORATORY
P.O. Box 3200, Amarillo TX 79116. 806/353-7478. **Physical address:** 6610 Amarillo Boulevard West, Amarillo TX. **Toll-free phone:** 888/646-5624. **Fax:** 806/359-0636. **Contact:** Robert W. Sprowls, Associate ABC Director. **Description:** A diagnostic laboratory that performs medical testing on animals to assist veterinarians with diagnosis and prognosis. Test fields include chemistry, hematology, urology, toxicology, serology, histology, bacteriology, and necropsies. **Common positions include:** Chemist; Clinical Lab Technician; Computer Operator; Human Resources Manager; Medical Records Technician; Microbiologist; Pathologist; Secretary; Toxicologist. **Educational backgrounds include:** Chemistry; Veterinary Medicine. **Benefits:** 401(k); Dental Insurance; Life Insurance; Medical Insurance; Pension Plan. **Office hours:** Monday - Friday, 8:00 a.m. - 5:00 p.m.; Saturday, 8:00 a.m. - 12:00 p.m. **Other area locations:** College Station TX. **Executive Director:** A. Konrad Eugster.

For more information on career opportunities in biotechnology, pharmaceuticals, and scientific R&D:

Associations

AMERICAN ASSN. FOR CLINICAL CHEMISTRY
2101 L Street NW, Suite 202, Washington DC 20037-1526. 202/857-0717. Toll-free phone: 800/892-1400. World Wide Web address: http://www.aacc.org.

AMERICAN ASSOCIATION OF COLLEGES OF PHARMACY
1426 Prince Street, Alexandria VA 22314-2841. 703/739-2330. World Wide Web address: http://www.aacp.org.

AMERICAN ASSOCIATION OF PHARMACEUTICAL SCIENTISTS
1650 King Street, Suite 200, Alexandria VA 22314-2747. 703/548-3000. World Wide Web address: http://www.aaps.org.

THE AMERICAN COLLEGE OF CLINICAL PHARMACY (ACCP)
3101 Broadway, Suite 380, Kansas City MO 64111. 816/531-2177. World Wide Web address: http://www.accp.com.

AMERICAN INST. OF BIOLOGICAL SCIENCES
1444 I Street NW, Suite 200, Washington DC 20005. 202/628-1500. Fax: 202/628-1509.

AMERICAN SOCIETY FOR BIOCHEMISTRY AND MOLECULAR BIOLOGY
9650 Rockville Pike, Bethesda MD 20814-3996. 301/530-7145. Fax: 301/571-1824. World Wide Web address: http://www.faseb.org/asbmb.

AMERICAN SOCIETY FOR CELL BIOLOGY
9650 Rockville Pike, Bethesda MD 20814-3992. 301/530-7153. Fax: 301/530-7139. World Wide Web address: http://www.ascb.org/ascb.

AMERICAN SOCIETY FOR CLINICAL LABORATORY SCIENCE
7910 Woodmont Avenue, Suite 530, Bethesda MD 20814. 301/657-2768. Fax: 301/657-2909. World Wide Web address: http://www.ascls.org.

AMERICAN SOCIETY OF HEALTH-SYSTEM PHARMACISTS
7272 Wisconsin Avenue, Bethesda MD 20814. 301/657-3000. World Wide Web address: http://www.ashp.org.

BIOTECHNOLOGY INDUSTRY ORGANIZATION
1625 K Street NW, Suite 1100, Washington DC 20006-1604. 202/857-0244. Fax: 202/857-0237. World Wide Web address: http://www.bio.org.

INTERNATIONAL SOCIETY FOR PHARMACEUTICAL ENGINEERING
3816 West Linebaugh Avenue, Suite 412, Tampa FL 33624. 813/960-2105. World Wide Web address: http://www.ispe.org.

Online Services

MEDZILLA
E-mail address: info@medzilla.com. World Wide Web address: http://www.medzilla.com.

Visit our exciting job and career site at www.careercity.com

BUSINESS SERVICES AND NON-SCIENTIFIC RESEARCH

You can expect to find the following types of companies in this chapter:
Adjustment and Collection Services • Cleaning, Maintenance, and Pest Control Services • Credit Reporting • Detective, Guard, and Armored Car Services • Miscellaneous Equipment Rental and Leasing • Secretarial and Court Reporting Services

Some helpful information: The average salary for custodians and janitorial staff is under $20,000, while general maintenance workers can earn up to $35,000 annually (particularly if they have a related skill, such as electronics repair). Security guards who are specially trained and work for manufacturing companies often earn $10.00 - 12.00 per hour (nearly twice what general guards earn). Accountants and credit officers that do financial service work for client companies generally earn between $25,000 and $50,000 annually, depending on the nature of their work and the size of the client company.

ACS, INC.
2828 North Haskell, Dallas TX 75204. 214/841-6111. **Contact:** Human Resources. **World Wide Web address:** http://www.acs-inc.com. **Description:** A full-service provider of data processing, computer outsourcing, facilities management, electronic transaction processing, and telecommunications services. The firm owns several data centers across the United States and a telecommunications network that encompasses leading edge technologies. The company uses many different computer platforms including IBM, Amdahl, Hewlett-Packard, Tandem, and UNIX-based systems.

ACE AMERICA'S CASH EXPRESS INC.
1231 Greenway Drive, Suite 800, Irving TX 75038. 972/550-5000. **Fax:** 972/582-1410. **Contact:** Human Resources. **Description:** One of the largest check cashing companies in the United States, offering check cashing services for government and payroll checks. **Other U.S. locations:** Nationwide.

AUTOMATIC DATA PROCESSING (ADP)
2735 North Stemmons Freeway, Dallas TX 75207. 214/630-9311. **Toll-free phone:** 800/829-2775. **Fax:** 214/905-2828. **Contact:** Sandy Davis, Director of Human Resources. **World Wide Web address:** http://www.adp.com. **Description:** Provides computerized transaction processing, recordkeeping, data communications, and information services. ADP helps more than 300,000 clients improve their business performance by providing services such as payroll, payroll tax, and human resource information management; brokerage industry market data, back office, and proxy services; industry-specific services to auto and truck dealers; and computerized auto repair and replacement estimating for auto insurance companies and body repair shops. The company's four largest businesses. are Employer Services, Brokerage Services, Dealer Services, and Claims Services. **Common positions include:** Account Representative; Administrative Assistant; Customer Service Representative; Sales Manager; Sales Representative; Secretary; Typist/Word Processor. **Educational backgrounds include:** Accounting; Business Administration. **Benefits:** 401(k); Daycare Assistance; Dental Insurance; Disability Coverage; Life Insurance; Medical Insurance; Pension Plan; Savings Plan; Stock Purchase; Tuition Assistance. **Corporate headquarters location:** Roseland NJ. **Other U.S. locations:** Nationwide. **Listed on:** New York Stock Exchange. **Annual sales/revenues:** More than $100 million. **Number of employees at this location:** 500. **Number of employees nationwide:** 29,000.

BMS ENTERPRISES INC.
303 Arthur Street, Fort Worth TX 76107. 817/810-9200. **Fax:** 817/810-9226. **Contact:** Human Resources. **Description:** A high-tech restoration and cleaning firm with affiliate companies involved in providing environmental services. BMS Enterprises Inc. has specific technical expertise with electronics and wet document recovery. The company provides disaster restoration services following fire and water catastrophes. **Common positions include:** Accountant/Auditor; Advertising Clerk; Attorney; Biological Scientist; Budget Analyst; Chemical Engineer; Chemist; Computer Programmer; Cost Estimator; Emergency Medical Technician;

Financial Analyst; Geologist/Geophysicist; Human Resources Manager; Public Relations Specialist; Services Sales Representative. **Educational backgrounds include:** Accounting; Biology; Business Administration; Chemistry; Computer Science; Engineering; Finance; Geology. **Benefits:** 401(k); Dental Insurance; Life Insurance; Medical Insurance. **Corporate headquarters location:** This Location. **Listed on:** Privately held. **Number of employees at this location:** 200. **Number of employees nationwide:** 600.

THE DWYER GROUP INC.
1010 North University Parks Drive, Waco TX 76707. 254/745-2444. **Contact:** Human Resources. **World Wide Web address:** http://www.dwyergroup.com. **Description:** An international provider of specialty services through a group of service-based franchisers. **Subsidiaries include:** Rainbow International Carpet Dyeing & Cleaning Company has more than 480 franchises in the U.S., 30 franchises in Canada, and more than 120 franchise operations in 16 foreign countries. Rainbow specializes in indoor restoration and cleaning services including upholstery and drapery cleaning, carpet dyeing and cleaning, ceiling cleaning, deodorization, and comprehensive fire and water damage restoration and cleanup; Mr. Rooter Corporation is a complete residential and commercial plumbing service company, with a total of 240 franchises in the U.S. and five foreign countries; General Business Services, Inc. (GBS) and E.K. Williams & Company provide small business owners with business counseling, tax planning, tax research, tax return preparation, recordkeeping systems, computer services, and financial management planning. GBS has a total of 320 franchises in the U.S. and Canada. E.K. Williams has more than 185 franchises located throughout the U.S.; Aire Serv Heating & Air Conditioning, Inc. is a franchiser of heating, ventilation, and air conditioning maintenance and repair services. The primary client base for its franchisees includes residential and light commercial applications. Aire Serv has nearly 40 U.S. franchises; Mr. Electric, an electrical contracting service franchise has one U.S. franchise.

MBNA INFORMATION SERVICES
16001 North Dallas Parkway, Dallas TX 75001. 972/233-7101. **Toll-free phone:** 800/527-3890. **Contact:** Human Resources. **Description:** MBNA Information Services, a subsidiary of MBNA American Bank, is an information processing company serving financial institutions and merchant plans nationwide. MBNA Information Services also provides printing, data processing, and mailing services to businesses in a number of industries. **Corporate headquarters location:** This Location. **Parent company:** MBNA Corporation (Newark DE) was formed in 1990 out of the credit card operations of MNC, Inc. The company is a world leader in issuing Gold MasterCard cards, and one of the world's largest lenders through bank credit cards. MBNA is also a leading issuer of affinity credit cards. Other operations of the company include home equity and personal loans, and accepting deposits. Other subsidiaries of MBNA Corporation include MBNA American Bank, N.A., a national bank; and MBNA Marketing Systems.

PINKERTON SECURITY COMPANY
7610 Stemmons Freeway, Suite 140, Dallas TX 75247. 214/631-5934. **Recorded jobline:** 800/585-2460. **Contact:** Personnel Administrator. **World Wide Web address:** http://www.pinkertons.com. **Description:** One of the oldest and largest non-governmental security service organizations in the world. The company's principal business is providing security, investigative, and consulting services to a multitude of commercial, industrial, institutional, governmental, and residential clients. The company operates through more than 125 offices in the United States, Canada, and Great Britain. Major services include industrial and nuclear plant security, institutional security, commercial and residential building security, retail security, construction security, patrol and inspection services, community security, sports and special events services, K-9 patrol services, courier services, inventory services, investigation services, security consultation, and equipment evaluation. **NOTE:** Entry-level positions and part-time jobs are offered. **Common positions include:** Security Officer. **Educational backgrounds include:** College Degree; High School Diploma/GED. **Benefits:** 401(k); Dental Insurance; Life Insurance; Medical Insurance. **Corporate headquarters location:** Westlake Village CA. **Other U.S. locations:** Nationwide. **Parent company:** Securitas AB. **Annual sales/revenues:** More than $100 million. **Number of employees at this location:** 700. **Number of employees nationwide:** 50,000. **Number of projected hires for 2000 - 2001 at this location:** 250.

RIA
2395 Midway Road, Carrollton TX 75006. 972/250-7000. **Fax:** 972/250-7763. **Contact:** Tom Parson, Technical Recruiting Manager. **World Wide Web address:** http://www.riahome.com. **Description:** One of the world's largest providers of solutions for tax research, compliance, and information. **Parent company:** Thomson Tax and Accounting.

WARRANTECH CORPORATION
150 Westpark Way, Suite 200, Euless TX 76040. 817/283-7267. **Contact:** Human Resources. **World Wide Web address:** http://www.warrantech.com. **Description:** Provides extended service contracts and limited warranties to retailers, distributors, and manufacturers of automobiles, recreational vehicles, automotive components, home appliances, home entertainment products, computers and peripherals, and office and communications equipment. **Benefits:** Incentive Plan; Profit Sharing; Stock Option. **Corporate headquarters location:** This Location. **Other U.S. locations:** Stamford CT. **Number of employees nationwide:** 240.

Note: Because addresses and telephone numbers of smaller companies can change rapidly, we recommend you call each company to verify the information below before inquiring about job opportunities. Mass mailings are not recommended.

Additional small employers:

ADJUSTMENT AND COLLECTION SERVICES

CMI Group Inc.
4200 International Pkwy, Carrollton TX 75007-1912. 972/862-4200.

Commercial Recovery Systems
PO Box 28989, Dallas TX 75228-0989. 214/324-9575.

Cygnet Financial Services Inc.
PO Box 940569, Plano TX 75094-0569. 972/633-7271.

Nationscredit Corporation
PO Box 150279, Fort Worth TX 76108-0279. 817/367-5300.

CREDIT REPORTING SERVICES

Chex Systems Inc.
12005 Ford Rd, Ste 650, Dallas TX 75234-7230. 972/247-5100.

Experian Corporation
PO Box 2106, Allen TX 75013-2106. 972/390-3000.

DETECTIVE, GUARD, AND ARMORED CAR SERVICES

Accu-Guard Inc.
8585 N Stemmons Fwy, Dallas TX 75247-3836. 214/637-6410.

Advance Security
1425 W Pioneer Dr, Ste 209, Irving TX 75061-7132. 972/254-1513.

Allied Security Inc.
1140 Empire Central Dr, Dallas TX 75247-4322. 214/631-6928.

American Commercial Security Services
2300 Valley View Ln, Irving TX 75062-1721. 972/570-3999.

American Protective Services
9441 LBJ Fwy, Dallas TX 75243-4545. 972/238-5994.

Ameritex Guard Services
811 S Central Expy, Richardson TX 75080-7415. 972/231-6395.

Ameritex Guard Services
PO Box 226776, Dallas TX 75222-6776. 214/688-0331.

Armored Transport Texas
PO Box 223646, Dallas TX 75222-3646. 214/631-5355.

Burns International Security Services
8150 Brookriver Dr, Dallas TX 75247-4068. 214/638-1666.

Burns International Security Services
6707 Brentwood Stair Rd, Fort Worth TX 76112-3335. 817/492-8001.

Burns International Security Services
PO Box 749, Glen Rose TX 76043-0749. 254/897-5434.

Citadel Security Corp.
111 S Terry St, Malakoff TX 75148-9207. 903/489-3662.

D&L Security Services
1420 W Mockingbird Ln, Dallas TX 75247-4931. 214/634-0146.

Fort Knox Protection Inc.
111 Executive Way, Ste 102, Desoto TX 75115-2388. 972/298-6991.

Guardsmark Inc.
1327 Empire Central Dr, Dallas TX 75247-4065. 972/263-0145.

Loomis Fargo Co.
1655 Vilbig Rd, Dallas TX 75208-1326. 214/742-4473.

Pinkerton's Security & Investigation Services
4150 International Plz, Fort Worth TX 76109-4892. 817/731-7590.

Ruiz Protective Services
11029 Shady Trl, Ste 117, Dallas TX 75229-5621. 214/357-0820.

Security Forces Inc.
332 W Pipeline Rd, Hurst TX 76053-5636. 817/285-9191.

Silver Star Security Inc.
1616 Gateway Blvd, Richardson TX 75080-3529. 972/235-8910.

Supreme Security Inc.
1616 Gateway Blvd, Richardson TX 75080-3529. 972/235-8844.

Triad Protective Services Inc.
1925 E Belt Line Rd, Carrollton TX 75006-5801. 972/416-6169.

Truth Verification Inc.
PO Box 35712, Dallas TX 75235-0712. 214/631-4444.

US Security Associates Inc.
718 S Polk St, Ste 720, Amarillo TX 79101-2310. 806/376-1193.

Wackenhut Corporation
1111 W Mockingbird Ln, Dallas TX 75247-5028. 214/634-8691.

Wackenhut Corporation
3002 Gilmer Rd, Ste 5, Longview TX 75604-1412. 903/759-9341.

Wells Fargo Guard Services
3610 Avenue Q, Ste 224, Lubbock TX 79412-1248. 806/765-0006.

Wells Fargo Guard Services
8150 Brookriver Dr, Dallas TX 75247-4068. 214/638-4906.

MISC. EQUIPMENT RENTAL AND LEASING

A1 Rental
711 N Beach St, Fort Worth TX 76111-5944. 817/831-3121.

SECRETARIAL AND COURT REPORTING SERVICES

Team Texas
1600 Airport Fwy, Ste 208, Bedford TX 76022-6881. 817/354-7785.

SECURITY SYSTEMS SERVICES

Access Protection Systems
6500 Greenville Ave, Dallas TX 75206-1014. 214/696-1824.

ADT Security Services Inc.
1375 River Bend Dr, Dallas TX 75247-4915. 214/638-3000.

Brinks Incorporated
8880 Esters Blvd, Irving TX 75063-2419. 972/871-3500.

Firstwatch Corporation
PO Box 36304, Dallas TX 75235-1304. 214/630-6636.

Security Tech Holding Corp.
15182 Marsh Ln, Dallas TX 75234. 214/351-7100.

Smith Alarm Systems
7777 John W. Carpenter Fwy, Dallas TX 75247-4828. 214/631-3300.

West Star Security Services
4221 W John Carpenter Fwy, Irving TX 75063-2924. 972/916-6100.

For more information on career opportunities in miscellaneous business services and non-scientific research:

Associations

AMERICAN SOCIETY OF APPRAISERS
P.O. Box 17265, Washington DC 20041. 703/478-2228. Toll-free phone: 800/ASA-VALU. Fax: 703/742-8471. World Wide Web address: http://www.appraisers.org. An international, nonprofit, independent appraisal organization. ASA teaches, tests, and awards designations.

EQUIPMENT LEASING ASSOCIATION OF AMERICA
4301 North Fairfax Drive, Suite 550, Arlington VA 22203. 703/527-8655. World Wide Web address: http://www.elaonline.com.

INSTITUTE OF BUSINESS FORECASTING
P.O. Box 670159, Flushing NY 11367-0159. 718/463-3914. World Wide Web address: http://www.ibf.org. Disseminates information and offers products and services to help businesses with their forecasting and planning needs.

NATIONAL ASSOCIATION OF PERSONNEL SERVICES
3133 Mt. Vernon Avenue, Alexandria VA 22305. 703/684-0180. Fax: 703/684-0071. World Wide Web address: http://www.napsweb.org. Provides federal legislative protection, education, certification, and business products and services to its member employment service agencies.

NATIONAL FUNERAL DIRECTORS ASSOCIATION
13625 Bishop's Drive, Brookfield WI 53005-6607. Toll-free phone: 800/228-6332. Fax: 262/789-6977. E-mail address: nfda@nfda.org. World Wide Web address: http://www.proaccess.net/vts/nfda_vts/html/about_nfda.html. Founded in 1882, this organization represents 15,000 members nationwide and promotes quality service in the funeral home industry.

Online Services

PLANT MAINTENANCE RESOURCE CENTER
World Wide Web address: http://www.plant-maintenance.com. A great resource for maintenance professionals offering links to maintenance consultants and vendors; information on conferences; and articles on maintenance.

CHARITIES AND SOCIAL SERVICES

You can expect to find the following types of organizations in this chapter:
Social and Human Service Agencies • Job Training and Vocational
Rehabilitation Services • Nonprofit Organizations

Some helpful information: *The average annual salary range for social workers is $25,000 - $35,000, with casework supervisors and managers earning $30,000 - $40,000 per year. Salaries are similar or lower for workers in charitable organizations, although executives may earn a great deal more ($75,000 or higher would not be uncommon).*

ABILENE REGIONAL MENTAL HEALTH & MENTAL RETARDATION CENTER
2616 South Clack, Abilene TX 79606. 915/690-5100. **Fax:** 915/690-5136. **Contact:** Personnel. **Description:** An outpatient counseling facility for mentally challenged individuals.

AMERICAN HEART ASSOCIATION (AHA)
7272 Greenville Avenue, Dallas TX 75231. 214/373-6300. **Fax:** 214/706-1191. **Contact:** Human Resources Department. **World Wide Web address:** http://www.americanheart.org. **Description:** One of the oldest and largest national, nonprofit, voluntary health associations dedicated to reducing disability and death from cardiovascular diseases and stroke. AHA-funded research has yielded such discoveries as CPR, bypass surgery, pacemakers, artificial heart valves, microsurgery, life-extending drugs, and new surgical techniques to repair heart defects. The AHA's interactive public education programs emphasize quitting smoking; controlling high blood pressure; eating a low-fat, low-cholesterol diet; and maintaining a physically active lifestyle. The AHA also teaches the warning signs of heart attack and stroke, and what to do if they occur. The association trains about 5 million Americans per year in emergency care procedures. Founded in 1924. **Special programs:** Internships. **Corporate headquarters location:** This Location. **Other U.S. locations:** Nationwide.

BIG SKY RANCH
2234 Amy Lynn Avenue, Abilene TX 79603. 915/676-5671. **Contact:** Peter Brown, Administrator. **Description:** A group home for mentally challenged individuals.

BOY SCOUTS OF AMERICA
1325 West Walnut Hill Lane, P.O. Box 152079, Irving TX 75015-2079. 972/580-2000. **Contact:** Professional Selection and Placement. **World Wide Web address:** http://www.bsa.scouting.org. **Description:** The national scouting organization for young men. Boy Scouts of America has more than 300 local councils nationwide. **Common positions include:** Administrator; Customer Service Representative; Human Service Worker; Sales Representative. **Educational backgrounds include:** Bachelor of Arts; Business Administration; College Degree; Liberal Arts; Management/Planning; Master of Arts; MBA; Ph.D.; Social Science. **Benefits:** 401(k); Dental Insurance; Disability Coverage; Life Insurance; Medical Insurance; Pension Plan. **Special programs:** Internships. **Corporate headquarters location:** This Location. **Other U.S. locations:** Nationwide. **Listed on:** Privately held. **Number of employees nationwide:** 4,000.

DAY CARE ASSOCIATION/FORT WORTH AND TARRANT
P.O. Box 7935, Fort Worth TX 76111. 817/838-0055. **Contact:** Human Resources. **Description:** A nonprofit daycare association. The organization's primary function is assisting low-income families in finding affordable daycare.

E.O.A.C.
500 Franklin Avenue, Waco TX 76701. 254/753-0331. **Contact:** Employment. **Description:** This is the central office of E.O.A.C. Overall, the organization offers Head Start programs for three and four year olds; charter school for children ages five years through third grade; Youth in Action, an alcohol and drug prevention program for teenagers; assistance with rent and utilities payments; and a variety of services for the homeless.

THE GLADNEY CENTER
2300 Hemphill Street, Fort Worth TX 76110. 817/926-3304. **Contact:** Human Resources. **World Wide Web address:** http://www.gladney.org. **Description:** A nonprofit adoption agency,

providing services to young women who seek adoptive parents for their infant; individuals seeking to adopt; and adoptees. Founded in 1887.

GOODWILL INDUSTRIES
2800 North Hampton Road, Dallas TX 75212. 214/638-2800. **Contact:** Human Resources. **World Wide Web address:** http://www.goodwill.org. **Description:** A nonprofit provider of employment training for the disabled and the poor, operating 1,400 thrift stores nationwide. **Other U.S. locations:** Nationwide.

HARMONY FAMILY SERVICES
P.O. Box 6579, Abilene TX 79608. 915/677-4663. **Contact:** Personnel. **Description:** A social services agency that offers many programs including a residential treatment center for runaway and homeless youths.

MEALS ON WHEELS
1416 West Eighth Avenue, Room 106, Amarillo TX 79101. 806/374-1521. **Contact:** Personnel. **Description:** Delivers meals to homebound senior citizens.

PANHANDLE COMMUNITY SERVICES
P.O. Box 763, Clarendon TX 79226. 806/874-2573. **Contact:** Human Resources. **Description:** Offers housing, energy, transportation, and food banks for homeless and low-income families.

TOWN NORTH YMCA
4332 Northaven Road, Dallas TX 75229. 214/357-8431. **Contact:** Human Resources. **World Wide Web address:** http://www.ymca.com. **Description:** One of the nation's largest and most comprehensive nonprofit service organizations. The YMCA provides health and fitness; social and personal development; sports and recreation; education and career development; and camps and conferences to children, teens, adults, senior citizens, families, disabled individuals, refugees and foreign nationals, YMCA residents, and community residents through a broad range of specific programs. **Other U.S. locations:** Nationwide.

UNITED WAY OF METROPOLITAN DALLAS
901 Ross Avenue, Dallas TX 75202. 214/978-0000. **Contact:** Human Resources. **World Wide Web address:** http://www.unitedwaydallas.com. **Description:** A nonprofit organization that helps to meet the health and human-care needs of Dallas area residents. Overall, the United Way includes approximately 1,900 organizations. **Common positions include:** Accountant; Administrative Assistant; Chief Financial Officer; Controller; Event Planner; Human Resources Manager; Marketing Manager; Marketing Specialist; Systems Manager; Webmaster. **Educational backgrounds include:** Business Administration; Microsoft Office; Microsoft Word; Public Administration; Spreadsheets. **Benefits:** 403(b); Casual Dress - Fridays; Dental Insurance; Disability Coverage; Flexible Schedule; Life Insurance; Medical Insurance; Sick Days (11+); Vacation Days (10 - 20). **Special programs:** Internships. **Office hours:** Monday - Friday, 8:15 a.m. - 5:00 p.m. **Corporate headquarters location:** Alexandria VA. **President:** Ed McDunn. **Facilities Manager:** Richard Orozco. **Information Systems Manager:** Brenda Cooper. **Annual sales/revenues:** $21 - $50 million. **Number of employees at this location:** 75. **Number of projected hires for 2000 - 2001 at this location:** 20.

YMCA OF METROPOLITAN FORT WORTH
540 Lamar Street, Fort Worth TX 76102. 817/332-3281. **Contact:** Human Resources. **World Wide Web address:** http://www.ymca.com. **Description:** One of the nation's largest and most comprehensive nonprofit service organizations. The YMCA provides health and fitness; social and personal development; sports and recreation; education and career development; and camps and conferences to children, teens, adults, senior citizens, families, disabled individuals, refugees and foreign nationals, YMCA residents, and community residents through a broad range of specific programs. **Other U.S. locations:** Nationwide.

For more information on career opportunities in charities and social services:

Associations

ADVOCACY INSTITUTE
1707 L Street NW, Suite 400, Washington DC 20036. 202/659-8475.

ALLIANCE FOR CHILDREN AND FAMILIES
11700 West Lake Park Drive, Milwaukee WI 53224. 414/359-1040. World Wide Web address: http://www.alliance1.org. Membership required.

AMERICAN COUNCIL OF THE BLIND
1155 15th Street NW, Suite 1004, Washington DC 20005. 202/467-5081. Toll-free phone: 800/424-8666. World Wide Web address: http://www.acb.org. Membership required. Offers an annual

conference, a monthly magazine, scholarships, and employment listings.

AMERICAN LUNG ASSOCIATION
1740 Broadway, New York NY 10019. Toll-free phone: 800/586-4872. World Wide Web address: http://www.lungusa.org. Focused on preventing and curing lung disease through research, education, and fundraising.

CATHOLIC CHARITIES USA
1731 King Street, Suite 200, Alexandria VA 22314. 703/549-1390. World Wide Web address: http://www.catholiccharitiesusa.org. Membership required.

CLINICAL SOCIAL WORK FEDERATION
P.O. Box 3740, Arlington VA 22203. 703/522-3866. A lobbying organization. Offers newsletters and a conference every two years to member organizations.

NATIONAL ASSOCIATION OF SOCIAL WORKERS
750 First Street NE, Suite 700, Washington DC 20002-4241. 202/408-8600. World Wide Web address: http://www.socialworkers.org.

NATIONAL COUNCIL ON ALCOHOLISM AND DRUG DEPENDENCE
12 West 21st Street, New York NY 10010. 212/206-6770. Toll-free phone: 800/622-2255. Fax: 212/645-1690. Provides counseling and treatment for those suffering from alcohol and drug addictions. The association also educates the public in an attempt to prevent addictions.

NATIONAL COUNCIL ON FAMILY RELATIONS
3989 Central Avenue NE, Suite 550, Minneapolis MN 55421. 612/781-9331. Fax: 612/781-9348. Membership required. Publishes two quarterly journals. Offers an annual conference and newsletters.

THE NATIONAL COUNCIL ON THE AGING
409 Third Street SW, Suite 200, Washington DC 20024. Toll-free phone: 800/424-9046. World Wide Web address: http://www.ncoa.org. Ensures the well-being of the nation's elderly by improving both public and private policies and educating the public.

NATIONAL FEDERATION OF THE BLIND
1800 Johnson Street, Baltimore MD 21230. 410/659-9314. World Wide Web address: http://www.nfb.org. Membership of 50,000 in 600 local chapters. Publishes a quarterly magazine.

NATIONAL MULTIPLE SCLEROSIS SOCIETY
733 Third Avenue, New York NY 10017. 212/986-3240. Toll-free phone: 800/344-4867. World Wide Web address: http://www.nmss.org. Publishes *InsideMS* magazine.

NATIONAL ORGANIZATION FOR HUMAN SERVICE EDUCATION
Brookdale Community College, 765 Newman Springs Road, Lyncroft NJ 07738. 732/842-1900x546.

Directories

NON-PROFITS AND EDUCATION JOB FINDER
Planning/Communications, 7215 Oak Avenue, River Forest IL 60305. 708/366-5200. World Wide Web address: http://www.jobfindersonline.com. Provides over 2,200 sources with which to find a job in the competitive nonprofit/education sectors. Sources include online job and resume databases, directories, mailing lists, job matching services, and salary negotiation surveys. Organized by profession and state.

Newsletters

CEO UPDATE
101 South Whiting Street, Suite 305, Alexandria VA 22304. 703/370-6700. World Wide Web address: http://www.associationjobs.com. A bimonthly newsletter which lists job openings at associations and nonprofit organizations, with salaries of at least $50,000 per year.

Online Services

COOLWORKS
World Wide Web address: http://www.coolworks.com. This Website includes information on volunteer openings. The site also provides links to 22,000 job openings in national parks, summer camps, ski areas, river areas, ranches, fishing areas, cruise ships, and resorts.

NONPROFIT JOBS
World Wide Web address: http://www.philanthropy-journal.org. The *Philanthropy Journal*'s site lists jobs in nonprofit associations and philanthropic occupations.

SOCIALSERVICE.COM
World Wide Web address: http://www.socialservice.com. Provides links to local job sites as well as detailed job listings searchable by geographic area.

For information about the JobBank List Service visit www.adamsjobbank.com

CHEMICALS/RUBBER AND PLASTICS

You can expect to find the following types of companies in this chapter:
Adhesives, Detergents, Inks, Paints, Soaps, Varnishes • Agricultural Chemicals and Fertilizers • Carbon and Graphite Products • Chemical Engineering Firms Industrial Gases

Some helpful information: The average salary for rubber and plastics manufacturing workers is approximately $20,000 - $25,000 annually. Entry-level chemists generally earn between $20,000 and $30,000, and chemists with advanced degrees can earn over $50,000 annually in the private sector.

AC MOLDING COMPOUND
2700 South Westmoreland Road, Dallas TX 75233. 214/330-8671. **Contact:** Lee Hicks, General Manager. **Description:** Manufactures a wide variety of resins, plastics, and glass-reinforced plastics for use in the electronics industry, as well as plastic tableware products used in the food service industry. **Corporate headquarters location:** This Location.

AMERICAN EXCELSIOR COMPANY
900 Avenue H East, Arlington TX 76005. 817/640-2161. **Fax:** 817/649-5714. **Contact:** Mr. Bob Vesey, Branch Manager. **World Wide Web address:** http://www.amerexcel.com. **Description:** Engaged in the production of environmentally sound, water-soluble packaging materials, foam protective shipping pads, fabricated polyurethane foam, and shaped packaging. **Common positions include:** Blue-Collar Worker Supervisor; Cost Estimator; Customer Service Representative; Industrial Production Manager; Quality Control Supervisor. **Educational backgrounds include:** Business Administration; Marketing. **Benefits:** Dental Insurance; Life Insurance; Medical Insurance; Profit Sharing. **Number of employees at this location:** 30. **Number of employees nationwide:** 600.

CAPROCK MANUFACTURING, INC.
2303 120th Street, Lubbock TX 79423. 806/745-6454. **Contact:** Human Resources. **World Wide Web address:** http://www.caprock-mfg.com. **Description:** A plastic injection molding company that manufactures plastic parts for cellular phones including phone windows and battery cases. **NOTE:** Second and third shifts are offered. **Common positions include:** Advertising Clerk; Buyer; Controller; Customer Service Representative; Design Engineer; General Manager; Human Resources Manager; Manufacturing Engineer; Production Manager; Purchasing Agent/Manager; Quality Control Supervisor; Secretary. **Educational backgrounds include:** Accounting; Art/Design; Business Administration; Chemistry; Communications; Computer Science; Engineering; Finance; Mathematics; Public Relations. **Benefits:** 401(k); Dental Insurance; Disability Coverage; Life Insurance; Medical Insurance; Savings Plan. **Corporate headquarters location:** This Location. **Listed on:** Privately held. **President:** Ryan Provenzano. **Number of employees at this location:** 150.

CARROLL COMPANY
2900 West Kingsley Road, Garland TX 75041. 972/278-1304. **Toll-free phone:** 800/527-5722. **Fax:** 972/840-0678. **Recorded jobline:** 972/278-1304x600. **Contact:** Shirley Wren, Human Resources Manager. **World Wide Web address:** http://www.carrollco.com. **Description:** A manufacturer of institutional cleaning products. **NOTE:** Entry-level positions and second and third shifts are offered. **Common positions include:** Account Manager; Account Rep.; Accountant; Administrative Assistant; Blue-Collar Worker Supervisor; Buyer; Chemist; Computer Programmer; Controller; Credit Manager; Customer Service Rep.; Database Manager; Electrician; Graphic Artist; Human Resources Manager; Industrial Engineer; Marketing Manager; Production Manager; Purchasing Agent; Sales Exec.; Sales Manager; Secretary; Video Production Coordinator. **Educational backgrounds include:** Accounting; Art/Design; Marketing. **Benefits:** 401(k); Dental Insurance; Disability Coverage; Employee Discounts; Life Insurance; Medical Insurance; Public Transit Available; Tuition Assistance. **Corporate headquarters location:** This Location. **Other U.S. locations:** Carson CA; Santa Fe Springs CA; Walbridge OH. **Listed on:** Privately held. **President/CEO:** Kyle Ogden. **Number of employees at this location:** 165. **Number of employees nationwide:** 260.

CHEMICAL LIME COMPANY
P.O. Box 985004, Fort Worth TX 76185. 817/732-8164. **Contact:** Mr. Ken Cage, Director of Human Resources. **World Wide Web address:** http://www.chemicallime.com. **Description:** A

manufacturer and distributor of chemical lime products. The company's principal products are high calcium limestone, dolomite limestone, dolomite glass flux, high calcium quicklime, dolomitic quicklime, calcium hydrated lime, and dolomitic hydrated lime under the trade name Type S Hydrated Lime for use in the construction industry. **Common positions include:** Accountant/Auditor; Chemist; Civil Engineer; Computer Programmer; Electrical/Electronics Engineer; Financial Analyst; Geologist/Geophysicist; Industrial Engineer; Mechanical Engineer; Mining Engineer; Operations/Production Manager; Quality Control Supervisor; Systems Analyst; Transportation/Traffic Specialist. **Educational backgrounds include:** Accounting; Business Administration; Chemistry; Computer Science; Engineering; Geology. **Benefits:** Dental Insurance; Disability Coverage; Life Insurance; Medical Insurance; Profit Sharing; Savings Plan; Tuition Assistance. **Corporate headquarters location:** This Location.

CRYOVAC
1301 West Magnolia Avenue, Iowa Park TX 76367-1410. 940/592-2111. **Contact:** Human Resources Department. **Description:** Manufactures plastic bags. **Parent company:** W.R. Grace & Company is one of the largest producers of specialty chemicals, as well as a provider of specialized health care. The major divisions of W.R. Grace include Grace Packaging, Grace Davison, Grace Construction Products, Grace Dearborn, Grace Container & Specialty Polymers, and Grace Health Care.

CYRO INDUSTRIES
101 East Park Boulevard, Suite 1039, Plano TX 75074. 972/424-6830. **Contact:** Human Resources. **E-mail address:** human-resources@cyro.com. **World Wide Web address:** http://www.cyro.com. **Description:** This location is a sales office. Overall, Cyro Industries is a leading manufacturer of acrylic sheet, acrylic molding, and extusion compounds. **Corporate headquarters location:** Rockaway NJ. **Other U.S. locations:** Nationwide.

CYTEC FIBERITE INC.
4300 Jackson Street, Greenville TX 75402. 903/454-2004. **Contact:** Human Resources. **World Wide Web address:** http://www.cytec.com. **Description:** This location manufactures graphite composite materials. Overall, Cytec Fiberite is a specialty chemical and coated products manufacturer. **Corporate headquarters location:** Winona MN.

FINA OIL & CHEMICAL COMPANY
6000 Legacy Drive, Plano TX 75024-3601. 972/801-2000. **Contact:** Human Resources. **World Wide Web address:** http://www.fina.com. **Description:** Explores for crude oil and natural gas; markets natural gas; refines, supplies, transports, and markets petroleum products; manufactures and markets specialty chemicals, primarily petrochemicals and plastics including polypropylene, polystyrene, styrene monomer, high-density polyethylene, and aromatics; licenses certain chemical processes; and manufactures and markets paints and coatings. **Corporate headquarters location:** This Location.

GAF MATERIALS CORPORATION
2600 Singleton Boulevard, Dallas TX 75212. 214/637-1060. **Contact:** Human Resources. **World Wide Web address:** http://www.gaf.com. **Description:** A multiproduct manufacturer with sales in both consumer and industrial markets. The company's product line includes building, roofing, and insulation materials for the construction trades; specialty chemicals and plastics; and reprographic products. **Common positions include:** Accountant/Auditor; Blue-Collar Worker Supervisor; Customer Service Representative; Electrical/Electronics Engineer; Industrial Engineer; Manufacturer's/Wholesaler's Sales Rep.; Operations/Production Manager; Production Worker; Purchasing Agent/Manager; Quality Control Supervisor. **Educational backgrounds include:** Accounting; Business Administration; Engineering; Manufacturing Management. **Benefits:** 401(k); Dental Insurance; Disability Coverage; Life Insurance; Medical Insurance; Pension Plan; Tuition Assistance. **Corporate headquarters location:** Wayne NJ. **Other U.S. locations:** Nationwide. **Listed on:** Privately held. **Number of employees at this location:** 235.

M.A. HANNA COLOR
9001 South Freeway, Fort Worth TX 76140. 817/293-1555. **Contact:** Ms. Mardell Everett, Personnel Manager. **Description:** Formulates color and additive systems for the plastics industry in a variety of product forms, from dry powder blends and concentrates to small-lot pre-color compounds. M.A. Hanna Color serves a broad variety of end markets such as packaging, housewares, consumer durables, automotive, medical, toys and recreation, electrical/electronics, and furniture. The company develops formulations with metal oxides, pearlescents, and organic pigments by using processing chemistry including slip and blowing agents, ultraviolet light stabilizers, and antistats. Each facility is equipped with a color-matching

lab with color computers and instrumentation to support product development efforts. M.A. Hanna Color invests in statistical process control and in technologies linking extrusion equipment with process control computers, in order to deliver precise color-matching and batch-to-batch consistency. **Corporate headquarters location:** Suwanee GA. **Other U.S. locations:** Nationwide.

INDUSTRIAL MOLDING CORPORATION
616 East Slaton Road, Lubbock TX 79404. 806/474-1000. **Contact:** Amy Willingham, Personnel Manager. **World Wide Web address:** http://www.indmolding.com. **Description:** An injection molding company. **Corporate headquarters location:** This Location.

JAMAK FABRICATION, INC.
1401 North Bowie Drive, Weatherford TX 76086. 817/594-8771. **Fax:** 817/594-8324. **Contact:** Human Resources. **World Wide Web address:** http://www.jamak.com. **Description:** Manufactures synthetic silicone rubber products. **Parent company:** JMK International. **Number of employees at this location:** 300. **Number of employees worldwide:** 700.

JONES BLAIR COMPANY
P.O. Box 35286, Dallas TX 75235. 214/353-1661. **Contact:** Personnel. **Description:** A manufacturer of paints, resins, elastomers, and powder coatings. **Common positions include:** Chemical Engineer; Chemist; Industrial Engineer; Industrial Production Manager; Management Trainee; Operations/Production Manager. **Educational backgrounds include:** Chemistry; Engineering. **Benefits:** 401(k); Disability Coverage; Employee Discounts; Life Insurance; Medical Insurance; Tuition Assistance. **Corporate headquarters location:** This Location. **Other U.S. locations:** Chattanooga TN. **Listed on:** Privately held. **Number of employees at this location:** 250. **Number of employees nationwide:** 450.

KELLY-SPRINGFIELD TIRE COMPANY
P.O. Box 4670, Tyler TX 75712-4670. 903/535-1500. **Contact:** Human Resources. **World Wide Web address:** http://www.kelly-springfield.com. **Description:** Manufactures tires and inner tubes. **Common positions include:** Accountant/Auditor; Blue-Collar Worker Supervisor; Buyer; Chemist; Computer Programmer; Electrical/Electronics Engineer; Industrial Engineer; Management Trainee; Mechanical Engineer; Purchasing Agent/Manager. **Educational backgrounds include:** Business Administration; Engineering. **Benefits:** 401(k); Dental Insurance; Life Insurance; Medical Insurance. **Corporate headquarters location:** Cumberland MD. **Other U.S. locations:** Freeport IL; Fayetteville NC. **Parent company:** Goodyear Tire & Rubber Company. **Listed on:** New York Stock Exchange.

LUBRICATION ENGINEERS INC.
P.O. Box 7128, Fort Worth TX 76111. 817/834-6321. **Physical address:** 3851 Airport Freeway, Fort Worth TX 76111. **Contact:** Karen May, Personnel Director. **Description:** Produces a variety of industrial lubricants including lubrication oils, greases, transmission fluids, synthetic fuels, and oil supplements. **Corporate headquarters location:** This Location.

MOHAWK LABORATORIES
2730 Carl Road, Irving TX 75062. 972/438-0551. **Contact:** Human Resources Department. **Description:** Operates two laboratories that manufacture specialty cleaning and polishing chemicals.

NCH CORPORATION
2727 Chemsearch Boulevard, Irving TX 75062. **Toll-free phone:** 800/527-9919. **Fax:** 972/438-0707. **Recorded jobline:** 972/721-6116. **Contact:** Human Resources. **World Wide Web address:** http://www.nch.com. **Description:** Manufactures and supplies specialty chemicals, water treatment products, fasteners, welding supplies, plumbing and electronic parts, and safety supplies to a worldwide customer base. Founded in 1919. **NOTE:** Entry-level positions and part-time jobs are offered. **Company slogan:** World class products and services. **Common positions include:** Account Representative; Accountant; Administrative Assistant; Advertising Clerk; Applications Engineer; Assistant Manager; Attorney; Auditor; Biochemist; Blue-Collar Worker Supervisor; Chemist; Clerical Supervisor; Clinical Lab Technician; Computer Engineer; Computer Operator; Computer Programmer; Computer Support Technician; Cost Estimator; Credit Manager; Customer Service Representative; Database Administrator; Desktop Publishing Specialist; Draftsperson; Editorial Assistant; Electrician; Environmental Engineer; General Manager; Graphic Artist; Graphic Designer; Human Resources Manager; Industrial Production Manager; Intellectual Property Lawyer; Internet Services Manager; Management Trainee; Market Research Analyst; Marketing Manager; Marketing Specialist; MIS Specialist; Multimedia Designer; Network/Systems Administrator; Operations Manager; Paralegal; Production

Manager; Purchasing Agent/Manager; Quality Control Supervisor; Sales Manager; Sales Representative; Secretary; Technical Writer/Editor; Telecommunications Manager; Typist/Word Processor; Webmaster. **Educational backgrounds include:** Accounting; Art/Design; Business Administration; Chemistry; Communications; Liberal Arts; Marketing. **Benefits:** 401(k); Adoption Assistance; Credit Union; Dental Insurance; Disability Coverage; Employee Discounts; Financial Planning Assistance; Flexible Schedule; Job Sharing; Life Insurance; Medical Insurance; Profit Sharing; Public Transit Available; Telecommuting; Tuition Assistance; Vacation Days (6 - 10). **Special programs:** Internships; Training. **Corporate headquarters location:** This Location. **Other U.S. locations:** El Segundo CA; Atlanta GA; Chicago IL; Paramus NJ; Seattle WA. **International locations:** Asia; Australia; Europe; South America. **Listed on:** New York Stock Exchange. **Stock exchange symbol:** NCH. **Executive Director:** Lester Levy. **Annual sales/revenues:** More than $100 million. **Number of employees at this location:** 600. **Number of employees nationwide:** 6,000. **Number of employees worldwide:** 10,700.

OCCIDENTAL CHEMICAL CORPORATION
P.O. Box 809050, Dallas TX 75380-9050. 972/404-3800. **Contact:** James F. Reder, Senior Consultant - Staffing. **World Wide Web address:** http://www.oxychem.com. **Description:** Manufactures commodity and specialty chemicals. The company has approximately 25 manufacturing facilities nationwide. **NOTE:** The company does most of its hiring through Texas employment agencies and local colleges. **Common positions include:** Accountant/Auditor; Chemical Engineer; Electrical/Electronics Engineer; Mechanical Engineer. **Educational backgrounds include:** Accounting; Engineering. **Benefits:** 401(k); Dental Insurance; Disability Coverage; Life Insurance; Medical Insurance; Pension Plan; Tuition Assistance. **Corporate headquarters location:** Los Angeles CA. **Other U.S. locations:** Nationwide. **Parent company:** Occidental Petroleum Corporation. **Listed on:** New York Stock Exchange. **Annual sales/revenues:** More than $100 million. **Number of employees at this location:** 400. **Number of employees nationwide:** 5,000.

POLY-AMERICA INC.
2000 West Marshall Drive, Grand Prairie TX 75051. 972/647-4374. **Fax:** 972/337-7410. **Recorded jobline:** 972/337-7107. **Contact:** Human Resources Department. **World Wide Web address:** http://www.poly-america.com. **Description:** A leading producer of polyethylene construction film and trash bags and a leading supplier of geomembrane liners. **Corporate headquarters location:** This location. **Other U.S. locations:** Cottage Grove MN; Las Vegas NV; Columbia SC; Mt. Belview TX. **Number of employees this location:** 1,000. **Number of employees nationwide:** 1,570.

REGAL INTERNATIONAL INC.
P.O. Box 1237, Corsicana TX 75151. 903/872-3091. **Toll-free phone:** 800/442-6316. **Contact:** Human Resources. **World Wide Web address:** http://www.regalrubber.com. **Description:** A diversified manufacturer of rubber products for oilfield, offshore marine, industrial, and custom applications. **Corporate headquarters location:** This location.

RIBELIN SALES INC.
P.O. Box 461673, Garland TX 75046-1673. 972/272-1594. **Contact:** Human Resources. **World Wide Web address:** http://www.ribelin.com. **Description:** Ribelin Sales Inc. is a wholesale distributor of raw materials for the paint and coating industry. Founded in 1936.

THE SHERWIN-WILLIAMS COMPANY
P.O. Box 38469, Dallas TX 75238-0469. 214/553-2950. **Physical address:** 10440 East NW Highway, Dallas TX. **Fax:** 214/553-3903. **Contact:** Division Recruiting Manager. **World Wide Web address:** http://www.sherwin-williams.com. **Description:** This location is engaged in the manufacturing, selling, and distributing of coatings and related products. Overall, Sherwin-Williams operates in six business segments: Retail Stores, Coatings, Chemicals, Packaging Products, Specialty Products, and International. Products include Sherwin-Williams, Dutch Boy, Martin Senour, Baltimore, and Kem paints, as well as related packaging. **Common positions include:** Management Trainee. **Corporate headquarters location:** Cleveland OH. **Other U.S. locations:** Nationwide. **Number of employees nationwide:** 23,000.

STYROCHEM INTERNATIONAL
3607 North Sylvania, Fort Worth TX 76111. 817/759-4400. **Contact:** Estella Hernandez, Human Resources Manager. **World Wide Web address:** http://www.styrochem.com. **Description:** Manufactures raw plastic beads. **Common positions include:** Administrator; Blue-Collar Worker Supervisor; Buyer; Chemist; Claim Representative; Customer Service Representative; Draftsperson; Electrical/Electronics Engineer; General Manager; Human Resources Manager; Insurance Agent/Broker; Manufacturer's/Wholesaler's Sales Rep.;

Marketing Specialist; Mechanical Engineer; Operations/Production Manager; Purchasing Agent/Manager; Quality Control Supervisor; Transportation/Traffic Specialist. **Educational backgrounds include:** Business Administration; Chemistry; Communications; Engineering; Marketing; Mathematics. **Benefits:** Dental Insurance; Disability Coverage; Life Insurance; Medical Insurance; Pension Plan; Savings Plan.

TEXAS EASTMAN
P.O. Box 7444, Longview TX 75607. 903/237-5000. **Contact:** Human Resources. **Description:** Manufactures more than 40 chemical and plastic products. The company primarily uses propane and ethane to create its products. **Parent company:** Eastman Chemicals. **Number of employees at this location:** 2,250.

TEXAS REFINERY CORPORATION
P.O. Box 711, Fort Worth TX 76101. 817/332-1161. **Contact:** Jan Peel, Personnel Director. **Description:** Manufactures specialty lubricant products and building maintenance products such as roof coatings. **Common positions include:** Chemist; Credit Manager; Manufacturer's/Wholesaler's Sales Rep. **Educational backgrounds include:** Chemistry. **Number of employees at this location:** 275.

VIRGINIA KMP CORPORATION
4100 Platinum Way, Dallas TX 75237. 214/330-7731. **Contact:** Vice President of Operations. **Description:** Manufactures and sells chemicals, filter dryers, refrigeration accumulators, and air conditioners.

WELLMARK INTERNATIONAL
12200 Denton Drive, Dallas TX 75234. 972/243-2321. **Contact:** Human Resources Specialist. **Description:** An international producer of a wide range of insecticide products including strips, flea and tick collars, and agricultural insecticides and dips. **Corporate headquarters location:** Bensonville IL. **Parent company:** Central Garden and Pet. **Operations at this facility include:** Divisional Headquarters.

Note: Because addresses and telephone numbers of smaller companies can change rapidly, we recommend you call each company to verify the information below before inquiring about job opportunities. Mass mailings are not recommended.

Additional small employers:

AGRICULTURAL CHEMICALS

Ennis Agri-Tech Inc.
PO Box 237, Ennis TX 75120-0237. 972/878-4400.

Letco
1212 Harrison Ave, Arlington TX 76011-7332. 817/312-2000.

CARBON BLACK

Cabot Corporation
PO Box 5001, Pampa TX 79066-5001. 806/669-8100.

Richardson Carbon & Gas Co.
PO Box 3118, Borger TX 79008-3118. 806/274-7213.

CHEMICALS AND ALLIED PRODUCTS WHOLESALE

Ecolab Inc.
2305 Sherwin St, Garland TX 75041-1222. 972/278-6121.

Share Corporation
3605 W Houston St, Paris TX 75460-3529. 903/785-0486.

Tech Spray
PO Box 949, Amarillo TX 79105-0949. 806/372-8523.

CLEANING, POLISHING, AND SANITATION PREPARATIONS

Arden Corporation
10901 Airport Blvd, Amarillo TX 79111-1202. 806/335-1147.

Certified Laboratories
PO Box 152170, Irving TX 75015-2170. 972/438-0290.

Magnolia Enterprises
PO Box 59089, Dallas TX 75229-1089. 972/247-7111.

National Chemsearch
PO Box 152170, Irving TX 75015-2170. 972/438-0211.

Zep Manufacturing Company
PO Box 645, Desoto TX 75123-0645. 214/228-3388.

INDUSTRIAL GASES

Air Liquide America Corp.
13546 N Central Expy, Dallas TX 75243-1108. 972/995-2790.

Air Products and Chemicals
209 West Texas Street, Mesquite TX 75149-4241. 214/339-0098.

INDUSTRIAL INORGANIC CHEMICALS

Celanese Americas Corporation
PO Box 937, Pampa TX 79066-0937. 806/665-1801.

Darco Activated Carbon
PO Box 790, Marshall TX 75671-0790. 903/938-9211.

MISC. RUBBER AND PLASTIC PRODUCTS

Atco
PO Box 430, Ferris TX 75125-0430. 972/225-8178.

PAINTS, VARNISHES, AND RELATED PRODUCTS

Kelly Moore Paint
PO Box 1507, Hurst TX 76053-1507. 817/268-3131.

Chemicals/Rubber and Plastics/103

Sherwin-Williams Company
2802 W Miller Rd, Garland TX
75041-1211. 972/271-2541.

Spraylat Corporation
PO Box 1337, Gainesville TX
76241-1337. 940/665-9590.

PLASTIC MATERIALS WHOLESALE

Plastican Incorporated
2651 Santa Anna Ave, Dallas
TX 75228-1688. 214/328-2721.

Ticona LLC
1601 LBJ Fwy, Dallas TX
75234-6034. 972/443-4000.

PLASTIC MATERIALS, SYNTHETICS, AND ELASTOMERS

Coroplast Inc.
4501 Spring Valley Rd, Dallas
TX 75244-3706. 972/392-2241.

Life-Like Products Inc.
1600 W Highway 287 Bypass,
Waxahachie TX 75165-5068.
972/937-6512.

United States Brass Corp.
PO Box 1031, Commerce TX
75429-1031. 903/886-2580.

PLASTIC PRODUCTS

AEP Industries Inc.
6250 N Interstate Highway,
Waxahachie TX 75165-5602.
972/576-8193.

Belco Manufacturing Co. Inc.
PO Box 210, Belton TX 76513-0210. 254/933-9000.

Cantex Inc.
PO Box 340, Mineral Wells TX
76068-0340. 940/325-3344.

Centron International Inc.
PO Box 490, Mineral Wells TX
76068-0490. 940/325-1341.

Constar Inc.
2210 Saint Germain Road,
Dallas TX 75212-4811.
214/688-0714.

Creative Manufacturing Inc.
1016 W Harris Rd, Arlington TX
76001-6806. 817/465-1452.

Dexas International Inc.
2221 Luna Rd, Carrollton TX
75006-6505. 972/484-8413.

Ennis Extruded Products
PO Box 340, Ennis TX 75120-0340. 972/875-1770.

ER Carpenter LP
PO Box 1007, Temple TX
76503-1007. 254/778-8991.

Fibergrate Corporation
PO Box 208, Stephenville TX
76401-0208. 254/965-3148.

Genpak Corporation
1101 W Harrison Rd, Longview
TX 75604-5610. 903/297-4445.

Homco Inc.
1400 Lavon Dr, McKinney TX
75069-7307. 972/238-0453.

ITW Meritex
PO Box 5508, Arlington TX
76005-5508. 817/640-5668.

Koral Industries Inc.
PO Box 1270, Ennis TX 75120-1270. 972/875-6555.

Kysor/Needham
PO Box 14248, Fort Worth TX
76117-0248. 817/281-5121.

Marco Company
PO Box 123439, Fort Worth TX
76121-3439. 817/244-8300.

Master Shield Building Products
1202 N Bowie Dr, Weatherford
TX 76086-1539. 817/596-7090.

Medical Plastic Co.
PO Box 38, Gatesville TX
76528-0038. 254/865-7221.

Molded Products Company
PO Box 37169, Fort Worth TX
76117-8169. 817/428-3636.

Nova Design International
4809 Brentwood Stair Rd, Fort
Worth TX 76103-1737.
817/457-4685.

Paramount Packaging
800 Jordan Valley Rd, Longview
TX 75604-5221. 903/297-3242.

Pescor Plastics Inc.
3300 W Bolt St, Fort Worth TX
76110-5816. 817/926-5471.

Ring Can
2107 Franklin Dr, Fort Worth
TX 76106-2206. 817/625-7214.

Ropak Southwest Inc.
1501 E Dallas St, Mansfield TX
76063-2405. 817/473-0259.

Sherman Plastics Inc.
4201 S Highway 75, Sherman
TX 75090-9305. 903/870-7080.

Southern Plastics Inc.
PO Box 2949, Kilgore TX
75663-2949. 903/984-6229.

Supreme Plastics Inc.
PO Box 1007, Gladewater TX
75647-1007. 903/844-9400.

Tallyho Plastics Inc.
PO Box 990, Jacksonville TX
75766-0990. 903/586-2263.

Tekni-Plex Inc.
4700 S Westmoreland Rd,
Dallas TX 75237-1629.
214/337-4711.

Texstar Plastics
925 Avenue H E, Arlington TX
76011-7721. 972/647-1366.

Thermo-Serv Inc.
3901 Pipestone Rd, Dallas TX
75212-6017. 214/631-0307.

Trinity Plastics Inc.
901 E Industrial Ave, Fort
Worth TX 76131-2715.
817/230-2020.

RUBBER PRODUCTS

Fineline Packaging
1416 Upfield Dr, Carrollton TX
75006-6915. 972/242-2711.

Pactiv Corporation
4501 E State Highway 31,
Corsicana TX 75110-9762.
903/872-6540.

UNSUPPORTED PLASTIC PRODUCTS

Eastman Kodak Company
18325 Waterview Pkwy, Dallas
TX 75252-8026. 972/994-1200.

Pak-Sher Co.
2500 N Longview St, Kilgore TX
75662-6840. 903/984-8596.

For more information on career opportunities in the chemicals/rubber and plastics industries:

Associations

AMERICAN ASSOCIATION FOR CLINICAL CHEMISTRY
2101 L Street NW, Suite 202, Washington DC
20037-1526. 202/857-0717. Toll-free phone: 800/892-1400. World Wide Web address: http://www.aacc.org. International scientific/medical society of individuals involved with clinical chemistry and other clinical lab science-related disciplines.

AMERICAN CHEMICAL SOCIETY
Career Services, 1155 16th Street NW, Washington DC 20036. 202/872-4600. World Wide Web address: http://www.acs.org.

AMERICAN INSTITUTE OF CHEMICAL ENGINEERS
3 Park Avenue, New York NY 10016. 212/591-7338. Toll-free phone: 800/242-4363. World Wide Web address: http://www.aiche.org. Provides leadership in advancing the chemical engineering profession as it meets the needs of society.

CHEMICAL MANUFACTURERS ASSOCIATION
1300 Wilson Boulevard, Arlington VA 22209. 703/741-5000. World Wide Web address: http://www.cmahq.com. A trade association that develops and implements programs and services and advocates public policy that benefits the industry and society.

THE ELECTROCHEMICAL SOCIETY
65 South Main Street, Pennington NJ 08534. 609/737-1902. An international educational society dealing with electrochemical issues. Also publishes monthly journals.

SOAP AND DETERGENT ASSOCIATION
475 Park Avenue South, New York NY 10016. 212/725-1262. World Wide Web address: http://www.sdahq.org. A trade association and research center.

SOCIETY OF PLASTICS ENGINEERS
P.O. Box 403, Brookfield CT 06804-0403. 203/775-0471. World Wide Web address: http://www.4spe.org. Dedicated to helping members attain higher professional status through increased scientific, engineering, and technical knowledge.

THE SOCIETY OF THE PLASTICS INDUSTRY, INC.
1801 K Street NW, Suite 600K, Washington DC 20006. 202/974-5200. Promotes the development of the plastics industry and enhances public understanding of its contributions while meeting the needs of society.

Directories

CHEMICALS DIRECTORY
Cahners Business Information, 275 Washington Street, Newton MA 02458. 617/964-3030. World Wide Web address: http://www.cahners.com.

DIRECTORY OF CHEMICAL PRODUCERS
SRI International, 333 Ravenswood Avenue, Menlo Park CA 94025. 650/326-6200. World Wide Web address: http://www.sri.com.

Magazines

CHEMICAL & ENGINEERING NEWS
American Chemical Society, 1155 16th Street NW, Washington DC 20036. 202/872-4600. World Wide Web address: http://www.acs.org.

CHEMICAL MARKET REPORTER
Schnell Publishing Company, 2 Rector Street, 26th Floor, New York NY 10004. 212/791-4267. Toll-free phone: 877/550-3839.

CHEMICAL WEEK
888 Seventh Avenue, 26th Floor, New York NY 10106. 212/621-4900. World Wide Web address: http://www.chemweek.com.

For information about the JobBank List Service visit www.adamsjobbank.com

COMMUNICATIONS: TELECOMMUNICATIONS AND BROADCASTING

You can expect to find the following types of companies in this chapter:
*Cable/Pay Television Services • Communications Equipment •
Radio and Television Broadcasting Systems • Telephone, Telegraph, and other Message Communications*

Some helpful information: *The average salary range for telecommunications equipment repairers is $20,000 - $25,000. Experienced telephone/cable mechanics and broadcast technicians earn $35,000, on average, per year. Experienced electronics engineers earn an average of $50,000 - $60,000 annually..*

ALCATEL USA INC.
1225 North Alma Road, Richardson TX 75081. 972/996-5000. **Contact:** Human Resources Department. **World Wide Web address:** http://www.usa.alcatel.com. **Description:** Manufactures telecommunications equipment including fiberoptic transmission systems and optical networks. **Corporate headquarters location:** This Location. **Other U.S. locations:** St. Louis MO; Raleigh NC. **Parent company:** Alcatel Alsthom (Paris, France). **Listed on:** NASDAQ.

ALCATEL USA INC.
1000 Coit Road, Mail Stop 210, Plano TX 75075-5813. 972/519-3000. **Contact:** Human Resources. **World Wide Web address:** http://www.usa.alcatel.com. **Description:** Manufactures telecommunications equipment including fiberoptic transmission systems and optical networks. **Corporate headquarters location:** Richardson TX. **Other U.S. locations:** St. Louis MO; Raleigh NC. **Parent company:** Alcatel Alsthom (Paris, France). **Listed on:** NASDAQ.

ANDREW CORPORATION
2701 Mayhill Road, Denton TX 76208. 940/891-0965. **Fax:** 940/381-3158. **Contact:** Tim Dee, Human Resources Manager. **World Wide Web address:** http://www.andrew.com. **Description:** A manufacturer of telecommunications equipment including Earth station satellite, cellular, and microwave antennas; towers; shelters; cables; and associated equipment. **Common positions include:** Accountant/Auditor; Blue-Collar Worker Supervisor; Budget Analyst; Buyer; Civil Engineer; Construction and Building Inspector; Cost Estimator; Customer Service Representative; Designer; Draftsperson; Electrical/Electronics Engineer; Electrician; Financial Analyst; General Manager; Human Resources Manager; Industrial Engineer; Industrial Production Manager; Licensed Practical Nurse; Management Analyst/Consultant; Mechanical Engineer; Operations/Production Manager; Purchasing Agent/Manager; Quality Control Supervisor; Registered Nurse; Software Engineer; Structural Engineer; Technical Writer/Editor; Transportation/Traffic Specialist. **Educational backgrounds include:** Accounting; Business Administration; Communications; Computer Science; Engineering; Finance; Liberal Arts; Marketing. **Benefits:** 401(k); Dental Insurance; Disability Coverage; Employee Discounts; Life Insurance; Medical Insurance; Pension Plan; Profit Sharing; Savings Plan; Tuition Assistance. **Special programs:** Internships. **Corporate headquarters location:** Orland Park IL. **Other U.S. locations:** Torrance CA; Austin TX; Dallas TX; Garland TX; Richardson TX; Bothell WA. **Listed on:** New York Stock Exchange. **Number of employees at this location:** 600. **Number of employees nationwide:** 3,000.

A.H. BELO CORPORATION
THE DALLAS MORNING NEWS
P.O. Box 655237, Dallas TX 75265. 214/977-6600. **Contact:** Mr. Lee Smith, Employment Manager. **World Wide Web address:** http://www.belo.com. **Description:** A.H. Belo Corporation owns and operates newspapers and network-affiliated television stations in seven U.S. metropolitan areas. *The Dallas Morning News* (also at this location) has a circulation of 550,000 during the week and 800,000 on Sunday. A.H. Belo traces its roots to *The Galveston Daily News*, which was first published in 1842. **Subsidiaries include:** DFW Printing Company, Inc.; DFW Suburban Newspapers, Inc.

CONTINENTAL ELECTRONICS CORPORATION
P.O. Box 270879, Dallas TX 75227-0879. 214/381-7161. **Contact:** Employment. **World Wide Web address:** http://www.contelec.com. **Description:** A manufacturer and distributor of radio and television transmitters and machinery. **Common positions include:** Accountant/Auditor;

Assistant Manager; Blue-Collar Worker Supervisor; Buyer; Computer Programmer; Credit Manager; Customer Service Representative; Department Manager; Draftsperson; Electrical/Electronics Engineer; Human Resources Manager; Manufacturer's/Wholesaler's Sales Rep.; Mechanical Engineer; Operations/Production Manager; Purchasing Agent/Manager; Quality Control Supervisor; Technical Writer/Editor. **Educational backgrounds include:** Accounting; Business Administration; Engineering; Marketing. **Benefits:** 401(k); Dental Insurance; Disability Coverage; Life Insurance; Medical Insurance; Tuition Assistance. **Corporate headquarters location:** Houston TX. **Parent company:** Tech-Sym Corporation. **Listed on:** New York Stock Exchange. **Number of employees at this location:** 250.

CORNING CABLE SYSTEMS
9275 Denton Highway, Keller TX 76248. 817/431-1521. **Contact:** Human Resources. **World Wide Web address:** http://www.corningcablesystems.com. **Description:** Manufactures fiberoptic, copper cable, and hardware communications solutions to a worldwide network of public and private networks and OEMS. **Parent company:** Corning Incorporated. **Number of employees worldwide:** 14,000.

D.F.W. COMMUNICATIONS
2413 Gravel Drive, Fort Worth TX 76118. 817/589-7322. **Contact:** Human Resources. **Description:** Sells and services two-way radios.

DECIBEL PRODUCTS INC.
8635 Stemmons Freeway, Dallas TX 75247. 214/634-8502. **Fax:** 214/819-4262. **Contact:** Human Resources. **World Wide Web address:** http://www.decibelproducts.com. **Description:** Manufactures and distributes telecommunications products including cables, connectors, and sway brace kits. **Common positions include:** Accountant/Auditor; Buyer; Electrical/Electronics Engineer; Industrial Engineer; Mechanical Engineer; Quality Control Supervisor; Technical Writer/Editor. **Educational backgrounds include:** Engineering. **Benefits:** 401(k); Dental Insurance; Disability Coverage; Life Insurance; Medical Insurance; Pension Plan; Profit Sharing; Savings Plan; Tuition Assistance. **Corporate headquarters location:** Beachwood OH. **Parent company:** Allen Telecom Systems. **Number of employees at this location:** 600.

ERICSSON INC.
PRIVATE RADIO SYSTEMS
4757 Irving Boulevard, Suite 108, Dallas TX 75247. 214/267-6907. **Contact:** Human Resources. **World Wide Web address:** http://www.ericsson.com. **Description:** Designs and manufactures advanced telecommunications equipment for wired and mobile communications in public and private networks. **Common positions include:** Electrical/Electronics Engineer; Software Engineer. **Educational backgrounds include:** Computer Science; Engineering. **Benefits:** 401(k); Daycare Assistance; Dental Insurance; Disability Coverage; Life Insurance; Medical Insurance; Pension Plan; Savings Plan; Tuition Assistance. **Corporate headquarters location:** Sweden. **Other U.S. locations:** New York NY; Lynchburg VA. **Listed on:** New York Stock Exchange. **Number of employees nationwide:** 5,000.

FUJITSU NETWORK COMMUNICATIONS (FNC)
2801 Telecom Parkway, Richardson TX 75082. 972/690-6000. **Contact:** Recruiting. **World Wide Web address:** http://www.fnc.fujitsu.com. **Description:** This location is engaged in the repair of cellular telephones. Overall, FNC develops and manufactures broadband transmission and switching technologies to deliver voice, video, and data capabilities.

GTE CORPORATION
VERIZON
1255 Corporate Drive, Irving TX 75038. 972/507-5000. **Contact:** Human Resources Department. **World Wide Web address:** http://www.verizone.com. **Description:** Provides a wide variety of communications services ranging from local telephone services for the home and office to highly-complex voice and data services for industry. Verizon is one of the largest publicly-held telecommunications companies in the world, one of the largest U.S.-based local telephone companies, and one of the largest cellular-service providers in the United States. **NOTE:** This location now operates as Verizon. **Corporate headquarters location:** New York NY.

GTE SOUTHWEST INC.
VERIZON
P.O. Box 152013, Irving TX 75015-2013. 972/717-7700. **Physical address:** 500 East John Carpenter Freeway, Irving TX. **Contact:** Human Resources. **World Wide Web address:** http://www.verizon.com. **Description:** Provides a wide variety of communications services

ranging from local telephone services for the home and office to highly complex voice and data services for industry. Verizon is one of the largest publicly-held telecommunications companies in the world, one of the largest U.S.-based local telephone companies, and one of the largest cellular service providers in the United States. **NOTE:** This location now operates as Verizon. **Corporate headquarters location:** New York NY.

GENERAL CABLE COMPANY
800 East Second Street, Bonham TX 75418. 903/583-2181. **Contact:** Human Resources. **World Wide Web address:** http://www.generalcable.com. **Description:** This location produces commercial cable for telephone companies. Overall, the company's business units include the Electrical Group, the Telecommunications and Electronics Group, the Consumer Products Group, and the Manufacturing Group. The Electrical Group operates under the business units General Cable/Guardian, which manufactures and distributes a full line of copper building wire, tray cable, power cable, and other cable products; Carol Cable Electrical, which manufactures industrial, power, mining, and control cable, THHN building wire, entertainment cable, rubber portable cord, and cordsets insulated with plastic and thermosetting compounds; and Capital Wire and Cable, which manufactures insulated wire and cable using both aluminum and copper conductors. The Telecommunications and Electronics Group operates under the business units Outside Products, which markets wire and cable designed for use in the outside plant network; Premise Products, which manufactures wire products that support the central office and commercial premise markets; and Electronics, which manufactures computer and control cables, IBM cabling products, ethernet, coaxial, twin axial, and fire alarm cables. The Consumer Products Group operates under the business units Carol Cable, which manufactures extension cords, portable lights, and home office power supplies; General/Capital Wire Retail, which sells building wire to the retail market; and the OEM Engineered Cordsets Division, which manufactures cord and cordsets for data processing equipment, tools, floor care products, and other appliances. The Manufacturing Group provides specialized support and expertise in the areas of purchasing, transportation, engineering, labor relations, manufacturing, and environmental and safety support. **Corporate headquarters location:** Highland Heights KY.

KFDA-TV
NEWS CHANNEL 10
P.O. Box 10, Amarillo TX 79105. 806/383-1010. **Contact:** Human Resources. **World Wide Web address:** http://www.newschannel10.com. **Description:** A CBS-affiliated television broadcasting station.

KLBK-TV
7403 South University Avenue, Lubbock TX 79423. 806/745-2345. **Contact:** Human Resources Department. **World Wide Web address:** http://www.klbk.com. **Description:** Operates two television broadcasting stations: ABC 28 and CBS 13.

KRLD/TEXAS STATE NETWORKS
1080 Ballpark Way, Arlington TX 76011. 817/543-5400. **Fax:** 817/543-5570. **Contact:** Human Resources. **World Wide Web address:** http://www.krld.com. **Description:** An all-news radio station.

KVII-TV
One Broadcast Center, Amarillo TX 79101. 806/373-1787. **Contact:** Human Resources Department. **World Wide Web address:** http://www.kvii.com. **Description:** An ABC-affiliated television station.

KVIL-AM/FM 103.7
9400 North Central Expressway, Suite 1600, Dallas TX 75231. 214/691-1037. **Fax:** 214/891-7975. **Contact:** Human Resources Department. **World Wide Web address:** http://www.kvil.com. **Description:** An adult contemporary radio station broadcasting on both AM and FM frequencies. **Common positions include:** Assistant Manager; Assistant Program Officer; Copywriter; Program Manager; Promotion Manager; Radio/TV Announcer/Broadcaster; Transportation Specialist. **Parent company:** Infinity Broadcasting Corporation of Texas.

KXXV-TV
P.O. Box 2522, Waco TX 76702. 254/754-2525. **Contact:** Human Resources. **World Wide Web address:** http://www.kxxv.com. **Description:** An ABC-affiliated television station.

LUCENT TECHNOLOGIES INC.
3000 Skyline Drive, Mesquite TX 75149. 972/284-2000. **Contact:** Human Resources Department. **World Wide Web address:** http://www.lucent.com. **Description:** This location manufactures electronic power components for the communications industry. Overall, Lucent Technologies Inc. manufactures communications products including switching, transmission, fiberoptic cable, wireless systems, and operations systems, to supply the needs of telephone companies and other communications services providers. **Corporate headquarters location:** Murray Hill NJ. **Other U.S. locations:** Nationwide.

MARCONI COMMUNICATIONS
P.O. Box 919, Bedford TX 76095. 817/267-3141. **Contact:** Employee Relations Manager. **World Wide Web address:** http://www.marconicomms.com. **Description:** Provides services and equipment for the Internet, enterprise networks, and telecommunications systems. **Corporate headquarters location:** Pittsburgh PA. **Parent company:** Marconi plc (London, England).

MOTOROLA, INC.
5555 North Beach Street, Fort Worth TX 76137. 817/245-6000. **Contact:** Human Resources Manager. **World Wide Web address:** http://www.mot.com. **Description:** This location manufactures pagers. Overall, Motorola manufactures communications equipment and electronic products including car radios, cellular phones, semiconductors, computer systems, cellular infrastructure equipment, pagers, cordless phones, and LAN systems. **Common positions include:** Computer Programmer; Electrical/Electronics Engineer; Industrial Engineer; Mechanical Engineer; Quality Control Supervisor; Software Engineer; Systems Analyst. **Educational backgrounds include:** Computer Science; Engineering; Physics. **Benefits:** 401(k); Dental Insurance; Disability Coverage; Employee Discounts; Life Insurance; Medical Insurance; Pension Plan; Profit Sharing; Savings Plan; Tuition Assistance. **Special programs:** Internships. **Corporate headquarters location:** Schaumburg IL. **Other U.S. locations:** Nationwide. **International locations:** Worldwide. **Listed on:** NASDAQ. **Number of employees at this location:** 107,000.

NEC AMERICA INC.
1525 West Walnut Hill Lane, Irving TX 75038. 972/580-9100. **Contact:** Human Resources Department. **World Wide Web address:** http://www.nec.com. **Description:** Manufactures communications systems and equipment, computers, industrial electronic systems, electronic devices, and home electronic products.

NOKIA MOBILE PHONES INC.
6000 Connection Drive, Irving TX 75039. 972/894-5000. **Contact:** Human Resources. **World Wide Web address:** http://www.nokia.com. **Description:** A leading manufacturer and supplier of mobile phones as well as a supplier of mobile, broadband, and IP networks. **Number of employees worldwide:** 56,000.

PAGENET
14911 Quorum Drive, Dallas TX 75240. 972/801-8000. **Contact:** Human Resources. **World Wide Web address:** http://www.pagenet.com. **Description:** A leading provider of wireless messaging and information services across the U.S. and Canada. **Corporate headquarters location:** This Location. **Subsidiaries include:** Vast Solutions.

RF MONOLITHICS, INC.
4347 Sigma Road, Dallas TX 75244. 972/233-2903. **Contact:** Human Resources. **World Wide Web address:** http://www.rfm.com. **Description:** Designs, develops, manufactures, and sells a broad range of radio frequency components and modules for the low-power wireless, high-frequency timing, and telecommunications markets. The company's products are based on surface acoustic wave reduced power consumption. The company markets its line of more than 500 resonators, filters, delay lines, and related modules to original equipment manufacturers worldwide. **Corporate headquarters location:** This Location. **Listed on:** NASDAQ. **Stock exchange symbol:** RFMI.

SUSQUEHANNA RADIO CORP.
3500 Maple Avenue, Suite 1600, Dallas TX 75219. 214/526-2400. **Fax:** 214/520-4343. **Contact:** Human Resources. **World Wide Web address:** http://www.dfwradio.com. **Description:** Operates four radio stations in the Dallas - Forth Worth area including 99.5 The Wolf, Big Talk 570, Merge 93.3 Net, and The Ticket Sports Radio. **Corporate headquarters**

location: York PA. **Other U.S. locations:** Anniston AL; Atlanta GA; Indianapolis IN; Cincinnati OH; Houston TX.

VERTEX COMMUNICATIONS CORPORATION
2600 Longview Street, Kilgore TX 75662. 903/984-0555. **Fax:** 903/984-7769. **Contact:** Ann Jerden, Manager of Personnel. **World Wide Web address:** http://www.vertexcomm.com. **Description:** Designs and manufactures satellite Earth station antennas which use domestic, international, and military radio frequencies. The company also offers a complete line of standard antenna products. **NOTE:** Entry-level positions are offered. **Common positions include:** Buyer; Civil Engineer; Computer Programmer; Design Engineer; Draftsperson; Electrical/Electronics Engineer; Mechanical Engineer; MIS Specialist; Operations/Production Manager; Software Engineer; Structural Engineer; Systems Analyst; Technical Writer/Editor; Transportation/Traffic Specialist. **Educational backgrounds include:** Accounting; Computer Science; Engineering; Finance; Marketing. **Benefits:** 401(k); Dental Insurance; Disability Coverage; Life Insurance; Medical Insurance; Pension Plan; Profit Sharing; Savings Plan; Tuition Assistance. **Corporate headquarters location:** This Location. **Other U.S. locations:** Torrance CA; State College PA. **Listed on:** NASDAQ. **Annual sales/revenues:** $21 - $50 million. **Number of employees at this location:** 400. **Number of employees nationwide:** 575. **Number of employees worldwide:** 605.

WORLDCOM INC.
2400 North Glenville Drive, Richardson TX 75082. 972/729-7000. **Contact:** Human Resources. **World Wide Web address:** http://www.wcom.com. **Description:** One of the world's largest suppliers of local, long distance, and international telecommunications services, and a global Internet service provider. **Corporate headquarters location:** Clinton MS. **Other U.S. locations:** Nationwide. **International locations:** Worldwide. **Parent company:** MCI Communications Corporation. **Listed on:** NASDAQ. **Stock exchange symbol:** WCOM. **Annual sales/revenues:** More than $100 million.

Note: Because addresses and telephone numbers of smaller companies can change rapidly, we recommend you call each company to verify the information below before inquiring about job opportunities. Mass mailings are not recommended.

Additional small employers:

CABLE/PAY TELEVISION SERVICES

AT&T Cable Services
1565 Chenault St, Dallas TX 75228-5468. 972/840-2288.

AT&T Corp.
1565 Chenault St, Dallas TX 75228-5468. 214/328-2882.

Cablevision
PO Box 7852, Waco TX 76714-7852. 254/776-2996.

Charter Communications Inc.
PO Box 2666, Fort Worth TX 76113-2666. 817/737-4795.

TCI Cablevision
1565 Chenault St, Dallas TX 75228-5468. 214/320-7431.

TCI Cablevision
PO Box 120, Arlington TX 76004. 817/265-7766.

COMMUNICATIONS EQUIPMENT

ADC Telecommunications Inc.
2240 Campbell Creek Blvd, Richardson TX 75082. 972/680-6900.

Alcatel
1227 W Marshall Ave, Longview TX 75604-5110. 903/236-5200.

Chorum Technologies Inc.
1155 E Collins Blvd 200, Richardson TX 75081-2304. 972/238-1770.

Ericsson Inc.
740 E Campbell Rd, Richardson TX 75081-6708. 214/925-8800.

Ericsson Inc.
815 Enterprise Blvd, Allen TX 75013-2771. 972/359-2080.

Ericsson Inc.
715 N Glenville, D17 Milstop, Richardson TX 75081. 972/583-5431.

Gardiner Communications Corp.
3605 Security St, Garland TX 75042-7629. 214/348-4747.

Intecom Inc.
PO Box 911790, Dallas TX 75391-1790. 972/855-8000.

Octel Communications Corp.
3410 Midcourt Rd, Ste 115,
Carrollton TX 75006-5178. 972/733-2700.

Spectrapoint Wireless LLC
1125 E Collins Blvd, Richardson TX 75081-2304. 972/852-7068.

Teknekron Infoswitch Corp.
4425 Cambridge Rd, Fort Worth TX 76155-2629. 817/267-3025.

Transition Technology
PO Box 2168, Hurst TX 76053-2168. 817/285-8011.

RADIO BROADCASTING STATIONS

Heaven 97 AM Radio
7901 John W. Carpenter Fwy, Dallas TX 75247-4832. 214/630-3011.

Infinity Broadcasting Corp.
5956 Sherry Ln, Dallas TX 75225-6531. 214/691-1075.

Mesquite FM Radio Broadcasting Station
2500 Memorial Blvd, Mesquite TX 75149-3702. 972/285-0297.

Radio Disney
13725 Montfort Dr, Dallas TX
75240-4455. 972/991-9200.

WBAP-KSCS Radio Inc.
2221 E Lamar Blvd, Ste 400,
Arlington TX 76006-7419.
817/695-1820.

TELEGRAPH AND OTHER MESSAGE COMMUNICATIONS

GTE Communications Corp.
6665 N MacArthur Blvd, Irving
TX 75039-2443. 972/465-4000.

Super One
1801 W Parker Rd, Plano TX
75023-7502. 972/612-8441.

TELEPHONE COMMUNICATIONS

Airtouch Paging of Texas
12221 Merit Dr, Ste 800, Dallas
TX 75251-2242. 972/860-3210.

Airtouch Paging of Texas
1720 Lakepointe Dr, Lewisville
TX 75057-6408. 972/860-3292.

Allegiance Telecom Inc.
1950 N Stemmons Fwy, Dallas
TX 75207-3107. 214/261-7100.

Allied Riser Communications
1700 Pacific Ave, Ste 400,
Dallas TX 75201-4679.
214/210-3000.

Americom Handset Processing
9001 Sterling St, Ste B, Irving
TX 75063-2422. 972/929-3721.

AT&T Corp.
5525 LBJ Fwy, Ste 600, Dallas
TX 75240-6241. 972/851-4556.

AT&T Corp.
6303 Forest Park Rd, Dallas TX
75235-5450. 214/654-8880.

Avantel Telecommunications
1201 E Arapaho Rd, Richardson
TX 75081-2442. 972/918-2522.

Caprock Communications Corp.
15601 Dallas Pkwy, Ste 700,
Dallas TX 75248. 214/720-7782.

Cisco Systems Inc.
14875 Landmark Blvd, Dallas
TX 75240-6786. 972/364-8700.

Excel Telecommunications
PO Box 650582, Dallas TX
75265-0582. 214/863-8000.

Gateway Technologies Inc.
PO Box 815749, Dallas TX
75381-5749. 972/241-1535.

Global Interactive Communications
1901 N Glenville Dr,
Richardson TX 75081-1957.
972/669-6000.

GTE Southwest Incorporated
1824 N 1st St, Garland TX
75040-4704. 972/487-5701.

GTE Southwest Incorporated
2303 S Fm 1417, Sherman TX
75092-4814. 903/870-5253.

GTE Southwest Incorporated
PO Box 1997, Texarkana TX
75504-1997. 903/798-4201.

INP-Skytel Local Paging
1101 Resource Dr, Plano TX
75074-7037. 972/543-6504.

Integrated Business Solutions
5420 LBJ Fwy, Dallas TX
75240-6222. 972/405-0224.

Intellicall Inc.
2155 Chenault Dr, Ste 410,
Carrollton TX 75006-5087.
972/416-0022.

Ionex Telecommunications Inc.
5710 LBJ Fwy, Ste 215, Dallas
TX 75240-6392. 972/392-4601.

Logistics Services
13500 Independence Pkw, Fort
Worth TX 76178-4010.
817/490-4311.

Max-Tel Communications Inc.
PO Box 280, Alvord TX 76225-0280. 940/427-2149.

Metrocall
6340 LBJ Fwy, Ste 100, Dallas
TX 75240-6402. 972/687-2000.

National Auto Cellular
1730 Briercroft Ct, Carrollton
TX 75006-6400. 972/466-5000.

Network Long Distance
PO Box 3529, Longview TX
75606-3529. 903/758-9350.

Nextlink Communications Inc.
2653 Summit Ave, Plano TX
75074-7432. 972/516-5599.

Nortel Networks Inc.
2100 Lakeside Blvd, Richardson
TX 75082-4302. 972/234-5300.

NTS Communications Inc.
PO Box 10730, Lubbock TX
79408-3730. 806/797-0687.

Oncor Communications Inc.
1412 Main St, Ste 2600, Dallas
TX 75202-4006. 214/653-1247.

Oncor Communications Inc.
3530 Forest Ln, Ste 200, Dallas
TX 75234-7933. 214/350-5060.

Pathnet Inc.
1661 Gateway Blvd,
Richardson TX 75080-3530.
972/690-9933.

Poka Lambro Telephone Coop
PO Box 1340, Tahoka TX
79373-1340. 806/924-7234.

Radio Paging Service
PO Box 10127, Lubbock TX
79408-3127. 806/762-0811.

Southwestern Bell Telephone
17330 Preston Rd, Dallas TX
75252-5728. 972/733-2000.

Southwestern Bell Telephone
15660 Dallas Pkwy, Ste 101,
Dallas TX 75248-3352.
972/774-4774.

Southwestern Bell Telephone
2200 N Greenville Ave,
Richardson TX 75082-4412.
972/454-6206.

Southwestern Bell Telephone
1405 Main St, Rm 501,
Lubbock TX 79401-3225.
806/321-6444.

Southwestern Bell Telephone
1116 Houston St, Rm 900, Fort
Worth TX 76102-6416.
817/884-8332.

Southwestern Bell Telephone
PO Box 480, Wichita Falls TX
76307-0480. 940/766-7011.

Southwestern Bell Telephone
1255 Tavaros Ave, Rm 202,
Dallas TX 75218-4018.
214/324-7883.

Web America Networks Incorporated
17250 Dallas Parkway, Dallas
TX 75248-1146. 972/738-6000.

Weblink Wireless Inc.
7001 I-40 W, Amarillo TX
79106-2610. 806/324-6000.

TELEVISION BROADCASTING STATIONS

KDFW-TV Channel 4
400 N Griffin St, Dallas TX
75202-1901. 214/720-4444.

KERA Channel 13
3000 Harry Hines Blvd, Dallas
TX 75201-1087. 214/871-1390.

WB33 KDAF-TV
8001 John W. Carpenter Fwy,
Dallas TX 75247-4718.
972/445-5333.

WFAA Channel 8
PO Box 655237, Dallas TX
75265-5237. 214/748-9631.

For more information on career opportunities in the communications industries:

Associations

ACADEMY OF TELEVISION ARTS & SCIENCES
5220 Lankershim Boulevard, North Hollywood CA 91601. 818/754-2800. World Wide Web address: http://www.emmys.org.

AMERICAN DISC JOCKEY ASSOCIATION
10882 Demarr Road, White Plains MD 20695. 301/705-5150. Fax: 301/843-7284. World Wide Web address: http://www.adja.org. A membership organization for professional disc jockeys that publishes a newsletter of current events and new products.

AMERICAN WOMEN IN RADIO AND TELEVISION, INC.
1650 Tysons Boulevard, Suite 200, McLean VA 22102. 703/506-3290. World Wide Web address: http://www.awrt.org. A national, nonprofit professional organization for the advancement of women who work in electronic media and related fields. Services include *News and Views,* a fax newsletter transmitted biweekly to members; *Careerline,* a national listing of job openings available to members only; and the AWRT Foundation, which supports charitable and educational programs and annual awards.

THE COMPETITIVE TELECOMMUNICATIONS ASSOCIATION (COMPTEL)
1900 M Street NW, Suite 800, Washington DC 20036. 202/296-6650. World Wide Web address: http://www.comptel.org. A national association providing a wide variety of resources including telecommunications trade shows.

INTERNATIONAL TELEVISION ASSOCIATION
9202 North Meridian Street, Suite 200, Annapolis IN 46360. 317/816-6269. World Wide Web address: http://www.itva.org. Membership required.

NATIONAL ASSOCIATION OF BROADCASTERS
1771 N Street NW, Washington DC 20036. 202/429-5300, ext. 5490. Fax: 202/429-5343. World Wide Web address: http://www.nab.org. Provides employment information.

NATIONAL CABLE TELEVISION ASSOCIATION
1724 Massachusetts Avenue NW, Washington DC 20036-1969. 202/775-3669. Fax: 202/775-3695. World Wide Web address: http://www.ncta.com. A trade association. Publications include *Cable Television Developments, Secure Signals,* and *Kids and Cable.*

PROMAX INTERNATIONAL
2029 Century Park East, Suite 555, Los Angeles CA 90067. 310/788-7600. Fax: 310/788-7616. A nonprofit organization for radio, film, television, video, and other broadcasting professionals. Ask for the jobline.

RADIO-TELEVISION NEWS DIRECTORS ASSOCIATION
1000 Connecticut Avenue NW, Suite 615, Washington DC 20036. 202/659-6510. Fax: 202/223-4007. World Wide Web address: http://www.rtnda.org.

U.S. TELEPHONE ASSOCIATION
1401 H Street NW, Suite 600, Washington DC 20005. 202/326-7300. World Wide Web address: http://www.usta.org. A trade association for local telephone companies.

Magazines

ELECTRONIC MEDIA
Crain Communications, 740 North Rush Street, Chicago IL 60611-2590. 312/649-5200.

Online Services

BROADCAST PROFESSIONALS FORUM
Go: BPForum. A CompuServe discussion group for professionals in radio and television.

CPB JOBLINE
World Wide Web address: http://www.cpb.org/jobline/index.html. The Corporation for Public Broadcasting, a nonprofit company, operates this site which provides a list of job openings in the public radio and television industries.

JOURNALISM FORUM
Go: Jforum. A CompuServe discussion group for journalists in print, radio, or television.

ON-LINE DISC JOCKEY ASSOCIATION
World Wide Web address: http://www.odja.com. Provides members with insurance, Internet advertising, a magazine, and networking resources. This site also posts job opportunities.

COMPUTER HARDWARE, SOFTWARE, AND SERVICES

You can expect to find the following types of companies in this chapter:
Computer Components and Hardware Manufacturers • Consultants and Computer Training Companies • Internet and Online Service Providers • Networking and Systems Services • Repair Services/Rental and Leasing • Resellers, Wholesalers, and Distributors • Software Developers/Programming Services • Web Technologies

Some helpful information: *The average salary for entry-level computer professionals (such as programmers, systems analysts, software developers and engineers) ranges between $25,000 and $40,000, with salary remaining largely dependent upon experience and performance. Experienced computer specialists frequently earn over $50,000 per year, and those in management can receive $75,000 and up.*

ACS TECHNOLOGY SOLUTIONS
3030 LBJ Freeway, Suite 910, Lock Box 2, Dallas TX 75234. 972/243-1020. **Contact:** Human Resources Administrator. **World Wide Web address:** http://www.acsts.com. **Description:** An international computer consulting firm offering information technology and software consulting services. Founded in 1975. **Corporate headquarters location:** This Location.

ANALYSTS INTERNATIONAL CORPORATION (AiC)
3030 LBJ Freeway, Suite 820, Dallas TX 75234. 972/243-2001. **Fax:** 972/243-7468. **Contact:** Human Resources. **World Wide Web address:** http://www.analysts.com. **Description:** An international computer consulting firm. The company assists clients in a variety of industries in developing systems using different programming languages and software. Founded in 1966. **Corporate headquarters location:** Minneapolis MN. **Other U.S. locations:** Nationwide. **International locations:** Canada; England. **Listed on:** NASDAQ. **Stock exchange symbol:** ANLY. **Number of employees nationwide:** 5,000.

ANDERSEN CONSULTING
901 Main Street, Suite 5400, Dallas TX 75202. 214/853-1000. **Fax:** 214/853-2000. **Contact:** Human Resources. **World Wide Web address:** http://www.andersenconsulting.com. **Description:** Provides services to help organizations effectively apply technology to their business advantage. By combining general business knowledge with information systems skills, the company develops solutions that help clients in various industries manage technology. **Corporate headquarters location:** Chicago IL. **Other U.S. locations:** Nationwide.

BANCTEC, INC.
4851 LBJ Freeway, Dallas TX 75244. 972/341-4000. **Contact:** Human Resources Department. **E-mail address:** jobs@banctec.com. **World Wide Web address:** http://www.banctec.com. **Description:** Engaged in systems integration and specializes in document management solutions. The company also provides network support services and develops image management software. **Common positions include:** Manufacturing Engineer. **Office hours:** Monday - Friday, 8:30 a.m. - 5:30 p.m. **Corporate headquarters location:** This Location. **Listed on:** New York Stock Exchange. **Stock exchange symbol:** BTC. **Number of employees worldwide:** 4,000.

BANCTEC, INC.
2701 East Grauwyler Road, Irving TX 75061. 972/579-6000. **Fax:** 972/579-6877. **Contact:** Human Resources Manager. **E-mail address:** jobs@banctec.com. **World Wide Web address:** http://www.banctec.com. **Description:** Engaged in systems integration and specializes in document management solutions. The company also provides network support services and develops image management software. **Common positions include:** Accountant/Auditor; Blue-Collar Worker Supervisor; Branch Manager; Budget Analyst; Buyer; Clerical Supervisor; Computer Programmer; Customer Service Representative; Draftsperson; Electrical/Electronics Engineer; Electrician; Financial Analyst; General Manager; Human Resources Manager; Management Analyst/Consultant; Mechanical Engineer; Purchasing Agent/Manager; Quality Control Supervisor; Software Engineer; Systems Analyst; Technical Writer/Editor. **Educational backgrounds include:** Accounting; Business Administration; Computer Science; Engineering; Marketing; Mathematics. **Benefits:** 401(k); Dental Insurance; Disability Coverage; Employee Discounts; Life Insurance; Medical Insurance; Spending Account; Tuition Assistance.

Corporate headquarters location: Dallas TX. Listed on: New York Stock Exchange. Stock exchange symbol: BTC. Number of employees worldwide: 4,000.

CALYX SOFTWARE
718 North Buckner Boulevard, Building 416, Suite 104, Dallas TX 75218. 214/320-3668. Contact: Human Resources. World Wide Web address: http://www.calyxsoftware.com. Description: Designs and markets POINT for Windows, a processing application for mortgage professionals and POINTMan, a processing application for loan agents. Corporate headquarters location: San Jose CA.

CERNER CORPORATION
8235 Douglas Avenue, Suite 1000, Dallas TX 75225. 214/369-4210. Contact: Human Resources. World Wide Web address: http://www.cerner.com. Description: Designs, installs, and supports software systems for the health care industry worldwide including hospitals, HMOs, clinics, physicians' offices, and integrated health organizations. All Cerner Corporation applications are structured around a single architectural design, Health Network Architecture (HNA), which allows information to be shared among clinical disciplines and across multiple facilities. Founded in 1979. NOTE: All hiring is conducted through the corporate headquarters. Interested jobseekers should direct resumes to Human Resources, Cerner Corporation, 2800 Rockcreek Parkway, Kansas City MO 64117. Other U.S. locations: Irvine CA; Atlanta GA; Burlington MA; Southfield MI; Herndon VA; Bellevue WA. Listed on: NASDAQ. Stock exchange symbol: CERN. Annual sales/revenues: More than $100 million. Number of employees worldwide: 2,650.

COMPAQ COMPUTER CORPORATION
5310 Harvest Hill Road, Suite 200, Dallas TX 75240. 972/702-4000. Contact: Human Resources. World Wide Web address: http://www.compaq.com. Description: This location is a sales and service office. Overall, Compaq Computer Corporation designs, manufactures, sells, and services computers and associated peripheral equipment, software, and supplies. Applications and programs include scientific research, computation, communications, education, data analysis, industrial control, time sharing, commercial data processing, graphic arts, word processing, health care, instrumentation, engineering, and simulation. Corporate headquarters location: Houston TX. Other U.S. locations: Nationwide. Annual sales/revenues: More than $100 million.

COMPUCOM SYSTEMS, INC.
7171 Forest Lane, Dallas TX 75230. 214/265-3600. Contact: Human Resources. World Wide Web address: http://www.compucom.com. Description: A leading PC integration services company providing product procurement, advanced configuration, network integration, and support services. Common positions include: Accountant/Auditor; Buyer; Computer Operator; Computer Programmer; Customer Service Representative; Software Engineer; Systems Analyst. Educational backgrounds include: Business Administration; Computer Science. Corporate headquarters location: This Location. Other U.S. locations: Nationwide. Number of employees at this location: 800. Number of employees nationwide: 1,600.

COMPUTER ASSOCIATES INTERNATIONAL, INC.
909 Las Colinas Boulevard East, Irving TX 75039. 972/556-7100. Contact: Lavena Sipes, Human Resources Manager. E-mail address: careers@ca.com. World Wide Web address: http://www.cai.com. Description: This location develops and sells software, and offers support services. Overall, Computer Associates International is one of the world's leading developers of client/server and distributed computing software. The company develops, markets, and supports enterprise management, database and applications development, business applications, and consumer software products for a broad range of mainframe, midrange, and desktop computers. Computer Associates International serves major business, government, research, and educational organizations. Founded in 1976. Common positions include: Administrative Manager; Clerical Supervisor; Computer Programmer; Customer Service Representative; Data Processor; Financial Services Sales Representative; Human Resources Manager; Manufacturer's/Wholesaler's Sales Rep.; Marketing Specialist; Quality Control Supervisor; Sales Representative; Services Sales Representative; Software Engineer; Support Personnel; Systems Analyst; Technical Writer/Editor. Educational backgrounds include: Accounting; Business Administration; Computer Science; Finance; Human Resources; Marketing. Benefits: 401(k); Dental Insurance; Disability Coverage; Employee Discounts; Life Insurance; Medical Insurance; Savings Plan; Smoke-free; Tuition Assistance. Special programs: Co-ops; Internships. Corporate headquarters location: Islandia NY. Other U.S. locations: Nationwide. Listed on: New York Stock Exchange. Stock exchange symbol: CA. Annual

sales/revenues: More than $100 million. **Number of employees at this location:** 400. **Number of employees worldwide:** 18,000.

COMPUTER ASSOCIATES INTERNATIONAL, INC.
300 Crescent Court, Suite 1200, Dallas TX 75201-7832. 214/981-1000. **Fax:** 214/981-1255. **Contact:** Personnel. **E-mail address:** careers@ca.com. **World Wide Web address:** http://www.cai.com. **Description:** One of the world's leading developers of client/server and distributed computing software. The company develops, markets, and supports enterprise management, database and applications development, business applications, and consumer software products for a broad range of mainframe, midrange, and desktop computers. Computer Associates International serves major business, government, research, and educational organizations. Founded in 1976. **Common positions include:** Accountant/Auditor; Blue-Collar Worker Supervisor; Buyer; Chemical Engineer; Chemist; Designer; Draftsperson; Electrical/Electronics Engineer; Human Resources Manager; Mechanical Engineer; Public Relations Specialist; Purchasing Agent/Manager; Quality Control Supervisor; Registered Nurse. **Educational backgrounds include:** Accounting; Business Administration; Chemistry; Computer Science; Engineering; Finance; Marketing; Physics. **Benefits:** 401(k); Dental Insurance; Disability Coverage; Life Insurance; Medical Insurance; Pension Plan; Profit Sharing; Tuition Assistance. **Corporate headquarters location:** Islandia NY. **Other U.S. locations:** Nationwide. **Listed on:** New York Stock Exchange. **Stock exchange symbol:** CA. **Annual sales/revenues:** More than $100 million. **Number of employees worldwide:** 18,000.

COMPUTER HORIZONS CORPORATION
2655 Villa Creek, Suite 280, Dallas TX 75234-7316. 972/488-0011. **Fax:** 972/406-0544. **Contact:** Human Resources. **World Wide Web address:** http://www.computerhorizons.com. **Description:** Offers contract staffing, outsourcing, re-engineering, and network management. **Corporate headquarters location:** Mountain Lakes NJ.

COMPUTER SCIENCES CORPORATION (CSC)
5525 LBJ Freeway, Dallas TX 75240. 972/386-0020. **Fax:** 972/386-0315. **Contact:** Human Resources. **World Wide Web address:** http://www.csc.com. **Description:** This location develops and markets software for financial institutions. Overall, CSC helps clients in industry and government use information technology to achieve strategic and operational objectives. The company tailors solutions from a broad suite of integrated service and technology offerings including e-business strategies and technologies, management and IT consulting, systems development and integration, application software, and IT and business process outsourcing. Founded in 1959. **Corporate headquarters location:** El Segundo CA.

DMR CONSULTING GROUP, INC.
13355 Noel Road, Suite 815, One Galleria Tower, Dallas TX 75240. 972/503-3700. **Toll-free phone:** 800/259-0012. **Fax:** 972/371-0400. **Contact:** Human Resources. **World Wide Web address:** http://www.dmr.com. **Description:** Provides computer consulting services including outsourcing and systems integration. **Common positions include:** Account Manager; Account Representative; Applications Engineer; Computer Operator; Computer Programmer; Database Manager; IT Specialist; MIS Specialist; Operations Manager; Project Manager; Software Engineer; Systems Analyst; Systems Manager; Technical Writer/Editor; Telecommunications Manager. **Benefits:** 401(k); Dental Insurance; Disability Coverage; Financial Planning Assistance; Life Insurance; Pension Plan; Profit Sharing; Savings Plan; Tuition Assistance.

EDS (ELECTRONIC DATA SYSTEMS CORPORATION)
5400 Legacy Drive, Mail Slot H4-GB-35, Plano TX 75024. 972/605-2700. **Fax:** 800/562-6241. **Contact:** Human Resources. **E-mail address:** careers@eds.com. **World Wide Web address:** http://www.eds.com. **Description:** Provides consulting, systems development, systems integration, and systems management services for large-scale and industry-specific applications. Founded in 1962. **NOTE:** Entry-level positions are offered. **Common positions include:** Applications Engineer; Computer Programmer; Database Manager; Financial Analyst; Software Engineer; Systems Analyst; Systems Manager. **Educational backgrounds include:** Accounting; Business Administration; Communications; Computer Science; Engineering; Finance; Marketing. **Benefits:** Dental Insurance; Employee Discounts; Life Insurance; Medical Insurance. **Special programs:** Internships; Training. **Corporate headquarters location:** This Location. **Listed on:** New York Stock Exchange; London Stock Exchange. **Stock exchange symbol:** EDS. **Annual sales/revenues:** More than $100 million.

ENTEX INFORMATION SERVICES
7171 Forest Lane, Dallas TX 75230. **Contact:** Human Resources. **World Wide Web address:** http://www.entex.com. **Description:** Provides systems integration, help desk, and PC repair

services to *Fortune* 1000 companies and federal clients. The company also resells hardware and software products. Founded in 1993. **Corporate headquarters location:** Rye Brook NY.

EXECUTRAIN OF TEXAS
12201 Merit Drive, Suite 350, Dallas TX 75251. 972/387-1212. **Contact:** Human Resources. **E-mail address:** info@executrain.com. **World Wide Web address:** http://www.executrain.com/dallas. **Description:** Trains businesses in the use of computer software and offers IT certification. **Corporate headquarters location:** Alpharetta GA. **Other U.S. locations:** Nationwide. **International locations:** Worldwide.

GE CAPITAL IT SOLUTIONS
5400 LBJ Freeway, Suite 1280, Dallas TX 75240. 972/419-3200. **Contact:** Human Resources. **World Wide Web address:** http://www.gecits.ge.com. **Description:** A nationwide reseller of computer products and services to commercial, governmental, and educational users. The company's products and services include value-added systems, systems integration, networking services, support, maintenance, facilities management, outsourcing, software and business consulting services, and rental services. GE Capital IT Solutions markets its computer products and business services through its offices in approximately 70 cities nationwide.

HEWLETT-PACKARD COMPANY
3000 Waterview Parkway, Richardson TX 75080. 972/497-4000. **Contact:** Human Resources. **World Wide Web address:** http://www.hp.com. **Description:** This location builds supercomputers. Overall, Hewlett-Packard is engaged in the design and manufacture of measurement and computation products and systems used in business, industry, engineering, science, health care, and education. Principal products are integrated instrument and computer systems (including hardware and software), peripheral products, and electronic medical equipment and systems. **NOTE:** Jobseekers should send resumes to Employment Response Center, Event #2498, Hewlett-Packard Company, Mail Stop 20-APP, 3000 Hanover Street, Palo Alto CA 94304-1181. **Common positions include:** Accountant/Auditor; Electrical/Electronics Engineer; Financial Analyst; Software Engineer; Technical Writer/Editor. **Educational backgrounds include:** Computer Science; Engineering. **Benefits:** 401(k); Dental Insurance; Disability Coverage; Life Insurance; Medical Insurance; Tuition Assistance. **Special programs:** Internships. **Corporate headquarters location:** Palo Alto CA. **Listed on:** New York Stock Exchange. **Number of employees at this location:** 700. **Number of employees worldwide:** 93,000.

I-CONCEPTS
2607 Walnut Hill Lane, Suite 200, Dallas TX 75229. 214/956-7770. **Contact:** Human Resources. **Description:** Develops software for the insurance industry.

IBM CORPORATION
1605 LBJ Freeway, Dallas TX 75234. 972/280-4000. **Toll-free phone:** 800/426-4968. **Recorded jobline:** 800/964-4373. **Contact:** IBM Staffing Services. **World Wide Web address:** http://www.ibm.com. **Description:** This location is a regional sales and marketing office. Overall, IBM is a developer, manufacturer, and marketer of advanced information processing products including computers and microelectronic technology, software, networking systems, and information technology-related services. **NOTE:** Jobseekers should send a resume to IBM Staffing Services, 1DPA/051, 3808 Six Forks Road, Raleigh NC 27609. **Corporate headquarters location:** Armonk NY. **International locations:** Worldwide. **Subsidiaries include:** IBM Credit Corporation; IBM Instruments, Inc.; IBM World Trade Corporation. **Number of employees at this location:** 3,000.

IBM CORPORATION
15303 Dallas Parkway, Suite 1350, Addison TX 75001. 972/661-1900. **Recorded jobline:** 800/964-4373. **Contact:** Human Resources. **World Wide Web address:** http://www.ibm.com. **Description:** A developer, manufacturer, and marketer of advanced information processing products including computers and microelectronic technology, software, networking systems, and information technology-related services. **NOTE:** Jobseekers should send a resume to IBM Staffing Services, 1DPA/051, 3808 Six Forks Road, Raleigh NC 27609. **Corporate headquarters location:** Armonk NY. **International locations:** Worldwide. **Subsidiaries include:** IBM Credit Corporation; IBM Instruments, Inc.; IBM World Trade Corporation.

ICS COMPUTER SYSTEMS CORPORATION
2301 North Central Expressway, Suite 158, Plano TX 75075. 972/509-8000. **Contact:** Human Resources. **Description:** A computer reseller.

I.T. PARTNERS, INC.
2735 Villa Creek Drive, Suite 175, Dallas TX 75234. 972/484-5300. **Fax:** 972/484-5605. **Contact:** Human Resources. **World Wide Web address:** http://www.itpartners.net. **Description:** Offers computer consulting services, software training, network implementation, and Web services (Web hosting and development).

INTERPHASE CORPORATION
13800 Senlac Drive, Dallas TX 75234. 214/654-5000. **Toll-free phone:** 800/777-3722. **Fax:** 214/654-5500. **Contact:** Pat Flatbush, Human Resources Manager. **E-mail address:** resumes@iphase.com. **World Wide Web address:** http://www.iphase.com. **Description:** A developer, manufacturer, and marketer of networking and mass storage controllers, as well as stand alone networking devices for computer systems. Networking products are primarily sold to original equipment manufacturers, value-added resellers, systems integrators, and large end users. **Common positions include:** Design Engineer; Electrical/Electronics Engineer; Software Engineer. **Educational backgrounds include:** Computer Science; Engineering. **Benefits:** 401(k); Dental Insurance; Disability Coverage; Life Insurance; Medical Insurance; Pension Plan; Tuition Assistance; Vision Insurance. **Corporate headquarters location:** This Location. **Listed on:** NASDAQ. **Annual sales/revenues:** Less than $5 million. **Number of employees at this location:** 200.

INTERVOICE, INC.
17811 Waterview Parkway, Dallas TX 75252. 972/454-8000. **Fax:** 972/454-8408. **Contact:** Human Resources. **World Wide Web address:** http://www.intervoice.com. **Description:** Develops, sells, and services interactive voice response systems that allow individuals to access a computer database using a telephone keypad, computer keyboard, or human voice. Applications are functioning in industries including insurance, banking, higher education, government, utilities, health care, retail distribution, transportation, and operator services. **Corporate headquarters location:** This Location.

ITAC SYSTEMS, INC.
3113 Benton Street, Garland TX 75042. 972/494-3073. **Fax:** 972/494-4159. **Contact:** Human Resources. **World Wide Web address:** http://www.mousetrak.com. **Description:** Manufactures the mouse-trak trackball, a computer peripheral product. Founded in 1993. **NOTE:** Entry-level positions are offered. **Common positions include:** Account Manager; Accountant/Auditor; Administrative Assistant; Controller; Credit Manager; Customer Service Representative; Database Manager; Design Engineer; Electrical/Electronics Engineer; Finance Director; Human Resources Manager; Internet Services Manager; Manufacturing Engineer; Marketing Specialist; Mechanical Engineer; Operations/Production Manager; Production Manager; Purchasing Agent/Manager; Sales Executive; Sales Manager; Systems Manager; Vice President of Operations; Webmaster. **Educational backgrounds include:** Accounting; Computer Science; Engineering; Marketing. **Benefits:** 401(k); Dental Insurance; Disability Coverage; Life Insurance; Medical Insurance; Tuition Assistance. **Corporate headquarters location:** This Location. **Listed on:** Privately held. **Annual sales/revenues:** Less than $5 million. **Number of employees at this location:** 25.

JRA INFORMATION SERVICES, INC.
13714 Gamma Road, Suite 120, Dallas TX 75244-4469. 972/702-8900. **Fax:** 972/702-0916. **Contact:** Human Resources. **E-mail address:** resume@jrainfo.com. **World Wide Web address:** http://www.jrainfo.com. **Description:** Provides computer consulting and technical consulting services. Founded in 1983.

KANEB SERVICES, INC.
2435 North Central Expressway, Suite 700, Richardson TX 75080. 972/699-4000. **Contact:** Human Resources. engaged in the worldwide marketing, refining, manufacturing, exploration, production, transportation, and research and development of petroleum and chemical products. Other products include fabricated plastics, films, food bags, housewares, garbage bags, and building materials. The company also has subsidiaries involved in real estate development and mining operations. **World Wide Web address:** http://www.kaneb.com. **Description:** A holding company whose subsidiaries are engaged in various technical applications as well as in the refining of petroleum products. **Corporate headquarters location:** This Location. **Subsidiaries include:** InformaTech's Medical Services Division provides information technology services for medical information systems and applications. InformaTech's Information Technology Division is engaged in network design and installation, secure network architecture, seat management, custom computer design, and cabling; Kaneb Pipe Line Partners, LP owns and operates several thousand miles of pipeline, transports refined petroleum products, and terminals independent liquids. Kaneb Pipe Line operates more than

60 facilities in the United States and the United Kingdom. **Listed on:** New York Stock Exchange.

LINX DATA TERMINALS, INC.
625 Digital Drive, Suite 100, Plano TX 75075. 972/964-7090. **Contact:** Human Resources. **World Wide Web address:** http://www.linxdata.com. **Description:** A manufacturer of networked data collection terminals and host connectivity software.

LUMINANT WORLDWIDE CORPORATION
13737 Noel Road, Suite 1400, Dallas TX 75240. 972/581-7000. **Contact:** Human Resources. **World Wide Web address:** http://www.luminant.com. **Description:** Provides e-business consulting services and solutions. **Corporate headquarters location:** This location. **Other U.S. locations:** San Francisco CA; Denver CO; Washington DC; Atlanta GA; Chicago IL; New York NY; Seattle WA.

MERLIN SOFTWARE SERVICES, INC.
1800 Jay Ell Drive, Suite 100, Richardson TX 75081. 972/235-9551. **Contact:** Human Resources. **World Wide Web address:** http://www.merlinss.com. **Description:** Designs and installs software. The company also provides training services. Founded in 1979.

MICRO COMPUTER SYSTEMS, INC.
2300 Valley View Lane, Suite 800, Irving TX 75062. 972/659-1514. **Fax:** 972/659-1624. **Contact:** Human Resources. **World Wide Web address:** http://www.mcsdallas.com. **Description:** Develops software including Local Area Network (LAN) communication systems and configuration utilities for EISA computers.

MICROGRAFX, INC.
505 Millennium Drive, Allen TX 75013. 972/234-1769. **Fax:** 972/994-6036. **Contact:** Human Resources. **World Wide Web address:** http://www.micrografx.com. **Description:** Develops, markets, and supports a line of graphic application software products for IBM PCs and compatibles running under the Microsoft Windows operating environment. Products are designed for both business and professional use and include professional illustration, basic drawing and charting products, data-driven graphics, image editing, and reusable clip-art libraries. Micrografx, Inc. also offers systems software products designed to enhance the Windows and OS/2 operating environments. **Common positions include:** Account Representative; Applications Engineer; Computer Programmer; Sales Representative; Software Engineer; Systems Analyst. **Educational backgrounds include:** Business Administration; Computer Science; Engineering; Finance; Marketing. **Benefits:** 401(k); Dental Insurance; Disability Coverage; Employee Discounts; Life Insurance; Medical Insurance; Tuition Assistance. **Corporate headquarters location:** This Location. **International locations:** Australia; Italy; Japan; United Kingdom. **Listed on:** NASDAQ. **Annual sales/revenues:** $5 - $10 million. **Number of employees at this location:** 200. **Number of employees worldwide:** 300.

MILGO SOLUTIONS INC.
1100 Jupiter Road, Suite 190, Plano TX 75074. 972/509-4700. **Contact:** Personnel. **E-mail address:** milgo_staffing@milgo.com. **World Wide Web address:** http://www.milgo.com. **Description:** This location is a sales and technical service office. Overall, Milgo Solutions manufactures data communications equipment including WANs, LANs, and access products. The company also offers related services including project management, installation, consultation, network integration, maintenance, disaster recovery, and training. **NOTE:** Please send resumes to Staffing Department, Milgo Solutions Inc., 1619 North Harrison Parkway, Mail Stop D251, Sunrise FL 33323-2802.

MYND CORPORATION
7800 North Simmons Freeway, Suite 800, Dallas TX 75247. 214/637-1540. **Contact:** Human Resources. **World Wide Web address:** http://www.mynd.com. **Description:** Develops software for the life insurance and financial industries, and provides related support services. **Corporate headquarters location:** Columbia SC. **International locations:** Worldwide.

NCR CORPORATION
450 East John Carpenter Freeway, Irving TX 75062. 972/650-2710. **Contact:** Joy Maffeo, Human Resources Consultant. **E-mail address:** joy.maffeo@dallastx.ncr.com. **World Wide Web address:** http://www.ncr.com. **Description:** This location is a sales and service office. Overall, NCR Corporation is a worldwide provider of computer products and services. The company provides computer solutions to three targeted industries: retail, financial, and communication. NCR Computer Systems Group develops, manufactures, and markets computer systems. NCR

Financial Systems Group is an industry leader in financial delivery systems, relationship banking data warehousing solutions, and payments systems/item processing. NCR Retail Systems Group is a world leader in end-to-end retail solutions serving the food, general merchandise, and hospitality industries. NCR Worldwide Services provides data warehousing services solutions; end-to-end networking services; and designs, implements, and supports complex open systems environments. NCR Systemedia Group develops, produces, and markets a complete line of information products to satisfy customers' information technology needs including transaction processing media, auto identification media, business form communication products, managing documents and media, and a full line of integrated equipment solutions. **Educational backgrounds include:** Business Administration; Computer Science. **Benefits:** 401(k); Dental Insurance; Disability Coverage; Life Insurance; Medical Insurance; Pension Plan; Savings Plan; Tuition Assistance. **Corporate headquarters location:** Dayton OH. **Other U.S. locations:** Nationwide. **Listed on:** New York Stock Exchange. **Annual sales/revenues:** More than $100 million. **Number of employees nationwide:** 19,000. **Number of employees worldwide:** 38,000.

NETWORK ASSOCIATES, INC.
4099 McEwen Road, Suite 500, Dallas TX 75244. 972/308-9960. **Contact:** Human Resources. **World Wide Web address:** http://www.nai.com. **Description:** Designs, manufactures, markets, and supports software-based analysis and monitoring tools primarily for managing enterprisewide computer networks. Products include McAfee anti-virus, Gauntlet firewall, PGP encryption, Sniffer network analyzers, and Magic Help Desk applications. Founded in 1989. **Annual sales/revenues:** $51 - $100 million. **Number of employees nationwide:** 2,800.

OPENCONNECT SYSTEMS INC.
2711 LBJ Freeway, Suite 800, Dallas TX 75234. 972/484-5200. **Contact:** Human Resources. **World Wide Web address:** http://www.oc.com. **Description:** A leading provider of e-business solutions. Founded in 1981. **Corporate headquarters location:** This location. **Listed on:** Privately held.

PER-SE TECHNOLOGIES, INC.
9441 LBJ Freeway, Suite 400, Dallas TX 75243. 972/664-6900. **Contact:** Human Resources. **Description:** A leading provider of comprehensive business management services, financial and clinical software, and Internet solutions to physicians and other healthcare professionals. **Corporate headquarters location:** Atlanta GA.

POLICY MANAGEMENT SYSTEMS CORPORATION (PMSC)
12001 North Central Expressway, Suite 500, Dallas TX 75243. 972/778-7000. **Contact:** Personnel. **World Wide Web address:** http://www.pmsc.com. **Description:** This location is a sales office. Overall, Policy Management Systems Corporation develops and licenses standardized insurance software systems and provides automation and administrative support and information services to the insurance industry worldwide. The company also provides professional support services, which include implementation and integration assistance, consulting and education services, and information and outsourcing services. **Common positions include:** Computer Programmer; Insurance Agent/Broker; Systems Analyst. **Educational backgrounds include:** Computer Science. **Benefits:** 401(k); Dental Insurance; Disability Coverage; Employee Discounts; Life Insurance; Medical Insurance; Tuition Assistance. **Special programs:** Internships. **Corporate headquarters location:** Columbia SC. **Listed on:** New York Stock Exchange. **Number of employees nationwide:** 4,300.

RVSI ACUITY CIMATRIX
6311 North O'Connor Road, Suite N50, Irving TX 75039. 972/869-7684. **Contact:** Human Resources. **World Wide Web address:** http://www.rvsi.com. **Description:** Provides data collection integrators with complete solutions including scanning components, networking, software tools, and support services. Customers are primarily involved in materials handling and factory automation environments, and include systems integrators, original equipment manufacturers, value-added resellers, and end users performing in-house systems integration. Products and related services fall into four major categories: omnidirectional scanning systems, intelligent fixed position line scanners, data collection terminals, and networking products. RVSI's foreign subsidiaries are located in Canada, Belgium, England, France, and Germany. **NOTE:** Send resumes to Human Resources, 5 Shawmut Road, Canton MA 02021. **Benefits:** 401(k). **Corporate headquarters location:** Canton MA.

RAYTHEON SYSTEMS COMPANY
P.O. Box 660023, Dallas TX 75266. 972/272-0515. **Contact:** Human Resources. **E-mail address:** resume@rayjobs.com. **World Wide Web address:** http://www.raytheon.com.

Description: This location develops high-technology software. Overall, Raytheon Systems designs, manufactures, and installs state-of-the-art communications and integrated command-and-control systems for military and industrial customers worldwide. **Parent company:** Raytheon Company is a diversified, international, multi-industry technology-based company ranked among the 100 largest U.S. industrial corporations. Raytheon has 110 facilities in 28 states and the District of Columbia. Overseas facilities and representative offices are located in 26 countries, principally in Europe, the Middle East, and the Pacific Rim. The company's four business segments include Electronics, Major Appliances, Aircraft Products, and Energy and Environmental. **Listed on:** New York Stock Exchange.

SOFTWARE SPECTRUM INC.
2140 Merritt Drive, Garland TX 75041. 972/840-6600. **Fax:** 972/864-3219. **Contact:** Human Resources. **World Wide Web address:** http://www.softwarespectrum.com. **Description:** A reseller of microcomputer software and services to businesses and government agencies. Software Spectrum also offers technical support and volume software license services. **Common positions include:** Accountant/Auditor; Advertising Clerk; Blue-Collar Worker Supervisor; Buyer; Collector; Computer Programmer; Credit Manager; Customer Service Representative; Electrical/Electronics Engineer; Human Resources Manager; Operations/Production Manager; Public Relations Specialist; Purchasing Agent/Manager; Quality Control Supervisor; Services Sales Representative; Systems Analyst; Technical Writer/Editor. **Educational backgrounds include:** Accounting; Art/Design; Business Administration; Communications; Computer Science; Economics; Engineering; Finance; Liberal Arts; Marketing. **Benefits:** 401(k); Dental Insurance; Disability Coverage; Employee Discounts; Life Insurance; Medical Insurance; Profit Sharing. **Corporate headquarters location:** This Location. **Other U.S. locations:** Nationwide. **International locations:** Worldwide. **Subsidiaries include:** Spectrum Integrated Services. **Listed on:** NASDAQ. **Number of employees at this location:** 500. **Number of employees nationwide:** 575.

SOURCE MEDIA, INC.
One Lincoln Center, 5400 LBJ Freeway, Suite 680, Dallas TX 75240. 972/701-5400. **Contact:** Ms. Avis Novak, Human Resources Manager. **World Wide Web address:** http://www.srcm.com. **Description:** Operates the Interactive Channel, an online television browser and programming service. The Interactive Channel is broadcast over cable television networks, and provides on-demand information covering education, news, sports, entertainment, and shopping. **Corporate headquarters location:** This Location. **Listed on:** NASDAQ. **Stock exchange symbol:** SRCM.

S2 SYSTEMS, INC.
15301 Dallas Parkway, Suite 600, Addison TX 75001. 972/458-3800. **Contact:** Human Resources. **World Wide Web address:** http://www.s2systems.com. **Description:** A provider of data communications middleware and related professional services that bridge the gap between open distributed systems and legacy mainframe and midrange systems used for online applications. **Corporate headquarters location:** Marlborough MA. **Parent company:** Stratus Computer, Inc. offers a broad range of computer platforms, application solutions, middleware, and professional services for critical online operations. Other Stratus Computer subsidiaries include Shared Systems Corporation, a provider of software and professional services to the financial services, retail, and health care industries; and Isis Distributed Systems, Inc., a developer of advanced messaging middleware products that enable businesses to develop reliable, high-performance distributed computing applications involving networked desktop computers and shared systems.

TANDY WIRE AND CABLE COMPANY
3500 McCart Avenue, Fort Worth TX 76110. 817/415-1500. **Contact:** Marianne Wiestner, Human Resources Manager. **Description:** Engaged in the manufacture of wire and cable including computer cable. **Common positions include:** Blue-Collar Worker Supervisor; Customer Service Representative; Draftsperson; Electrical/Electronics Engineer; Systems Analyst. **Educational backgrounds include:** Business Administration; Engineering. **Benefits:** Dental Insurance; Employee Discounts; Life Insurance; Medical Insurance; Profit Sharing; Savings Plan; Tuition Assistance. **Parent company:** Tandy Corporation. **Listed on:** New York Stock Exchange.

THINKSPARK
4835 LBJ Freeway, Suite 900, Dallas TX 75244. 972/392-0955. **Contact:** Human Resources. **World Wide Web address:** http://www.thinkspark.com. **Description:** Offers services in four main areas: Database Services, which includes database administration and monitoring services; E-Business Solutions, which includes knowledge management, enterprise resource

planning, and e-commerce; System Services, which includes systems integration and interface design; and Education Services. Founded in 1987.

2021 INTERACTIVE
15944 Midway Road, Addison TX 75001. 972/392-2553. **Contact:** Human Resources. **World Wide Web address:** http://www.2021.com. **Description:** Performs custom computer programming for multilevel marketing firms.

UNITED STATES DATA CORPORATION (USDATA)
2435 North Central Expressway, Suite 100, Richardson TX 75080-2722. 972/680-9700. **Fax:** 972/680-9324. **Contact:** Personnel Administrator. **World Wide Web address:** http://www.usdata.com. **Description:** Develops, markets, and supports application-enabler software products that customers configure to implement a wide range of real-time monitoring, analysis, information management, and control solutions in worldwide industrial automation markets. USData also develops, markets, and supports integrated hardware, software, and systems solutions for automated identification and data collection applications that are sold to a broad base of customers throughout North America. The company also acts as a full-service distributor and value-added remarketer for manufacturers of bar code equipment. **Common positions include:** Computer Programmer; Designer; Electrical/Electronics Engineer; Industrial Engineer; Manufacturer's/Wholesaler's Sales Rep.; Mathematician; Mechanical Engineer; Petroleum Engineer; Software Engineer; Systems Analyst; Technical Writer/Editor. **Educational backgrounds include:** Business Administration; Computer Science; Engineering; Marketing. **Benefits:** 401(k); Dental Insurance; Life Insurance; Medical Insurance; Tuition Assistance. **Special programs:** Internships. **Corporate headquarters location:** This Location. **Other U.S. locations:** Atlanta GA; Chicago IL; Boston MA; Seattle WA. **Listed on:** Privately held. **Number of employees at this location:** 200. **Number of employees nationwide:** 300.

UNIVIEW TECHNOLOGIES
17300 North Dallas Parkway, Dallas TX 75248. 214/503-8880. **Fax:** 214/503-8515. **Contact:** Human Resources. **Description:** Provides Internet connection services.

VANGARD TECHNOLOGY
624 Krona Drive, Suite 160, Plano TX 75074. 972/424-2800. **Contact:** Human Resources. **Description:** Provides businesses with networking computer systems hardware and software.

WORLDCOM INC.
2400 North Glenville Drive, Richardson TX 75082. 972/729-7000. **Contact:** Human Resources. **World Wide Web address:** http://www.wcom.com. **Description:** One of the world's largest suppliers of local, long distance, and international telecommunications services, and a global Internet service provider. **Corporate headquarters location:** Clinton MS. **Other U.S. locations:** Nationwide. **International locations:** Worldwide. **Parent company:** MCI Communications Corporation. **Listed on:** NASDAQ. **Stock exchange symbol:** WCOM. **Annual sales/revenues:** More than $100 million.

Note: Because addresses and telephone numbers of smaller companies can change rapidly, we recommend you call each company to verify the information below before inquiring about job opportunities. Mass mailings are not recommended.

Additional small employers:

COMPUTER FACILITIES MANAGEMENT SERVICES

CSSI Computer Support Services
125 E John Carpenter Fwy, Irving TX 75062-2324. 972/869-3966.

Perot Systems Corporation
PO Box 809022, Dallas TX 75380-9022. 972/340-5000.

COMPUTER MAINTENANCE

Computer Mechanics
2012 Plymouth Rock Dr,
Richardson TX 75081-3945. 972/497-9335.

IT Services Inc.
12221 Merit Dr, Ste 650, Dallas TX 75251-2235. 972/980-9803.

PC Service
2800 Story Rd W, Ste 200, Irving TX 75038. 972/257-8855.

COMPUTER PROCESSING SERVICES

Alliance Data Systems Corp.
17201 Waterview Pkwy, Dallas TX 75252-8004. 972/643-4078.

CSC Logic
9330 LBJ Fwy, Ste 500, Dallas TX 75243-3435. 972/783-3509.

Electrical Generation Technology
806 S Saint Paul St, Dallas TX 75201-6226. 214/742-1178.

Electronic Data Systems
105 W Bethany Dr, Ste 200, Allen TX 75013-3712. 972/396-4000.

Electronic Data Systems
4490 Alpha Rd, Dallas TX 75244-4505. 972/715-5207.

Input of Texas Inc.
813 Greenview Dr, Grand Prairie TX 75050-2439. 972/988-3282.

Telequest Quality Verification
1250 E Copeland Rd, Arlington TX 76011-1345. 817/460-5700.

UST Delivery Systems Inc.
PO Box 89000, Dallas TX 75287. 214/821-9767.

COMPUTER SOFTWARE, PROGRAMMING, AND SYSTEMS DESIGN

ACS Retail Solutions Inc.
1111 W Mockingbird Ln, Dallas TX 75247-5028. 214/252-2100.

Adea Inc.
4835 LBJ Fwy, Ste 800, Dallas TX 75244-6056. 972/960-9626.

Akili Systems Group Inc.
2001 Bryan St, Ste 1500, Dallas TX 75201-3015. 214/978-9700.

Analysts International Corp.
3 Village Cir, Ste 205, Roanoke TX 76262-7940. 817/491-1390.

Antrim Corporation
101 E Park Blvd, Fl 12, Plano TX 75074-5483. 972/422-1022.

Argo Data Resource Corporation
12770 Coit Rd, Ste 600, Dallas TX 75251-1359. 972/866-3300.

Banctec Technologies
14240 Midway Rd, Dallas TX 75244-3609. 972/982-2938.

Compupros Inc.
16479 Dallas Pkwy, Ste 800, Addison TX 75001-6805. 972/250-4504.

Corporate Systems Inc.
PO Box 31780, Amarillo TX 79120-1780. 806/376-4223.

CTI Limited Inc.
5400 LBJ Fwy, Ste 910, Dallas TX 75240-1015. 972/776-3600.

Cybernet Solutions Inc.
PO Box 720667, Dallas TX 75372-0667. 214/265-9700.

Decision Consultants Inc.
5000 Quorum Dr, Ste 410, Dallas TX 75240-7068. 972/386-8777.

Electronic Catalog Service
6400 Legacy Dr, Plano TX 75024-3609. 972/604-2000.

Electronic Data Systems Corp.
PO Box 470487, Dallas TX 75247. 214/689-7400.

Empenta Inc.
7825 McCallum Blvd, Dallas TX 75252-8142. 972/267-2327.

EXE Technologies Inc.
8787 N Stemmons Fwy, Dallas TX 75247-3702. 972/233-3761.

Flashnet Communications
1812 N Forest Park Blvd, Fort Worth TX 76102-5807. 817/820-0068.

Harbinger Enterprise Solutions
PO Box 841374, Dallas TX 75284-1374. 972/643-3000.

Headway Corporate Resources
3838 Oak Lawn Ave, Ste 300, Dallas TX 75219-4504. 214/692-9141.

I2 Technologies Inc.
11701 Luna Rd, Dallas TX 75234-6072. 214/860-6000.

Ibertech Inc.
1320 Tennis Dr, Bedford TX 76022-6352. 817/252-9499.

ICL Retail Systems
5429 LBJ Fwy, Dallas TX 75240-2607. 972/716-8300.

Infinium Software Inc.
500 S Taylor St, Amarillo TX 79101-2442. 806/342-0477.

Intellimark Inc.
8701 W Bedford Euless Rd, Hurst TX 76053-3804. 817/276-3000.

Lacerte Software Corporation
13155 Noel Rd, Fl 22, Dallas TX 75240-5090. 972/490-8500.

Latron Holdings Inc.
1111 W Mockingbird Ln, Dallas TX 75247-5028. 214/905-2300.

Level One Communications Inc.
2340 E Trinity Mills Rd, Carrollton TX 75006-1942. 972/418-2956.

Mercury Interactive Corp.
PO Box 200876, Dallas TX 75320-0876. 408/822-5200.

Metapatah Software International
1755 N Collins Blvd, Richardson TX 75080-3562. 972/644-6886.

Metasolv Software Inc.
5560 Tennyson Pkwy, Plano TX 75024-3532. 972/403-8300.

Newdata Strategies
16415 Addison Rd, Ste 500, Dallas TX 75248. 972/735-0001.

PDX
101 Jim Wright Fwy S, Fort Worth TX 76108-2202. 817/246-6760.

Pegasus Systems Inc.
3811 Turtle Creek Blvd, Dallas TX 75219-4461. 214/528-5656.

Peoplesoft Inc.
5420 LBJ Fwy, Ste 1500, Dallas TX 75240. 972/866-3000.

Professional Data Solutions
PO Box 6115, Temple TX 76503-6115. 254/771-7100.

Realpage Inc.
4000 International Pkwy, Carrollton TX 75007-1913. 972/820-3000.

Responsive Services International
1220 Broadway St, Fl 9, Lubbock TX 79401-3201. 806/763-1586.

Sabre Decision Technologies
1 Kirkwood Dr, Southlake TX 76092-2100. 817/264-7841.

SAP America Inc.
600 Las Colinas Blvd E, Irving TX 75039-5627. 972/868-2000.

Sterling Commerce
750 W John Carpenter Fwy, Irving TX 75039-2500. 469/524-2000.

Sterling Commerce
15301 Dallas Pkwy, StE 400, Addison TX 75001-4670. 972/788-5270.

Tandem Telecom
1255 W 15th St, Ste 8030, Plano TX 75075-7299. 972/423-5383.

Technical Management Group
6100 Western Pl, Ste 105, Fort Worth TX 76107-4662. 817/762-8400.

Tivoli Systems Inc.
14643 Dallas Pkwy, Dallas TX 75240-8800. 214/860-3800.

MISC. COMPUTER RELATED SERVICES

Abacus Technical Service
2201 N Central Expy, Richardson TX 75080-2754. 972/644-4105.

Beryl Corp.
3600 Harwood Rd A, Bedford TX 76021-4012. 817/355-5040.

Cap Gemini America Inc.
14755 Preston Rd, Ste 310,

Dallas TX 75240-7886.
972/776-5600.

CSC Consulting Systems Integration
3811 Turtle Creek Blvd, Dallas TX 75219-4461. 214/520-0555.

DSI Service
12005 Ford Rd, Ste 750, Dallas TX 75234-7284. 972/241-9001.

Nortel Networks Inc.
2375A N Glenville Dr, Richardson TX 75082-4315. 972/684-1000.

Objectspace Inc.
14850 Quorum Dr, Ste 500, Dallas TX 75240-7045. 972/934-2496.

Red Leaf Enterprises Inc.
PO Box 123797, Fort Worth TX 76121-3797. 817/732-7486.

Systems Resources Consulting
5001 Spring Valley, Dallas TX 75244-3946. 972/934-4400.

Yahoo!
2914 Taylor St, Dallas TX 75226-1908. 214/748-6660.

For more information on career opportunities in the computer industry:

Associations

AMERICAN SOCIETY FOR INFORMATION SCIENCE
8720 Georgia Avenue, Suite 501, Silver Spring MD 20910-3602. 301/495-0900. Fax: 301/495-0810. World Wide Web address: http://www.asis.org. Offers *Challenging Careers in Information: Join the Information Age*, which covers education and job opportunities.

ASSOCIATION FOR COMPUTING MACHINERY
1515 Broadway, 17th Floor, New York NY 10036. 212/869-7440. World Wide Web address: http://www.acm.org. Membership required.

ASSOCIATION FOR MULTIMEDIA COMMUNICATIONS
P.O. Box 10645, Chicago IL 60610. 312/409-1032. E-mail address: amc@amcomm.org. World Wide Web address: http://www.amcomm.org. A multimedia and Internet association.

ASSOCIATION FOR WOMEN IN COMPUTING
41 Sutter Street, Suite 1006, San Francisco CA 94104. 415/905-4663. E-mail address: awc@awc-hq.org. World Wide Web address: http://www.awc-hq.org. A nonprofit organization promoting women in computing professions.

BLACK DATA PROCESSING ASSOCIATES
8401 Corporate Drive, Suite 405, Lanham MD 20785. Toll-free phone: 800/727-BDPA. E-mail address: nbdpa@ix.netcom.com. World Wide Web address: http://www.bdpa.org. An organization of information technology professionals serving the minority community.

THE CENTER FOR SOFTWARE DEVELOPMENT
111 West St. John, Suite 200, San Jose CA 95113. 408/494-8378. E-mail address: info@center.org. World Wide Web address: http://www.center.org. A nonprofit organization providing technical and business resources for software developers.

COMMERCIAL INTERNET EXCHANGE ASSOCIATION (CIX)
P.O. Box 1726, Herndon VA 20172-1726. 703/709-8200. E-mail address: helpdesk@cix.org. World Wide Web address: http://www.cix.org. A nonprofit trade association of data internetworking service providers.

ELECTRONIC PUBLISHING ASSOCIATION LLC
One Rodney Square, 10th Floor, 10th & King Streets, Wilmington DE 19801. World Wide Web address: http://www.epaonline.com. An international association of companies that publish electronically using such formats as CD-ROM, DVD-ROM, and the Internet.

HTML WRITERS GUILD
World Wide Web address: http://www.hwg.org. An international organization of Web page writers and Internet professionals.

INFORMATION TECHNOLOGY ASSOCIATION OF AMERICA
1616 North Fort Myer Drive, Suite 1300, Arlington VA 22209. 703/522-5055. World Wide Web address: http://www.itaa.org.

INTERNET ALLIANCE
1825 Eye Street, Suite 400, P.O. Box 65782, Washington DC 20006. 202/955-8091. World Wide Web address: http://www.isa.net.

MULTIMEDIA DEVELOPMENT GROUP
520 Third Street, Suite 257, San Francisco CA 94107. 415/512-3556. Fax: 415/512-3569. E-mail address: geninfo@mdg.org. A nonprofit trade association dedicated to the business and market development of multimedia companies.

THE OPEN GROUP
29-B Montvale Avenue, Woburn MA 01801. 781/376-8200. World Wide Web address: http://www.opengroup.org. A consortium concerned with open systems technology in the information systems industry. Membership required.

SOCIETY FOR INFORMATION MANAGEMENT
401 North Michigan Avenue, Chicago IL 60611-4267. 312/644-6610. E-mail address: info@simnet.org. World Wide Web address: http://www.simnet.org. A forum for information technology professionals.

SOFTWARE & INDUSTRY INFORMATION ASSOCIATION (SIAA)
1730 M Street NW, Suite 700, Washington DC 20036. 202/452-1600. World Wide Web address: http://www.siaa.net.

SOFTWARE DEVELOPMENT FORUM
953 Industrial Avenue, Suite 117, Palo Alto CA 94303. 650/856-3706. E-mail address: info@sdforum.org. World Wide Web address: http://www.sdforum.org. An independent, nonprofit organization for software industry professionals.

SOFTWARE SUPPORT PROFESSIONALS ASSOCIATION
11858 Bernardo Plaza Court, Suite 101C, San Diego CA 92128. Toll-free phone: 877/ASK-SSPA. World Wide Web address: http://www.supportgate.com. A forum for service and support professionals in the software industry.

USENIX ASSOCIATION
2560 Ninth Street, Suite 215, Berkeley CA 94710. 510/528-8649. World Wide Web address: http://www.usenix.org. An advanced computing systems professional association for engineers, systems administrators, scientists, and technicians.

WORLD WIDE WEB TRADE ASSOCIATION
World Wide Web address: http://www.web-star.com/wwwta.html. An association promoting responsible use of the World Wide Web.

Career Fairs

EXPO INTERNATIONAL, INC.
101 West 23rd Street, Suite 2390, New York NY 10011. 212/655-4505. Fax: 212/655-4501. World Wide Web address: http://www.tech-expo.com. One of the nation's leading technical career fairs.

Magazines

COMPUTER-AIDED ENGINEERING
Penton Media, Inc., 1100 Superior Avenue, Cleveland OH 44114. 216/696-7000. World Wide Web address: http://www.penton.com/cae.

DATAMATION
Earthweb Inc., 10 Post Office Square, Suite 600 South, Boston MA 02109. World Wide Web address: http://www.datamation.com.

IDC REPORT
International Data Corporation, 5 Speen Street, Framingham MA 01701. 508/872-8200.

Online Services

COMPUTER CONSULTANTS
Go: Consult. A CompuServe discussion group for computer professionals interested in networking and business development.

COMPUTER JOBS STORE
World Wide Web address: http://www.computerjobs.com. Over 5,000 job listings are available on this site which is updated every hour. The site also offers salary information and links to other sites.

COMPUTERWORLD
World Wide Web address: http://www.computerworld.com. A weekly online newspaper for information sciences professionals. Features the latest news and employment opportunities. *Computerworld* conducts a job search by skills, job level (entry-level or experienced), job title, company, and your choice of three cities and three states. One feature of this site is "Career Central," a service which e-mails you when a job matches the skills you have submitted online. This site also has corporate profiles, an events calendar, *Computerworld*'s publications, an index of graduate schools, and other informative and educational resources.

DICE.COM
World Wide Web address: http://www.dice.com. Offers listings for over 100,000 jobs in the high-tech field.

IDEAS JOB NETWORK
World Wide Web address: http://www.ideasjn.com. Offers job listings in the field of computer engineering.

INFOWORKS USA
World Wide Web address: http://www.infoworksusa.com. Provides job listings, profiles of member companies, and a skills quiz.

IT JOBS
World Wide Web address: http://www.internet-solutions.com/itjobs/us/usselect.htm. This Website provides links to companies that have job openings in the information technology industry.

JOBSERVE
World Wide Web address: http://www.jobserve.com. Provides information on job openings in the field of information technology for companies throughout Europe. The site also offers links to numerous company Web pages, resume posting services, and a directory of recruiters.

MACTALENT
World Wide Web address: http://www.mactalent.com. Updated daily with job postings for computer professionals with specialized Mac skills.

SELECTJOBS
World Wide Web address: http://www.selectjobs.com. Post a resume and search the job database by region, discipline, special requirements, and skills on *SelectJOBS*. Once your search criteria has been entered, this site will automatically e-mail you when a job opportunity matches your requests.

THE SOFTWARE JOBS HOMEPAGE
World Wide Web address: http://www.softwarejobs.com. This Website offers a searchable database of openings for jobseekers looking in the software and information technology industries. The site is run by Allen Davis & Associates.

Visit our exciting job and career site at www.careercity.com

EDUCATIONAL SERVICES

You can expect to find the following types of facilities in this chapter:
Business/Secretarial/Data Processing Schools • Colleges/Universities/Professional Schools • Community Colleges/Technical Schools/Vocational Schools • Elementary and Secondary Schools • Preschool and Child Daycare Services

Some helpful information: *The average salary range for teachers (grades K-12) is $30,000 - $40,000 annually, though salaries vary significantly between states. Instructors at colleges typically earn approximately $30,000 annually. Educational administrators earn approximately $50,000 - $70,000 per year. Assistant and associate college professors earn between $35,000 and $55,000 on average, and full professors can receive considerably more. Deans normally receive salaries commensurate with that of full professors in the same discipline.*

ABILENE CHRISTIAN UNIVERSITY
ACU Station, Box 29106, Abilene TX 79699-9106. 915/674-2000. **Contact:** Personnel. **World Wide Web address:** http://www.acu.edu. **Description:** A university with 117 undergraduate programs, 39 graduate fields of study, and one doctoral program in theology. Approximately 4,500 students are enrolled in the university.

AMARILLO COLLEGE
P.O. Box 447, Amarillo TX 79178. 806/371-5000. **Contact:** Human Resources. **Description:** A two-year community college. Approximately 7,300 students are enrolled at this location. Amarillo College has three other campuses throughout Amarillo.

THE ART INSTITUTE OF DALLAS
Two NorthPark, 8080 Park Lane, Dallas TX 75231. 214/692-8080. **Fax:** 214/692-6541. **Contact:** Personnel Office. **World Wide Web address:** http://www.aid.aii.edu. **Description:** A two-year accredited institute with associate degree programs in art, fashion, photography, interior design, and music and video production. **Common positions include:** Accountant/Auditor; Administrator; Commercial Artist; Customer Service Representative; Department Manager; Instructor/Trainer; Services Sales Representative. **Educational backgrounds include:** Accounting; Art/Design; Business Administration; Communications; Liberal Arts; Marketing. **Benefits:** Disability Coverage; Life Insurance; Medical Insurance; Pension Plan; Profit Sharing; Tuition Assistance.

BAYLOR UNIVERSITY
P.O. Box 97053, 2nd Floor, Clifton Robinson Tower, 700 University Parks Drive, Waco TX 76798. 254/710-2219. **Fax:** 254/710-3819. **Contact:** Personnel Director. **World Wide Web address:** http://www.baylor.edu. **Description:** One of the largest Baptist universities in the nation. Baylor has over 13,000 students enrolled in a wide range of undergraduate and graduate programs. Founded in 1845.

BROOKHAVEN COLLEGE
3939 Valley View Lane, Farmers Branch TX 75244. 972/860-4813. **Contact:** Human Resources Department. **World Wide Web address:** http://www.dcccd.edu. **Description:** A two-year community college offering a full range of transferable, freshman- and sophomore-level college courses. The college serves the northern portion of Dallas County including North Dallas, Carrollton, Farmers Branch, Addison, Lewisville, Flower Mound, and The Colony. Brookhaven College serves 2,400 international students representing more than 100 countries and 65 languages. Founded in 1978. **Corporate headquarters location:** This Location.

CISCO JUNIOR COLLEGE
841 North Judge Ely, Abilene TX 79601. 915/673-4567. **Contact:** Personnel. **World Wide Web address:** http://www.cisco.cc.tx.us. **Description:** A junior college. **NOTE:** Jobseekers should address inquiries to Personnel Department, Rural Route 3, Box 3, Cisco TX 76837.

COLLIN COUNTY COMMUNITY COLLEGE DISTRICT
P.O. Box 8001, McKinney TX 75070-8001. 972/881-5660. **Physical address:** 2200 West University Drive, McKinney TX 75070-8001. **Fax:** 972/985-3778. **Recorded jobline:** 972/881-5627. **Contact:** Brenda McNeacon, Director of Human Resources. **World Wide Web address:**

http://www.ccccd.edu. **Description:** A community college offering courses in computer science, humanities, international studies, fine arts, mathematics/natural science, health sciences, education, and engineering. **Common positions include:** Clerical Supervisor; Computer Programmer; Customer Service Representative; Education Administrator; Human Resources Manager; Librarian; Library Technician; Purchasing Agent/Manager; Systems Analyst; Teacher/Professor. **Educational backgrounds include:** Business Administration; Computer Science. **Benefits:** Dental Insurance; Disability Coverage; Life Insurance; Medical Insurance; Pension Plan; Tuition Assistance. **Special programs:** Internships. **Corporate headquarters location:** This Location.

DALLAS BAPTIST UNIVERSITY
3000 Mountain Creek Parkway, Dallas TX 75211-9299. 214/333-7100. **Contact:** Personnel. **World Wide Web address:** http://www.dbu.edu. **Description:** An accredited university offering 34 undergraduate majors and eight master's programs.

DALLAS CHRISTIAN COLLEGE
2700 Christian Parkway, Dallas TX 75234. 972/241-3371. **Contact:** Dr. Mike Young, Academic Dean. **World Wide Web address:** http://www.dallas.edu. **Description:** Offers undergraduate programs in religious studies. Degree programs include pastoral ministry, youth ministry, education, music, and counseling.

DALLAS COUNTY COMMUNITY COLLEGE DISTRICT
701 Elm Street, Dallas TX 75202. 214/860-2135. **Contact:** Human Resources. **World Wide Web address:** http://www.dcccd.edu. **Description:** A community college district. **Common positions include:** Accountant/Auditor; Administrator; Buyer; Education Administrator; Instructor/Trainer; Systems Manager. **Educational backgrounds include:** Accounting; Art/Design; Biology; Business Administration; Chemistry; Communications; Computer Science; Economics; Education; Engineering; Finance; Geology; Liberal Arts; Marketing; Mathematics; Physics. **Benefits:** Dental Insurance; Disability Coverage; Life Insurance; Medical Insurance; Pension Plan. **Corporate headquarters location:** This Location.

DALLAS PUBLIC SCHOOLS
3700 Ross Avenue, Dallas TX 75204. 972/925-3700. **Contact:** Personnel. **Description:** Administrative offices for the local school district. Dallas Public Schools comprises 154 elementary schools and 63 middle and high schools.

DEVRY INSTITUTE OF TECHNOLOGY
4800 Regent Boulevard, Irving TX 75063. 972/929-6777x250. **Fax:** 972/929-2871. **Contact:** Mr. R. Glyn Williams, Human Resources Manager. **E-mail address:** gwilliams@dal.devry.edu. **World Wide Web address:** http://www.dal.devry.edu. **Description:** A fully-accredited college offering baccalaureate degrees in business and technology. **Common positions include:** Education Administrator; Electrical/Electronics Engineer; Teacher/Professor; Telecommunications Manager. **Educational backgrounds include:** Computer Science; Engineering. **Benefits:** 401(k); Dental Insurance; Disability Coverage; Life Insurance; Medical Insurance; Public Transit Available; Tuition Assistance. **Corporate headquarters location:** Oakbrook Terrace IL. **Listed on:** New York Stock Exchange. **Stock exchange symbol:** DV. **Number of employees at this location:** 200. **Number of employees nationwide:** 3,000.

EASTFIELD COLLEGE
3737 Motley Drive, Mesquite TX 75150. 972/860-7100. **Contact:** Human Resources. **World Wide Web address:** http://www.efc.dcccd.edu. **Description:** A community college.

EL CENTRO COLLEGE
801 Main Street, Dallas TX 75212. 214/860-2037. **Contact:** Human Resources. **World Wide Web address:** http://www.dcccd.edu. **Description:** A two-year community college. El Centro College operates as part of the Dallas County Community College District which is comprised of seven area colleges.

FLIGHTSAFETY INTERNATIONAL, INC.
8900 Trinity Boulevard, Hurst TX 76053. 817/276-7500. **Fax:** 817/276-7501. **Contact:** Phyllis Lovelace, Manager of Human Resources. **World Wide Web address:** http://www.flightsafety.com. **Description:** FlightSafety International provides high-technology training to operators of aircraft and ships. Total training systems are used including sophisticated simulators and training devices, computer-based training, and professional instructors. The company's worldwide clients include corporations, airlines, the military, and government agencies. **Common positions include:** Computer Programmer; Operations/Production

Manager; Software Engineer; Systems Analyst; Technical Writer/Editor. **Educational backgrounds include:** Art/Design; Computer Science. **Benefits:** 401(k); Dental Insurance; Disability Coverage; Life Insurance; Medical Insurance; Pension Plan. **Corporate headquarters location:** Flushing NY. **Other U.S. locations:** Nationwide. **Listed on:** New York Stock Exchange. **Number of employees at this location:** 150. **Number of employees nationwide:** 2,000.

HARDIN-SIMMONS UNIVERSITY
HSU Box 16030, Abilene TX 79698. 915/670-1507. **Physical address:** 2200 South Hickory Street, Abilene TX. **Fax:** 915/670-5874. **Contact:** Earl T. Garrett, Director of Human Resources. **World Wide Web address:** http://www.hsutx.edu. **Description:** A Southern Baptist university offering both graduate and undergraduate degrees. **Common positions include:** Accountant/Auditor; Administrative Manager; Blue-Collar Worker Supervisor; Budget Analyst; Clerical Supervisor; Computer Programmer; Counselor; Education Administrator; Fundraising Specialist; Human Resources Manager; Librarian; Library Technician; Licensed Practical Nurse; Public Relations Specialist; Registered Nurse; Reporter; Systems Analyst; Teacher/Professor. **Educational backgrounds include:** Accounting; Art/Design; Biology; Business Administration; Chemistry; Communications; Computer Science; Economics; Finance; Geology; Liberal Arts; Marketing; Mathematics; Physical Therapy; Physics; Religion. **Benefits:** 403(b); Cafeteria; Dental Insurance; Disability Coverage; Employee Discounts; Life Insurance; Medical Insurance; Pension Plan; Tuition Assistance. **Corporate headquarters location:** This Location. **Number of employees at this location:** 300.

McKINNEY INDEPENDENT SCHOOL DISTRICT
One Duvall Street, McKinney TX 75069. 972/569-6400. **Contact:** Personnel. **Description:** Administrative offices of McKinney's school district, which is comprised of 10 elementary schools, two middle schools, and one high school.

McMURRY UNIVERSITY
McMurry Station, P.O. Box 308, Abilene TX 79697. 915/793-3800. **Contact:** Human Resources. **World Wide Web address:** http://www.mcm.edu. **Description:** A four-year university offering undergraduate degrees. Approximately 1,425 students attend McMurry University.

MIDWESTERN STATE UNIVERSITY
3410 Taft Boulevard, Wichita Falls TX 76308. 940/397-4221. **Fax:** 940/397-4780. **Contact:** Steve Holland, Director of Personnel. **E-mail address:** steve.holland@nexus.mwsu.edu. **World Wide Web address:** http://www.mwsu.edu. **Description:** A state university with approximately 6,000 students enrolled in its undergraduate and graduate degree programs. **Common positions include:** Accountant/Auditor; Buyer; Computer Programmer; Counselor; Education Administrator; Electrician; Human Resources Manager; Librarian; Library Technician; Property and Real Estate Manager; Public Relations Specialist; Radiological Technologist; Registered Nurse; Systems Analyst; Teacher/Professor. **Educational backgrounds include:** Accounting; Art/Design; Biology; Business Administration; Chemistry; Communications; Computer Science; Economics; Engineering; Finance; Geology; Marketing; Mathematics; Ph.D.; Physics. **Benefits:** 401(k); Dental Insurance; Disability Coverage; Employee Discounts; Life Insurance; Medical Insurance; Pension Plan; Savings Plan; Tuition Assistance. **Corporate headquarters location:** This Location. **President:** Dr. Louis J. Rodriguez. **Facilities Manager:** Al Hooten. **Number of employees at this location:** 900.

NORTH LAKE COLLEGE
5001 North MacArthur Boulevard, Irving TX 75038. 972/273-3000. **Contact:** Human Resources Department. **World Wide Web address:** http://www.dcccd.edu/nlc. **Description:** A two-year community college offering technical occupational courses as well as general studies. Approximately 6,200 students are enrolled. North Lake College operates as part of the Dallas County Community College District.

RICHLAND COLLEGE
12800 Abrams Road, Dallas TX 75243-2199. 972/238-6240. **Contact:** Personnel Director. **World Wide Web address:** http://www.rlc.dcccd.edu. **Description:** A junior college offering one- and two-year associate's degrees and certificates to approximately 12,500 students. Richland College operates as part of the Dallas County Community College District.

SOUTH PLAINS COLLEGE
1401 South College Avenue, Levelland TX 79336. 806/894-9611. **Fax:** 806/894-6880. **Contact:** Human Resources. **World Wide Web address:** http://www.spc.cc.tx.us. **Description:**

A two-year, state funded college. South Plains College offers majors in education, arts and sciences, nursing, and continuing education. The college has an enrollment of approximately 5,400 students.

SOUTHERN METHODIST UNIVERSITY
P.O. Box 750232, Dallas TX 75275-0232. 214/768-1111. **Contact:** Employment Office. **World Wide Web address:** http://www.smu.edu. **Description:** A university offering bachelor's, master's, professional, and doctoral degrees to approximately 9,700 students. **Common positions include:** Accountant/Auditor; Administrator; Attorney; Biological Scientist; Blue-Collar Worker Supervisor; Buyer; Chemist. **Benefits:** Dental Insurance; Disability Coverage; Employee Discounts; Life Insurance; Medical Insurance; Pension Plan; Tuition Assistance. **Special programs:** Internships. **Corporate headquarters location:** This Location. **Number of employees at this location:** 1,820.

SOUTHWESTERN ADVENTIST UNIVERSITY
100 Hillcrest Drive, P.O. Box 567, Keene TX 76059. 817/477-2543. **Contact:** Personnel Department. **World Wide Web address:** http://www.swau.edu. **Description:** A college affiliated with the Seventh Day Adventist Church and offering 40 undergraduate programs and two graduate level programs. Over 1,100 students are enrolled.

SOUTHWESTERN BAPTIST THEOLOGICAL SEMINARY
P.O. Box 22000, Fort Worth TX 76122. 817/923-1921. **Contact:** Office of Church/Minister Relations. **World Wide Web address:** http://www.swbts.edu. **Description:** A seminary college offering a variety of religious training programs.

TARLETON STATE UNIVERSITY
Mail Stop T-510, Tarleton Station, Stephenville TX 76402. 254/968-9905. **Fax:** 254/968-9590. **Contact:** Ms. Mary Chenault, Human Resources Assistant. **World Wide Web address:** http://www.tarleton.edu. **Description:** A four-year, state university offering bachelor's and master's degrees to approximately 6,300 students. Tarleton State University operates as part of the Texas A&M University System. **Common positions include:** Accountant/Auditor; Buyer; Clerical Supervisor; Computer Programmer; Counselor; Designer; Editor; Education Administrator; Electrician; Financial Analyst; General Manager; Human Resources Manager; Instructor/Trainer; Librarian; Library Technician; Management Analyst/Consultant; Psychologist; Public Relations Specialist; Registered Nurse; Research Assistant; Systems Analyst; Teacher/Professor; Technical Writer/Editor. **Educational backgrounds include:** Accounting; Biology; Business Administration; Chemistry; Communications; Computer Science; Hydrogeology; Liberal Arts; Marketing. **Benefits:** 403(b); Dental Insurance; Disability Coverage; Life Insurance; Medical Insurance; Pension Plan; Savings Plan. **Corporate headquarters location:** College Station TX. **Number of employees at this location:** 675.

TARRANT COUNTY JUNIOR COLLEGE
1500 Houston Street, Fort Worth TX 76102. 817/515-5100. **Contact:** Human Resources. **World Wide Web address:** http://www.tcjc.cc.tx.us. **Description:** A two-year college offering associate's degrees and certificates. **Common positions include:** Accountant/Auditor; Clerical Supervisor; Teacher/Professor. **Benefits:** Dental Insurance; Life Insurance; Medical Insurance; Pension Plan; Tuition Assistance. **Corporate headquarters location:** This Location. **Operations at this facility include:** Administration.

TEXAS A&M UNIVERSITY/COMMERCE
East Texas Station, Commerce TX 75429. 903/886-5668. **Fax:** 903/886-5670. **Recorded jobline:** 903/886-5665. **Contact:** Human Resources. **World Wide Web address:** http://www.tamu-commerce.edu. **Description:** A university that offers a wide range of undergraduate degree programs, master's degree programs, and doctoral and professional programs. **Corporate headquarters location:** College Station TX.

TEXAS CHRISTIAN UNIVERSITY
P.O. Box 298200, Fort Worth TX 76129. 817/257-7790. **Contact:** John Weif, Director of Employee Relations. **World Wide Web address:** http://www.tcu.edu. **Description:** A university offering undergraduate and graduate programs to approximately 7,000 students. **Common positions include:** Blue-Collar Worker Supervisor; Cashier; Construction Trade Worker; Dispatcher; Heating/AC/Refrigeration Technician; Library Technician; Payroll Clerk; Postal Clerk/Mail Carrier; Printing Press Operator; Secretary; Teacher/Professor; Typist/Word Processor. **Educational backgrounds include:** Accounting; Art/Design; Biology; Business Administration; Chemistry; Communications; Computer Science; Economics; Engineering; Finance; Geology; Liberal Arts; Marketing; Mathematics; Physics. **Benefits:** Dental Insurance;

Disability Coverage; Employee Discounts; Life Insurance; Medical Insurance; Pension Plan; Tuition Assistance. **Corporate headquarters location:** This Location. **Number of employees at this location:** 1,300.

TEXAS TECH UNIVERSITY
P.O. Box 41097, Lubbock TX 79409-1097. 806/742-2011. **Contact:** Jim Brown, Personnel Director. **World Wide Web address:** http://www.ttu.edu. **Description:** A state university. The university offers undergraduate and graduate degrees in liberal arts, law, applied health, and medicine. **Benefits:** Dental Insurance; Disability Coverage; Life Insurance; Medical Insurance; Pension Plan; Savings Plan. **Corporate headquarters location:** This Location.

TEXAS WESLEYAN UNIVERSITY
1201 Wesleyan Street, Fort Worth TX 76105. 817/531-4403. **Fax:** 817/531-4402. **Contact:** Human Resources. **World Wide Web address:** http://www.txwesleyan.edu. **Description:** A small, private university affiliated with the United Methodist Church. Texas Wesleyan University offers a variety of undergraduate and graduate degrees to approximately 3,000 students. Founded in 1890. **Common positions include:** Accountant/Auditor; Administrative Manager; Administrator; Biological Scientist; Blue-Collar Worker Supervisor; Chemist; Clerical Supervisor; Computer Programmer; Construction Contractor; Counselor; Dietician/Nutritionist; Economist; Education Administrator; Financial Analyst; Food Scientist/Technologist; Librarian; Library Technician; Mathematician; Paralegal; Psychologist; Public Relations Specialist; Registered Nurse; Systems Analyst; Teacher/Professor. **Educational backgrounds include:** Accounting; Art/Design; Biology; Business Administration; Chemistry; Communications; Computer Science; Economics; Finance; Liberal Arts; Marketing; Mathematics; Physics. **Benefits:** Dental Insurance; Disability Coverage; Employee Discounts; Life Insurance; Medical Insurance; Pension Plan; Tuition Assistance. **Corporate headquarters location:** This Location. **Number of employees at this location:** 285.

TEXAS WOMAN'S UNIVERSITY (TWU)
P.O. Box 425739, Denton TX 76204-3739. 940/898-3555. **Fax:** 940/898-3566. **Contact:** Lois Morris, Assistant Manager of Employment. **World Wide Web address:** http://www.twu.edu. **Description:** A university offering bachelor's, master's, and doctoral degrees. Founded in 1903. **Common positions include:** Accountant/Auditor; Computer Programmer; Counselor; Dispatcher; Electrician; Financial Analyst; Human Resources Manager; Librarian; Purchasing Agent/Manager; Receptionist; Registered Nurse; Secretary; Systems Analyst; Typist/Word Processor. **Educational backgrounds include:** Accounting; Business Administration; Computer Science; Finance; Marketing; Mathematics. **Benefits:** Dental Insurance; Disability Coverage; Life Insurance; Medical Insurance; Pension Plan. **Special programs:** Internships. **Corporate headquarters location:** This Location. **Other U.S. locations:** Dallas TX; Houston TX. **Number of employees at this location:** 1,000. **Number of employees nationwide:** 1,400.

UNIVERSITY OF NORTH TEXAS
P.O. Box 311010, Denton TX 76203. 940/565-2281. **Contact:** Personnel Department. **World Wide Web address:** http://www.unt.edu. **Description:** A university offering undergraduate, graduate, and doctoral programs of study in numerous fields. Approximately 25,000 students attend the university.

UNIVERSITY OF NORTH TEXAS HEALTH SCIENCE AT FORT WORTH
3500 Camp Bowie Boulevard, Suite 735, Fort Worth TX 76107-2699. 817/735-2690. **Contact:** Human Resources Services. **World Wide Web address:** http://www.hsc.unt.edu. **Description:** A health science education center. **Common positions include:** Accountant/Auditor; Biological Scientist; Biomedical Engineer; Buyer; Chemist; Claim Representative; Clinical Lab Technician; Computer Programmer; Graphic Artist; Library Technician; Licensed Practical Nurse; Receptionist; Registered Nurse; Science Technologist; Secretary; Systems Analyst; Typist/Word Processor. **Educational backgrounds include:** Accounting; Biology; Business Administration; Computer Science; Education; Mathematics. **Benefits:** Dental Insurance; Disability Coverage; Employee Discounts; Life Insurance; Medical Insurance; Pension Plan. **Corporate headquarters location:** This Location. **Number of employees at this location:** 1,000.

UNIVERSITY OF TEXAS AT ARLINGTON
1225 West Mitchell Street, Suite 112, Box 19176, Arlington TX 76019. 817/272-2011. **Fax:** 817/272-5798. **Contact:** Human Resources. **World Wide Web address:** http://www.uta.edu. **Description:** A state university offering 55 bachelor's, 60 master's, and 19 doctoral degrees to approximately 20,000 students. Founded in 1895. **Common positions include:** Accountant/Auditor; Administrative Manager; Administrative Worker/Clerk; Administrator; Aerospace Engineer; Architect; Attorney; Automotive Mechanic; Biomedical Engineer; Blue-

Collar Worker Supervisor; Budget Analyst; Buyer; Chemical Engineer; Chemist; Civil Engineer; Clerical Supervisor; Computer Programmer; Construction and Building Inspector; Counselor; Customer Service Representative; Electrical/Electronics Engineer; Electrician; Environmental Engineer; Financial Analyst; Geologist/Geophysicist; Health Services Manager; Human Resources Manager; Industrial Engineer; Librarian; Library Technician; Licensed Practical Nurse; Management Trainee; Materials Engineer; Mathematician; Mechanical Engineer; Pharmacist; Physician; Property and Real Estate Manager; Public Relations Specialist; Registered Nurse; Science Technologist; Services Sales Representative; Social Worker; Software Engineer; Systems Analyst; Teacher/Professor; Technical Writer/Editor; Wholesale and Retail Buyer. **Educational backgrounds include:** Accounting; Business Administration; Communications; Computer Science; Engineering; Finance; Health Care; Liberal Arts. **Benefits:** Dental Insurance; Disability Coverage; Life Insurance; Medical Insurance; Pension Plan. **Special programs:** Internships. **Corporate headquarters location:** Austin TX. **Number of employees at this location:** 4,000.

UNIVERSITY OF TEXAS AT DALLAS
2601 North Floyd Street, Richardson TX 75080-0688. 972/883-2221. **Contact:** Dorothy Miller, Human Resources Specialist. **World Wide Web address:** http://www.utdallas.edu. **Description:** A state university offering programs at the undergraduate, graduate, and doctoral levels. Enrollment at the university is approximately 10,000. **NOTE:** Part-time jobs are offered. **Common positions include:** Accountant; Administrative Assistant; Auditor; Biochemist; Biological Scientist; Budget Analyst; Computer Engineer; Computer Operator; Computer Programmer; Computer Support Technician; Counselor; Customer Service Representative; Database Administrator; Database Manager; Dietician/Nutritionist; Electrician; Finance Director; Financial Analyst; Graphic Artist; Graphic Designer; Help-Desk Technician; Human Resources Manager; Librarian; MIS Specialist; Molecular Biologist; Multimedia Designer; Psychologist; Purchasing Agent/Manager; Secretary; Software Engineer; Systems Analyst; Technical Writer/Editor; Typist/Word Processor. **Educational backgrounds include:** Accounting; Biology; C/C++; Education; Finance; HTML; MBA; Microsoft Office; Microsoft Word. **Benefits:** 401(k); Casual Dress - Fridays; Dental Insurance; Life Insurance; Medical Insurance. **Number of employees at this location:** 2,075.

UNIVERSITY OF TEXAS AT TYLER
3900 University Boulevard, Tyler TX 75799. 903/566-7234. **Fax:** 903/566-8368. **Contact:** Human Resources. **World Wide Web address:** http://www.uttyl.edu. **Description:** A state university offering undergraduate and graduate programs of study.

Note: Because addresses and telephone numbers of smaller companies can change rapidly, we recommend you call each company to verify the information below before inquiring about job opportunities. Mass mailings are not recommended.

Additional small employers:

CHILD DAYCARE SERVICES

Children's Choice Learning Center
2417 Mahon St, Dallas TX 75201-1915. 214/880-0485.

COLLEGES, UNIVERSITIES, AND PROFESSIONAL SCHOOLS

Amber University
1700 Eastgate Dr, Garland TX 75041-5511. 972/279-6511.

Austin College
900 N Grand Ave, Sherman TX 75090-4440. 903/813-2000.

East Texas Baptist University
1209 N Grove St, Marshall TX 75670-1423. 903/935-7963.

Jarvis Christian College
PO Box 1470, Hawkins TX 75765-1470. 903/769-2174.

LeTourneau University
PO Box 7001, Longview TX 75607-7001. 903/753-0231.

Lubbock Christian School
5601 19th St, Lubbock TX 79407-2031. 806/792-3221.

Paul Quinn College
3837 Simpson Stuart Rd, Dallas TX 75241-4331. 214/376-1000.

Southwestern Adventist University
PO Box 567, Keene TX 76059-0567. 817/645-3921.

Temple College
2600 S 1st St, Temple TX 76504-7435. 254/298-8282.

University of Dallas
1845 E Northgate Dr, Irving TX 75062-4736. 972/721-5000.

Wiley College
711 Wiley Ave, Marshall TX 75670-5151. 903/938-8341.

ELEMENTARY AND SECONDARY SCHOOLS

Abernathy Independent School District
505 7th St, Abernathy TX 79311-3318. 806/298-2563.

Abilene High School
2800 N 6th St, Abilene TX 79603-7125. 915/677-1731.

Alba-Golden Independent School District
Rural Route 2, Box 212H, Alba TX 75410-9802. 903/768-2472.

Aledo Independent School District
412 S Fm 1187, Aledo TX 76008-4407. 817/441-8327.

Allen High School
601 E Main St, Allen TX 75002-3007. 972/727-0400.

Allen Independent School District
PO Box 13, Allen TX 75013-0001. 972/727-0510.

AM Aikin Elementary School
3100 Pine Mill Rd, Paris TX 75460-4937. 903/737-7443.

Amarillo Independent School District
7200 W Interstate 40, Amarillo TX 79106-2528. 806/354-4200.

Annie Rainwater Elementary School
1408 E Frankford Rd, Carrollton TX 75007-5624. 972/323-6550.

Arlington Heights Senior High School
4501 W Rosedale St, Fort Worth TX 76107-5427. 817/377-7200.

Arlington High School
818 W Park Row Dr, Arlington TX 76013-3903. 817/460-2541.

Bailey Junior High School
2411 Winewood St, Arlington TX 76013-3333. 817/460-3933.

Barnett Junior High School
2101 Harwood Rd, Arlington TX 76018-3101. 817/468-1952.

Barton Elementary School
2931 Conflans Rd, Irving TX 75061-4171. 972/986-9191.

Bear Creek Elementary School
401 Bear Creek Dr, Euless TX 76039-2091. 817/267-6713.

Belton High School
600 Lake Rd, Belton TX 76513-1406. 254/933-4600.

Belton Independent School District
PO Box 148, Belton TX 76513-0148. 254/933-4740.

Big Sandy Elementary School
PO Box 598, Big Sandy TX 75755-0598. 903/636-5287.

Billy Ryan Senior High School
5101 E McKinney St, Denton TX 76208-4630. 940/566-7926.

Birdville Independent School District
6125 E Belknap St, Fort Worth TX 76117-4204. 817/831-5700.

Blooming Grove Independent School District
PO Box 258, Blooming Grove TX 76626-0258. 903/695-2536.

Boles Junior High School
3900 SW Green Oaks Blvd, Arlington TX 76017-4110. 817/483-5216.

Borger Independent School District
PO Box 1177, Borger TX 79008-1177. 806/273-6481.

Bowie Independent School District
PO Box 1168, Bowie TX 76230-1168. 940/872-1151.

Breckenridge Independent School District
PO Box 1738, Breckenridge TX 76424-1738. 254/559-2278.

Brewer High School
1000 S Cherry Ln, Fort Worth TX 76108-3215. 817/367-1242.

Briarhill Middle School
2100 Briarhill Blvd, Lewisville TX 75077-3174. 972/221-0988.

Bridgeport Independent School District
2107 15th St, Bridgeport TX 76426-2052. 940/683-5124.

Brownfield Independent School District
601 Tahoka Rd, Brownfield TX 79316-3631. 806/637-2591.

Bruceville-Eddy Independent School District
PO Box 99, Eddy TX 76524-0099. 254/859-5832.

Bryan Adams High School
2101 Millmar Dr, Dallas TX 75228-3375. 972/502-4900.

Buffalo Independent School District
PO Drawer C, Buffalo TX 75831-0168. 903/322-3765.

Bullard Junior High School
PO Box 250, Bullard TX 75757-0250. 903/894-6639.

Burkburnett High School
109 Cramer St, Burkburnett TX 76354. 940/569-1411.

Burleson High School
100 NW John Jones Dr, Burleson TX 76028-5648. 817/447-5700.

Burleson Junior High School
316 SW Thomas St, Burleson TX 76028-4610. 817/447-5750.

Canyon Creek Christian Academy
2800 Custer Pkwy, Richardson TX 75080-1633. 972/231-4753.

Canyon High School
910 9th Ave, Canyon TX 79015-4340. 806/656-6181.

Carroll Independent School District
801 Shady Oaks Dr, Southlake TX 76092-5014. 817/481-8068.

Carroll McMath Middle School
1900 Jason Dr, Denton TX 76205-0702. 940/382-7409.

Carrollton Elementary School
1805 Pearl St, Carrollton TX 75006-6123. 972/323-6603.

Carrollton-Farmers Branch Independent School District
PO Box 115186, Carrollton TX 75011-5186. 972/466-6100.

Cayuga Independent School District
PO Box 427, Cayuga TX 75832-0427. 903/928-2102.

Cedar Hill High School
1 Longhorn Blvd, Cedar Hill TX 75104-2748. 972/291-4273.

Chandler Elementary School
711 N Longview St, Kilgore TX 75662-5413. 903/984-2534.

Chapel Hill High School
13172 State Highway 64 E, Tyler TX 75707-5340. 903/566-2311.

Charlie C. McKamy Elementary School
3443 Briargrove Ln, Dallas TX 75287-6001. 972/323-6520.

Chisum Independent School District
3250 S Church St, Paris TX 75462-8909. 903/737-2830.

Christian Pantego Academy
2201 W Park Row Dr, Arlington TX 76013-7414. 817/460-3315.

Clark High School
523 W Spring Creek Pkwy, Plano TX 75023-4602. 972/519-8800.

Cleburne Independent School District
103 S Walnut St, Cleburne TX 76031-5422. 817/556-5600.

Colleyville Elementary School
5800 Colleyville Blvd, Colleyville TX 76034-6052. 817/485-5641.

Educational Services/131

Colleyville Heritage High School
5401 Heritage Ave, Colleyville TX 76034-5919. 817/358-4700.

Colony High School
4301 Blair Oaks Dr, Lewisville TX 75056-2718. 972/625-9000.

Community High School
PO Box 400, Nevada TX 75173-0400. 972/853-2192.

Community Independent School District
PO Box 400, Nevada TX 75173-0400. 972/853-2474.

Cooper High School
3639 Sayles Blvd, Abilene TX 79605-7050. 915/691-1000.

Copperas Cove High School
PO Box 580, Copperas Cove TX 76522-0580. 254/547-2534.

Coronado Senior High School
3307 Vicksburg Ave, Lubbock TX 79410-2321. 806/766-0600.

Corprew Intermediate School
PO Box 1117, Mount Pleasant TX 75456-1117. 903/575-2050.

Corsicana High School
3701 W State Highway 22, Corsicana TX 75110-2463. 903/874-8211.

Creekview High School
3201 Old Denton Rd, Carrollton TX 75007-3957. 972/939-4000.

Dallas Christian School
PO Box 28295, Dallas TX 75228-0295. 972/270-5495.

Dallas Independent School District
3700 Ross Ave, Dallas TX 75204-5476. 214/989-8000.

David G. Burnet Elementary School
3200 Kinkaid Dr, Dallas TX 75220-1623. 214/904-1220.

Decatur Elementary School
1300 Deer Park Rd, Decatur TX 76234-4403. 940/627-3332.

Denison Independent School District
1201 S Rusk Ave, Denison TX 75020-6340. 903/462-7037.

Denton High School
1007 Fulton St, Denton TX 76201-2851. 940/382-9611.

Denton State School
PO Box 368, Denton TX 76202-0368. 940/891-0342.

Dewitt Perry Middle School
1709 E Belt Line Rd, Carrollton TX 75006-6305. 972/323-6625.

Dowell Middle School
301 Ridge Rd, McKinney TX 75070-6416. 972/569-6500.

Dumas Junior High School
PO Box 697, Dumas TX 79029-0697. 806/935-4155.

Dumas Senior High School
300 S Klein Ave, Dumas TX 79029-3744. 806/935-6461.

Duncanville Independent School District
802 S Main St, Duncanville TX 75137-2316. 972/708-2000.

Eagle Mountain Saginaw Independent School District
PO Box 79160, Fort Worth TX 76179-0160. 817/232-0123.

East Texas Christian Academy
PO Box 8201, Tyler TX 75711-8201. 903/561-8642.

Eastern Hills Senior High School
5701 Shelton St, Fort Worth TX 76112-3929. 817/496-7600.

Eastland Independent School District
PO Box 31, Eastland TX 76448-0031. 254/631-5120.

Edgewood Independent School District
Hwy 80 E, Edgewood TX 75117. 903/896-4332.

EM Daggett Elementary School
958 Page Ave, Fort Worth TX 76110-2627. 817/922-6880.

Ennis Intermediate School
2301 W Ennis Pkwy, Ennis TX 75119-8542. 972/875-8560.

Estacado High School
1504 E Itasca St, Lubbock TX 79403-3120. 806/766-1400.

Everman Independent School District
1 Bulldog Dr, Fort Worth TX 76140. 817/568-3500.

Ewell D. Walker Special Education School
12532 Nuestra Dr, Dallas TX 75230-1718. 972/502-6000.

Farmsville Independent School District
PO Box 472, Farmersville TX 75442-0472. 972/782-6601.

Faubion Middle School
2000 Doe Rollins St, McKinney TX 75069-3208. 972/569-6168.

Fort Worth Country Day School
4200 Country Day Ln, Fort Worth TX 76109-4201. 817/732-7718.

Fort Worth Independent School District
100 N University Dr, Fort Worth TX 76107-1360. 817/871-2000.

Fort Worth State School
5000 Campus Dr, Fort Worth TX 76119-5921. 817/534-4831.

Fossil Ridge High School
4101 Thompson Rd, Keller TX 76248-6902. 817/337-3400.

Foster Middle School
410 S Green St, Longview TX 75601-7533. 903/753-1692.

Frankston Independent School District
PO Box 428, Frankston TX 75763-0428. 903/876-2556.

Friendship High School
PO Box 100, Wolfforth TX 79382-0100. 806/866-4440.

Friona High School
909 E 11th St, Friona TX 79035-1416. 806/247-2747.

Garland Independent School District
PO Box 469026, Garland TX 75046-9026. 972/494-8201.

George W. Carver Learning Center
3719 Greenleaf St, Dallas TX 75212-1522. 214/689-1540.

George W. Trett Elementary School
1811 Gross Rd, Dallas TX 75228-4765. 214/319-0120.

Gladewater High School
2201 W Gay Ave, Gladewater TX 75647-4357. 903/845-5591.

Glenhope Elementary School
6600 Glenhope Cir N, Colleyville TX 76034-5688. 817/251-0540.

Granbury High School
2000 W Pearl St, Granbury TX 76048-1888. 817/579-2230.

Grand Prairie High School
101 Highschool Dr, Grand Prairie TX 75050-3740. 972/264-5711.

Grand Prairie Independent School District
PO Box 531170, Grand Prairie TX 75053-1170. 972/264-6141.

Grapevine Elementary School
1801 Hall Johnson Rd,
Grapevine TX 76051-5705.
817/421-8449.

Grapevine Independent School District
3051 Ira E. Woods Ave,
Grapevine TX 76051-3817.
817/481-5575.

Greenhill School
4141 Spring Valley Rd, Addison TX 75001-3615. 972/661-1211.

Greenville High School
3515 Lions Lair St, Greenville TX 75402. 903/457-2550.

Greenville Middle School
3611 Texas St, Greenville TX 75401-5046. 903/457-2620.

Groesbeck High School
PO Box 559, Groesbeck TX 76642-0559. 254/729-5933.

H. Grady Spruce High School
9733 Old Seagoville Rd, Dallas TX 75217-7799. 972/892-5500.

Halstead Elementary School
PO Box 580, Copperas Cove TX 76522-0580. 254/547-3440.

Hamilton Park Elementary School
8301 Towns St, Dallas TX 75243-3658. 214/699-2380.

Harmony Independent School District
Rural Route 4, Box 652, Gilmer TX 75644-9470. 903/725-5493.

Henderson High School
PO Box 728, Henderson TX 75653-0728. 903/657-1483.

Henderson Independent School District
PO Box 1728, Henderson TX 75653-1728. 903/657-1491.

Hereford Senior High School
200 Avenue F, Hereford TX 79045-4408. 806/363-7620.

Heritage Elementary School
4500 Heritage Ave, Colleyville TX 76034-4841. 817/545-6894.

HF Stevens Middle School
940 N Crowley Rd, Crowley TX 76036-3738. 817/297-5840.

Hico School District
PO Box 218, Hico TX 76457-0218. 254/796-2181.

Highland Middle School
1001 E Bailey Boswell Rd, Fort Worth TX 76131-3514. 817/847-5143.

Highland Park Independent School District
PO Box 30430, Amarillo TX 79120-0430. 806/335-2821.

Highland Park Middle School
3555 Granada Ave, Dallas TX 75205-2235. 214/523-2900.

Hockaday School
11600 Welch Rd, Dallas TX 75229-2913. 214/363-6311.

Hood Middle School
7625 Hume Dr, Dallas TX 75227-8803. 214/381-8700.

Hooks Independent School District
PO Box 39, Hooks TX 75561-0039. 903/547-6077.

Hutcheson Junior High School
2101 Browning Dr, Arlington TX 76010-5949. 817/460-6572.

Iowa Park Independent School District
PO Box 898, Iowa Park TX 76367-0898. 940/592-4193.

Irving Independent School District
PO Box 152637, Irving TX 75015-2637. 972/273-6000.

Jacksonville High School
PO Box 631, Jacksonville TX 75766-0631. 903/586-3661.

James Bowie Middle School
3001 E 12th Ave, Amarillo TX 79104-2521. 806/371-5580.

Janie Stark Elementary School
12400 Josey Ln, Dallas TX 75234-6419. 972/247-7153.

Jasper High School
6800 Archgate Dr, Plano TX 75024-5214. 972/519-8887.

JC Cannaday Elementary School
2701 Chisolm Trail, Mesquite TX 75150-4829. 972/279-9694.

JL Long Middle School
6116 Reiger Ave, Dallas TX 75214-4599. 972/502-4700.

John Tyler High School
1120 N Northwest Loop, Tyler TX 75702-3617. 903/531-6000.

Joshua High School
PO Box 40, Joshua TX 76058-0040. 817/641-2285.

Keller Independent School District
304 Lorine St, Keller TX 76248-3435. 817/337-3200.

Killeen Independent School District
PO Box 967, Killeen TX 76540-0967. 254/526-8361.

La Vega Independent School District
3100 Bellmead Dr, Waco TX 76705-3033. 254/799-4963.

La Vega Primary School
900 Ashleman St, Waco TX 76705-2957. 254/799-6229.

Lakeview Centennial High School
3505 Hayman Dr, Garland TX 75043-1920. 972/494-8592.

Lakeview Middle School
4300 Keys Dr, Lewisville TX 75056-3203. 972/625-9040.

Lakewood Elementary School
3000 Hillbrook St, Dallas TX 75214-3412. 214/841-5250.

Lamar Middle School
4000 Timber Creek Rd, Flower Mound TX 75028-2102. 972/539-0886.

Lancaster High School
822 W Pleasant Run Rd, Lancaster TX 75146-1446. 972/227-2418.

Las Colinas Elementary School
2200 Kinwest Pkwy, Irving TX 75063-3429. 972/869-3996.

LD Bell High School
1601 Brown Trail, Hurst TX 76054-3703. 817/282-2551.

Leila Cowart Elementary School
1515 S Ravinia Dr, Dallas TX 75211-5742. 214/331-7870.

Lewisville High School
1098 W Main St, Lewisville TX 75067-3518. 972/221-3535.

LG Pinkston High School
2200 Dennison St, Dallas TX 75212-2460. 972/502-2700.

Liberty Christian School
1500 S Bonnie Brae St, Denton TX 76207-2017. 940/484-9733.

Liberty Junior High School
10330 Lawler Rd, Dallas TX 75243-2634. 972/238-6760.

Little Elm High School
500 Lobo Ln, Little Elm TX 75068-5220. 972/292-1840.

Longview High School
PO Box 3268, Longview TX 75606-3268. 903/663-1301.

Educational Services/133

Lubbock High School
Rural Route 6, PO Box 400,
Lubbock TX 79423-9530.
806/863-2282.

Lubbock Public Schools
1628 19th St, Lubbock TX
79401-4832. 806/766-1000.

Lubbock Senior High School
2004 19th St, Lubbock TX
79401-4606. 806/766-1444.

Lyles Middle School
4655 S Country Club Rd,
Garland TX 75043-1846.
972/494-8648.

Mabank High School
124 E Market St, Mabank TX
75147-8377. 903/887-9333.

MacArthur High School
3700 N MacArthur Blvd, Irving
TX 75062-3639. 972/255-2171.

Madison Middle School
3145 Barrow St, Abilene TX
79605-6926. 915/692-5661.

Mann Middle School
2545 Mimosa Dr, Abilene TX
79603-2131. 915/672-8493.

Mansfield High School
1071 Turner Warnell Rd,
Arlington TX 76001-8501.
817/473-5752.

Marcus High School
5707 Morriss Rd, Flower
Mound TX 75028-3730.
972/539-1591.

Mayfield Workman Junior High School
701 E Arbrook Blvd, Arlington
TX 76014-3240. 817/465-4741.

McKinney High School
1400 Wilson Creek Pkwy,
McKinney TX 75069-5320.
972/548-6100.

Meadowbrook Middle School
2001 Ederville Rd S, Fort Worth
TX 76103-1510. 817/531-6250.

Merkel High School
S 3rd & Ash Sts, Merkel TX
79536. 915/928-5511.

Mesquite Independent School District
405 E Davis St, Mesquite TX
75149-4701. 972/288-6411.

Mexia State School
PO Box 1132, Mexia TX 76667-1132. 254/562-2821.

Midlothian Independent School District
925 S 9th St, Midlothian TX
76065-3636. 972/775-8296.

Midway High School
800 N Hewitt Dr, Hewitt TX
76643-2970. 254/666-5151.

Monterey Senior High School
3211 47th St, Lubbock TX
79413-4112. 806/766-0700.

Montgomery Elementary School
2807 Amber Ln, Dallas TX
75234-3542. 972/241-2594.

Mount Vernon Independent School District
PO Box 98, Mount Vernon TX
75457-0098. 903/537-2546.

Mt. Pleasant High School
PO Box 1117, Mount Pleasant
TX 75456-1117. 903/572-1891.

Naaman Forest High School
4843 Naaman Forest Blvd,
Garland TX 75040-2732.
972/494-8670.

Nichols Junior High School
2201 Ascension Blvd, Arlington
TX 76006-5587. 817/460-7161.

Nimitz High School
100 W Oakdale Rd, Irving TX
75060-6833. 972/259-3621.

Nolan High School
4501 Bridge St, Fort Worth TX
76103-1160. 817/457-2920.

Nolan Middle School
505 E Jasper Dr, Killeen TX
76541-8940. 254/634-4646.

North Dallas High School
3120 N Haskell Ave, Dallas TX
75204-1568. 214/559-1900.

North Garland High School
2109 W Buckingham Rd,
Garland TX 75042-5031.
972/494-8451.

North Mesquite High School
18201 LBJ Fwy, Mesquite TX
75150-4124. 972/279-6721.

North Side High School
2211 McKinley Ave, Fort Worth
TX 76106-7739. 817/740-5300.

Northwest Independent School District
Rural Rte 1, Box 39A, Justin TX
76247-9801. 940/648-2611.

Oakridge School
5900 W Pioneer Pkwy,
Arlington TX 76013-2840.
817/451-4994.

OD Wyatt High School
2400 E Seminary Dr, Fort Worth
TX 76119-5502. 817/531-6300.

Palestine High School
1600 S Loop 256, Palestine TX
75801-5847. 903/731-8005.

Palo Duro High School
1400 N Grant St, Amarillo TX
79107-3951. 806/381-7132.

Paradise Independent School District
Rural Rte 2, Box 646, Paradise
TX 76073-9802. 940/969-2501.

Paris High School
2400 Jefferson Rd, Paris TX
75460-7825. 903/737-7400.

Pascal High School
3001 Forest Park Blvd, Fort
Worth TX 76110-2828.
817/922-6600.

PE Wallace Middle School
PO Box 1117, Mount Pleasant
TX 75456-1117. 903/575-2040.

Pearl C. Anderson Middle School
3400 Garden Ln, Dallas TX
75215-4865. 214/565-6400.

Pewitt Independent School District
PO Box 1106, Omaha TX
75571-1106. 903/884-2136.

Pine Tree Senior High School
PO Box 5878, Longview TX
75608-5878. 903/295-5031.

Plano East Senior High School
3000 Los Rios Blvd, Plano TX
75074-3513. 972/519-8600.

Plano Independent School District
2700 W 15th St, Plano TX
75075-7524. 972/519-8100.

Plano Senior High School
2200 Independence Pkwy,
Plano TX 75075-3143. 972/519-8500.

Plano West Senior High School
5601 W Parker Rd, Plano TX
75093-7727. 972/519-8770.

Queen City Independent School District
PO Box 128, Queen City TX
75572-0128. 903/796-8256.

Quitman Independent School District
1101 E Goode St, Quitman TX
75783-1651. 903/763-4593.

Red Oak High School
PO Box 9000, Red Oak TX
75154-9000. 972/617-3535.

Richardson Independent School District
400 S Greenville Ave,

Richardson TX 75081-4181. 972/301-3333.

Rio Vista Independent School District
PO Box 369, Rio Vista TX 76093-0369. 817/373-2241.

Robert E. Lee High School
411 E Southeast Loop 323, Tyler TX 75701-9633. 903/531-3900.

Rockwall High School
901 Yellow Jacket Ln, Rockwall TX 75087-4839. 972/771-7339.

Roosevelt Independent School District
Rural Route 1, Box 402, Lubbock TX 79403-9643. 806/842-3282.

Rosemeade Elementary School
3550 Kimberly Dr, Carrollton TX 75007-2986. 972/323-6665.

Rutherford Elementary School
1607 Sierra Dr, Mesquite TX 75149-6135. 972/285-0151.

Sabine Independent School District
Rural Rte 1, Box 189, Gladewater TX 75647-9723. 903/984-8564.

Salado High School
PO Box 98, Salado TX 76571-0098. 254/947-5479.

Sam Houston High School
2000 Sam Houston Dr, Arlington TX 76014-1660. 817/459-8200.

Sanford Independent School District
PO Drawer 1290, Fritch TX 79036-1290. 806/857-3125.

Seagraves High School
PO Box 1505, Seagraves TX 79359-1505. 806/546-2520.

Seymour Independent School District
409 W Idaho St, Seymour TX 76380-1650. 940/888-3525.

Shallowater School District
1100 Avenue K, Shallowater TX 79363-5768. 806/832-4531.

Sheffield Elementary School
18111 Kelly Blvd, Dallas TX 75287-5642. 972/323-6621.

Shepton High School
5505 W Plano Pkwy, Plano TX 75093-4837. 972/519-8900.

Sherman High School
2201 E Lamar St, Sherman TX 75090-6501. 903/893-8101.

Sims Elementary School
PO Box 1117, Mount Pleasant TX 75456-1117. 903/572-2218.

Solomon Schechter Academy
18011 Hillcrest Rd, Dallas TX 75252-5863. 972/248-3032.

South Garland High School
600 Colonel Dr, Garland TX 75043-2302. 972/494-8424.

South Grand Prairie High School
301 W Warrior Trl, Grand Prairie TX 75052-5718. 972/264-4731.

South Oak Cliff High School
3601 South Marsalis Ave, Dallas TX 75216-5964. 214/932-7000.

South West High School
4100 Altamesa Blvd, Fort Worth TX 76133-5420. 817/370-5800.

Springtown Independent School District
101 E 2nd St, Springtown TX 76082-2457. 817/220-7243.

Story Elementary School
PO Box 440, Palestine TX 75802-0440. 903/731-8015.

Sulphur Springs Independent School District
631 Connally St, Sulphur Springs TX 75482-2401. 903/885-2153.

Sweetwater High School
1506 Ragland St, Sweetwater TX 79556-2430. 915/235-4371.

Sweetwater Middle School
305 Lamar Street, Sweetwater TX 79556-5208. 915/236-6303.

TA Howard Middle School
7501 Calender Rd, Arlington TX 76001-7750. 817/561-3828.

Tahoka Elementary School
PO Box 1230, Tahoka TX 79373-1230. 806/998-4350.

Tascosa High School
3921 Westlawn St, Amarillo TX 79102-1795. 806/354-4500.

Taylor High School
3101 N Main St, Taylor TX 76574-1206. 512/352-6326.

Temple High School
415 North 31st Street, Temple TX 76504-2426. 254/791-6300.

Texarkana Arkansas School
PO Box 10509050, Texarkana TX 75505. 870/772-3371.

Texas High School
2112 Kennedy Ln, Texarkana TX 75503-2533. 903/794-3891.

Thomas Jefferson High School
4001 Walnut Hill Ln, Dallas TX 75229-6239. 972/502-7300.

Thompson Elementary School
2915 Scott Mill Rd, Carrollton TX 75007-5321. 972/323-6618.

Thompson Elementary School
5700 Bexar St, Dallas TX 75215-5200. 214/565-6450.

Trimble Technical Senior High School
1003 W Cannon St, Fort Worth TX 76104-3030. 817/871-3400.

Trinity Christian Academy
17001 Addison Rd, Addison TX 75001-5027. 972/931-8325.

Trinity Valley School
7500 Dutch Branch Rd, Fort Worth TX 76132-4110. 817/321-0100.

Troup High School
PO Box 578, Troup TX 75789-0578. 903/842-3065.

Troy Independent School District
PO Box 409, Troy TX 76579-0409. 254/938-2595.

TW Browne Middle School
3333 Sprague Dr, Dallas TX 75233-3123. 972/502-2500.

Tye Elementary School
PO Box 430, Merkel TX 79536-0430. 915/692-3809.

Tyler Independent School District
PO Box 2035, Tyler TX 75710-2035. 903/531-3500.

Union Grove Independent School District
PO Box 1447, Gladewater TX 75647-1447. 903/845-5509.

Ursuline Academy of Dallas
4900 Walnut Hill Ln, Dallas TX 75229-6542. 214/363-6551.

Van Alstyne Independent School District
PO Box 518, Van Alstyne TX 75495-0518. 903/482-6617.

Vines High School
1401 Highedge Dr, Plano TX 75075-7520. 972/519-8270.

Vivian Fowler Primary School
PO Box 1117, Mount Pleasant TX 75456-1117. 903/572-2161.

Waco High School
2020 N 42nd St, Waco TX
76710-3012. 254/776-1150.

Walter Lois Curtis Middle
School
1530 Rivercrest Blvd, Allen TX
75002-4547. 972/727-0340.

Waxahachie High School
1000 N Highway 77,
Waxahachie TX 75165-1754.
972/937-6800.

Waxahachie Independent
School District
411 N Gibson St, Waxahachie
TX 75165-3007. 972/923-4631.

Weatherford High School
1007 S Main St, Weatherford
TX 76086-5357. 817/598-2858.

West Rusk Independent School
District
PO Box 168, New London TX
75682-0168. 903/895-4503.

Western Hills High School
3600 Boston Ave, Fort Worth
TX 76116-6928. 817/560-5600.

Westwood Junior High School
7630 Arapaho Rd, Dallas TX
75248-4343. 972/448-2800.

Whitney High School
PO Box 518, Whitney TX
76692-0518. 254/694-3457.

Whitney Independent School
District
PO Box 518, Whitney TX
76692-0518. 254/694-2254.

Wichita Falls School District
4611 Cypress Ave, Wichita
Falls TX 76310-2540. 940/720-3000.

Wichita Falls School District
1615 Midwestern Pkwy,
Wichita Falls TX 76302-1521.
940/720-3153.

Wilmer Hutchins High School
5520 Langdon Rd, Dallas TX
75241-7148. 972/225-6143.

Wilmer Hutchins Independent
School District
3820 E Illinois Ave, Dallas TX
75216-4194. 214/376-7311.

Wilson Junior High School
4402 31st St, Lubbock TX
79410-2404. 806/766-0799.

Winters Independent School
District
603 N Heights St, Winters TX
79567-4003. 915/754-5574.

Woodrow Wilson High School
100 S Glasgow Dr, Dallas TX
75214-4580. 972/502-4400.

WT White High School
4505 Ridgeside Dr, Dallas TX
75244-7524. 972/308-8915.

WW Samuell High School
8928 Palisade Dr, Dallas TX
75217-2063. 972/892-5100.

Wylie High School
PO Box 490, Wylie TX 75098-0490. 972/442-2218.

NIOR COLLEGES AND
TECHNICAL INSTITUTES

Central Texas College
PO Box 1800, Killeen TX
76540-1800. 254/526-1331.

Collin County Community
College
2200 W University Dr,
McKinney TX 75070-2906.
972/548-6790.

Dallas County Community
College
701 Elm St, Coppell TX 75019.
214/860-2470.

El Centro College
4343 Highway 67, Mesquite TX
75150-2018. 972/860-7709.

Frank Phillips College
PO Box 5118, Borger TX
79008-5118. 806/274-5311.

Hill College
PO Box 619, Hillsboro TX
76645-0619. 254/582-2555.

McLennan Community College
1400 College Dr, Waco TX
76708-1402. 254/299-8000.

Navarro College
1900 John Arden Dr,
Waxahachie TX 75165-5220.
972/937-7612.

Navarro College
3200 W 7th Ave, Corsicana TX
75110-4818. 903/874-6501.

North Central Texas College
1525 W California St,
Gainesville TX 76240-4636.
940/668-7731.

North Central Texas College
1500 N Corinth St, Denton TX
76208-5408. 940/498-6282.

North East Texas Community
College
PO Box 1307, Mount Pleasant
TX 75456-9991. 903/572-1911.

Panola College
1109 W Panola St, Carthage TX
75633-2341. 903/693-2000.

Paris Junior College
2400 Clarksville St, Paris TX
75460-6258. 903/785-7661.

Texarkana College
2500 N Robison Rd, Texarkana
TX 75599-0002. 903/838-4541.

Texas State Technical College
PO Box 1269, Marshall TX
75671-1269. 903/935-1010.

Trinity Valley Community
College
500 S Prairieville St, Athens TX
75751-2734. 903/675-6200.

Vernon Regional Junior College
4400 College Dr, Vernon TX
76384-4005. 940/552-6291.

Weatherford College
308 E Park Ave, Weatherford
TX 76086-5618. 817/594-5471.

Western Texas College
6200 College Ave, Snyder TX
79549-6105. 915/573-8511.

For more information on career opportunities in educational services:

Associations

AMERICAN ASSOCIATION FOR HIGHER
EDUCATION
One DuPont Circle, Suite 360, Washington DC
20036. 202/293-6440. World Wide Web address:
http://www.aahe.org.

AMERICAN ASSOCIATION OF SCHOOL
ADMINISTRATORS
1801 North Moore Street, Arlington VA 22209.
703/528-0700. Fax: 703/841-1543. World Wide
Web address: http://www.aasa.org. An
organization of school system leaders. The
$244.00 membership includes a national
conference on education; programs and seminars;
The School Administrator, a monthly magazine;
Leadership News, a monthly newspaper; *Leaders'
Edge, Back Fence,* and *Edge City,* quarterly
publications; and a catalog of other publications
and audiovisuals.

AMERICAN FEDERATION OF TEACHERS
555 New Jersey Avenue NW, Washington DC

20001. 202/879-4400. World Wide Web address: http://www.aft.org.

COLLEGE AND UNIVERSITY PERSONNEL ASSOCIATION
1233 20th Street NW, Suite 301, Washington DC 20036. 202/429-0311. World Wide Web address: http://www.cupa.org. An organization of higher education human resource professionals. Membership is required and is available for students.

NATIONAL ASSOCIATION FOR COLLEGE ADMISSION COUNSELING
1631 Prince Street, Alexandria VA 22314. 703/836-2222. World Wide Web address: http://www.nacac.com. An education association of school counselors and admissions officers who assist students in making the transition from high school to post-secondary education.

NATIONAL ASSOCIATION OF BIOLOGY TEACHERS
11250 Roger Bacon Drive, Suite 19, Reston VA 20190. 703/471-1134. Toll-free phone: 800/406-0775. Fax: 703/435-5582. E-mail address: nabter@aol.com. World Wide Web address: http://www.nabt.org. A professional organization for biology and life science educators.

NATIONAL ASSOCIATION OF COLLEGE AND UNIVERSITY BUSINESS OFFICERS
2501 M Street NW, Suite 400, Washington DC 20037. 202/861-2500. World Wide Web address: http://www.nacubo.org. Association for those involved in the financial administration and management of higher education. Membership required.

NATIONAL COMMISSION FOR COOPERATIVE EDUCATION (NCCE)
360 Huntington Avenue, 384 CP, Boston MA 02115. 617/373-3770. E-mail address: ncce@lynx.neu.edu. Offers free information to students interested in learning more about cooperative education programs.

NATIONAL COUNCIL FOR THE SOCIAL STUDIES
3501 Newark Street NW, Washington DC 20016. 202/966-7840. Fax: 202/966-2061. World Wide Web address: http://www.ncss.org. Offers publications, conferences, Internet resources, and information on awards and grants to 20,000 educators nationwide.

NATIONAL COUNCIL OF TEACHERS OF ENGLISH
1111 West Kenyon Road, Urbana IL 61801. 217/328-3870. Toll-free phone: 800/369-6283. Fax: 217/328-9645. World Wide Web address: http://ncte.org. Fosters professional growth for English teachers. The organization has 80,000 members worldwide and publishes a newspaper and related journals.

NATIONAL SCIENCE TEACHERS ASSOCIATION
1840 Wilson Boulevard, Arlington VA 22201-3000. 703/243-7100. World Wide Web address: http://www.nsta.org. Organization committed to the improvement of science education at all levels, preschool through college. Publishes five journals, a newspaper, and a number of special publications. Also conducts national and regional conventions.

NATIONAL SOCIETY FOR EXPERIENTIAL EDUCATION (NSEE)
1703 North Beauregard Street, 4th Floor, Alexandria VA 22311-1714. 703/575-5475. E-mail address: info@nsee.org. World Wide Web address: http://www.nsee.org. A membership organization offering publications, conferences, and a resource center. Among the society's publications is *The Experienced Hand: A Student Manual for Making the Most of an Internship.*

TEACHERS OF ENGLISH TO SPEAKERS OF OTHER LANGUAGES, INC. (TESOL)
700 South Washington Street, Suite 200, Alexandria VA 22314. 703/836-0774. Fax: 703/836-7864. E-mail address: tesol@tesol.edu. World Wide Web address: http://www.tesol.edu. An advocacy group that develops programs, services, and products which promote the professional development of both students and teachers of English as a second or foreign language.

Directories

NON-PROFITS & EDUCATION JOB FINDER
Planning/Communications, 7215 Oak Avenue, River Forest IL 60305. 708/366-5200. World Wide Web address: http://www.jobfindersonline.com. Provides Websites, BBS listings, job and resume databases, newspapers, magazines, and salary surveys.

WASHINGTON EDUCATION ASSOCIATION DIRECTORY
Council for Advancement and Support of Education, 1307 New York Avenue, Suite 1000, Washington DC 20005-4701. 202/328-5900. World Wide Web address: http://www.case.org.

Magazines

AMERICAN LANGUAGE REVIEW
6363 Wilshire Boulevard, Suite 214, Los Angeles CA 90048. 323/658-7620. Fax: 323/658-7530. World Wide Web address: http://www.alr.org. Subscription: $19.95 per year for six issues.

THE ENGLISH TEACHER: AN INTERNATIONAL JOURNAL
Assumption University, Huamark, Bangkapi, Bangkok 10240 Thailand. Contact: John Joseph Courtney, Managing Editor. World Wide Web address: http://elt.au.edu/info.html. Subscription: $35.00 per year for three issues.

TRANSITIONS ABROAD
Transitions Abroad Publishing Inc., P.O. Box 1300, Amherst MA 01004-1300. 413/256-3414. Fax: 413/256-0373. E-mail address: info@transabroad.com. World Wide Web address: http://www.transabroad.com. Discusses international teaching programs and opportunities. The Website also details several related publications.

Online Services

ACADEMIC EMPLOYMENT NETWORK
World Wide Web address: http://www.academploy.com. This site offers information for the educational professional, and allows you to search for positions nationwide. It also has information on other sites of interest, educational products, certification requirements by state, and relocation services.

ACADEMIC POSITION NETWORK
World Wide Web address: http://www.apnjobs.com. Updated daily with employment listings for national and international positions.

THE CHRONICLE OF HIGHER EDUCATION
World Wide Web address: http://chronicle.com/jobs. This Website provides job listings from the weekly published newspaper *The Chronicle of Higher Education*.

DAVE'S ESL CAFE
World Wide Web address: http://www.eslcafe.com. A site for English as a Second Language (ESL) and English as a Foreign Language (EFL) students and teachers. Services include an ESL bookstore, a job center, and many other links.

EDUCATION FORUM
Go: Edforum. This CompuServe discussion group is open to educators of all levels.

HIGHEREDJOBS ONLINE
World Wide Web address: http://www.higheredjobs.com. This site is searchable by type of position, state, or a specific institution.

JOBWEB SCHOOL DISTRICTS SEARCH
World Wide Web address: http://www.jobweb.org/search/schools. Provides a search engine for school districts across the country. The site is run by the National Association of Colleges and Employers and it also provides information on colleges and career fairs.

LIBRARY & INFORMATION SCIENCE JOBSEARCH
World Wide Web address: http://carousel.lis.uiuc.edu/~jobs.

THE PRIVATE SCHOOL EMPLOYMENT NETWORK
World Wide Web address: http://www.privateschooljobs.com. Offers private school openings. There is a $25.00 fee to post a resume on the site.

VISUAL NATION ARTS JOBS LINKS
World Wide Web address: http://www.visualarts.com. Provides links to other sites that post academic and arts job openings and information.

ELECTRONIC/INDUSTRIAL ELECTRICAL EQUIPMENT

You can expect to find the following types of companies in this chapter:
Electronic Machines and Systems • Semiconductor Manufacturers

Some helpful information: The average annual salary of electricians is approximately $25,000 - $30,000. Precision assemblers of electronic products generally earn between $15,000 and $22,000. Electrical and electronics engineers can earn upwards of $50,000 annually.

AMTECH CORPORATION
19111 Dallas Parkway, Suite 300, Dallas TX 75287. 972/733-6600. **Fax:** 972/733-6699. **Contact:** Human Resources Manager. **World Wide Web address:** http://www.amtech.com. **Description:** Manufactures electronic identification equipment used for toll and traffic management, parking, and security applications. **Common positions include:** Computer Programmer; Editor; Electrical/Electronics Engineer; Software Engineer; Technical Writer/Editor. **Educational backgrounds include:** Business Administration; Engineering; Marketing. **Benefits:** 401(k); Dental Insurance; Life Insurance. **Corporate headquarters location:** This Location. **Parent company:** Intermec. **Listed on:** NASDAQ. **Number of employees at this location:** 300.

ARROW ELECTRONICS
3220 Commander Drive, Carrollton TX 75006. 972/380-6464. **Toll-free phone:** 800/238-7286. **Contact:** Human Resources. **World Wide Web address:** http://www.arrow.com. **Description:** A distributor of electronic components, systems, and related items through a network in North America, Europe, and Asia. The company operates 150 marketing facilities, 10 primary distribution centers, and over 4,000 remote computer terminals that supply components to about 125,000 original equipment manufacturers and commercial customers. Semiconductors account for more than half of Arrow Schweber's sales. **Corporate headquarters location:** Melville NY. **Subsidiaries include:** Arrow CMS; Arrow Richey; Arrow Bell; Arrow Semiconductor; Arrow/Zeus Electronics; Marubun/Arrow USA, LLC.

AVNET, INC.
11333 Pagemill Road, Dallas TX 75243. 214/343-5000. **Toll-free phone:** 800/459-1225. **Fax:** 214/343-5054. **Contact:** Human Resources. **World Wide Web address:** http://www.avnet.com. **Description:** This location is engaged in the distribution of company-manufactured electronics products. Overall, Avnet, Inc. is one of the nation's largest distributors of electronic components and computer products for industrial and military customers. The company also produces and distributes electronic, electrical, and video communications products. **Common positions include:** Account Manager; Accountant/Auditor; Bookkeeper; Computer Programmer; Human Resources Manager; Inventory Control Specialist; Manufacturer's/Wholesaler's Sales Rep.; Marketing Specialist; Services Sales Representative; Stock Clerk; Warehouse/Distribution Worker. **Educational backgrounds include:** Accounting; Business Administration; Engineering; Finance; Liberal Arts; Marketing. **Benefits:** 401(k); Dental Insurance; Employee Discounts; Life Insurance; Medical Insurance; Pension Plan; Savings Plan; Tuition Assistance. **Corporate headquarters location:** Chandler AZ. **Listed on:** American Stock Exchange; New York Stock Exchange.

AVO INTERNATIONAL
4271 Bronze Way, Dallas TX 75237. 214/333-3201. **Contact:** Manager of Human Resources. **World Wide Web address:** http://www.avointl.com. **Description:** Manufactures test equipment and measurement instruments for electric power applications. **Corporate headquarters location:** This Location. **Parent company:** TBG.

COLLMER SEMICONDUCTOR, INC.
P.O. Box 702708, Dallas TX 75370. 972/233-1589. **Physical address:** 14368 Proton Road, Dallas TX. **Fax:** 972/381-9991. **Contact:** Human Resources. **World Wide Web address:** http://www.collmer.com. **Description:** Manufactures and distributes semiconductors.

DALLAS SEMICONDUCTOR
4401 South Beltwood Parkway, Dallas TX 75244-3292. 972/371-4000. **Contact:** Human Resources. **World Wide Web address:** http://www.dalsemi.com. **Description:** Manufactures semiconductors. **NOTE:** Entry-level positions are offered. **Common positions include:**

Administrative Assistant; Applications Engineer; Customer Service Representative; Database Administrator; Design Engineer; Electrical/Electronics Engineer; Internet Services Manager; Marketing Manager; Marketing Specialist; Mechanical Engineer; MIS Specialist; Software Engineer; Systems Manager; Webmaster. **Educational backgrounds include:** Computer Science; Engineering; Physics. **Benefits:** 401(k); Dental Insurance; Disability Coverage; Life Insurance; Medical Insurance; Profit Sharing. **Corporate headquarters location:** This Location. **Listed on:** New York Stock Exchange. **Number of employees at this location:** 1,500.

DATAMATIC.COM, LTD.
715 North Glenville Drive, Suite 450, Richardson TX 75075. 972/234-5000. **Toll-free phone:** 800/880-2878. **Fax:** 972/234-1134. **Contact:** Human Resources. **E-mail address:** hr@datamatic.com. **World Wide Web address:** http://www.datamatic.com. **Description:** Supplies data collection and meter-reading products to investor-owned utilities and municipalities. Founded in 1977. **Office hours:** Monday - Friday, 8:00 a.m. - 5:00 p.m.

FAS TECHNOLOGIES
10480 Markison Road, Dallas TX 75230. 214/553-9991. **Fax:** 214/553-9919. **Contact:** Human Resources Manager. **E-mail address:** personnel@fas.com. **World Wide Web address:** http://www.fas.com. **Description:** Manufactures semiconductor processing equipment. Founded in 1988. **Common positions include:** Administrative Assistant; Buyer; Customer Service Representative; Electrical/Electronics Engineer; Mechanical Engineer; Software Engineer; Technical Writer/Editor. **Educational backgrounds include:** Engineering. **Benefits:** Dental Insurance; Employee Discounts; Life Insurance; Medical Insurance; Tuition Assistance. **Corporate headquarters location:** This Location. **International locations:** Japan. **Subsidiaries include:** FAS-Asia, Ltd. **Listed on:** Privately held.

HONEYWELL MICROSWITCH
830 East Arapaho Road, Richardson TX 75081. 972/470-4271. **Contact:** Jim Francis, Personnel Director. **World Wide Web address:** http://www.honeywell.com. **Description:** Manufactures several different optoelectronics and fiberoptic systems and components including light-emitting and sensing devices/systems; and optical switches and isolators applicable to data transmission and automation of the computer industry and the military worldwide. **Common positions include:** Accountant/Auditor; Buyer; Computer Programmer; Customer Service Representative; Draftsperson; Electrical/Electronics Engineer; Human Resources Manager; Industrial Engineer; Mechanical Engineer; Operations/Production Manager; Quality Control Supervisor. **Educational backgrounds include:** Accounting; Engineering; Physics. **Benefits:** Dental Insurance; Disability Coverage; Employee Discounts; Life Insurance; Medical Insurance; Pension Plan; Savings Plan; Tuition Assistance. **Parent company:** Honeywell is engaged in the research and development, manufacture, and sale of advanced technology products and services in satellite technology. **Listed on:** New York Stock Exchange.

HOWELL INSTRUMENTS, INC.
P.O. Box 985001, Fort Worth TX 76185-5001. 817/336-7411x223. **Physical address:** 3479 West Vickery Boulevard, Fort Worth TX 76107. **Fax:** 817/336-7874. **Contact:** Nell Whaylen, Personnel Manager. **E-mail address:** nmwhaylen@howellinst.com. **World Wide Web address:** http://www.howellinst.com. **Description:** Manufacturer of turbine engine instrumentation and test equipment for military and commercial applications. **NOTE:** Entry-level positions are offered. **Common positions include:** Computer Programmer; Sales Engineer; Software Engineer. **Educational backgrounds include:** Computer Science; Engineering. **Benefits:** Dental Insurance; Disability Coverage; Life Insurance; Medical Insurance; Pension Plan; Profit Sharing; Public Transit Available. **Corporate headquarters location:** This Location. **Listed on:** Privately held. **President/CEO:** John Howell. **Facilities Manager:** H.G. White. **Annual sales/revenues:** $11 - $20 million.

LITTON ELECTRO-OPTICAL SYSTEMS
3414 Herrmann Drive, Garland TX 75041. 972/840-5600. **Contact:** Human Resources. **Description:** Manufactures a diverse line of military equipment and electro-optical systems including guided-missile launchers, optical sighting and fire control equipment, laser range finders, night-vision sights, and systems for weapons and high-intensity searchlights. **NOTE:** Entry-level positions and second and third shifts are offered. **Common positions include:** Accountant/Auditor; Administrator; Blue-Collar Worker Supervisor; Buyer; Computer Programmer; Department Manager; Draftsperson; Electrical/Electronics Engineer; Financial Analyst; Human Resources Manager; Industrial Engineer; Mechanical Engineer; Operations/Production Manager; Physicist; Purchasing Agent/Manager; Quality Control Supervisor; Systems Analyst. **Educational backgrounds include:** Accounting; Business Administration; Chemistry; Computer Science; Engineering; Marketing; Physics. **Benefits:**

401(k); Dental Insurance; Disability Coverage; Life Insurance; Medical Insurance; Pension Plan; Stock Option; Tuition Assistance. **Other U.S. locations:** Tempe AZ. **Parent company:** Litton Industries. **Listed on:** New York Stock Exchange. **Number of employees at this location:** 550.

MICROPAC INDUSTRIES INC.
725 East Walnut Street, Garland TX 75040. 972/272-3571. **Contact:** Human Resources. **Description:** Manufactures semiconductors.

NATIONAL SEMICONDUCTOR CORPORATION
1111 West Bardin Road, Arlington TX 76017. 817/468-6300. **Contact:** Human Resources. **Description:** Designs, develops, and manufactures microprocessors, consumer products, integrated circuits, memory systems, computer products, telecommunication systems, and high-speed bipolar circuits. **Corporate headquarters location:** Santa Clara CA. **International locations:** Scotland.

OPTEK TECHNOLOGY INC.
1215 West Crosby Road, Carrollton TX 75006. 972/323-2200. **Contact:** Personnel Manager. **World Wide Web address:** http://www.optekinc.com. **Description:** Produces fiber optic, log-wavelength, light-emitting diodes; hybrid components; gallium arsenide and gallium aluminum arsenide circuits; and related products. **Common positions include:** Accountant/Auditor; Buyer; Ceramics Engineer; Chemical Engineer; Computer Programmer; Credit Manager; Customer Service Representative; Draftsperson; Electrical/Electronics Engineer; Financial Analyst; Human Resources Manager; Metallurgical Engineer; Purchasing Agent/Manager; Quality Control Supervisor; Technical Writer/Editor. **Educational backgrounds include:** Accounting; Chemistry; Computer Science; Engineering; Finance; Physics. **Benefits:** 401(k); Disability Coverage; Life Insurance; Medical Insurance; Tuition Assistance.

RAYTHEON SYSTEMS COMPANY
P.O. Box 6056, Greenville TX 75403-6056. 903/455-3450. **Contact:** Human Resources. **World Wide Web address:** http://www.raytheon.com. **Description:** This location manufactures electronic equipment for the military and commercial electronics industries. Military products include reconnaissance and surveillance equipment; command, control, and communications equipment; navigation and control systems; and aircraft maintenance and navigation systems. Nonmilitary products include mass media storage equipment, medical imaging devices, and data handling products. Overall, Raytheon Systems designs, manufactures, and installs state-of-the-art communications and integrated command-and-control systems for military and industrial customers worldwide. **Parent company:** Raytheon Company is a diversified, multi-industry company ranked among the 100 largest U.S. industrial corporations. Raytheon has 110 facilities in 28 states and the District of Columbia. Overseas facilities and representative offices are located in 26 countries, principally in Europe, the Middle East, and the Pacific Rim. The company's four business segments include Electronics, Major Appliances, Aircraft Products, and Energy and Environmental. **Listed on:** New York Stock Exchange.

RAYTHEON SYSTEMS COMPANY
P.O. Box 831359, Richardson TX 75083-1359. 972/470-2000. **Toll-free phone:** 800/933-5359. **Fax:** 972/301-5991. **Contact:** Lonnie Duke, Professional Recruiter. **E-mail address:** lonnie@koyote.com. **World Wide Web address:** http://www.raytheon.com. **Description:** Engaged in the design, manufacture, and installation of state-of-the-art communications and integrated command-and-control systems for military and industrial customers worldwide. **NOTE:** Entry-level positions are offered. **Common positions include:** Electrical/Electronics Engineer; Software Engineer; Technical Writer/Editor. **Educational backgrounds include:** C/C++; Computer Science; Software Development. **Benefits:** 401(k); Casual Dress - Daily; Dental Insurance; Disability Coverage; Employee Discounts; Life Insurance; Medical Insurance; Pension Plan; Public Transit Available; Savings Plan. **Special programs:** Co-ops. **Office hours:** Monday - Friday, 7:30 a.m. - 5:00 p.m. **Parent company:** Raytheon Company is a diversified, multi-industry company ranked among the 100 largest U.S. industrial corporations. Raytheon has 110 facilities in 28 states and the District of Columbia. Overseas facilities and representative offices are located in 26 countries, principally in Europe, the Middle East, and the Pacific Rim. The company's four business segments include Electronics, Major Appliances, Aircraft Products, and Energy and Environmental. **Listed on:** New York Stock Exchange. **Number of employees at this location:** 1,000.

REXEL INC.
P.O. Box 9085, Addison TX 75001. 972/387-3600. **Contact:** Human Resources. **World Wide Web address:** http://www.rexel.com. **Description:** One of the world's largest distributors of electrical parts and supplies. **NOTE:** Resumes should be sent to Human Resources, 6700 LBJ

Freeway, Suite 3200, Dallas TX 75240. **Common positions include:** Accountant/Auditor; Administrator; Credit Manager; Department Manager; Financial Analyst; Human Resources Manager; Management Trainee; Marketing Specialist; Operations/Production Manager. **Educational backgrounds include:** Accounting; Business Administration; Communications; Liberal Arts; Marketing. **Benefits:** Dental Insurance; Disability Coverage; Employee Discounts; Life Insurance; Medical Insurance; Pension Plan; Profit Sharing; Savings Plan; Tuition Assistance. **Corporate headquarters location:** This Location. **Parent company:** Pinault-Printemps-Redoute.

ROBINSON NUGENT DALLAS, INC.
2640 Tarna Drive, Dallas TX 75229. 972/241-1738. **Contact:** Virginia Graver, Human Resources Manager. **World Wide Web address:** http://www.robinsonnugent.com. **Description:** Manufactures electronic connectors. **NOTE:** Second and third shifts are offered. **Educational backgrounds include:** Chemistry; Engineering. **Benefits:** 401(k); Casual Dress - Fridays; Dental Insurance; Disability Coverage; Life Insurance; Medical Insurance; Pension Plan; Tuition Assistance. **Corporate headquarters location:** New Albany IN. **Listed on:** NASDAQ. **Facilities Manager:** Chris Smelcer. **Number of employees at this location:** 180.

ROCHESTER GAUGES, INC.
P.O. Box 29242, Dallas TX 75229. 972/241-2161. **Contact:** Barbara Nitishin, Corporate Human Resources Generalist. **Description:** A manufacturer of gauges, thermometers, and measuring devices. **NOTE:** Entry-level positions are offered. **Common positions include:** Blue-Collar Worker Supervisor; Customer Service Representative; Manufacturer's/Wholesaler's Sales Rep.; Mechanical Engineer; MIS Specialist. **Educational backgrounds include:** Engineering. **Benefits:** 401(k); Dental Insurance; Disability Coverage; Life Insurance; Medical Insurance; Pension Plan; Public Transit Available; Savings Plan; Tuition Assistance. **Corporate headquarters location:** This Location. **Listed on:** Privately held. **Annual sales/revenues:** $21 - $50 million. **Number of employees at this location:** 300. **Number of employees nationwide:** 500.

SGS-THOMSON MICROELECTRONICS
1310 Electronics Drive, Carrollton TX 75006. 972/466-6000. **Contact:** Human Resources Department. **Description:** This location manufactures microchips. Overall, SGS-THOMSON Microelectronics designs, develops, manufactures, and markets a broad range of semiconductor integrated circuits and discrete devices used in a variety of microelectronic applications. These applications include telecommunications systems, computer systems, consumer products, automotive products, and industrial automation and control systems. Founded in 1987. **Corporate headquarters location:** Montgomeryville PA. **Listed on:** New York Stock Exchange. **Stock exchange symbol:** STM.

SIEMENS ELECTROCOM L.P.
2910 Avenue F, Arlington TX 76011-5276. 817/640-5690. **Contact:** Human Resources. **World Wide Web address:** http://www.siemenselectrocom.com. **Description:** Designs, manufactures, integrates, and services high-speed automated document processing, materials handling, mobile data, and voice communication systems. Primary customers are the U.S. Postal Service and other government agencies.

TECCOR ELECTRONICS INC.
1801 Hurd Drive, Irving TX 75038. 972/580-1515. **Contact:** Human Resources Department. **Description:** Manufactures electronic power controls and related equipment. A second plant (also at this location) manufactures semiconductor power devices, solid state relays, and a variety of silicon chips and rectifiers. **Common positions include:** Accountant/Auditor; Administrator; Blue-Collar Worker Supervisor; Buyer; Ceramics Engineer; Chemical Engineer; Chemist; Computer Programmer; Customer Service Representative; Department Manager; Draftsperson; Electrical/Electronics Engineer; Industrial Engineer; Purchasing Agent/Manager; Quality Control Supervisor; Sales Executive; Systems Analyst. **Educational backgrounds include:** Accounting; Business Administration; Chemistry; Engineering; Marketing. **Benefits:** Dental Insurance; Disability Coverage; Employee Discounts; Life Insurance; Medical Insurance; Pension Plan; Profit Sharing; Savings Plan; Tuition Assistance. **Corporate headquarters location:** This Location. **Listed on:** New York Stock Exchange.

TELEDYNE BROWN ENGINEERING
GEOTECH INSTRUMENTS
10755 Sanden Drive, Dallas TX 75238. 214/221-0000. **Contact:** Human Resources. **World Wide Web address:** http://www.tbe.com. **Description:** Manufactures earthquake monitoring equipment.

TEXAS INSTRUMENTS, INC. (TI)
EDUCATIONAL & PRODUCTIVITY SOLUTIONS BUSINESS
P.O. Box 660199, Dallas TX 75243. **Fax:** 972/917-1335. **Contact:** Human Resources. **E-mail address:** epsjobs@ti.com. **World Wide Web address:** http://www.ti.com. **Description:** Texas Instruments (TI) is one of the world's largest suppliers of semiconductor products. TI's defense electronics business is a leading supplier of avionics, infrared, and weapons guidance systems to the U.S. Department of Defense and U.S. allies. The company is also a technology leader in high-performance notebook computers and model-based software development tools. TI sensors monitor and regulate pressure and temperature in products ranging from automobiles to air conditioning systems. **Common positions include:** Computer Programmer; Electrical/Electronics Engineer; Industrial Engineer; Mechanical Engineer; Systems Analyst. **Educational backgrounds include:** Computer Science; Engineering. **Benefits:** Dental Insurance; Disability Coverage; Life Insurance; Medical Insurance; Pension Plan; Profit Sharing; Savings Plan; Tuition Assistance. **Corporate headquarters location:** This Location. **Listed on:** New York Stock Exchange. **Annual sales/revenues:** More than $100 million. **Number of employees at this location:** 25,000. **Number of employees nationwide:** 56,000.

THERMALLOY INC.
P.O. Box 810839, Dallas TX 75381-0839. 972/243-4321. **Contact:** Personnel. **World Wide Web address:** http://www.thermalloy.com. **Description:** Produces a variety of electronics components and systems, plastics, and machined products including ceramic electrical products, electronic semiconductor equipment, semiconductor insulating covers, screw machine products, plastic injected molding products for electronics use, and printed circuit board guides. **Corporate headquarters location:** This Location.

ULTRAK INC.
1301 Waters Ridge Drive, Lewisville TX 75057. 972/353-6500. **Contact:** Human Resources. **World Wide Web address:** http://www.ultrak.com. **Description:** Manufactures security surveillance equipment.

WARREN ELECTRIC
P.O. Box 540247, Dallas TX 75334-0247. 214/902-5500. **Contact:** Personnel. **Description:** A supplier of electrical appliances and equipment.

ZIMMERMAN SIGN COMPANY
9846 Highway 31 East, Tyler TX 75705. 903/535-7400. **Contact:** Human Resources Manager. **Description:** Manufactures electric signs. **Common positions include:** Accountant/Auditor; Blue-Collar Worker Supervisor; Budget Analyst; Buyer; Cost Estimator; Customer Service Representative; Designer; Draftsperson; Human Resources Manager; Purchasing Agent/Manager; Quality Control Supervisor; Systems Analyst. **Educational backgrounds include:** Accounting; Art/Design; Business Administration; Computer Science; Engineering; Marketing. **Benefits:** Disability Coverage; Life Insurance; Medical Insurance. **Corporate headquarters location:** This Location. **Other U.S. locations:** Jacksonville TX; Longview TX. **Operations at this facility include:** Administration; Manufacturing; Sales; Service. **Number of employees at this location:** 50. **Number of employees nationwide:** 400.

Note: Because addresses and telephone numbers of smaller companies can change rapidly, we recommend you call each company to verify the information below before inquiring about job opportunities. Mass mailings are not recommended.

Additional small employers:

AEROSPACE AND/OR NAUTICAL SYSTEMS AND INSTRUMENTS

EFW Inc.
PO Box 136969, Fort Worth TX 76136-0969. 817/234-6600.

Raytheon E-Systems Inc.
PO Box 154580, Waco TX 76715-4580. 254/799-5533.

Raytheon Systems Company
13532 N Central Expy, Dallas TX 75243-1108. 972/344-3831.

S-Tec Corporation
1 S-Tec Way, Mineral Wells TX 76067-9236. 940/325-9406.

ELECTRIC LIGHTING AND WIRING EQUIPMENT

Corbett Lighting Inc.
2816 Commodore Dr, Carrollton TX 75007-4612. 972/241-8800.

Crouse-Hinds
Rural Route 5, Box 6, Amarillo TX 79118-9805. 806/358-4585.

EGS Electrical Group
2150 W South Loop, Stephenville TX 76401-3922. 254/968-6071.

Genlyte Controls
2413 South Shiloh Road, Garland TX 75041-1344. 972/840-1640.

Philips Lighting Co.
3010 Clarksville Street, Paris TX 75460-7913. 903/784-7453.

Electronic/Industrial Electrical Equipment/143

Probity Electronics Inc.
1700 Capital Ave, Plano TX
75074-8155. 972/398-3111.

ELECTRICAL ENGINE EQUIPMENT

Delphi Energy & Engineering Management Systems
PO Box 97504, Wichita Falls
TX 76307-7504. 940/855-7190.

Federal Parts Corporation
9249 King James Dr, Dallas TX
75247-3603. 214/631-5942.

Mini-Tune
2700 Lone Star Dr, Dallas TX
75212-6209. 214/951-0010.

Unison Industries Inc.
2155 Eagle Pkwy, Fort Worth
TX 76177-2311. 817/264-3100.

USA Harness Inc.
PO Box 793, Winnsboro TX
75494-0793. 903/342-3767.

ELECTRICAL EQUIPMENT WHOLESALE

Andrew Corporation
2601 Telecom Pkwy,
Richardson TX 75082-3521.
972/952-9700.

Brandon & Clark Inc.
PO Box 3159, Lubbock TX
79452-3159. 806/747-3861.

Simplex Time Recorder
8300 Esters Blvd, Ste 950,
Irving TX 75063-2292. 972/621-1900.

ELECTRICAL EQUIPMENT, MACHINERY, AND SUPPLIES

Caddx Controls Inc.
1420 N Main St, Gladewater TX
75647-4518. 903/845-6941.

Chatham Technologies Inc.
12221 Merit Dr, Ste 400, Dallas
TX 75251-2201. 972/991-5559.

Texas Instruments Incorporated
PO Box 801, McKinney TX
75070-0801. 972/542-3301.

Tocom Inc.
1330 Capital Pkwy, Carrollton
TX 75006-3647. 972/323-4000.

ELECTRICAL INDUSTRIAL APPARATUS

ABB Control Inc.
1206 Hatton Rd, Wichita Falls
TX 76302-3099. 940/397-7000.

Crouzet Corporation
3237 Commander Dr,
Carrollton TX 75006-2506.
972/250-1647.

Cutler-Hammer
1102 Avenue T, Grand Prairie
TX 75050-1118. 972/606-5900.

Industrial Technology Inc.
6100 Columbia Rd, Mineral
Wells TX 76067-9240.
940/325-3000.

Mantek
PO Box 660196, Dallas TX
75266-0196. 972/438-0361.

Panja Corporation
11995 Forestgate Dr, Dallas TX
75243-5449. 972/644-3048.

ELECTRONIC COMPONENTS AND ACCESSORIES

Cuplex Interconnect
1140 Pagemill Rd, Dallas TX
75243. 214/503-9988.

Dynamic Details Inc.
1500 Highway 66, Garland TX
75040-6727. 972/276-0333.

MTI
1920 Diplomat Dr, Dallas TX
75234-8913. 972/243-6767.

Sanmina Corporation
1250 American Pkwy,
Richardson TX 75081-2931.
972/669-1125.

ELECTRONIC PARTS AND EQUIPMENT WHOLESALE

All Components Inc.
13717 Beta Rd, Dallas TX
75244-4513. 972/233-0203.

Allied Electronics Inc.
PO Box 1544, Fort Worth TX
76101-1544. 817/595-3500.

Bearcom Operating LP
PO Box 559001, Dallas TX
75355. 214/340-8876.

Mouser Electronics Inc.
PO Box 714, Mansfield TX
76063-0714. 817/483-0165.

NEC America Inc.
1555 W Walnut Hill Ln, Irving
TX 75038-3702. 972/751-7000.

Source Inc.
PO Box 890184, Dallas TX
75389-0184. 972/450-2600.

Texas Instruments Inc.
PO Box 660246, Dallas TX
75266-0246. 214/480-6281.

Texas Instruments Inc.
PO Box 10508, Lubbock TX
79408-3508. 806/741-4880.

Uniden America Corporation
4700 Amon Carter Blvd, Fort
Worth TX 76155-2297.
817/858-3300.

Williams Communications Stations
5151 Belt Line Rd, Ste 100,
Dallas TX 75240-7545.
972/991-3388.

Wiltel
19111 Dallas Pkwy, Ste 100,
Dallas TX 75287-6912.
972/349-5200.

MISC. ELECTRONIC COMPONENTS

Boeing Corinth Company
7801 S Stemmons Fwy, Lake
Dallas TX 75065-2356.
940/497-7600.

Mexia Fabricators
PO Box 458, Wortham TX
76693-0458. 254/765-3304.

Micrometals/Texas Inc.
4825 Derrick Dr, Abilene TX
79601-6701. 915/677-8753.

Precision Cable Manufacturing Corp.
PO Box 1448, Rockwall TX
75087-1448. 972/771-1233.

Regal Research & Manufacturing Co.
2020 Copper St, Garland TX
75042-6656. 972/494-0359.

SEMICONDUCTORS AND RELATED DEVICES

Benchmarq Microelectronics
17919 Waterview Pkwy, Dallas
TX 75252-8011. 972/437-9195.

Memc Southwest Inc.
PO Box 9600, Sherman TX
75091-9600. 903/891-5000.

Micron Technology Inc.
500 W Renner Road,
Richardson TX 75080-1324.
972/994-3600.

Raytheon Service Company
2501 S Highway 121,
Lewisville TX 75067-8122.
972/462-4111.

Triquint Semiconductor Texas
PO Box 833938, Dallas TX
75243. 972/994-8200.

SWITCHGEAR AND SWITCHBOARD APPARATUS

Aztec Manufacturing Company
PO Box 668, Crowley TX
76036-0668. 817/297-4361.

For more information on career opportunities in the electronic/industrial electrical equipment industry:

Associations

AMERICAN CERAMIC SOCIETY
P.O. Box 6136, Westerville OH 43086-6136. 614/890-4700. World Wide Web address: http://www.acers.org. Provides ceramics industry information. Membership required.

ELECTROCHEMICAL SOCIETY
65 South Main Street, Pennington NJ 08534. 609/737-1902. World Wide Web address: http://www.electrochem.org. An international society which holds bi-annual meetings internationally and periodic meetings through local sections.

ELECTRONIC INDUSTRIES ASSOCIATION
2500 Wilson Boulevard, Arlington VA 22201. 703/907-7500. World Wide Web address: http://www.eia.org.

ELECTRONICS TECHNICIANS ASSOCIATION
602 North Jackson Street, Greencastle IN 46135. 765/653-4301. World Wide Web address: http://www.eta-sda.com. Offers published job-hunting advice from the organization's officers and members. Also offers educational material and certification programs.

FABLESS SEMICONDUCTOR ASSOCIATION
Three Lincoln Centre, 5430 LBJ Freeway, Suite 280, Dallas TX 75240-6636. 972/866-7579. Fax: 972/239-2292. World Wide Web address: http://www.fsa.org. A semiconductor industry association.

INSTITUTE OF ELECTRICAL AND ELECTRONICS ENGINEERS, INC. (IEEE)
305 East 47th Street, 9th Floor, New York NY 10017. 212/705-8900. Toll-free customer service line: 800/678-4333. World Wide Web address: http://www.ieee.org.

INTERNATIONAL SOCIETY OF CERTIFIED ELECTRONICS TECHNICIANS
2708 West Berry Street, Fort Worth TX 76109. 817/921-9101. World Wide Web address: http://www.iscet.org.

NATIONAL ELECTRONICS SERVICE DEALERS ASSOCIATION
2708 West Berry Street, Fort Worth TX 76109. 817/921-9061. World Wide Web address: http://www.nesda.com. Provides newsletters and directories to members.

SEMICONDUCTOR EQUIPMENT AND MATERIALS INTERNATIONAL
805 East Middlefield Road, Mountain View CA 94043-4080. 650/964-5111. E-mail address: semihq@semi.org. World Wide Web address: http://www.semi.org. An international trade association concerned with the semiconductor and flat-panel display industries. Membership required.

Career Fairs

JOB EXPO INTERNATIONAL, INC.
175 Fifth Avenue, Suite 2390, New York NY 10010. 212/655-4505. Fax: 212/655-4501. World Wide Web address: http://www.tech-expo.com. One of the nation's leading technical career fairs.

Online Services

SEMICONDUCTOR JOBS
World Wide Web address: http://www.semiconductorjobs.com. Provides links to job postings related to the semiconductor industry.

Visit our exciting job and career site at www.careercity.com

ENVIRONMENTAL AND WASTE MANAGEMENT SERVICES

You can expect to find the following types of companies in this chapter:
Environmental Engineering Firms • Sanitary Services

Some helpful information: *The average salary for entry-level sanitation workers is $20,000 - $25,000 annually, with experienced workers earning an average of $30,000 per year. Environmental engineers can earn upwards of $40,000 annually.*

ADS ENVIRONMENTAL SERVICES INC.
10715 Plano Road, Suite 200, Dallas TX 75238. 214/340-5696. **Fax:** 214/343-2848. **Contact:** Human Resources Department. **World Wide Web address:** http://www.adsenv.com. **Description:** Provides diagnostic testing services of water and wastewater, flow monitoring, and sewer system evaluation. Founded in 1974. **Parent company:** ADS Corporation.

APPLIED EARTH SCIENCES
2833 Trinity Square, Suite 149, Carrollton TX 75006. 972/416-7171. **Fax:** 972/416-7175. **Contact:** Human Resources. **Description:** Provides environmental testing services on soil and water.

CENTEX WASTE MANAGEMENT, INC.
P.O. Box 475, McGregor TX 76657. 254/840-3604. **Contact:** Personnel. **World Wide Web address:** http://www.wm.com. **Description:** Engaged in residential and commercial refuse collection. **Corporate headquarters location:** Houston TX. **Other U.S. locations:** Nationwide.

DUNCAN DISPOSAL
1408 North Martin Luther King Boulevard, Lubbock TX 79403. 806/762-2650. **Contact:** Personnel. **Description:** Provides waste disposal services.

GEO-MARINE, INC.
550 East 15th Street, Plano TX 75074. 972/423-5480. **Contact:** Human Resources. **World Wide Web address:** http://www.geo-marine.com/gmi. **Description:** An environmental engineering and consulting firm.

SAFETY-KLEEN CORPORATION
1722 Cooper Creek Road, Denton TX 76208. 940/383-2611. **Contact:** Personnel. **World Wide Web address:** http://www.safety-kleen.com. **Description:** This location is a recycling center for hazardous waste. Overall, the company offers treatment, recycling, and disposal services.

For more information on career opportunities in environmental and waste management services:

Associations

AIR & WASTE MANAGEMENT ASSOCIATION
One Gateway Center, 3rd Floor, Pittsburgh PA 15222. 412/232-3444. E-mail address: info@awma.org. World Wide Web address: http://www.awma.org. A nonprofit, technical and educational organization providing a neutral forum where all points of view regarding environmental management issues can be addressed.

AMERICAN ACADEMY OF ENVIRONMENTAL ENGINEERS
130 Holiday Court, Suite 100, Annapolis MD 21401. 410/266-3311. World Wide Web address: http://www.aaee.net. Publishes *Environmental Engineer*, a quarterly magazine addressing policies and technical issues.

ENVIRONMENTAL INDUSTRY ASSOCIATIONS
4301 Connecticut Avenue NW, Suite 300, Washington DC 20008. 202/244-4700. World Wide Web address: http://www.envasns.org.

INSTITUTE OF CLEAN AIR COMPANIES
1660 L Street NW, Suite 1100, Washington DC 20036. 202/457-0911. World Wide Web address: http://www.icac.com. A national association of companies involved in stationary source air pollution control.

WATER ENVIRONMENT FEDERATION
601 Wythe Street, Alexandria VA 22314. 703/684-2452. World Wide Web address: http://www.wef.org. Provides educational and technical information regarding water quality, and also has a job site.

Magazines

JOURNAL OF THE AIR & WASTE MANAGEMENT ASSOCIATION
One Gateway Center, 3rd Floor, Pittsburgh PA 15222. 412/232-3444. Toll-free phone: 800/275-5851. World Wide Web address: http://www.awma.org.

Newsletters

SOLID WASTE DIGEST
SOLID WASTE MARKET: REVIEW, TRENDS, & FORECAST
Chartwell Information Publishers, 805 Cameron Street, Alexandria VA 22314. 703/519-3630. Fax: 703/519-7881. World Wide Web address: http://www.wasteinfo.com.

Online Services

ECOLOGIC
World Wide Web address: http://www.eng.rpi.edu/dept/union/pugwash/ecojobs.htm. This Website provides links to a variety of environmental job resources. This site is run by the Rensselaer Student Pugwash.

ENVIRONMENTAL JOBS SEARCH PAGE/UBIQUITY
World Wide Web address: http://ourworld.compuserve.com/homepages/ubikk/env4.htm. This Website includes internships, tips, and links to other databases of environmental job openings.

INTERNATIONAL & ENVIRONMENTAL JOB BULLETINS
World Wide Web address: http://www.sas.upenn.edu/African_Studies/Publications/International_Environmental_16621.html. Provides a wealth of information on bulletins, magazines, and resources for jobseekers who are looking to get into the environmental field. Most of these resources are on a subscription basis and provide job openings and other information. This information was compiled by Dennis F. Desmond.

LINKS TO SOURCES OF INFORMATION ON ENVIRONMENTAL JOBS
World Wide Web address: http://www.utexas.edu/ftp/student/scb/joblinks.html. Provides links to numerous sites that offer job openings and information in the environmental field. The site is run by the University of Texas at Austin.

WATER ENVIRONMENT WEB
World Wide Web address: http://www.wef.org. A service of the Water Environment Federation.

FABRICATED/PRIMARY METALS AND PRODUCTS

You can expect to find the following types of companies in this chapter:
*Aluminum and Copper Foundries • Die-Castings • Iron and Steel Foundries
Steel Works, Blast Furnaces, and Rolling Mills*

Some helpful information: *The average salary of a metalworking machine operator is between $20,000 and $25,000 annually. Trained setup operators generally earn more than standard operators. Machinery installation workers earn an average of $25,000 per year. Tool and die makers earn between $28,000 and $35,000 on average (very skilled precision workers may earn $40,000 or more annually).*

AIR SYSTEMS COMPONENTS (ASC)
1200 Executive Drive East, Suite 90, Richardson TX 75081. 972/907-0791. **Fax:** 972/234-0354. **Contact:** Human Resources Department. **Description:** Engaged in sheet metal fabrication of heating and air conditioning components for the residential and commercial markets. **NOTE:** Entry-level positions are offered. **Common positions include:** Accountant/Auditor; Computer Programmer; Customer Service Representative; Design Engineer; Designer; Draftsperson; Human Resources Manager; Industrial Engineer; Mechanical Engineer; Operations/Production Manager; Systems Analyst; Typist/Word Processor; Video Production Coordinator. **Educational backgrounds include:** Business Administration; Engineering; Marketing. **Benefits:** 401(k); Dental Insurance; Disability Coverage; Employee Discounts; Life Insurance; Medical Insurance; Profit Sharing; Public Transit Available; Savings Plan; Tuition Assistance. **Corporate headquarters location:** This Location. **Other U.S. locations:** AZ; OK. **Parent company:** Tomkins plc. **Listed on:** New York Stock Exchange. **Annual sales/revenues:** More than $100 million. **Number of employees at this location:** 100. **Number of employees nationwide:** 1,600.

AMERIMAX BUILDING PRODUCTS, INC.
14651 Dallas Parkway, Suite 330, Dallas TX 75240. 972/701-4900. **Fax:** 972/701-4960. **Contact:** Patti Perez, Human Resources Manager. **Description:** Fabricates building products of aluminum, steel, and vinyl. The company sells its products to manufacturers of recreational vehicles and prefabricated housing, retail building products suppliers, construction firms, and others. Amerimax's facilities include 15 fabrication plants located throughout the United States. Founded in 1954. **Common positions include:** Accountant/Auditor; Agricultural Engineer; Branch Manager; Computer Programmer; Customer Service Representative; Human Resources Manager; Management Trainee; Mechanical Engineer; Operations/Production Manager; Purchasing Agent/Manager. **Educational backgrounds include:** Accounting; Business Administration; Engineering; Marketing. **Benefits:** 401(k); Dental Insurance; Disability Coverage; Life Insurance; Medical Insurance; Pension Plan; Savings Plan; Tuition Assistance; Vision Insurance. **Corporate headquarters location:** This Location. **Listed on:** New York Stock Exchange. **Number of employees at this location:** 55. **Number of employees nationwide:** 750.

BWAY CORPORATION
3737 Miller Park Drive, Garland TX 75042. 972/535-1100. **Fax:** 972/535-1110. **Contact:** Cindy Berch, Human Resources Manager/Safety Director. **Description:** Manufactures steel containers such as aerosol cans, pails, paint cans, and food cans. The company also produces a variety of stumped metal products including ammunition boxes. **NOTE:** Second and third shifts are offered. **Common positions include:** Buyer; Controller; Electrician; Human Resources Manager; Industrial Engineer; Operations/Production Manager; Plant Manager; Purchasing Agent/Manager; Quality Control Supervisor; Sales Representative; Secretary. **Educational backgrounds include:** Business Administration; Engineering. **Benefits:** 401(k); Dental Insurance; Disability Coverage; Life Insurance; Medical Insurance; Profit Sharing. **Corporate headquarters location:** Atlanta GA. **Other U.S. locations:** Nationwide. **Listed on:** NASDAQ; New York Stock Exchange. **Stock exchange symbol:** BWAY. **Facilities Manager:** Charles Drake. **Number of employees at this location:** 80.

CHAPARRAL STEEL COMPANY
300 Ward Road, Midlothian TX 76065. 972/775-8241. **Contact:** Human Resources. **World Wide Web address:** http://www.chaparralsteel.com. **Description:** A steel works company. Founded in 1975. **Parent company:** TXI.

G.H. HENSLEY INDUSTRIES, INC.
P.O. Box 29779, Dallas TX 75229. 972/241-2321. **Contact:** Tom McCormack, Personnel Director. **Description:** Operates a steel foundry producing steel castings and construction equipment parts. **Corporate headquarters location:** This Location.

KEYSTONE CONSOLIDATED INDUSTRIES, INC.
5430 LBJ Freeway, Suite 1740, Dallas TX 75240. 972/458-0028. **Contact:** Human Resources. **Description:** A steel works and blast furnace producer.

KOCH-GLITSCH, INC.
4900 Singleton Boulevard, Dallas TX 75212. 214/631-3841. **Contact:** Chip Davis, Manager of Human Resources. **World Wide Web address:** http://www.koch-glitsch.com. **Description:** Fabricates metal plates and sheet metal and manufactures petroleum refinery processing equipment, pollution control equipment, and mesh products used in the automotive industry.

LEWIS & LAMBERT METAL
P.O. Box 14439, Haltom City TX 76117. 817/834-7146. **Contact:** Personnel. **World Wide Web address:** http://www.lewisandlambert.com. **Description:** A leader in sheet metal installation and fabrication.

THE LOFLAND COMPANY
P.O. Box 35446, Dallas TX 75235. 214/631-5250. **Fax:** 214/637-1110. **Contact:** Gail Wachtendorf, Personnel Manager. **Description:** A steel fabricator and distributor of construction materials. **Corporate headquarters location:** This Location. **Other U.S. locations:** Little Rock AR; Keithville LA; Fort Worth TX; Waxahachie TX. **Number of employees nationwide:** 260.

LONE STAR STEEL COMPANY
P.O. Box 803546, Dallas TX 75380-3546. 972/386-3981. **Contact:** Personnel. **Description:** Manufactures steel tubular goods used for oil and gas drilling. **Corporate headquarters location:** This Location.

TEXAS STEEL COMPANY
3901 Hemphill Street, Fort Worth TX 76110. 817/923-4611. **Contact:** Rhonda Jones, Personnel Supervisor. **Description:** Manufactures carbon, stainless steel, alloy castings, and other metal products for use in construction. **Corporate headquarters location:** This Location.

THORNTON STEEL COMPANY INC.
2700 West Pafford, Fort Worth TX 76110. 817/926-3324. **Fax:** 817/926-0758. **Contact:** Hiring. **Description:** A structural steel fabricator. **Common positions include:** Computer Operator; Structural Engineer. **Educational backgrounds include:** Accounting; Business Administration; Engineering. **Corporate headquarters location:** This Location. **Number of employees at this location:** 15.

VULCRAFT
P.O. Box 186, Grapeland TX 75844-0186. 936/687-4665. **Contact:** Human Resources. **World Wide Web address:** http://www.vulcraft.com. **Description:** Manufactures steel joists and steel decking. **Parent company:** Nucor Corporation is a steel and steel products manufacturer with mills in North and South Carolina, Nebraska, Texas, Utah, and Arizona. Products include hot-rolled and cold-finished steel shapes, girders, and beams.

Note: Because addresses and telephone numbers of smaller companies can change rapidly, we recommend you call each company to verify the information below before inquiring about job opportunities. Mass mailings are not recommended.

Additional small employers:

FABRICATED STRUCTURAL METAL PRODUCTS

AEP Span
PO Box 150449, Dallas TX 75315-0449. 214/827-1740.

Alpine Engineered Products
2820 N Great Southwest Pk,

Grand Prairie TX 75050-6472. 972/660-4422.

APW Enclosure Systems LP
3801 Regency Crest Dr, Garland TX 75041-6194. 214/343-1400.

Atrium Aluminum Products
2101 East Union Bower Rd, Irving TX 75061-8811. 972/438-4787.

Builder's Best Inc.
201 Broiles Dr, Jacksonville TX 75766. 903/586-8283.

Fabricated/Primary Metals and Products/149

Challenge Door of Texas Co.
902 Hillcrest Dr N, Sulphur Springs TX 75482-2084. 903/885-0660.

Chatham Enterprises Inc.
3233 W Kingsley Rd, Garland TX 75041-2205. 972/271-5525.

Danvid Company Inc.
1813 Kelly Blvd, Carrollton TX 75006-5511. 972/416-8140.

FWT Incorporated
PO Box 8597, Fort Worth TX 76124-0597. 817/255-3060.

Golden Manufacturing Inc.
322 S Barnes Dr, Garland TX 75042-7342. 972/272-6371.

H&S Manufacturing Co.
PO Box 1515, Rowlett TX 75030-1515. 972/475-4747.

Hirschfeld Steel Co. Inc.
PO Box 3695, Abilene TX 79604-3695. 915/676-1421.

Humanetics II Inc.
1700 Columbian Club Dr, Carrollton TX 75006-5517. 972/416-1304.

Imperial Fabricating Company
PO Box 616, Decatur TX 76234-0616. 940/627-1700.

Kaufman Steel
PO Box 269, Kaufman TX 75142-0269. 972/932-2157.

Lane Company
120 Fairview St, Arlington TX 76010-7221. 817/261-9116.

M&M Manufacturing Company
PO Box 9739, Fort Worth TX 76147-2739. 817/336-2311.

Magni-Fab Southwest Co.
PO Box 578, Howe TX 75459-0578. 903/532-5533.

Metal Buildings Supply Texas
PO Box 20, Grapevine TX 76099-0020. 817/488-8511.

Metl-Span Corp.
1497 N Kealy St, Lewisville TX 75057-2650. 972/221-6656.

Norris Cylinder Company
PO Box 7486, Longview TX 75607-7486. 903/757-7633.

Philips Inc.
PO Box 1240, Clarksville TX 75426-1240. 903/427-2256.

Reliant Building Products
3010 LBJ Fwy, Ste 400, Dallas TX 75234-7749. 972/919-1000.

Rooftop Systems Inc.
1811 Trinity Valley Dr, Carrollton TX 75006-6510. 972/247-7447.

SBS
PO Box 40409, Fort Worth TX 76140-0409. 817/572-4029.

Simpson Strong-Tie Company
1720 Couch Dr, McKinney TX 75069-7326. 972/542-0326.

Scott Manufacturing
PO Box 10232, Lubbock TX 79408-3232. 806/866-9591.

Special Products Manufacturing
2455 Interstate 30, Rockwall TX 75087-9715. 972/771-8851.

United States Aluminum Corporation
200 Singleton Rd, Waxahachie TX 75165-5012. 972/937-9651.

W&W Steel Company
PO Box 2219, Lubbock TX 79408-2219. 806/765-5781.

FABRICATED WIRE PRODUCTS

Cargill Steel & Wire
1915 John Connally Dr, Carrollton TX 75006-5420. 972/416-2822.

Meadow Steel
7000 Will Rogers Blvd, Fort Worth TX 76140-6010. 817/293-9641.

IRON AND STEEL FOUNDRIES

Columbus Metals Supply
PO Box 1043, Temple TX 76503-1043. 254/773-9055.

Consolidated Casting Corp.
1501 S I 45, Hutchins TX 75141. 972/225-7305.

EBAA Iron Inc.
PO Box 877, Eastland TX 76448-0877. 254/629-1737.

Frazier & Frazier Industries
PO Box 279, Coolidge TX 76635-0279. 254/786-2293.

Oil City Iron Works Inc.
PO Box 1560, Corsicana TX 75151-1560. 903/872-6571.

Smith Steel Casting Company
PO Box 969, Marshall TX 75671-0969. 903/935-5266.

METAL FORGINGS

Crosby Lebus Manufacturing
PO Box 271, Longview TX 75606-0271. 903/759-4424.

Trinity Forge Inc.
947 Trinity Drive, Mansfield TX 76063-2730. 817/473-1515.

NONFERROUS ROLLING AND DRAWING OF METALS

Airmax
PO Box 2704, Longview TX 75606-2704. 903/843-5666.

Alcoa Mill Products
300 Alumax Drive, Texarkana TX 75501-0209. 903/832-8471.

BICC General Corp.
910 10th Street, Suite A, Plano TX 75074-6802. 972/423-6565.

BICC General Corp.
PO Box 430, Scottsville TX 75688-0430. 903/938-8151.

Extruders Inc.
PO Box 1719, Wylie TX 75098-1719. 972/442-3535.

International Extrusion Corp.
202 Singleton Road, Waxahachie TX 75165-5012. 972/937-7032.

Snow Coil
PO Box 2704, Longview TX 75606-2704. 903/984-0838.

Western Extrusions Corporation
PO Box 810219, Dallas TX 75381-0219. 972/245-7515.

SCREW MACHINE PRODUCTS

Cisco Precision Components
PO Box 531290, Grand Prairie TX 75053-1290. 972/988-0454.

SMELTING AND REFINING OF NONFERROUS METALS

Alcoa
PO Box 472, Rockdale TX 76567-0472. 512/446-5811.

Alcoa Building Products
1601 Commerce Drive, Denison TX 75020-1905. 903/463-6095.

American Smelting & Refining Co.
PO Box 30200, Amarillo TX 79120-0200. 806/383-2201.

STEEL WIRE, NAILS, AND SPIKES

Sherman Wire
PO Box 729, Sherman TX 75091-0729. 903/893-0191.

STEEL WORKS, BLAST FURNACES, AND ROLLING MILLS

Basden Steel Corporation
PO Box 1061, Burleson TX 76097-1061. 817/295-6100.

Ennis Steel Industries Inc.
PO Box 1360, Ennis TX 75120-1360. 972/878-0400.

Lone Star Steel Company
PO Box 1000, Lone Star TX 75668-1000. 903/656-6521.

WHOLESALE METALS SERVICE CENTERS AND OFFICES

Davis Iron Works Inc.
PO Box 99, Hewitt TX 76643-0099. 254/666-1000.

O'Neal Steel Inc.
3730 Forest Ln, Garland TX 75042-6927. 972/487-6441.

Ryerson Steel
PO Box 655960, Dallas TX 75265-5960. 214/637-4710.

The Altair Company
PO Box 853900, Richardson TX 75085-3900. 972/231-5176.

For more information on career opportunities in the fabricated/primary metals and products industries:

Associations

ASM INTERNATIONAL: THE MATERIALS INFORMATION SOCIETY
9639 Kinsman Road, Materials Park OH 44073. 440/338-5151. World Wide Web address: http://www.asm-intl.org. Gathers, processes, and disseminates technical information to foster the understanding and application of engineered materials.

THE ALUMINUM ASSOCIATION, INC.
900 19th Street NW, Suite 300, Washington DC 20036. 202/862-5100. Fax: 202/862-5164. World Wide Web address: http://www.aluminum.org. A trade association for U.S. producers and recyclers of primary aluminum. Member companies operate over 200 plants throughout the nation.

AMERICAN FOUNDRYMEN'S SOCIETY
505 State Street, Des Plaines IL 60016. 847/824-0181. World Wide Web address: http://www.afsinc.org.

AMERICAN IRON AND STEEL INSTITUTE
1101 17th Street NW, Suite 1300, Washington DC 20036. 202/452-7100. Fax: 202/463-6573. World Wide Web address: http://www.steel.org.

AMERICAN WELDING SOCIETY
550 NW LeJeune Road, Miami FL 33126. 305/443-9353. World Wide Web address: http://www.aws.org.

ASSOCIATION OF IRON AND STEEL ENGINEERS
3 Gateway Center, Suite 1900, Pittsburgh PA 15222-1004. 412/281-6323. World Wide Web address: http://www.aise.org.

STEEL FOUNDERS' SOCIETY OF AMERICA
205 Park Street, Barrington IL 60010. 847/382-8240. World Wide Web address: http://www.sfsa.org.

Directories

DIRECTORY OF STEEL FOUNDRIES AND BUYER'S GUIDE
Steel Founders' Society of America, 455 State Street, Des Plaines IL 60016. 847/299-9160. World Wide Web address: http://www.sfsa.org.

Magazines

AMERICAN METAL MARKET
350 Hudson Street, New York NY 10014. 212/519-7550.

IRON & STEEL ENGINEER
Association of Iron and Steel Engineers, 3 Gateway Center, Suite 1900, Pittsburgh PA 15222-1004. 412/281-6323. World Wide Web address: http://www.aise.org.

MODERN METALS
Trend Publishing, One East Drive, Suite 401, Chicago IL 60611. 312/654-2300.

FINANCIAL SERVICES

You can expect to find the following types of companies in this chapter:
Consumer Finance and Credit Agencies • Investment Specialists • Mortgage Bankers and Loan Brokers • Security and Commodity Brokers, Dealers, and Exchanges

Some helpful information: Salary depends heavily on a broker's production and experience in the field. Average compensation for experienced brokers and financial managers ranges between $40,000 and $100,000 per year, depending on the size of the firm. Many successful brokers earn considerably more. The average salary for junior stock and research analysts can be as high as $70,000 if the candidate has an M.B.A. and a bit of experience, and senior analysts and managing directors can earn over $150,000 annually.

AMERICREDIT CORPORATION
801 Cherry Street, Suite 3900, Fort Worth TX 76102. 817/302-7000. **Fax:** 817/302-7934. **Contact:** Human Resources. **E-mail address:** hr@americredit.com. **World Wide Web address:** http://www.americredit.com. **Description:** A national consumer finance company specializing in the purchasing, securitizing, and servicing of automobile loans. **Benefits:** 401K; Dental Insurance; Life Insurance; Medical Insurance; Stock Options. **Corporate headquarters location:** This location. **Other U.S. locations:** Nationwide.

ASSOCIATES FIRST CAPITAL GROUP
dba THE ASSOCIATES
P.O. Box 660237, Dallas TX 75266-0237. 972/652-4000. **Fax:** 972/652-7420. **Contact:** Human Resources Department. **World Wide Web address:** http://www.theassociates.com. **Description:** A diversified financial services company providing various consumer finance, commercial leasing, credit card, insurance, and related services. **Common positions include:** Accountant/Auditor; Adjuster; Attorney; Budget Analyst; Buyer; Claim Representative; Clerical Supervisor; Computer Programmer; Credit Clerk and Authorizer; Credit Manager; Customer Service Representative; Department Manager; Employment Interviewer; Financial Analyst; Financial Services Sales Representative; Marketing Manager; Paralegal; Payroll Clerk; Purchasing Agent/Manager; Receptionist; Secretary; Securities Sales Representative; Systems Analyst; Technical Writer/Editor; Typist/Word Processor. **Educational backgrounds include:** Accounting; Business Administration; Communications; Computer Science; Economics; Finance; Marketing; Mathematics. **Benefits:** 401(k); Dental Insurance; Disability Coverage; Employee Discounts; Fitness Program; Life Insurance; Medical Insurance; Pension Plan; Profit Sharing; Savings Plan; Tuition Assistance. **Special programs:** Internships. **Corporate headquarters location:** This Location. **Other U.S. locations:** Nationwide. **Parent company:** Ford Motor Company. **Number of employees at this location:** 3,500. **Number of employees nationwide:** 17,000.

BANK ONE SECURITIES
1600 Redbud Boulevard, McKinney TX 75069. 972/647-1111. **Contact:** Human Resources. **World Wide Web address:** http://www.bankone.com. **Description:** Provides financial services in the areas of stocks, bonds, and mutual funds. **Parent company:** Bank One Corporation (Chicago IL).

BEAR, STEARNS & COMPANY, INC.
300 Crescent Court, Suite 200, Dallas TX 75201. 214/979-7900. **Contact:** Human Resources. **World Wide Web address:** http://www.bearstearns.com. **Description:** A leading worldwide investment banking, securities trading, and brokerage firm. The firm's business includes corporate finance, mergers and acquisitions, public finance, institutional equities, fixed income sales and trading, foreign exchange, future sales and trading, derivatives, and asset management. **Corporate headquarters location:** New York NY. **Other U.S. locations:** Nationwide. **Parent company:** The Bear Stearns Companies Inc. **Listed on:** New York Stock Exchange. **Annual sales/revenues:** More than $100 million. **Number of employees nationwide:** 7,800.

CENTEX CORPORATION
P.O. Box 199000, Dallas TX 75219. 214/981-5000. **Contact:** Human Resources. **World Wide Web address:** http://www.centex.com. **Description:** In addition to a wide range of contracting and construction services, Centex Corporation is a mortgage banker through its subsidiary, CTX

Mortgage Company. **Corporate headquarters location:** This Location. **Listed on:** New York Stock Exchange. **Annual sales/revenues:** More than $100 million.

CITY FINANCIAL
901 North Polk Street, Suite 309, De Soto TX 75115. 972/228-5688. **Contact:** Human Resources. **Description:** Specializes in the financing of small personal loans. **Corporate headquarters location:** Baltimore MD.

CONTINENTAL CREDIT CORPORATION
706 10th Street, Wichita Falls TX 76301. 940/766-3122. **Contact:** Human Resources. **Description:** Specializes in the financing of small personal loans.

CONTINENTAL CREDIT CORPORATION
217 North Kentucky Street, McKinney TX 75069. 972/542-2916. **Contact:** Human Resources. **Description:** Provides financing for small personal loans.

CREDIT CHOICE
300 North Travis Street, Sherman TX 75090. 903/892-1281. **Contact:** Human Resources. **Description:** Specializes in personal loans.

DAIN RAUSCHER
2711 North Haskell Avenue, Suite 2400, Dallas TX 75204. 214/989-1000. **Contact:** Human Resources. **World Wide Web address:** http://www.dainrauscher.com. **Description:** A financial consulting and securities firm. The company also provides real estate syndication and property investment services, as well as data processing services. **Corporate headquarters location:** Minneapolis MN. **Listed on:** American Stock Exchange; New York Stock Exchange.

DIAMOND SHAMROCK, INC.
P.O. Box 300, Amarillo TX 79105. 806/324-4601. **Contact:** Human Resources. **Description:** This location is the credit card center, servicing over 500,000 accounts. Overall, Diamond Shamrock, Inc. is a regional petroleum refining, transporting, and marketing company. The company operates 3,800 miles of pipeline, six terminals, and approximately 2,000 stores in eight southwestern states. Diamond Shamrock, Inc. also owns two refineries in Texas, and is engaged in crude oil refining; wholesale marketing; retail marketing; and the storing, manufacturing, and marketing of gas liquids, petrochemicals, and ammonia fertilizer. **Corporate headquarters location:** San Antonio TX.

A.G. EDWARDS & SONS
2305 Cedars Spring Road, Suite 300, Dallas TX 75201. 214/954-1999. **Contact:** Human Resources. **World Wide Web address:** http://www.agedwards.com. **Description:** An investment firm offering bonds, money market accounts, mutual funds, IRAs, annuities, estate planning, and related services. Founded in 1887. **Corporate headquarters location:** St. Louis MO.

FIDELITY INVESTMENTS
400 East Las Colinas Boulevard, Irving TX 75039. 972/584-7000. **Fax:** 972/584-7275. **Recorded jobline:** 972/584-6622. **Contact:** Human Resources. **World Wide Web address:** http://www.fidelity.com. **Description:** One of the nation's leading investment counseling and mutual fund/discount brokerage firms. **NOTE:** Entry-level positions and second and third shifts are offered. **Common positions include:** Account Representative; Accountant; Administrative Assistant; Computer Operator; Computer Programmer; Customer Service Representative; Database Manager; Financial Analyst; Management Trainee; MIS Specialist; Operations Manager; Project Manager; Sales Representative; Secretary; Software Engineer; Systems Analyst; Systems Manager; Telecommunications Manager. **Educational backgrounds include:** Business Administration; Computer Science; Finance. **Benefits:** 401(k); Dental Insurance; Disability Coverage; Employee Discounts; Financial Planning Assistance; Flexible Schedule; Life Insurance; Medical Insurance; Pension Plan; Profit Sharing; Tuition Assistance. **Special programs:** Internships. **Internship information:** The company has an MIS internship program. Applications must be submitted by March 1st via e-mail or in writing. **Corporate headquarters location:** Boston MA. **Other U.S. locations:** Nationwide. **Listed on:** Privately held.

THE FINANCE COMPANY
2201 South W.S. Young Drive, Suite 106C, Killeen TX 76543. 254/526-8390. **Contact:** Human Resources. **Description:** Engaged primarily in buying and servicing installment contracts originated by used car dealers. Most of The Finance Company's income comes from interest charged on contracts and from the discounts at which it purchases contracts. The company also

receives revenue from the commissions received on ancillary products, such as credit insurance, limited physical damage insurance, and product warranties offered by the company and underwritten by third-party vendors.

FIRST SOUTHWEST COMPANY
1700 Pacific Avenue, Suite 500, Dallas TX 75201-4652. 214/953-4000. **Fax:** 214/953-4050. **Contact:** Personnel. **World Wide Web address:** http://www.firstsw.com. **Description:** Offers a complete line of investment services including public, private, and corporate banking; funds management; trading of debt and equity securities; institutional sales; and clearing. **Corporate headquarters location:** This location. **Other U.S. locations:** Fayetteville AR; Miami FL; Orlando FL.

FIRST UNION SECURITIES INC.
500 North Akard Street, 1515 Lincoln Plaza, Dallas TX 75201. 214/740-3200. **Contact:** Human Resources. **World Wide Web address:** http://www.firstunionsec.com. **Description:** Provides a broad range of financial services including asset management, lending, trust services, and investment banking. **Parent company:** First Union Corporation. **Listed on:** New York Stock Exchange.

FORD MOTOR CREDIT COMPANY
P.O. Box 833830, Richardson TX 75083. 972/669-0022. **Contact:** Human Resources. **World Wide Web address:** http://www.fordcredit.com. **Description:** One of the largest providers of financial services in the United States, providing financing for all types of automobiles. **Parent company:** Ford Motor Company is engaged in the design, development, manufacture, and sale of cars, trucks, tractors, and related components and accessories. The company has manufacturing, assembly, and sales affiliates in 29 countries outside the United States. Ford Motor Company's two core businesses are the Automotive Group and the Financial Services Group (Ford Motor Credit, The Associates, USL Capital, and First Nationwide). Ford is also engaged in a number of other businesses including electronics, glass, electrical, and fuel-handling products; plastics; climate-control systems; automotive services and replacement parts; vehicle leasing and rental; and land development.

JEFFERIES & COMPANY, INC.
13355 Noel Road, Suite 1400, Dallas TX 75240. 972/701-3000. **Contact:** Human Resources. **World Wide Web address:** http://www.jefco.com. **Description:** Engaged in equity, convertible debt and taxable fixed income securities brokerage and trading, and corporate finance. Jefferies & Company is one of the leading national firms engaged in the distribution and trading of blocks of equity securities primarily in the third market. **Parent company:** Jefferies Group, Inc. is a holding company which, through its primary subsidiaries Jefferies & Company, Investment Technology Group, Inc., Jefferies International Limited, and Jefferies Pacific Limited, is engaged in securities brokerage and trading, corporate finance, and other financial services.

MERRILL LYNCH
P.O. Box 1720, Amarillo TX 79105-1720. 806/376-4861. **Contact:** Hiring Manager. **World Wide Web address:** http://www.ml.com. **Description:** Brokers in securities, option contracts, commodities, financial futures contracts, and insurance. The company also deals with corporate and municipal securities and investment banking. **NOTE:** Please call for specific information on where to mail a resume. **Other U.S. locations:** Nationwide.

PAINEWEBBER INC.
2200 Ross Avenue, Suite 5000, Dallas TX 75201-2777. 214/978-6000. **Contact:** Branch Manager. **World Wide Web address:** http://www.painewebber.com. **Description:** One of the world's largest investment services firms. PaineWebber assists corporations, governments, and individuals in meeting their long-term financial needs. The company also has operations in equity and fixed-income securities. **Corporate headquarters location:** New York NY.

SEI INVESTMENTS COMPANY
8585 North Stemmons Freeway, Suite 900, South Tower, Dallas TX 75247. 214/689-3200. **Contact:** Human Resources. **World Wide Web address:** http://www.seic.com. **Description:** An investment services firm that operates in two business markets: trust and banking, and fund/sponsor investments. The company also provides an online investment accounting system for trust departments. **Corporate headquarters location:** Wayne PA.

SOUTHWEST SECURITIES GROUP, INC.
1201 Elm Street, Suite 3500, Dallas TX 75270-2180. 214/651-1800. **Contact:** Human Resources. **World Wide Web address:** http://www.southwestsecurities.com. **Description:** A

holding company with subsidiaries engaged in providing securities brokerage, investment banking, and investment advisory services. Founded in 1972. **Corporate headquarters location:** This Location. **Other U.S. locations:** Chicago IL; Albuquerque NM; Santa Fe NM. **Subsidiaries include:** Brokers Transaction Services, Inc.; NorAm Investment Services, Inc. (also at this location); Southwest Securities, Inc. (also at this location); Sovereign Securities, Inc. (also at this location); SW Capital Corporation (also at this location); SWST Computer Corporation (also at this location); Westwood Management Corporation. **Listed on:** New York Stock Exchange. **Stock exchange symbol:** SWS. **President/CEO:** David Glatstein. **Annual sales/revenues:** More than $100 million. **Number of employees worldwide:** 550.

TRADESTAR INVESTMENTS
8201 Preston Road, Suite 270, Dallas TX 75225. **Toll-free phone:** 800/622-5484. **Contact:** Human Resources. **Description:** A regional brokerage firm.

WORLD FINANCE
1009 Gilmer Street, Sulphur Springs TX 75482. 903/885-0811. **Contact:** Human Resources. **Description:** Provides financing for small personal loans.

WORLD FINANCE
1708 NW 28th Street, Fort Worth TX 76106. 817/625-7281. **Contact:** Human Resources. **Description:** Provides financing for small personal loans.

Note: Because addresses and telephone numbers of smaller companies can change rapidly, we recommend you call each company to verify the information below before inquiring about job opportunities. Mass mailings are not recommended.

Additional small employers:

CREDIT AGENCIES AND INSTITUTIONS

Auto One Acceptance Corp.
5550 LBJ Fwy, Ste 901, Dallas TX 75240-1411. 972/661-1234.

Citicorp North America
1400 Trammel Crow Ct, Dallas TX 75201. 214/953-3800.

Federal Home Loan Bank
PO Box 619026, Dallas TX 75261-9026. 214/944-8100.

First USA Merchant Services
PO Box 650370, Dallas TX 75265-0370. 512/623-1000.

Nationscredit Consumer Corp.
PO Box 561688, Dallas TX 75356-1688. 972/506-5000.

Paymentech Inc.
PO Box 650370, Dallas TX 75265-0370. 214/849-3000.

Sallie Mae
777 N Twin Creek Dr, Killeen TX 76543-4236. 254/554-4500.

Transamerica Mortgage Co.
1201 Elm St, Ste 400, Dallas TX 75270-2121. 214/698-1500.

INVESTMENT ADVISORS

American Express Financial Advisors
3213 W Pioneer Pkwy, Arlington TX 76013-4620. 817/226-2583.

American Express Financial Advisors
801 E Campbell Rd, Ste 250, Richardson TX 75081-1887. 972/437-9311.

Basic Capital Management Inc.
10670 N Central Expy, Dallas TX 75231-2111. 214/692-4700.

CSC Financial Services
5525 LBJ Fwy, Dallas TX 75240-6241. 972/341-6988.

Hudson Advisors LLC
600 N Pearl St, Dallas TX 75201-2812. 214/754-8400.

LOAN BROKERS

Meritech Mortgage Services
PO Box 121549, Fort Worth TX 76121-1549. 817/665-7200.

MORTGAGE BANKERS

Accubanc Mortgage Corporation
PO Box 809089, Dallas TX 75380-9089. 972/458-9200.

Amresco Inc.
700 N Pearl Street, Ste 2400, Dallas TX 75201-2832. 214/953-7700.

Capstead Mortgage Corporation
2711 North Haskell Avenue, Dallas TX 75204-2943. 214/874-2323.

Countrywide Home Loans Inc.
5151 Belt Line Rd, Dallas TX 75240-7507. 972/980-4100.

CWF Home Loans
6400 Legacy Dr, Plano TX 75024-3609. 972/608-6000.

EMC Mortgage Corporation
PO Box 141358, Irving TX 75014-1358. 972/444-2800.

Fannie Mae
PO Box 650043, Dallas TX 75265-0043. 972/773-4663.

Firstplus Financial Inc.
1600 Viceroy Dr, Dallas TX 75235-2306. 214/599-6300.

Freddie Mac
12222 Merit Dr, Ste 700, Dallas TX 75251-3284. 972/702-2000.

Landmark Mortgage
2901 Dallas Pkwy, Ste 100, Plano TX 75093-5981. 972/398-7700.

New America Financial Inc.
3131 Turtle Creek Blvd, Dallas TX 75219-5426. 214/599-2300.

PMI Mortgage
1341 W Mockingbird Ln, Dallas TX 75247-6913. 214/267-5300.

Sebring Capital Corporation
4000 Intl Pkwy, Ste 3000, Carrollton TX 75007. 972/862-5000.

SECURITY BROKERS AND DEALERS

HMC/Morningstar LP
200 Crescent Ct, Ste 1600, Dallas TX 75201-1829. 214/740-7300.

Morgan Stanley Dean Witter
PO Box 809058, Dallas TX 75380-9058. 972/774-6500.

Salomon Smith Barney
200 Crescent Ct, Ste 1200, Dallas TX 75201-7837. 214/855-7900.

For more information on career opportunities in financial services:

Associations

ASSOCIATION FOR FINANCIAL PROFESSIONALS (AFP)
7315 Wisconsin Avenue, Suite 600-W, Bethesda MD 20814. 301/907-2862. World Wide Web address: http://www.AFPonline.org.

THE BOND MARKET ASSOCIATION
40 Broad Street, 12th Floor, New York NY 10004. 212/809-7000. Publishes an annual report and several newsletters.

FINANCIAL EXECUTIVES INSTITUTE
P.O. Box 1938, Morristown NJ 07962-1938. 973/898-4600. World Wide Web address: http://www.fei.org. Fee and membership required. Publishes biennial member directory. Provides member referral service.

INSTITUTE OF FINANCIAL EDUCATION
55 West Monroe Street, Suite 2800, Chicago IL 60603-5014. Toll-free phone: 800/946-0488. World Wide Web address: http://www.theinstitute.com.

NATIONAL ASSOCIATION OF BUSINESS ECONOMISTS
1233 20th Street NW, Suite 505, Washington DC 20036. 202/463-6223. World Wide Web address: http://www.nabe.com.

NATIONAL ASSOCIATION OF CREDIT MANAGEMENT
8840 Columbia 100 Parkway, Columbia MD 21045. 410/740-5560. World Wide Web address: http://www.nacm.org. Publishes a business credit magazine.

NATIONAL ASSOCIATION OF TAX PRACTITIONERS
720 Association Drive, Appleton WI 54914-1483. Toll-free phone: 800/558-3402. E-mail address: natp@natptax.com. World Wide Web address: http://www.natptax.com. A membership organization that offers newsletters and nationwide workshops.

SECURITIES INDUSTRY ASSOCIATION
120 Broadway, 35th Floor, New York NY 10271. 212/608-1500. Contact: Phil Williams, Membership. E-mail address: info@sia.com. World Wide Web address: http://www.sia.com.

Directories

DIRECTORY OF AMERICAN FINANCIAL INSTITUTIONS
Thomson Business Publications, 4709 West Golf Road, 6th Floor, Skokie IL 66076-1253. Sales: 800/321-3373.

MOODY'S BANK AND FINANCE MANUAL
Financial Information Services, 60 Madison Avenue, 6th Floor, New York NY 10010. Toll-free phone: 800/342-5647. World Wide Web address: http://www.moodys.com.

Magazines

BARRON'S: NATIONAL BUSINESS AND FINANCIAL WEEKLY
Barron's, 200 Liberty Street, New York NY 10281. 212/416-2700.

FINANCIAL PLANNING
Securities Data Publishing, 1290 Avenue of the Americas, 36th Floor, New York NY 10104. 212/765-5311.

FUTURES: THE MAGAZINE OF COMMODITIES AND OPTIONS
250 South Wacker Drive, Suite 1150, Chicago IL 60606. Toll-free phone: 888/898-5514. World Wide Web address: http://www.futuresmag.com.

Online Services

ACCOUNTING & FINANCE JOBS
World Wide Web address: http://www.accountingjobs.com. Provides national and international job listings and offers links to related sites.

BLOOMBERG.COM
World Wide Web address: http://www.bloomberg.com. Provides national and some international job postings.

FINANCIAL, ACCOUNTING, AND INSURANCE JOBS PAGE
World Wide Web address: http://www.nationjob.com/financial. This Website provides a list of financial, accounting, and insurance job openings.

JOBS IN CORPORATE FINANCE
World Wide Web address: http://www.cob.ohio-state.edu/dept/fin/jobs/corpfin.htm. Provides information and resources for jobseekers looking to work in the field of corporate finance.

NATIONAL BANKING NETWORK: RECRUITING FOR BANKING AND FINANCE
World Wide Web address: http://www.banking-financejobs.com. Offers a searchable database of job openings in financial services and banking. The database is searchable by region, keyword, and job specialty.

Visit our exciting job and career site at www.careercity.com

FOOD AND BEVERAGES/ AGRICULTURE

You can expect to find the following types of companies in this chapter:
Crop Services and Farm Supplies • Dairy Farms • Food Manufacturers/Processors and Agricultural Producers • Tobacco Products

Some helpful information: *Farmers and agricultural workers earn, on average, $20,000 - $25,000 annually (though employees of large commercial farms may earn more). Earnings tend to fluctuate according to the season and government subsidy. Food inspectors earn approximately $30,000 - $35,000 annually, while general manufacturing salaries tend to be lower ($25,000 per year is average).*

AMERICAN PRODUCTS COMPANY, INC.
10741 Miller Road, Dallas TX 75238. 214/343-4816. **Fax:** 214/343-9462. **Contact:** Human Resources Department. **Description:** Produces a complete range of bakery products. **Common positions include:** Manufacturer's/Wholesaler's Sales Rep.; Operations/Production Manager. **Benefits:** Credit Union; Dental Insurance; Life Insurance; Medical Insurance; Pension Plan. **Corporate headquarters location:** St. Paul MN. **Other U.S. locations:** Kingswood TX; San Antonio TX. **Parent company:** Best Brands, Inc.

ATTEBURY GRAIN INC.
P.O. Box 162688, Fort Worth TX 76161. 817/624-4171. **Contact:** Superintendent. **Description:** Produces and stores grain.

BEST MAID
P.O. Box 1809, Fort Worth TX 76101-1809. 817/335-5494. **Contact:** Personnel Manager. **Description:** Manufactures and distributes pickled fruits and vegetables.

BUNGE FOODS GROUP
P.O. Box 163289, Fort Worth TX 76161-3289. 817/625-2331. **Contact:** Personnel. **Description:** Produces shortening and margarine. **Common positions include:** Accountant/Auditor; Blue-Collar Worker Supervisor; Customer Service Representative; Department Manager; Electrical/Electronics Engineer; Food Scientist/Technologist; Industrial Engineer; Manufacturer's/Wholesaler's Sales Rep.; Mechanical Engineer. **Educational backgrounds include:** Engineering. **Corporate headquarters location:** St. Louis MO. **Parent company:** Bunge Corporation.

C&C BAKERY INC.
515 Jones Street, Fort Worth TX 76102. 817/212-2000. **Contact:** Rachel Gerragauch, Accounts Receivable Coordinator. **Description:** Produces Mexican-style foods including tortilla chips, corn-flour tortillas, and taco shells.

CACTUS FEEDERS INC.
P.O. Box 3050, Amarillo TX 79116. 806/373-2333. **Contact:** Kevin Hazelwood, Director of Employment Development. **Description:** Feeds and prepares cattle for delivery to meat packing plants and slaughterhouses.

CAMPBELL SOUP COMPANY
P.O. Box 9016, Paris TX 75461-9016. 903/737-2282. **Contact:** Human Resources. **World Wide Web address:** http://www.campbellsoup.com. **Description:** This location manufactures and cans soup. Overall, Campbell Soup Company manufactures commercial soups, juices, pickles, frozen foods, canned beans, canned pasta products, spaghetti sauces, and baked goods. The company's products are distributed worldwide. U.S. brand names include Campbell's, Vlasic, V8, Chunky, Home Cookin', Prego, Pepperidge Farm, LeMenu, and Swanson. European foods are sold under brand names such as Pleybin, Biscuits Delacre, Freshbake, Groko, Godiva, and Betis. **Common positions include:** Accountant/Auditor; Biological Scientist; Chemist; Electrical/Electronics Engineer; Electrician; Food Scientist/Technologist; Human Resources Manager; Industrial Production Manager; Management Trainee; Mechanical Engineer; Purchasing Agent/Manager; Registered Nurse. **Educational backgrounds include:** Accounting; Biology; Chemistry; Engineering; Technology. **Benefits:** 401(k); Dental Insurance; Disability Coverage; Employee Discounts; Life Insurance;

Food and Beverages/Agriculture/157

Medical Insurance; Pension Plan; Savings Plan; Tuition Assistance. **Corporate headquarters location:** Camden NJ. **Other U.S. locations:** Sacramento CA; Maxton NC; Napoleon OH. **Subsidiaries include:** Arnotts Biscuits of Australia. **Listed on:** New York Stock Exchange. **Number of employees at this location:** 1,600. **Number of employees nationwide:** 49,000.

CARGILL INC.
P.O. Box 79370, Saginaw TX 76179. 817/847-3400. **Contact:** Personnel. **World Wide Web address:** http://www.cargill.com. **Description:** This facility processes and distributes flour and grain. Overall, Cargill Inc., with its subsidiaries and its affiliates, is involved in nearly 50 individual lines of business. The company deals in commodity trading, handling, transporting, processing, and risk management. Cargill is a major trader of grains and oilseeds, as well as a marketer of other agricultural and non-agricultural commodities. As a transporter, the company moves bulk commodities using a network of rail and road systems, inland waterways, and ocean-going routes combining its own fleet and transportation services purchased from outside sources. Agricultural products include a wide variety of feed, seed, fertilizers, and other goods and services for producers worldwide. Cargill is also a leader in producing and marketing seed varieties and hybrids. Cargill Central Research aims to develop new agricultural products that address the needs of customers around the world. The company also provides financial and technical services. Cargill's Financial Markets Division supports Cargill and its subsidiaries with financial products and services including financial instrument trading, emerging markets instrument trading, value investing, and money management. Cargill's worldwide food processing businesses supply products ranging from basic ingredients used in food production to name brands. The company also operates a number of industrial businesses including the production of steel, industrial-grade starches, ethanol, and salt products. **Corporate headquarters location:** Minneapolis MN. **Listed on:** Privately held. **Number of employees worldwide:** 80,000.

COCA-COLA BOTTLING COMPANY OF NORTH TEXAS
P.O. Box 132008, Dallas TX 75313. 214/357-1781. **Physical address:** 6011 Lemmon Avenue, Dallas TX 75209. **Recorded jobline:** 214/902-2634. **Contact:** Human Resources. **Description:** This location houses executive offices. Overall, Coca-Cola Bottling Company of North Texas is a regional subsidiary of Coca-Cola Enterprises. **Common positions include:** Accountant/Auditor; Blue-Collar Worker Supervisor; Financial Analyst; Services Sales Representative. **Educational backgrounds include:** Accounting; Business Administration; Finance. **Benefits:** 401(k); Dental Insurance; Disability Coverage; Employee Discounts; Life Insurance; Medical Insurance; Pension Plan; Savings Plan; Tuition Assistance. **Special programs:** Internships. **Corporate headquarters location:** Atlanta GA. **Other U.S. locations:** Nationwide. **Parent company:** Coca-Cola Enterprises Inc. is in the liquid, nonalcoholic refreshment business, which includes traditional carbonated soft drinks, still and sparkling waters, juices, isotonics, and teas. The company operates in 38 states, the District of Columbia, the U.S. Virgin Islands, the Islands of Tortola and Grand Cayman, and the Netherlands. **Listed on:** New York Stock Exchange.

CONAGRA BEEF COMPANY
P.O. Box 524, Dumas TX 79029. 806/966-5103. **Contact:** Personnel. **Description:** A meat processing and packing facility.

DALLAS CITY PACKING INC.
3049 Morrell Avenue, Dallas TX 75203. 214/948-3901. **Contact:** David Myers, Personnel. **Description:** A meat packing plant.

DARLING INTERNATIONAL INC.
251 O'Connor Ridge Boulevard, Suite 300, Irving TX 75038. 972/717-0300. **Contact:** Mike Campbell, Director of Human Resources. **Description:** Processes animal by-products including fats and proteins. **Common positions include:** Accountant/Auditor; Agricultural Engineer; Computer Programmer; Management Trainee; Systems Analyst. **Educational backgrounds include:** Accounting; Business Administration; Computer Science; Marketing. **Benefits:** 401(k); Dental Insurance; Disability Coverage; Medical Insurance; Pension Plan; Tuition Assistance. **Corporate headquarters location:** This Location. **Listed on:** Privately held. **Number of employees at this location:** 50. **Number of employees nationwide:** 1,450.

DR. PEPPER/7-UP COMPANY
P.O. Box 869077, Plano TX 75086-9077. 972/673-7000. **Physical address:** 5301 Legacy Drive, Plano TX 75024. **Contact:** Personnel. **World Wide Web address:** http://www.drpepper.com. **Description:** This location houses the company's U.S. headquarters. Overall, Dr. Pepper/7-Up Company manufactures, markets, and distributes soft drink syrups,

concentrates, and extracts to bottlers. A food service segment distributes products to restaurants and convenience stores. The premier beverages segment makes Welch's carbonated drinks.

EARTHGRAINS COMPANY
3500 Manor Way, Dallas TX 75235. 214/357-1754. **Fax:** 214/350-1137. **Contact:** Jerry I. Riano, Director of Human Resources. **Description:** Produces a variety of baked goods. **Common positions include:** Accountant/Auditor; Blue-Collar Worker Supervisor; Branch Manager; Buyer; Chemist; Clerical Supervisor; Credit Manager; Electrician; Human Resources Manager; Industrial Production Manager; Operations/Production Manager. **Benefits:** Dental Insurance; Employee Discounts; Life Insurance; Medical Insurance; Pension Plan. **Corporate headquarters location:** St. Louis MO. **Listed on:** New York Stock Exchange. **Number of employees at this location:** 420.

FLEMING COMPANY
P.O. Box 469012, Garland TX 75046-9028. 972/840-4400. **Contact:** Personnel. **Description:** A wholesale distributor of a wide variety of groceries, meats, dairy and delicatessen products, frozen foods, fresh produce, and general merchandise.

FLOWERS BAKING COMPANY
3521 East Avenue E, Arlington TX 76011-5236. 817/640-8752. **Contact:** Personnel. **Description:** Bakes and distributes a variety of bread products.

FRIONA INDUSTRIES
P.O. Box 15568, Amarillo TX 79105-5568. 806/374-1811. **Fax:** 806/374-1324. **Contact:** Dave Delaney, General Manager. **Description:** Owns and operates cattle feed lots.

FRITO-LAY, INC.
P.O. Box 225458, Dallas TX 75222-5458. 817/861-1784. **Contact:** Staffing. **World Wide Web address:** http://www.fritolay.com. **Description:** A worldwide manufacturer and wholesaler of a wide range of snack products including Fritos Corn Chips, Doritos Tortilla Chips, Lays Potato Chips, Ruffles Potato Chips, Cracker Jack Popcorn, Chee-tos, and Smartfood Popcorn. **Common positions include:** Chemical Engineer; Computer Programmer; Electrical/Electronics Engineer; Financial Analyst; Mechanical Engineer; Purchasing Agent/Manager. **Educational backgrounds include:** Business Administration; Engineering; Finance. **Benefits:** 401(k); Dental Insurance; Disability Coverage; Employee Discounts; Life Insurance; Medical Insurance; Savings Plan; Tuition Assistance. **Special programs:** Internships. **Corporate headquarters location:** Plano TX. **Other U.S. locations:** Nationwide. **Parent company:** PepsiCo, Inc. (Purchase NY) consists of Frito-Lay Company, Pepsi-Cola Company, and Tropicana Products, Inc. **Listed on:** New York Stock Exchange. **Number of employees at this location:** 2,000. **Number of employees nationwide:** 29,000.

FRITO-LAY, INC.
P.O. Box 569100, Dallas TX 75356-9100. 972/579-2111. **Physical address:** 701 North Wildwood, Irving TX 75061. **Contact:** Human Resources. **World Wide Web address:** http://www.fritolay.com. **Description:** A worldwide manufacturer and wholesaler of a wide range of snack products including Fritos Corn Chips, Doritos Tortilla Chips, Lays Potato Chips, Ruffles Potato Chips, Cracker Jack Popcorn, Chee-tos, and Smartfood Popcorn. **Special programs:** Internships. **Corporate headquarters location:** Plano TX. **Other U.S. locations:** Nationwide. **Parent company:** PepsiCo, Inc. (Purchase NY) consists of Frito-Lay Company, Pepsi-Cola Company, and Tropicana Products, Inc. **Listed on:** New York Stock Exchange. **Number of employees nationwide:** 29,000.

FRITO-LAY, INC.
P.O. Box 660634, Dallas TX 75266-0634. 972/334-7000. **Physical address:** 7701 Legacy Drive, Plano TX 75024-4099. **Fax:** 972/334-2019. **Contact:** Staffing. **World Wide Web address:** http://www.fritolay.com. **Description:** A worldwide manufacturer and wholesaler of a wide range of snack products including Fritos Corn Chips, Lays Potato Chips, Doritos Tortilla Chips, Ruffles Potato Chips, Cracker Jack Popcorn, Chee-tos, and Smartfood Popcorn. **Special programs:** Internships. **Corporate headquarters location:** This Location. **Other U.S. locations:** Nationwide. **Parent company:** PepsiCo, Inc. (Purchase NY) consists of Frito-Lay Company, Pepsi-Cola Company, and Tropicana Products, Inc. **Listed on:** New York Stock Exchange. **Number of employees nationwide:** 29,000.

FRITO-LAY, INC.
3203 Avenue B, Lubbock TX 79404. 806/762-7700. **Contact:** Human Resources Director. **World Wide Web address:** http://www.fritolay.com. **Description:** A worldwide manufacturer

and wholesaler of a wide range of snack products including Fritos Corn Chips, Lays Potato Chips, Doritos Tortilla Chips, Ruffles Potato Chips, Chee-tos, and Smartfood Popcorn. **Corporate headquarters location:** Plano TX. **Other U.S. locations:** Nationwide. **Parent company:** PepsiCo, Inc. (Purchase NY) consists of Frito-Lay Company, Pepsi-Cola Company, and Tropicana Products, Inc. **Listed on:** New York Stock Exchange. **Number of employees nationwide:** 29,000.

HOLLY SUGAR CORPORATION
P.O. Drawer 1778, Hereford TX 79045. 806/364-2590. **Contact:** Human Resources Manager. **World Wide Web address:** http://www.hollysugar.com. **Description:** This location grows, harvests, and processes sugar beets, which are then used to produce granulated sugar. Sugar is packaged at this location year round. Overall, Holly Sugar produces sugar and sugar products such as beet pulp and molasses. **Parent company:** Imperial Holly Corporation (Sugar Land TX). **Number of employees at this location:** 350.

HORMEL FOODS CORPORATION
700 Highlander Boulevard, Suite 540, Arlington TX 76015. 817/465-4772. **Contact:** Office Manager. **World Wide Web address:** http://www.hormel.com. **Description:** One of the leading processors and marketers of branded, value-added meat and food products. Principal products of the company are branded, processed meat and food entrees which are sold fresh, frozen, cured, smoked, cooked, and canned. These include sausages, hams, franks, bacon, canned luncheon meats, shelf-stable microwaveable entrees, stews, chili, hash, meat spreads, and frozen processed products. The majority of the company's products are sold under the Hormel brand name. Other trademarks of the company include Farm Fresh, Little Sizzlers, Quick Meal, Kid's Kitchen, Chi-Chi's, House of Tsang, Mary Kitchen, Dinty Moore, Light & Lean, Chicken by George, Black Label, and SPAM. **Corporate headquarters location:** Austin MN. **Other U.S. locations:** CA; GA; IA; KS; NE; OK; WI. **International locations:** Australia; England; Japan; Korea; Panama; Philippines. **Subsidiaries include:** Dan's Prize, Inc.; Dubuque Foods; Farm Fresh Catfish Company; Jennie-O Foods. **Listed on:** New York Stock Exchange. **Number of employees nationwide:** 10,000.

IBP INC.
P.O. Box 30500, Amarillo TX 79187. 806/335-1531. **Contact:** Human Resources Department. **World Wide Web address:** http://www.ibpinc.com. **Description:** A slaughterhouse and meat packing plant.

INTERNATIONAL HOME FOODS INC.
P.O. Box 1867, Fort Worth TX 76101. 817/336-5581. **Contact:** Personnel. **Description:** Produces ranch-style beans.

KINGS LIQUOR INC.
6659 Camp Bowie Boulevard, Fort Worth TX 76116. 817/732-0661. **Contact:** Harry Labovitz, Personnel Director. **Description:** A liquor distiller, distributor, and retailer.

KRAFT FOODS, INC.
2340 Forest Lane, Garland TX 75042. 972/272-7511. **Contact:** Stan Mitchel, Human Resources Supervisor. **Description:** This location produces a variety of food products including barbecue sauce, mayonnaise, tartar sauce, Miracle Whip, Catalina dressing, and salad products. Overall, Kraft Foods, Inc. is one of the largest producers of packaged grocery products in North America. Major brands include Jell-O, Post, Kool-Aid, Crystal Light, Entenmann's, Miracle Whip, Stove Top, and Shake 'n Bake. Kraft markets a number of products under the Kraft brand name including natural and processed cheeses, and dry packaged dinners. The company's products are supplied to more than 100 countries worldwide. **Parent company:** Philip Morris Companies is a holding company whose principal wholly-owned subsidiaries are Philip Morris Inc. (Philip Morris U.S.A.), Philip Morris International Inc., Kraft Foods, Inc., Miller Brewing Company, and Philip Morris Capital Corporation. The Oscar Mayer unit markets processed meats, poultry, lunch combinations, and pickles under the Oscar Mayer, Louis Rich, Lunchables, and Claussen brand names. Kraft Foods Ingredients Corporation manufactures private-label and industrial food products for sale to other food processing companies. In the tobacco industry, Philip Morris U.S.A. and Philip Morris International together form one of the largest international cigarette operations in the world. U.S. brand names include Marlboro, Parliament, Virginia Slims, Benson & Hedges, and Merit. Miller Brewing Company brews beer under brand names including Molson Ice, Miller Genuine Draft, Miller High Life, Sharp's, Red Dog, Miller Lite, Icehouse, Foster's Lager, and Lowenbrau. Philip Morris Capital Corporation is engaged in financial services and real estate. **Listed on:** New York Stock Exchange. **Number of employees nationwide:** 155,000.

LEON'S TEXAS CUISINE
P.O. Box 1850, McKinney TX 75070-1850. 972/529-5050. **Fax:** 972/529-2244. **Contact:** Cindy Stephens, Human Resources Director. **E-mail address:** cindy@texascuisine.com. **World Wide Web address:** http://www.texascuisine.com. **Description:** Produces corndogs and other southwestern-style items which are sold and distributed to retail grocery stores nationwide. **NOTE:** Entry-level positions are offered. **Common positions include:** Administrative Assistant; Controller; Customer Service Representative; Electrician; Human Resources Manager; Marketing Manager; Mechanical Engineer; Purchasing Agent/Manager; Quality Control Supervisor; Sales Manager; Sales Representative; Secretary; Transportation/Traffic Specialist. **Benefits:** 401(k); Casual Dress - Fridays; Dental Insurance; Employee Discounts; Life Insurance; Medical Insurance; Sick Days (6 - 10); Vacation Days (1 - 5). **Corporate headquarters location:** This Location. **Subsidiaries include:** Shoreline Restaurant Corporation. **Number of employees at this location:** 150.

LIPTON FOODS
1729 Irving Boulevard, Dallas TX 75207. 214/741-5481. **Contact:** Personnel Supervisor. **Description:** A producer of margarine and nondairy spreads.

MILLER BREWING COMPANY
7001 South Freeway, Fort Worth TX 76134. 817/551-3200. **Contact:** Personnel Department. **World Wide Web address:** http://www.millerbrewing.com. **Description:** This location brews a variety of beer brands. Overall, Miller Brewing Company produces and distributes beer and other malt beverages. Principal beer brands include Miller Lite, Lite Ice, Miller Genuine Draft, Miller Genuine Draft Light, Miller High Life, Miller Reserve, Lowenbrau, Milwaukee's Best, Meister Brau, Red Dog, and Icehouse. Miller also produces Sharp's, a non-alcoholic beer. **Corporate headquarters location:** Milwaukee WI. **Subsidiaries include:** Jacob Leinenkugel Brewing Company (Chippewa Falls WI) brews Leinenkugel's Original Premium, Leinenkugel's Light, Leinie's Ice, Leinenkugel's Limited, Leinenkugel's Red Lager, and four seasonal beers: Leinenkugel's Genuine Bock, Leinenkugel's Honey Weiss, Leinenkugel's Autumn Gold, and Leinenkugel's Winter Lager. Molson Breweries U.S.A., Inc. (Reston VA) imports Molson beers from Canada, as well as Australia's Foster's Lager and many other brands. Miller is also majority owner of Celis Brewery Inc. (Austin TX). **Parent company:** Philip Morris Companies Inc. (New York).

MINUTE MAID COMPANY
8400 Imperial Drive, Waco TX 76712. **Contact:** Human Resources. **Description:** This location manufactures Powerade, Nestea, Fruitopia, and Minute Maid brand juice products. **NOTE:** This firm does not accept unsolicited resumes. Please only respond to advertised openings.

MRS. BAIRD'S BAKERIES
P.O. Box 417, Dallas TX 75221. 214/526-7201. **Contact:** Sharon King, Personnel Director. **Description:** Bakes bread and other goods. The company operates 11 facilities located throughout Texas. **Corporate headquarters location:** This Location.

NORTH CENTRAL DISTRIBUTORS INC.
2445 Santa Ana, Dallas TX 75228. 214/328-2821. **Contact:** Personnel. **Description:** A distributor of tobacco products.

OWENS COUNTRY SAUSAGE INC.
P.O. Box 830249, Richardson TX 75083. 972/235-7181. **Contact:** Human Resources. **World Wide Web address:** http://www.owensinc.com. **Description:** Produces sausage and other pork products. **Corporate headquarters location:** This Location.

PEPSI-COLA COMPANY
4532 Highway 67, Mesquite TX 75150. 214/324-8500. **Contact:** Human Resources. **World Wide Web address:** http://www.pepsico.com. **Description:** Bottles and distributes Pepsi-Cola beverages including the brand names Pepsi-Cola, Mountain Dew, Mug Root Beer, and Slice. **Parent company:** PepsiCo, Inc. (Purchase NY) consists of The Frito-Lay Company, Pepsi-Cola Company, and Tropicana Products, Inc.

PILGRIM'S PRIDE CORPORATION
P.O. Box 93, Pittsburg TX 75686-0093. 903/855-1000. **Contact:** Human Resources. **Description:** Produces chicken products and eggs for the restaurant, institutional, food service, grocery, and wholesale markets. The company's operations include breeding, hatching, growing, processing, packaging, and preparing poultry. Pilgrim's Pride Corporation also produces animal feeds and ingredients. The company is one of the largest producers of chicken

products in the United States and Mexico. The company's primary domestic distribution is handled through restaurants and retailers in central, southwestern, and western United States, and through the food service industry throughout the country. **Common positions include:** Accountant/Auditor; Blue-Collar Worker Supervisor; Computer Programmer; Credit Manager; Customer Service Representative; Food Scientist/Technologist; Human Resources Manager; Management Trainee; Manufacturer's/Wholesaler's Sales Rep. **Benefits:** 401(k); Daycare Assistance; Disability Coverage; ESOP; Life Insurance; Medical Insurance; Tuition Assistance. **Corporate headquarters location:** This Location. **Other U.S. locations:** AR; AZ; OK. **Listed on:** New York Stock Exchange.

PILGRIM'S PRIDE CORPORATION
P.O. Box 1656, Mount Pleasant TX 75455. 903/575-1000. **Contact:** Human Resources. **Description:** This location manufactures animal feeds and prepared foods, and operates two slaughterhouses. Overall, Pilgrim's Pride Corporation produces chicken products and eggs for the restaurant, institutional, food service, grocery, and wholesale markets. The company's operations include breeding, hatching, growing, processing, packaging, and preparing poultry. Pilgrim's Pride Corporation also produces animal feeds and ingredients. The company is one of the largest producers of chicken products in the United States and Mexico. The company's primary domestic distribution is handled through restaurants and retailers in central, southwestern, and western United States, and through the food service industry throughout the country. **Corporate headquarters location:** Pittsburg TX. **Other U.S. locations:** AR; AZ; OK. **Listed on:** New York Stock Exchange.

PLAINS COTTON COOPERATIVE ASSOCIATION
P.O. Box 2827, Lubbock TX 79408. 806/763-8011. **Physical address:** 3301 East 50th Street, Lubbock TX 79404. **Contact:** Mr. Lee Phenix, Personnel Manager. **World Wide Web address:** http://www.pcca.com. **Description:** A marketing firm that buys and sells cotton. Plains Cotton Cooperative Association acts as the liaison between buyers and sellers by marketing raw cotton worldwide. The company sells to cotton merchants and textile mills.

PLANTATION FOODS INC.
P.O. Box 20788, Waco TX 76702. 254/799-6211. **Contact:** Human Resources. **World Wide Web address:** http://www.plantation-foods.com. **Description:** A turkey processor.

THE QUAKER OATS COMPANY
13745 Jupiter Road, Dallas TX 75238. 214/340-0370. **Contact:** Personnel Director. **World Wide Web address:** http://www.quakeroats.com. **Description:** This location is a distribution center. Overall, The Quaker Oats Company is best known for Old Fashioned Quaker Oats. Other products include Van Camps' canned pork and beans, and specialty products such as Beanee Weenee canned beans and wieners. The Quaker Oats Company is also the primary producer of Gatorade, one of the leading sports beverages in the United States. **Corporate headquarters location:** Chicago IL. **Listed on:** New York Stock Exchange.

REPUBLIC BEVERAGE COMPANY
P.O. Box 536389, Grand Prairie TX 75053. 972/595-6100. **Contact:** Personnel Representative. **World Wide Web address:** http://www.republicbeverage.com. **Description:** A wine and alcohol wholesaler and distributor.

RODRIGUEZ FESTIVE FOODS
P.O. Box 4369, Fort Worth TX 76106. 817/624-2123. **Contact:** Pam Harris, Personnel Director. **Description:** Produces a line of frozen Mexican foods.

SCHEPPS DAIRY INC.
P.O. Box 279000, Dallas TX 75227. 214/824-8163. **Contact:** Personnel. **Description:** A producer and distributor of dairy products.

SEED RESOURCE, INC.
P.O. Box 326, Tulia TX 79088. 806/995-3882. **Contact:** Gary Regner, Manager. **Description:** Distributes forage seed including Sorghum Sudans, alfalfa, turf grass seed, and wheat seed. The company also produces wheat. **Parent company:** AgriBioTech, Inc. (ABT) is a specialized distributor of forage (hay crops) and turf grass seed. The forage and turf grass seed industry supplies seed to the forage and turf cash crop sectors. The company also distributes non-seed products including Bloatenz Plus, a liquid bloat preventative administered to the drinking water of cattle, permitting them to graze on alfalfa safely; and PDS-1000, marketed in conjunction with Bloatenz Plus, is a microprocessor-controlled precision dispensing system designed to dispense solutions into the drinking water of livestock at a preset dosage rate.

Other subsidiaries of ABT include Scott Seed Company; Hobart Seed Company; Halsey Seed Company; and Sphar & Company. Combined, these companies cover the following distribution territories: IN; KY; NM; NY; OK; OR; PA; TX; WA.

SIMEUS FOODS INTERNATIONAL
812 South Fifth Avenue, Mansfield TX 76063. 817/473-1562. **Contact:** Human Resources. **Description:** Manufactures food products for restaurants.

SOUTHWEST COCA-COLA BOTTLING COMPANY
6101 Avenue A, Lubbock TX 79404. 806/472-3200. **Contact:** Human Resources. **World Wide Web address:** http://www.coca-cola.com. **Description:** A bottling company packaging Coca-Cola, Barq's, and Dr. Pepper. **Parent company:** Coca-Cola Enterprises, Inc. is in the liquid non-alcoholic refreshment business, which includes traditional carbonated soft drinks, still and sparkling waters, juices, isotonics, and teas. The company operates in 38 states, the District of Columbia, the U.S. Virgin Islands, the Islands of Tortola and Grand Cayman, and the Netherlands. Coca-Cola Enterprises operates 268 facilities, approximately 24,000 vehicles, and over 860,000 vending machines, beverage dispensers, and coolers used to market, distribute, and produce the company's products.

SUIZA FOODS
2515 McKinney Avenue, Suite 1200, Dallas TX 75201. 214/303-3400. **Fax:** 214/303-3499. **Contact:** Human Resources. **World Wide Web address:** http://www.suizafoods.com. **Description:** Manufactures and distributes fresh milk and related dairy products, shelf-stable and refrigerated food and beverage products, frozen food products, coffee, and plastic containers. **Corporate headquarters location:** This Location. **Annual sales/revenues:** More than $100 million.

SUPREME BEEF PROCESSORS
5219 Second Avenue, Dallas TX 75210. 214/428-1761. **Contact:** Sandi Wheeler, Personnel Director. **Description:** A beef processing plant.

TYSON FOODS INC.
P.O. Box 648, Carthage TX 75633. 903/693-7101. **Contact:** Personnel. **Description:** This location is a poultry processing plant. Overall, Tyson Foods Inc. is one of the world's largest fully integrated producers, processors, and marketers of poultry-based food products. The company also produces other entrees and convenience food items. Products include Tyson Holly Farms Fresh Chicken, Weaver, Louis Kemp Crab, Lobster Delights, Healthy Portion, Beef Stir Fry, Crab Delights Stir Fry, Chicken Fried Rice Kits, Pork Chops with Cinnamon Apples, Salmon Grill Kits, Fish'n Chips Kits, and Rotisserie Chicken. **Common positions include:** Accountant/Auditor; Agricultural Engineer; Agricultural Scientist; Architect; Biological Scientist; Blue-Collar Worker Supervisor; Branch Manager; Budget Analyst; Clerical Supervisor; Computer Programmer; Construction and Building Inspector; Construction Contractor; Cost Estimator; Counselor; Customer Service Representative; Draftsperson; Electrical/Electronics Engineer; Electrician; Emergency Medical Technician; Financial Analyst; Food Scientist/Technologist; General Manager; Human Resources Manager; Industrial Engineer; Industrial Production Manager; Insurance Agent/Broker; Licensed Practical Nurse; Management Trainee; Mechanical Engineer; Purchasing Agent/Manager; Quality Control Supervisor; Registered Nurse; Software Engineer; Systems Analyst; Veterinarian. **Educational backgrounds include:** Accounting; Business Administration; Engineering. **Benefits:** 401(k); Dental Insurance; Disability Coverage; Employee Discounts; Life Insurance; Medical Insurance; Pension Plan; Profit Sharing; Savings Plan. **Special programs:** Internships. **Corporate headquarters location:** Springdale AR. **Listed on:** American Stock Exchange; NASDAQ; New York Stock Exchange. **Number of employees at this location:** 900.

U.S. FOODSERVICE
P.O. Box 28928, Dallas TX 75228. 214/388-7700. **Toll-free phone:** 800/827-7926. **Contact:** Human Resources. **World Wide Web address:** http://www.usfoodservice.com. **Description:** An institutional food production and distribution company with clients in the restaurant and health care industries. **Corporate headquarters location:** Columbia MD.

U.S. FOODSERVICE
P.O. Box 2804, Lubbock TX 79408. 806/747-5204. **Contact:** Human Resources. **World Wide Web address:** http://www.usfoodservice.com. **Description:** An institutional food production and distribution company with clients in the restaurant and health care industries. **Corporate headquarters location:** Columbia MD. **Other U.S. locations:** Nationwide.

Food and Beverages/Agriculture/163

U.S. FOODSERVICE
4202 Dan Morton Drive, Suite 106, Dallas TX 75236. 972/780-2310. **Fax:** 972/283-6123. **Contact:** Human Resources. **World Wide Web address:** http://www.usfoodservice.com. **Description:** An institutional food production and distribution company with clients in the restaurant and health care industries. **Corporate headquarters location:** Columbia MD. **Other U.S. locations:** Nationwide.

VANDERVOORT DAIRY
900 South Main Street, Fort Worth TX 76104. 817/332-7551. **Contact:** Personnel. **Description:** A large producer of ice cream and other dairy products.

Note: Because addresses and telephone numbers of smaller companies can change rapidly, we recommend you call each company to verify the information below before inquiring about job opportunities. Mass mailings are not recommended.

Additional small employers:

ALCOHOL WHOLESALE

Ben E. Keith Company
PO Box 36629, Dallas TX 75235-1629. 214/634-1500.

Budweiser Beer
7001 Will Rodgers Blvd, Fort Worth TX 76140. 817/568-4000.

Coors Distributing Company
3508 Avenue F, Arlington TX 76011-5225. 817/649-5626.

Coors Distributing Company
PO Box 162869, Fort Worth TX 76161-2869. 817/838-1600.

Glazers Wholesale Drug Company
PO Box 542648, Dallas TX 75354-2648. 214/357-1245.

Glazers Wholesale Drug Company
PO Box 809013, Dallas TX 75380-9013. 972/702-0900.

Miller Brewing Company
PO Box 3062, Fort Worth TX 76113-3062. 817/877-5960.

Miller Brewing Company
PO Box 566187, Dallas TX 75356-6187. 214/630-0777.

Oley Distributing Co. Inc.
PO Box 4389, Fort Worth TX 76164-0389. 817/625-8251.

United Distillers & Vinters North America
5080 Spectrum Dr, Addison TX 75001-4648. 972/716-7700.

BAKERY PRODUCTS

Dallas Baked Snacks
3433 Morse Dr, Dallas TX 75236-1119. 214/331-7084.

Earthgrains Baking Company
PO Box 9019, Paris TX 75461-9019. 903/785-6401.

Earthgrains Baking Company
1950 Texas Ave, Lubbock TX 79405-1117. 806/747-3244.

Earthgrains Refrigerated Dough Products
PO Box 110457, Carrollton TX 75011-0457. 972/416-4395.

Flowers Baking Co.
PO Box 360, Tyler TX 75710-0360. 903/595-2421.

Lil' Dutch Maid Cookies
5425 N 1st St, Abilene TX 79603-6424. 915/691-5425.

Mrs. Baird's Bakeries
PO Box 937, Fort Worth TX 76101-0937. 817/293-6230.

Mrs. Baird's Bakeries
PO Box 1496, Lubbock TX 79408-1496. 806/763-9304.

Mrs. Baird's Bakeries
PO Box 5086, Abilene TX 79608-5086. 915/692-3141.

Pioneer Frozen Foods Inc.
627 Big Stone Gap Rd, Duncanville TX 75137-2223. 972/298-4281.

BEEF

Oppliger Land & Cattle
PO Box 669, Farwell TX 79325-0669. 505/389-5321.

BEVERAGES

Abtex Beverage Corporation
650 Colonial Dr, Abilene TX 79603-3104. 915/673-7171.

Coca-Cola Bottling Company
8161 Moberly Ln, Dallas TX 75227-2322. 214/388-6000.

Coca-Cola Enterprises
PO Box 2008, Dallas TX 75221-2008. 214/902-2943.

Coca-Cola Enterprises Inc.
1512 Lamar St, Wichita Falls TX 76301-7035. 940/766-3251.

Coca-Cola Enterprises Inc.
PO Box 15050, Amarillo TX 79105-5050. 806/376-5421.

Coca-Cola Enterprises Inc.
PO Box 1441, Abilene TX 79604-1441. 915/672-3232.

Dr. Pepper-7Up Bottling
2304 Center Blvd, Irving TX 75062. 972/579-1024.

Dr. Pepper-7Up Bottling
PO Box 655024, Irving TX 75062. 972/445-0801.

Dr. Pepper-7Up Bottling
2817 Braswell Dr, Fort Worth TX 76111-1814. 817/926-8151.

North Texas Coca-Cola Company
PO Box 163349, Fort Worth TX 76161-3349. 817/232-8600.

Republic Beverages
10777 Shady Trail, Dallas TX 75220-1330. 214/358-1463.

Southwest Fountain Supply
PO Box 655024, Dallas TX 75265-5024. 972/721-8197.

CHIPS AND SNACKS

Frito-Lay Inc.
PO Drawer 4, Addison TX 75001-0004. 972/376-7405.

Frito-Lay Inc.
948 Avenue HE, Arlington TX 76011-7722. 817/649-3266.

Leo's Foods Inc.
3200 Northern Cross Blvd, Fort

Worth TX 76137-3601.
817/834-3200.

Mission Foods
1159 Cottonwood Ln, Irving TX
75038-6107. 972/232-5000.

Mission Foods
4000 Dan Morton Dr, Dallas TX
75236-1399. 972/709-1217.

Tom's Foods Inc.
3001 E State Highway 31,
Corsicana TX 75110-9048.
903/874-6553.

COFFEE

Folger's Coffee Company
PO Box 3125, Sherman TX
75091-3125. 903/893-5166.

CROP SERVICES

Birdsong Peanuts
PO Box 698, Gorman TX
76454-0698. 254/734-2266.

Dallas Fresh Express
2500 S Good Latimer Expy,
Dallas TX 75215-1419.
214/421-1947.

River Ranch Southwest Inc.
PO Box 803148, Dallas TX
75380-3148. 972/385-5900.

DAIRY FARMS

Oak Farms Dairies
PO Box 910067, Dallas TX
75391-0067. 214/941-0302.

RJ Smelley Company Inc.
4750 Cattlebaron Dr, Fort
Worth TX 76108-9351.
817/448-8520.

DAIRY PRODUCTS

Americana Foods Ltd.
3333 Dan Morton Dr, Dallas TX
75236-1066. 972/709-7100.

Bell Dairy Products Inc.
PO Box 2588, Lubbock TX
79408-2588. 806/765-8333.

Dairy Farmers of America Inc.
RR 1, Box 69, Stephenville TX
76401-9801. 254/968-6040.

Dannon Yogurt
1300 W Peter Smith St, Fort
Worth TX 76104-2116.
817/332-1264.

Morningstar Foods Inc.
300 Industrial Dr E, Sulphur
Springs TX 75482-4800.
903/885-0881.

Southwest Ice Cream
1220 N Tennessee St,
McKinney TX 75069-2116.
972/542-9391.

FARM SUPPLIES WHOLESALE

Texas Farm Bureau
PO Box 2689, Waco TX 76702-2689. 254/772-3030.

FLORICULTURE AND NURSERY PRODUCTS

Color Spot
2901 S 12th St, Waco TX
76706-3505. 254/752-9711.

Gandy's Nursery Inc.
PO Box 337, Ben Wheeler TX
75754-0337. 903/833-5869.

Mill Creek Farm Nursery
Rural Route 9, Box 9184,
Winnsboro TX 75494-9809.
903/857-2222.

Powell Farms
Rural Route 3, Box 1058, Troup
TX 75789-9160. 903/842-3123.

Rainbow Plant Sales
6115 Garcia Ln, Fort Worth TX
76140-7825. 817/572-0727.

FOOD CROPS

Valasico
PO Box 639, Hillsboro TX
76645-0639. 254/582-3458.

FOOD PREPARATIONS

Aramark School Nutrition Service
3501 Avenue G, Lubbock TX
79404-2339. 806/766-1225.

BBU Inc.
7301 South Fwy, Fort Worth TX
76134-4004. 817/615-3149.

CPC Baking Business
10701 Harry Hines Blvd, Dallas
TX 75220-1311. 214/956-2030.

Prime Deli Corporation
1301A Ridgeview St, Lewisville
TX 75057-6016. 972/219-7110.

FOOD WHOLESALE

Abilene Distribution Co. Inc.
PO Box 2938, Abilene TX
79604-2938. 915/692-1440.

Affiliated Foods Inc.
PO Box 30300, Amarillo TX
79120-0300. 806/372-3851.

Alliant Foodservice
PO Box 469024, Garland TX
75046-9024. 972/487-6200.

American Food Service
PO Box 802332, Dallas TX
75380-2332. 972/385-5800.

Ameriserve Food Distribution
1603 N Garden Ridge Blvd,
Lewisville TX 75077-2156.
972/318-0909.

Ameriserve Food Distribution
PO Box 9016, Addison TX
75001-9016. 972/364-2000.

Ameriserve Food Distribution
1201 John Burgess Dr, Fort
Worth TX 76140-6218.
817/551-5704.

Ameriserve Food Distribution
3901 Scientific Dr, Arlington TX
76014-4515. 817/557-0100.

Baby Fresh Produce Inc.
PO Box 7273, Dallas TX 75209-0273. 214/528-3237.

Ben E. Keith Company
PO Box 1588, Amarillo TX
79105-1588. 806/376-6257.

Ben E. Keith Company
PO Box 2628, Fort Worth TX
76113-2628. 817/332-9171.

Ben E. Keith Corporation
PO Box 270985, Dallas TX
75227-0985. 214/388-5411.

Borden Dairy
PO Box 1739, Dallas TX 75221-1739. 214/565-0332.

Coca-Cola Bottling Co.
3200 W Gentry Pkwy, Tyler TX
75702-1311. 903/597-9325.

Country Fresh Meats
PO Box 910, Plainview TX
79073-0910. 806/293-5181.

Dynamic Foods
1001 E 33rd St, Lubbock TX
79404-1816. 806/747-2777.

Fleming
PO Box 1530, Lubbock TX
79408-1530. 806/747-3674.

Freedman Food Services
PO Box 561067, Dallas TX
75356-1067. 214/331-8712.

Fresh Advantage
PO Box 535789, Grand Prairie
TX 75053-5789. 972/988-8553.

Frito-Lay Inc.
4701 Pylon St, Fort Worth TX
76106-1919. 817/625-7007.

Frosty Acres
4151 Blue Mound Rd, Fort
Worth TX 76106-1926.
817/625-8921.

General Mills Inc.
106 Clove Ln, Euless TX 76039-7905. 817/858-0920.

Gourmet Award Foods
5101 Highland Place Dr, Dallas TX 75236-1449. 972/298-2957.

Intraco Inc.
8201 Preston Rd, Ste 520, Dallas TX 75225-6210. 214/750-7345.

John Soules Foods Inc.
PO Box 4579, Tyler TX 75712-4579. 903/592-9800.

Lance Inc.
2735 Villa Creek Dr, Dallas TX 75234-7454. 972/247-1433.

Loggins Meat Co. Inc.
PO Box 164, Tyler TX 75710-0164. 903/595-1011.

Lone Star Donut Co.
PO Box 225979, Dallas TX 75222-5979. 214/946-2185.

Marketing Management Inc.
4717 Fletcher Ave, Fort Worth TX 76107-6826. 817/731-4176.

Martin-Brower Company LLC
1350 Avenue S, Ste 110, Grand Prairie TX 75050-1256. 972/647-2666.

MBM
7301 Trinity Blvd, Fort Worth TX 76118-6930. 817/595-4794.

McLane Company Inc.
PO Box 6115, Temple TX 76503-6115. 254/771-7500.

McLane High Plains Inc.
PO Box 5550, Lubbock TX 79408-5550. 806/766-2900.

Multifoods
5225 Investment Dr, Dallas TX 75236-1422. 972/709-3001.

Nabisco Inc.
PO Box 3988, Lubbock TX 79452-3988. 806/745-5675.

Ozarka Spring Water
2000 Westridge Dr, Irving TX 75038-2900. 972/580-0997.

Ozarka Spring Water
4250 Cambridge Rd, Fort Worth TX 76155-2626. 817/354-2900.

Pritchard Brokerage Co.
PO Box 12010, Lubbock TX 79452-2010. 806/745-7404.

Proficient Food Company
7301 Trinity Blvd, Fort Worth TX 76118-6930. 817/589-9679.

R&R Acquisition Inc.
100 Anderson Pl, Olney TX 76374-2322. 940/564-3549.

Resource Project Management
2324 Gateway Dr, Irving TX 75063-2725. 972/550-1822.

Sygma Network Inc.
2301 Centennial Dr, Arlington TX 76011-6606. 817/633-5701.

Sysco Food Services of Dallas
PO Box 814229, Dallas TX 75381-4229. 972/233-9700.

Texas-American Foodservice
1301 Northpark Dr, Fort Worth TX 76102-1003. 817/332-5807.

Tree of Life
105 Bluebonnet, Cleburne TX 76031-8956. 817/641-6678.

Watson Foodservice
PO Box 5910, Lubbock TX 79408-5910. 806/747-2678.

GRAIN MILL PRODUCTS

Morrison Milling Company
PO Box 719, Denton TX 76202-0719. 940/387-6111.

Pillsbury Company
3400 Texoma Dr, Denison TX 75020-1006. 903/465-5650.

GRAINS

Pioneer Hi-Bred International
Rural Rte 3, Box 125, Plainview TX 79072-9305. 806/293-5231.

HOGS

Premium Standard Farms
HC 3 Box 322, Dalhart TX 79022-9408. 806/377-6289.

Texas Farms Co.
4200 S Main St, Perryton TX 79070-9700. 806/435-5935.

MEAT AND POULTRY PROCESSING

Beltex Corporation
3801 N Grove St, Fort Worth TX 76106-3720. 817/624-1136.

Decker Food Co.
PO Box 472587, Garland TX 75047-2587. 972/278-6192.

Doskocil Food Service Co.
6350 Browning Ct, Fort Worth TX 76180-6013. 817/656-5507.

Kennedy Sausage Co.
PO Box 235, Weatherford TX 76086-0235. 817/594-3316.

Quality Sausage Company Ltd.
1925 Lone Star Dr, Dallas TX 75212-6302. 214/634-3400.

Rosani Foods
4114 Mint Way, Dallas TX 75237-1606. 214/331-1010.

Sadler's Smokehouse
PO Box 1088, Henderson TX 75653-1088. 903/657-5581.

Wright Brand Foods Inc.
PO Box 1779, Vernon TX 76385-1779. 940/553-1811.

PREPARED FEEDS AND INGREDIENTS FOR ANIMALS

Gore's Inc.
PO Box 1000, Comanche TX 76442-1000. 915/356-3045.

Hi-Pro
PO Box 519, Friona TX 79035-0519. 806/250-2791.

Martindale Feed Mill
PO Box 249, Valley View TX 76272-0249. 940/726-3276.

Vigortone Agricultural Products Inc.
1050 Vigortone Blvd, Weatherford TX 76086-1554. 817/594-9628.

PRESERVED FRUITS AND VEGETABLES

Delta Dailyfood
2200 Redbud Blvd, McKinney TX 75069-8217. 972/562-5300.

KPR Foods
7401 Will Rogers Blvd, Fort Worth TX 76140-6019. 817/568-9000.

Mrs. Crockett's Kitchens Inc.
8821G Forum Way, Fort Worth TX 76140-5009. 817/293-8164.

Ocean Spray Cranberries Inc.
419 Industrial Dr E, Sulphur Springs TX 75482-4883. 903/885-8676.

State Fair Foods Inc.
PO Box 561223, Dallas TX 75356-1223. 817/427-7700.

SUGAR AND CONFECTIONERY PRODUCTS

Kennedy Gourmet
1313 Energy Dr, Kilgore TX 75662-5539. 903/986-3227.

M&M Mars
PO Box 7955, Waco TX 76714-7955. 254/776-2100.

Russell Stover Candies Inc.
PO Box 613, Corsicana TX 75151-0613. 903/874-0008.

For more information on career opportunities in the food, beverage, and agriculture industries:

Associations

AMERICAN ASSOCIATION OF CEREAL CHEMISTS (AACC)
3340 Pilot Knob Road, St. Paul MN 55121. 651/454-7250. E-mail address: aacc@scisoc.org. World Wide Web address: http://www.scisoc.org/aacc. Dedicated to the dissemination of technical information and continuing education in cereal science.

AMERICAN CROP PROTECTION ASSOCIATION
1156 15th Street NW, Suite 400, Washington DC 20005. 202/296-1585. World Wide Web address: http://www.acpa.org.

AMERICAN FROZEN FOOD INSTITUTE
2000 Corporate Ridge, Suite 1000, McLean VA 22102. 703/821-0770. Fax: 703/821-1350. World Wide Web address: http://www.affi.org. A national trade association representing the interests of the frozen food industry.

AMERICAN SOCIETY OF AGRICULTURAL ENGINEERS
2950 Niles Road, St. Joseph MI 49085-9659. 616/429-0300. World Wide Web address: http://www.asae.org.

AMERICAN SOCIETY OF BREWING CHEMISTS
3340 Pilot Knob Road, St. Paul MN 55121-2097. 651/454-7250. World Wide Web address: http://www.scisoc.org/asbc. Founded in 1934 to improve and bring uniformity to the brewing industry on a technical level.

CIES - THE FOOD BUSINESS FORUM
5549 Lee Highway, Arlington VA 22207. 703/534-8880. World Wide Web address: http://www.ciesnet.com. A global food business network. Membership is on a company basis. Members learn how to manage their businesses more effectively and gain access to information and contacts.

DAIRY MANAGEMENT, INC.
10255 West Higgins Road, Suite 900, Rosemont IL 60018. 847/803-2000. World Wide Web address: http://www.dairyinfo.com. A federation of state and regional dairy promotion organizations that develop and execute effective programs to increase consumer demand for U.S.-produced milk and dairy products.

INTERNATIONAL ASSOCIATION OF FOOD INDUSTRY SUPPLIERS
1451 Dolley Madison Boulevard, McLean VA 22101. 703/761-2600. Fax: 703/761-4334. Contact: Dorothy Brady. E-mail address: info@iafis.org. World Wide Web address: http://www.iafis.org. A trade association whose members are suppliers to the food, dairy, liquid processing, and related industries.

MASTER BREWERS ASSOCIATION OF THE AMERICAS (MBAA)
2421 North Mayfair Road, Suite 310, Wauwatosa WI 53226. 414/774-8558. World Wide Web address: http://www.mbaa.com. Promotes, advances, improves, and protects the professional interests of brew and malt house production and technical personnel. Disseminates technical and practical information.

NATIONAL BEER WHOLESALERS' ASSOCIATION
1100 South Washington Street, Alexandria VA 22314-4494. 703/683-4300. Fax: 703/683-8965. Contact: Karen Craig.

NATIONAL CATTLEMEN'S BEEF ASSOCIATION
P.O. Box 3469, Englewood CO 80155. 303/694-0305. World Wide Web address: http://www.beef.org. Operates to improve the economic, political, and social interests of the U.S. cattle industry.

NATIONAL FOOD PROCESSORS ASSOCIATION
1350 I Street NW, Suite 300, Washington DC 20005. 202/639-5900. World Wide Web address: http://www.nfpa-food.org.

NATIONAL SOFT DRINK ASSOCIATION
1101 16th Street NW, Washington DC 20036. 202/463-6732. World Wide Web address: http://www.nsda.org.

USA POULTRY AND EGG EXPORT COUNCIL
2300 West Park Place Boulevard, Suite 100, Stone Mountain GA 30087. 770/413-0006. Fax: 770/413-0007. E-mail address: info@usapeec.org. World Wide Web address: http://www.usapeec.org.

Directories

THOMAS FOOD INDUSTRY REGISTER
Thomas Publishing Company, Five Penn Plaza, New York NY 10001. 212/290-7341. World Wide Web address: http://www.tfir.com.

Magazines

FROZEN FOOD AGE
Bill Communications, 355 Park Avenue South, New York NY 10010-1789. 212/592-6200.

Online Servises

CHEFJOBSNETWORK
World Wide Web address: http://www.chefjobsnetwork.com. Posts job openings for chefs, pastry chefs, bakers, sous chefs, restaurant managers, and other foodservice positions. Members can register, free of charge, for a job search agent.

For information about the JobBank List Service visit www.adamsjobbank.com

GOVERNMENT

You can expect to find the following types of agencies in:
Courts • Executive, Legislative, and General Government • Public
(Firefighters, Military, Police) • United States Postal Service

Some helpful information: *Salaries for public agency workers vary largely by city. The average starting salary for police officers and firefighters is $25,000 and experienced officers can exceed $40,000 per year. Sheriffs in large metropolitan areas can earn considerably more. Postal clerks generally earn between $25,000 and $40,000 annually, and mail handlers between $20,000 and $35,000. Enlisted military personnel receive between $25,000 and $35,000 per year, in addition to a monthly allowance for those living off-base. A highly-ranked officer may receive a base salary of over $40,000.*

ABILENE, CITY OF
P.O. Box 60, Abilene TX 79604. 915/676-6347. **Recorded jobline:** 915/676-6247. **Contact:** Human Resources. **World Wide Web address:** http://www.abilenetx.com. **Description:** Administrative offices for the city of Abilene.

DALLAS, CITY OF
1500 Marilla Street, Room 6AN, Dallas TX 75201. 214/670-3120. **Fax:** 214/670-5855. **Recorded jobline:** 214/670-5908. **Contact:** Human Resources. **E-mail address:** dalcvsrv@airmail.net. **World Wide Web address:** http://www.ci.dallas.tx.us. **Description:** Administrative offices for the city of Dallas. This location also hires seasonally. **NOTE:** Second and third shifts are offered. **Common positions include:** Account Representative; Accountant; Administrative Assistant; Administrative Manager; Architect; Attorney; Auditor; Blue-Collar Worker Supervisor; Budget Analyst; Buyer; Chemist; Chief Financial Officer; Child Care Center Director; Civil Engineer; Claim Representative; Clerical Supervisor; Computer Operator; Computer Programmer; Computer Technician; Controller; Counselor; Customer Service Representative; Design Engineer; Draftsperson; Electrician; Environmental Engineer; Finance Director; Fund Manager; General Manager; Human Resources Manager; Landscape Architect; Librarian; Marketing Manager; Mechanical Engineer; Paralegal; Purchasing Agent/Manager; Radio/TV Announcer/Broadcaster; Secretary; Social Worker; Telecommunications Manager; Typist/Word Processor; Veterinarian. **Educational backgrounds include:** Accounting; Business Administration; Communications; Computer Science; Economics; Finance; HTML; MBA; Microsoft Office; Microsoft Word; Novell; Software Development; Software Tech. Support. **Benefits:** 401(k); Casual Dress - Fridays; Dental Insurance; Disability Coverage; Life Insurance; Medical Insurance; Pension Plan; Public Transit Available; Sick Days (11 +); Tuition Assistance; Vacation Days (1 - 5). **Special programs:** Summer Jobs; Training. **Corporate headquarters location:** This Location. **Information Systems Manager:** Dan McFarland. **Purchasing Manager:** Lea Davis. **Number of employees at this location:** 14,000. **Number of projected hires for 2000 - 2001 at this location:** 1,500.

DALLAS POLICE DEPARTMENT
2014 Main Street, Room 201, Dallas TX 75201. 214/670-4407. **Toll-free phone:** 800/527-2948. **Fax:** 214/670-5093. **Contact:** Seth Terao, Recruiting Sergeant. **World Wide Web address:** http://www.ci.dallas.tx.us/dpd. **Description:** Provides law enforcement services. **NOTE:** The department requires 45 semester hours from an accredited college or university with an average of "C" or better. Entry-level positions and second and third shifts are offered. **Common positions include:** Police/Law Enforcement Officer. **Benefits:** 401(k); Dental Insurance; Disability Coverage; Life Insurance; Medical Insurance; Pension Plan; Savings Plan; Tuition Assistance; Vision Insurance.

DALLAS PUBLIC WORKS AND TRANSPORTATION DEPARTMENT
320 East Jefferson Boulevard, Room 208, Dallas TX 75203. 214/948-4200. **Contact:** Human Resources Division. **Description:** Administrative offices for the Dallas Public Works and Transportation department. **Common positions include:** Budget Analyst; Property and Real Estate Manager; Surveyor. **Educational backgrounds include:** Business Administration; Engineering; Finance. **Benefits:** 401(k); Disability Coverage; Life Insurance; Medical Insurance; Pension Plan; Tuition Assistance. **Operations at this facility include:** Administration; Divisional Headquarters. **Number of employees at this location:** 775.

CITY OF DALLAS SHERIFF'S DEPARTMENT
133 North Industrial Boulevard, Dallas TX 75207. 214/749-8641. **Contact:** Human Resources Department. **Description:** Enforces justice, public order, and safety for the city of Dallas.

PLANO, CITY OF
1520 Avenue K, Plano TX 75074. 972/941-7000. **Contact:** Human Resources. **World Wide Web address:** http://www.ci.plano.tx.us. **Description:** Administrative offices for the city of Plano.

ROBERTSON UNIT
12071 FM 3522, Abilene TX 79601. 915/548-9035. **Contact:** Joyce Lee, Human Resources Manager. **Description:** A maximum security prison.

TEXAS DEPARTMENT OF TRANSPORTATION
P.O. Box 150, Abilene TX 79604. 915/676-6800. **Toll-free phone:** 800/893-6817. **Recorded jobline:** 800/893-6848. **Contact:** Employment. **World Wide Web address:** http://www.dot.state.tx.us. **Description:** Designs, builds, and maintains roads and highways throughout the state of Texas.

U.S. ENVIRONMENTAL PROTECTION AGENCY (EPA)
1445 Ross Avenue, Dallas TX 75202-2733. 214/665-6444. **Contact:** Personnel Services. **World Wide Web address:** http://www.epa.gov. **Description:** As part of Region 6, this location of the EPA serves Arkansas, Louisiana, New Mexico, Oklahoma, and Texas. The EPA is dedicated to improving and preserving the quality of the environment, both national and global, and protecting human health and the productivity of natural resources. The agency is committed to ensuring that federal environmental laws are implemented and enforced effectively; U.S. policy, both foreign and domestic, fosters the integration of economic development and environmental protection so that economic growth can be sustained over the long term; and public and private decisions affecting energy, transportation, agriculture, industry, international trade, and natural resources fully integrate considerations of environmental quality. Founded in 1970. **Benefits:** Daycare Assistance; Fitness Program; Flextime Plan; Incentive Plan; Leave Time; Retirement Plan. **Special programs:** Internships. **Corporate headquarters location:** Washington DC. **Other U.S. locations:** San Francisco CA; Denver CO; Atlanta GA; Chicago IL; Kansas City KS; Boston MA; New York NY; Philadelphia PA; Seattle WA. **Number of employees nationwide:** 19,000.

WACO, CITY OF
P.O. Box 2570, Waco TX 76702-2570. 254/750-5600. **Contact:** Personnel. **Description:** Administrative offices for the city of Waco.

Note: Because addresses and telephone numbers of smaller companies can change rapidly, we recommend you call each company to verify the information below before inquiring about job opportunities. Mass mailings are not recommended.

Additional small employers:

ADMINISTRATION OF ECONOMIC PROGRAMS

Department of Economic Development
320 E Jefferson Blvd, Dallas TX 75203-2668. 214/958-4331.

United States Census Bureau
6303 Harry Hines Blvd, Dallas TX 75235-5270. 214/640-4400.

ADMINISTRATION OF PUBLIC HEALTH PROGRAMS

Department of Public Health
1109 Kemper St, Lubbock TX 79403-2523. 806/744-3577.

Department of Public Health
2408 S 37th St, Temple TX 76504-7168. 254/778-6744.

Department of Public Health
PO Box 2501, Tyler TX 75710-2501. 903/595-3585.

Food & Drug Administration
3310 Live Oak St, Dallas TX 75204-6153. 214/655-5315.

ADMINISTRATION OF SOCIAL AND MANPOWER PROGRAMS

Department of Health & Human Services
3303 Mineola Hwy, Tyler TX 75702-1126. 903/595-4841.

Social Security Administration
1301 Young St, Rm 640, Dallas TX 75202-5433. 214/767-0853.

Texas Department of Human Services
1540 New York Ave, Arlington TX 76010-4722. 817/461-8273.

COURTS

Dallas County District Court
600 Commerce St, Dallas TX 75202-4616. 214/653-7131.

Tarrant County Court
401 W Belknap St, Fort Worth TX 76102-1913. 817/884-1400.

EXECUTIVE, LEGISLATIVE, AND GENERAL GOVERNMENT

Addison, Town of
PO Box 144, Addison TX 75001-0144. 972/450-7000.

Amarillo, City of
PO Box 1971, Amarillo TX
79186-0001. 806/378-3011.

Bell, County of
PO Box 768, Belton TX 76513-
0768. 254/939-3521.

Borger, City of
PO Box 5250, Borger TX
79008-5250. 806/273-0900.

Bowie, County of
PO Box 248, New Boston TX
75570-0248. 903/628-2571.

Breckenridge, City of
105 N Rose Ave, Breckenridge
TX 76424-3531. 254/559-8287.

Carrollton, City of
PO Box 110535, Carrollton TX
75011-0535. 972/466-3000.

Cass, County of
PO Box 152, Linden TX 75563-
0152. 903/756-5067.

Cedar Hill, City of
PO Box 96, Cedar Hill TX
75106-0096. 972/291-5100.

Cleburne, City of
PO Box 657, Cleburne TX
76033-0657. 817/645-0901.

Collin, County of
210 S McDonald St, McKinney
TX 75069-5655. 972/548-4100.

Coppell, City of
PO Box 478, Coppell TX
75019-0478. 972/462-0022.

Copperas Cove, City of
PO Drawer 1449, Copperas
Cove TX 76522. 254/547-4221.

Corsicana, City of
200 N 12th St, Corsicana TX
75110-4616. 903/654-4800.

Dawson, County of
PO Box 1268, Lamesa TX
79331-1268. 806/872-7474.

Denton, City of
215 E McKinney St, Denton TX
76201-4229. 940/566-8200.

Duncanville, City of
PO Box 380280, Duncanville
TX 75138-0280. 972/780-5000.

Euless, City of
201 N Ector Dr, Euless TX
76039-3543. 817/685-1400.

Flower Mound, Town of
2121 Cross Timbers Rd, Flower
Mound TX 75028-2602.
972/539-6006.

Gaines, County of
PO Box 847, Seminole TX
79360-0847. 915/758-5411.

Gainesville, City of
200 S Rusk St, Gainesville TX
76240-4851. 940/668-4500.

Gregg, County of
101 E Methvin St, Longview TX
75601-7200. 903/236-8420.

Haltom, City of
PO Box 14246, Fort Worth TX
76117-0246. 817/222-7786.

Hunt, County of
PO Box 1097, Greenville TX
75403-1097. 903/408-4120.

Hutchinson, County of
PO Box 850, Stinnett TX 79083-
0850. 806/878-2428.

Irving, City of
PO Box 152288, Irving TX
75015-2288. 972/721-2600.

Johnson, County of
2 N Main St, Cleburne TX
76031-5573. 817/556-6300.

Lamesa, City of
601 S 1st St, Lamesa TX 79331-
6247. 806/872-2124.

Lancaster, City of
PO Box 940, Lancaster TX
75146-0940. 972/227-2111.

Longview, City of
PO Box 1952, Longview TX
75606-1952. 903/237-1000.

Mesquite, City of
PO Box 850137, Mesquite TX
75185-0137. 972/288-7711.

Pampa, City of
PO Box 2499, Pampa TX
79066-2499. 806/669-5750.

Paris, City of
PO Box 9037, Paris TX 75461-
9037. 903/785-7511.

Plainview, City of
901 Broadway St, Plainview TX
79072-7317. 806/296-1100.

Richardson, City of
PO Box 830309, Richardson TX
75083-0309. 972/238-4100.

Rusk, County of
115 N Main St, Rm 103,
Henderson TX 75652-3147.
903/657-0307.

Stephenville, City of
298 W Washington St,
Stephenville TX 76401-4257.
254/965-7887.

Sulphur Springs, City of
125 Davis St S, Sulphur Springs
TX 75482-2717. 903/885-7541.

Tarrant, County of
100 W Weatherford St, Fort
Worth TX 76102-2115.
817/884-1111.

Taylor, County of
300 Oak St, Abilene TX 79602-
1581. 915/674-1235.

Temple, City of
PO Box 987, Temple TX 76503-
0987. 254/298-5631.

Texarkana, City of
PO Box 1967, Texarkana TX
75504-1967. 903/798-3900.

Titus, County of
100 W 1st St, Ste 200, Mount
Pleasant TX 75455-4443.
903/572-8723.

Weatherford, City of
PO Box 255, Weatherford TX
76086-0255. 817/598-4221.

Wichita, County of
900 7th St, Wichita Falls TX
76301-2402. 940/766-8100.

Yoakum, County of
PO Box 516, Plains TX 79355-
0516. 806/456-2422.

**FINANCE, TAXATION, AND
MONETARY POLICY BODIES**

United States Customs Service
PO Box 619050, Dallas TX
75261-9050. 972/574-2170.

**HOUSING AND URBAN
DEVELOPMENT PROGRAMS**

**LAND, MINERAL, AND
WILDLIFE CONSERVATION
PROGRAMS**

**Department of Parks &
Recreation**
PO Box 152288, Irving TX
75015-2288. 972/721-2501.

**Department of Parks &
Recreation**
PO Box 469002, Garland TX
75046-9002. 972/205-3589.

**Department of Parks &
Recreation**
4700 Drexel Dr, Dallas TX
75205-3107. 214/521-4161.

**PUBLIC ENVIRONMENTAL
QUALITY PROGRAMS**

Brazos River Authority
PO Box 7555, Waco TX 76714-
7555. 254/776-1441.

170/The Dallas Fort-Worth JobBank

Central Waste Water Treatment Plant
1020 Sargent Rd, Dallas TX 75203-4656. 214/670-7425.

Trinity River Authority
PO Box 531196, Grand Prairie TX 75053-1196. 972/262-5186.

PUBLIC ORDER AND SAFETY

Abilene Police Department
PO Box 174, Abilene TX 79604-0174. 915/676-6600.

Amarillo Fire Department
400 S Van Buren St, Amarillo TX 79101-1354. 806/378-3061.

Bedford Police Department
2000 Forest Ridge Dr, Bedford TX 76021-5713. 817/952-2100.

Belton Sheriff's Department
PO Box 749, Belton TX 76513-0749. 254/933-5400.

Bowie County Correctional Facility
105 W Front St, Texarkana TX 75501-5610. 903/798-3515.

Bureau of Prisons
PO Box 27066, Fort Worth TX 76127-0066. 817/782-4048.

Buster Cole State Jail
3801 Silo Rd, Bonham TX 75418-5817. 903/583-1100.

Carrollton Fire Department
PO Box 11035, Carrollton TX 75011. 972/446-3600.

Collin County Sheriff's Department
4300 Community Blvd, McKinney TX 75070-2402. 972/547-5100.

Cottrell House
7929 Military Pkwy, Dallas TX 75227-4016. 214/388-5498.

Crockett State School
PO Box 411, Crockett TX 75835-0411. 936/544-5917.

Dalhart Prison
PO Box 4000, Dalhart TX 79022-9340. 806/249-8655.

Dallas Fire Department
2014 Main St, Ste 401, Dallas TX 75201-4439. 214/670-4319.

Dallas Police Department
3723 Valley View Ln, Dallas TX 75244-4902. 972/484-3620.

Denton County Correctional Facility
127 N Woodrow Ln, Denton TX 76205-6325. 940/898-5700.

Denton County Sheriff's Department
127 N Woodrow Ln, Denton TX 76205-6325. 940/898-5600.

Department of Public Safety
PO Box 420, Lubbock TX 79408-0420. 806/747-4491.

Department of Public Safety
PO Box 130040, Tyler TX 75713-0040. 903/566-9740.

Drug Enforcement Administration
1880 Regal Row, Dallas TX 75235-2302. 214/640-0801.

Eastham Unit
PO Box 16, Lovelady TX 75851-0016. 936/636-7321.

Ellis County Sheriff's Department
300 S Jackson St, Waxahachie TX 75165-3750. 972/923-4900.

Euless Police Department
205 N Ector Dr, Euless TX 76039-3543. 817/685-1555.

Federal Bureau of Investigation
1801 N Lamar St, Ste 300, Dallas TX 75202-1739. 214/720-2200.

Ferguson Unit
Rural Route 2, Box 20, Midway TX 75852-9711. 936/348-3751.

Formby State Jail
970 Country Road AA, Plainview TX 79072. 806/296-2448.

Fort Worth Police Department
2500 N Houston St, Fort Worth TX 76106-7147. 817/871-6454.

Gainesville State School
4701 East Farm Road 678, Gainesville TX 76240. 940/665-0701.

Garland Fire Department
1019 Austin St, Garland TX 75040-5608. 972/205-2275.

Garland Police Department
217 N 5th St, Garland TX 75040-6313. 972/205-2010.

Hughes Prison
Rural Route 2, Box 44, Gatesville TX 76597-0001. 254/865-6663.

Hutchins State Jail
1500 E Langdon Rd, Dallas TX 75241-7136. 972/225-1304.

Hutto Correctional Center
PO Box 1063, Taylor TX 76574-1063. 512/352-3502.

Immigration & Naturalization Service
7701 N Stemmons Fwy, Dallas TX 75247-4232. 214/767-7020.

Irving Police Department
PO Box 152288, Irving TX 75015-2288. 972/721-2650.

Irving Youth Commission
6095 Lobby Box, Ste 503, Irving TX 75062. 972/554-1904.

Johnson County Sheriff's Department
1800 Ridgemar Dr, Cleburne TX 76031-1353. 817/556-6060.

Killeen Fire Department
201 S 28th St, Killeen TX 76541-6220. 254/634-3131.

Killeen Police Department
402 N 2nd St, Killeen TX 76541-5207. 254/526-8311.

Lewisville Police Department
184 N Valley Pkwy, Lewisville TX 75067-3429. 972/219-3600.

Limestone County Detention Center
910 N Tyus St, Groesbeck TX 76642-2011. 254/729-8615.

Longview City Police Department
PO Box 1952, Longview TX 75606-1952. 903/237-1199.

Lubbock County Jail
2025 N Akron Ave, Lubbock TX 79415-1118. 806/775-1800.

Marlin Youth Commission
PO Box 5000, Marlin TX 76661-5000. 254/883-9223.

McLennan County Jail
3201 E Highway 6, Waco TX 76705-3734. 254/757-2555.

Murray Unit
1916 Highway 36 Bypass North, Gatesville TX 76596-0001. 254/865-2000.

Neal Prison
9055 Spur 591, Amarillo TX 79107-9696. 806/383-1175.

Plano Police Department
909 14th St, Plano TX 75074-5803. 972/424-5678.

Richardson Police Department
PO Box 831078, Richardson TX 75083-1078. 972/238-3800.

Smith County Sheriff's Department
PO Box 90, Tyler TX 75710-0090. 903/535-0911.

Government/171

Tarrant County Juvenile Probation
2701 Kimbo Rd, Fort Worth TX 76111-3007. 817/838-4600.

Telford Prison
PO Box 9200, New Boston TX 75570-9200. 903/628-3171.

Texas Highway Patrol
1617 E Crest Dr, Waco TX 76705-1555. 254/867-4628.

Texas Youth Commission
400 Haynes Rd, Roanoke TX 76262-6155. 817/491-9387.

Tulia Unit
HC 3, Box 5C, Tulia TX 79088-9512. 806/995-4109.

Tyler Police Department
711 W Ferguson St, Tyler TX 75702-5612. 903/531-1015.

Tyler Youth Commission
3800 Paluxy Dr, Ste 415, Tyler TX 75703-1662. 903/561-8312.

US Attorney's Office
1100 Commerce St, Fl 3, Dallas TX 75242-1027. 214/659-8600.

US Attorney's Office
801 Cherry St, Ste 1700, Fort Worth TX 76102-6817. 817/252-5200.

Wallace Unit
1681 S Farm Rd, Colorado City TX 79512. 915/728-2162.

REGULATORY ADMINISTRATION OF TRANSPORTATION

Department of Public Works
PO Box 860358, Plano TX 75086-0358. 972/964-4130.

Department of Public Works
PO Box 8005, Dallas TX 75205. 214/987-5402.

Fort Worth Highway Department
PO Box 6868, Fort Worth TX 76115-0868. 817/292-6510.

Office of Flight Standards
2601 Meacham Blvd, Fort Worth TX 76137-4204. 817/222-5200.

Texas Department of Transportation
PO Box 771, Lubbock TX 79408-0771. 806/745-4411.

Texas Department of Transportation
100 S Loop Dr, Bellmead TX 76704-2858. 254/867-2854.

Texas Department of Transportation
PO Box 900, Childress TX 79201-0900. 940/937-2571.

Texas Highway Department
PO Box 2708, Amarillo TX 79105-2708. 806/356-3200.

Waco Highway Department
PO Box 1010, Waco TX 76703-1010. 254/867-2700.

REGULATORY ADMINISTRATION OF UTILITIES

Department of Energy
PO Box 30020, Amarillo TX 79120-0020. 806/477-3000.

UNITED STATES POSTAL SERVICE

United States Postal Service
194 Civic Cir, Lewisville TX 75067-3424. 972/221-2755.

United States Postal Service
401 Dallas Fort Worth Tpke, Dallas TX 75260. 214/760-4401.

United States Postal Service
2211 N Robison Rd, Texarkana TX 75501-3248. 903/838-9537.

United States Postal Service
2336 S Mobberly Ave, Longview TX 75602-3864. 903/753-7644.

United States Postal Service
232 SW Johnson Ave, Burleson TX 76028-9998. 817/295-8158.

United States Postal Service
825 Precinct Line Rd, Hurst TX 76053-9998. 817/284-3464.

United States Postal Service
101 Belmont St, Fort Worth TX 76179-9998. 817/232-0808.

United States Postal Service
6640 Abrams Rd, Dallas TX 75231-7210. 214/553-8894.

United States Postal Service
6051 Davis Blvd, Fort Worth TX 76180-9998. 817/281-1831.

United States Postal Service
PO Box 9998, Wichita Falls TX 76301. 940/766-6247.

United States Postal Service
PO Box 9998, Temple TX 76501. 254/773-0792.

United States Postal Service
470 W State Highway 6, Waco TX 76712-3973. 254/757-6516.

United States Postal Service
2901 W Parker Rd, Plano TX 75023-8019. 972/964-7743.

United States Postal Service
PO Box 9998, Greenville TX 75401. 903/455-5363.

United States Postal Service
341 Pine St, Abilene TX 79601-5943. 915/673-6485.

For more information about career opportunities in the government:

Associations

INTERNATIONAL ASSOCIATION OF CHIEFS OF POLICE
515 North Washington Street, Alexandria VA 22314. 703/836-6767. World Wide Web address: http://www.theiacp.org. Represents police chiefs and other law enforcement officials.

NATIONAL CRIME PREVENTION COUNCIL
One Prospect Street, Amsterdam NY 12010. 518/842-4388. Fax: 800/995-5121.

Directories

GOVERNMENT JOB FINDER
Planning/Communications, 7215 Oak Avenue, River Forest IL 60305. 708/366-5200. World Wide Web address: http://www.jobfindersonline.com. Provides information on several online and offline services.

Government Agency Websites

U.S. DEPARTMENT OF AGRICULTURE
World Wide Web address: http://www.usda.gov.

U.S. DEPARTMENT OF COMMERCE
World Wide Web address: http://www.doc.gov.

U.S. DEPARTMENT OF EDUCATION
World Wide Web address: http://www.ed.gov.

U.S. DEPARTMENT OF ENERGY
World Wide Web address: http://www.hr.doe.gov.

U.S. DEPARTMENT OF HEALTH AND HUMAN SERVICES
World Wide Web address: http://www.hhs.gov.

U.S. DEPARTMENT OF HOUSING & URBAN DEVELOPMENT
World Wide Web address: http://www.hud.gov.

U.S. DEPARTMENT OF INTERIOR
World Wide Web address: http://www.doi.gov.

U.S. DEPARTMENT OF JUSTICE
World Wide Web address: http://www.usdoj.gov.

U.S. DEPARTMENT OF LABOR
World Wide Web address: http://www.dol.gov.

U.S. DEPARTMENT OF STATE
World Wide Web address: http://www.state.gov.

U.S. DEPARTMENT OF TREASURY
World Wide Web address: http://www.ustreas.gov.

U.S. DEPARTMENT OF VETERAN AFFAIRS
World Wide Web address: http://www.va.gov.

U.S. POSTAL SERVICE
World Wide Web address: http://www.usps.gov.

Online Services

CORPORATE GRAY ONLINE
World Wide Web address: http://www.greentogray.com. This site is offered as a career resource for military personnel leaving the service.

FEDERAL JOB OPPORTUNITIES BOARD
World Wide Web address: ftp://fjob.opm.gov/jobs. A Telnet bulletin board that allows jobseekers to search for government jobs by department, agency, or state. The site includes information about the application process as well as opportunities overseas.

FEDERAL JOBS CENTRAL
World Wide Web address: http://www.fedjobs.com. Federal Jobs Central offers a subscription to a 64-page biweekly publication containing over 3,500 job listings; online listings that are accessible by occupation, salary, and location; and a service that pairs you with the job you are seeking. This site's services require a fee.

FEDERAL JOBS DIGEST
World Wide Web address: http://www.jobsfed.com. An excellent site for jobseekers hoping to work for the government, this site offers over 3,500 opportunities in fields such as engineering, medical, administration, management, secretarial, computer services, and law enforcement. The site also includes employment links to government agencies. For a fee, you can let *FJD*'s matching service perform the job hunt for you.

FEDWORLD
World Wide Web address: http://www.fedworld.gov. Provides a wealth of information on all aspects of the government. Besides an employment link to federal job opportunities, this site also offers access to all government agencies and many government documents.

FEDERAL JOBS.NET (CAREER CENTER)
World Wide Web address: http://www.federaljobs.net. Provides approximately 2 million federal and 850,000 postal job openings in all 50 states, which can be searched by agency. The site also gives details on how to apply for federal jobs, and strategies to help you win the job.

4GOVERNMENT.COM
World Wide Web address: http://www.4government.com. Provides a wealth of information on governments (federal, state, and local) as well as international entities like the World Bank, World Trade Organization, World Court, NATO, and the European Union.

GOVSPOT.COM
World Wide Web address: http://www.govspot.com. Simplifies the search for the best government Websites, documents, facts and figures, news, and political information.

GOVTJOBS.COM
World Wide Web address: http://www.govtjobs.com. Provides a list of job openings in the public sector. Jobs can be searched by pre-determined categories. This site also includes information on executive search firms, and lists joblines to call for the latest government openings.

JOBS IN GOVERNMENT
World Wide Web address: http://www.jobsingovernment.com. E-mail address: info@jobsingovernment.com. A helpful search engine for individuals seeking employment in government or the public sector. The site offers profile based searches for thousands of open positions, the ability to post and e-mail resumes, and information about current topics and resources in government.

LAW ENFORCEMENT EMPLOYMENT
World Wide Web address: http://www.officer.com/jobs.htm. This site does not provide job listings, rather it provides links to law enforcement sites that do list openings and related job information.

USA JOBS
World Wide Web address: http://www.usajobs.opm.gov. This site, run by the Office of Personnel Management, lets you select a job by experience level, labor type, agency, or job title. The site allows you to fill out an online application, and provides general information on applying for work within the government.

HEALTH CARE: SERVICES, EQUIPMENT, AND PRODUCTS

You can expect to find the following types of companies in this chapter:
Dental Labs and Equipment • Home Health Care Agencies • Hospitals and Medical Centers • Medical Equipment Manufacturers and Wholesalers • Offices and Clinics of Health Practitioners • Residential Treatment Centers/Nursing Homes • Veterinary Services

Some helpful information: Doctors earn an average of $150,000 annually, with large variations depending on specialty (general practitioners may earn less than $100,000, while some surgeons earn as much as $250,000 or more). Dentists' salaries average about $120,000. Entry level workers in residential care and home health care generally earn approximately $22,000 - $25,000, with more experienced workers and managerial staff earning $30,000 - $40,000. Experienced veterinarians in private practice earn an average of $50,000 per year. Jobs in hospital administration generally begin at $50,000 for qualified candidates. Nurses' starting salaries range from $25,000 - $35,000, and experienced practitioners can earn as much as $60,000 annually (the average range, however, is $30,000 - $45,000).

ALL SAINTS EPISCOPAL HOSPITAL
1400 Eighth Avenue, Fort Worth TX 76104. 817/926-2544. **Contact:** Human Resources. **Description:** A hospital with over 500 beds.

AUGUST HEALTH CARE
4320 West 19th Street, Lubbock TX 79407. 806/795-7147. **Contact:** Personnel Department. **Description:** A nursing home. **Number of employees at this location:** 100.

BAPTIST ST. ANTHONY HEALTH SYSTEM
1600 Wallace Boulevard, Amarillo TX 79106. 806/376-4411. **Contact:** Human Resources Manager. **E-mail address:** hr@bsahs.com. **World Wide Web address:** http://www.bsahs.com. **Description:** A 255-bed general hospital. Baptist St. Anthony Health System also offers home health services, a hospice program, a rehabilitation/skilled nursing facility, a senior health center and a sports and occupational health center. **Common positions include:** Clerical Supervisor; Food Service Manager; Laboratory Technician; Nurse; Physical Therapist; Registered Nurse; Retail Manager; Secretary. **Number of employees at this location:** 1,000.

BAYLOR MEDICAL CENTER AT GARLAND
2300 Marie Curie Boulevard, Garland TX 75042. 972/487-5000. **Contact:** Human Resources. **World Wide Web address:** http://www.bhcs.com/garland. **Description:** A 206-bed acute care medical and surgical center. **Parent company:** Baylor Health Care System.

BAYLOR MEDICAL CENTER IRVING
1901 North MacArthur Boulevard, Irving TX 75061. 972/579-8100. **Contact:** Human Resources Department. **World Wide Web address:** http://www.bhcs.com/irving. **Description:** A 288-bed, full-service hospital. The hospital employs specialists in the areas of oncology, neurosurgery, neurology, cardiology, and gastroenterology. **Parent company:** Baylor Health Care System.

BAYLOR/RICHARDSON MEDICAL CENTER
401 West Campbell Road, Richardson TX 75080. 972/498-4737. **Fax:** 972/498-4978. **Recorded jobline:** 972/498-4875. **Contact:** Employment Coordinator. **World Wide Web address:** http://www.bhcs.com/richardson. **Description:** A 174-bed, nonprofit medical, surgical, and psychiatric hospital. Hospital specialties include family medicine, pediatrics, women's services, oncology, emergency medicine, cardiology, radiology and imaging, chemical dependency, skilled nursing, respiratory therapy, and home health. **Common positions include:** Accountant/Auditor; Buyer; Claim Representative; Clerical Supervisor; Collector; Counselor; Dietician/Nutritionist; EEG Technologist; EKG Technician; Human Resources Manager; Licensed Practical Nurse; Medical Records Technician; Nuclear Medicine

Technologist; Occupational Therapist; Pharmacist; Physical Therapist; Public Relations Specialist; Purchasing Agent/Manager; Radiological Technologist; Recreational Therapist; Registered Nurse; Respiratory Therapist; Social Worker; Speech-Language Pathologist; Surgical Technician; Systems Analyst. **Educational backgrounds include:** Health Care; M.D./Medicine. **Benefits:** 401(k); 403(b); Dental Insurance; Disability Coverage; Employee Discounts; Life Insurance; Medical Insurance; Tuition Assistance. **Parent company:** Baylor Health Care System. **Operations at this facility include:** Administration. **Number of employees at this location:** 680.

BAYLOR SENIOR HEALTH CENTER
820 West Arapaho Road, Suite 200, Richardson TX 75080. 972/498-4500. **Contact:** Human Resources. **World Wide Web address:** http://www.bhcs.com. **Description:** An outpatient facility that offers comprehensive primary care services to senior citizens. Founded in 1995. **Parent company:** Baylor Health Care System.

BAYLOR UNIVERSITY MEDICAL CENTER
3500 Gaston Avenue, Dallas TX 75246. 214/820-2525. **Contact:** Personnel. **World Wide Web address:** http://www.bhcs.com. **Description:** A full-service, tertiary, teaching hospital. As the flagship hospital of the Baylor Health Care System, Baylor University Medical Center is comprised of five connecting hospitals. Hospital departments include family medicine, neurosurgery, obstetrics, gynecology, oncology, opthamology, orthopaedic surgery, pathology, pediatrics, physical rehabilitation, plastic and reconstructive surgery, psychiatry, radiology, urology, and anesthesiology. **NOTE:** This location also houses the Baylor Rehabilitation Center. The center can be reached at 214/826-7030. **Common positions include:** Accountant/Auditor; Biomedical Engineer; Blue-Collar Worker Supervisor; Buyer; Computer Programmer; Customer Service Representative; Dietician/Nutritionist; General Manager; Human Resources Manager; Marketing Specialist; Purchasing Agent/Manager; Technical Writer/Editor. **Educational backgrounds include:** Accounting; Biology; Business Administration; Chemistry; Communications; Computer Science; Engineering; Finance; Liberal Arts; Marketing. **Benefits:** Daycare Assistance; Dental Insurance; Disability Coverage; Employee Discounts; Life Insurance; Medical Insurance; Pension Plan; Retirement Plan; Tuition Assistance. **Parent company:** Baylor Health Care System.

CENTRAL TEXAS VETERANS HEALTHCARE SYSTEM
4800 Memorial Drive, Waco TX 76711. 254/752-6581. **Contact:** Personnel. **World Wide Web address:** http://www.va.gov. **Description:** A medical center. From 54 hospitals in 1930, the VA health care system has grown to include more than 170 medical centers; more than 360 outpatient, community, and outreach clinics; 130 nursing home care units; and more than 35 domiciliaries. The VA operates at least one medical center in each of the 48 contiguous states, Puerto Rico, and the District of Columbia. With approximately 76,000 medical center beds, the VA treats nearly one million patients in VA hospitals; 75,000 in nursing home care units; and 25,000 in domiciliaries. The VA's outpatient clinics register approximately 24 million visits per year. **NOTE:** Central Texas Veterans Healthcare System hires current or former federal employees, veterans, and disabled veterans. Central Texas Veterans Healthcare System is currently under hiring constraints. Applications from the general public are not accepted. **Parent company:** U.S. Department of Veterans Affairs.

CHILDREN'S MEDICAL CENTER OF DALLAS
1935 Motor Street, Dallas TX 75235. 214/539-2161. **Fax:** 214/539-6099. **Contact:** Human Resource Services. **World Wide Web address:** http://www.childrens.com. **Description:** A private, 322-bed, children's medical center operating through 50 specialty clinics. **Common positions include:** Claim Representative; Clinical Lab Technician; Computer Programmer; Customer Service Representative; EEG Technologist; EKG Technician; Emergency Medical Technician; Human Resources Manager; Medical Records Technician; Nuclear Medicine Technologist; Occupational Therapist; Pharmacist; Physical Therapist; Psychologist; Public Relations Specialist; Radiological Technologist; Registered Nurse; Respiratory Therapist; Social Worker; Speech-Language Pathologist; Surgical Technician; Systems Analyst. **Educational backgrounds include:** Business Administration; Communications; Computer Science; Health Care. **Listed on:** Privately held. **Number of employees at this location:** 2,100.

CHRISTUS ST. JOSEPH'S HEALTH SYSTEM
P.O. Box 9070, Paris TX 75461. 903/737-3253. **Physical address:** 820 Clarksbill Street, Paris TX 75460. **Fax:** 903/737-3887. **Contact:** Human Resources. **World Wide Web address:** http://www.stjosephs.com. **Description:** A 216-bed, nonprofit, acute care hospital that provides comprehensive heart programs, inpatient and outpatient dialysis, rehabilitation services,

Health Care: Services, Equipment, and Products/175

oncology, radiation therapy, and nuclear medicine services. **Number of employees at this location:** 800.

COLUMBIA/HCA
6565 North MacArthur, Suite 350, Irving TX 75039. 972/401-8750. **Contact:** Human Resources. **World Wide Web address:** http://www.columbia-hca.com. **Description:** This location is a regional administrative office. Overall, Columbia/HCA owns several hundred surgical centers and hospitals. Founded in 1992. **Other U.S. locations:** Nationwide. **Number of employees at this location:** 5,000.

COOK CHILDREN'S MEDICAL CENTER
801 Seventh Avenue, Fort Worth TX 76104-2733. 817/885-4419. **Fax:** 817/885-3947. **Recorded jobline:** 817/885-4414. **Contact:** Kay Kirby, Employment Specialist. **World Wide Web address:** http://www.cookchildrens.org. **Description:** A pediatric health care center. Founded in 1985. **NOTE:** Entry-level positions and second and third shifts are offered. **Common positions include:** Accountant; Applications Engineer; Buyer; Certified Nurses Aide; Chief Financial Officer; Computer Operator; Computer Programmer; Counselor; Customer Service Representative; Database Manager; Dietician/Nutritionist; EEG Technologist; EKG Technician; Emergency Medical Technician; Financial Analyst; Fund Manager; Human Resources Manager; Librarian; Licensed Practical Nurse; Marketing Specialist; Medical Records Technician; MIS Specialist; Nuclear Medicine Technologist; Occupational Therapist; Pharmacist; Physical Therapist; Physician; Psychologist; Public Relations Specialist; Radiological Technologist; Registered Nurse; Respiratory Therapist; Secretary; Social Worker; Speech-Language Pathologist; Surgical Technician; Systems Analyst; Systems Manager; Typist/Word Processor; Webmaster. **Educational backgrounds include:** Accounting; Computer Science; Health Care; Marketing; Nutrition; Public Relations. **Benefits:** 403(b); Dental Insurance; Disability Coverage; Employee Discounts; Flexible Schedule; Life Insurance; Medical Insurance; Public Transit Available; Tuition Assistance. **Listed on:** Privately held. **Facilities Manager:** Harry Delks. **Annual sales/revenues:** More than $100 million. **Number of employees at this location:** 2,000.

DALLAS-FORT WORTH MEDICAL CENTER
2709 Hospital Boulevard, Grand Prairie TX 75051. 972/641-5000. **Contact:** Human Resources. **World Wide Web address:** http://www.dfmedicalcenter.com. **Description:** A full-service, acute care hospital with 160 beds.

DE SOTO ANIMAL HOSPITAL
201 Lyndalyn, De Soto TX 75115. 972/223-4840. **Contact:** Human Resources. **Description:** Provides general medical and surgical services to domestic animals. Other services include radiology, dentistry, behavior counseling, allergy testing, and boarding.

DOCTORS HOSPITAL
9440 Poppy Drive, Dallas TX 75218. 214/324-6297. **Fax:** 214/324-6547. **Recorded jobline:** 214/324-6700. **Contact:** Human Resources. **World Wide Web address:** http://www.tenethealth.com. **Description:** A hospital. Founded in 1959. **NOTE:** Interested jobseekers should submit an application or send their resume to the Human Resources Office at 1151 North Buckner Boulevard, Suite 107, Dallas TX 75218. **Common positions include:** Dietician/Nutritionist; EEG Technologist; EKG Technician; Electrician; Human Resources Manager; Medical Records Technician; Nuclear Medicine Technologist; Pharmacist; Physical Therapist; Purchasing Agent/Manager; Radiological Technologist; Recreational Therapist; Registered Nurse; Respiratory Therapist; Social Worker; Surgical Technician. **Educational backgrounds include:** Health Care; Nursing. **Benefits:** 401(k); Dental Insurance; Disability Coverage; Employee Discounts; Life Insurance; Medical Insurance; Tuition Assistance. **Special programs:** Internships. **Other U.S. locations:** Nationwide. **Listed on:** New York Stock Exchange. **Number of employees at this location:** 900.

EAST TEXAS MEDICAL CENTER
1000 South Beckam Avenue, Tyler TX 75701. 903/597-0351. **Recorded jobline:** 903/531-8016. **Contact:** Human Resources. **E-mail address:** employment@etmc.org. **World Wide Web address:** http://www.etmc.org. **Description:** A 454-bed general hospital. Services include acute care rehabilitation, cardiovascular care, diagnostic services, neurological services, obstetrical services, and a Level I trauma center.

GARLAND COMMUNITY HOSPITAL
2696 West Walnut Street, Garland TX 75042. 972/276-7116. **Fax:** 972/487-2592. **Personnel phone:** 972/487-2405. **Contact:** Human Resources. **World Wide Web address:**

http://www.garlancommunityhosp.com. **Description:** A 113-bed hospital specializing in industrial and behavioral medicine, orthopedics, plastic surgery, and surgical weight loss programs. Founded in 1975. **Parent company:** Tenet HealthSystem. **CEO:** Mr. Gene Miller.

HARRINGTON CANCER CENTER
1500 Wallace Boulevard, Amarillo TX 79106. 806/359-4673. **Toll-free phone:** 800/274-HOPE. **Fax:** 806/354-5881. **Contact:** Personnel Department. **E-mail address:** jobs@harringtoncc.org. **World Wide Web address:** http://www.harringtoncc.org. **Description:** Provides various services to cancer patients who formerly had to travel hundreds of miles for treatment. Medical specialties include radiation services, medical oncology, blood diseases and hematology, supportive care, a women's center, and cancer prevention and education. **NOTE:** All applicants must fill out a job application to be considered for employment. Applications can be picked up in the Personnel Department or obtained online.

HARRIS METHODIST FORT WORTH HOSPITAL
1301 Pennsylvania Avenue, Fort Worth TX 76104. 817/882-2882. **Fax:** 817/882-2865. **Recorded jobline:** 800/477-7876. **Contact:** Human Resources. **World Wide Web address:** http://www.texashealth.org. **Description:** A 606-bed, tertiary care facility that also houses a multidisciplinary cancer center. **NOTE:** Entry-level positions, part-time jobs, and second and third shifts are offered. **Common positions include:** Biomedical Engineer; Clinical Lab Technician; Nuclear Medicine Technologist; Occupational Therapist; Pharmacist; Physical Therapist; Radiological Technologist; Registered Nurse; Respiratory Therapist; Social Worker; Speech-Language Pathologist; Surgical Technician. **Educational backgrounds include:** Health Care. **Benefits:** 401(k); Dental Insurance; Disability Coverage; Financial Planning Assistance; Life Insurance; Medical Insurance; On-Site Daycare; Pension Plan; Public Transit Available; Tuition Assistance. **Special programs:** Internships. **Office hours:** Monday - Friday, 8:00 a.m. - 5:00 p.m. **Parent company:** Harris Methodist Health System.

HEALTHSOUTH MEDICAL CENTER
2124 Research Row, Dallas TX 75235. 214/358-8363. **Contact:** Human Resources. **World Wide Web address:** http://www.healthsouth.com. **Description:** A comprehensive, medical rehabilitation hospital specializing in orthopedic surgery. HealthSouth also operates an outpatient facility. **Common positions include:** Accountant/Auditor; Biomedical Engineer; Clinical Lab Technician; Counselor; Dietician/Nutritionist; Electrician; Human Resources Manager; Licensed Practical Nurse; Mechanical Engineer; Medical Records Technician; Occupational Therapist; Physical Therapist; Purchasing Agent/Manager; Registered Nurse; Respiratory Therapist; Speech-Language Pathologist; Systems Analyst. **Educational backgrounds include:** Nursing; Physical Therapy. **Benefits:** 401(k); Dental Insurance; Disability Coverage; Life Insurance; Medical Insurance; Profit Sharing; Tuition Assistance. **Corporate headquarters location:** Birmingham AL. **Other U.S. locations:** Nationwide. **Listed on:** New York Stock Exchange. **Number of employees at this location:** 345. **Number of employees nationwide:** 15,065.

HENDERSON MEMORIAL HOSPITAL
300 Wilson Street, Henderson TX 75652. 903/655-6533. **Toll-free phone:** 800/329-7541. **Fax:** 903/655-3661. **Recorded jobline:** 903/655-3773. **Contact:** Human Resources. **World Wide Web address:** http://www.hmhmychoice.com. **Description:** A private, nonprofit, acute care hospital. **NOTE:** Entry-level positions and second and third shifts are offered. **Common positions include:** Account Representative; Accountant; Adjuster; Administrative Assistant; Biomedical Engineer; Certified Nurses Aide; Claim Representative; Clerical Supervisor; Clinical Lab Technician; Computer Operator; Counselor; Customer Service Representative; Dietician/Nutritionist; Education Administrator; EEG Technologist; EKG Technician; Emergency Medical Technician; Environmental Engineer; Financial Analyst; Food Scientist/Technologist; Licensed Practical Nurse; Licensed Vocational Nurse; Medical Records Technician; Operations Manager; Pharmacist; Physical Therapist; Physician; Purchasing Agent/Manager; Quality Control Supervisor; Radiological Technologist; Recreational Therapist; Registered Nurse; Respiratory Therapist; Restaurant/Food Service Manager; Secretary; Social Worker; Surgical Technician; Systems Analyst; Systems Manager; Typist/Word Processor. **Educational backgrounds include:** Accounting; Biology; Business Administration; Chemistry; Health Care; Nursing. **Benefits:** 403(b); Dental Insurance; Disability Coverage; Employee Discounts; Flexible Schedule; Life Insurance; Medical Insurance; Pension Plan; Tuition Assistance. **Special programs:** Apprenticeships; Internships. **Office hours:** Monday - Friday, 7:30 a.m. - 5:00 p.m. **Corporate headquarters location:** This Location. **Listed on:** Privately held. **CEO:** George Roberts. **Annual sales/revenues:** $21 - $50 million. **Number of employees at this location:** 385.

HENDRICK HEALTH SYSTEM
1242 North 19th Street, Abilene TX 79601-2316. 915/670-2000. **Contact:** Human Resources. **E-mail address:** hrdept@hendrickhealth.org. **World Wide Web address:** http://www.hendrickhealth.org. **Description:** Operates a 525-bed, general hospital. Founded in 1924. **Common positions include:** Accountant/Auditor; Database Manager; Marketing Specialist; Medical Assistant; Medical Records Technician; Medical Secretary; MIS Specialist; Nurse; Pharmacist; Pharmacy Technician; Physical Therapist; Surgical Technician. **Parent company:** Baptist General Convention of Texas.

HUGULEY MEMORIAL MEDICAL CENTER
11801 South Freeway, P.O. Box 6337, South Fort Worth TX 76115-0337. 817/551-2703. **Fax:** 817/551-2455. **Contact:** Human Resources. **Description:** A 220-bed acute care facility. Huguley Memorial Medical Center also owns Willow Creek (Arlington TX), a mental health facility. **Common positions include:** Accountant/Auditor; Buyer; Clerical Supervisor; Clinical Lab Technician; Counselor; Customer Service Representative; Dietician/Nutritionist; Emergency Medical Technician; Licensed Practical Nurse; Medical Records Technician; Nuclear Medicine Technologist; Occupational Therapist; Pharmacist; Physical Therapist; Recreational Therapist; Registered Nurse; Respiratory Therapist; Social Worker; Speech-Language Pathologist; Surgical Technician. **Educational backgrounds include:** Nursing. **Benefits:** 403(b); Credit Union; Dental Insurance; Disability Coverage; Employee Discounts; Life Insurance; Medical Insurance; Savings Plan; TSAs; Tuition Assistance. **Special programs:** Internships. **Corporate headquarters location:** Orlando FL. **Number of employees at this location:** 1,700. **Number of employees nationwide:** 1,400.

IHS HOSPITAL AT DALLAS
7955 Harry Heinz Boulevard, Dallas TX 75235. 214/637-0000. **Fax:** 214/905-0566. **Contact:** Ruby Williams, Human Resources Manager. **World Wide Web address:** http://www.ihs-inc.com. **Description:** A long-term, acute care hospital. **NOTE:** Entry-level positions and part-time jobs are offered. **Common positions include:** Accountant; Administrative Assistant; Certified Nurses Aide; Certified Occupational Therapy Assistant; Controller; Dietician/Nutritionist; Medical Records Technician; Occupational Therapist; Pharmacist; Physical Therapist; Registered Nurse; Respiratory Therapist; Secretary; Social Worker; Speech-Language Pathologist. **Educational backgrounds include:** Business Administration; Finance; Health Care; Marketing; Microsoft Word; Nutrition.

JOHNSON & JOHNSON MEDICAL, INC.
2500 East Arbrook Boulevard, Arlington TX 76014. 817/262-3900. **Contact:** Human Resources. **E-mail address:** resume@medus.jnj.com. **World Wide Web address:** http://www.jnjmedical.com. **Description:** Manufactures and markets an extensive line of disposable packs and gowns, surgical products, decontamination and disposal systems, latex gloves, and surgical antiseptics. **Common positions include:** Accountant/Auditor; Biological Scientist; Buyer; Chemical Engineer; Chemist; Clinical Lab Technician; Computer Programmer; Human Resources Manager; Industrial Production Manager; Operations/Production Manager; Purchasing Agent/Manager; Quality Control Supervisor; Software Engineer; Systems Analyst. **Educational backgrounds include:** Accounting; Biology; Business Administration; Chemistry; Computer Science; Engineering; Finance; Marketing. **Benefits:** 401(k); Dental Insurance; Disability Coverage; Employee Discounts; Life Insurance; Medical Insurance; Pension Plan; Tuition Assistance. **Special programs:** Internships. **Corporate headquarters location:** This Location. **Other U.S. locations:** Irvine CA; Southington CT; Tampa FL; El Paso TX; Jacksonville TX; Sherman TX. **Parent company:** Johnson & Johnson (New Brunswick NJ). **Number of employees at this location:** 400. **Number of employees nationwide:** 2,500.

JORDAN HEALTH SERVICES
P.O. Box 889, Mount Vernon TX 75457. 903/537-2376. **Contact:** John McAuley, Human Resources Manager. **Description:** A diversified home health care agency. **Common positions include:** Licensed Practical Nurse; Occupational Therapist; Physical Therapist; Registered Nurse; Respiratory Therapist; Social Worker; Speech-Language Pathologist. **Educational backgrounds include:** Health Care. **Benefits:** 401(k); Disability Coverage; Life Insurance; Medical Insurance. **Corporate headquarters location:** This Location. **Listed on:** Privately held. **Annual sales/revenues:** $21 - $50 million. **Number of employees at this location:** 500.

LONGVIEW REGIONAL MEDICAL CENTER
P.O. Box 14000, Longview TX 75607. 903/758-1818. **Fax:** 903/232-3888. **Recorded jobline:** 903/232-3726. **Contact:** Human Resources. **World Wide Web address:** http://www.triadhospitals.com. **Description:** A 164-bed, acute care, medical center providing cardiovascular, pediatric, dialysis, intensive care, intermediate care, outpatient care, and

laboratory services. Founded in 1980. **NOTE:** Entry-level positions, part-time jobs, and second and third shifts are offered. **Common positions include:** Administrative Assistant; Certified Nurses Aide; Clerical Supervisor; Clinical Lab Technician; Computer Technician; Dietician/Nutritionist; EKG Technician; Emergency Medical Technician; Licensed Practical Nurse; Medical Records Technician; Medical Secretary; Nuclear Medicine Technologist; Nurse Practitioner; Pharmacist; Physician Assistant; Radiological Technologist; Registered Nurse; Respiratory Therapist; Secretary; Social Worker; Speech-Language Pathologist; Surgical Technician; Typist/Word Processor. **Educational backgrounds include:** Health Care; Microsoft Office; Microsoft Word; Spreadsheets. **Benefits:** 401(k); Dental Insurance; Disability Coverage; Life Insurance; Medical Insurance; Pension Plan; Profit Sharing; Tuition Assistance. **Corporate headquarters location:** Dallas TX. **Other U.S. locations:** Nationwide. **Parent company:** Triad Hospitals, Inc. **Listed on:** NASDAQ. **CEO:** Vicki Romero. **Number of employees at this location:** 730.

LUBBOCK METHODIST HOSPITAL
3615 19th Street, Lubbock TX 79410. 806/725-1011. **Contact:** Personnel. **Description:** A 760-bed hospital.

MEDICAL CENTER OF PLANO
3901 West 15th Street, Plano TX 75075. 972/596-6800. **Recorded jobline:** 972/596-5300. **Contact:** Human Resources. **Description:** A 300-bed medical center providing acute and residential care.

MEDICAL CITY DALLAS HOSPITAL
7777 Forest Lane, Building B, Suite 250, Dallas TX 75230. 972/566-7070. **Toll-free phone:** 800/224-4733. **Recorded jobline:** 888/344-5627. **Contact:** Professional Recruiter. **E-mail address:** MedCityHR@lonestarhealth.com. **World Wide Web address:** http://www.medicalcityhospital.com. **Description:** A full-service hospital. **NOTE:** Entry-level positions, part-time jobs, and second and third shifts are offered. **Common positions include:** Accountant; Administrative Assistant; Certified Nurses Aide; Chief Financial Officer; Computer Operator; Computer Technician; Controller; Customer Service Representative; Dietician/Nutritionist; EEG Technologist; EKG Technician; Librarian; Licensed Practical Nurse; Marketing Manager; Medical Records Technician; Network/Systems Administrator; Nuclear Medicine Technologist; Occupational Therapist; Pharmacist; Physical Therapist; Physical Therapy Assistant; Purchasing Agent/Manager; Radiological Technologist; Registered Nurse; Respiratory Therapist; Secretary; Social Worker; Speech-Language Pathologist; Statistician; Surgical Technician; Vice President; Vice President of Finance. **Educational backgrounds include:** Accounting; Biology; Business Administration; Computer Science; Finance; Health Care; Microsoft Word; Nursing; Nutrition; Spreadsheets. **Benefits:** 401(k); Daycare Assistance; Dental Insurance; Disability Coverage; Employee Discounts; Flexible Schedule; Life Insurance; Medical Insurance; Retirement Plan; Sick Days (6 - 10); Tuition Assistance; Vacation Days (16+). **Special programs:** Internships; Summer Jobs; Training. **CEO:** Steve Corbeil.

MESQUITE COMMUNITY HOSPITAL
3500 Interstate 30, Mesquite TX 75150. 972/698-3300. **Fax:** 972/698-2580. **Recorded jobline:** 972/698-2463. **Contact:** Debbie Ottwell, Executive Assistant. **World Wide Web address:** http://www.mesquitecommunityhosp.com. **Description:** A 172-bed hospital. Founded in 1978.

METHODIST MEDICAL CENTER
1441 North Beckley Avenue, Dallas TX 75203. 214/947-8181. **Contact:** Human Resources Department. **World Wide Web address:** http://www.mhd.com/mmc.html. **Description:** A 463-bed teaching and referring hospital. Founded in 1927. **Parent company:** Methodist Hospitals of Dallas.

MIRACLE HOME HEALTH CARE
1515 Willis Lane, Keller TX 76248. 972/436-5229. **Fax:** 972/221-1076. **Contact:** Human Resources. **Description:** A home health care agency. **Common positions include:** Bookkeeper; Claim Representative; Computer Operator; Data Entry Clerk; Nurse; Occupational Therapist; Physical Therapist; Receptionist; Secretary; Social Worker.

NORTHWEST TEXAS HEALTHCARE SYSTEM
P.O. Box 1110, Amarillo TX 79175-0001. 806/354-1000. **Contact:** Human Resources. **World Wide Web address:** http://www.nwths.com. **Description:** Operates Northwest Texas Hospital and The Pavilion. Northwest Texas Hospital offers more than 25 medical specialties and sub-specialties. The Pavilion is a full-service mental health care facility that provides a

comprehensive range of services to people of all ages. **NOTE:** Please check the Website for a listing of open positions. **Number of employees at this location:** 1,700.

NURSEFINDERS
3141 Hood Street, Suite 620, Dallas TX 75219. 214/520-8770. **Contact:** Human Resources. **World Wide Web address:** http://www.nursefinders.com. **Description:** A home health care agency. **Common positions include:** Home Health Aide; Licensed Practical Nurse; Registered Nurse. **Other U.S. locations:** Nationwide.

NURSES TODAY INCORPORATED
4230 LBJ Freeway, Suite 110, Dallas TX 75244. 972/233-9966. **Toll-free phone:** 800/830-7616. **Fax:** 972/233-5354. **Contact:** Beth Goucher, Human Resources Manager. **World Wide Web address:** http://www.nursestoday.com. **Description:** Provides home health care and case management services. Founded in 1982. **NOTE:** Part-time jobs are offered. **Common positions include:** Administrative Assistant; Certified Nurses Aide; Home Health Aide; Licensed Practical Nurse; Medical Assistant; Physical Therapist; Registered Nurse. **Educational backgrounds include:** Health Care. **Benefits:** Casual Dress - Fridays; Credit Union; Flexible Schedule; Job Sharing; Public Transit Available; Sick Days (1 - 5); Telecommuting; Vacation Days (10 - 20). **Office hours:** Monday - Friday, 8:00 a.m. - 5:00 p.m. **Corporate headquarters location:** This Location. **Listed on:** Privately held. **CEO:** Anita Porco. **Facilities Manager:** Luisa Morton. **Information Systems Manager:** Debbie Penny. **Annual sales/revenues:** Less than $5 million.

OMEGA OPTICAL COMPANY, INC.
13515 North Stemmons Freeway, Dallas TX 75234. 972/241-4141. **Contact:** Personnel Manager. **Description:** A manufacturer of prescription optical lenses and ophthalmic products. **Common positions include:** Accountant/Auditor; Blue-Collar Worker Supervisor; Clerical Supervisor; Computer Programmer; Credit Manager; Customer Service Representative; Electrician; General Manager; Human Resources Manager; Operations/Production Manager; Quality Control Supervisor; Systems Analyst. **Educational backgrounds include:** Accounting; Business Administration. **Benefits:** 401(k); Dental Insurance; Disability Coverage; Employee Discounts; Life Insurance; Medical Insurance. **Corporate headquarters location:** This Location. **Parent company:** Benson Eyecare. **Number of employees at this location:** 600.

183 ANIMAL HOSPITAL
1010 West Airport Freeway, Irving TX 75062. 972/579-0115. **Contact:** Human Resources. **Description:** Provides general medical and surgical services along with diagnostic testing, radiography, and dentistry for small animals.

ORTHOFIX INC.
250 East Arapaho Road, Richardson TX 75081. 972/918-8300. **Fax:** 972/918-8311. **Contact:** Human Resources. **World Wide Web address:** http://www.orthofix.com. **Description:** Develops, manufactures, markets, and distributes medical devices to promote bone healing. Products are primarily used by orthopedic surgeons. **Common positions include:** Chemical Engineer; Customer Service Representative; Electrical/Electronics Engineer; Mechanical Engineer; Services Sales Representative. **Benefits:** 401(k); Dental Insurance; Disability Coverage; Life Insurance; Medical Insurance; Profit Sharing; Savings Plan; Tuition Assistance. **Parent company:** Orthofix International N.V. (Henly, England). **Operations at this facility include:** Administration; Divisional Headquarters; Manufacturing; Research and Development; Sales; Service. **Listed on:** NASDAQ. **Annual sales/revenues:** $21 - $50 million. **Number of employees at this location:** 240. **Number of employees worldwide:** 350.

PALO PINTO GENERAL HOSPITAL
400 SW 25th Avenue, Mineral Wells TX 76067. 940/328-6390. **Fax:** 940/328-6389. **Contact:** Barbara Stagner, Director of Human Resources. **Description:** A 99-bed, nonprofit, acute care hospital. **NOTE:** Entry-level positions, part-time jobs, and second and third shifts are offered. **Common positions include:** Administrative Assistant; Certified Nurses Aide; Chief Financial Officer; Computer Support Technician; Dietician/Nutritionist; Home Health Aide; Human Resources Manager; Licensed Practical Nurse; Marketing Specialist; Medical Assistant; Medical Records Technician; MIS Specialist; Nuclear Medicine Technologist; Nurse Practitioner; Occupational Therapist; Pharmacist; Physical Therapist; Physical Therapy Assistant; Physician; Public Relations Specialist; Purchasing Agent/Manager; Radiological Technologist; Registered Nurse; Respiratory Therapist; Secretary; Social Worker; Speech-Language Pathologist; Surgical Technician. **Educational backgrounds include:** Business Administration; Chemistry; Finance; Health Care; Marketing; Nutrition. **Benefits:** 403(b); Dental Insurance; Disability Coverage; Employee Discounts; Life Insurance; Medical Insurance; Savings Plan; Tuition Assistance.

Operations at this facility include: Administration; Service. **Annual sales/revenues:** $21 - $50 million. **Number of employees at this location:** 420.

PAMPA MEDICAL CENTER
One Medical Plaza, Pampa TX 79065. 806/665-3721. **Contact:** Personnel. **Description:** A 107-bed acute care hospital.

PARKLAND HEALTH & HOSPITAL SYSTEM
PARKLAND MEMORIAL HOSPITAL
5201 Harry Hines Boulevard, Dallas TX 75235. 214/590-8266. **Fax:** 214/590-2767. **Contact:** Employment Services. **World Wide Web address:** http://www.pmh.org. **Description:** Parkland Health & Hospital System is comprised of Parkland Memorial Hospital (also at this location), Community Oriented Private Care, Parkland Community Health Plan, and The Parkland Foundation. Parkland Memorial Hospital is the primary teaching hospital of The University of Texas Southwestern Medical School. The 997-bed hospital specializes in such areas as epilepsy treatment, arrhythmia management, and diagnostic cardiology. **Common positions include:** Accountant/Auditor; Administrator; Biological Scientist; Biomedical Engineer; Blue-Collar Worker Supervisor; Buyer; Chemist; Civil Engineer; Claim Representative; Computer Programmer; Credit Manager; Customer Service Representative; Department Manager; Dietician/Nutritionist; Electrician; Financial Analyst; Human Resources Manager; Management Trainee; Public Relations Specialist; Purchasing Agent/Manager; Quality Control Supervisor; Systems Analyst. **Educational backgrounds include:** Accounting; Biology; Business Administration; Chemistry; Computer Science; Engineering. **Benefits:** Disability Coverage; Employee Discounts; Life Insurance; Medical Insurance; Pension Plan; Savings Plan; Tuition Assistance. **Parent company:** Parkland Health & Hospital System includes Parkland Memorial Hospital, Community Oriented Primary Care, Parkland Community Health Plan, Inc., and the Parkland Foundation.

PEARLE VISION, INC.
2534 Royal Lane, Dallas TX 75229. 972/277-5000. **Fax:** 972/277-5944. **Contact:** Human Resources. **World Wide Web address:** http://www.pearlevision.com. **Description:** Manufactures and retails prescription eyewear. **Common positions include:** Accountant/Auditor; Advertising Clerk; Attorney; Computer Programmer; Customer Service Representative; Department Manager; Financial Analyst; Human Resources Manager; Management Trainee; Manufacturer's/Wholesaler's Sales Rep.; Marketing Specialist; Purchasing Agent/Manager; Systems Analyst. **Educational backgrounds include:** Accounting; Business Administration; Computer Science; Finance; Marketing; Merchandising. **Benefits:** Dental Insurance; Disability Coverage; Employee Discounts; Life Insurance; Medical Insurance; Profit Sharing; Savings Plan; Tuition Assistance. **Corporate headquarters location:** This Location. **Parent company:** Grand Met USA. **Listed on:** London Stock Exchange.

PLAZA MEDICAL CENTER
900 Eighth Avenue, Fort Worth TX 76104. 817/336-2100. **Contact:** Human Resources. **Description:** A 298-bed hospital offering in-patient medical and surgical care, emergency services, a neuroscience center, various women's services, several educational opportunities, and support groups. **Common positions include:** Dietician/Nutritionist; Nuclear Medicine Technologist; Pharmacist; Physical Therapist; Registered Nurse; Respiratory Therapist. **Educational backgrounds include:** Health Care; Nursing. **Benefits:** 401(k); Dental Insurance; Disability Coverage; Employee Discounts; Life Insurance; Medical Insurance; Pension Plan; Profit Sharing; Savings Plan; Tuition Assistance. **Number of employees at this location:** 700.

PROVIDENCE HEALTH CENTER
6901 Medical Parkway, Waco TX 76712. 254/751-4000. **Fax:** 254/751-4909. **Contact:** Human Resources. **World Wide Web address:** http://www.providence-waco.org. **Description:** A 170-bed, acute care hospital. Founded in 1905. **Corporate headquarters location:** This location. **Parent company:** Providence Healthcare Network (also at this location) consists of Providence Health Center, Providence Home Care, De Paul Center, St. Catherine Center, Providence Clinics, Providence Foundation, and Providence Health Alliance.

QUEST MEDICAL, INC.
ATRION CORPORATION
One Allentown Parkway, Allen TX 75002-4211. 972/390-9800. **Contact:** Human Resources. **Description:** Develops, manufactures, markets, sells, and distributes proprietary products for the healthcare industry. **Corporate headquarters location:** This Location. **Parent company:** Atrion Corporation (also at this location) is a holding company that designs, develops, manufactures, markets, sells, and distributes proprietary products and components for the

healthcare industry. Other subsidiaries of the company include Atrion
Halkey-Roberts. **Listed on:** NASDAQ. **Stock exchange symbol:** QMED.
at this location: 250.

RHD MEMORIAL MEDICAL CENTER
7 Medical Parkway, Dallas TX 75234. 972/247-1000. **Contact:** Personnel
address: http://www.rhdmemorial.com. **Description:** A 160-bed, ac
hospital. **Parent company:** Tenet HealthSystem.

ROYAL OPTICAL U.S. VISION
1334 Inwood Road, Dallas TX 75247. 214/630-5791. **Contact:** Personnel Department.
Description: Manufactures frames, grinds lenses, and distributes a line of eyewear.

ST. PAUL MEDICAL CENTER
5909 Harry Hines Boulevard, Dallas TX 75235. 214/879-1000. **Contact:** Human Resources
Department. **Description:** A not-for-profit, 600-bed medical center. St. Paul Medical Center is
affiliated with the University of Texas Southwestern Medical Center of Dallas.

JOHN PETER SMITH HEALTH NETWORK
1500 South Main Street, Fort Worth TX 76104. 817/921-3431. **Contact:** Human Resources.
Description: An acute care hospital with over 160 beds.

STERN REED ASSOCIATES
4203 Beltway, Suite 5, Addison TX 75001. 817/640-8341. **Contact:** Human Resources.
Description: A dental laboratory that makes dental prosthetics. **Benefits:** 401(k); Incentive Plan;
Stock Option. **Other U.S. locations:** Houston TX; Tyler TX. **Parent company:** National Dentex
Corporation is one of the largest operators of dental laboratories in the United States. These
dental laboratories provide a full range of custom-made dental prosthetic appliances, divided
into three main groups: restorative products (crowns and bridges); reconstructive products
(partial and full dentures); and cosmetic products (porcelain veneers and ceramic crowns). Each
lab is operated as a stand-alone facility under the direction of a local manager. All sales and
marketing activities are done through each lab's own direct sales force. **Listed on:** NASDAQ.

STERN TYLER
1918 East Front Street, Tyler TX 75702. 903/597-3198. **Contact:** Human Resources.
Description: A dental laboratory that makes dental prosthetics. **Benefits:** 401(k); Incentive Plan;
Stock Option. **Other U.S. locations:** Arlington TX; Houston TX. **Parent company:** National
Dentex Corporation is one of the largest operators of dental laboratories in the United States.
These dental laboratories provide a full range of custom-made dental prosthetic appliances,
divided into three main groups: restorative products (crowns and bridges); reconstructive
products (partial and full dentures); and cosmetic products (porcelain veneers and ceramic
crowns). Each lab is operated as a stand-alone facility under the direction of a local manager.
All sales and marketing activities are done through each lab's own direct sales force. **Listed on:**
NASDAQ.

TENET HEALTHCARE CORPORATION
P.O. Box 809088, Dallas TX 75380-9088. 972/789-2324. **Fax:** 972/980-2685. **Contact:** Mary
McClain, Manager of Recruitment. **World Wide Web address:** http://www.tenethealth.com.
Description: A multibillion-dollar, multi-hospital corporation that, in conjunction with its
subsidiaries, owns or operates approximately 130 healthcare facilities nationwide. **Common
positions include:** Accountant/Auditor; Administrative Manager; Computer Programmer;
Human Resources Manager; Public Relations Specialist; Systems Analyst. **Benefits:** 401(k);
Credit Union; Dental Insurance; Disability Coverage; Employee Discounts; Life Insurance;
Medical Insurance; Tuition Assistance. **Corporate headquarters location:** Santa Monica CA.
Other U.S. locations: Nationwide. **Listed on:** New York Stock Exchange; Pacific Stock
Exchange. **Number of employees at this location:** 300. **Number of employees nationwide:**
68,000.

TEXAS HEALTH RESOURCES
8440 Walnut Hill Lane, Dallas TX 75231. 214/345-4251. **Toll-free phone:** 800/749-6877. **Fax:**
214/345-4003. **Recorded jobline:** 214/345-7863. **Contact:** Linda Ochoa, Employment
Manager. **World Wide Web address:** http://www.texashealth.org. **Description:** One of the
largest nonprofit health care systems in Texas. Texas Health Resources consists of a nursing
home, 11 acute care hospitals, clinics, and home health services. **NOTE:** Part-time jobs and
second and third shifts are offered. **Common positions include:** Accountant; Administrative
Assistant; Administrative Manager; AS400 Programmer Analyst; Assistant Manager; Attorney;

...or; Blue-Collar Worker Supervisor; Certified Nurses Aide; Certified Occupational Therapy ...sistant; Claim Representative; Clerical Supervisor; Computer Operator; Computer ...rogrammer; Computer Support Technician; Computer Technician; Customer Service Representative; Database Administrator; Database Manager; Dietician/Nutritionist; EEG Technologist; EKG Technician; Emergency Medical Technician; Finance Director; Financial Analyst; Home Health Aide; Human Resources Manager; Licensed Practical Nurse; Medical Assistant; Medical Records Technician; MIS Specialist; Network/Systems Administrator; Nuclear Medicine Technologist; Nurse Practitioner; Occupational Therapist; Paralegal; Pharmacist; Physical Therapist; Physical Therapy Assistant; Physician; Project Manager; Radiological Technologist; Registered Nurse; Respiratory Therapist; Secretary; Social Worker; Speech-Language Pathologist; Surgical Technician; Systems Analyst; Systems Manager. **Educational backgrounds include:** Health Care; Microsoft Word; Novell; Spreadsheets. **Benefits:** 401(k); Dental Insurance; Disability Coverage; Life Insurance; Medical Insurance; On-Site Daycare. **Corporate headquarters location:** This Location. **Other area locations:** Greenville TX; Kaufman TX; Plano TX; Winnsboro TX. **Number of employees nationwide:** 16,000.

TEXAS MEDICAL AND SURGICAL ASSOCIATES
8440 Walnut Hill Lane, Dallas TX 75231. 214/345-5740. **Contact:** Personnel. **Description:** A private clinic. **Office hours:** Monday - Friday, 8:30 a.m. - 5:00 p.m.

TEXOMA MEDICAL CENTER (TMC)
P.O. Box 890, Denison TX 75021. 903/416-4050. **Physical address:** 1000 Memorial Drive, Denison TX 75020. **Fax:** 903/415-4087. **Recorded jobline:** 800/566-1211. **Contact:** Joni Horn, Employment Coordinator. **World Wide Web address:** http://www.thcs.org. **Description:** Texoma Medical Center (TMC) is an acute care hospital with 300 beds. TMC offers general medical and surgical services, intensive care, and pediatric care. Founded in 1965. **NOTE:** Second and third shifts are offered. **Common positions include:** Accountant; Administrative Assistant; Buyer; Certified Nurses Aide; Clerical Supervisor; Clinical Lab Technician; Computer Operator; Controller; Customer Service Representative; Database Manager; Dietician/Nutritionist; EEG Technologist; EKG Technician; Electrician; Human Resources Manager; Licensed Practical Nurse; Marketing Specialist; Medical Records Technician; Nuclear Medicine Technologist; Occupational Therapist; Pharmacist; Physical Therapist; Radiological Technologist; Registered Nurse; Respiratory Therapist; Secretary; Speech-Language Pathologist; Surgical Technician; Systems Analyst; Systems Manager. **Educational backgrounds include:** Computer Science; Health Care. **Benefits:** 403(b); Dental Insurance; Disability Coverage; Job Sharing; Life Insurance; Medical Insurance; Pension Plan; Profit Sharing; Tuition Assistance. **Special programs:** Co-ops; Summer Jobs. **Corporate headquarters location:** This Location. **Other U.S. locations:** Durant OK; Bonham TX; Sherman TX; Trenton TX; Whitewright TX. **Subsidiaries include:** Times Medical Equipment. **Parent company:** Texoma Healthcare Systems, Inc. (also at this location). **President/CEO:** Arthur L. Hohenberger. **Number of employees nationwide:** 1,200.

TRI-CITY HOSPITAL
7525 Scyene Road, Dallas TX 75227. 214/381-7171. **Contact:** Human Resources Department. **Description:** A 131-bed, acute care hospital.

UNITED REGIONAL HEALTHCARE SYSTEMS
1504 Eighth Street, Wichita Falls TX 76301. 940/764-7000. **Toll-free phone:** 800/221-9750. **Fax:** 940/723-8223. **Recorded jobline:** 940/764-7802. **Contact:** Patra Linderkamp, Recruitment Coordinator. **World Wide Web address:** http://www.urhcs.org. **Description:** A licensed, 300-bed, acute care facility.

UNIVERSITY MEDICAL CENTER
602 Indiana Avenue, Lubbock TX 79415. 806/743-3111. **Recorded jobline:** 806/743-3352. **Contact:** Human Resources Manager. **World Wide Web address:** http://www.teamumc.org. **Description:** A 354-bed hospital operating through The Children's Hospital, The Southwest Cancer Center, Level I Trauma Center, a Pre-Hospital Emergency Service, a Burn Intensive Care Unit, and Community Outreach Programs. **Common positions include:** Accountant/Auditor; Buyer; Clerical Supervisor; Clinical Lab Technician; Computer Programmer; Dietician/Nutritionist; EEG Technologist; EKG Technician; Health Services Manager; Licensed Practical Nurse; Medical Records Technician; Nuclear Medicine Technologist; Occupational Therapist; Pharmacist; Physical Therapist; Registered Nurse; Respiratory Therapist; Restaurant/Food Service Manager; Social Worker; Speech-Language Pathologist; Surgical Technician; Systems Analyst. **Educational backgrounds include:** Accounting; Business Administration; Health Care. **Benefits:** 401(k); Dental Insurance; Employee Discounts; Life

Insurance; Medical Insurance; Profit Sharing. **Special programs:** Internships. **Operations at this facility include:** Administration; Service. **Number of employees at this location:** 1,850.

UNIVERSITY OF TEXAS HEALTH CENTER AT TYLER
11937 U.S. Highway 271, Tyler TX 75708-3154. 903/877-7740. **Recorded jobline:** 903/877-7071. **Contact:** Employment Services. **World Wide Web address:** http://www.uthct.edu. **Description:** A nonprofit hospital engaged in patient care, education, and research. **Common positions include:** Accountant/Auditor; Biological Scientist; Budget Analyst; Buyer; Chemist; Clerical Supervisor; Clinical Lab Technician; Computer Programmer; Dietician/Nutritionist; EEG Technologist; EKG Technician; Electrician; Hotel Manager; Human Resources Manager; Librarian; Library Technician; Licensed Practical Nurse; Meteorologist; Nuclear Medicine Technologist; Occupational Therapist; Pharmacist; Physical Therapist; Physician; Radiological Technologist; Registered Nurse; Respiratory Therapist; Social Worker; Surgical Technician; Systems Analyst. **Educational backgrounds include:** Health Care. **Benefits:** Dental Insurance; Disability Coverage; Employee Discounts; Life Insurance; Medical Insurance; Tuition Assistance. **Number of employees at this location:** 1,300.

UNIVERSITY OF TEXAS SOUTHWESTERN MEDICAL CENTER AT DALLAS
5323 Harry Hines Boulevard, Dallas TX 75390. 214/648-3111. **Fax:** 214/648-9874. **Contact:** Human Resources. **World Wide Web address:** http://www.swmed.edu. **Description:** An academic medical center affiliated with Southwestern Medical School, Southwestern Graduate School of Biomedical Sciences, and Southwestern Allied Health Sciences School. **NOTE:** Entry-level positions are offered. **Common positions include:** Accountant; Administrative Assistant; Administrative Manager; AS400 Programmer Analyst; Attorney; Auditor; Biochemist; Biological Scientist; Biomedical Engineer; Budget Analyst; Computer Operator; Computer Programmer; Computer Support Technician; Counselor; Database Administrator; Database Manager; Electrician; Emergency Medical Technician; Financial Analyst; Intellectual Property Lawyer; Librarian; Medical Assistant; Network/Systems Administrator; Nurse Practitioner; Psychologist; Purchasing Agent/Manager; Radiological Technologist; Registered Nurse; Secretary; Systems Analyst; Systems Manager. **Educational backgrounds include:** Accounting; AS400 Certification; Biology; Business Administration; C/C++; Chemistry; Computer Science; Finance; Health Care; HTML; Internet; MCSE; Novell; PowerBuilder; Software Tech. Support; Visual Basic. **Benefits:** 403(b); Dental Insurance; Disability Coverage; Financial Planning Assistance; Life Insurance; Medical Insurance; Pension Plan; Public Transit Available; Savings Plan; Sick Days (11+); Vacation Days (11 - 15). **Special programs:** Internships. **Number of employees at this location:** 5,000.

VA MEDICAL CENTER
6010 Amarillo Boulevard West, Amarillo TX 79106. 806/355-9703. **Contact:** Human Resources. **World Wide Web address:** http://www.va.gov. **Description:** A medical center operated by the U.S. Department of Veterans Affairs. From 54 hospitals in 1930, the VA health care system has grown to include 171 medical centers; more than 364 outpatient, community, and outreach clinics; 130 nursing home care units; and 37 domiciliaries. The VA operates at least one medical center in each of the 48 contiguous states, Puerto Rico, and the District of Columbia. With approximately 76,000 medical center beds, the VA treats nearly 1 million patients in VA hospitals; 75,000 in nursing home care units; and 25,000 in domiciliaries. The VA's outpatient clinics register approximately 24 million visits per year. **NOTE:** The VA Medical Center hires current or former federal employees, veterans, and disabled veterans. The VA Medical Center is currently under hiring constraints. Applications from the general public are not accepted. **Corporate headquarters location:** Washington DC.

VA NORTH TEXAS HEALTHCARE SYSTEM
4500 South Lancaster Road, Dallas TX 75216. 214/742-8387. **Contact:** Personnel. **World Wide Web address:** http://www.va.gov. **Description:** This location houses administrative offices. From 54 hospitals in 1930, the VA health care system has grown to include 171 medical centers; more than 364 outpatient, community, and outreach clinics; 130 nursing home care units; and 37 domiciliaries. The VA operates at least one medical center in each of the 48 contiguous states, Puerto Rico, and the District of Columbia. With approximately 76,000 medical center beds, the VA treats nearly one million patients in VA hospitals; 75,000 in nursing home care units; and 25,000 in domiciliaries. The VA's outpatient clinics register approximately 24 million visits per year. **Common positions include:** Accountant/Auditor; Attorney; Clerical Supervisor; Clinical Lab Technician; Computer Programmer; Counselor; Dental Assistant/Dental Hygienist; Dental Lab Technician; Dentist; Designer; Dietician/Nutritionist; Education Administrator; EEG Technologist; EKG Technician; Electrical/Electronics Engineer; Electrician; Emergency Medical Technician; Environmental Engineer; Financial Analyst; Human Resources Manager; Human Service Worker; Industrial

Engineer; Librarian; Library Technician; Licensed Practical Nurse; Management Analyst/Consultant; Management Trainee; Materials Engineer; Mechanical Engineer; Medical Records Technician; Nuclear Engineer; Nuclear Medicine Technologist; Occupational Therapist; Operations/Production Manager; Pharmacist; Physical Therapist; Physician; Physicist; Psychologist; Public Relations Specialist; Purchasing Agent/Manager; Radiological Technologist; Recreational Therapist; Registered Nurse; Respiratory Therapist; Social Worker; Sociologist; Software Engineer; Speech-Language Pathologist; Surgical Technician; Systems Analyst. **Benefits:** 401(k); Dental Insurance; Disability Coverage; Employee Discounts; Life Insurance; Medical Insurance; Pension Plan; Savings Plan; Tuition Assistance. **Special programs:** Internships. **Corporate headquarters location:** Washington DC.

VENCOR HOSPITAL OF DALLAS
9525 Greenville Avenue, Dallas TX 75243. 214/355-2600. **Contact:** Business Office. **Description:** A 609-bed, acute care hospital.

VERNON WICHITA FALLS STATE HOSPITAL
P.O. Box 300, Wichita Falls TX 76307. 940/689-5878. **Fax:** 940/689-5735. **Recorded jobline:** 940/552-9901x4030. **Contact:** Staffing. **Description:** A nonprofit, forensic and mental health hospital. **Common positions include:** Certified Nurses Aide; Dietician/Nutritionist; Electrician; Human Resources Manager; Licensed Practical Nurse; Occupational Therapist; Pharmacist; Psychiatrist; Psychologist; Registered Nurse; Secretary; Social Worker; Typist/Word Processor. **Educational backgrounds include:** Health Care. **Benefits:** Disability Coverage; Medical Insurance; Pension Plan; Sick Days (11+); Vacation Days (6 - 10). **Special programs:** Internships. **Corporate headquarters location:** Austin TX. **Other area locations:** Vernon Campus, P.O. Box 2231, Vernon TX 76385-2231, 940/552-9901. **Parent company:** Texas Department of Mental Health. **CEO:** James E. Smith. **Number of employees at this location:** 2,000.

VISITING NURSE ASSOCIATION
1440 West Mockingbird Lane, Suite 500, Dallas TX 75247. 214/689-0000. **Fax:** 214/631-8106. **Contact:** Human Resources. **Description:** Provides in-home health care and health-related social services. Services include nursing, Eldercare, and Meals on Wheels. **Common positions include:** Dietician/Nutritionist; Licensed Practical Nurse; Occupational Therapist; Physical Therapist; Registered Nurse. **Other U.S. locations:** Nationwide.

WADLEY REGIONAL MEDICAL CENTER
1000 Pine Street, Texarkana TX 75501. 903/798-7160. **Fax:** 903/798-7177. **Recorded jobline:** 903/798-7161. **Contact:** Jan Loveall, Employment Coordinator. **E-mail address:** loveall@wadleyrmc.com. **World Wide Web address:** http://www.wadleyrmc.com. **Description:** A nonprofit, acute care hospital with 448 beds. The services offered at Wadley Regional Medical Center include a skilled nursing facility, a Cancer Treatment & Diagnostic Imaging Center, a day surgery center, and a Community Oriented Medical Plan Clinic. Founded in 1959. **NOTE:** Second and third shifts are offered. **Company slogan:** To improve the health and healthcare of those we serve. **Common positions include:** Accountant; Certified Nurses Aide; Chief Financial Officer; Customer Service Representative; Daycare Worker; Dietician/Nutritionist; EEG Technologist; EKG Technician; Electrical/Electronics Engineer; Electrician; Emergency Medical Technician; Nuclear Medicine Technologist; Pharmacist; Registered Nurse; Respiratory Therapist; Social Worker; Speech-Language Pathologist; Surgical Technician. **Educational backgrounds include:** Health Care. **Benefits:** 401(k); 403(b); Dental Insurance; Disability Coverage; Employee Discounts; Life Insurance; Medical Insurance; On-Site Daycare; Pension Plan; Tuition Assistance. **Special programs:** Summer Jobs. **CEO:** Hugh Hallgren. **Number of employees at this location:** 1,200.

ZALE LIPSHY UNIVERSITY HOSPITAL
UNIVERSITY OF TEXAS SOUTHWESTERN MEDICAL CENTER CAMPUS
5151 Harry Hines Boulevard, Dallas TX 75235-7786. 214/590-3150. **Fax:** 214/590-3193. **Recorded jobline:** 214/590-3484. **Contact:** Human Resources. **E-mail address:** response@zluh.org. **World Wide Web address:** http://www.zluh.org. **Description:** A private, nonprofit, adult referral hospital for specialized tertiary care. The facilities consist of 152 hospital beds (20 intensive care unit beds, 89 medical/surgical beds, 22 rehabilitation beds, and 21 psychiatric beds) and 12 operating room suites for specialized surgical care in the areas of neurological surgery, orthopedics, urology, gynecology, otorhinolaryngology (ear, nose, and throat), ophthalmology, cardiothoracic surgery, oral and maxillofacial surgery, vascular surgery, and plastic and reconstructive surgery. Founded in 1989. **NOTE:** Second and third shifts are offered. **Common positions include:** Accountant/Auditor; Biomedical Engineer; Buyer; Certified Nurses Aide; Chemist; Chief Financial Officer; Clinical Lab Technician; Computer Programmer;

Health Care: Services, Equipment, and Products

Dietician/Nutritionist; Electrician; Financial Analyst; Health Services Manager; Medical Records Technician; Nuclear Medicine Technologist; Occupational Therapist; Pharmacist; Physical Therapist; Radiological Technologist; Registered Nurse; Respiratory Therapist; Restaurant/Food Service Manager; Secretary; Social Worker; Surgical Technician; Systems Analyst. **Educational backgrounds include:** Accounting; Business Administration; Computer Science; Health Care. **Benefits:** 403(b); Dental Insurance; Disability Coverage; Employee Discounts; Incentive Plan; Life Insurance; Medical Insurance; Pension Plan; Tuition Assistance. **Annual sales/revenues:** More than $100 million. **Number of employees at this location:** 600.

Note: Because addresses and telephone numbers of smaller companies can change rapidly, we recommend you call each company to verify the information below before inquiring about job opportunities. Mass mailings are not recommended.

Additional small employers:

DENTISTS' OFFICES AND CLINICS

Monarch Dental Associates Inc.
4201 Spring Valley Rd, Dallas TX 75244-3631. 972/437-4795.

DOCTORS' OFFICES AND CLINICS

Amarillo Diagnostic Clinic
6700 W 9th Ave, Amarillo TX 79106-1701. 806/358-0200.

Arlington Cancer Center
906 W Randol Mill Rd, Arlington TX 76012-2510. 817/261-4906.

Arlington Medical Associates
1300 S Fielder Rd, Arlington TX 76013-2348. 817/277-2221.

Clinics of North Texas
PO Box 97521, Wichita Falls TX 76307-7521. 940/766-8690.

De Paul Center
301 Londonderry Dr, Waco TX 76712-7915. 254/776-5970.

Diagnostic Clinic Longview
707 Hollybrook Dr, Longview TX 75605-2410. 903/757-6042.

Heritage Southwest Medical Group
7610 N Stemmons Fwy, Dallas TX 75247-4231. 214/631-7700.

Medical Clinic of North Texas
800 W Arbrook Blvd, Arlington TX 76015-4327. 817/277-7133.

Neurocare Network
816 S Fleishel Ave, Tyler TX 75701-2016. 903/597-3472.

North Texas Surgery Center
7992 W Virginia Dr, Dallas TX 75237-3764. 972/283-2400.

Opthmalogist Associates
1201 Summit Ave, Fort Worth TX 76102-4413. 817/335-5435.

Promedco of Temple Inc.
1905 SW HK Dodgen Loop, Temple TX 76502-1814. 254/778-2123.

Radiology Associates of Tarrant County
PO Box 2927, Fort Worth TX 76113-2927. 817/336-8684.

Southern Clinic
2602 Saint Michael Dr, Texarkana TX 75503-2372. 903/614-6000.

Southwestern Medical Center
5323 Harry Hines Blvd, Dallas TX 75390-7208. 214/648-3407.

Stephenville Medical & Surgical
150 River North Blvd, Stephenville TX 76401-1803. 254/968-6051.

Texarkana Regional Dialysis Center
PO Box 1409, Texarkana TX 75504-1409. 903/792-7151.

Trinity Clinic
520 Douglas Blvd, Tyler TX 75702-8307. 903/593-1721.

HEALTH AND ALLIED SERVICES

American Medical Response Inc.
2603 Inwood Rd, Dallas TX 75235-7423. 214/353-7610.

Carter Blood Care Center
2205 Highway 121, Bedford TX 76021-5950. 214/351-8111.

Concentra Health Services Inc.
3010 LBJ Fwy, Ste 400, Dallas TX 75234-7749. 972/484-2700.

Diagnostic Health Services Inc.
2777 N Stemmons Fwy, Dallas TX 75207-2277. 214/634-0403.

Harris Methodist Hospital
611 Ryan Plaza Dr, Arlington TX 76011-4018. 817/462-7000.

HOME HEALTH CARE SERVICES

American Hospice Inc.
12900 Senlac Dr, Ste 100, Dallas TX 75234-9232. 972/406-2742.

Attentive Home Health Care
PO Box 689, Desoto TX 75123-0689. 972/230-6195.

Cherokee Home Health Care Inc.
615A E Rusk St, Jacksonville TX 75766-5017. 903/586-3173.

Concentra Managed Care Inc.
3220 Keller Springs Rd, Carrollton TX 75006-5049. 972/725-1450.

Crown of Texas Hospice Ltd.
1000 S Jefferson St, Amarillo TX 79101-3232. 806/372-7696.

Doctors Nursing Service Inc.
2101 Kemp Blvd, Wichita Falls TX 76309-4313. 940/322-4357.

Girling Health Care Inc.
6060 N Central Expy, Dallas TX 75206-5209. 214/824-3621.

Girling Health Care Inc.
4849 Granville Ave, Ste 1560, Dallas TX 75206. 214/828-4811.

Harris Home Health Services
6000 Western Pl, Ste 118, Fort Worth TX 76107-4654. 817/570-8100.

Healthcor Holdings Inc.
8150 N Central Expy, Dallas TX 75206-1815. 972/233-7744.

Hi Plains Hospital & Nursing Home
PO Box 1260, Hale Center TX 79041-1260. 806/839-2471.

Hillcrest Home Care
PO Box 5100, Waco TX 76708-0100. 254/202-5100.

Home Health of Tarrant County
923 Pennsylvania Ave, Fort Worth TX 76104-2254. 817/338-9595.

Home Health Plus
8700 N Stemmons Fwy, Dallas TX 75247-3729. 214/630-9070.

Home Health Services of Dallas
2929 Carlisle St, Ste 375A, Dallas TX 75204-4047. 214/720-4473.

Interim Healthcare Lubbock Inc.
166 S Willis St, Abilene TX 79605-1734. 915/677-2047.

Jackson Healthcare Systems
PO Box 3945, Temple TX 76505-3945. 254/778-4210.

Magnolia Home Health Care Inc.
PO Box 1084, Paris TX 75461-1084. 903/784-6185.

PT Home Service
8200 Brookriver Dr, Grand Prairie TX 75050. 972/263-9619.

Quality Home Health Care Inc.
2626 Hilltop Dr, Ste 2, Sherman TX 75090-2248. 903/892-9281.

Signature Home Care
2006 N Highway 360, Grand Prairie TX 75050-1423. 972/714-7800.

Signature Home Care
PO Box 1135, Lewisville TX 75067-1135. 972/420-8711.

Symphony Diagnostic Services
9535 Forest Ln, Ste 114, Dallas TX 75243-5958. 972/644-7442.

TLC Inc.
3415 Custer Rd, Ste 132, Plano TX 75023-7555. 972/422-1375.

Visiting Nurse Association
PO Box 91, Texarkana TX 75504-0091. 903/794-3102.

Wichita Home Health
1100 Alma St, Wichita Falls TX 76301-5702. 940/322-7113.

HOSPITALS AND MEDICAL CENTERS

Arlington Memorial Hospital
800 W Randol Mill Rd, Arlington TX 76012-2504. 817/548-6100.

Atlanta Memorial Hospital
PO Box 1049, Atlanta TX 75551-1049. 903/796-4151.

Baylor Medical Center
805 W Lampasas St, Ennis TX 75119-4535. 972/875-6221.

Baylor Medical Center
1405 W Jefferson St, Waxahachie TX 75165-2231. 972/923-7000.

Bowie Memorial Hospital
705 E Greenwood Ave, Bowie TX 76230-3135. 940/872-1126.

Brownfield Regional Medical Center
705 E Felt St, Brownfield TX 79316-3439. 806/637-3551.

Campbell Memorial Hospital
713 E Anderson St, Weatherford TX 76086-5705. 817/596-8751.

Childress Regional Medical Center
PO Box 1030, Childress TX 79201-1030. 940/937-6371.

Columbia Medical Center of Arlington
3301 Matlock Rd, Arlington TX 76015-2908. 817/472-4800.

Columbia Medical Center of Dallas SW
2929 S Hampton Rd, Dallas TX 75224-3026. 214/330-4611.

Columbia Medical Center of Lancaster
2600 W Pleasant Run Rd, Lancaster TX 75146-1100. 972/223-9600.

Columbia Medical Center of Lewisville
500 W Main St, Lewisville TX 75057-3641. 972/420-1000.

Columbia North Texas Medical Center
4500 Medical Center Dr, McKinney TX 75069-1650. 972/547-8000.

Coryell Memorial Hospital
1507 W Main St, Gatesville TX 76528-1024. 254/865-8251.

Covenant Hospital
1900 College Ave, Levelland TX 79336-6508. 806/894-4963.

Crosbyton Clinic Hospital
710 W Main St, Crosbyton TX 79322-2143. 806/675-2382.

Darnell Army Hospital
Bldg 36000, Fort Hood TX 76544. 254/288-8000.

Decatur Community Hospital
2000 S Fm 51, Decatur TX 76234-3702. 817/430-0863.

Denton Community Hospital
207 N Bonnie Brae St, Denton TX 76201-3727. 940/898-7000.

East Texas Medical Center-Athens
2000 S Palestine St, Athens TX 75751-5610. 903/675-2216.

East Texas Medical Center-Carthage
PO Box 549, Carthage TX 75633-0549. 903/693-3841.

East Texas Medical Center-Clarksville
PO Box 1270, Clarksville TX 75426-1270. 903/427-3851.

East Texas Medical Center-Jacksonville
501 S Ragsdale St, Jacksonville TX 75766-2434. 903/586-3000.

East Texas Medical Center-Rusk
PO Box 317, Rusk TX 75785-0317. 903/683-2273.

Eastland Memorial Hospital
PO Box 897, Eastland TX 76448-0897. 254/629-2601.

Edwards Cancer Center
PO Box 669, Bedford TX 76095-0669. 817/685-4000.

Gainesville Memorial Hospital
1016 Ritchey St, Gainesville TX 76240-3539. 940/665-1751.

Glen Oaks Hospital
301 Division St, Greenville TX 75402-4199. 903/454-6000.

Golden Plains Community Hospital
200 S McGee St, Borger TX 79007-4022. 806/273-2851.

Good Shepherd Medical Center
700 E Marshall Ave, Longview TX 75601-5572. 903/236-2000.

Harris Methodist Hospital
1608 Hospital Pkwy, Bedford TX 76022-6913. 817/355-7700.

Harris Methodist Hospital
PO Box 1399, Stephenville TX 76401-1399. 254/965-3115.

HealthSouth of Texarkana Inc.
515 W 12th St, Texarkana TX 75501-4416. 903/793-0088.

HealthSouth Plano Rehabilitation Hospital
2800 W 15th St, Plano TX 75075-7526. 972/612-9000.

HealthSouth Rehabilitation Hospital
3200 Matlock Rd, Arlington TX 76015-2911. 817/468-4000.

Health Care: Services, Equipment, and Products/187

HealthSouth Rehabilitation Hospital
1212 W Lancaster Ave, Fort Worth TX 76102-4510. 817/870-2336.

Hereford Regional Medical Center
PO Box 1858, Hereford TX 79045-1858. 806/364-2141.

Highland Medical Center
2412 50th St, Lubbock TX 79412-2504. 806/795-8251.

Hillcrest Baptist Medical Center
PO Box 5100, Waco TX 76708-0100. 254/202-2000.

Hopkins County Memorial Hospital
PO Box 275, Sulphur Springs TX 75483-0275. 903/885-7671.

Johns Community Hospital
305 Mallard Ln, Taylor TX 76574-1208. 512/352-7611.

King's Daughters Hospital
1901 SW Dodgen Loop, Temple TX 76502-1814. 254/771-8600.

Lake Granbury Medical Center
1310 Paluxy Rd, Granbury TX 76048-5655. 817/573-2683.

Lake Pointe Medical Center
PO Box 1550, Rowlett TX 75030-1550. 972/412-2273.

Lake Whitney Medical Center
PO Box 458, Whitney TX 76692-0458. 254/694-3165.

Lamb Healthcare Center
1500 S Sunset Ave, Littlefield TX 79339-4899. 806/385-6411.

Linden Municipal Hospital
PO Box 32, Linden TX 75563-0032. 903/756-5561.

Mansfield General Hospital
1802 Highway 157 N, Mansfield TX 76063-3923. 817/473-6101.

Marshall Regional Medical Center
PO Box 1599, Marshall TX 75671-1599. 903/935-9311.

McCuistion Regional Medical Center
865 Deshong Dr, Paris TX 75462-2006. 903/737-1111.

Medical Arts Hospital
1600 N Bryan Ave, Lamesa TX 79331-3145. 806/872-2183.

Methodist Hospital Plainview
2601 Dimmitt Rd, Plainview TX 79072-1833. 806/296-5531.

Metroplex Hospital
2201 S Clear Creek Rd, Killeen TX 76549-4110. 254/526-7523.

Mother Frances Hospital Region
PO Box 6457, Tyler TX 75711-6457. 903/593-8441.

Mother Francis Memorial Hospital
PO Box 4070, Palestine TX 75802-4070. 903/729-6981.

Muleshoe Area Medical Center
708 S 1st St, Muleshoe TX 79347-3627. 806/272-4524.

Nocona General Hospital
100 Park Rd, Nocona TX 76255-3616. 940/825-3235.

North Texas Hospital for Children
7777 Forest Ln, Dallas TX 75230-2505. 972/566-8888.

Northeast Community Hospital
1301 Airport Fwy, Bedford TX 76021-6624. 817/868-5740.

Northeast Medical Inc.
PO Drawer C, Bonham TX 75418-0180. 903/583-8585.

Ochiltree General Hospital
3101 Garrett Dr, Perryton TX 79070-5323. 806/435-3606.

Olney-Hamilton Hospital
PO Box 158, Olney TX 76374-0158. 940/564-5521.

Pavilion Counseling Center
1501 Coulter Dr, Amarillo TX 79106-1770. 806/354-1810.

Plains Memorial Hospital
PO Box 278, Dimmitt TX 79027-0278. 806/647-2191.

Presbyterian Hospital of Dallas
8200 Walnut Hill Ln, Dallas TX 75231-4426. 214/345-6789.

Presbyterian Hospital of Greenville
PO Drawer 1059, Greenville TX 75403-1059. 903/408-5000.

Presbyterian Hospital of Plano
6200 W Parker Rd, Plano TX 75093-7939. 972/608-8000.

Red River Hospital
1505 8th St, Wichita Falls TX 76301-3106. 940/322-3171.

Richards Memorial Hospital
PO Box 1010, Rockdale TX 76567-1010. 512/446-2513.

Rolling Plains Memorial Hospital
PO Box 690, Sweetwater TX 79556-0690. 915/235-1701.

Roy H. Laird Memorial Hospital
1612 S Henderson Blvd, Kilgore TX 75662-3518. 903/984-3505.

Scott & White Memorial Hospital
2401 S 31st St, Temple TX 76508-0001. 254/724-2111.

St. Paul Home Health
7920 Elmbrook Dr, Dallas TX 75247-6900. 214/634-7600.

Stephens Memorial Hospital
200 S Geneva St, Breckenridge TX 76424-4702. 254/559-2241.

Teague Veterans Center
1901 S 1st St, Temple TX 76504-7451. 254/778-4811.

Terrell State Hospital
PO Box 70, Terrell TX 75160-9000. 972/563-6452.

Texas Scottish Rite Hospital
PO Box 190567, Dallas TX 75219-0567. 214/521-3168.

The Cedar Hospital
2000 Old Hickory Trl, Desoto TX 75115-2242. 972/298-7323.

Titus Regional Medical Center
2001 N Jefferson Ave, Mount Pleasant TX 75455-2386. 903/577-6000.

Trinity Medical Center
4343 N Josey Ln, Carrollton TX 75010-4608. 972/492-1010.

Trinity Mother Frances
421 S Beckham Ave, Tyler TX 75702-8309. 903/533-8494.

Trinity Valley Medical Center
2900 S Loop 256, Palestine TX 75801-6958. 903/731-1000.

VA Medical Center
1016 Ward St, Marlin TX 76661-2175. 254/883-3511.

Vencor Hospital
1000 N Cooper St, Arlington TX 76011-5540. 817/543-0200.

Vencor Hospital
7800 Oakmont Blvd, Fort Worth TX 76132-4203. 817/346-0094.

Vernon State Hospital
PO Box 2231, Vernon TX 76385-2231. 940/552-9901.

Walls Regional Hospital
201 Walls Dr, Cleburne TX 76031-1008. 817/641-2551.

Wilbarger General Hospital
920 Hillcrest Dr, Vernon TX 76384-3132. 940/552-9351.

Wilson Jones Regional Health Systems
500 N Highland Ave, Sherman TX 75092-7354. 903/870-4611.

W.J. Mangold Memorial Hospital
PO Box 37, Lockney TX 79241-0037. 806/652-3373.

Wood County Central Hospital
PO Drawer 1000, Quitman TX 75783. 903/763-4505.

MEDICAL EQUIPMENT

Advanced Neuromodulation Systems
6501 Windcrest Dr, Ste 100, Plano TX 75024-3064. 972/309-8000.

Allegiance Corporation
200 McKnight, Jacksonville TX 75766. 903/586-6502.

Argon Medical
PO Box 1970, Athens TX 75751-1970. 903/675-9321.

Avcor Health Care Products
PO Box 40500, Fort Worth TX 76140-0500. 817/551-0595.

B. Braun/McGaw Inc.
1601 Wallace Dr, Ste 150, Carrollton TX 75006-6690. 972/245-2243.

Benedict Optical Inc.
651 E Corporate Dr, Lewisville TX 75057-6403. 972/221-4141.

Blacksheep Inc.
3220 W Gentry Pkwy, Tyler TX 75702-1311. 903/592-3853.

Medtronic Midas
3001 Race St, Fort Worth TX 76111-4117. 817/838-2351.

Retractable Technologies Inc.
PO Box 9, Little Elm TX 75068-0009. 972/221-8734.

Rex Midas Pneumatic Tools
2925 Race St, Fort Worth TX 76111-4134. 800/433-7080.

Safety Clothing Manufacturing
PO Box 1030, Atlanta TX 75551-1030. 903/796-4111.

Spenco Medical Corporation
PO Box 2501, Waco TX 76702-2501. 254/772-6000.

MEDICAL EQUIPMENT AND SUPPLIES WHOLESALE

Kinetic Concepts
2132 113th St, Grand Prairie TX 75050-1240. 972/647-4477.

Milcare Inc.
4425 W Airport Fwy, Ste 200, Irving TX 75062. 972/594-8300.

PSS World Medical Inc.
1419 Dunn Dr, Carrollton TX 75006-6909. 972/245-0908.

Siemens Medical Systems Inc.
2002 N Highway 360, Grand Prairie TX 75050-1423. 972/622-2461.

NURSING AND PERSONAL CARE FACILITIES

All Saints-Bishop Davies Center
2712 Hurstview Dr, Hurst TX 76054-2402. 817/281-6708.

Alta Mesa Nursing Center Inc.
5300 Alta Mesa Blvd, Fort Worth TX 76133-5924. 817/346-1800.

Ashford Hall
2021 Shoaf Dr, Irving TX 75061-2553. 972/579-1919.

Bell Haven Nursing Center
1002 Medical Dr, Killeen TX 76543-3525. 254/634-0374.

Bellmire Healthcare Facility
1101 Rock St, Bowie TX 76230-3115. 940/872-2283.

Bivins Memorial Home
1001 Wallace Blvd, Amarillo TX 79106-1735. 806/355-7453.

Brentwood Place
8069 Scyene Cir, Bldg 1, Dallas TX 75227-5534. 214/388-0609.

Briarcliff Health Center
4400 Walnut St, Greenville TX 75401-5586. 903/455-8729.

Briarcliff Health Center
3403 S Vine Ave, Tyler TX 75701-8539. 903/581-5714.

Broadway Plaza Health Center
5301 Bryant Irvin Rd, Fort Worth TX 76132-4030. 817/346-9407.

Brookhaven Nursing Home Center
1855 Cheyenne Dr, Carrollton TX 75010-2201. 972/394-7141.

Buckner Ryburn Nursing Center
4810 Samuell Blvd, Dallas TX 75228-6831. 214/388-0426.

Capital Senior Living Inc.
14160 Dallas Pkwy, Ste 300, Dallas TX 75240-4383. 972/770-5600.

Carriage House Manor Inc.
PO Box 914, Sulphur Springs TX 75483-0914. 903/885-3589.

Christian Care Center
1000 Wiggins Pkwy, Mesquite TX 75150-7465. 972/686-3100.

Clarksville Nursing Center
300 E Baker St, Clarksville TX 75426-5034. 903/427-2236.

Clifton Lutheran Sunset Home
PO Box 71, Clifton TX 76634-0071. 254/675-8637.

Collins Care Center
3100 S Rigsbee Dr, Plano TX 75074-7008. 972/423-6217.

Colonial Manor Nursing Center
2035 Granbury St, Cleburne TX 76031-1601. 817/645-9134.

Colonial Manor Nursing Center
930 S Baxter Ave, Tyler TX 75701-2209. 903/597-2068.

Colonial Park Nursing Home
PO Box 1869, Marshall TX 75671-1869. 903/935-7886.

Cotru Inc.
PO Box 4704, Wichita Falls TX 76308-0704. 940/692-8977.

Covenant Home Health Care
4709 66th St, Lubbock TX 79414-4841. 806/797-8125.

Craig Retirement Community
5500 W 9th Ave, Amarillo TX 79106-4162. 806/352-7244.

Creekview Retirement Center
123 Lions Club Park Rd, Lancaster TX 75146-3108. 972/227-1205.

Crest View Manor
PO Box 2239, Waco TX 76703-2239. 254/753-0291.

Crestwood Nursing Home
PO Box 368, Wills Point TX 75169-0368. 903/873-2542.

Dallas Metro Care Services
2822 Wimbledon Ct, Garland TX 75041-6601. 972/278-9727.

Dallas Metro Care Services
14255 Haymeadow Dr, Dallas TX 75240-2827. 972/239-6643.

Dallas Nursing & Rehabilitation Center
11301 Dennis Rd, Dallas TX 75229-2305. 972/247-4866.

Health Care: Services, Equipment, and Products/189

Denton Rehabilitation Center
2229 N Carroll Blvd, Denton TX 76201-1833. 940/387-8508.

Elmwood Nursing Center
221 Virginia Ave, Marlin TX 76661-2160. 254/883-5548.

Farwell Convalescent Center
PO Box 890, Farwell TX 79325-0890. 806/481-9027.

Forum Healthcare
7827 Park Ln, Dallas TX 75225-2032. 214/369-9905.

Four Seasons Nursing Centers
3326 Burgoyne St, Dallas TX 75233-1304. 214/330-9291.

Four Seasons Nursing Centers
7625 Glenview Dr, Fort Worth TX 76180-8331. 817/284-1427.

Four States Care Center
8 E Midway Dr, Texarkana TX 75501-5884. 903/838-9526.

Glen Rose Nursing Home
PO Box 2099, Glen Rose TX 76043-2099. 254/897-2215.

Glenview Nursing Home
3526 W Erwin St, Tyler TX 75702-6519. 903/593-6441.

Golden Acres
2525 Centerville Rd, Dallas TX 75228-2634. 214/327-4503.

Grace Presbyterian Village
550 E Ann Arbor Ave, Dallas TX 75216-6767. 214/376-1701.

Grandbury Care Center
301 S Park St, Granbury TX 76048-1800. 817/573-3726.

Greens Manor
401 Owen Ln, Waco TX 76710-5558. 254/772-8900.

Hansford Manor
707 Roland St, Spearman TX 79081-3441. 806/659-2535.

Harvest Senior Services Inc.
600 Maple Ave, Burleson TX 76028-5810. 817/295-8118.

Heartland Health Care
2001 Forest Ridge Dr, Bedford TX 76021-5712. 817/571-6804.

Heritage Manor Plano
1621 Coit Rd, Plano TX 75075-6141. 972/596-7930.

Heritage Nursing Home
PO Box 728, Quitman TX 75783-0728. 903/763-2284.

Heritage Oaks Nursing Center
1112 Gibbins Rd, Arlington TX 76011-5618. 817/274-2584.

Heritage Park
3208 Thunderbird Ln, Plano TX 75075-2321. 972/422-2214.

Heritage Place
825 W Kearney St, Mesquite TX 75149-3206. 972/288-7668.

Heritage Village
1111 Rockingham Ln, Richardson TX 75080-4309. 972/231-8833.

Heritage Western Hills
8001 Western Hills Blvd, Fort Worth TX 76108-3524. 817/246-4953.

Hilltop Haven
PO Box 39, Gunter TX 75058-0039. 903/433-2415.

Holiday Lodge Nursing Home
1301 Eden Dr, Longview TX 75605-4102. 903/753-7651.

Lakeside Care Center
4306 24th St, Lubbock TX 79410-1818. 806/793-2555.

Life Care Center of Plano
3800 W Park Blvd, Plano TX 75075-3542. 972/612-1700.

Manor Oaks Nursing Home
Rural Route 1, Box 7, Rockdale TX 76567-9799. 512/446-5893.

Mansfield Nursing Center
1402 E Broad St, Mansfield TX 76063-1806. 817/477-2176.

Mariner Health
4825 Wellesley Ave, Fort Worth TX 76107-6148. 817/732-6608.

New Boston Nursing Center
210 Rice St, New Boston TX 75570-2929. 903/628-5551.

North Dallas Rehabilitation Hospital
8383 Meadow Rd, Dallas TX 75231-3701. 214/891-0880.

Oak Brook Health Care Center
107 Stacy Dr, Whitehouse TX 75791-3755. 903/839-5050.

Park Haven Healthcare Center
2108 15th St, Bridgeport TX 76426-2055. 940/683-5023.

Park Place Nursing Home
PO Box 2430, Palestine TX 75802-2430. 903/729-3246.

Post Oak Health & Rahabilitation
1518 S Sam Rayburn Fwy, Sherman TX 75090-8736. 903/893-5553.

Prairie House Living Center
1301 Mesa Dr, Plainview TX 79072-3905. 806/293-4855.

Progressive Care Centers
424 S Adams St, Fort Worth TX 76104-1003. 817/338-0354.

Quality Care of Waco Inc.
2501 Maple Ave, Waco TX 76707-1337. 254/752-0311.

Quality Convalescent Center
1000 6th Ave, Fort Worth TX 76104-2808. 817/336-2586.

Regency Manor Nursing Center
3011 W Adams Ave, Temple TX 76504-2873. 254/773-1626.

Regency Nursing & Rehabilitation
17440 Dallas Pkwy, Dallas TX 75287-7336. 972/381-0200.

Regis/St. Elizabeth Centers
PO Box 1909, Waco TX 76703-1909. 254/756-5441.

Renfro Nursing Home Inc.
1413 W Main St, Waxahachie TX 75165-2241. 972/937-2298.

Ridgecrest Retirement Center
1900 W Highway 6, Waco TX 76712-9729. 254/776-9681.

Robinson Nursing & Development Center
305 S Andrews Dr, Waco TX 76706-5705. 254/662-4010.

Rockwall Nursing Care Center
206 Storrs St, Rockwall TX 75087-4036. 972/771-5000.

Rose Haven Retreat
PO Box 240, Atlanta TX 75551-0240. 903/796-4127.

Rowlett Nursing Center
9300 Hwy 66, Rowlett TX 75088. 972/475-4700.

Shady Oaks Nursing Center
1000 E US Highway 82, Sherman TX 75090-1704. 903/893-9636.

Skyview Living Center
1680 S Edmonds Ln, Lewisville TX 75067-5803. 972/436-4538.

Stonegate Nursing Center
4201 Stonegate Blvd, Fort Worth TX 76109-9503. 817/924-5440.

Sweetbriar of Taylor
PO Box 831, Taylor TX 76574-0831. 512/352-3684.

Sweetwater Healthcare
1600 Josephine St, Sweetwater TX 79556-3599. 915/236-6653.

Texas Choice Communities
PO Box 1066, Henderson TX
75653-1066. 903/657-6506.

Town Hall Estates Nursing
PO Box 588, Cleburne TX
76033-0588. 817/641-9843.

Vitas Healthcare Corp.
5001 LBJ Fwy, Ste 1050, Dallas
TX 75244-6134. 972/661-2004.

Ware Memorial Care Center
400 W 14th Ave, Amarillo TX
79101-4140. 806/373-0471.

Western Hill Nursing Home
Rural Rte 5, Box 26, Comanche
TX 76442-9702. 915/356-2571.

Westgate Nursing Home
PO Box 1999, Hereford TX
79045-1999. 806/364-0661.

Westview Manor
414 Johnson Dr, McGregor TX
76657-1426. 254/840-3281.

Whitehall Nursing Center Inc.
PO Box 998, Crockett TX
75835-0998. 936/544-2163.

Williamsburg Village Nursing Center
941 Scotland Dr, Desoto TX
75115-2058. 972/572-2700.

Woodland Springs Nursing Center
1010 Dallas St, Waco TX
76704-1711. 254/752-9774.

Woodridge Convalescent Center
1500 Autumn Dr, Grapevine TX
76051-3103. 817/481-3622.

OFFICES AND CLINICS OF HEALTH PRACTITIONERS

North Texas Medical Group
1500 S Main St, Fort Worth TX
76104-4917. 817/927-3982.

Sundance Rehabilitation Corp.
15851 Dallas Pkwy, Ste 240,
Addison TX 75001-3360.
972/770-7955.

Trinity Rehab Inc.
4514 Travis St, Ste 330, Dallas
TX 75205-4186. 972/889-1133.

RESIDENTIAL CARE

Baylor Institute For Rehabilitation
3505 Gaston Ave, Dallas TX
75246-2094. 214/826-7030.

Buckner Baptist Children's Home
5200 S Buckner Blvd, Dallas TX
75227-2006. 214/321-4515.

Buckner Baptist Village
4800 Samuell Blvd, Dallas TX
75228-6831. 214/381-2171.

Buckner Retirement Services
600 N Pearl St, Ste 1900, Dallas
TX 75201-2896. 214/758-8000.

Cartmell Home For the Aged
2212 W Reagan St, Palestine TX
75801-2222. 903/727-8500.

Children's Home of Lubbock
PO Box 2824, Lubbock TX
79408-2824. 806/762-0481.

Cook Children's Home Health
1522 Pennsylvania Ave, Fort
Worth TX 76104-2027.
817/820-8433.

Emerald Point Home
1601 N Angon, Cleburne TX
76031. 817/558-1121.

Ennis Care Center
1200 S Hall St, Ennis TX 75119-
6318. 972/875-9051.

Forum At Park Lane
7831 Park Ln, Dallas TX 75225-
2000. 214/369-9902.

Lighthouse For the Blind
912 W Broadway St, Fort Worth
TX 76104-1115. 817/332-3341.

Presbyterian Manor
4600 Taft Blvd, Wichita Falls
TX 76308-4935. 940/691-1710.

Professional Care Center
1950 Record Crossing Rd,
Dallas TX 75235-6223.
214/630-1491.

Skyview Living Center
PO Box 154486, Waco TX
76715-4486. 254/799-6291.

Skyview Living Center
1519 Scripture St, Denton TX
76201-3915. 940/383-3576.

Waco Center For Youth
3501 N 19th St, Waco TX
76708-2007. 254/756-2171.

SPECIALTY OUTPATIENT FACILITIES

Covenant Medical System
4010 22nd St, Lubbock TX
79410-1116. 806/725-5627.

Dalby Correctional Facility
805 N Avenue F, Post TX
79356-9304. 806/495-2111.

Disability Services of the Southwest
5701 Westcreek Dr, Fort Worth
TX 76133-3301. 817/292-4209.

Heart Texas Regional Medical Center
PO Box 890, Waco TX 76703-
0890. 254/752-3451.

Lifenet Community Behavioral Healthcare
10405 E Northwest Hwy,
Dallas TX 75238-4619.
214/221-5433.

Lubbock Memorial Health
PO Box 2828, Lubbock TX
79408-2828. 806/766-0310.

Pride
PO Box 35546, Dallas TX
75235-0546. 214/351-6600.

Sammons Cancer Center
3500 Gaston Ave, Dallas TX
75246-2096. 214/820-3535.

Southern Rehabilitation Centers
10610 Metric Dr, Ste 175,
Dallas TX 75243-5594.
972/398-1572.

Tyler Rehabilitation Hospital
3131 Troup Hwy, Tyler TX
75701-8350. 903/510-7000.

West Texas Rehabilitation Center Inc.
4601 Hartford St, Abilene TX
79605-4603. 915/793-3400.

For more information on career opportunities in the health care industry:

Associations

AMBULATORY INFORMATION MANAGEMENT ASSOCIATION
27212 Calaroga Avenue, Hayward CA 94545.
510/293-5688. Contact: Martha Feinberg,
Membership Coordinator. E-mail address:
info@aim4.org. World Wide Web address:
http://www.aim4.org.

AMERICAN ACADEMY OF ALLERGY, ASTHMA, & IMMUNOLOGY
611 East Wells Street, Milwaukee WI 53202.
414/272-6071. World Wide Web address:
http://www.aaaai.org.

AMERICAN ACADEMY OF FAMILY PHYSICIANS
11400 Tomahawk Creek Parkway, Leawood KS
66211. 913/906-6000. World Wide Web address:

http://www.aafp.org. Promotes continuing education for family physicians.

AMERICAN ACADEMY OF NEUROLOGY
1080 Montreal Avenue, St. Paul MN 55116. 651/695-1940.

AMERICAN ACADEMY OF NURSE PRACTITIONERS
P.O. Box 12846, Austin TX 78711. 512/442-4262. Fax: 512/442-6469. World Wide Web address: http://www.aanp.org.

AMERICAN ACADEMY OF OPHTHALMOLOGY
655 Beech Street, San Francisco CA 94109. 415/561-8500. World Wide Web address: http://www.eyenet.org.

AMERICAN ACADEMY OF PEDIATRIC DENTISTRY
211 East Chicago Avenue, Suite 700, Chicago IL 60611-2616. 312/337-2169. World Wide Web address: http://www.aapd.org.

AMERICAN ACADEMY OF PERIODONTOLOGY
737 North Michigan Avenue, Suite 800, Chicago IL 60611-2690. 312/573-3218. World Wide Web address: http://www.perio.org.

AMERICAN ACADEMY OF PHYSICAL MEDICINE AND REHABILITATION
One IBM Plaza, Suite 2500, Chicago IL 60611. 312/464-9700. Fax: 312/464-0227. World Wide Web address: http://www.aapmr.org.

AMERICAN ACADEMY OF PHYSICIAN ASSISTANTS
950 North Washington Street, Alexandria VA 22314-1552. 703/836-2272. World Wide Web address: http://www.aapa.org. Promotes the use of physician assistants.

AMERICAN ASSOCIATION FOR CLINICAL CHEMISTRY
2101 L Street NW, Suite 202, Washington DC 20037. 202/857-0717. World Wide Web address: http://www.aacc.org. A nonprofit association for clinical, chemical, medical, and technical doctors.

AMERICAN ASSOCIATION FOR HEALTH EDUCATION
1900 Association Drive, Reston VA 20191-1599. 703/476-3437. Fax: 703/476-6638. World Wide Web address: http://www.aahperd.org/aahe/aahe-main.html.

AMERICAN ASSOCIATION FOR RESPIRATORY CARE
11030 Ables Lane, Dallas TX 75229. 972/243-2272. World Wide Web address: http://www.aarc.org. Promotes the art and science of respiratory care, while focusing on the needs of the patients.

AMERICAN ASSOCIATION OF COLLEGES OF OSTEOPATHIC MEDICINE
5550 Friendship Boulevard, Suite 310, Chevy Chase MD 20815. 301/968-4100. World Wide Web address: http://www.aacom.org. Provides application processing services for colleges of osteopathic medicine.

AMERICAN ASSOCIATION OF COLLEGES OF PODIATRIC MEDICINE
1350 Piccard Drive, Suite 322, Rockville MD 20850-4307. 301/990-7400. Fax: 301/990-2807. World Wide Web address: http://www.aacpm.org. Provides applications processing services for colleges of podiatric medicine.

AMERICAN ASSOCIATION OF DENTAL SCHOOLS
1625 Massachusetts Avenue NW, Suite 600, Washington DC 20036-2212. 202/667-9433. Fax: 202/667-0642. E-mail address: aads@aads.jhu.edu. World Wide Web address: http://www.aads.jhu.edu. Represents all 54 of the dental schools in the U.S. as well as individual members. This organization addresses research, education, and public health.

AMERICAN ASSOCIATION OF HEALTHCARE CONSULTANTS
11208 Waples Mill Road, Suite 109, Fairfax VA 22030. 703/691-2242. World Wide Web address: http://www.aahc.net.

AMERICAN ASSOCIATION OF HOMES AND SERVICES FOR THE AGING
901 E Street NW, Suite 500, Washington DC 20004. 202/783-2242. World Wide Web address: http://www.aahsa.org.

AMERICAN ASSOCIATION OF MEDICAL ASSISTANTS
20 North Wacker Drive, Suite 1575, Chicago IL 60606. 312/899-1500. World Wide Web address: http://www.aama-ntl.org.

AMERICAN ASSOCIATION OF NURSE ANESTHETISTS
222 South Prospect Avenue, Park Ridge IL 60068-4001. 847/692-7050. World Wide Web address: http://www.aana.com

AMERICAN ASSOCIATION OF ORAL AND MAXILLOFACIAL SURGEONS
9700 West Bryn Mawr Avenue, Rosemont IL 60018-5701. 847/678-6200. World Wide Web address: http://www.aaoms.org.

AMERICAN ASSOCIATION OF ORTHODONTISTS
401 North Lindbergh Boulevard, St. Louis MO 63141-7816. Toll-free phone: 800/222-9969.

AMERICAN CHIROPRACTIC ASSOCIATION
1701 Clarendon Boulevard, Arlington VA 22209. 703/276-8800. World Wide Web address: http://www.amerchiro.org. A national, nonprofit professional membership organization offering educational services (through films, booklets, texts, and kits), regional seminars and workshops, and major health and education activities that provide information on public health, safety, physical fitness, and disease prevention.

AMERICAN COLLEGE OF HEALTH CARE ADMINISTRATORS
1800 Diagonal Road, Suite 355, Alexandria VA 22314. 703/739-7900. World Wide Web address: http://www.achca.org. A professional membership society for individual long-term care professionals. Sponsors educational programs, supports research, and produces a number of publications.

AMERICAN COLLEGE OF HEALTHCARE EXECUTIVES
One North Franklin Street, Suite 1700, Chicago IL 60606-3491. 312/424-2800. World Wide Web

address: http://www.ache.org. Offers credentialing and educational programs. Publishes *Hospital & Health Services Administration* (a journal), and *Healthcare Executive* (a magazine.

AMERICAN COLLEGE OF MEDICAL PRACTICE EXECUTIVES
104 Inverness Terrace East, Englewood CO 80112-5306. 303/799-1111. World Wide Web address: http://www.mgma.com/acmpe.

AMERICAN COLLEGE OF OBSTETRICIANS AND GYNECOLOGISTS
409 12th Street SW, P.O. Box 96920, Washington DC 20090-6920. World Wide Web address: http://www.acog.org.

AMERICAN COLLEGE OF PHYSICIAN EXECUTIVES
4890 West Kennedy Boulevard, Suite 200, Tampa FL 33609-2575. 813/287-2000. Fax: 813/287-8993. World Wide Web address: http://www.acpe.org.

AMERICAN DENTAL ASSOCIATION
211 East Chicago Avenue, Chicago IL 60611. 312/440-2500. World Wide Web address: http://www.ada.org.

AMERICAN DENTAL HYGIENISTS' ASSOCIATION
444 North Michigan Avenue, Suite 3400, Chicago IL 60611. 312/440-8900. World Wide Web address: http://www.adha.org.

AMERICAN DIABETES ASSOCIATION
1701 North Beauregard Street, Alexandria VA 22311. Toll-free phone: 800/232-3472. World Wide Web address: http://www.diabetes.org. A nonprofit health organization dedicated to researching, preventing, and finding a cure for diabetes.

AMERICAN DIETETIC ASSOCIATION
216 West Jackson Boulevard, Suite 800, Chicago IL 60606. 312/899-0040. Toll-free phone: 800/877-1600. World Wide Web address: http://www.eatright.org. Promotes optimal nutrition to improve public health and well-being.

AMERICAN HEALTH INFORMATION MANAGEMENT ASSOCIATION
233 North Michigan Avenue, Suite 2150, Chicago IL 60601. 312/787-2672. World Wide Web address: http://www.ahima.org.

AMERICAN HEALTHCARE RADIOLOGY ADMINISTRATORS
111 Boston Post Road, Suite 105, Sudbury MA 01776. Toll-free phone: 800/334-2472. Fax: 978/443-8046. World Wide Web address: http://www.ahraonline.org.

AMERICAN HOSPITAL ASSOCIATION
One North Franklin Street, Chicago IL 60606. 312/422-3000. World Wide Web address: http://www.aha.org.

AMERICAN LUNG ASSOCIATION
1740 Broadway, New York NY 10019. Toll-free phone: 800/586-4872. World Wide Web address: http://www.lungusa.org. Focused on preventing and curing lung disease through research, education, and fundraising.

AMERICAN MEDICAL ASSOCIATION
515 North State Street, Chicago IL 60610. 312/464-5000. World Wide Web address: http://www.ama-assn.org. An organization for medical doctors.

AMERICAN MEDICAL INFORMATICS ASSOCIATION
4915 St. Elmo Avenue, Suite 401, Bethesda MD 20814. 301/657-1291. World Wide Web address: http://www.amia.org.

AMERICAN MEDICAL TECHNOLOGISTS
710 Higgins Road, Park Ridge IL 60068. 847/823-5169. World Wide Web address: http://www.amt1.com.

AMERICAN MEDICAL WOMEN'S ASSOCIATION
801 North Fairfax Street, Suite 400, Alexandria VA 22314. 703/838-0500. Fax: 703/549-3864. E-mail address: info@amwa-doc.org. World Wide Web address: http://www.amwa-doc.org. Supports the advancement of women in medicine.

AMERICAN NURSES ASSOCIATION
600 Maryland Avenue SW, Suite 100W, Washington DC 20024. 202/554-4444. World Wide Web address: http://www.nursingworld.org.

AMERICAN OCCUPATIONAL THERAPY ASSOCIATION, INC.
4720 Montgomery Lane, Bethesda MD 20824-1220. 301/652-2682. Toll-free phone: 800/377-8555. Fax: 301/652-7711. World Wide Web address: http://www.aota.org.

AMERICAN OPTOMETRIC ASSOCIATION
243 North Lindbergh Boulevard, St. Louis MO 63141. 314/991-4100. Offers publications, discounts, and insurance programs for members.

AMERICAN ORGANIZATION OF NURSE EXECUTIVES
One North Franklin Street, 34th Floor, Chicago IL 60606. 312/422-2800. World Wide Web address: http://www.aone.org.

AMERICAN ORTHOPAEDIC ASSOCIATION
6300 North River Road, Suite 505, Rosemont IL 60018. 847/318-7330. World Wide Web address: http://www.aoassn.org.

AMERICAN PHYSICAL THERAPY ASSOCIATION
1111 North Fairfax Street, Alexandria VA 22314. 703/684-2782. World Wide Web address: http://www.apta.org. Small fee required for information.

AMERICAN PODIATRIC MEDICAL ASSOCIATION
9312 Old Georgetown Road, Bethesda MD 20814-1698. 301/571-9200. World Wide Web address: http://www.apma.org.

AMERICAN PSYCHIATRIC ASSOCIATION
World Wide Web address: http://www.psych.org. Professional association for mental health professionals.

AMERICAN PUBLIC HEALTH ASSOCIATION
1015 15th Street NW, Suite 300, Washington DC 20005. 202/789-5600. World Wide Web address: http://www.apha.org.

AMERICAN SOCIETY OF ANESTHESIOLOGISTS
520 North NW Highway, Park Ridge IL 60068.

Health Care: Services, Equipment, and Products/193

847/825-5586. World Wide Web address: http://www.asahq.org.

AMERICAN SPEECH LANGUAGE HEARING ASSOCIATION
10801 Rockville Pike, Rockville MD 20852. Toll-free phone: 800/498-2071. World Wide Web address: http://www.asha.org. Professional, scientific, and credentialing association for audiologists; speech-language pathologists; and speech, language, and hearing scientists.

AMERICAN VETERINARY MEDICAL ASSOCIATION
1931 North Meacham Road, Suite 100, Schaumburg IL 60173. 847/925-8070. World Wide Web address: http://www.avma.org. Provides a forum for the discussion of important issues in the veterinary profession.

ASSOCIATION OF AMERICAN MEDICAL COLLEGES
2450 N Street NW, Washington DC 20037-1126. 202/828-0400. World Wide Web address: http://www.aamc.org.

ASSOCIATION OF UNIVERSITY PROGRAMS IN HEALTH ADMINISTRATION
730 11th Street NW, Washington DC 20001. 202/638-1448.

ASTHMA & ALLERGY FOUNDATION OF AMERICA
1233 20th Street NW, Suite 402, Washington DC 20036. Toll-free phone: 800/727-8462. World Wide Web address: http://www.aafa.org. A nonprofit health organization focused on assisting those suffering from asthma and/or allergies. The organization publishes *BreathingEasier*, a newsletter that provides allergy and asthma sufferers with current information about their diseases.

HEALTHCARE FINANCIAL MANAGEMENT ASSOCIATION
2 Westbrook Corporate Center, Suite 700, Westchester IL 60154-5700. 708/531-9600. World Wide Web address: http://www.hfma.org.

HEALTHCARE INFORMATION AND MANAGEMENT SYSTEMS SOCIETY
230 East Ohio Street, Suite 500, Chicago IL 60611. 312/664-4467. World Wide Web address: http://www.himss.org.

NATIONAL ASSOCIATION FOR CHIROPRACTIC MEDICINE
15427 Baybrook Drive, Houston TX 77062. 281/280-8262. World Wide Web address: http://www.chiromed.org.

NATIONAL COALITION OF HISPANIC HEALTH AND HUMAN SERVICES ORGANIZATIONS
1501 16th Street NW, Washington DC 20036. 202/387-5000. World Wide Web address: http://www.cossmho.org. Strives to improve the health and well-being of Hispanic communities throughout the United States.

NATIONAL HOSPICE ORGANIZATION
1700 Diagonal Road, Suite 300, Alexandria VA 22314. 703/243-5900. World Wide Web address: http://www.nho.org. Educates and advocates for the principles of hospice care to meet the needs of the terminally ill.

NATIONAL MEDICAL ASSOCIATION
1012 10th Street NW, Washington DC 20001. 202/347-1895. World Wide Web address: http://www.nmanet.org.

NATIONAL MENTAL HEALTH ASSOCIATION
1021 Prince Street, Alexandria VA 22314-2971. Toll-free phone: 800/969-6642. World Wide Web address: http://www.nmha.org. Focuses on preventing mental illness, improving mental health services, and educating the public on symptoms of and treatments for mental illnesses.

Magazines

AMERICAN MEDICAL NEWS
American Medical Association, 515 North State Street, Chicago IL 60610. 312/670-7827.

HEALTHCARE EXECUTIVE
American College of Health Care Executives, One North Franklin Street, Suite 1700, Chicago IL 60606-3491. 312/424-2800.

MODERN HEALTHCARE
Crain Communications, 740 North Rush Street, Chicago IL 60611. 312/649-5350. World Wide Web address: http://www.modernhealthcare.com.

NURSEFAX
Springhouse Corporation, 1111 Bethlehem Pike, Springhouse PA 19477. 215/646-8700. World Wide Web address: http://www.springnet.com. This is a jobline service designed to be used in conjunction with *Nursing* magazine.

Online Services

AMIA/MEDSIG
Go: MedSIG. A CompuServe forum for health care professionals to discuss and exchange information about topics in medicine.

ACADEMIC PHYSICIAN AND SCIENTIST
Gopher://aps.acad-phy-sci.com. A great resource for jobseekers interested in administrative or clinical positions at teaching hospitals.

AMERICA'S HEALTH CARE SOURCE
World Wide Web address: http://www.healthcaresource.com.

HEALTH CARE JOB STORE
World Wide Web address: http://www.healthcarejobstore.com.

HEALTH CARE JOBS ONLINE JOB BULLETIN BOARD
World Wide Web address: http://www.hcjobsonline.com. This Website is for jobseekers who are looking for job opportunities in the health care industry.

HEALTH CAREER WEB
World Wide Web address: http://www.healthcareerweb.com. Offers career articles and advice, an e-mail service for jobseekers, and links to career books.

MEDICAL-ADMART
World Wide Web address: http://www.medical-admart.com. This site lists health care/medical publications and provides links to their sites.

MEDSEARCH AMERICA
World Wide Web address: http://www.medsearch.com. Offers national and international job searches, career forums, a resume builder, resume posting, recruiters' sites, listings of professional associations, and employer profiles. Over 4,000 job openings are posted on Medsearch America.

MEDZILLA
E-mail address: info@medzilla.com. World Wide Web address: http://www.medzilla.com. Lists job openings for professionals in the fields of biotechnology, health care, medicine, and science related industries.

NURSING NETWORK FORUM
Go: Custom 261. A CompuServe bulletin board for nurses that provides periodic "live" discussions with special guests.

NURSING SPECTRUM CAREER FITNESS ONLINE
World Wide Web address: http://www.nursingspectrum.com. Provides a schedule of nationwide nursing events, a chat area, health care policy information, and educational resources.

PHYSICIAN'S EMPLOYMENT
World Wide Web address: http://www.physemp.com. Lists over 2,000 job openings for physicians, nurses, and allied health professionals.

SALUDOS WEB CAREER GUIDE: HEALTH CARE
World Wide Web address: http://www.saludos.com/cguide/hcguide.html. Provides information for jobseekers looking in the health care field. The site includes links to several health care associations and other sites that are sources of job openings in health care. This site is run by Saludos Hispanos.

Visit our exciting job and career site at www.careercity.com

HOTELS AND RESTAURANTS

You can expect to find the following types of companies in this chapter:
Casinos • Dinner Theaters • Hotel/Motel Operators • Resorts • Restaurants

Some helpful information: *Hotel workers, such as clerks, food service workers, and housekeepers, generally earn approximately $20,000 or less per year. Excluding tips, restaurant waitstaff and bartenders normally earn between $10,000 and $20,000 per year. Entry-level management candidates with degrees from hotel or restaurant management schools earn an average of $20,000 - $25,000 on their first job, and experienced management personnel at first class hotels or large restaurant chains can earn as much as $100,000 or more annually.*

BFX HOSPITALITY GROUP, INC.
226 Bailey Avenue, Suite 101, Fort Worth TX 76107. 817/332-4761. **Fax:** 817/877-0420. **Contact:** Personnel. **Description:** Owns and operates hotels and restaurants. **Corporate headquarters location:** This location. **Subsidiaries include:** American Food Classics Inc.; Hotels of Distinction. **Listed on:** American Stock Exchange. **Stock exchange symbol:** BFX.

BLACK-EYED PEA RESTAURANT U.S.A., INC.
2212 Arlington Downs Road, Suite 204, Arlington TX 76011. 817/633-6992. **Contact:** Human Resources. **Description:** A full-service restaurant chain specializing in homestyle cooking. Black-Eyed Pea operates over 130 locations nationwide. **Common positions include:** Restaurant/Food Service Manager. **Benefits:** Dental Insurance; Disability Coverage; Life Insurance; Medical Insurance; Profit Sharing; Savings Plan; Stock Option; Tuition Assistance. **Corporate headquarters location:** This Location. **Other U.S. locations:** AR; DC; GA; IN; KS; MD; NC; NM; OK; SC; TN; VA. **Parent company:** Unigate plc. **Operations at this facility include:** Administration; Research and Development.

BRINKER INTERNATIONAL INC.
6820 LBJ Freeway, Dallas TX 75240. 972/980-9917. **Fax:** 972/770-9593. **Contact:** Corporate Recruiting. **World Wide Web address:** http://www.brinker.com. **Description:** Operates full-service, casual dining restaurants including Chili's Grill & Bar, Cozymel's, On the Border, Romano's Macaroni Grill, and Spageddie's Italian Foods. In total, Brinker International operates 150 restaurants. **Common positions include:** Accountant/Auditor; Architect; Attorney; Buyer; Computer Programmer; Construction Contractor; Designer; General Manager; Management Trainee; Property and Real Estate Manager; Systems Analyst. **Educational backgrounds include:** Accounting; Computer Science; Finance; Hotel Administration. **Benefits:** 401(k); Daycare Assistance; Dental Insurance; Disability Coverage; Employee Discounts; Life Insurance; Medical Insurance; Profit Sharing; Public Transit Available; Stock Option; Tuition Assistance. **Corporate headquarters location:** This Location. **Other U.S. locations:** Nationwide. **Listed on:** New York Stock Exchange. **Annual sales/revenues:** More than $100 million. **Number of employees at this location:** 750. **Number of employees nationwide:** 65,000.

CEC ENTERTAINMENT INC.
dba CHUCK E. CHEESE
4441 West Airport Freeway, Irving TX 75062. 972/258-8507. **Fax:** 972/258-8545. **Contact:** Human Resources. **E-mail address:** careers@cecentertainment.com. **World Wide Web address:** http://www.chuckecheese.com. **Job page:** http://www.cec-careers.com. **Description:** Operates over 350 Chuck E. Cheese's pizza and amusement franchises throughout the United States and Canada. **Common positions include:** Account Representative; Attorney; Claim Representative; Computer Programmer; Construction Contractor; General Manager; Human Resources Manager; Operations/Production Manager; Paralegal; Property and Real Estate Manager; Purchasing Agent/Manager; Restaurant/Food Service Manager; Systems Analyst. **Educational backgrounds include:** Accounting; Business Administration; Computer Science; Finance; Marketing. **Benefits:** 401(k); Daycare Assistance; Dental Insurance; Disability Coverage; Employee Discounts; Life Insurance; Medical Insurance. **Corporate headquarters location:** This Location. **Listed on:** NASDAQ.

CARLSON RESTAURANTS WORLDWIDE INC.
7540 LBJ Freeway, Dallas TX 75251. 972/450-5400. **Fax:** 972/776-5468. **Contact:** Employee Relations. **World Wide Web address:** http://www.tgifridays.com. **Description:** Operates the TGI Friday's chain of casual-dining restaurants, which has over 500 locations. **Corporate**

headquarters location: This Location. **Parent company:** Carlson Companies, Inc. (Minneapolis MN).

CULINAIRE INTERNATIONAL, INC.
2121 San Jacinto Street, Suite 3100, Dallas TX 75201. 214/754-1880. **Contact:** Human Resources. **E-mail address:** recruit@culinaireintl.com. **World Wide Web address:** http://www.culinaireintl.com. **Description:** Provides the food and beverage services for a wide variety of corporate clients. **Corporate headquarters location:** This location.

DAVE & BUSTER'S, INC.
2481 Manana Drive, Dallas TX 75220. 214/357-9588. **Contact:** Human Resources. **World Wide Web address:** http://www.daveandbusters.com. **Description:** An operator of 12 restaurant/entertainment complexes. Each location houses eating venues and amusement facilities including billiards, video games, and virtual reality games. Founded in 1982. **Corporate headquarters location:** This Location. **Other area locations:** Houston TX. **Other U.S. locations:** Ontario CA; Denver CO; Hollywood FL; Atlanta GA; Chicago IL; North Bethesda MD; Detroit MI; Cincinnati OH; Philadelphia PA.

EL CHICO RESTAURANTS, INC.
12200 Stemmons Freeway, Suite 100, Dallas TX 75234. 972/241-5500. **Fax:** 972/888-8150. **Contact:** Corporate Recruiter. **World Wide Web address:** http://www.elchico.com. **Description:** Operates a chain of full-service restaurants. **Common positions include:** Management Trainee; Restaurant/Food Service Manager. **Educational backgrounds include:** Business Administration; Chemistry; Marketing; Restaurant Management. **Corporate headquarters location:** This Location. **Parent company:** Consolidated Restaurants Inc. (also at this location). **Operations at this facility include:** Administration; Manufacturing; Research and Development.

EMBASSY SUITES HOTEL
4250 Ridgemont Drive, Abilene TX 79606. 915/698-1234. **Contact:** Human Resources. **World Wide Web address:** http://www.embassy-suites.com. **Description:** A 176-room hotel.

FOUR SEASONS RESORT AND CLUB
4150 North MacArthur Boulevard, Irving TX 75038. 972/717-0700. **Fax:** 972/717-2578. **Recorded jobline:** 972/717-2544. **Contact:** Human Resources. **World Wide Web address:** http://www.fourseasons.com. **Description:** A 357-room resort offering two championship golf courses, 12 tennis courts, a spa, and a conference center. The 18-hole TPC championship golf course is the site of the annual GTE Byron Nelson Classic on the PGA Tour. The 176,000 square-foot sports club and spa has a racquet sports center, indoor and outdoor pools and tracks, and complete personal training facilities. The 20,000 square-foot conference center includes 26 multipurpose meeting and function rooms. **NOTE:** Entry-level positions, part-time jobs, and second and third shifts are offered. **Educational backgrounds include:** Hotel Administration. **Benefits:** 401(k); Dental Insurance; Disability Coverage; Flexible Schedule; Free Meals; Life Insurance; Medical Insurance; Profit Sharing; Sick Days (6 - 10); Vacation Days (6 - 10). **Special programs:** Training; Summer Jobs. **Corporate headquarters location:** Toronto, Canada. **Other U.S. locations:** Nationwide. **International locations:** Worldwide.

FURR'S/BISHOP'S CAFETERIAS
3001 East George Bush Highway, Richardson TX 75082. 972/808-2923. **Contact:** Human Resources. **Description:** Operates a national chain of cafeteria-style restaurants.

HARVEY HOTEL/DFW AIRPORT
4545 West John Carpenter Freeway, Irving TX 75063. 972/929-4500. **Fax:** 972/929-0733. **Contact:** Human Resources. **Description:** A 500-room hotel featuring a business center. **NOTE:** Entry-level positions and second and third shifts are offered. **Common positions include:** Accountant/Auditor; Administrative Assistant; Auditor; General Manager; Human Resources Manager; Management Trainee; Marketing Manager; Sales Manager; Systems Manager. **Educational backgrounds include:** Accounting; Business Administration; Communications; Marketing; Public Relations. **Benefits:** 401(k); Dental Insurance; Disability Coverage; Employee Discounts; Flexible Schedule; Life Insurance; Medical Insurance; Savings Plan. **Special programs:** Internships; Training. **Corporate headquarters location:** Addison TX. **Listed on:** New York Stock Exchange. **Number of employees at this location:** 350.

HYATT REGENCY DALLAS AT REUNION
300 Reunion Boulevard, Dallas TX 75207. 214/651-1234. **Contact:** Mark Spinelli, Human Resources Manager. **World Wide Web address:** http://www.hyatt.com. **Description:** A luxury

hotel offering an 18-story atrium that houses dining and entertainment facilities including a pool, a fully-equipped fitness center, tennis and basketball courts, three restaurants, and a revolving rooftop lounge. **Corporate headquarters location:** Chicago IL. **Other U.S. locations:** Nationwide. **Parent company:** Hyatt Hotel Corporation.

JACK IN THE BOX
7700 Bent Branch Drive, Suite 130, Irving TX 75063. 972/263-4403. **Contact:** Human Resources. **World Wide Web address:** http://www.jackinthebox.com. **Description:** Operates Jack-in-the-Box restaurants primarily in the western and southwestern United States. **Corporate headquarters location:** San Diego CA. **Other U.S. locations:** Houston TX. **International locations:** Hong Kong; Mexico.

MARRIOTT SOUTH CENTRAL REGIONAL OFFICE
5151 Beltline Road, Suite 500, Dallas TX 75240. 972/385-1600. **Contact:** Regional Director. **World Wide Web address:** http://www.marriott.com. **Description:** This location houses the regional office for the hotel chain. Overall, Marriott Corporation is a nationwide, diversified food service, retail merchandising, and hospitality company, doing business in more than 25 United States airports, as well as operating restaurants under various names nationwide. **Common positions include:** Human Resources Manager. **Educational backgrounds include:** Culinary Arts/Cooking; Hospitality. **Benefits:** Dental Insurance; Disability Coverage; Employee Discounts; Life Insurance; Medical Insurance; Pension Plan; Profit Sharing; Savings Plan; Tuition Assistance. **Special programs:** Internships. **Corporate headquarters location:** Washington DC. **Operations at this facility include:** Regional Headquarters. **Listed on:** New York Stock Exchange.

METROMEDIA RESTAURANT GROUP
6500 International Parkway, Suite 1000, Plano TX 75093. 972/588-5000. **Fax:** 972/588-5467. **Contact:** Julie Bottoms, Corporate Recruiter. **Description:** One of the largest, full-service, restaurant chain operators in the nation. The company operates 1,200 restaurants in 45 states and two countries including Bennigan's, Bonanza, and Ponderosa. **NOTE:** Entry-level positions and second and third shifts are offered. **Common positions include:** Accountant; Administrative Assistant; Attorney; Auditor; Budget Analyst; Buyer; Chief Financial Officer; Claim Representative; Computer Programmer; Controller; Customer Service Representative; Database Manager; Financial Analyst; Food Scientist/Technologist; Human Resources Manager; MIS Specialist; Paralegal; Purchasing Agent/Manager; Quality Control Supervisor; Secretary; Systems Analyst; Typist/Word Processor; Video Production Coordinator. **Educational backgrounds include:** Accounting; Business Administration; Finance; Liberal Arts. **Benefits:** 401(k); Dental Insurance; Disability Coverage; Employee Discounts; Fitness Program; Flexible Schedule; Life Insurance; Medical Insurance; Profit Sharing; Savings Plan; Tuition Assistance. **Corporate headquarters location:** This Location. **Listed on:** Privately held. **Annual sales/revenues:** $51 - $100 million. **Number of employees at this location:** 450.

MOTEL 6
14651 Dallas Parkway, Suite 500, Dallas TX 75240. 972/386-6161. **Contact:** Cheryl Beuttas, Director of Corporate Human Resources. **World Wide Web address:** http://www.motel6.com. **Description:** This location houses the administrative offices. Overall, Motel 6 operates a chain of motels. **Common positions include:** Administrative Assistant; Auditor; Customer Service Representative; General Manager; Human Resources Generalist; Instructor/Trainer; IT Specialist; Management Trainee; Marketing Specialist. **Educational backgrounds include:** Accounting; Business Administration; Computer Science; Liberal Arts. **Benefits:** 401(k); Disability Coverage; Life Insurance; Medical Insurance; Pension Plan; Tuition Assistance. **Corporate headquarters location:** This Location. **Parent company:** Accor (Paris, France). **Operations at this facility include:** Administration. **Number of employees at this location:** 275. **Number of employees nationwide:** 17,000.

MOTEL 6
4951 West Stamford Street, Abilene TX 79603. 915/672-8462. **Contact:** Manager. **World Wide Web address:** http://www.motel6.com. **Description:** One of over 50 Texas locations of the motel chain. **Corporate headquarters location:** Dallas TX. **Parent company:** Accor (Paris, France). **Number of employees nationwide:** 17,000.

OMNI HOTELS
420 Decker Drive, Suite 200, Irving TX 75062-3952. 972/730-6664. **Fax:** 972/871-5669. **Contact:** Alison Brody, Corporate Recruiting Manager. **World Wide Web address:** http://www.omnihotels.com. **Description:** Operates an international chain of hotels, motels, and resorts. **NOTE:** Entry-level positions are offered. **Common positions include:**

Accountant/Auditor; Computer Programmer; Credit Manager; Electrician; Financial Analyst; General Manager; Hotel Manager; Human Resources Manager; Management Trainee; MIS Specialist; Public Relations Specialist; Purchasing Agent/Manager; Quality Control Supervisor; Restaurant/Food Service Manager; Systems Analyst; Technical Writer/Editor; Typist/Word Processor. **Educational backgrounds include:** Accounting; Finance; Hospitality; Liberal Arts; Marketing; Mathematics. **Benefits:** 401(k); Dental Insurance; Disability Coverage; Employee Discounts; Job Sharing; Life Insurance; Medical Insurance; Pension Plan; Profit Sharing; Savings Plan; Tuition Assistance. **Special programs:** Internships; Training. **Corporate headquarters location:** This Location. **Other U.S. locations:** Nationwide. **Parent company:** TRT Holdings, Inc. **Operations at this facility include:** Administration. **Listed on:** Privately held. **Annual sales/revenues:** More than $100 million. **Number of employees at this location:** 30. **Number of employees nationwide:** 7,000. **Number of employees worldwide:** 8,000.

OMNI RICHARDSON HOTEL
701 East Campbell Road, Richardson TX 75081. 972/231-9600. **Contact:** Human Resources. **World Wide Web address:** http://www.omnihotels.com. **Description:** A 342-room hotel with two restaurants, meeting facilities, and a fitness center. **Corporate headquarters location:** Irving TX. **Parent company:** Omni Hotels.

PANCHO'S MEXICAN BUFFET, INC.
P.O. Box 7407, Fort Worth TX 76111. 817/831-0081. **Physical address:** 3500 Noble Street, Fort Worth TX. **Contact:** Human Resources. **Description:** This location houses administrative offices. Overall, Pancho's Mexican Buffet operates a chain of Mexican restaurants with a buffet-style format. Pancho's Mexican Buffet operates 72 restaurants throughout Texas, Arizona, Louisiana, New Mexico, and Oklahoma. Founded in 1966. **Corporate headquarters location:** This Location. **Listed on:** NASDAQ. **Stock exchange symbol:** PAMX.

PIZZA INN INC.
5050 Quorum Drive, Suite 500, Dallas TX 75240. 972/701-9955. **Contact:** Sandra Feinglas, Assistant to Chief Operating Officer. **Description:** Engaged primarily in operating and franchising restaurants serving pizza and complimentary foods and beverages. Pizza Inn operates more than 740 restaurants in 33 states, Mexico, Puerto Rico, Japan, the Philippines, and South Africa. **Common positions include:** Accountant/Auditor; Advertising Clerk; Architect; Computer Programmer; Draftsperson; General Manager; Human Resources Manager; Management Trainee; Marketing Specialist; Operations/Production Manager. **Benefits:** Dental Insurance; Disability Coverage; Life Insurance; Medical Insurance. **Operations at this facility include:** Administration; Sales. **Listed on:** American Stock Exchange.

SULLINS & ASSOCIATES, INC.
McDONALD'S CORPORATION
122 South 12th Street, Suite 105, Corsicana TX 75110. 903/872-5611. **Fax:** 903/872-5613. **Contact:** Human Resources. **World Wide Web address:** http://www.sullinsandassociates.com. **Description:** A leader in the fast-food industry, McDonald's offers quick-service meals, specializing in hamburgers. **Common positions include:** Branch Manager; General Manager; Management Trainee; Restaurant/Food Service Manager. **Educational backgrounds include:** Business Administration; Communications. **Benefits:** Dental Insurance; Employee Discounts; Life Insurance; Medical Insurance. **Special programs:** Internships. **Other area locations:** Ennis TX; Greenville TX; Palestine TX; Terrell TX; Waxahachie TX. **Operations at this facility include:** Administration. **Number of employees at this location:** 300.

WYATT'S CAFETERIAS INC.
16970 Dallas Parkway, Suite 701, Dallas TX 75248. 972/248-4145. **Fax:** 972/248-8116. **Contact:** Human Resources Director. **Description:** A cafeteria chain with 68 locations in five states. **Common positions include:** Accountant/Auditor; Claim Representative; Food Scientist/Technologist; General Manager; Management Trainee; Restaurant/Food Service Manager. **Educational backgrounds include:** Business Administration. **Benefits:** Dental Insurance; Employee Discounts; ESOP; Life Insurance; Medical Insurance; Pension Plan. **Corporate headquarters location:** This Location. **Operations at this facility include:** Administration; Research and Development. **Listed on:** Privately held. **Number of employees at this location:** 60. **Number of employees nationwide:** 3,500.

WYNDHAM ANATOLE HOTEL
2201 Stemmons Freeway, Dallas TX 75207. 214/748-1200. **Contact:** Employment Manager. **Description:** A luxury convention hotel with over 1,600 rooms. **Common positions include:** Accountant/Auditor; Chef/Cook/Kitchen Worker; Department Manager; Hotel Manager; Operations/Production Manager; Restaurant/Food Service Manager; Services Sales

Representative. **Educational backgrounds include:** Business Administration; Liberal Arts; Marketing. **Benefits:** 401(k); Dental Insurance; Employee Discounts; Life Insurance; Medical Insurance; Tuition Assistance. **Corporate headquarters location:** 1950 Stemmons Freeway, Suite 6001, Dallas TX. **Operations at this facility include:** Service. **Number of employees at this location:** 1,500.

Note: Because addresses and telephone numbers of smaller companies can change rapidly, we recommend you call each company to verify the information below before inquiring about job opportunities. Mass mailings are not recommended.

Additional small employers:

DRINKING PLACES

Logan's Roadhouse
8310 I-40 W, Amarillo TX 79106-1500. 806/467-8015.

Million Dollar Saloon
6848 Greenville Ave, Dallas TX 75231-6404. 214/363-4506.

On the Border Cafe
1350 Northwest Hwy, Garland TX 75041-5850. 972/686-7867.

On the Border Cafe
1801 N Lamar St, Dallas TX 75202-1748. 214/855-0296.

The Fare West
3021 W Northwest Hwy, Dallas TX 75220-5940. 214/956-7941.

The Lodge
10530 Spangler Rd, Dallas TX 75220-2308. 972/506-9229.

EATING PLACES

50th Street Caboose Restaurant
5027 50th St, Lubbock TX 79414-3420. 806/796-2240.

American Kitchen
1709 Nest Pl, Plano TX 75093-6032. 972/758-0591.

Angeluna
215 E 4th St, Fort Worth TX 76102-4020. 817/334-0080.

Applebee's
614 N Valley Mills Dr, Waco TX 76710-6047. 254/751-9084.

Applebee's
1009 N Central Expy, Plano TX 75075-8806. 972/881-1100.

Applebee's
1610 E Belt Line Rd, Richardson TX 75081-4620. 972/238-9591.

Applebee's
3790 Belt Ln, Dallas TX 75244. 972/243-8025.

Applebee's
5110 Summerhill Rd, Texarkana TX 75503-1824. 903/792-9476.

Applebee's
6645 NE Loop 820, Fort Worth TX 76180-6040. 817/788-9797.

Applebee's
707 S Interstate 35 E, Denton TX 76205-8101. 940/591-9353.

Applebee's
2700 E Central Texas Expy, Killeen TX 76543-5331. 254/526-9711.

Art Bar Cafe
2803 Main St, Dallas TX 75226-1502. 214/939-0077.

Bennigan's
4900 W Park Blvd, Plano TX 75093-2332. 972/964-1036.

Bennigan's
4000 S Cooper St, Arlington TX 76015-4125. 817/467-3363.

Big Texan Steak Ranch
PO Box 37000, Amarillo TX 79120-7000. 806/372-6000.

Black Eyed Pea
900 Airport Fwy, Hurst TX 76054-3250. 817/428-1096.

Blue Goose Cantina
2905 Greenville Ave, Dallas TX 75206-6240. 214/823-6786.

Burger King
Century Plaza 2, Ste 210, Abilene TX 79606. 915/695-0311.

Burger King
4215 Beltwood Pkwy, Dallas TX 75244-3227. 214/320-3031.

Burger King
6100 Southwest Blvd, Fort Worth TX 76109-3930. 817/731-1845.

Calico County Restaurant
3220 Church St, Amarillo TX 79109-1540. 806/358-2021.

Caterair Holdings Corporation
524 East Lamar Boulevard, Arlington TX 76011-3929. 817/792-2170.

Cheddars
39640 LBJ Hwy, Dallas TX 75237. 972/780-1200.

Cheddars
12355 Greenville Ave, Dallas TX 75243-3511. 972/235-5595.

Cheddars
812 Six Flags Dr, Arlington TX 76011-5122. 817/640-6073.

Cheddars
1937 Airport Freeway, Bedford TX 76021-5732. 817/540-0778.

Cheddars
4830 Little Road, Arlington TX 76017-1054. 817/572-2966.

Chili's Grill & Bar
2624 North Josey Ln, Carrollton TX 75007-5516. 972/466-1350.

Chili's Grill & Bar
3421 West Airport Freeway, Irving TX 75062-5924. 972/255-2727.

Chili's Grill & Bar
1129 S Stemmons Fwy, Lewisville TX 75067-5359. 972/221-8521.

Chili's Grill & Bar
3230 Knox St, Dallas TX 75205-4032. 214/520-1555.

Chili's Grill & Bar
191 Walnut Hill Village, Dallas TX 75220-4941. 214/352-9327.

Chili's Grill & Bar
7567 Greenville Avenue, Dallas TX 75231-3801. 214/361-4371.

Chili's Grill & Bar
9239 Skillman Street Dallas TX 75243-7328. 214/553-0444.

Chili's Grill & Bar
924 East Copeland Rd, Arlington TX 76011-4944. 817/261-3891.

Chili's Grill & Bar
1540 S University Dr, Fort Worth TX 76107-6500. 817/429-2002.

Chili's Grill & Bar
5288 S Hulen St, Fort Worth TX
76132-1912. 817/572-1195.

Cozymel's
5021 W Park Blvd, Plano TX
75093-2514. 972/964-2809.

Cozymel's
1300 E Copeland Rd, Arlington
TX 76011-4952. 817/469-9595.

Cracker Barrel
3302 Saint Michael Dr,
Texarkana TX 75503-2354.
903/832-3282.

Cracker Barrel
4691 Gemini Ct, Arlington TX
76016. 817/624-8050.

Cracker Barrel
4008 N I 35, Denton TX 76207.
940/382-5277.

Cracker Barrel
4275 Interstate 35 N, Waco TX
76705-7021. 254/799-4729.

Dave & Buster's
10727 Composite Dr, Dallas TX
75220-1207. 214/353-0649.

Del Fresco's
5251 Spring Valley Rd, Dallas
TX 75240-3007. 972/490-9000.

Dobbs International Services
3301 N 22nd Ave, Dallas TX
75261. 972/574-5634.

Don Pablo's Restaurant
1933 Airport Fwy, Bedford TX
76021-5732. 817/685-8868.

Don Pablo's Restaurant
5601 S Hulen St, Fort Worth TX
76132-2260. 817/346-3787.

El Chico
1028 Central Fwy, Wichita Falls
TX 76306-6166. 940/322-1455.

El Fenix Mexican Restaurants
3904 Towne Crossing Blvd,
Mesquite TX 75150-6122.
972/279-8900.

Fifty Yard Line
PO Box 54212, Lubbock TX
79453-4212. 806/745-3991.

Food Concepts International
2520 State Hwy 35E, Lewisville
TX 75067. 972/316-3600.

Food Concepts International
824 Airport Fwy, Hurst TX
76054-6234. 817/514-9355.

Front Row In Arlington
1000 Ballpark Way, Ste 401,
Arlington TX 76011-5170.
817/265-5191.

Golden Corral Corporation
420 W Southwest Loop 323,
Tyler TX 75701-9404. 903/534-0281.

Good Eats
2225 S Stemmons Fwy,
Lewisville TX 75067-8760.
972/315-5998.

Good Eats
1101 N Central Expy, Plano TX
75075-7116. 972/516-3287.

Hard Rock Cafe
2601 McKinney Ave, Dallas TX
75204-8696. 214/855-0007.

Harrigan's
3801 50th St, Lubbock TX
79413-3807. 806/792-4648.

Host Marriot
3301 S 22nd Ave, Dallas TX
75261. 972/574-5605.

Houston's Restaurant
8141 Walnut Hill Ln, Dallas TX
75231-4366. 214/691-8991.

Houston's Restaurant
5318 Belt Line Rd, Dallas TX
75240-7606. 972/960-1752.

Humperdink's
4959 N O'Connor Rd, Irving TX
75062-2719. 972/717-5515.

Humperdink's
1601 N Central Expy,
Richardson TX 75080-3504.
972/690-4867.

Humperdink's
700 Six Flags Dr, Arlington TX
76011-6327. 817/640-8553.

J. Christen's Grill
4650 W Airport Fwy, Irving TX
75062-5825. 972/513-0116.

Joe's Crab Shack
5802W W Loop 289, Lubbock
TX 79424-1127. 806/797-8600.

Josie's Restaurant Inc.
318 N University Ave, Lubbock
TX 79415-2318. 806/744-6262.

La Hacienda Ranch
5250 Highway 121, Colleyville
TX 76034-5927. 817/318-7500.

La Madeline Inc.
6060 N Central Expy, Dallas TX
75206-5209. 214/696-6962.

Landry's Seafood Restaurant
8300 I-40 W, Amarillo TX
79106-1500. 806/351-0349.

Las Colinas Entertainment
4504 Winewood Ct, Colleyville
TX 76034-4877. 817/868-0081.

Lombardi's of Las Vegas Inc.
211 N Record St, Ste 325,
Dallas TX 75202-3368.
314/748-5566.

LSG/Skychef
PO Box 610405, Dallas TX
75261-0405. 972/615-6128.

LSG/Skychef
524 E Lamar Blvd, Ste 200,
Arlington TX 76011-3901.
817/792-2100.

Luby's
1350 N Hampton Rd, Dallas TX
75208-1306. 214/946-0862.

McDonald's
4439 Lemmon Ave, Ste 1,
Dallas TX 75219-2143.
214/520-2596.

McDonald's
PO Box 1623, Mount Pleasant
TX 75456-1623. 903/572-5380.

McDonald's
PO Box 699, Marshall TX
75671-0699. 903/938-7745.

McDonald's
2102 E Highway 190, Killeen
TX 76541-7362. 254/699-1659.

Medieval Times
PO Box 567706, Dallas TX
75356-7706. 214/761-1801.

Mesa Southwest Restaurants
1003 N Beckley Ave, Desoto
TX 75115-4208. 972/228-2181.

Mexican Inn Cafe
4200 S Cooper St, Ste 200A,
Arlington TX 76015-4139.
817/467-0505.

Mi Piaci Restaurant
14854 Montfort Dr, Dallas TX
75240-7518. 972/934-8424.

Monsouni Inc.
4215 Beltwood Pkwy, Dallas
TX 75244-3227. 972/458-8300.

Mr. Gatti's of Amarillo
4412 S Western St, Amarillo TX
79109-6007. 806/355-5601.

Multi Restaurants Group
8008 Cedar Springs Rd, Dallas
TX 75235-2852. 214/353-3959.

Nelon's Fast Foods Inc.
PO Box 5949, Texarkana TX
75505-5949. 903/793-4100.

Ninfa's Mexican Restaurant
220 S 3rd St, Waco TX 76701-2221. 254/757-2050.

Old San Francisco Steak House
10965 Composite Dr, Dallas TX
75220-1211. 214/357-0484.

Hotels and Restaurants/201

Olive Garden
5921 W Waco Dr, Waco TX 76710-6356. 254/751-1667.

Olive Garden
4121 I-40 W, Amarillo TX 79109-1530. 806/355-9973.

Olive Garden
5702 Slide Rd, Lubbock TX 79414-4106. 806/791-3575.

Olive Garden
3210 S Clack St, Abilene TX 79606-2200. 915/691-0388.

Olive Garden
3816 Towne Crossing Blvd, Mesquite TX 75150-6124. 972/270-1582.

Olive Garden
9079 Vantage Point Dr, Dallas TX 75243-3581. 972/234-3292.

Olive Garden
4604 S Cooper St, Arlington TX 76017-5826. 817/472-9733.

Olive Garden
8020 Bedford Euless Rd, Bedford TX 76022. 817/581-9511.

Olive Garden
4700 SW Loop 820, Fort Worth TX 76109-4419. 817/377-8091.

Olive Garden
925 Alta Mere Dr, Fort Worth TX 76114-4001. 817/732-0618.

Olive Garden
3916 Kemp Blvd, Wichita Falls TX 76308-2141. 940/692-4714.

On the Border Cafe
4320 W Waco Dr, Waco TX 76710-7043. 254/399-9986.

On the Border Cafe
4400 Belt Line Rd, Addison TX 75001-4513. 972/788-4400.

On the Border Cafe
1890 S Stemmons Fwy, Lewisville TX 75067-6321. 972/315-8520.

On the Border Cafe
1505 N Central Expy, Ste 9, Plano TX 75075-7022. 972/881-2257.

Outback Steakhouse
3510 W Airport Fwy, Irving TX 75062-5922. 972/399-1477.

Outback Steakhouse
2211 S Stemmons Fwy, Lewisville TX 75067-8760. 972/315-5772.

Outback Steakhouse
1509 N Central Expy, Plano TX 75075-7022. 972/516-4100.

Outback Steakhouse
3903 Towne Crossing Blvd, Mesquite TX 75150-6121. 972/686-0555.

Outback Steakhouse
1031 W Highway 114, Grapevine TX 76051-3988. 817/329-4949.

Papa's BBQ
2231 W Northwest Hwy, Dallas TX 75220-4304. 214/956-9038.

Papacitas Mexican Restaurant
305 W Loop 281, Longview TX 75605-4426. 903/663-1700.

Pappadeaux Seafood
725 S Central Expy, Dallas TX 75201-6001. 972/235-1181.

Pappadeaux Seafood
3520 Oak Lawn Ave, Dallas TX 75219-4308. 214/521-4700.

Pappadeaux Seafood
1304 E Copeland Rd, Arlington TX 76011-4952. 817/543-0544.

Pappas Bros. Steakhouse
10477 Lombardy Ln, Dallas TX 75220-4349. 214/366-2000.

Pappasito's Cantina
723 S Central Expy, Richardson TX 75080-7410. 972/480-8595.

Pappasito's Cantina
10433 Lombardy Ln, Dallas TX 75220-4349. 214/350-1970.

Pappasito's Cantina
2704 West Fwy, Fort Worth TX 76102-7111. 817/877-5546.

Perfect Pizza Ltd.
2661 Buffalo Gap Rd, Abilene TX 79605-6105. 915/692-6326.

PF Chang's China Bistro
225 Northpark Ctr, Dallas TX 75225-2205. 214/265-8669.

PF Chang's China Bistro
18323 Dallas Pkwy, Dallas TX 75287-5204. 972/818-3336.

Pizza Hut
14841 Dallas Pkwy, Dallas TX 75240-7552. 972/338-7700.

Pizza Hut
227 W University Dr, Denton TX 76201-1837. 940/383-1670.

Rainforest Cafe
3000 Grapevine Mills Pkwy, Grapevine TX 76051-2008. 972/539-5001.

Razzoo's Cajan Cafe
13949 N Central Expy, Dallas TX 75243-1007. 972/235-3700.

Red Lobster
5034 50th St, Lubbock TX 79414-3421. 806/792-4805.

Red Lobster
4205 W Airport Fwy, Irving TX 75062-5916. 972/659-0104.

Red Lobster
3906 Towne Crossing Blvd, Mesquite TX 75150-6122. 972/613-1444.

Red Lobster
7800 Bedford Euless Rd, Hurst TX 76053. 817/281-7540.

Romano's Macaroni Grill
4535 Belt Line Rd, Addison TX 75001-4516. 972/386-3831.

Romano's Macaroni Grill
5858 W Northwest Hwy, Dallas TX 75225-3201. 214/265-0770.

Romano's Macaroni Grill
1670 Interstate 20 W, Arlington TX 76017-5840. 817/784-1197.

Saltgrass Inc.
2484 S Stemmons Fwy, Lewisville TX 75067-8755. 972/316-0086.

Sneaky Pete's
3101 Sagebrush Dr, Flower Mound TX 75022-2731. 972/434-2500.

Snuffer's Restaurant
3526 Greenville Ave, Dallas TX 75206-5630. 214/826-6850.

Spaghetti Warehouse Inc.
1815 N Market St, Dallas TX 75202-1895. 214/651-8475.

Spaghetti Warehouse Inc.
600 E Exchange Ave, Fort Worth TX 76106-8246. 817/625-4171.

Stagecoach Inn
PO Box 97, Salado TX 76571-0097. 254/947-5111.

Star Canyon Inc.
3102 Oak Lawn Ave, Ste 144, Dallas TX 75219-4257. 214/520-7827.

Steak & Ale
721 N Watson Rd, Arlington TX 76011-5163. 817/640-6088.

Steak & Ale
4650 Little Rd, Arlington TX 76017-1038. 817/483-5108.

Texas Roadhouse of Tampa Inc.
2815 La Salle Ave, Waco TX 76706-3845. 254/662-1177.

TGI Friday's
4300 Franklin Ave, Waco TX 76710-6906. 972/450-5411.

TGI Friday's
5100 Belt Line Rd, Dallas TX 75240-7559. 972/386-5824.

TGI Friday's
3200 E Airfield Dr, Dallas TX 75261-4904. 972/574-0420.

TGI Friday's
8605 Airport Fwy, Fort Worth TX 76180-7254. 817/498-2527.

The Fare
5030 Greenville Ave, Dallas TX 75206-4006. 214/369-4070.

Tippin's Pie Pantry
3321 S Cooper St, Arlington TX 76015-2345. 817/467-7437.

Trail Dust Steak House
10841 Composite Dr, Dallas TX 75220-1209. 214/357-3862.

Trail Dust Steak House
2300 E Lamar Blvd, Arlington TX 76006-7412. 817/640-6411.

Turtle Creek Restaurants LLC
5641 Dyer St, Dallas TX 75206-5003. 214/739-4948.

Uncle Julio's
1125 N Union Bower Rd, Irving TX 75061-5825. 972/554-3616.

Uncle Julio's
4125 Lemmon Ave, Dallas TX 75219-3739. 214/520-6620.

Uncle Julio's
7557 Greenville Ave, Dallas TX 75231-3801. 214/987-9900.

Uncle Julio's
5301 Camp Bowie Blvd, Fort Worth TX 76107-4838. 817/377-2777.

Voltaire Restaurants
5150 Keller Springs Rd, Richardson TX 75080. 972/239-8988.

Weiss Enterprises Inc.
PO Box 150406, Dallas TX 75315-0406. 214/565-1511.

HOTELS AND MOTELS

Arlington Marriott
1500 Convention Center Dr, Arlington TX 76011-5116. 817/261-8200.

Clarion Hotel
1981 N Central Expy, Richardson TX 75080-3509. 972/644-4000.

Crowne Plaza
7050 N Stemmons Fwy, Dallas TX 75247-5100. 214/630-8500.

Dallas Marriott Suites
2493 N Stemmons Fwy, Dallas TX 75207-2601. 214/905-0050.

Dallas Parkway Hilton Hotel
4801 LBJ Fwy, Dallas TX 75244-6002. 972/661-3600.

Days Inn-Arlington
910 N Collins St, Arlington TX 76011-6024. 817/261-8444.

Depalma Hotel Corp.
5701 S Broadway Ave, Tyler TX 75703-4350. 903/561-5800.

Dominion Equity Corporation
1106 N Highway 360, Grand Prairie TX 75050-2559. 972/641-6641.

Doubletree Hotel
8250 N Central Expy, Dallas TX 75206-1803. 214/691-8700.

Doubletree Hotel
5410 LBJ Fwy, Dallas TX 75240-6206. 972/934-8400.

Embassy Suites
4650 W Airport Fwy, Irving TX 75062-5825. 972/790-0093.

Embassy Suites
13131 N Central Expy, Dallas TX 75243-1140. 972/234-3300.

Embassy Suites Market Center
2727 N Stemmons Fwy, Dallas TX 75207-2211. 214/630-5332.

Embassy Suites Outdoor World
2401 Bass Pro Dr, Grapevine TX 76051-2043. 972/724-2600.

Fairmont Hotel
1717 N Akard St, Dallas TX 75201-2344. 214/720-2020.

Four Points Hotel
5301 N State Line Ave, Texarkana TX 75503-5301. 903/792-3222.

Gateway Inn Motel
PO Box 1299, Graham TX 76450-1299. 940/549-5041.

Hilton Arlington
2401 E Lamar Blvd, Arlington TX 76006-7503. 817/640-3322.

Hilton DFW Lakes
1800 E Highway 26, Grapevine TX 76051-2044. 817/481-8444.

Hilton-Waco
113 S University Parks Dr, Waco TX 76701-2241. 254/754-8484.

Holiday Inn
4440 W Airport Fwy, Irving TX 75062-5821. 972/399-1010.

Holiday Inn
4441 W State Highway 114, Irving TX 75063. 972/929-8181.

Holiday Inn
1515 N Beckley Ave, Desoto TX 75115-2600. 972/224-9100.

Holiday Inn
4070 N Central Expy, Dallas TX 75204-3101. 214/827-0880.

Holiday Inn
10650 N Central Expy, Dallas TX 75231-2102. 214/373-6000.

Holiday Inn
3300 W Mockingbird Ln, Dallas TX 75235-5906. 214/357-8500.

Holiday Inn
1507 N Watson Rd, Arlington TX 76006-6065. 817/640-7712.

Holiday Inn
3005 Airport Fwy, Bedford TX 76021-6011. 817/267-3181.

Holiday Inn Select
11350 LBJ Fwy, Dallas TX 75238-3127. 214/341-5400.

Hotel Adolphus
1321 Commerce St, Dallas TX 75202-4211. 214/742-8200.

Hotel Crescent Court
400 Crescent Ct, Dallas TX 75201-1888. 214/871-3200.

Ironside Motor Inn
404 S Fort Hood St, Killeen TX 76541-6839. 254/526-4632.

ITT Sheraton Corporation
2150 Market Center Blvd, Dallas TX 75207-3321. 214/653-1166.

La Meridien Dallas
650 N Pearl St, Dallas TX 75201-2848. 214/979-9000.

Lake Kiowa Lodge
107 Kiowa Dr S, Gainesville TX 76240-9539. 940/665-1055.

Lane Hospitality Inc.
1011 S Akard St, Dallas TX 75215-1063. 214/421-1083.

Lubbock Plaza Hotel
3201 S Loop 289, Lubbock TX 79423-1320. 806/797-3241.

Marriott Hotel
PO Box 612427, Irving TX 75063. 972/929-8800.

Hotels and Re[staurants]

Marriott Hotel
14901 Dallas Pkwy, Dallas TX 75240-7551. 972/661-2800.

Marriott Hotel
PO Box 612427, Dallas TX 75261-2427. 972/453-0600.

Marriott Solana
5 Village Cir, Roanoke TX 76262-5901. 817/430-3848.

Melrose Hotel
3015 Oak Lawn Ave, Dallas TX 75219-4134. 214/521-5151.

Omni Dallas Hotel Parkwest
1590 LBJ Fwy, Dallas TX 75234-6031. 972/869-4300.

Omni Mandalay Hotel
221 Las Colinas Blvd E, Irving TX 75039-5504. 972/556-0800.

Radisson Hotel Denton
2211 S Interstate 35 E, Denton TX 76205-8188. 940/565-8499.

Ramada Airport
14180 Dallas Pkwy, Ste 700, Dallas TX 75240-4374. 972/490-9600.

Ramada Inn Market Center Inc.
1055 Regal Row, Dallas TX 75247-4404. 214/634-8550.

Ramada Plaza
1701 Commerce St, Fort Worth TX 76102-6511. 817/335-7000.

RE Management Co.
215 E Wall St, Grapevine TX 76051-5304. 817/481-5177.

Renaissance Dallas North
4099 Valley View Ln, Dallas TX 75244-5002. 972/385-9000.

Rough Creek Lodge
1435 Private Road 1256, Iredell TX 76649-3505. 254/965-7634.

Sheraton Grand Hotel
PO Box 619765, Dallas TX 75261-9765. 972/929-8400.

Sheraton Hotel
2101 N Stemmons Fwy, Dallas TX 75207-3004. 214/747-3000.

Sheraton Hotel
7750 LBJ Fwy, Dallas T[X] 75251-1202. 972/233-4[4..]

Sheraton Hotel Brookhollow
1241 W Mockingbird Ln, Dalla[s] TX 75247-4901. 214/630-7000.

Sheraton Park Central Hotel
12720 Merit Dr, Dallas TX 75251-1206. 972/385-3000.

Stockyards Hotel Inc.
PO Box 4558, Fort Worth TX 76164-0558. 817/625-6427.

Stouffer Renaissance Dallas Hotel
2222 N Stemmons Fwy, Dallas TX 75207-2802. 214/631-2222.

TRT Development Company Inc.
420 Decker Dr, Ste 100, Irving TX 75062-3952. 972/443-1300.

Wyndham Hotels & Resorts
1950 N Stemmons Fwy, Dallas TX 75207-3107. 214/863-1000.

For more information on career opportunities in hotels and restaurants:

Associations

AMERICAN HOTEL AND MOTEL ASSOCIATION
1201 New York Avenue NW, Suite 600, Washington DC 20005-3931. 202/289-3100. World Wide Web address: http://www.ahma.com. Provides lobbying services and educational programs, maintains and disseminates industry data, and produces a variety of publications.

THE EDUCATIONAL FOUNDATION OF THE NATIONAL RESTAURANT ASSOCIATION
250 South Wacker Drive, Suite 1400, Chicago IL 60606. 312/715-1010. World Wide Web address: http://www.edfound.org. Offers educational products, including textbooks, manuals, instruction guides, manager and employee training programs, videos, and certification programs.

NATIONAL RESTAURANT ASSOCIATION
1200 17th Street NW, Washington DC 20036. 202/331-5900. World Wide Web address: http://www.restaurant.org.

Directories

DIRECTORY OF CHAIN RESTAURANT OPERATORS
Lebhar-Friedman, Inc., 425 Park Avenue, New York NY 10022. 212/756-5000. World Wide Web address: http://www.lf.com.

DIRECTORY OF HIGH-VOLUME INDEPENDENT RESTAURANTS
Lebhar-Friedman, Inc., 425 Park Avenue, New York NY 10022. 212/756-5000. World Wide Web address: http://www.lf.com.

Magazines

CORNELL HOTEL AND RESTAURANT ADMINISTRATION QUARTERLY
Elsevier Science, Inc., P.O. Box 945, New York NY 10159-0945. 212/633-3730. World Wide Web address: http://www.sha.cornell.edu/publications/hraq/.

NATION'S RESTAURANT NEWS
Lebhar-Friedman, Inc., 425 Park Avenue, New York NY 10022. 212/756-5000. World Wide Web address: http://www.lf.com.

Online Services

COOLWORKS
World Wide Web address: http://www.coolworks.com. This Website provides links to 22,000 job openings at resorts, summer camps, ski areas, river areas, ranches, fishing areas, and cruise ships. This site also includes information on volunteer openings.

ESCOFFIER ONLINE
World Wide Web address: http://www.escoffier.com/nonscape/employ.shtml.

HOSPITALITY NET VIRTUAL JOB EXCHANGE
World Wide Web address: http://www.hospitalitynet.nl/job.

JOBNET: HOSPITALITY INDUSTRY
World Wide Web address: http://www.westga.edu:80/~coop/joblinks/subject/hospitality.html. This Website provides links to job openings and information for hotels.

For information about the JobBank List Service visit www.adamsjobbank.com

INSURANCE

You will find the following types of companies in this chapter:
Commercial Property/Casualty Insurers • Health Maintenance Organizations (HMOs) • Medical/Life Insurance Companies

Compensation: The average salary of an entry-level actuary ranges between $22,000 and $30,000 (higher salaries are awarded to those who have completed their actuary exams), and experienced actuaries earn an average of $50,000 - $60,000 annually. Insurance agents and brokers can expect approximately $22,000 - $28,000 during training, and after several years the average salary range is $40,000 - $70,000. Experienced agents with a strong sales record can earn over $100,000 annually. Insurance underwriters earn approximately $30,000 - $55,000 per year.

BLUE CROSS BLUE SHIELD OF TEXAS
P.O. Box 655730, Dallas TX 75265-5730. 972/766-6336. **Physical address:** 901 South Central Expressway, Richardson TX 75080. **Fax:** 972/766-6102. **Recorded jobline:** 972/766-5364. **Contact:** Michael Jarvis, Director of Employment. **World Wide Web address:** http://www.bcbstx.com. **Description:** A health and life insurance company. **Common positions include:** Accountant/Auditor; Actuary; Attorney; Budget Analyst; Buyer; Claim Representative; Claims Investigator; Clerical Supervisor; Computer Programmer; Credit Manager; Customer Service Representative; Financial Analyst; Health Services Manager; Instructor/Trainer; Licensed Practical Nurse; Mathematician; Paralegal; Physician; Public Relations Specialist; Purchasing Agent/Manager; Registered Nurse; Software Engineer; Statistician; Supervisor; Systems Analyst; Technical Writer/Editor; Underwriter/Assistant Underwriter. **Educational backgrounds include:** Accounting; Computer Science; Liberal Arts; Mathematics. **Benefits:** 401(k); Dental Insurance; Disability Coverage; EAP; Employee Discounts; Life Insurance; Medical Insurance; Pension Plan; Savings Plan; Tuition Assistance. **Corporate headquarters location:** This Location. **Number of employees at this location:** 5,000.

CNA COMMERCIAL INSURANCE
P.O. Box 219011, Dallas TX 75221-9011. 214/220-1300. **Toll-free phone:** 877/261-6680. **Fax:** 214/220-1690. **Contact:** Human Resources Department. **World Wide Web address:** http://www.cna.com. **Description:** This location specializes in commercial insurance policies including worker's compensation. Overall, the company is a property and casualty insurance writer offering commercial and personal policies. **Corporate headquarters location:** Chicago IL.

CHUBB GROUP OF INSURANCE COMPANIES
1445 Ross Avenue, Suite 4200, Dallas TX 75202. 214/754-0777. **Contact:** Janie Brown, Personnel Manager. **World Wide Web address:** http://www.chubb.com. **Description:** A property and casualty insurer with more than 115 offices in 30 countries worldwide. Chubb Group of Insurance Companies offers a broad range of specialty services designed for individuals and businesses, serving industries including high-tech, financial institutions, and general manufacturers. Founded in 1882. **Number of employees worldwide:** 10,000.

CRUM & FORSTER INSURANCE
6404 International Parkway, Suite 1000, Plano TX 75093. 972/380-3000. **Contact:** Human Resources. **World Wide Web address:** http://www.cfins.com. **Description:** Offers property and casualty insurance to commercial customers.

GENERALCOLOGNE RE
8144 Walnut Hill Lane, Suite 1250, Dallas TX 75231-3309. 214/691-3000. **Contact:** Human Resources. **World Wide Web address:** http://www.gcre.com. **Description:** Provides property and casualty reinsurance to primary insurers on a direct basis.

GILES INSURANCE AGENCY
2002 North Galloway Avenue, Suite A, Mesquite TX 75149. 972/288-9810. **Contact:** Human Resources. **Description:** Offers automobile and homeowners insurance policies.

INSPIRE INSURANCE SOLUTIONS
300 Burnett Street, Fort Worth TX 76113. 817/332-7761. **Contact:** Human Resources. **World Wide Web address:** http://www.nspr.com. **Description:** Provides administrative and consulting services to property and casualty insurance companies. **Corporate headquarters location:** This Location. **Listed on:** NASDAQ. **Stock exchange symbol:** NSPR.

LAWYERS TITLE INSURANCE CORPORATION
7557 Rambler Road, Suite 1200, Dallas TX 75231. 214/720-7600. **Contact:** Human Resources. **World Wide Web address:** http://www.ltic.com. **Description:** Provides title insurance and other real estate-related services on commercial and residential transactions in the United States, Canada, the Bahamas, Puerto Rico, and the U.S. Virgin Islands. Lawyers Title Insurance Corporation also provides search and examination services and closing services for a broad-based customer group that includes lenders, developers, real estate brokers, attorneys, and home buyers. This location covers Kansas, New Mexico, Oklahoma, and Texas. **Corporate headquarters location:** Richmond VA. **Other U.S. locations:** Pasadena CA; Tampa FL; Chicago IL; Boston MA; Troy MI; White Plains NY; Westerville OH; Memphis TN. **Subsidiaries include:** Datatrace Information Services Company, Inc. (Richmond VA) markets automated public record information for public and private use. Genesis Data Systems, Inc. (Englewood CO) develops and markets computer software tailored specifically to the title industry. Lawyers Title Exchange Company operates out of 10 of the Lawyers Title Insurance Corporation's regional offices and functions as an intermediary for individual and corporate investors interested in pursuing tax-free property exchanges. **Parent company:** Lawyers Title Corporation. **Listed on:** NASDAQ.

NATIONAL FOUNDATION LIFE INSURANCE COMPANY
110 West Seventh Street, Suite 300, Fort Worth TX 76102. 817/878-3300. **Contact:** Human Resources. **Description:** A life insurance company. **Common positions include:** Accountant/Auditor; Actuary; Attorney; Claim Representative; Clerical Supervisor; Computer Programmer; Human Resources Manager; Paralegal; Purchasing Agent/Manager; Systems Analyst; Underwriter/Assistant Underwriter. **Educational backgrounds include:** Accounting; Business Administration; Computer Science. **Benefits:** 401(k); Dental Insurance; Disability Coverage; Life Insurance; Medical Insurance. **Corporate headquarters location:** This Location. **Number of employees at this location:** 225.

REPUBLIC UNDERWRITERS INSURANCE COMPANY
2727 Turtle Creek Boulevard, Dallas TX 75219. 214/559-1222. **Contact:** Larry Westerfield, Director of Human Resources. **Description:** Offers a broad range of property and liability insurance. **Special programs:** Internships.

SOUTHWESTERN LIFE INSURANCE
P.O. Box 2699, Dallas TX 75221. 214/954-7703. **Contact:** Human Resources Department. **Description:** A life insurance company.

STATE FARM MUTUAL INSURANCE COMPANY
P.O. Box 799100, Dallas TX 75379-9100. 972/732-5000. **Contact:** Human Resources. **World Wide Web address:** http://www.statefarm.com. **Description:** Offers automobile, health, homeowners, life, and renters insurance. **Corporate headquarters location:** Bloomington IL. **Number of employees nationwide:** 67,000.

TRAVELERS PROPERTY CASUALTY COMPANY
P.O. Box 660456, Dallas TX 75266. 972/866-4748. **Physical address:** 7920 Beltline Road, Dallas TX 75240. **Contact:** Susan Oliver, Human Resources Coordinator. **World Wide Web address:** http://www.travelers.com. **Description:** Offers a wide range of insurance products to commercial customers including workers' compensation, property, liability, and surety bonds. The company also provides homeowners and auto insurance to consumers. **Corporate headquarters location:** Hartford CT.

UNITED AMERICAN INSURANCE COMPANY
P.O. Box 8080, McKinney TX 75070-8080. 972/529-5085. **Contact:** Human Resources Department. **Description:** Offers health and life insurance.

UNITED INSURANCE COMPANIES INC.
4001 McEwen, Suite 200, Dallas TX 75244. 972/392-6700. **Fax:** 972/392-6737. **Contact:** Human Resources. **Description:** Offers health and life insurance. **NOTE:** Entry-level positions are offered. **Common positions include:** Accountant/Auditor; Actuary; Claim Representative; Clerical Supervisor; Computer Programmer; Customer Service Representative; MIS Specialist;

Systems Analyst; Typist/Word Processor; Underwriter/Assistant Underwriter. **Educational backgrounds include:** Accounting; Computer Science; Health Care. **Benefits:** 401(k); Daycare Assistance; Dental Insurance; Disability Coverage; Employee Discounts; Life Insurance; Medical Insurance; Profit Sharing; Tuition Assistance. **Special programs:** Training. **Corporate headquarters location:** This Location. **Other U.S. locations:** Glendale AZ; Lakewood CO; St. Petersburg FL; Norcross GA; Oklahoma City OK; Sioux Falls SD. **Listed on:** NASDAQ. **Number of employees at this location:** 400. **Number of employees nationwide:** 780.

WAUSAU INSURANCE COMPANIES
P.O. Box 152800, Irving TX 75015-2800. 972/650-1955. **Contact:** Human Resources. **Description:** Offers casualty, property, and group insurance products to commercial customers through 100 service offices located nationwide. **NOTE:** Entry-level positions are offered. **Common positions include:** Accountant/Auditor; Adjuster; Attorney; Customer Service Representative; Data Analyst; Human Resources Manager; Insurance Agent/Broker; Safety Engineer; Underwriter/Assistant Underwriter. **Educational backgrounds include:** Business Administration; Economics; Engineering; Finance; Liberal Arts. **Benefits:** 401(k); Dental Insurance; Disability Coverage; Life Insurance; Medical Insurance; Pension Plan; Telecommuting; Tuition Assistance. **Corporate headquarters location:** Wausau WI. **Other U.S. locations:** Nationwide. **Annual sales/revenues:** More than $100 million. **Number of employees at this location:** 150. **Number of employees nationwide:** 5,500.

Note: Because addresses and telephone numbers of smaller companies can change rapidly, we recommend you call each company to verify the information below before inquiring about job opportunities. Mass mailings are not recommended.

Additional small employers:

INSURANCE AGENTS, BROKERS, AND SERVICES

Allied North America
12770 Coit Rd, Ste 750, Dallas TX 75251-1339. 972/455-1400.

Allstate Insurance Company
8711 Freeport Pkwy, Irving TX 75063-2578. 972/915-5171.

American Southwest Insurance Managers
PO Box 869018, Plano TX 75086-9018. 972/398-4100.

Century 2000
8008 Slide Rd, Ste 3, Lubbock TX 79424-2828. 806/794-1666.

CGU Corp.
5910 N Central Expy, Dallas TX 75206-5125. 214/739-3919.

CGU Corp.
9229 LBJ Fwy, Ste 200, Dallas TX 75243-3454. 972/783-6100.

Cranford Insurance Services
PO Box 53067, Lubbock TX 79453-3067. 806/798-2665.

Crawford & Company
1210 River Bend Dr, Dallas TX 75247-4969. 214/631-7560.

Cuna Mutual Insurance Group
4455 LBJ Fwy, Ste 1008, Dallas TX 75244. 972/661-8485.

Cunningham Lindsey Inc.
PO Box 569430, Dallas TX 75356-9430. 214/630-3730.

Farmers Insurance Group
200 Chisholm Pl, Plano TX 75075-6939. 972/484-7188.

GPA
300 Municipal Dr, Richardson TX 75080-3541. 972/238-7900.

HCC Aviation Insurance Group
PO Box 797408, Dallas TX 75379-7408. 972/447-2000.

Healthtexas Provider Network
2625 Elm St, Dallas TX 75226-1400. 214/820-7717.

Invesco North American Holdings
5400 LBJ Fwy, Ste 700, Dallas TX 75240-1032. 972/715-7400.

John Hancock Mutual Life Insurance Company
1661 Gateway Blvd, Richardson TX 75080-3530. 972/699-6500.

Leader Insurance Company
4100 Harry Hines Blvd, Dallas TX 75219-3207. 214/526-3876.

Liberty Mutual Insurance
PO Box 152067, Irving TX 75015-2067. 972/550-7899.

Mass Group Marketing Inc.
704 E 15th St, Plano TX 75074-5712. 972/881-2255.

Nationwide Mutual Insurance Co.
4320 S Western St, Amarillo TX 79109-6008. 806/351-1566.

PFL Life Insurance Center
PO Box 982010, Fort Worth TX 76182-8010. 817/656-6110.

Prudential Insurance Corp.
4100 Alpha Rd, Ste 400, Dallas TX 75244-4327. 972/263-3861.

State National Companies
8200 Anderson Blvd, Fort Worth TX 76120-3620. 817/265-2000.

Transport Insurance Company
4100 Harry Hines Blvd, Dallas TX 75219-3207. 214/520-4520.

US Risk Insurance Group Inc.
10210 N Central Expwy, Dallas TX 75206. 214/265-7090.

Zurich American Insurance Group
9330 LBJ Fwy, Ste 1200, Dallas TX 75243-3446. 972/231-7001.

INSURANCE COMPANIES

Aetna Health Plan
PO Box 569440, Dallas TX 75356-9440. 972/470-7610.

Allstate Insurance Company
222 Las Colinas Blvd W, Irving TX 75039-5421. 972/869-6200.

American Amicable Life Insurance
PO Box 2549, Waco TX 76702-2549. 254/297-2777.

American Hallmark Insurance
14651 Dallas Pkwy, Ste 900,

Dallas TX 75240-8808. 972/934-2400.

American Health & Life Insurance
307 W 7th St, Ste 400, Fort Worth TX 76102-5192. 817/348-7500.

American Income Life Insurance Co.
PO Box 2608, Waco TX 76702-2608. 254/751-8600.

American International Group
8144 Walnut Hill Ln, Dallas TX 75231-4388. 214/932-2788.

Associates Financial Life Insurance
250 E Carpenter Fwy, Irving TX 75062-2710. 972/652-3800.

Central Security Life Insurance Co.
PO Box 833879, Richardson TX 75083-3879. 972/699-2770.

Chicago Title Insurance Co.
2001 Bryan St, Ste 1700, Dallas TX 75201-3009. 214/720-4000.

Cigna Property Casualty Companies
PO Box 152041, Irving TX 75015-2041. 972/751-3500.

Continental Insurance Co.
PO Box 960, Dallas TX 75221. 214/220-1421.

Employers General Insurance Group
PO Box 219010, Dallas TX 75221-9010. 214/665-6100.

EW Blanch Co.
500 N Akard St, Ste 450, Dallas TX 75201-3320. 214/756-7000.

Farmers Mutual Insurance
PO Box 6106, Temple TX 76503-6106. 254/773-2181.

FDIC
PO Box 214155, Dallas TX 75201. 214/754-0098.

Fireman's Fund Insurance Co.
PO Box 2519, Dallas TX 75221. 214/220-4000.

Frontier General Insurance
PO Box 230, Fort Worth TX 76101-0230. 817/732-2111.

Geico Insurance
PO Box 650253, Dallas TX 75265-0253. 972/701-8700.

General Agents Insurance of America
PO Box 2933, Fort Worth TX 76113-2933. 817/336-2500.

Great Southern Life Insurance Co.
PO Box 219040, Dallas TX 75221-9040. 214/954-8100.

Insurance Investors Life Insurance
1300 W Mockingbird Ln, Dallas TX 75247-4921. 214/638-9206.

Kemper Insurance Companies
PO Box 749033, Dallas TX 75374. 972/364-5100.

LSW
PO Box 569080, Dallas TX 75356-9080. 214/638-7100.

Lumbermen's Mutual Casualty Co.
12377 Merit Dr, Ste 1400, Dallas TX 75251-2290. 972/980-9856.

New York Life Insurance Co.
12201 Merit Dr, Ste 1000, Dallas TX 75251-2213. 972/387-2929.

Ohio State Life Insurance Co.
PO Box 219061, Dallas TX 75221-9061. 816/512-3626.

Old American County Mutual Fire Insurance
PO Box 802325, Dallas TX 75380-2325. 972/661-0400.

Pacificare of Texas Inc.
5001 LBJ Fwy, Dallas TX 75244-6120. 214/631-5312.

Pioneer American Insurance Co.
PO Box 240, Waco TX 76703-0240. 817/753-0123.

Rodney D. Young Insurance Agency
PO Box 224467, Dallas TX 75222-4467. 214/333-4002.

Saint Paul Companies
PO Box 90608, Arlington TX 76006-9608. 817/695-1400.

Texas Life Insurance Company
PO Box 830, Waco TX 76703-0830. 254/752-6521.

TIG Insurance Company
PO Box 152870, Irving TX 75015-2870. 972/831-5000.

TIG Reinsurance Company
PO Box 152870, Irving TX 75015-2870. 203/977-8000.

Union Standard Insurance Co.
PO Box 152180, Irving TX 75015-2180. 972/719-2400.

United Benefit Life Insurance Co.
3909 Hulen St, Ste 300, Fort Worth TX 76107-7253. 817/732-0399.

USPA & IRA
4100 S Hulen St, Fort Worth TX 76109-4953. 817/731-8621.

Voyager Indemnity Insurance Co.
PO Box 901045, Fort Worth TX 76101-2045. 817/390-1700.

For more information on career opportunities in insurance:

Associations

ALLIANCE OF AMERICAN INSURERS
3025 Highland Parkway, Suite 800, Downers Grove IL 60515. 630/724-2100. World Wide Web address: http://www.allianceai.org.

AMERICAN COUNCIL OF LIFE INSURANCE
1001 Pennsylvania Avenue NW, Suite 500, Washington DC 20004-2599. 202/624-2000. A nonprofit trade association representing the life insurance industry.

HEALTH INSURANCE ASSOCIATION OF AMERICA
555 13th Street NW, Suite 600E, Washington DC 20004. 202/824-1600. World Wide Web address: http://www.hiaa.org.

INSURANCE INFORMATION INSTITUTE
110 William Street, New York NY 10038. 212/669-9200. World Wide Web address: http://www.iii.org. Provides information on property/casualty insurance issues.

NATIONAL ASSOCIATION OF INSURANCE AND FINANCIAL ADVISORS (NAIFA)
1922 F Street NW, Washington DC 20006. 202/331-6000. Fax: 202/385-9607. World Wide Web address: http://www.naifa.org. A trade organization representing insurance and finance professionals throughout the United States.

NATIONAL ASSOCIATION OF PROFESSIONAL INSURANCE AGENTS
400 North Washington Street, Alexandria VA 22314. 703/836-9340. World Wide Web address: http://www.pianet.com.

SOCIETY OF ACTUARIES
475 North Martingale Road, Suite 800, Schaumburg IL 60173. 847/706-3500. World Wide Web address: http://www.soa.org.

Career Fairs

CAREER FAIRS INTERNATIONAL
World Wide Web address: http://www.career-fairs.com. Organizes career fairs in the fields of accounting, banking, finance, and insurance.

Directories

INSURANCE ALMANAC
Underwriter Printing and Publishing Company, 50 East Palisade Avenue, Englewood NJ 07631. 201/569-8808. Available at libraries.

INSURANCE PHONE BOOK
Douglas Publications, 2807 North Parham Road, Suite 200, Richmond VA 23294. Toll-free phone: 800/521-8110. World Wide Web address: http://www.douglaspublications.com. New editions available every other year. Also available at libraries.

NATIONAL DIRECTORY OF HEALTH PLANS
American Association of Health Plans, 1129 20th Street NW, Suite 600, Washington DC 20036. 202/778-3200. World Wide Web address: http://www.aahp.org.

Magazines

BEST'S REVIEW
A.M. Best Company, Ambest Road, Oldwick NJ 08858. 908/439-2200. World Wide Web address: http://www.ambest.com. Monthly.

INSURANCE JOURNAL
Wells Publishing, 9191 Towne Centre Drive, Suite 550, San Diego, CA 92122-1231. 858/455-7717. World Wide Web address: http://www.insurancejrnl.com. A biweekly magazine covering the insurance industry for the western United States.

Online Services

FINANCIAL, ACCOUNTING, AND INSURANCE JOBS PAGE
World Wide Web address: http://www.nationjob.com/financial. This Website provides a list of financial, accounting, and insurance job openings.

THE INSURANCE CAREER CENTER
World Wide Web address: http://connectyou.com/talent. Offers job openings, career resources, and a resume database for jobseekers looking to get into the insurance field.

INSURANCE NATIONAL SEARCH
World Wide Web address: http://www.insurancerecruiters.com/insjobs/jobs.htm. Provides a searchable database of job openings in the insurance industry. The site is run by Insurance National Search, Inc.

LEGAL SERVICES

You can expect to find the following types of companies in this chapter:
Law Firms • Legal Service Agencies

Some helpful information: The average salary for a law school graduate after a year on the job is between $40,000 and $50,000 (lawyers in private practice generally earn more than federally employed lawyers). Experienced lawyers and firm associates can earn $80,000 and up (partners can earn considerably more). The average salary range for experienced paralegals is $30,000 - $35,000.

ACKELS & ACKELS LLP
2777 Stemmons Freeway, Suite 879, Dallas TX 75207. 214/267-8600. **Fax:** 214/267-8605. **Contact:** Office Manager. **Description:** A law firm that specializes in civil, criminal, and commercial litigation, and also practices personal injury, juvenile, and entertainment law.

JOHN ATWOOD LAW OFFICE
3500 Oak Lawn, Suite 400, Dallas TX 75219. 214/523-9520. **Contact:** Personnel Department. **Description:** A law firm specializing in corporate, real estate, administrative, and taxation law.

BAILEY AND WILLIAMS
7502 Greenville Avenue, Suite 500, Dallas TX 75231. 214/890-4006. **Contact:** Personnel. **Description:** A law firm specializing in litigation. **Common positions include:** Attorney; Paralegal. **Benefits:** Dental Insurance; Life Insurance; Medical Insurance; Pension Plan. **Corporate headquarters location:** This Location. **Operations at this facility include:** Service.

BAKER BOTTS LLP
2001 Ross Avenue, Suite 600, Dallas TX 75201-2980. 214/953-6500. **Contact:** Personnel. **World Wide Web address:** http://www.bakerbotts.com. **Description:** A law firm providing services in almost all areas of civil law. **Common positions include:** Attorney; Librarian; Secretary; Typist/Word Processor. **Educational backgrounds include:** Business Administration; Liberal Arts. **Benefits:** Dental Insurance; Disability Coverage; Life Insurance; Medical Insurance; Pension Plan; Profit Sharing; Travel Allowance; Tuition Assistance. **Corporate headquarters location:** Houston TX. **Other U.S. locations:** Washington DC; New York NY; Austin TX. **International locations:** Baku, Azerbaijan; London, England; Moscow, Russia.

BARON & BUDD, P.C.
3102 Oak Lawn Avenue, Suite 1100, Dallas TX 75219-4281. 214/521-3605. **Contact:** Personnel. **World Wide Web address:** http://www.baronbudd.com. **Description:** A plaintiffs' law firm specializing in toxic tort litigation.

BICKEL & BREWER
1717 Main Street, Suite 4800, Dallas TX 75201. 214/653-4000. **Contact:** Human Resources. **World Wide Web address:** http://www.bickelbrewer.com. **Description:** A law firm specializing in corporate litigation including bankruptcy.

CANTEY & HANGER, LLP
801 Cherry Street, Suite 2100, Burnett Plaza, Fort Worth TX 76102. 817/877-2800. **Contact:** Personnel. **World Wide Web address:** http://www.canteyhanger.com. **Description:** A law firm specializing in corporate law.

CRENSHAW DUPREE & MILAM
P.O. Box 1499, Lubbock TX 79408. 806/762-5281. **Contact:** Human Resources. **Description:** A defense law firm.

FRED MISKO, JR., P.C.
3811 Turtle Creek Boulevard, Suite 1900, Dallas TX 75231. 214/443-8000. **Contact:** Personnel. **World Wide Web address:** http://www.misko.com. **Description:** A trial practice specializing in personal injury law.

NOVAKOV DAVIS
750 North St. Paul Street, Suite 2000, Dallas TX 75201-3286. 214/922-9221. **Contact:** Human Resources. **Description:** A law firm specializing in corporate, IPO, estate, and real estate law.

THOMPSON & KNIGHT LLP
1700 Pacific Avenue, Suite 3300, Dallas TX 75201. 214/969-1700. **Contact:** Human Resources Department. **World Wide Web address:** http://www.tklaw.com. **Description:** A law firm specializing in a wide variety of law disciplines including bankruptcy, corporate, intellectual property, real estate, and environmental.

WINSTEAD SECHREST & MINICK P.C.
5400 Renaissance Tower, 1201 Elm Street, Dallas TX 75270. 214/745-5211. **Contact:** Patty Stewart, Human Resources Manager. **World Wide Web address:** http://www.winstead.com. **Description:** A law firm offering services in a variety of practice areas including environmental, insurance, real estate, and tax.

OFFICES OF NORMAN A. ZABLE, P.C.
16633 Dallas Parkway, Suite 700, LB 18, Addison TX 75001. 972/386-6900. **Contact:** Human Resources Department. **Description:** A civil law practice specializing in business and bankruptcy law.

Note: Because addresses and telephone numbers of smaller companies can change rapidly, we recommend you call each company to verify the information below before inquiring about job opportunities. Mass mailings are not recommended.

Additional small employers:

LEGAL SERVICES

Arter & Hadden
1717 Main St, Ste 4100, Dallas TX 75201-7302. 214/761-2100.

Barrett Burke Wilson Castle
15000 Surveyor Blvd, Ste 100, Addison TX 75001. 972/386-5040.

Cooper & Scully PC
900 Jackson St, Ste 100, Dallas TX 75202-4452. 214/712-9500.

Cowles & Thompson
901 Main St, Ste 4000, Dallas TX 75202-3746. 214/672-2000.

Dehay and Elliston LLP
901 Main St, Ste 3500, Dallas TX 75202-3736. 214/210-2400.

EDS Legal Affairs
7540 LBJ Fwy, Ste 300, Dallas TX 75251-1007. 972/448-1127.

Fulbright & Jaworski LLP
2200 Ross Ave, Ste 2800, Dallas TX 75201-2750. 214/855-8000.

Gardere & Wynne
1601 Elm St, Ste 3000, Dallas TX 75201-4761. 214/999-3000.

Gibson Dunn & Crutcher LLP
1717 Main St, Ste 5400, Dallas TX 75201-7367. 214/698-3100.

Heard Linebarger Graham
2323 Bryan St, Ste 1720, Dallas TX 75201-2644. 214/880-0089.

Hughes & Luce LLP
1717 Main St, Ste 2800, Dallas TX 75201-4685. 214/939-5500.

Jackson Walker LLP
901 Main St, Ste 6000, Dallas TX 75202-3797. 214/953-6000.

Jenkins & Gilcrist
1445 Ross Ave, Ste 3200, Dallas TX 75202-2785. 214/855-4500.

Locke Liddell & Sapp LLP
2200 Ross Ave, Ste 2200, Dallas TX 75201-2748. 214/740-8000.

Patton Boggs
2100 Ross Ave, Ste 3000, Dallas TX 75201-2704. 214/871-2141.

Strasburger & Price LLP
901 Main St, Ste 4300, Dallas TX 75202-3724. 214/651-4300.

Vinson & Elkins LP
2001 Ross Ave, Ste 3700, Dallas TX 75201-2965. 214/220-7700.

Windle Turley & Associates PC
6440 N Central Expy, Dallas TX 75206-4123. 214/691-4025.

Winstead Sechrest & Minick PC
1201 Elm St, Ste 5400, Dallas TX 75270-2199. 214/745-5400.

Worsham Forsythe Wooldridge LLP
1601 Bryan St, Fl 30, Dallas TX 75201-3401. 214/979-3000.

For more information on career opportunities in legal services:

Associations

AMERICAN BAR ASSOCIATION
750 North Lake Shore Drive, Chicago IL 60611. 312/988-5000. World Wide Web address: http://www.abanet.org.

FEDERAL BAR ASSOCIATION
2215 M Street NW, Washington DC 20037. 202/785-1614. World Wide Web address: http://www.fedbar.org.

NATIONAL ASSN. OF LEGAL ASSISTANTS
1516 South Boston Avenue, Suite 200, Tulsa OK 74119-4013. 918/587-6828. World Wide Web address: http://www.nala.org. An educational association. Memberships are available.

NATIONAL CRIME PREVENTION COUNCIL
One Prospect Street, Amsterdam NY 12010. 518/842-4388. Fax: 800/995-5121. Works to promote greater awareness in local neighborhoods in order to decrease crime.

NATIONAL FEDERATION OF PARALEGAL ASSOCIATIONS
P.O. Box 33108, Kansas City MO 64114-0108. 816/941-4000. World Wide Web address:

http://www.paralegals.org. Offers magazines, seminars, and Internet job listings.

NATIONAL PARALEGAL ASSOCIATION
Box 406, Solebury PA 18963. 215/297-8333. Fax: 215/297-8358. World Wide Web address: http://www.nationalparalegal.org.

Directories

MARTINDALE-HUBBELL LAW DIRECTORY
121 Chanlon Road, New Providence NJ 07974. 800/526-4902. World Wide Web address: http://www.martindale.com. A directory consisting exclusively of the names of legal employers. In all, listings for over 900,000 lawyers and law firms are available. In addition to information regarding firms and practices, the information includes biographies of many individual lawyers. Thus, you can search for firm names, law schools attended, and field of law.

Newsletters

LAWYERS WEEKLY USA
Lawyers Weekly, Inc., 41 West Street, Boston MA 02111. Toll-free phone: 800/444-5297. World Wide Web address: http://www.lawyersweekly.com. A newsletter that profiles law firms, provides general industry information, and provides information on jobs nationwide.

Online Services

COURT REPORTERS FORUM
Go: CrForum. A CompuServe networking forum that includes information from the *Journal of Court Reporting.*

LAW NEWS NETWORK
World Wide Web address: http://www.lawjobs.com. Lists jobs and recruiters primarily in California, Connecticut, District of Columbia, Florida, Georgia, New Jersey, New York, Pennsylvania, and Texas.

LEGAL EXCHANGE
Jump to: Legal Exchange. A debate forum for lawyers and other legal professionals, offered through Prodigy.

LEGAL INFORMATION NETWORK
Keyword: LIN. An America Online networking resource for paralegals, family law specialists, social security specialists, and law students.

For information about the JobBank List Service visit www.adamsjobbank.com

MANUFACTURING: MISCELLANEOUS CONSUMER

You can expect to find the following types of companies in this chapter:
Art Supplies • Batteries • Cosmetics and Related Products • Household Appliances and Audio/Video Equipment • Jewelry, Silverware, and Plated Ware
Miscellaneous Household Furniture and Fixtures • Musical Instruments
Tools • Toys and Sporting Goods

Some helpful information: The average salary of machinery operators is approximately $20,000 - $25,000, while machine repairers earn approximately $20,000 - $28,000 annually. Inspectors, testers, and graders earn between $25,000 and $40,000. Manufacturing supervisors earn $30,000 per year on average, though many earn more.

ACTION COMPANY
P.O. Box 8008, McKinney TX 75069. 972/542-8600. **Fax:** 972/562-7300. **Contact:** Human Resources. **Description:** Manufactures leather riding saddles.

AMERICAN PERMANENT WARE COMPANY
729 Third Avenue, Dallas TX 75226. 214/421-7366. **Fax:** 214/565-0976. **Contact:** Personnel. **Description:** Manufactures stainless steel hardware and kitchen utensils.

AMERICAN RECREATION PRODUCTS INC.
2125 West Broad Street, Mineola TX 75773. 903/569-3882. **Fax:** 903/569-0990. **Contact:** Human Resources. **Description:** Manufactures sleeping bags and dog beds.

ARROW INDUSTRIES
2625 Beltline Road, Carrollton TX 75006. 972/416-6500x238. **Contact:** Kyle Marlin, Vice President of Human Resources. **World Wide Web address:** http://www.arrowindustries.com. **Description:** A private label manufacturer, processor, and packager of polyethylene bags, household aluminum foil, paper plates, charcoal, lighter fluid, beans, rice, popcorn, and spices. **Common positions include:** Accountant/Auditor; Blue-Collar Worker Supervisor; Computer Programmer; Department Manager; Human Resources Manager; Manufacturer's/Wholesaler's Sales Rep.; Mechanical Engineer; Operations/Production Manager; Purchasing Agent/Manager; Quality Control Supervisor; Transportation/Traffic Specialist. **Educational backgrounds include:** Accounting; Business Administration; Computer Science; Engineering; Marketing. **Benefits:** Dental Insurance; Life Insurance; Medical Insurance; Profit Sharing. **Corporate headquarters location:** This Location. **Operations at this facility include:** Administration; Manufacturing; Sales.

ATLAS MATCH CORPORATION (AMC)
1801 South Airport Circle, Euless TX 76040. 817/267-1500. **Fax:** 817/354-7478. **Contact:** Personnel. **World Wide Web address:** http://www.atlasmatch.com. **Description:** Manufactures a wide variety of matchbooks with advertisements.

CARLTON MANUFACTURING
P.O. Box 539, Mount Vernon TX 75457. 903/537-4591. **Contact:** Human Resources. **Description:** Manufactures wooden household furniture.

DALLAS WOODCRAFT
2829 Sea Harbour Road, Dallas TX 75212. 214/631-2782. **Contact:** Personnel. **Description:** Manufactures wooden picture frames.

DART CONTAINER CORPORATION
850 Solon Road, Waxahachie TX 75165. 972/937-7270. **Contact:** Human Resources. **World Wide Web address:** http://www.dartcontainer.com. **Description:** Manufactures and wholesales single-use cups, plates, and beverage coolers.

DESIGN SOURCE
P.O. Box 420406, Dallas TX 75342-1068. 214/742-8234. **Contact:** Human Resources. **Description:** A manufacturer of wooden and upholstered furniture for the home.

FIRST COMPANY, INC.
8273 Moverly Lane, Dallas TX 75227. 214/388-5751. **Contact:** Personnel. **Description:** Manufactures air conditioners.

FOSSIL, INC.
2280 North Greenville Avenue, Richardson TX 75082-4412. 214/348-7400. **Contact:** Human Resources. **World Wide Web address:** http://www.fossil.com. **Description:** Manufactures watches, leather accessories, T-shirts, and sunglasses.

INTERCRAFT-BURNES COMPANY
One Intercraft Plaza, Taylor TX 76574. 512/352-8500. **Contact:** Gary Hall, Vice President of Human Resources. **World Wide Web address:** http://www.intercraft.com. **Description:** A manufacturer of picture frames sold to volume purchasers. **Common positions include:** Accountant/Auditor; Blue-Collar Worker Supervisor; Buyer; Customer Service Representative; Financial Analyst; Human Resources Manager; Industrial Engineer; Industrial Production Manager; Management Trainee; Manufacturer's/Wholesaler's Sales Rep.; Mechanical Engineer; Operations/Production Manager; Purchasing Agent/Manager. **Educational backgrounds include:** Accounting; Business Administration; Engineering; Finance; Marketing. **Benefits:** 401(k); Dental Insurance; Disability Coverage; Employee Discounts; Life Insurance; Medical Insurance; Pension Plan; Savings Plan; Tuition Assistance. **Corporate headquarters location:** Freeport IL. **Other U.S. locations:** Statesville NC. **Parent company:** Newell Company. **Listed on:** New York Stock Exchange. **Number of employees at this location:** 700. **Number of employees nationwide:** 1,600.

JOSTENS, INC.
P.O. Box AC, Denton TX 76202-1836. 940/891-0434. **Contact:** Human Resources. **Description:** This location manufactures jewelry which is sold to consumers through independent contract salespeople. Overall, Jostens, Inc.'s primary business segments are School Products, Recognition, and Jostens Learning. The School Products segment is comprised of five businesses: Printing and Publishing, Jewelry, Graduation Products, U.S. Photography, and Jostens Canada. Products include yearbooks, commercial printing, desktop publishing curriculum kits, class rings, graduation accessories, diplomas, trophies, plaques and other awards, school pictures, group photographs for youth camps and organizations, and senior graduation portraits. This segment serves schools, colleges, and alumni associations in the United States and Canada through 1,100 independent sales representatives. Jostens also maintains an international sales force in approximately 50 countries for American schools and military installations. The Recognition segment provides products and services that reflect achievements in service, sales, quality, productivity, attendance, safety, and retirements. It also produces awards for championship team accomplishments and affinity products for associations. This segment serves companies, professional and amateur sports teams, and special interest associations through an independent sales force of approximately 100 people. Jostens Learning produces educational software for kids in kindergarten through grade 12, offering software-based curriculum in reading, mathematics, language arts, science programs, and early childhood instruction, as well as programs for at-risk learning and home learning. As one of the nation's largest providers of curriculum software, Jostens Learning serves more than 4 million students in 10,000 schools nationwide. Customers may purchase programs to meet specific instructional needs, add products in a modular approach, or choose to implement a comprehensive schoolwide solution.

JUMPKING INC.
901 West Miller Road, Garland TX 75041. 972/271-5867. **Contact:** Human Resources. **World Wide Web address:** http://www.jumpking.com. **Description:** Manufactures trampolines and related accessories.

KIMBERLY-CLARK CORPORATION
P.O. Box 619100, Dallas TX 75261. 972/281-1200. **Contact:** Human Resources. **World Wide Web address:** http://www.kimberly-clark.com. **Description:** Manufactures and markets products for personal, business, and industrial uses throughout the world. The name brands of Kimberly-Clark Corporation include Kleenex facial and bathroom tissue, Huggies diapers and baby wipes, Pull-Ups training pants, Kotex and New Freedom feminine care products, Depend and Poise incontinence care products, Hi-Dri household towels, Kimguard sterile wrap, Kimwipes industrial wipers, and Classic business and correspondence papers. Most of the company's products are made using advanced technologies in absorbency, fibers, and nonwovens. Kimberly-Clark Corporation has extensive overseas operations in Europe and Asia. **Corporate headquarters location:** This Location. **Annual sales/revenues:** More than $100 million.

LASTING PRODUCTS
2115 West Valley View Lane, Farmers Branch TX 75234. 972/247-9696. **Contact:** Personnel Director. **Description:** Manufactures decorative home products made of wood, metal, ceramic, and glass.

LEVOLOR HOME FASHIONS
P.O. Box 154186, Waco TX 76704. 254/799-5523. **Contact:** Human Resources. **World Wide Web address:** http://www.levolor.com. **Description:** Manufactures window dressings including wooden and mini-blinds.

MARY KAY, INC.
16251 Dallas Parkway, Dallas TX 75001. 972/687-6300. **Contact:** Human Resources. **World Wide Web address:** http://www.marykay.com. **Description:** Manufactures and distributes cosmetics and other health and beauty aids. Production and development is conducted at a facility in Texas, while distribution is carried out by approximately 300,000 direct sales consultants. Products are sold in 16 countries.

NASH MANUFACTURING COMPANY, INC.
315 West Ripy Street, Fort Worth TX 76110. 817/926-5225. **Contact:** Personnel. **Description:** Manufactures sports and athletic equipment including skateboards and water skis.

NATIONAL BANNER COMPANY
11938 Harry Hines Boulevard, Dallas TX 75234. 972/241-2131. **Contact:** Human Resources. **World Wide Web address:** http://www.nationalbanner.com. **Description:** Manufactures and wholesales flags, banners, and pennants.

PRO-LINE CORPORATION
2121 Panoramic Circle, Dallas TX 75212. 214/631-4247. **Contact:** Human Resources. **Description:** Manufactures hair care products including relaxers, botanicals, and perm repair products. **Corporate headquarters location:** This Location.

RUBBERMAID, INC.
7121 Shelby Avenue, Greenville TX 75401. 903/455-0011. **Contact:** Human Resources. **World Wide Web address:** http://www.rubbermaid.com. **Description:** This location manufactures household products such as plastic food storage containers. Overall, Rubbermaid manufactures and sells rubber and plastic products for the consumer and commercial markets. Products include over 2,500 items for home organization, kitchen and bath, household repairs/do-it-yourself, and agricultural, industrial, and institutional use. **Corporate headquarters location:** Wooster OH.

SAMSILL CORPORATION
4301 Mansfield Highway, Fort Worth TX 76119. 817/535-0203. **Contact:** Human Resources. **Description:** Manufactures office products such as plastic binders and sheet protectors.

SKEETER PRODUCTS INC.
P.O. Box 230, Kilgore TX 75663-0230. 903/984-0541. **Contact:** Human Resources. **World Wide Web address:** http://www.skeeterboats.com. **Description:** Manufactures fishing boats.

STANLEY MECHANICS TOOLS
12827 Valley Branch Lane, Dallas TX 75234. 972/247-1367. **Contact:** Human Resources Department. **Description:** Manufactures hand tools such as socket wrenches.

SWEETHEART CUP COMPANY, INC.
4444 West Ledbetter Drive, Dallas TX 75236. 214/339-3131. **Contact:** Human Resources. **World Wide Web address:** http://www.sweetheart.com. **Description:** Manufactures and distributes a variety of food serviceware including plates, cups, bowls, drinking straws, and ice cream cones, as well as containers for use in packaging food and dairy products. **Common positions include:** Blue-Collar Worker Supervisor; Department Manager; Electrician; Millwright; Printing Press Operator. **Educational backgrounds include:** Business Administration; Engineering; Liberal Arts. **Corporate headquarters location:** Chicago IL. **Number of employees at this location:** 850. **Number of employees nationwide:** 8,000.

TANDYCRAFTS, INC.
1400 Everman Parkway, Fort Worth TX 76140-5006. 817/551-9600. **Contact:** Human Resources. **World Wide Web address:** http://www.tandycrafts.com. **Description:** A leading manufacturer and marketer of various consumer products including frames and wall decor,

office supplies, home furnishings, and gift products. Founded in 1975. **Benefits:** 401(k); Employee Discounts; Medical Insurance. **Corporate headquarters location:** This Location. **Subsidiaries include:** Joshua's Christian Stores; Sav-On Office Supplies; Tandy Leather. **Listed on:** New York Stock Exchange.

TEMPO/INFINITI LIGHTING
P.O. Box 421403, Dallas TX 75342-1403. 214/742-2685. **Contact:** Human Resources. **Description:** Manufactures household floor and table lamps.

TEMTEX INDUSTRIES INC.
5400 LBJ Freeway, Suite 1375, Dallas TX 75240. 972/726-7175. **Contact:** Human Resources. **Description:** Manufactures ceramic logs for fireplaces. **Corporate headquarters location:** This Location.

TEXAS RECREATION CORPORATION
P.O. Box 539, Wichita Falls TX 76307. 940/322-4463. **Contact:** Human Resources. **Description:** Manufactures soft foam products including pool flotation devices.

UNIVEX INTERNATIONAL
1000 Jewel Drive, Waco TX 76712. 972/660-7400. **Contact:** Human Resources. **World Wide Web address:** http://www.univex.com. **Description:** Manufactures audiotape and videotape albums and loose-leaf binders. **Common positions include:** Advertising Clerk; Blue-Collar Worker Supervisor; Clerical Supervisor; Cost Estimator; Customer Service Representative; Environmental Engineer; General Manager; Industrial Production Manager; Management Trainee; Manufacturer's/Wholesaler's Sales Rep.; Operations/Production Manager; Purchasing Agent/Manager; Quality Control Supervisor. **Benefits:** 401(k). **Corporate headquarters location:** Denver CO. **Other U.S. locations:** Colorado Springs CO. **Listed on:** Privately held. **Number of employees at this location:** 80. **Number of employees nationwide:** 200.

Note: Because addresses and telephone numbers of smaller companies can change rapidly, we recommend you call each company to verify the information below before inquiring about job opportunities. Mass mailings are not recommended.

Additional small employers:

COSMETICS AND RELATED PRODUCTS

Beauticontrol Inc.
PO Box 815189, Dallas TX 75381-5189. 972/458-0601.

Glycolique
PO Box 841058, Dallas TX 75284-1058. 972/241-7546.

HOUSEHOLD APPLIANCES

Clark United
3000 W Commerce St, Dallas TX 75212-4807. 214/630-3337.

Lasko Metal Products Inc.
1700 Meacham Blvd, Fort Worth TX 76106-2109. 817/625-6381.

HOUSEHOLD AUDIO AND VIDEO EQUIPMENT

Graham Magnetics
1715 4th St, Graham TX 76450-2927. 940/549-4500.

HOUSEHOLD FURNITURE

American Leather Inc.
3700 Eagle Place Dr, Dallas TX 75236-1464. 972/296-9599.

Mayo Brothers
PO Box 5338, Texarkana TX 75505-5338. 903/838-0518.

Smith Furniture Manufacturing Co.
PO Box 7973, Waco TX 76714-7973. 254/772-2760.

Southern Traditions
PO Box 751, Mexia TX 76667-0751. 254/562-9344.

Towne Square Furniture Inc.
PO Box 419, Hillsboro TX 76645-0419. 254/582-7444.

JEWELRY, SILVERWARE, AND PLATED WARE

Prime Art & Jewel
2930 N Stemmons Fwy, Dallas TX 75247-6103. 214/688-0088.

MISC. FURNITURE AND FIXTURES

CH Industries Inc.
PO Box 29923, Dallas TX 75229-0923. 972/245-2444.

Royal Windows Inc.
3109 E Randol Mill Rd,
Arlington TX 76011-6835. 817/640-4433.

Rubbermaid, Inc.
400 Commerce Blvd, Cleburne TX 76031-1360. 817/641-4444.

Tucker Housewares
721 111th St, Arlington TX 76011-7616. 817/640-5621.

POWER-DRIVEN HAND TOOLS

Stanley Tools
2801 Production Blvd, Wichita Falls TX 76302-5920. 940/767-0555.

TOYS AND SPORTING GOODS

Adams Golf Inc.
2801 E Plano Pkwy, Plano TX 75074-7418. 972/673-9000.

Backyard Adventures
14201 Interstate 27, Amarillo TX 79119-2547. 806/622-1220.

Hebb Industries Inc.
PO Box 1698, Whitehouse TX 75791-1698. 903/534-3832.

For more information on career opportunities in consumer manufacturing:

Associations

ASSOCIATION FOR MANUFACTURING EXCELLENCE
380 West Palatine Road, Wheeling IL 60090. 847/520-3282. World Wide Web address: http://www.ame.org.

ASSOCIATION FOR MANUFACTURING TECHNOLOGY
7901 Westpark Drive, McLean VA 22102. 703/893-2900. World Wide Web address: http://www.mfgtech.org. Offers research services.

ASSOCIATION OF HOME APPLIANCE MANUFACTURERS
1111 19th Street NW, Suite 402, Washington DC 20036. 202/872-5955. World Wide Web address: http://www.aham.org.

NATIONAL ASSOCIATION OF MANUFACTURERS
1331 Pennsylvania Avenue NW, Suite 600, Washington DC 20004. 202/637-3000. World Wide Web address: http://www.nam.org. A lobbying association for manufacturers.

NATIONAL HOUSEWARES MANUFACTURERS ASSOCIATION
6400 Schafer Court, Suite 650, Rosemont IL 60018. 847/292-4200. World Wide Web address: http://www.housewares.org. Offers shipping discounts and other services.

SOCIETY OF MANUFACTURING ENGINEERS
P.O. Box 930, One SME Drive, Dearborn MI 48121. 313/271-1500. World Wide Web address: http://www.sme.org. Offers educational events and educational materials on manufacturing.

Directories

AMERICAN MANUFACTURER'S DIRECTORY
InfoUSA, 5711 South 86th Circle, Omaha NE 68127. Toll-free phone: 800/555-5211. World Wide Web address: http://www.infousa.com. Made by the same company that created *American Big Business Directory*, *American Manufacturer's Directory* lists over 531,000 manufacturing companies of all sizes and industries. The directory contains product and sales information, company size, and a key contact name for each company.

APPLIANCE MANUFACTURER ANNUAL DIRECTORY
Appliance Manufacturer, 5900 Harper Road, Suite 105, Solon OH 44139. 440/349-3060. $25.00.

HOUSEHOLD & PERSONAL PRODUCTS INDUSTRY BUYERS GUIDE
Rodman Publishing Group, 17 South Franklin Turnpike, Ramsey NJ 07446. 201/825-2552. World Wide Web address: http://www.happi.com.

Magazines

APPLIANCE
Dana Chase Publications, 1110 Jorie Boulevard, Oak Brook IL 60522-9019. 630/990-3484. World Wide Web address: http://www.appliance.com.

COSMETICS INSIDERS REPORT
Advanstar Communications, 131 West First Street, Duluth MN 55802-2065. Toll-free phone: 800/346-0085. World Wide Web address: http://www.advanstar.com. $189.00 for a one year subscription; 24 issues annually. Features timely articles on cosmetics marketing and research.

Online Services

CAREER PARK - MANUFACTURING JOBS
World Wide Web address: http://www.careerpark.com/jobs/manulist.html. This Website provides a list of current job openings in the manufacturing industry. The site is run by Parker Advertising Service, Inc.

MANUFACTURING: MISCELLANEOUS INDUSTRIAL

You can expect to find the following types of companies in this chapter:
Ball and Roller Bearings • Commercial Furniture and Fixtures • Fans, Blowers, and Purification Equipment • Industrial Machinery and Equipment • Motors and Generators/Compressors and Engine Parts • Vending Machines

Some helpful information: *The average salary of industrial machinery operators is approximately $20,000 - $25,000, while machine repairers earn $22,000 - $35,000 annually. Manufacturing supervisors earn $30,000 per year on average, though many earn more. Entry-level industrial engineers earn between $35,000 and $45,000 per year, and experienced engineers earn $50,000 and up.*

ABCO INDUSTRIES INC.
P.O. Box 268, Abilene TX 79604. 915/677-2011. **Fax:** 915/673-3232. **Contact:** Charlotte Murch, Personnel Director. **World Wide Web address:** http://www.abcoboilers.com. **Description:** Manufactures industrial boilers.

AIR SYSTEMS COMPONENTS (ASC)
800 Airport Road, Terrell TX 75160. 972/563-2605. **Fax:** 972/551-5128. **Contact:** Human Resources. **Description:** Manufactures air system registers, grills, and diffusers. **Corporate headquarters location:** Richardson TX. **Number of employees nationwide:** 1,600.

BOOTH, INC.
2007 Royal Lane, Dallas TX 75229. 972/488-1030. **Contact:** Human Resources Department. **World Wide Web address:** http://www.booth-inc.com. **Description:** An industrial manufacturing company specializing in the production of soft drink fountain equipment.

THE BRINKMANN CORPORATION
4215 McEwen Road, Dallas TX 75244. 972/387-4939. **Contact:** Milly S. Hall, Executive Vice President. **World Wide Web address:** http://www.thebrinkmanncorp.com. **Description:** A diversified manufacturer producing items such as meat smokers, spotlights, and metal detectors. **Common positions include:** Accountant/Auditor; Advertising Clerk; Blue-Collar Worker Supervisor; Computer Programmer; Credit Manager; Customer Service Representative; Financial Analyst; Human Resources Manager; Manufacturer's/Wholesaler's Sales Rep.; Mechanical Engineer; Operations/Production Manager; Purchasing Agent/Manager; Systems Analyst; Transportation/Traffic Specialist. **Educational backgrounds include:** Accounting; Business Administration; Engineering; Finance; Marketing. **Benefits:** Employee Discounts; Life Insurance; Medical Insurance. **Corporate headquarters location:** This Location.

CONVEYORS, INC.
P.O. Box 50817, Fort Worth TX 76105. 817/477-3155. **Contact:** Personnel. **Description:** A manufacturer and retailer of conveyors and conveyor equipment.

EAGLE-PICHER INDUSTRIES, INC.
1802 East 50th Street, Lubbock TX 79404. 806/747-4663. **Contact:** Human Resources. **World Wide Web address:** http://www.epcorp.com. **Description:** Manufactures and distributes Caterpillar brand industrial machinery and other industrial equipment. **Corporate headquarters location:** Cincinnati OH. **Number of employees at this location:** 460.

FERGUSON MANUFACTURING AND EQUIPMENT
4900 Harry Hines Boulevard, Dallas TX 75235. 214/631-3700. **Contact:** Personnel. **Description:** Manufactures and distributes construction machines and equipment.

FISHER CONTROLS INTERNATIONAL
310 East University, McKinney TX 75069. 972/542-5512. **Contact:** Human Resources. **Description:** Manufactures gas pressure regulators.

FLOWSERVE CORPORATION
222 West Las Colinas Boulevard, Suite 1500, Irving TX 75039. 972/443-6500. **Contact:** Human Resources. **World Wide Web address:** http://www.flowserve.com. **Description:**

Manufactures valves for the chemical and petroleum industries. **Corporate headquarters location:** This Location.

FORNEY CORPORATION
3405 Wiley Post Road, Carrollton TX 75006. 972/458-6100. **Contact:** Personnel. **Description:** Manufactures industrial boiler burners, and burner and process control equipment and systems. **Common positions include:** Accountant/Auditor; Designer; Draftsperson; Electrical/Electronics Engineer; Mechanical Engineer. **Educational backgrounds include:** Accounting; Engineering; Finance. **Benefits:** 401(k); Dental Insurance; Disability Coverage; Life Insurance; Medical Insurance; Tuition Assistance. **Parent company:** Kidde International, Inc. **Number of employees at this location:** 320.

GNB TECHNOLOGIES INC.
P.O. Box 819023, Dallas TX 75381-9023. 972/243-1011. **Contact:** Kevin Williams, Regional Human Resources Manager. **World Wide Web address:** http://www.gnb.com. **Description:** This location manufactures batteries for automobiles, trucks, farm equipment, and industrial uses. Overall, GNB Technologies has three divisions: Automotive Battery, Industrial Battery, and Resource Recycling, with primary operations in North America. **Common positions include:** Environmental Engineer; Human Resources Manager; Industrial Engineer; Quality Control Supervisor. **Educational backgrounds include:** Business Administration; Chemistry; Engineering. **Benefits:** 401(k); Dental Insurance; Disability Coverage; Life Insurance; Medical Insurance; Pension Plan; Profit Sharing; Tuition Assistance. **Number of employees at this location:** 350.

HOBART CORPORATION
8120 Jetstar Drive, Suite 100, Irving TX 75063. 972/915-3822. **Contact:** Human Resources. **Description:** Manufactures food equipment for restaurants and supermarkets. Products include slicers, mixers, scales, fryers, food cutters, and toasters. **Common positions include:** Accountant/Auditor; Electronics Technician; Manufacturer's/Wholesaler's Sales Rep. **Educational backgrounds include:** Accounting; Marketing. **Corporate headquarters location:** Troy OH. **Parent company:** Premark International.

HUCK INTERNATIONAL INC.
P.O. Box 8117, Waco TX 76714. 254/776-2000. **Contact:** Human Resources. **World Wide Web address:** http://www.huck.com. **Description:** Manufactures industrial fasteners.

HYCO TEXAS
600 West Beltline Road, Lancaster TX 75146-3019. 972/218-3100. **Contact:** Personnel. **Description:** Manufactures hydraulic cylinders for industrial purposes.

INGERSOLL-RAND COMPANY
P.O. Box 462288, Garland TX 75040. 972/495-8181. **Contact:** Human Resources. **World Wide Web address:** http://www.ingersoll-rand.com. **Description:** Manufactures compressors, pumps, and other nonelectrical industrial equipment and machinery. Ingersoll-Rand Company's products include air compression systems, antifriction systems, construction equipment, air tools, bearings, locks, tools, and pumps. The company operates 93 production facilities throughout the world.

JOHN DEERE COMPANY
4040 McEwen, Suite 200, Dallas TX 75244-5032. 972/385-1701. **Contact:** Human Resources. **World Wide Web address:** http://www.deere.com. **Description:** This office is the agricultural equipment sales office for the region. Overall, John Deere manufactures, distributes, and finances the sale of heavy equipment and machinery for use in the agricultural equipment and industrial equipment industries. The agricultural equipment sector manufactures tractors, soil, seeding, and harvesting equipment. The industrial equipment segment manufactures a variety of earth-moving equipment, tractors, loaders, and excavators; while the consumer products division manufactures a variety of tractors and products for the homeowner. Financial services, including personal and commercial lines of insurance, retail, and managed health care services, are also offered.

JOHNSON CONTROLS, INC.
3021 West Bend Drive, Irving TX 75063. 972/869-4494. **Contact:** Human Resources. **World Wide Web address:** http://www.johnsoncontrols.com. **Description:** Manufactures and markets automobile, marine, and commercial storage batteries for sale to private labels. **Common positions include:** Accountant/Auditor; Blue-Collar Worker Supervisor; Buyer; Customer Service Representative. **Educational backgrounds include:** Accounting; Business

Administration; Computer Science; Engineering; Finance. **Benefits:** Dental Insurance; Disability Coverage; Employee Discounts; Life Insurance; Medical Insurance; Pension Plan; Savings Plan; Stock Option; Tuition Assistance. **Corporate headquarters location:** Milwaukee WI. **Listed on:** New York Stock Exchange. **Number of employees at this location:** 300.

KEVCO
P.O. Box 947015, Fort Worth TX 76147-9015. 817/332-2758. **Contact:** Human Resources. **Description:** A national group of manufacturing and distribution companies supplying a wide array of products used mostly in the production of manufactured housing, modular housing, and RVs.

MADIX INC.
P.O. Box 729, Terrell TX 75160-0729. 972/524-5744. **Contact:** Human Resources. **World Wide Web address:** http://www.madixinc.com. **Description:** A manufacturer of store fixtures such as grocery store shelving.

MARTIN SPROCKET & GEAR INC.
P.O. Box 91588, Arlington TX 76015. 817/467-5181. **Contact:** Guy Young, Personnel Manager. **World Wide Web address:** http://www.martinsprocket.com. **Description:** Manufactures chain sprockets and gears. **Corporate headquarters location:** This Location. **Other U.S. locations:** Nationwide. **Listed on:** Privately held. **Number of employees nationwide:** 1,200.

MARTIN SPROCKET & GEAR INC.
P.O. Box 1038, Fort Worth TX 76101. 817/258-3000. **Contact:** Darrell Riddick, Personnel Manager. **World Wide Web address:** http://www.martinsprocket.com. **Description:** Manufactures, installs, and services conveyor equipment. **Common positions include:** Accountant/Auditor; Administrative Manager; Blue-Collar Worker Supervisor; Branch Manager; Buyer; Computer Programmer; Designer; Draftsperson; Electrician; Financial Analyst; General Manager; Human Resources Manager; Management Trainee; Manufacturer's/Wholesaler's Sales Rep.; Medical Records Technician; Operations/Production Manager; Purchasing Agent/Manager; Transportation/Traffic Specialist. **Educational backgrounds include:** Business Administration. **Benefits:** 401(k); Dental Insurance; Disability Coverage; Employee Discounts; Life Insurance; Medical Insurance; Pension Plan; Profit Sharing; Tuition Assistance. **Corporate headquarters location:** Arlington TX. **Other U.S. locations:** Nationwide. **Listed on:** Privately held. **Number of employees at this location:** 400. **Number of employees nationwide:** 1,200.

MILLIPORE CORPORATION
915 Enterprise Boulevard, Allen TX 75013-8003. 972/359-4000. **Contact:** Human Resources. **World Wide Web address:** http://www.millipore.com. **Description:** Manufactures pressure gauges used by pharmaceutical, agricultural, and oil and gas companies. **Corporate headquarters location:** Bedford MA.

NCH CORPORATION
2727 Chemsearch Boulevard, Irving TX 75062. **Toll-free phone:** 800/527-9919. **Fax:** 972/438-0707. **Recorded jobline:** 972/721-6116. **Contact:** Human Resources. **World Wide Web address:** http://www.nch.com. **Description:** Manufactures and supplies specialty chemicals, water treatment products, fasteners, welding supplies, plumbing and electronic parts, and safety supplies to a worldwide customer base. Founded in 1919. **NOTE:** Entry-level positions and part-time jobs are offered. **Company slogan:** World class products and services. **Common positions include:** Account Representative; Accountant; Administrative Assistant; Advertising Clerk; Applications Engineer; Assistant Manager; Attorney; Auditor; Biochemist; Blue-Collar Worker Supervisor; Chemist; Clerical Supervisor; Clinical Lab Technician; Computer Engineer; Computer Operator; Computer Programmer; Computer Support Technician; Cost Estimator; Credit Manager; Customer Service Representative; Database Administrator; Desktop Publishing Specialist; Draftsperson; Editorial Assistant; Electrician; Environmental Engineer; General Manager; Graphic Artist; Graphic Designer; Human Resources Manager; Industrial Production Manager; Intellectual Property Lawyer; Internet Services Manager; Management Trainee; Market Research Analyst; Marketing Manager; Marketing Specialist; MIS Specialist; Multimedia Designer; Network/Systems Administrator; Operations Manager; Paralegal; Production Manager; Purchasing Agent/Manager; Quality Control Supervisor; Sales Manager; Sales Representative; Secretary; Technical Writer/Editor; Telecommunications Manager; Typist/Word Processor; Webmaster. **Educational backgrounds include:** Accounting; Art/Design; Business Administration; Chemistry; Communications; Liberal Arts; Marketing. **Benefits:** 401(k); Adoption Assistance; Credit Union; Dental Insurance; Disability Coverage; Employee Discounts; Financial Planning Assistance; Flexible Schedule; Job Sharing; Life Insurance;

Medical Insurance; Profit Sharing; Public Transit Available; Telecommuting; Tuition Assistance; Vacation Days (6 - 10). **Special programs:** Internships; Training. **Corporate headquarters location:** This Location. **Other U.S. locations:** El Segundo CA; Atlanta GA; Chicago IL; Paramus NJ; Seattle WA. **International locations:** Asia; Australia; Europe; South America. **Listed on:** New York Stock Exchange. **Stock exchange symbol:** NCH. **Executive Director:** Lester Levy, Sr. **Annual sales/revenues:** More than $100 million. **Number of employees at this location:** 600. **Number of employees nationwide:** 6,000. **Number of employees worldwide:** 10,700.

PVI INDUSTRIES INC.
P.O. Box 7124, Fort Worth TX 76111. 817/335-9531. **Contact:** Personnel. **Description:** A manufacturer of commercial water heaters and boilers.

PARKER HANNIFIN CORPORATION
STRATOFLEX AEROSPACE/MILITARY CONNECTORS DIVISION
P.O. Box 10398, Fort Worth TX 76114. 817/738-6543. **Fax:** 817/738-0598. **Contact:** Human Resources. **World Wide Web address:** http://www.parker.com. **Description:** This location is a manufacturer of hose fittings and hose assemblies for the aerospace, military, and marine markets. Overall, the company makes motion control products including fluid power systems, electromechanical controls, and related components. The Motion and Control Group manufactures hydraulic pumps, power units, control valves, accumulators, cylinders, actuators, and automation devices to remove contaminants from air, fuel, oil, water, and other fluids. The Fluid Connectors Group manufactures connectors, tube and hose fittings, hoses, and couplers which transmit fluid. The Seal Group manufactures sealing devices, gaskets, and packing materials which insure leak-proof connections. The Automotive and Refrigeration Groups manufacture components for use in industrial and automotive air conditioning and refrigeration systems. **Common positions include:** Account Representative; Accountant; Blue-Collar Worker Supervisor; Buyer; Computer Programmer; Customer Service Representative; Draftsperson; Electrician; Human Resources Manager; Industrial Engineer; Manufacturing Engineer; Marketing Specialist; Mechanical Engineer; MIS Specialist; Operations/Production Manager; Quality Control Supervisor; Secretary; Systems Analyst. **Educational backgrounds include:** Business Administration; Engineering. **Benefits:** Dental Insurance; Disability Coverage; Life Insurance; Medical Insurance; Pension Plan; Profit Sharing; Savings Plan; Tuition Assistance. **Corporate headquarters location:** Cleveland OH. **Listed on:** New York Stock Exchange. **Number of employees at this location:** 425.

PERRY EQUIPMENT CORPORATION
P.O. Box 640, Mineral Wells TX 76068-0640. 940/325-2575. **Contact:** Doug Harcourt, Vice President of Human Resources. **Description:** Manufactures filtration separation cartridges, flow-measurement systems, and systems for the oil, gas, and chemical processing industries. **Common positions include:** Accountant/Auditor; Blue-Collar Worker Supervisor; Buyer; Chemical Engineer; Computer Programmer; Customer Service Representative; Designer; Draftsperson; Electrical/Electronics Engineer; General Manager; Industrial Engineer; Industrial Production Manager; Manufacturer's/Wholesaler's Sales Rep.; Mechanical Engineer; Operations/Production Manager; Purchasing Agent/Manager; Quality Control Supervisor; Systems Analyst; Transportation/Traffic Specialist. **Educational backgrounds include:** Accounting; Business Administration; Computer Science; Engineering; Marketing. **Benefits:** Disability Coverage; Life Insurance; Medical Insurance; Pension Plan; Profit Sharing; Tuition Assistance. **Corporate headquarters location:** This Location. **Other area locations:** Amarillo TX; Houston TX. **Listed on:** Privately held. **Number of employees at this location:** 500.

GUY SHADDOCK AND COMPANY
1616 Oak Lawn Avenue, Dallas TX 75207-3402. 214/744-9124. **Contact:** Human Resources. **Description:** Manufactures reproduction wooden furniture for home and office.

STEELCASE INC.
3131 McKinney Avenue, Suite 300, Dallas TX 75204-2442. 214/871-3044. **Contact:** Human Resources. **World Wide Web address:** http://www.steelcase.com. **Description:** Manufactures metal and wood office furniture.

STEVENS INTERNATIONAL
5500 Airport Freeway, Fort Worth TX 76117-5985. 817/831-3911. **Contact:** Personnel Department. **Description:** Manufactures machinery for the printing industry.

THIRD COAST TECHNOLOGIES (TCT)
1571 North Glenville Street, Richardson TX 75081. 972/238-9123. **Contact:** Human Resources. **Description:** Manufactures toner cartridges for copy machines.

THE TRANE COMPANY
P.O. Box 814609, Dallas TX 75381. 972/406-6000. **Fax:** 972/488-7415. **Contact:** Heather Etheridge, Human Resources Representative. **Description:** Engaged in the development, manufacture, and sale of air conditioning equipment designed for use in central air conditioning systems for commercial, institutional, industrial, and residential buildings. The Trane Company's products are designed to cool water, and to cool, heat, humidify, dehumidify, move, and filter air. Other products include similar systems for buses and rapid transit vehicles, refrigeration equipment for trucks, and pollution control equipment. **NOTE:** Entry-level positions are offered. **Common positions include:** Administrative Assistant; Credit Manager; Market Research Analyst; Mechanical Engineer; Project Manager; Systems Analyst; Typist/Word Processor. **Educational backgrounds include:** Accounting; Business Administration; Communications; Engineering. **Benefits:** 401(k); Dental Insurance; Disability Coverage; Life Insurance; Medical Insurance. **Special programs:** Apprenticeships; Training. **Corporate headquarters location:** La Crosse WI. **Parent company:** American Standard. **Number of employees at this location:** 200.

TRAULSEN & COMPANY, INC.
4401 Blue Mound Road, Fort Worth TX 76106. 817/625-9671. **Contact:** Susan Pereira, Human Resources Manager. **World Wide Web address:** http://www.traulsen.com. **Description:** Manufactures an extensive line of commercial refrigerators and freezers. **Corporate headquarters location:** This Location.

TRINITY INDUSTRIES, INC.
P.O. Box 568887, Dallas TX 75356-8887. 214/631-4420. **Contact:** Human Resources Department. **World Wide Web address:** http://www.trin.net. **Description:** Manufactures an assortment of railroad and construction equipment and replacement parts. Trinity Industries also offers related services for the transportation, construction, aerospace, commercial, and industrial markets. Products include railcars, gas processing systems, petroleum transportation systems, guard rails, bridge girders and beams, airport boarding bridges, barges, tug boats, military marine vessels, and precision welding products. Trinity Industries also makes concrete and aggregates and produces metal components for the petrochemical, industrial, processing, and power markets. **Common positions include:** Accountant/Auditor; Data Entry Clerk. **Educational backgrounds include:** Accounting; Business Administration; Computer Science; Engineering. **Benefits:** Daycare Assistance; Disability Coverage; Employee Discounts; Life Insurance; Medical Insurance; Pension Plan; Profit Sharing; Savings Plan; Tuition Assistance. **Corporate headquarters location:** This Location. **Listed on:** New York Stock Exchange.

TYLER PIPE INDUSTRIES, INC.
P.O. Box 2027, Tyler TX 75710. 903/882-5511. **Contact:** Human Resources. **World Wide Web address:** http://www.tylerpipe.com. **Description:** Manufactures and distributes soil and pipe fittings. Tyler Pipe Industries, Inc. is also a national producer of both plastic and iron piping for large-volume users.

VECTA
1800 South Great SW Parkway, Grand Prairie TX 75051. 972/641-2860. **Contact:** Human Resources. **World Wide Web address:** http://www.vecta.com. **Description:** Custom manufactures office furniture.

VIRGINIA KMP CORPORATION
4100 Platinum Way, Dallas TX 75237. 214/330-7731. **Contact:** Vice President of Operations. **Description:** Manufactures and sells chemicals, filter dryers, refrigeration accumulators, and air conditioners.

XEROX CORPORATION
1301 Ridgeview Drive, Lewisville TX 75057. 972/830-4000. **Contact:** Human Resources Department. **E-mail address:** xerox@isearch.com. **World Wide Web address:** http://www.xerox.com. **Description:** This location is a sales and service office. Overall, Xerox Corporation is a leader in the global document market providing document solutions that enhance business productivity. Xerox develops, manufactures, markets, sells, and services a full range of document processing products. **Corporate headquarters location:** Stamord CT.

Note: Because addresses and telephone numbers of smaller companies can change rapidly, we recommend you call each company to verify the information below before inquiring about job opportunities. Mass mailings are not recommended.

Additional small employers:

COMMERCIAL FURNITURE AND FIXTURES

ADNC Inc.
PO Box 6129, Temple TX 76503-6129. 254/773-1776.

Anderson Hickey Company
PO Box 80, Henderson TX 75653-0080. 903/657-9531.

Artco-Bell Corporation
PO Box 608, Temple TX 76503-0608. 254/778-1811.

Faubion Associates Inc.
PO Box 150159, Dallas TX 75315-0159. 214/565-1000.

Fixture Concepts
726 E Highway 121, Lewisville TX 75057-4159. 972/420-0955.

Full Vue Display Systems
3300 Enterprise Dr, Rowlett TX 75088-4085. 972/475-2954.

Furniture Contractors Inc.
2000 E Richmond Ave, Fort Worth TX 76104. 817/531-3682.

Inca Manufacturing Corporation
PO Box 897, Lewisville TX 75067-0897. 972/436-5581.

JSJ Seating Corporation
1 Industrial Park Rd, Belton TX 76513-1922. 254/939-3517.

Madix Store Fixtures
PO Box 729, Terrell TX 75160. 972/563-5744.

Rodgers-Wade Manufacturing Co.
PO Box 158, Paris TX 75461-0158. 903/785-1619.

Royal Seating Corp.
PO Box 753, Cameron TX 76520-0753. 254/697-6421.

Smith System Manufacturing Co.
PO Box 860415, Plano TX 75086-0415. 972/424-6591.

Tarrant Interiors Inc.
5000 South Fwy, Fort Worth TX 76115-3902. 817/922-5000.

Universal Display & Fixtures Co.
613 Easy St, Garland TX 75042-6812. 972/276-8335.

Weber Aircraft Inc.
2000 Weber Dr, Gainesville TX 76240-9699. 940/668-8541.

Woodland Furniture
PO Box 760, Forney TX 75126-0760. 972/564-1075.

COMMERCIAL LAUNDRY, DRY-CLEANING, AND PRESSING MACHINES

ELX Group-Washex Machinery
5000 Central Fwy N, Wichita Falls TX 76306-1502. 940/855-3990.

CONSTRUCTION MACHINERY AND EQUIPMENT

Alpine Engineered Products
2820 N GSW Pkwy, Grand Prairie TX 75050. 972/660-3940.

Condor
PO Box 21447, Waco TX 76702-1447. 254/420-5200.

Hanson Industries
1000 MacArthur Blvd, Grand Prairie TX 75050-7942. 972/260-3659.

Trencor Inc.
1400 E Highway 26, Grapevine TX 76051-3713. 817/424-1968.

CONVEYORS AND CONVEYING EQUIPMENT

BAE Automated Systems Inc.
2525 Carter Dr, Carrollton TX 75006-1310. 972/245-9411.

KWS Manufacturing Company
PO Box 1550, Joshua TX 76058-1550. 817/295-2247.

Mannesmann Dematic Rapistan
8600 N Royal Ln, Ste 100B, Irving TX 75063-2571. 972/929-2500.

ENGINE PARTS

Precise Hard Chrome
PO Box 1067, Temple TX 76503-1067. 254/778-4701.

FANS, BLOWERS, AND AIR PURIFICATION EQUIPMENT

AAF International
PO Box 1129, Hutchins TX 75141-1129. 972/225-8288.

Filtration Group Incorporated
1560 Hillguard Rd, Dallas TX 75243-5504. 214/341-2199.

Glasfloss Industries
PO Box 150469, Dallas TX 75315-0469. 214/741-7056.

FARM MACHINERY AND EQUIPMENT

Agco Corporation
PO Box 1120, Lockney TX 79241-1120. 806/652-3367.

Big Tex Trailer World Inc.
RR 6, Box 1369, Mount Pleasant TX 75455-9596. 903/575-0300.

Phoenix Fabricators & Erectors
PO Box 8257, Ennis TX 75120-8257. 972/875-9675.

Priefert Manufacturing Co.
PO Box 1540, Mount Pleasant TX 75456-1540. 903/572-1741.

INDUSTRIAL AND COMMERCIAL MACHINERY AND EQUIPMENT

Automatic Products Corp.
PO Box 461088, Garland TX 75046-1088. 972/272-6422.

Karlee Company
PO Box 461207, Garland TX 75046-1207. 972/272-0628.

SPM
7601 Wyatt Dr, Fort Worth TX 76108-2530. 817/246-2461.

MEASURING AND CONTROLLING EQUIPMENT

Delphi Energy & Engineering Management Systems
PO Box 97504, Wichita Falls TX 76307-7504. 940/855-7097.

Ludlow Measurements
PO Box 810, Sweetwater TX 79556-0810. 915/235-4947.

Y-Z Industries Inc.
206 Lubbock Hwy, Snyder TX 79549-1528. 915/573-8578.

METAL CUTTING OR FORMING TOOLS

Woodlawn Manufacturing Inc.
PO Box 788, Marshall TX 75671-0788. 903/938-1882.

METAL HARDWARE

Kwikset Corporation
2600 N Highway 75A, Denison TX 75020-9042. 903/463-1313.

METALWORKING MACHINERY

Delta Brands Inc.
2204 Century Center Blvd, Irving TX 75062-4999. 972/438-7150.

MISC. INDUSTRIAL MACHINE TOOLS

Varel International Inc.
PO Box 540157, Dallas TX 75354-0157. 972/242-1160.

MISC. INDUSTRIAL MACHINERY AND EQUIPMENT

Tote Kinetics
651 N Burleson Blvd, Burleson TX 76028-2911. 817/447-9110.

MISC. PIPE FITTINGS AND/OR VALVES

Dynamco Inc.
410 Industrial Blvd, McKinney TX 75069-7323. 972/548-9961.

Fisher Controls International
PO Box 1658, Sherman TX 75091-1658. 903/868-3200.

Fujikoki America Inc.
4040 Bronze Way, Dallas TX 75237-1081. 214/333-4266.

JCM Industries Inc.
PO Box 1220, Nash TX 75569-1220. 903/832-2581.

Nordstrom Valves Inc.
PO Box 501, Sulphur Springs TX 75483-0501. 903/885-3151.

Thermadyne Modern Engineering
PO Box 1007, Denton TX 76202-1007. 601/892-3500.

PLUMBING FIXTURE FITTINGS AND TRIM

Dearborn Brass
PO Box 1020, Tyler TX 75710-1020. 903/877-3468.

Weather-Matic
PO Box 180205, Dallas TX 75218-0205. 972/278-6131.

PUMPS AND PUMPING EQUIPMENT

Commercial Pump Service
10661 Newkirk St, Dallas TX 75220-2303. 214/357-1320.

WTG Turbine
PO Box 5487, Lubbock TX 79408-5487. 806/743-5700.

SERVICE INDUSTRY MACHINERY

H&K Dallas Inc.
PO Box 180729, Dallas TX 75218-0729. 214/821-2740.

TEXTILE MACHINERY

Poser Business Forms Inc.
2621 S Cooper St, Arlington TX 76015-2414. 817/261-6431.

Vesuvius USA Corporation
1812 E Duncan St, Tyler TX 75702-2409. 903/597-7237.

For more information on career opportunities in industrial manufacturing:

Associations

ASSOCIATION FOR MANUFACTURING EXCELLENCE
380 West Palatine Road, Wheeling IL 60090. 847/520-3282. World Wide Web address: http://www.ame.org.

ASSOCIATION FOR MANUFACTURING TECHNOLOGY
7901 Westpark Drive, McLean VA 22102. 703/893-2900. A trade association. World Wide Web address: http://www.mfgtech.org.

INSTITUTE OF INDUSTRIAL ENGINEERS
25 Technology Park, Norcross GA 30092. 770/449-0460. World Wide Web address: http://www.iienet.org. A nonprofit organization with 27,000 members. Conducts seminars and offers reduced rates on its books and publications.

NATIONAL ASSOCIATION OF MANUFACTURERS
1331 Pennsylvania Avenue NW, Suite 600, Washington DC 20004. 202/637-3000. World Wide Web address: http://www.nam.org. A lobbying association.

NATIONAL TOOLING & MACHINING ASSOCIATION
9300 Livingston Road, Fort Washington MD 20744. Toll-free phone: 800/248-6862. World Wide Web address: http://www.ntma.org. Reports on wages and operating expenses, produces monthly newsletters, and offers legal advice.

PRECISION MACHINED PRODUCTS ASSN.
6700 West Snowville Road, Brecksville OH 44141. 440/526-0300. Provides resource information.

SOCIETY OF MANUFACTURING ENGINEERS
P.O. Box 930, One SME Drive, Dearborn MI 48121. 313/271-1500. World Wide Web address: http://www.sme.org. Offers educational events and educational materials on manufacturing.

Directories

AMERICAN MANUFACTURER'S DIRECTORY
5711 South 86th Circle, P.O. Box 37347, Omaha NE 68127. Toll-free phone: 800/555-5211. World Wide Web address: http://www.infousa.com. Made by the same company that created *American Big Business Directory*, *American Manufacturer's Directory* lists over 531,000 manufacturing companies of all sizes and industries. The directory contains product and sales information, company size, and a key contact name for each company.

Online Services

CAREER PARK - MANUFACTURING JOBS
World Wide Web address: http://www.careerpark.com/jobs/manulist.html. This Website provides a list of current job openings in the manufacturing industry. The site is run by Parker Advertising Service, Inc.

Special Programs

BUREAU OF APPRENTICESHIP AND TRAINING
U.S. Department of Labor, 200 Constitution Avenue NW, Room N4649, Washington DC 20210. 202/219-5921.

For information about the JobBank List Service visit www.adamsjobbank.com

MINING/GAS/PETROLEUM/ENERGY RELATED

You can expect to find the following types of companies in this chapter:
Anthracite, Coal, and Ore Mining • Mining Machinery and Equipment •
Oil and Gas Field Services • Petroleum and Natural Gas

Some helpful information: Power plant operators average about $35,000 - $40,000 per year. Petroleum engineers average about $40,000 - $45,000, and mining engineers earn about $35,000 - $40,000 per year.

ATMOS ENERGY CORPORATION
P.O. Box 650205, Dallas TX 75265-0205. 972/934-9227. **Fax:** 972/855-4039. **Contact:** Manager of Compensation and Employment. **World Wide Web address:** http://www.atmosenergy.com. **Description:** Distributes natural gas and propane. **Common positions include:** Accountant/Auditor; Computer Programmer; Mechanical Engineer; Petroleum Engineer. **Educational backgrounds include:** Accounting; Computer Science; Engineering. **Benefits:** Dental Insurance; Disability Coverage; Life Insurance; Medical Insurance; Pension Plan; Profit Sharing. **Corporate headquarters location:** This Location. **Other U.S. locations:** CO; KY; LA. **Subsidiaries include:** Energas Company; Enermart Energy Services, Inc.; Greeley Gas Company; Trans Louisiana Gas Company; United Cities Gas Company; Western Kentucky Gas Company. **Listed on:** New York Stock Exchange. **Number of employees at this location:** 200. **Number of employees nationwide:** 1,700.

BP AMOCO
2300 West Plano Parkway, Plano TX 75075. **Contact:** Human Resources Department. **Description:** Engaged in all phases of the petroleum energy industry. **NOTE:** This firm does not accept unsolicited resumes. Please only respond to advertised openings.

CALTEX PETROLEUM CORPORATION
125 East John Carpenter Freeway, Irving TX 75062-2794. 972/830-1000. **Contact:** Professional Recruiter. **World Wide Web address:** http://www.caltex.com. **Description:** Refines crude oil and markets petroleum and convenience products for motorists. **Common positions include:** Accountant/Auditor; Chemical Engineer; Data Processor; Financial Analyst; Mechanical Engineer. **Parent company:** Caltex Petroleum Corporation is jointly owned ny Texaco and Chevron.

W.R. CHILDRESS OIL COMPANY
P.O. Box 7496, Fort Worth TX 76111. 817/834-1901. **Contact:** Melissa Paredez, Secretary. **Description:** Distributes petroleum and related products.

CODA ENERGY INC.
5735 Pineland Drive, Suite 300, Dallas TX 75231. 214/692-1800. **Contact:** Personnel. **Description:** Distributes petroleum and natural gas.

**COMPUTALOG
WIRELINE PRODUCTS, INC.**
500 Winscott Road, Fort Worth TX 76126. 817/249-1391. **Fax:** 817/249-7284. **Contact:** Human Resources Manager. **World Wide Web address:** http://www.computalog.com. **Description:** Manufactures, sells, and services oil well equipment for the oil field service industry. **Common positions include:** Accountant; Electrical/Electronics Engineer; Mechanical Engineer; Sales Engineer; Software Engineer. **Educational backgrounds include:** Accounting; Engineering; Geology. **Benefits:** 401(k); Dental Insurance; Disability Coverage; Life Insurance; Medical Insurance; Tuition Assistance. **Office hours:** Monday - Friday, 8:00 a.m. - 5:00 p.m. **Number of employees at this location:** 200. **Number of employees nationwide:** 430.

DIAMOND SHAMROCK, INC.
HCR 1, Box 36, Sunray TX 79086-9705. 806/935-2141. **Contact:** Tonja Bilbrey, Human Resources Director. **Description:** This location is an oil refinery. Overall, Diamond Shamrock is a regional petroleum refining, transporting, and marketing company. The company operates 3,800 miles of pipeline, six terminals, and approximately 2,000 stores in eight southwestern states. Diamond Shamrock is engaged in crude oil refining; wholesale marketing; retail marketing; and the storing, manufacturing, and marketing of gas liquids, petrochemicals, and ammonia fertilizer. The company also operates a credit card program with over 500,000 active

accounts. **Corporate headquarters location:** San Antonio TX. **Number of employees at this location:** 400.

ENSCO INTERNATIONAL INCORPORATED
1445 Ross Avenue, Suite 2700, Dallas TX 75202. 214/922-1500. **Contact:** Human Resources. **World Wide Web address:** http://www.enscous.com. **Description:** One of the world's largest offshore oil and gas drilling companies. **Corporate headquarters location:** This location. **Listed on:** New York Stock Exchange.

EXXONMOBIL CORPORATION
P.O. Box 819047, Dallas TX 75381. 972/851-8111. **Contact:** Human Resources. **World Wide Web address:** http://www.exxon.mobil.com. **Description:** This location is a research facility. Overall, ExxonMobil is an integrated oil company engaged in the worldwide marketing, refining, manufacturing, exploration, production, transportation, and research and development of petroleum and chemical products. Other products include fabricated plastics, films, food bags, housewares, garbage bags, and building materials. The company also has subsidiaries involved in real estate development and mining operations. **Corporate headquarters location:** Irving TX. **Listed on:** New York Stock Exchange. **Stock exchange symbol:** XOM. **Annual sales/revenues:** More than $100 million.

EXXONMOBIL CORPORATION
5959 Las Colinas Boulevard, Irving TX 75039-2298. 972/444-1000. **Fax:** 972/444-1350. **Contact:** Human Resources. **World Wide Web address:** http://www.exxon.mobil.com. **Description:** An integrated oil company engaged in the worldwide marketing, refining, manufacturing, exploration, production, transportation, and research and development of petroleum and chemical products. Other products include fabricated plastics, films, food bags, housewares, garbage bags, and building materials. The company also has subsidiaries involved in real estate development and mining operations. **Corporate headquarters location:** This Location. **Listed on:** New York Stock Exchange. **Stock exchange symbol:** XOM. **Annual sales/revenues:** More than $100 million.

FINA OIL & CHEMICAL COMPANY
6000 Legacy Drive, Plano TX 75024-3601. 972/801-2000. **Contact:** Human Resources. **World Wide Web address:** http://www.fina.com. **Description:** Explores for crude oil and natural gas; markets natural gas; refines, supplies, transports, and markets petroleum products; manufactures and markets specialty chemicals, primarily petrochemicals and plastics including polypropylene, polystyrene, styrene monomer, high-density polyethylene, and aromatics; licenses certain chemical processes; and manufactures and markets paints and coatings. **Corporate headquarters location:** This Location.

GAS EQUIPMENT COMPANY (GEC)
11616 Harry Hines Boulevard, P.O. Box 29242, Dallas TX 75229. 972/241-2333. **Toll-free phone:** 800/821-1829. **Contact:** Human Resources Department. **World Wide Web address:** http://www.gasequipment.com. **Description:** A wholesale distributor of in-process, transfer, and control equipment. **Common positions include:** Administrative Manager; Manufacturer's/Wholesaler's Sales Rep. **Educational backgrounds include:** Marketing. **Benefits:** 401(k); Dental Insurance; Disability Coverage; Employee Discounts; Life Insurance; Medical Insurance; Pension Plan; Public Transit Available; Savings Plan; Tuition Assistance. **Corporate headquarters location:** This Location. **Listed on:** Privately held. **Annual sales/revenues:** $21 - $50 million. **Number of employees at this location:** 30. **Number of employees nationwide:** 75.

GEER TANK TRUCKS INC.
P.O. Drawer J, Jacksboro TX 76458. 940/567-2677. **Contact:** Human Resources. **Description:** A crude oil purchaser. The company also hauls various substances including oil and saltwater.

HARBISON-FISCHER MANUFACTURING COMPANY
P.O. Box 2477, Fort Worth TX 76113-2477. 817/297-2211. **Physical address:** 901 North Crowley Road, Crowley TX 76036-3798. **Fax:** 817/297-4248. **Contact:** Leon Gregory, Personnel Director. **World Wide Web address:** http://www.hfpumps.com. **Description:** Manufactures subsurface oil well pumping equipment. **Common positions include:** Accountant/Auditor; Blue-Collar Worker Supervisor; Buyer; Claim Representative; Clerical Supervisor; Computer Programmer; Designer; Draftsperson; Electrician; General Manager; Human Resources Manager; Management Trainee; Metallurgical Engineer; Petroleum Engineer; Systems Analyst. **Educational backgrounds include:** Accounting; Business Administration; Engineering. **Benefits:** Bonus Award/Plan; Dental Insurance; Disability Coverage; Life

Insurance; Medical Insurance; Pension Plan; Savings Plan; Tuition Assistance. **Corporate headquarters location:** This Location. **Other area locations:** Odessa TX. **Subsidiaries include:** Challenger Tank (Whitehouse TX); National Steelcrafters (Eugene OR). **Number of employees at this location:** 270. **Number of employees nationwide:** 500.

HOLLY CORPORATION
100 Crescent Court, Suite 1600, Dallas TX 75201-6927. 214/871-3555. **Contact:** Human Resources. **Description:** A holding company that, through its subsidiaries, is engaged in the refining, transporting, terminalling, and marketing of petroleum products. **Subsidiaries include:** Montana Refining Company (Great Falls MT); Navajo Refining Company (Artesia NM). **Listed on:** American Stock Exchange. **Number of employees at this location:** 440.

HUNT OIL COMPANY
1445 Ross Avenue, Dallas TX 75202. 214/978-8022. **Fax:** 214/978-8911. **Contact:** Personnel. **Description:** Refines and distributes petroleum and natural gas. **Common positions include:** Accountant/Auditor; Clerical Supervisor; Computer Programmer; Draftsperson; Environmental Engineer; Financial Analyst; General Manager; Geologist/Geophysicist; Human Resources Manager; Paralegal; Petroleum Engineer; Purchasing Agent/Manager. **Educational backgrounds include:** Accounting; Business Administration; Computer Science; Engineering; Finance; Geology. **Benefits:** 401(k); Dental Insurance; Disability Coverage; Life Insurance; Medical Insurance; Pension Plan; Tuition Assistance. **Special programs:** Internships. **Corporate headquarters location:** This Location. **Listed on:** Privately held. **Number of employees at this location:** 600.

IRI INTERNATIONAL COMPANY
P.O. Box 1101, Pampa TX 79066-1101. 806/665-3701. **Fax:** 806/665-3216. **Contact:** Vice President of Human Resources. **Description:** Designs and manufactures a complete line of oil and gas drilling and workover rigs, related equipment, and accessories. Through its specialty steel division, the company produces a wide array of alloy steel forging and bar stock for use in industries ranging from aerospace to nuclear energy. Founded in 1925. **Common positions include:** Account Manager; Accountant; Civil Engineer; Computer Programmer; Controller; Design Engineer; Draftsperson; Electrician; Human Resources Manager; Industrial Engineer; Metallurgical Engineer; Purchasing Agent/Manager; Quality Control Supervisor; Sales Manager. **Educational backgrounds include:** Accounting; Engineering. **Benefits:** 401(k); Dental Insurance; Disability Coverage; Life Insurance; Medical Insurance; Profit Sharing; Tuition Assistance. **Corporate headquarters location:** This Location. **Other area locations:** Alice TX; Beaumont TX; Houston TX; Odessa TX. **International locations:** Moscow, Russia; United Kingdom. **Listed on:** New York Stock Exchange. **Annual sales/revenues:** More than $100 million. **Number of employees at this location:** 400. **Number of employees nationwide:** 600.

JRC HALLIBURTON ENERGY SERVICES, INC.
8432 South Interstate 35 W, Alvarado TX 76009. 817/790-2038. **Contact:** Human Resources Manager. **World Wide Web address:** http://www.halliburton.com. **Description:** Provides evaluation services in connection with the drilling and completion of gas and oil wells. The company also manufactures and sells the equipment and supplies required to perform well evaluation services. **Other U.S. locations:** Nationwide. **Parent company:** Halliburton Company.

KANEB SERVICES, INC.
2435 North Central Expressway, Suite 700, Richardson TX 75080. 972/699-4000. **Contact:** Human Resources. engaged in the worldwide marketing, refining, manufacturing, exploration, production, transportation, and research and development of petroleum and chemical products. Other products include fabricated plastics, films, food bags, housewares, garbage bags, and building materials. The company also has subsidiaries involved in real estate development and mining operations. **World Wide Web address:** http://www.kaneb.com. **Description:** A holding company whose subsidiaries are engaged in various technical applications as well as in the refining of petroleum products. **Corporate headquarters location:** This Location. **Subsidiaries include:** InformaTech's Medical Services Division provides information technology services for medical information systems and applications. InformaTech's Information Technology Division is engaged in network design and installation, secure network architecture, seat management, custom computer design, and cabling; Kaneb Pipe Line Partners, LP owns and operates several thousand miles of pipeline, transports refined petroleum products, and terminals independent liquids. Kaneb Pipe Line operates more than 60 facilities in the United States and the United Kingdom. **Listed on:** New York Stock Exchange.

LA GLORIA OIL AND GAS COMPANY
P.O. Box 840, Tyler TX 75710. 903/579-3400. **Contact:** Human Resources. **Description:** A wholesaler of petroleum products.

MAGUIRE OIL COMPANY
1201 Elm Street, Suite 4000, Dallas TX 75270. 214/741-5137. **Contact:** Debbe Karnes, Personnel Manager. **Description:** Produces and explores for petroleum and natural gas. **Common positions include:** Accountant/Auditor; Administrator; Geologist/Geophysicist; Petroleum Engineer. **Benefits:** Dental Insurance; Disability Coverage; Life Insurance; Medical Insurance; Profit Sharing; Tuition Assistance. **Corporate headquarters location:** This Location.

MAXUS ENERGY CORPORATION
717 North Harwood Street, Suite 3000, Dallas TX 75201. 214/953-2000. **Contact:** Director of Human Resources. **Description:** A crude oil and natural gas exploration and production company. Most oil production operations are located in Indonesia. Gas production is conducted primarily in Texas, Oklahoma, and the Gulf of Mexico. **Common positions include:** Accountant/Auditor; Computer Programmer; Geologist/Geophysicist; Petroleum Engineer; Systems Analyst. **Educational backgrounds include:** Accounting; Business Administration; Computer Science; Engineering; Geology. **Benefits:** 401(k); Dental Insurance; Disability Coverage; Life Insurance; Medical Insurance; Pension Plan; Tuition Assistance. **Corporate headquarters location:** This Location. **Listed on:** New York Stock Exchange. **Number of employees at this location:** 300.

MERIDIAN OIL INC.
801 Cherry Street, Suite 700, Fort Worth TX 76102. 817/347-2542. **Fax:** 817/347-2263. **Contact:** Linda Harris, Human Resources Supervisor. **Description:** A petroleum and natural gas exploration and production company. **Common positions include:** Accountant/Auditor; Administrative Manager; Architect; Assistant Manager; Blue-Collar Worker Supervisor; Chemical Engineer; Civil Engineer; Claim Representative; Clerical Supervisor; Computer Operator; Computer Programmer; Construction and Building Inspector; Construction Contractor; Credit Manager; Dispatcher; Draftsperson; Emergency Medical Technician; Employment Interviewer; Financial Analyst; General Manager; Geographer; Geologist/Geophysicist; Human Service Worker; Industrial Engineer; Interviewing Clerk; Mechanical Engineer; Metallurgical Engineer; Mining Engineer; New Accounts Clerk; Payroll Clerk; Petroleum Engineer; Postal Clerk/Mail Carrier; Public Relations Specialist; Purchasing Agent/Manager; Receptionist; Secretary; Software Engineer; Systems Analyst; Typist/Word Processor; Underwriter/Assistant Underwriter; Welder. **Educational backgrounds include:** Accounting; Biology; Business Administration; Communications; Computer Science; Economics; Engineering; Finance; Geology; Marketing; Mathematics; Physics. **Benefits:** Daycare Assistance; Dental Insurance; Disability Coverage; Life Insurance; Medical Insurance; Pension Plan; Savings Plan; Tuition Assistance. **Corporate headquarters location:** Houston TX. **Other area locations:** Midland TX. **Other U.S. locations:** Denver CO; Farmington NM. **Number of employees at this location:** 450. **Number of employees nationwide:** 2,000.

NORTON DRILLING COMPANY
5211 Brownfield Highway, Suite 230, Lubbock TX 79407. 806/785-8400. **Contact:** Human Resources. **Description:** Owns and operates 13 oil and gas drilling rigs and provides contract drilling services to the oil and gas industry.

ORYX ENERGY COMPANY
14311 Welch Road, Dallas TX 75244. 972/715-4000. **Contact:** Employment. **Description:** Explores for, acquires, develops, produces, and sells oil and natural gas worldwide. **Common positions include:** Accountant/Auditor; Attorney; Chemist; Computer Programmer; Draftsperson; Electrical/Electronics Engineer; Financial Analyst; Geologist/Geophysicist; Petroleum Engineer; Systems Analyst. **Educational backgrounds include:** Accounting; Computer Science; Engineering; Finance; Geology. **Benefits:** Dental Insurance; Disability Coverage; Life Insurance; Medical Insurance; Pension Plan; Savings Plan; Tuition Assistance. **Corporate headquarters location:** This Location. **International locations:** Algeria; Australia; Ecuador; Indonesia. **Listed on:** New York Stock Exchange.

PATTERSON DRILLING COMPANY, INC.
P.O. Drawer 1416, Snyder TX 79550. 915/573-1104. **Contact:** Human Resources. **Description:** Engaged in onshore drilling for oil and gas; and the exploration, development, and production of oil and gas. The company's operations are conducted primarily in Texas and New Mexico. **Corporate headquarters location:** This Location.

PHILLIPS COAL COMPANY
2929 North Central Expressway, Richardson TX 75080. 972/669-1200. **Contact:** Human Resources. **Description:** This location houses administrative offices. Overall, Phillips Coal Company is engaged in surface mining.

PIONEER NATURAL RESOURCES
5205 North O'Connor Boulevard, Suite 1400, Irving TX 75039-3747. 972/444-9001. **Contact:** Human Resources. **World Wide Web address:** http://www.pioneernrc.com. **Description:** Engaged in the exploration and production of petroleum oil and natural gas. **Educational backgrounds include:** AS400 Certification; Computer Science; Engineering. **Benefits:** 401(k); Bonus Award/Plan; Casual Dress - Daily; Dental Insurance; Disability Coverage; Flexible Schedule; Life Insurance; Medical Insurance; Sick Days (6 - 10); Vacation Days (10 - 20). **Corporate headquarters location:** This Location. **International locations:** Buenos Aires, Argentina; Calgary, Canada. **Listed on:** New York Stock Exchange. **Stock exchange symbol:** PXD. **Annual sales/revenues:** More than $100 million. **Number of employees nationwide:** 800. **Number of projected hires for 2000 - 2001 at this location:** 60.

PRIMROSE OIL COMPANY
P.O. Box 29665, Dallas TX 75229. 972/241-1100. **Toll-free phone:** 800/275-2772. **Contact:** Ryan Miller, Credit Manager. **World Wide Web address:** http://www.primrose.com. **Description:** Refines oil and distributes petroleum products. Primrose's five major product lines are Primrose Plus, Premium Select, Syn-O-Gen, EnviroBlend, and Odyssey 2000.

REPUBLIC SUPPLY COMPANY
5646 Milton Street, Suite 800, Dallas TX 75206. 214/987-9868. **Contact:** Personnel. **Description:** Distributes oil field supplies and industrial machinery. **Common positions include:** Accountant/Auditor; Clerical Supervisor; Computer Programmer; Cost Estimator; Credit Manager; Manufacturer's/Wholesaler's Sales Rep.; Operations/Production Manager; Purchasing Agent/Manager; Services Sales Representative. **Educational backgrounds include:** Accounting; Business Administration; Computer Science. **Benefits:** Life Insurance; Medical Insurance. **Corporate headquarters location:** This Location. **Listed on:** Privately held. **Number of employees at this location:** 30. **Number of employees nationwide:** 170.

SANTA FE INTERNATIONAL CORPORATION
2 Lincoln Centre, 5420 LBJ Freeway, Suite 1100, Dallas TX 75240. 972/701-7300. **Contact:** Human Resources. **World Wide Web address:** http://www.sfdrill.com. **Description:** An international offshore and land contract driller. Founded in 1946. **Corporate headquarters location:** This location. **Listed on:** New York Stock Exchange.

SOUTHWESTERN PETROLEUM CORPORATION (SWEPCO)
534 North Main Street, Fort Worth TX 76106. 817/332-2336. **Toll-free phone:** 800/US-SWEPCO. **Fax:** 817/877-4047. **Contact:** Human Resources. **World Wide Web address:** http://www.swepcousa.com. **Description:** Manufactures protective coatings and specialty lubricants for the energy industry. **Common positions include:** Chemist; Management Trainee; Manufacturer's/Wholesaler's Sales Rep.; Petroleum Engineer. **Educational backgrounds include:** Business Administration; Marketing. **Benefits:** 401(k); Life Insurance; Medical Insurance. **Corporate headquarters location:** This Location. **Subsidiaries include:** NV Southwestern Petroleum Europe, SA (Belgium); Southwestern Petroleum Canada Ltd. (Canada). **Listed on:** Privately held. **Number of employees at this location:** 100.

TRITON ENERGY CORPORATION
6688 North Central Expressway, Suite 1400, Dallas TX 75206. 214/691-5200. **Contact:** Human Resources. **World Wide Web address:** http://www.tritonenergy.com. **Description:** An international oil and gas exploration company. **Common positions include:** Accountant/Auditor; Administrative Assistant; Chemical Engineer; Computer Programmer; Financial Analyst; Geologist/Geophysicist. **Educational backgrounds include:** Engineering. **Benefits:** 401(k); Dental Insurance; Disability Coverage; Life Insurance; Medical Insurance; Pension Plan; Savings Plan; Tuition Assistance. **Special programs:** Internships. **Corporate headquarters location:** This Location. **International locations:** Argentina; China; Colombia; Ecuador; Guatemala; Indonesia; Italy; Malaysia; Thailand. **Listed on:** New York Stock Exchange.

UNION PACIFIC RESOURCES
P.O. Box 7, Fort Worth TX 76101. 817/321-6000. **Physical address:** 777 Main Street, Fort Worth TX 76102. **Contact:** Human Resources. **World Wide Web address:**

Mining/Gas/Petroleum/Energy Related/229

http://www.upr.com. **Description:** One of the nation's largest independent oil and gas exploration and production companies. **Corporate headquarters location:** This location.

WICHITA RIVER OIL
2626 Cole Avenue, Suite 501, Dallas TX 75204-1074. 214/871-2889. **Contact:** Personnel Department. **Description:** Involved in oil and gas exploration and extraction.

Note: Because addresses and telephone numbers of smaller companies can change rapidly, we recommend you call each company to verify the information below before inquiring about job opportunities. Mass mailings are not recommended.

Additional small employers:

COAL MINING

Monticello Mine
PO Box 1636, Mount Pleasant TX 75456-1636. 903/524-3461.

Northwestern Resources
PO Box 915, Jewett TX 75846-0915. 903/626-5485.

Texas Utilities Mining Co.
PO Box 1359, Tatum TX 75691-1359. 903/836-6513.

Winfield South Mine
PO Box 1636, Mount Pleasant TX 75456-1636. 903/524-1213.

COAL MINING SERVICES

TXU Mining
PO Box 800, Fairfield TX 75840-0800. 903/389-1521.

DRILLING OIL AND GAS WELLS

FWA Peterson Drilling
PO Box 130518, Tyler TX 75713-0518. 903/561-2049.

Hudson Leonard Drilling Co. Inc.
PO Box 1876, Pampa TX 79066-1876. 806/665-1816.

Martex Drilling Company
PO Box 2069, Marshall TX 75671-2069. 903/938-3574.

Ringo Drilling Co.
PO Box 2894, Abilene TX 79604-2894. 915/695-5600.

MISC. PIPELINES

Koch Pipelines Inc.
PO Box 548, Carthage TX 75633-0548. 903/693-2421.

OIL AND GAS FIELD MACHINERY AND EQUIPMENT

Bowen Tools
PO Box 1101, Pampa TX 79066-1101. 713/651-8002.

FMC Fluid Control
PO Box 1377, Stephenville TX 76401-1377. 254/968-2181.

Petrofac LLC
PO Box 131859, Tyler TX 75713-1859. 903/581-8755.

Weatherford International
1231 Greenway Dr, Ste 550, Irving TX 75038-2529. 972/751-5421.

OIL AND GAS FIELD SERVICES

Amerada Hess Corporation
PO Box 840, Seminole TX 79360-0840. 915/758-6700.

Bonner Hoffman Oil Well Services
PO Box 658, Seminole TX 79360-0658. 915/758-5858.

Brooks Well Servicing
PO Box 1240, Kilgore TX 75663-1240. 903/984-8528.

Five Star Consolidated
PO Box 1506, Denver City TX 79323-1506. 806/592-3113.

Lone Star Pipeline Company
301 S Harwood St, Dallas TX 75201-5600. 214/741-3711.

MND Energy Corporation
PO Box 790, Mineral Wells TX 76068-0790. 940/325-1321.

RRH Corporation
1445 Ross At Fld, Dallas TX 75202. 214/978-8000.

PETROLEUM AND NATURAL GAS

Bass Enterprises
201 Main St, Ste 300, Fort Worth TX 76102-3105. 817/390-8400.

Crescendo Resources LP
PO Box 400, Amarillo TX 79105-0400. 806/371-4400.

Cross Timbers Oil Company
810 Houston St, Ste 2000, Fort Worth TX 76102-6223. 817/870-2800.

Davoil Inc.
PO Box 122169, Fort Worth TX 76121-2169. 817/626-5483.

Denbury Resources Inc.
5100 Tennyson Pkwy, Plano TX 75024-3524. 972/673-2000.

Gulf-Petro Trading Company
PO Box 8163, Dallas TX 75205. 214/987-2211.

Marathon Oil Company
PO Box 130849, Tyler TX 75713-0849. 903/581-6820.

Mercury Exploration Company
1619 Pennsylvania Ave, Fort Worth TX 76104-2030. 817/332-9133.

North American Gas
5400 LBJ Fwy, Ste 500, Dallas TX 75240-1019. 972/701-9106.

Nova Resource
4925 Greenville Ave, Dallas TX 75206-4026. 972/530-3930.

Shell Western E&P Inc.
PO Drawer MM, Denver City TX 79323-1700. 806/592-2193.

Texaco Exploration and Production
PO Box 860, Levelland TX 79336-0860. 806/894-3118.

PETROLEUM AND PETROLEUM PRODUCTS WHOLESALE

Arco International Oil & Gas Co.
PO Box 26088, Plano TX 75026. 972/509-3000.

PETROLEUM REFINING

Borger Refinery
PO Box 271, Borger TX 79008-0271. 806/275-1202.

Pride Refining Inc.
PO Box 3237, Abilene TX 79604-3237. 915/674-8000.

For more information on career opportunities in the mining, gas, petroleum, and energy industries:

Associations

AMERICAN ASSOCIATION OF PETROLEUM GEOLOGISTS
P.O. Box 979, Tulsa OK 74101. 918/584-2555. World Wide Web address: http://www.aapg.org. International headquarters for petroleum geologists.

AMERICAN GEOLOGICAL INSTITUTE
4220 King Street, Alexandria VA 22302-1502. 703/379-2480. Fax: 703/379-7563. World Wide Web address: http://www.agiweb.org. Scholarships available. Publishes *Geotimes* (monthly) and *Careers in the Geosciences*, which details job opportunities and outlooks.

AMERICAN NUCLEAR SOCIETY
555 North Kensington Avenue, La Grange Park IL 60526. 708/352-6611. World Wide Web address: http://www.ans.org. Offers educational services.

AMERICAN PETROLEUM INSTITUTE
1220 L Street NW, Suite 900, Washington DC 20005. 202/682-8000. World Wide Web address: http://www.api.org. A trade association.

GEOLOGICAL SOCIETY OF AMERICA
3300 Penrose Place, P.O. Box 9140, Boulder CO 80301. 303/447-2020. World Wide Web address: http://www.geosociety.org. Membership of over 17,000. Offers sales items and publications. Also conducts society meetings.

NUCLEAR ENERGY INSTITUTE
1776 I Street NW, Suite 400, Washington DC 20006. 202/739-8000. World Wide Web address: http://www.nei.org. Provides a wide variety of information on nuclear energy issues.

SOCIETY FOR MINING, METALLURGY, AND EXPLORATION, INC.
8307 Shaffer Parkway, Littleton CO 80127. 303/973-9550. World Wide Web address: http://www.smenet.org.

SOCIETY OF EXPLORATION GEOPHYSICISTS
P.O. Box 702740, Tulsa OK 74170-2740. 918/497-5500. World Wide Web address: http://www.seg.org. A membership association. Offers publications.

SOCIETY OF PETROLEUM ENGINEERS
P.O. Box 833836, Richardson TX 75083. 972/952-9393. World Wide Web address: http://www.spe.org.

Directories

BROWN'S DIRECTORY OF NORTH AMERICAN & INTERNATIONAL GAS COMPANIES
Advanstar Communications, 7500 Old Oak Boulevard, Cleveland OH 44130. Toll-free phone: 800/225-4569. World Wide Web address: http://www.advanstar.com.

OIL AND GAS DIRECTORY
Geophysical Directory, Inc., P.O. Box 130508, Houston TX 77219. 713/529-8789.

Magazines

AMERICAN GAS
American Gas Association, 400 North Capitol Street NW, 4th Floor, Washington DC 20001. 202/824-7000.

GAS INDUSTRIES
Gas Industries News, Inc., 6300 North River Road, Suite 505, Rosemont IL 60018. 847/696-2394.

NATIONAL PETROLEUM NEWS
Adams Business Media, 2101 South Arlington Heights Road, Suite 150, Arlington Heights IL 60005. 847/427-9512. Fax: 847/427-2006. World Wide Web address: http://www.petroretail.net.

OIL AND GAS JOURNAL
PennWell Publishing Company, P.O. Box 1260, Tulsa OK 74101. 918/835-3161. World Wide Web address: http://www.ogjonline.com.

Online Services

NATIONAL CENTRE FOR PETROLEUM GEOLOGY AND GEOPHYSICS
World Wide Web address: http://www.ncpgg.adelaide.edu.au/ncpgg.html. This Website provides links to sites that post job openings in mining, petroleum, energy, and related fields.

OIL-LINK
World Wide Web address: http://www.oillink.com. Loaded with industry information, news, surveys, and links to all sorts of resources.

PETROLEUM & GEOSYSTEMS ENGINEERING
World Wide Web address: http://www.pe.utexas.edu/Dept/Reading/pejb.html. Offers a vast list of links to sites that post current job openings in petroleum and geosystems engineering and related fields. The site is run by the University of Texas at Austin. Links to many relevant associations are also offered.

PAPER AND WOOD PRODUCTS

You can expect to find the following types of companies in this chapter:
*Forest and Wood Products and Services • Lumber and Wood Wholesale
Millwork, Plywood, and Structural Members • Paper and Wood Mills*

Some helpful information: *The average annual salary range for a forester with a bachelor's degree is $19,000 - $25,000. Precision woodworkers generally earn approximately $20,000 per year (woodworkers that specialize in finished work and products such as decorative wood furniture may earn more).*

BATES CONTAINER INC.
P.O. Box 822028, North Richland Hills TX 76182-2028. 817/498-3200. **Contact:** Personnel Manager. **Description:** A manufacturer and distributor of corrugated containers.

BLUE RIDGE PAPER PRODUCTS
1901 Windsor Place, Fort Worth TX 76110. 817/926-6661. **Contact:** Personnel Department. **Description:** Manufactures polyethylene coated milk cartons. **Listed on:** New York Stock Exchange.

BOISE CASCADE CORPORATION
9708 Skillman Street, Suite 102, Dallas TX 75243. 214/341-9000. **Contact:** Personnel Director. **World Wide Web address:** http://www.bc.com. **Description:** An integrated paper and forest products company with operations located nationwide. The company manufactures and distributes paper and paper products, office products, and building products; and owns and manages timberland to support these operations. Boise Cascade is one of the largest pulp and paper producers in the United States. The company has the capacity to produce 3.2 million tons of uncoated and coated papers, newsprint, containerboard, and pulp each year. Founded in 1957. **Corporate headquarters location:** Boise ID.

INTERNATIONAL PAPER COMPANY
P.O. Box 870, Texarkana TX 75504-0870. 903/796-7101. **Contact:** Human Resources. **World Wide Web address:** http://www.internationalpaper.com. **Description:** This location manufactures folding cartons. Overall, International Paper is a manufacturer of pulp and paper, packaging, and wood products, as well as a range of specialty products. The company is organized into five business segments: Printing Papers, in which principal products include uncoated papers, coated papers, bristles, and pulp; Packaging, which includes industrial packaging, consumer packaging, and kraft and specialty papers; Distribution, which includes sales of printing papers, graphic arts equipment and supplies, packaging materials, industrial supplies, and office products; Specialty Products, which includes imaging products, specialty panels, nonwovens, chemicals, and minerals; and Forest Products, which includes logs and wood products. **Corporate headquarters location:** Purchase NY. **Number of employees worldwide:** 72,500.

MEAD PAPER
5215 North O'Connor Boulevard, Suite 200, Irving TX 75039. 972/868-9060. **Contact:** Human Resources. **World Wide Web address:** http://www.mead.com. **Description:** This location is a sales office. Overall, Mead Paper manufactures, sells, and markets pulp, paper, paperboard, shipping containers, packaging, lumber, school supplies, office supplies, stationery products, and electronic publishing and information retrieval systems.

REDI PACKAGING, INC.
905 Avenue T, Suite 312, Grand Prairie TX 75050. 972/602-9121. **Contact:** Personnel Director. **Description:** A manufacturer of corrugated paper, polypropylene, and polyethylene products.

SMURFIT-STONE CONTAINER CORPORATION
6701 South Freeway, Fort Worth TX 76134. 817/568-3400. **Contact:** Personnel. **World Wide Web address:** http://www.smurfit-stone.com. **Description:** This location manufactures corrugated fibreboard boxes. Overall, Smurfit-Stone Container Corporation is one of the world's leading paper-based packaging companies. The company's main products include corrugated containers, folding cartons, and multiwall industrial bags. The company is also one of the world's largest collectors and processors of recycled products that are then sold to a

worldwide customer base. Smurfit-Stone Container Corporation also operates several paper tube, market pulp, and newsprint production facilities. **Corporate headquarters location:** Chicago IL. **Other U.S. locations:** Nationwide. **International locations:** Worldwide.

TRIANGLE PACIFIC CORPORATION
16803 Dallas Parkway, Addison TX 75001. 972/931-3000. **Contact:** Human Resources. **World Wide Web address:** http://www.trianglepacific.com. **Description:** Manufactures hardwood dimension and flooring. Brand names include Bruce, Hartco, and Robbins flooring and cabinets. **Parent company:** Armstrong World Industries.

WILLAMETTE INDUSTRIES, INC.
BUSINESS FORMS DIVISION
8800 Sterling Street, Irving TX 75063. 972/929-8581. **Contact:** Human Resources. **World Wide Web address:** http://www.wii.com. **Description:** This location manufactures computer paper. Overall, Willamette Industries is a diversified, integrated forest products company with more than 100 plants and mills manufacturing containerboard, paper bags, fine paper, bleached hardwood market pulp, specialty printing papers, corrugated containers, business forms, cut sheet paper, paper bags, inks, lumber, plywood, particleboard, medium-density fiberboard, laminated beams, and value-added wood products. The company owns or controls over 1.7 million acres of forestland. **Common positions include:** Accountant/Auditor; Branch Manager; Department Manager; General Manager; Manufacturer's/Wholesaler's Sales Rep. **Educational backgrounds include:** Accounting; Business Administration. **Benefits:** Dental Insurance; Disability Coverage; Life Insurance; Medical Insurance; Pension Plan; Savings Plan; Stock Option; Tuition Assistance. **Corporate headquarters location:** Portland OR. **International locations:** France; Ireland; Mexico.

Note: Because addresses and telephone numbers of smaller companies can change rapidly, we recommend you call each company to verify the information below before inquiring about job opportunities. Mass mailings are not recommended.

Additional small employers:

CONVERTED PAPER AND PAPERBOARD PRODUCTS

Paragon Trade Brands Inc.
4920 Franklin Ave, Waco TX 76710-6918. 254/776-7570.

DIE-CUT PAPER AND PAPER PRODUCTS

Corporate Express
PO Box 709, Hutchins TX 75141-0709. 972/225-0600.

Smead Manufacturing Company
PO Box 447, McGregor TX 76657-0447. 254/840-5026.

INDUSTRIAL PAPER AND RELATED PRODUCTS WHOLESALE

Pollock Paper Distributors
PO Box 660005, Dallas TX 75266-0005. 972/263-2126.

LUMBER AND WOOD WHOLESALE

International Paper Company
PO Box 460, Henderson TX 75653-0460. 903/657-4575.

International Paper Company
PO Box 809024, Dallas TX 75380-9024. 972/934-6000.

Texas Plywood & Lumber Co. Inc.
PO Box 535429, Grand Prairie TX 75053-5429. 972/262-1331.

Universal Forest Products
PO Box 162089, Fort Worth TX 76161-2089. 817/232-2233.

MILLWORK, PLYWOOD, AND STRUCTURAL MEMBERS

Annona Manufacturing Company
PO Box 287, Annona TX 75550-0287. 903/697-3591.

Atrium Door & Window Company
PO Box 226957, Dallas TX 75222-6957. 214/634-9663.

Clifton Moulding Corp.
PO Box 77, Clifton TX 76634-0077. 254/675-8641.

Daven Products Company
1000 W Crosby Rd, Ste 120, Carrollton TX 75006-6924. 972/245-5457.

Premdoor Corporation
PO Box 1887, Greenville TX 75403-1887. 903/454-9500.

Summit Window & Door
4000 E State Highway 31,
Corsicana TX 75110-9693. 903/872-2426.

Trussway Ltd.
PO Box 125, Fort Worth TX 76101-0125. 817/589-1467.

PAPER BAGS

Arrow Industries
3401 Garden Brook Dr, Dallas TX 75234-2435. 972/620-2902.

Printpack Inc.
PO Box 534030, Grand Prairie TX 75053. 972/641-4421.

Super Sack Manufacturing Corp.
PO Box 245, Savoy TX 75479-0245. 903/965-7713.

PAPER MILLS

Gulf States Paper Corporation
PO Box 1129, Waco TX 76703-1129. 254/299-6500.

Southern Champion Tray Lp
949 S 6th Ave, Mansfield TX 76063-2726. 817/473-0232.

PAPERBOARD CONTAINERS AND BOXES

Acco Brands Inc.
1346 N Main St, Duncanville TX 75116-2312. 972/298-4225.

Central Texas Corrugated
PO Box 21539, Waco TX 76702-1539. 254/776-6902.

Gaylord Container Corporation
PO Box 38008, Dallas TX 75238-0008. 214/342-7200.

Green Bay Packaging
PO Box 303, Fort Worth TX 76101-0303. 817/551-1934.

Harris Packaging Corporation
PO Box 14437, Fort Worth TX 76117-0437. 817/429-6262.

International Paper Company
1655 S I 35 E, Carrollton TX 75006-7415. 972/446-9890.

Liberty Carton Corp.
PO Box 14989, Fort Worth TX 76117-0989. 817/577-6100.

Nekoosa Packaging Corp.
5800 N Interstate Highway, Waxahachie TX 75165-5717. 972/937-8804.

O'Grady Containers
PO Box 9737, Fort Worth TX 76147-2737. 817/338-4000.

Pactiv Corporation
2510 W Miller Rd, Garland TX 75041-1311. 972/278-8141.

Pactiv Corporation
9200 Old McGregor Rd, Waco TX 76712-6438. 254/776-8890.

Paris Packaging Inc.
PO Box 1155, Paris TX 75461-1155. 903/785-6411.

Simpkins Industries
2801 E Abram St, Arlington TX 76010-1402. 817/633-7311.

Smurfit-Stone Container Corp.
PO Box 534028, Grand Prairie TX 75053. 972/647-1333.

Smurfit-Stone Container Corp.
PO Box 1356, Tyler TX 75710-1356. 903/877-3421.

Temple-Inland Inc.
2605 E Belt Line Rd, Carrollton TX 75006-5444. 972/416-2691.

Waxahachie Folding
6200 N Interstate Highway, Waxahachie TX 75165-5602. 972/617-0111.

WOOD MILLS

Dean Lumber Co. Inc.
PO Box 610, Gilmer TX 75644-0610. 903/843-2457.

Snider Industries Inc.
PO Box 668, Marshall TX 75671-0668. 903/938-9221.

WOOD PALLETS AND SKIDS

Arrington Lumber & Pallet Co.
PO Box 1898, Jacksonville TX 75766-1898. 903/586-4070.

M&H Crates Inc.
Rural Route 7, Box 96, Jacksonville TX 75766-9117. 903/683-5351.

National Pallet Company
PO Box 560041, Dallas TX 75356-0041. 214/688-4108.

WOOD PRODUCTS

Texas Reel Co.
PO Box 10, Sherman TX 75091-0010. 903/893-8827.

For more information on career opportunities in the paper and wood products industries:

Associations

FOREST PRODUCTS SOCIETY
2801 Marshall Court, Madison WI 53705-2295. 608/231-1361. Fax: 608/231-2152. E-mail address: info@forestprod.org. World Wide Web address: http://www.forestprod.org. An international, nonprofit, educational association that provides an information network for all segments of the forest products industry, as well as an employment referral service.

NATIONAL PAPER TRADE ASSOCIATION
111 Great Neck Road, Great Neck NY 11021. 516/829-3070. World Wide Web address: http://www.papertrade.com. Offers management services to paper wholesalers, as well as books, seminars, and research services.

TECHNICAL ASSOCIATION OF THE PULP AND PAPER INDUSTRY
P.O. Box 105113, Atlanta GA 30348-5113. 770/446-1400. World Wide Web address: http://www.tappi.org. A nonprofit organization offering conferences and continuing education.

Directories

DIRECTORY OF THE WOOD PRODUCTS INDUSTRY
Miller Freeman, Inc., 600 Harrison Street, Suite 400, San Francisco CA 94107. 415/905-2200. World Wide Web address: http://www.woodwideweb.com.

INTERNATIONAL PULP AND PAPER DIRECTORY
Miller Freeman, Inc., 600 Harrison Street, Suite 400, San Francisco CA 94107. 415/905-2200. World Wide Web address: http://www.pulp-paper.com.

LOCKWOOD-POST'S DIRECTORY OF THE PULP, PAPER AND ALLIED TRADES
Miller Freeman, Inc., 600 Harrison Street, Suite 400, San Francisco CA 94107. 415/905-2200. World Wide Web address: http://www.pulp-paper.com/lpdisk.htm.

Magazines

PAPERBOARD PACKAGING
Advanstar Communications, 131 West First Street, Duluth MN 55802. 218/723-9200. World Wide Web address: http://www.advanstar.com.

PULP & PAPER
Miller Freeman, Inc., 600 Harrison Street, Suite 400, San Francisco CA 94107. 415/905-2200. World Wide Web address: http://www.mfi.com.

WOOD TECHNOLOGY
Miller Freeman, Inc., 600 Harrison Street, San Francisco CA 94107. 415/905-2200. World Wide Web address: http://www.woodtechmag.com.

For information about the JobBank List Service visit www.adamsjobbank.com

PRINTING AND PUBLISHING

You can expect to find the following types of companies in this chapter:
Book, Newspaper, and Periodical Publishers • Commercial Photographers
Commercial Printing Services • Graphic Designers

Some helpful information: *Printing press operators earn approximately $20,000 - $25,000 per year. The average salary range for an editorial assistant is $20,000 - $28,000, and associate editors earn around $30,000 annually. Managing editors and editorial directors generally earn $35,000 - $60,000 or more, depending on the size of the publishing house and years employed. Jobs in electronic publishing may pay considerably more.*

AMARILLO GLOBE TIMES
P.O. Box 2091, Amarillo TX 79166. 806/376-4488. **Fax:** 806/345-3370. **Contact:** Human Resources. **World Wide Web address:** http://www.amarillonet.com. **Description:** Publishes morning and afternoon daily papers. The Sunday edition has a circulation of approximately 74,000.

AMERICAN BANK NOTE COMPANY
5307 East Mockingbird Lane, Suite 705, Dallas TX 75206. 214/823-2700. **Fax:** 214/821-9026. **Contact:** Human Resources. **Description:** This location is a national sales office. Overall, the company is a printer of counterfeit-resistant documents and one of the largest security printers in the world. American Bank Note creates secure documents of value for governments and corporations worldwide. Products include currencies; passports; stock and bond certificates; bank, corporate, government, and traveler's checks; food coupons; gift vouchers and certificates; driver's licenses; product authentication labels; and vital documents. **Corporate headquarters location:** New York NY. **Other U.S. locations:** Burbank CA; Long Beach CA; San Francisco CA; Washington DC; Atlanta GA; Bedford Park IL; Needham MA; St. Louis MO; Horsham PA; Huntington Valley PA; Philadelphia PA; Pittsburgh PA. **Parent company:** American Bank Note Corporation also operates two other subsidiaries: American Bank Note Holographics, Inc., one of the world's largest producers of the laser-generated, three-dimensional images that appear on credit cards and products requiring proof of authenticity; and American Bank Note Company Brazil, one of Brazil's largest private security printers and a provider of personalized checks, financial transaction cards, and pre-paid telephone cards. **Listed on:** New York Stock Exchange.

AMERICAN WAY
P.O. Box 619640, Mail Drop 5598, DFW Airport TX 75261-9640. 817/967-1804. **Fax:** 817/967-1571. **Contact:** Personnel. **World Wide Web address:** http://www.americanair.com/away. **Description:** An in-flight magazine produced by American Airlines.

BANKERS DIGEST
9550 Forest Lane, Suite 125, Dallas TX 75243. 214/373-4544. **Contact:** Editor. **Description:** A trade magazine that provides Texas banking news. *Bankers Digest* has a circulation of 4,800. Founded in 1942.

A.H. BELO CORPORATION
THE DALLAS MORNING NEWS
P.O. Box 655237, Dallas TX 75265. 214/977-6600. **Contact:** Mr. Lee Smith, Employment Manager. **World Wide Web address:** http://www.dallasnews.com. **Description:** A.H. Belo Corporation owns and operates newspapers and network-affiliated television stations in seven U.S. metropolitan areas. One of its papers, *The Dallas Morning News* (also at this location), has a circulation of 550,000 during the week and 800,000 on Sunday. A.H. Belo traces its roots to *The Galveston Daily News*, which was first published in 1842. **Subsidiaries include:** DFW Printing Company, Inc.; DFW Suburban Newspapers, Inc.

CORSICANA DAILY SUN
P.O. Box 622, Corsicana TX 75151. 903/872-3931. **Contact:** Human Resources. **World Wide Web address:** http://www.corsicanadailysun.com. **Description:** Publishes a daily newspaper with a circulation of 7,100 during the week and 8,100 on Sunday.

DALLAS BUSINESS JOURNAL
10670 North Central Expressway, Suite 710, Dallas TX 75231. 214/696-5959. **Contact:** Personnel. **World Wide Web address:** http://www.bizjournals.com/dallas. **Description:** A weekly business periodical with a circulation of 18,000. **Parent company:** American City Business Journals Inc. (Charlotte NC) publishes 39 business journals in cities nationwide.

ENNIS BUSINESS FORMS
114 North East Main, Ennis TX 75119. 972/872-3100. **Contact:** Human Resources. **Description:** Produces business forms, checks, and other printed forms.

GTE DIRECTORIES
P.O. Box 619810, DFW Airport TX 75261-9810. 972/453-7000. **Contact:** Human Resources. **World Wide Web address:** http://www.gte.com. **Description:** This location prints GTE telephone directories. Overall, GTE provides a wide variety of communications services ranging from local telephone services for the home and office to highly complex voice and data services for industry. GTE is one of the largest publicly-held telecommunications companies in the world, one of the largest U.S.-based local telephone companies, and one of the largest cellular service providers in the United States. GTE's Telephone Operations division serves 17.4 million access lines in 28 states. **NOTE:** As of June 2000, GTE Corporation and Bell Atlantic Corporation were awaiting regulatory approval for a planned merger. The new company is expected to operate under the name Verizon. Please call this location for more information. **Corporate headquarters location:** Irving TX.

GREAT WESTERN DIRECTORIES
2400 Lakeview Drive, Suite 109, Amarillo TX 79109. 806/353-5155. **Contact:** Human Resources. **Description:** A publisher of telephone directories. **Corporate headquarters location:** This Location.

THE IMAGE BANK, INC.
2777 Stemmons Freeway, Suite 600, Dallas TX 75207. 214/863-4900. **Contact:** Human Resources. **World Wide Web address:** http://www.imagebank.com. **Description:** Stocks and sells photographs obtained from various photographers. **Corporate headquarters location:** This Location. **International locations:** Worldwide.

LEGAL DIRECTORIES PUBLISHING COMPANY, INC.
P.O. Box 189000, Dallas TX 75218-9000. 214/321-3238. **Contact:** Human Resources Department. **World Wide Web address:** http://www.legaldirectories.com. **Description:** One of the nation's largest publishers of state legal directories.

LUBBOCK AVALANCHE-JOURNAL
P.O. Box 491, Lubbock TX 79408. 806/762-8844. **Contact:** Personnel. **World Wide Web address:** http://www.lubbockonline.com. **Description:** A daily newspaper. The *Lubbock Avalanche-Journal* has a circulation of approximately 67,000 daily and 74,000 on Sundays.

McGRAW-HILL EDUCATIONAL & PROFESSIONAL PUBLISHING GROUP
220 East Danieldale Road, De Soto TX 75115. 972/224-1111. **Contact:** Human Resources Department. **World Wide Web address:** http://www.mcgraw-hill.com. **Description:** This location publishes text books. Overall, McGraw-Hill is a provider of information and services through books, magazines, newsletters, software, CD-ROMs, online data, fax, and TV broadcasting services. The company operates four network-affiliated TV stations and also publishes *Business Week* magazine and books for college, medical, international, legal, and professional markets. McGraw-Hill also offers financial services including *Standard & Poor's*, commodity items, and international and logistics management products and services.

MILLER FREEMAN INC.
IMPRESSIONS MAGAZINE
P.O. Box 612488, Dallas TX 75261-2488. 972/906-6500. **Contact:** Personnel Department. **World Wide Web address:** http://www.mfi.com. **Description:** Publishes a monthly trade magazine for the imprinted sportswear and textile screen printing industry. *Impressions Magazine* was first published in 1977 and has a circulation of 30,000.

MOTHERAL PRINTING COMPANY
P.O. Box 629, Fort Worth TX 76101. 817/335-1481. **Contact:** Personnel Department. **Description:** A commercial lithography and printing company. **Common positions include:** Bindery Worker; Blue-Collar Worker Supervisor; Customer Service Representative; Department Manager; Printing Press Operator. **Educational backgrounds include:** Business Administration;

Communications; Computer Science; Engineering. **Benefits:** Disability Coverage; Employee Discounts; Life Insurance; Medical Insurance; Pension Plan; Profit Sharing; Tuition Assistance. **Special programs:** Internships. **Corporate headquarters location:** This Location. **Operations at this facility include:** Administration; Manufacturing; Sales.

PADGETT PRINTING CORPORATION
1313 North Industrial Boulevard, Dallas TX 75207. 214/742-4261. **Contact:** Personnel. **Description:** A printing company. **Common positions include:** Accountant/Auditor; Bindery Worker; Customer Service Representative; Prepress Worker. **Benefits:** 401(k); Disability Coverage; Life Insurance; Medical Insurance; Profit Sharing; Savings Plan. **Corporate headquarters location:** This Location. **Listed on:** Privately held. **Number of employees at this location:** 110.

POLITICAL RESEARCH, INC.
16850 Dallas Parkway, Dallas TX 75248. 972/931-8827. **Contact:** Personnel Director. **Description:** A publisher of reference services on current state, federal, and international governments. Primary customers include educational institutions, libraries, government offices, and businesses. **Common positions include:** Accountant/Auditor; Customer Service Representative; Marketing Specialist; Purchasing Agent/Manager; Reporter; Researcher; Services Sales Representative; Technical Writer/Editor. **Educational backgrounds include:** Accounting; Economics; Liberal Arts; Marketing; Political Science. **Corporate headquarters location:** This Location. **Number of employees at this location:** 35.

QUEBECOR DALLAS
4800 Spring Valley Road, Dallas TX 75244. 972/233-3400. **Contact:** Human Resources. **Description:** A commercial printing company. Quebecor Dallas handles large print runs for commercial magazines including *Time* magazine and *Sports Illustrated* for the regional market. The company also prints retail inserts and catalogs.

SCHUTZMAN COMPANY
P.O. Box 1529, Dallas TX 75221-1529. 214/443-1600. **Contact:** Human Resources. **Description:** A commercial printing and lithography firm. **Common positions include:** Credit Manager; Customer Service Representative; Department Manager; Manufacturer's/Wholesaler's Sales Rep.; Operations/Production Manager. **Benefits:** Employee Discounts; Medical Insurance; Savings Plan. **Corporate headquarters location:** Houston TX. **Operations at this facility include:** Manufacturing; Sales; Service.

SHOPPER'S GUIDE
1302 Avenue T, Grand Prairie TX 75050. 972/641-7690. **Contact:** Personnel. **Description:** A weekly shopper's newspaper with a circulation of approximately 430,000.

THE SHOPPING NEWS
4808 South Buckner Boulevard, Suite A, Dallas TX 75227. 214/388-3431. **Contact:** Personnel Department. **Description:** A weekly consumer publication with a circulation of 101,000. Founded in 1955. **Common positions include:** Advertising Clerk. **Educational backgrounds include:** Art/Design. **Benefits:** 401(k); Dental Insurance; Life Insurance; Medical Insurance. **Number of employees at this location:** 30.

STAR-TELEGRAM
P.O. Box 1870, Fort Worth TX 76102. 817/390-7459. **Fax:** 817/336-3739. **Contact:** Lamildred Branch, Employment Coordinator. **World Wide Web address:** http://www.star-telegram.com. **Description:** Publishes a daily newspaper. **NOTE:** Entry-level positions are offered. **Common positions include:** Account Representative; Advertising Clerk; Blue-Collar Worker Supervisor; Budget Analyst; Buyer; Credit Manager; Customer Service Representative; Database Manager; Editor; Editorial Assistant; Graphic Artist; Human Resources Manager; Internet Services Manager; Production Manager; Reporter; Sales Executive; Sales Manager; Sales Representative; Secretary; Typist/Word Processor. **Educational backgrounds include:** Art/Design; Business Administration; Communications; Liberal Arts; Marketing. **Benefits:** 401(k); Dental Insurance; Disability Coverage; Employee Discounts; Life Insurance; Medical Insurance; Pension Plan; Tuition Assistance. **Special programs:** Internships. **Corporate headquarters location:** Orlando FL. **Parent company:** Walt Disney Company. **Listed on:** New York Stock Exchange. **Number of employees at this location:** 1,200.

TAYLOR PUBLISHING COMPANY
1550 West Mockingbird Lane, Dallas TX 75235. 214/819-8458. **Fax:** 214/819-8141. **Contact:** Stacey Young, Employment Supervisor. **World Wide Web address:** http://www.taylorpub.com.

Description: A publisher of yearbooks and specialty books. **Common positions include:** Accountant/Auditor; Adjuster; Collector; Computer Programmer; Editor; Investigator; Purchasing Agent/Manager; Systems Analyst. **Educational backgrounds include:** Business Administration; Computer Science; Liberal Arts. **Benefits:** 401(k); Dental Insurance; Employee Discounts; Life Insurance; Medical Insurance; Pension Plan; Tuition Assistance.

TRAVELHOST
10701 North Stemmons Freeway, Dallas TX 75220-2419. 972/556-0541. **Fax:** 972/402-0721. **Contact:** Mr. Chung-Ping Chang, Controller. **World Wide Web address:** http://www.travelhost.com. **Description:** A travel, business, and entertainment magazine published weekly. Founded in 1967.

UMR COMMUNICATIONS
P.O. Box 660275, Dallas TX 75266-0275. 214/630-6495. **Contact:** Personnel Department. **World Wide Web address:** http://www.umr.org. **Description:** Publishes religious articles including the *United Methodist Reporter* and the *National Christian Reporter*. Founded in 1847.

WACO TRIBUNE-HERALD/A COX NEWSPAPER
P.O. Box 2588, Waco TX 76702-2588. 254/757-5757. **Contact:** Human Resources. **World Wide Web address:** http://www.coxnews.com. **Description:** Publishes a daily newspaper.

WILLIAMSON PRINTING CORPORATION
6700 Denton Drive, Dallas TX 75235. 214/904-2670. **Toll-free phone:** 800/843-5423. **Fax:** 214/352-5698. **Recorded jobline:** 214/904-2603. **Contact:** Erica Sinch, Human Resources Administrator. **E-mail address:** jobs@twpc.com. **World Wide Web address:** http://www.twpc.com. **Description:** A commercial printing company. **NOTE:** Entry-level positions and second and third shifts are offered. **Common positions include:** Cost Estimator; Customer Service Representative; Graphic Artist; Sales Representative. **Educational backgrounds include:** Art/Design. **Benefits:** 401(k); Dental Insurance; Life Insurance; Medical Insurance; Tuition Assistance. **Special programs:** Summer Jobs. **Corporate headquarters location:** This Location. **Subsidiaries include:** Classic Color Corporation; Image Express; The Fulfillment Center. **Listed on:** Privately held. **CEO:** Jerry Williamson. **Number of employees nationwide:** 400.

Note: Because addresses and telephone numbers of smaller companies can change rapidly, we recommend you call each company to verify the information below before inquiring about job opportunities. Mass mailings are not recommended.

Additional small employers:

BLANK BOOKS AND BOOKBINDING

Big D Bindery Inc.
737 Regal Row, Dallas TX 75247-5211. 214/634-8060.

Deluxe Financial Services
PO Box 660257, Dallas TX 75266-0257. 214/631-7780.

Venture Encoding Service Inc.
4401 Cambridge Rd, Fort Worth TX 76155-2629. 817/283-9500.

VIP Samples
2800 112th St, Ste 100, Grand Prairie TX 75050-6495. 972/647-8888.

BOOKS, PERIODICALS, AND NEWSPAPERS WHOLESALE

ETD Kromar
PO Box 29666, Dallas TX 75229-0666. 972/501-5500.

Harcourt Inc.
1175 N Stemmons Fwy, Lewisville TX 75067-2516. 972/459-6000.

JA Majors Company
PO Box 819074, Dallas TX 75381-9074. 972/247-2929.

Texas Bookman
8450 Denton Dr, Dallas TX 75235-2506. 214/350-6648.

BUSINESS FORMS

Corporate Express Inc.
3403 Dan Morton Dr, Dallas TX 75236-1068. 972/225-0200.

Reynolds and Reynolds Co.
1010 E Avenue J, Grand Prairie TX 75050-2619. 972/647-1722.

Safeguard
8585 N Stemmons Fwy, Dallas TX 75247-3836. 214/905-3935.

Wallace Computer Services Inc.
PO Box 600, Marlin TX 76661-0600. 254/883-9281.

COMMERCIAL ART AND GRAPHIC DESIGN

CDS
2623 Manana Dr, Dallas TX 75220-1301. 214/357-7041.

COMMERCIAL PHOTOGRAPHY

Laser Tech Color Inc.
2010 Westridge Dr, Irving TX 75038-2900. 972/714-4800.

COMMERCIAL PRINTING

AdGraphics Commercial Printing
PO Box 1792, Longview TX 75606-1792. 903/237-7782.

AJ Bart Inc.
4130 Lindbergh Dr, Addison TX 75001-4344. 972/960-8300.

Branch Smith Publications
PO Box 1868, Fort Worth TX 76101-1868. 817/882-4110.

Buchanan Visual Communications
PO Box 814289, Dallas TX 75381-4289. 972/241-3311.

Dallas Tarrant Printing Inc.
PO Box 1850, Euless TX 76039-1850. 817/571-9966.

G&D Printing Inc.
PO Box 1184, Addison TX 75001-1184. 972/233-8404.

Global Group Inc.
4901 N Beach St, Fort Worth TX 76137-3404. 817/831-2631.

Graphic Arts
4601 Pylon St, Fort Worth TX 76106-1918. 817/625-1116.

Harland
4055 Corporate Dr, Ste 100, Grapevine TX 76051-2307. 817/329-7113.

Haughton Publishing
PO Box 180218, Dallas TX 75218-0218. 972/289-0705.

Heritage Press Inc.
8939 Premier Row, Dallas TX 75247-5418. 214/637-2700.

Jarvis Press Inc.
9112 Viscount Row, Dallas TX 75247-5414. 214/637-2340.

Lehigh Press Inc.
PO Box 110284, Carrollton TX 75011-0284. 972/446-1900.

Rediform Inc.
555 Airline Dr, Coppell TX 75019-4610. 972/393-8080.

Screencraft Advertising Inc.
PO Box 7612, Fort Worth TX 76111-0612. 817/834-5555.

Sprint Press Inc.
PO Box 9068, Fort Worth TX 76147-2068. 817/336-4639.

Uniscan Inc.
PO Box 550129, Dallas TX 75355-0129. 972/484-9878.

Voyager Expanded Learning
2200 Ross Ave, Ste 3800, Dallas TX 75201-2752. 214/631-0990.

Williamson Printing Corp.
PO Box 650500, Dallas TX 75265-0500. 214/352-1122.

MISC. PUBLISHING

Archipelago Productions
301 Commerce St, Ste 3700, Fort Worth TX 76102-4137. 817/334-7500.

Harmon Publishing Company
15400 Knoll Trail Dr, Dallas TX 75248-3467. 972/701-0244.

Publishing Concepts
12840 Hillcrest Rd, Dallas TX 75230-1528. 972/386-0100.

NEWSPAPERS: PUBLISHING AND/OR PRINTING

Abilene Reporter News
PO Box 30, Abilene TX 79604-0030. 915/673-4271.

Dallas Morning News
508 Young St, Dallas TX 75202-4893. 214/977-8222.

Denton Record-Chronicle
PO Box 369, Denton TX 76202-0369. 940/387-3811.

Longview News Journal
PO Box 1792, Longview TX 75606-1792. 903/757-3311.

Star Telegram Northeast
3201 Airport Fwy, Ste 108, Bedford TX 76021-6000. 817/685-3930.

Temple Daily Telegram
PO Box 6114, Temple TX 76503-6114. 254/778-4444.

Texarkana Gazette
PO Box 621, Texarkana TX 75504-0621. 903/794-3311.

Wichita Falls Times Record
PO Box 120, Wichita Falls TX 76307-0120. 940/767-8341.

PERIODICALS: PUBLISHING AND/OR PRINTING

Newpubco
111 Corporate Dr, Big Sandy TX 75755-2446. 903/636-4011.

Squadron/Signal Publications
1115 Crowley Dr, Carrollton TX 75006-1312. 972/242-1485.

Statabase
15850 Dallas Pkwy, Dallas TX 75248-3308. 972/991-6657.

PHOTOGRAPHIC EQUIPMENT AND SUPPLIES

Photronics
PO Box 655012, Dallas TX 75265-5012. 972/889-6273.

PRINTING TRADE SERVICES

Bowne of Dallas Inc.
1931 Market Center Blvd, Dallas TX 75207-3307. 214/651-1001.

Process Graphic Services Inc.
PO Box 535338, Grand Prairie TX 75053-5338. 972/601-6000.

Taxex Inc.
PO Box 2660, Waco TX 76702-2660. 254/799-4911.

For more information on career opportunities in printing and publishing:

Associations

AMERICAN BOOKSELLERS ASSOCIATION
828 South Broadway, Tarrytown NY 10591. 914/591-2665. World Wide Web address: http://www.bookweb.org. Publishes *American Bookseller*, *Bookselling This Week*, and *Bookstore Source Guide*.

AMERICAN INSTITUTE OF GRAPHIC ARTS
164 Fifth Avenue, New York NY 10010. 212/807-1990. World Wide Web address: http://www.aiga.org. A nationwide organization sponsoring programs and events for graphic designers and related professionals.

AMERICAN SOCIETY OF COMPOSERS, AUTHORS AND PUBLISHERS (ASCAP)
One Lincoln Plaza, New York NY 10023. 212/621-6000. World Wide Web address: http://www.ascap.com. A membership association which licenses members' work and pays members' royalties. Offers showcases and educational seminars and workshops. The society also has an events hotline: 212/621-6485.

AMERICAN SOCIETY OF NEWSPAPER EDITORS
11690-B Sunrise Valley Drive, Reston VA 20191. 703/453-1122. World Wide Web address: http://www.asne.org.

ASSOCIATION OF AMERICAN PUBLISHERS
71 Fifth Avenue, New York NY 10003. 212/255-

0200. Fax: 212/255-7007. World Wide Web address: http://www.publishers.org. A national trade association for the book publishing industry that provides industry updates and news of upcoming events.

ASSOCIATION OF GRAPHIC COMMUNICATIONS
330 Seventh Avenue, 9th Floor, New York NY 10001-5010. 212/279-2100. World Wide Web address: http://www.agcomm.org. Offers educational classes and seminars.

THE AUTHORS GUILD
330 West 42nd Street, 29th Floor, New York NY 10036. 212/563-5904. Fax: 212/564-5363. World Wide Web address: http://www.authorsguild.org. A membership organization for published authors that promotes free speech, fair compensation, and copyright protection.

BINDING INDUSTRIES OF AMERICA
70 East Lake Street, Suite 300, Chicago IL 60601. 312/372-7606. Offers credit collection, government affairs, and educational services.

THE CHICAGO BOOK CLINIC
825 Green Bay Road, Suite 270, Wilmette IL 60091. 847/256-8448. Fax: 847/256-8954. World Wide Web address: http://www.chicagobookclinic.org. A membership organization for professionals involved in all aspects of book publishing. The organization offers educational programs, publications, and special events throughout the year.

THE DOW JONES NEWSPAPER FUND, INC.
P.O. Box 300, Princeton NJ 08543-0300. 609/452-2820. World Wide Web address: http://www.dj.com/newsfund

ELECTRONIC PUBLISHING ASSOCIATION LLC
One Rodney Square, 10th Floor, 10th & King Streets, Wilmington DE 19801. World Wide Web address: http://www.epaonline.com. An international association of companies that publish electronically using such formats as CD-ROM, DVD-ROM, and the Internet.

GRAPHIC ARTISTS GUILD
90 John Street, Suite 403, New York NY 10038. 212/791-3400. World Wide Web address: http://www.gag.org. A union for artists.

THE GRAPHIC ARTS TECHNICAL FOUNDATION
200 Deer Run Road, Sewickley PA 15143-2600. 412/741-6860. World Wide Web address: http://www.gatf.org. Provides information, services, and training to those in graphic arts professions.

MAGAZINE PUBLISHERS OF AMERICA
919 Third Avenue, 22nd Floor, New York NY 10022. 212/752-0055. World Wide Web address: http://www.magazine.org. A membership association.

NATIONAL ASSOCIATION OF PRINTERS AND LITHOGRAPHERS
75 West Century Road, Paramus NJ 07652. 201/634-9600. World Wide Web address: http://www.napl.org. Membership required. Offers consulting services and a publication.

THE NATIONAL NEWSPAPER ASSOCIATION
1010 North Glebe Road, Suite 350, Arlington VA 22201. 703/907-7900. World Wide Web address: http://www.nna.org.

NATIONAL PRESS CLUB
529 14th Street NW, 13th Floor, Washington DC 20045. 202/662-7500. World Wide Web address: http://npc.press.org. Offers professional seminars, career services, and conference facilities, as well as members-only restaurants and a health club.

NEWSPAPER ASSOCIATION OF AMERICA
1921 Gallows Road, Suite 600, Vienna VA 22182. 703/902-1600. Fax: 703/902-1735. World Wide Web address: http://www.naa.org. Focuses on marketing, public policy, diversity, industry development, and newspaper operations.

PRINTING INDUSTRIES OF AMERICA
100 Dangerfield Road, Alexandria VA 22314. 703/519-8100. World Wide Web address: http://www.printing.org. Members are offered publications and insurance.

PUBLISHERS MARKETING ASSOCIATION
627 Aviation Way, Manhattan Beach CA 90266. Fax: 310/374-3342. A membership organization offering seminars and educational materials for professionals in the publishing industry.

TECHNICAL ASSOCIATION OF THE GRAPHIC ARTS
68 Lomb Memorial Drive, Rochester NY 14623. 716/475-7470. World Wide Web address: http://www.taga.org. Conducts an annual conference and offers newsletters.

WRITERS GUILD OF AMERICA WEST
7000 West Third Street, Los Angeles CA 90048. 310/550-1000. World Wide Web address: http://www.wga.org. A membership association which registers scripts.

Directories

EDITOR & PUBLISHER INTERNATIONAL YEARBOOK
Editor & Publisher Company, 11 West 19th Street, New York NY 10011. 212/675-4380. World Wide Web address: http://www.mediainfo.com. Offers newspapers to editors in both the United States and foreign countries.

GRAPHIC ARTS BLUE BOOK
A.F. Lewis & Company, Hudson Street, 4th Floor, New York NY 10014. 212/519-7398. $85.00. Lists manufacturers and dealers.

THE JOURNALISTS ROAD TO SUCCESS
The Dow Jones Newspaper Fund, P.O. Box 300, Princeton NJ 08543-0300. 609/452-2820. World Wide Web address: http://www.dj.com/newsfund

Magazines

AIGA JOURNAL OF GRAPHIC DESIGN
American Institute of Graphic Arts, 164 Fifth Avenue, New York NY 10010. 212/807-1990. World Wide Web address: http://www.aiga.org. $22.00. A 56-page magazine, published three times per year, that deals with contemporary issues.

THE EDITOR & PUBLISHER
Editor & Publisher Co., 11 West 19th Street, New York NY 10011. 212/675-4380. World Wide Web

address: http://www.mediainfo.com. A periodical focusing on the newspaper publishing industry.

GRAPHIS
141 Lexington Avenue, New York NY 10016. 212/532-9387. $90.00. Magazine covers portfolios, articles, designers, advertising, and photos.

PRINT
RC Publications, 104 Fifth Avenue, 19th Floor, New York NY 10011. 212/463-0600. Offers a graphic design magazine. $57.00 for subscription.

PUBLISHERS WEEKLY
245 West 17th Street, New York NY 10011. 212/463-6758. Toll-free phone: 800/278-2991. World Wide Web address: http://www.publishersweekly.com. Weekly magazine for book publishers and booksellers. Each issue includes a listing of job openings.

Special Book and Magazine Programs

CENTER FOR BOOK ARTS
28 West 27th Street, 3rd Floor, New York NY 10001. 212/481-0295. Offers bookbinding, printing, and papermaking workshops.

EMERSON COLLEGE WRITING AND PUBLISHING PROGRAM
100 Beacon Street, Boston MA 02116. 617/824-8500. World Wide Web address: http://www.emerson.edu.

THE NEW YORK UNIVERSITY SUMMER PUBLISHING PROGRAM
11 West 42nd Street, Room 400, New York NY 10036. 212/790-3232.

THE RADCLIFFE PUBLISHING COURSE
6 Ash Street, Cambridge MA 02138. 617/495-8678. Fax: 617/496-2333. E-mail address: rpc@radcliffe.edu.

THE STANFORD PROFESSIONAL PUBLISHING COURSE
Stanford Alumni Association, Bowman Alumni House, Stanford CA 97305-4005. 650/723-2027. Fax: 650/723-8597. E-mail address: publishing.courses@stanford.edu. World Wide Web address: http://www.stanfordproed.org.

UNIVERSITY OF DENVER PUBLISHING INSTITUTE
2075 South University Boulevard, #D-114, Denver CO 80210. 303/871-2570.

Online Services

JOBS FOR JOURNALISTS
World Wide Web address: http://ajr.newslink.org/newjoblink.html. Offers links to newspapers and magazines, news articles, and an e-mail notification section for jobseekers.

JOURNALISM FORUM
Go: Jforum. A CompuServe discussion group for journalists in print, radio, or television.

PHOTO PROFESSIONALS
Go: Photopro. A CompuServe forum for imaging professionals.

PROPUBLISHING FORUM
Go: Propub. CompuServe charges a fee for this forum which caters to publishing and graphic design professionals.

REAL ESTATE

You can expect to find the following types of companies in this chapter:
Land Subdividers and Developers • Real Estate Agents, Managers, and Operators • Real Estate Investment Trusts

Some helpful information: *Real estate salespersons and brokers earn an average of $50,000 annually (agents in their first year of sales, however, generally earn under $25,000). Experienced and successful agents that sell choice property (such as condominiums in large metropolitan areas) can earn over $200,000 annually.*

ADLETA & POSTON, REALTORS
5956 Sherry Lane, Suite 100, Dallas TX 75225. 214/696-0900. **Fax:** 214/369-6996. **Contact:** Lynda Adleta, Partner. **World Wide Web address:** http://www.adletaposton.com. **Description:** A residential real estate brokerage specializing in the executive market. **Common positions include:** Real Estate Agent; Receptionist; Secretary. **Benefits:** Medical Insurance; Profit Sharing. **Special programs:** Internships. **Corporate headquarters location:** This Location.

CENTURY 21 REAL ESTATE CORPORATION
3637 Highway 80, Mesquite TX 75150. 972/270-7521. **Contact:** Human Resources. **World Wide Web address:** http://www.century21.com. **Description:** A local branch of the national realty company specializing in residential and commercial properties. **Corporate headquarters location:** Parsippany NJ. **Parent company:** Cendant.

COLDWELL BANKER
3636 North MacArthur Boulevard, Suite 100, Irving TX 75062. 972/659-1525. **Contact:** Human Resources. **World Wide Web address:** http://www.coldwellbanker.com. **Description:** One of the largest residential real estate companies in the United States and Canada in terms of total home sales transactions. Coldwell Banker is also a leader in corporate relocation services. **NOTE:** This office hires agents only. **Corporate headquarters location:** Mission Viejo CA. **Other U.S. locations:** Nationwide.

COLDWELL BANKER
2801 Gateway Drive, Suite 180, Irving TX 75063. 972/582-9200. **Contact:** Hiring Manager. **World Wide Web address:** http://www.coldwellbanker.com. **Description:** One of the largest residential real estate companies in the United States and Canada in terms of total home sales transactions. Coldwell Banker is also a leader in corporate relocation services. **Corporate headquarters location:** Mission Viejo CA. **Other U.S. locations:** Nationwide.

GRUBB & ELLIS
14785 Preston Road, Suite 1000, Dallas TX 75240. 972/450-3300. **Contact:** Personnel. **World Wide Web address:** http://www.grubb-ellis.com. **Description:** A real estate services firm dealing primarily with commercial real estate including shopping centers, office buildings, and similar complexes. Founded in 1958. **Corporate headquarters location:** Northbrook IL.

LINCOLN PROPERTY COMPANY
500 North Akard Street, Suite 3300, Dallas TX 75201. 214/740-3300. **Contact:** Human Resources. **World Wide Web address:** http://www.lincolnpc.com. **Description:** A property management company with commercial, residential, and industrial properties.

McFARLAN REAL ESTATE
10100 North Central Expressway, Suite 200, Dallas TX 75231. 214/559-4599. **Contact:** Human Resources. **Description:** A commercial real estate agency. **Corporate headquarters location:** This Location.

TOWN EAST REALTORS
2220 Town East Boulevard, Mesquite TX 75150. 972/270-8673. **Contact:** Fern Hardin, Broker. **E-mail address:** towneastrealtors@att.worldnet.com. **Description:** A real estate agency.

TRAMMELL CROW COMPANY
3400 Trammell Crow Center, 2001 Ross Avenue, Dallas TX 75201-2997. 214/863-3000. **Contact:** Employment. **World Wide Web address:** http://www.trammellcrow.com. **Description:** A national real estate development and brokerage agency. Founded in 1948. **Common positions include:** Accountant/Auditor; Financial Analyst; Marketing Specialist;

Property and Real Estate Manager; Real Estate Agent. **Educational backgrounds include:** Accounting; Business Administration; Finance; Marketing; Real Estate. **Benefits:** Dental Insurance; Disability Coverage; Employee Discounts; Life Insurance; Medical Insurance; Savings Plan. **Special programs:** Internships.

WYNNE/JACKSON, INC.
600 North Pearl Street, Suite 650, Lock Box 149, Dallas TX 75201. 214/880-8600. **Contact:** Frank Murphy, Vice President. **Description:** A commercial real estate development and property management company. **Corporate headquarters location:** This Location.

Note: Because addresses and telephone numbers of smaller companies can change rapidly, we recommend you call each company to verify the information below before inquiring about job opportunities. Mass mailings are not recommended.

Additional small employers:

LAND SUBDIVIDERS AND DEVELOPERS

Musgrave Enterprises Inc.
PO Box 1743, Abilene TX 79604-1743. 915/673-6662.

Pulte Homes of Texas
1431 Greenway Dr, Ste 700, Irving TX 75038. 972/518-0177.

REAL ESTATE AGENTS AND MANAGERS

CB Richard Ellis Inc.
5400 LBJ Fwy, Ste 1100, Dallas TX 75240-1029. 972/458-4800.

Century 21
150 Westpark Way, Ste 120, Euless TX 76040-3704. 817/354-7653.

Fairfield Properties
PO Box 5407, Arlington TX 76005-5407. 817/640-9450.

Grubb & Ellis Company
PO Box 833, Richardson TX 75083. 972/684-2335.

Harwood Pacific Corporation
2651 N Harwood St, Ste 450, Dallas TX 75201-1564. 214/871-0871.

Kennedy-Wilson
9400 N Central Expy, Dallas TX 75231-5027. 214/871-6666.

Prentiss Properties Trust
3890 W Northwest Hwy, Dallas TX 75220-8108. 214/654-0886.

Preston Del Norte Home Owners
8131 LBJ Fwy, Ste 750, Dallas TX 75251-1329. 972/788-1286.

REAL ESTATE OPERATORS

CWS Communities LP
2310 LBJ Fwy, Ste 200, Dallas TX 75234-7338. 972/884-9340.

Hartex Property Group Inc.
13355 Noel Rd, Ste 1906, Dallas TX 75240-6643. 972/980-1111.

Marcrum Management Co.
2102 Roosevelt Dr, Ste K, Arlington TX 76013-5932. 817/548-7785.

McDougal Property
7008 Salem Ave, Ste 200, Lubbock TX 79424-2234. 806/797-3162.

Sabine Valley Properties Inc.
11255 Highway 80 W, Aledo TX 76008-3692. 817/560-8801.

Trammell Crow Residential Co.
717 N Harwood St, Ste 1200, Dallas TX 75201-6516. 214/922-8400.

Walden Residential Properties
5080 Spectrum Dr, Addison TX 75001-4648. 972/490-2600.

For more information on career opportunities in real estate:

Associations

INSTITUTE OF REAL ESTATE MANAGEMENT
430 North Michigan Avenue, Chicago IL 60611. 312/661-1930. World Wide Web address: http://www.irem.org.

INTERNATIONAL REAL ESTATE INSTITUTE
1224 North Nokomis, Alexandria MN 56308.

NATIONAL ASSOCIATION OF REAL ESTATE INVESTMENT TRUSTS
1875 Eye Street NW, Suite 600, Washington DC 20006. 202/739-9400. Toll-free phone: 800/3-NAREIT. Contact: Matt Lentz, Membership. World Wide Web address: http://www.nareit.com.

NATIONAL ASSOCIATION OF REALTORS
430 North Michigan Avenue, Chicago IL 60611. 312/329-8200. World Wide Web address: http://www.realtor.com.

Magazines

JOURNAL OF PROPERTY MANAGEMENT
Institute of Real Estate Management, 430 North Michigan Avenue, Chicago IL 60610. 312/329-6000. World Wide Web address: http://www.irem.org.

NATIONAL REAL ESTATE INVESTOR
PRIMEDIA Intertec, 6151 Powers Ferry Road NW, Suite 200, Atlanta GA 30339. 770/955-2500. World Wide Web address: http://www.nreionline.com.

Online Services

JOBS IN REAL ESTATE
World Wide Web address: http://www.cob.ohio-state.edu/dept/fin/jobs/realest.htm.

For information about the JobBank List Service visit www.adamsjobbank.com

RETAIL

You can expect to find the following types of companies in this chapter:
Catalog Retailers • Department Stores • Specialty Stores • Retail Bakeries • Supermarkets

Some helpful information: *The average salary of general sales staff is approximately $5.00 - $12.00 per hour (more if the salesperson earns a commission on successful sales). Store managers generally earn $24,000 - $45,000, district managers earn $40,000 - $70,000, and regional managers can earn as much as $100,000 or more.*

BABBAGE'S ETC.
2250 William D. Tate Avenue, Grapevine TX 76051. 817/424-2000. **Fax:** 817/424-2002. **Contact:** Human Resources. **World Wide Web address:** http://www.gamestop.com. **Description:** A national retailer of interactive games and accessories. Babbage's Etc. operates more than 475 stores in the U.S. and Puerto Rico under the Babbage's, Software Etc., Gamestop, SuperSoftware, and Planet X names. **Corporate headquarters location:** This Location.

W.O. BANKSTON LINCOLN MERCURY
4747 LBJ Freeway, Dallas TX 75244. 972/233-1441. **Contact:** Human Resources. **World Wide Web address:** http://www.bankstoplincoln.com. **Description:** A car dealer offering both new and used vehicles.

BESTWAY RENTAL, INC.
7800 Stemmons Freeway, Suite 320, Dallas TX 75247. 214/630-6655x 206. **Contact:** Payroll. **Description:** A rent-to-own furniture and appliance service.

BLOCKBUSTER ENTERTAINMENT GROUP
1201 Elm Street, Suite 2100, Dallas TX 75270. 214/854-3259. **Fax:** 214/854-3241. **Contact:** Tom Grissom, Manager of Recruiting. **E-mail address:** career@blockbuster.com. **World Wide Web address:** http://www.blockbuster.com. **Description:** Operates a chain of video rental and music retail stores. There are approximately 6,000 Blockbuster locations worldwide. **NOTE:** Entry-level positions are offered. **Common positions include:** Accountant/Auditor; Buyer; Computer Operator; Financial Analyst; Market Research Analyst; MIS Specialist; Systems Analyst. **Educational backgrounds include:** Accounting; Business Administration; Computer Science; Finance. **Benefits:** 401(k); Dental Insurance; Disability Coverage; Employee Discounts; Financial Planning Assistance; Life Insurance; Medical Insurance; Tuition Assistance. **Office hours:** Monday - Friday, 8:30 a.m. - 5:30 p.m. **Corporate headquarters location:** This Location. **Other U.S. locations:** Nationwide. **International locations:** Australia; Canada; United Kingdom. **Parent company:** Viacom. **Listed on:** New York Stock Exchange. **CEO:** John Antioco. **Annual sales/revenues:** More than $100 million. **Number of employees at this location:** 1,600. **Number of employees nationwide:** 58,000.

THE BOMBAY COMPANY, INC.
550 Bailey Avenue, Suite 700, Fort Worth TX 76107-2111. 817/870-1847. **Fax:** 817/348-7090. **Recorded jobline:** 817/339-3799. **Contact:** Human Resources. **World Wide Web address:** http://www.bombayco.com. **Description:** A specialty retailer of ready-to-assemble home furnishings, prints, and accessories. Products are sold through over 400 Bombay Company and Alex & Ivy Stores. **Common positions include:** Accountant/Auditor; Buyer; Customer Service Representative; Designer; Financial Analyst; Management Trainee; Retail Sales Worker; Secretary; Systems Analyst; Wholesale and Retail Buyer. **Educational backgrounds include:** Accounting; Art/Design; Business Administration; Finance; Liberal Arts; Marketing. **Benefits:** 401(k); Dental Insurance; Disability Coverage; Employee Discounts; Life Insurance; Medical Insurance; Profit Sharing; Stock Option; Tuition Assistance. **Special programs:** Internships. **Corporate headquarters location:** This Location. **Other U.S. locations:** Nationwide. **International locations:** Canada. **Listed on:** New York Stock Exchange. **Number of employees nationwide:** 8,000.

BRIDGESTONE/FIRESTONE, INC.
9901 East Valley Ranch Parkway, Suite 3020, Irving TX 75063. 972/869-2303. **Contact:** Steve Kratohvil, Human Resources Manager. **World Wide Web address:** http://www.bridgestone-firestone.com. **Description:** A zone office of the tire and automotive services company.

Common positions include: Automotive Mechanic; Retail Sales Worker. **Corporate headquarters location:** Rolling Meadows IL.

COMPUSA INC.
14951 North Dallas Parkway, Dallas TX 75240. 972/982-4000. **Contact:** Human Resources. **World Wide Web address:** http://www.compusa.com. **Description:** This location houses administrative offices. Overall, CompUSA Inc. operates more than 75 computer superstores in 40 metropolitan areas throughout the U.S. Each store offers more than 5,000 computer products including hardware, software, accessories, and related products, at discount prices to retail, business, governmental, and institutional customers. The stores also offers full-service technical departments as well as classroom facilities. **Common positions include:** Accountant/Auditor; Adjuster; Administrative Manager; Advertising Clerk; Attorney; Buyer; Clerical Supervisor; Collector; Computer Programmer; Credit Manager; Customer Service Representative; General Manager; Human Resources Manager; Investigator; Operations/Production Manager; Property and Real Estate Manager; Public Relations Specialist; Purchasing Agent/Manager; Services Sales Representative; Systems Analyst; Technical Writer/Editor; Wholesale and Retail Buyer. **Educational backgrounds include:** Accounting; Advertising; Business Administration; Computer Science; Finance. **Benefits:** 401(k); Dental Insurance; Disability Coverage; Employee Discounts; Life Insurance; Medical Insurance. **Corporate headquarters location:** This Location. **Other U.S. locations:** Nationwide. **Listed on:** New York Stock Exchange. **Number of employees at this location:** 620. **Number of employees nationwide:** 8,000. **Number of employees worldwide:** 17,300.

DUNLAP COMPANY
200 Greenleaf Street, Fort Worth TX 76107. 817/336-4985. **Contact:** Human Resources. **Description:** Operates a chain of department stores with over 50 locations. The stores operate under the Dunlaps, McClurkans, M.M. Cohn, Heironimus, Stripling & Cox, Porteus, and The White House names. Founded in 1892. **Corporate headquarters location:** This Location. **Other U.S. locations:** Nationwide. **Listed on:** Privately held. **CEO:** Edward Martin. **Number of employees nationwide:** 2,100.

EVANS PONTIAC GMC
12100 East NW Highway, Dallas TX 75218. 214/328-8411. **Contact:** Dick Manuel, Vice President. **World Wide Web address:** http://www.evanspontiacgmc.com. **Description:** A new and used car dealer.

F.F.P./NU-WAY OIL COMPANY, INC.
2801 Glenda Avenue, Fort Worth TX 76117. 817/838-4700. **Contact:** Controller. **Description:** Operates a chain of convenience stores that also offer drive-up gasoline pumps.

FIRST CASH, INC.
690 East Lamar Boulevard, Suite 400, Arlington TX 76011. 817/460-3947. **Contact:** Human Resources. **Description:** Acquires, establishes, and operates more than 140 pawnshops and retails previously-owned merchandise acquired in forfeited transactions. First Cash also operates more than 25 check-cashing stores. **Common positions include:** Cashier; Computer Programmer; Inventory Control Specialist. **Benefits:** 401(k); Casual Dress - Daily; Dental Insurance; Medical Insurance. **Corporate headquarters location:** This Location. **Other U.S. locations:** CA; DC; IL; MD; MO; OK; SC. **International locations:** Mexico. **Listed on:** NASDAQ. **Stock exchange symbol:** PAWN. **Number of employees at this location:** 800.

FOXWORTH-GALBRAITH
P.O. Box 799002, Dallas TX 75379-9002. 972/437-6100. **Contact:** Human Resources. **World Wide Web address:** http://www.foxgal.com. **Description:** One of the Southwest's largest retailers of lumber and building materials. Foxworth-Galbraith has more than 70 locations in Texas, New Mexico, Colorado, and Arizona. Founded in 1901. **Listed on:** Privately held.

FRIENDLY CHEVROLET COMPANY, INC.
P.O. Box 7066, Dallas TX 75209. 214/920-1900. **Contact:** Hiring Manager. **World Wide Web address:** http://www.friendlychevy.com. **Description:** A new and used automobile dealership.

JCPENNEY COMPANY, INC.
P.O. Box 10001, Dallas TX 75301. 972/431-1000. **Contact:** Human Resources. **World Wide Web address:** http://www.jcpenney.com. **Description:** This location houses administrative offices. Overall, JCPenney Company is a national retail merchandise sales and service corporation with department stores nationwide. JCPenney sells apparel, home furnishings, and leisure lines in catalogs and 1,900 stores. **Corporate headquarters location:** This Location.

Other U.S. locations: Nationwide. **Subsidiaries include:** JCPenney Life Insurance Company, which sells life, health, and credit insurance; and JCPenney National Bank. **Listed on:** New York Stock Exchange. **Annual sales/revenues:** More than $100 million.

JCPENNEY COMPANY, INC.
6002 Slide Road, P.O. Box 68611, Lubbock TX 79414. 806/792-6841. **Contact:** Human Resources. **World Wide Web address:** http://www.jcpenney.com. **Description:** One location of the department store chain that sells apparel, home furnishings, and leisure lines. **Corporate headquarters location:** Dallas TX. **Other U.S. locations:** Nationwide. **Listed on:** New York Stock Exchange. **Annual sales/revenues:** More than $100 million.

KROGER
3612 North Beltline Road, Irving TX 75062. 972/252-7413. **Contact:** Human Resources. **World Wide Web address:** http://www.kroger.com. **Description:** A supermarket. **Parent company:** The Kroger Company (Cincinnati OH) is a major supermarket and convenience store operator and food processor. The company operates over 1,250 supermarkets in 24 states and over 900 convenience stores in 16 states. The Kroger Company also has more than 35 food processing plants which supply over 4,000 private label products to its supermarkets.

LORD & TAYLOR
450 Northpark Center, Dallas TX 75225. 214/691-6600. **Contact:** Human Resources Manager. **World Wide Web address:** http://www.mayco.com/lt. **Description:** A full-line department store carrying clothing, accessories, home furnishings, and a wide range of other items. Founded in 1826. **NOTE:** Part-time jobs are offered. **Common positions include:** Sales Representative; Stock Clerk. **Benefits:** 401(k); Dental Insurance; Employee Discounts; Medical Insurance; Profit Sharing. **Office hours:** Monday - Friday, 10:00 a.m. - 9:00 p.m. **Corporate headquarters location:** New York NY. **Parent company:** The May Company. **Annual sales/revenues:** More than $100 million.

LORD & TAYLOR
15350 Dallas Parkway, Dallas TX 75248. 972/387-0588. **Contact:** Human Resources. **World Wide Web address:** http://www.mayco.com/lt. **Description:** A full-line department store carrying clothing, accessories, home furnishings, and a wide range of other items. Founded in 1826. **Corporate headquarters location:** New York NY. **Parent company:** The May Company. **Annual sales/revenues:** More than $100 million.

BRUCE LOWRIE CHEVROLET
711 SW Loop 820, Fort Worth TX 76134. 817/293-5811. **Contact:** Personnel. **World Wide Web address:** http://www.brucelowrie.com. **Description:** A new and used car dealership.

MASSEY CADILLAC
11501 East Northwest Highway, Dallas TX 75218. 214/348-2711. **Contact:** Personnel Department. **Description:** A new and used auto dealership. Massey Cadillac also offers maintenance and repair services.

MICHAEL'S STORES, INC.
P.O. Box 619566, Dallas TX 75261-9566. 972/409-1300. **Physical address:** 8000 Bent Branch Drive, Irving TX 75063. **Contact:** Human Resources. **World Wide Web address:** http://www.michaels.com. **Description:** A nationwide specialty retailer of art, crafts, and decorative items and supplies, offering over 30,000 items, from picture framing materials to seasonal and holiday merchandise. Michael's Stores operates approximately 180 stores nationwide. **Corporate headquarters location:** This Location. **Other U.S. locations:** Nationwide.

MINYARD FOOD STORES, INC.
P.O. Box 518, Coppell TX 75019. 972/393-8700. **Fax:** 972/304-3828. **Contact:** Personnel Department. **Description:** A retail grocery chain with over 80 stores. **Common positions include:** Computer Programmer; Management Trainee; Pharmacist; Systems Analyst. **Educational backgrounds include:** Computer Science; Pharmacology. **Benefits:** 401(k); Dental Insurance; Disability Coverage; Life Insurance; Medical Insurance. **Corporate headquarters location:** This Location. **Listed on:** Privately held. **Number of employees at this location:** 350. **Number of employees nationwide:** 6,100.

MONTGOMERY WARD & COMPANY, INC.
2700 East Pioneer Parkway, Arlington TX 76010. 817/633-1100. **Contact:** Personnel. **Description:** One of the oldest and largest retailers in the nation, Montgomery Ward &

Company operates specialty stores, distribution centers, and product service centers nationwide. The company focuses on apparel, fine jewelry, appliances, electronics, home products, and automotive services. **Common positions include:** Branch Manager; Department Manager; Human Resources Manager; Management Trainee; Operations/Production Manager; Services Sales Representative. **Educational backgrounds include:** Business Administration; Finance; Marketing; Merchandising. **Benefits:** Dental Insurance; Disability Coverage; Employee Discounts; Life Insurance; Medical Insurance; Pension Plan; Profit Sharing; Savings Plan. **Corporate headquarters location:** Chicago IL.

THE NEIMAN MARCUS GROUP, INC.
1618 Main Street, Dallas TX 75201. 214/573-5688. **Contact:** Crystal Curren, Manager of MDP Placement. **World Wide Web address:** http://www.neimanmarcus.com. **Description:** Operates two specialty retailing businesses: Neiman Marcus and Bergdorf Goodman. Combined, these two chains offer men's and women's apparel, fashion accessories, jewelry, fine china, and moderately-priced crystal and silver. **Corporate headquarters location:** This Location. **Subsidiaries include:** NM Direct is a direct marketing company which advertises primarily through the use of such specialty catalogs as Neiman Marcus and Horchow.

NICHOLS FORD
2401 East Interstate 20 at Campus Drive, Fort Worth TX 76119. 817/535-3673. **Contact:** Personnel Administrator. **World Wide Web address:** http://www.nicholsford.com. **Description:** A new and used car dealership.

PARK PLACE MID-CITIES
3737 Airport Freeway, Bedford TX 76021. 817/571-3737. **Contact:** Personnel Department. **Description:** A new and used car dealership.

PARK PLACE MOTORCARS
4023 Oak Lawn Avenue, Dallas TX 75219. 214/526-8701. **Toll-free phone:** 800/336-7073. **Fax:** 214/443-8270. **Contact:** Human Resources. **World Wide Web address:** http://www.parkplacetexas.com. **Description:** A new and preowned car dealership for Mercedes-Benz, Porsche, Lexus, and Audi automobiles. **NOTE:** Entry-level positions are offered. **Common positions include:** Administrative Assistant; Assistant Manager; Chief Financial Officer; Clerical Supervisor; Computer Operator; Computer Programmer; Controller; Finance Director; General Manager; Human Resources Manager; Management Analyst/Consultant; Management Trainee; Quality Control Supervisor; Sales Executive; Sales Manager; Sales Representative; Secretary; Typist/Word Processor. **Educational backgrounds include:** Accounting; Business Administration; Finance. **Benefits:** 401(k); Dental Insurance; Disability Coverage; Employee Discounts; Life Insurance; Medical Insurance; Savings Plan. **Corporate headquarters location:** This Location. **Other area locations:** Houston TX; Plano TX. **Number of employees at this location:** 230. **Number of employees nationwide:** 430.

PEARLE VISION, INC.
2534 Royal Lane, Dallas TX 75229. 972/277-5000. **Fax:** 972/277-5944. **Contact:** Human Resources. **Description:** Manufactures and retails prescription eyewear. **Common positions include:** Accountant/Auditor; Advertising Clerk; Attorney; Computer Programmer; Customer Service Representative; Department Manager; Financial Analyst; Human Resources Manager; Management Trainee; Manufacturer's/Wholesaler's Sales Rep.; Marketing Specialist; Purchasing Agent/Manager; Systems Analyst. **Educational backgrounds include:** Accounting; Business Administration; Computer Science; Finance; Marketing; Merchandising. **Benefits:** Dental Insurance; Disability Coverage; Employee Discounts; Life Insurance; Medical Insurance; Profit Sharing; Savings Plan; Tuition Assistance. **Corporate headquarters location:** This Location. **Parent company:** Grand Met USA. **Listed on:** London Stock Exchange.

PIER 1 IMPORTS
P.O. Box 961020, Fort Worth TX 76161-0020. 817/878-8000. **Contact:** Tawny McCarty, Staffing Manager. **World Wide Web address:** http://www.pier1.com. **Description:** This location houses administrative offices. Overall, Pier 1 Imports is engaged in the specialty retailing of handcrafted decorative home furnishings and accessories imported from approximately 45 countries around the world. **Common positions include:** Accountant/Auditor; Assistant Manager; Computer Programmer; Distribution Manager; Management Trainee; Real Estate Agent; Retail Merchandiser; Transportation/Traffic Specialist. **Educational backgrounds include:** Accounting; Business Administration; Communications; Finance; Liberal Arts; Merchandising. **Benefits:** Accident/Emergency Insurance; Dental Insurance; Disability Coverage; Employee Discounts; Life Insurance; Medical Insurance; Retirement Plan; Stock Option; Tuition Assistance; Vision Plan. **Corporate headquarters location:** This Location.

Other U.S. locations: Nationwide. Listed on: New York Stock Exchange. Number of employees at this location: 520. Number of employees nationwide: 8,500.

PIONEER OIL COMPANY
P.O. Box 1838, Fort Worth TX 76101. 817/531-3776. **Fax:** 817/531-2271. **Contact:** Hiring Manager. **Description:** Owns and operates a chain of self-service gas stations. **Common positions include:** Accountant/Auditor; Clerical Supervisor; General Manager; Management Trainee; Property and Real Estate Manager. **Educational backgrounds include:** Business Administration. **Benefits:** Dental Insurance; Life Insurance; Medical Insurance; Pension Plan. **Corporate headquarters location:** This Location. **Other U.S. locations:** AR; KS; MS; TN. **Listed on:** Privately held. **Number of employees at this location:** 10.

THE RADIOSHACK CORPORATION
100 Throckmorton Street, Suite 1800, Fort Worth TX 76102. 817/415-3700. **Contact:** Jeff Bland, Senior Director. **World Wide Web address:** http://www.radioshack.com. **Description:** Sells a wide variety of consumer electronic parts and equipment through more than 7,000 stores nationwide. **Common positions include:** Accountant/Auditor; Advertising Clerk; Computer Programmer; Customer Service Representative; Services Sales Representative; Systems Analyst. **Educational backgrounds include:** Accounting; Computer Science. **Benefits:** Dental Insurance; Employee Discounts; Life Insurance; Medical Insurance; Pension Plan; Tuition Assistance. **Corporate headquarters location:** This Location. **Listed on:** New York Stock Exchange. **Annual sales/revenues:** More than $100 million.

RENT-A-CENTER
5700 Tennyson Parkway, 3rd Floor, Plano TX 75024. 972/801-1100. **Toll-free phone:** 800/275-2696. **Fax:** 972/943-0112. **Contact:** Staffing. **World Wide Web address:** http://www.rentacenter.com. **Description:** Rents furniture, appliances, stereos, and other furnishings and equipment. **Special programs:** Internships. **Corporate headquarters location:** This Location. **Other U.S. locations:** Nationwide. **Annual sales/revenues:** More than $100 million. **Number of employees at this location:** 500. **Number of employees nationwide:** 7,000.

SAKS FIFTH AVENUE
13550 Dallas Parkway, Dallas TX 75240. 972/458-7000. **Contact:** Human Resources Manager. **World Wide Web address:** http://www.saksincorporated.com. **Description:** One location of the upscale department store chain. **Corporate headquarters location:** New York NY.

SHOWCASE CHEVROLET
P.O. Box 801089, Dallas TX 75380. 972/233-3500. **Contact:** Victor Mullino, Office Manager. **World Wide Web address:** http://www.showcasechev.com. **Description:** A new and used car dealership. **NOTE:** Salespeople should apply in person and expect to fill out an application.

SOUTHLAND CORPORATION
P.O. Box 711, Dallas TX 75221. 214/828-7011. **Fax:** 214/841-6688. **Contact:** Beth Marquardt, Staff Personnel Manager. **World Wide Web address:** http://www.7eleven.com. **Description:** Owns and operates 7-Eleven convenience stores. **Common positions include:** Accountant/Auditor; Management Trainee. **Benefits:** Daycare Assistance; Dental Insurance; Disability Coverage; Life Insurance; Medical Insurance; Profit Sharing. **Corporate headquarters location:** This Location. **Listed on:** NASDAQ. **Number of employees at this location:** 870. **Number of employees nationwide:** 35,000.

SPORTS SUPPLY GROUP, INC.
P.O. Box 7726, 1901 Diplomat Drive, Farmers Branch TX 75234. 972/484-9484. **Contact:** Human Resources. **World Wide Web address:** http://www.sportsgroup.com. **Description:** A catalog retailer of sporting goods and recreational products. **Corporate headquarters location:** This Location. **Listed on:** New York Stock Exchange. **Stock exchange symbol:** GYM.

STEAKLY CHEVROLET-GEO-SUBARU INC.
6411 East NW Highway, Dallas TX 75231. 214/363-8341. **Contact:** Personnel. **Description:** A new and used car dealership.

STRIPLING & COX
6370 Camp Bowie Boulevard, Fort Worth TX 76116. 817/738-7361. **Contact:** Human Resources. **Description:** A department store offering men's and women's apparel and home furnishings.

TOM THUMB FOOD & PHARMACY

14303 Inwood Road, Dallas TX 75244. 972/661-9700. **Contact:** Training & Development. **World Wide Web address:** http://www.tomthumb.com. **Description:** A supermarket. **Common positions include:** Customer Service Representative; Management Trainee; Pharmacist; Restaurant/Food Service Manager; Retail Sales Worker. **Educational backgrounds include:** Accounting; Business Administration; Communications; Economics; Finance; Liberal Arts; Marketing. **Benefits:** Dental Insurance; Disability Coverage; Life Insurance; Medical Insurance; Stock Option; Tuition Assistance. **Special programs:** Internships. **Corporate headquarters location:** Houston TX. **Parent company:** Randalls. **Listed on:** Privately held. **Number of employees nationwide:** 20,000.

TOYOTA OF DALLAS INC.

2610 Forest Lane, Dallas TX 75234. 972/241-6655. **Fax:** 972/243-3706. **Contact:** Paula Beaver, Controller. **World Wide Web address:** http://www.toyotaofdallas.com. **Description:** Specializes in the retail sale of new and used Toyota automobiles. **Common positions include:** Accountant/Auditor; Credit Manager; Customer Service Representative; Department Manager; General Manager; Management Trainee; Operations/Production Manager; Retail Sales Worker; Technician. **Benefits:** Employee Discounts; Medical Insurance; Profit Sharing. **Corporate headquarters location:** This Location.

TROY AIKMAN AUTO MALL

P.O. Box 121819, Fort Worth TX 76121-1819. 817/560-0500. **Fax:** 817/560-7982. **Contact:** Personnel Office. **World Wide Web address:** http://www.troyaikmanautomall.com. **Description:** A new and used car dealership specializing in Chevrolet and Chrysler-Plymouth-Jeep lines. Founded in 1996. **NOTE:** Entry-level positions are offered. **Common positions include:** Administrative Assistant; Automotive Mechanic; Controller; Finance Director; General Manager; Human Resources Manager; Receptionist; Sales Executive; Sales Manager. **Educational backgrounds include:** Accounting; Business Administration; Finance. **Benefits:** 401(k); Dental Insurance; Disability Coverage; Employee Discounts; Life Insurance; Medical Insurance. **Special programs:** Apprenticeships; Training. **Office hours:** Monday - Friday, 8:30 a.m. - 9:00 p.m.; Saturday, 8:30 a.m. - 7:00 p.m. **Corporate headquarters location:** This Location. **General Manager:** Jim Hardick. **Facilities Manager:** Jim Kappler. **Number of employees at this location:** 200.

ZALE CORPORATION

901 West Walnut Hill Lane, Mail Station 5B-12, Irving TX 75038. 972/580-4000. **Fax:** 972/580-5266. **Contact:** Manager of Corporate Staffing. **E-mail address:** careers@zalecorp.com. **World Wide Web address:** http://www.zalecorp.com. **Description:** A specialty retail firm engaged in the selling of fine jewelry and related products. **NOTE:** Entry-level positions are offered. **Common positions include:** Accountant/Auditor; Administrative Assistant; Architect; Attorney; Buyer; Computer Programmer; Customer Service Representative; Financial Analyst; Human Resources Manager; MIS Specialist; Property and Real Estate Manager; Systems Analyst; Typist/Word Processor. **Educational backgrounds include:** Accounting; Communications; Computer Science; Finance; Marketing. **Benefits:** 401(k); Daycare Assistance; Dental Insurance; Disability Coverage; Employee Discounts; Life Insurance; Medical Insurance; Profit Sharing; Savings Plan; Tuition Assistance. **Special programs:** Internships. **Corporate headquarters location:** This Location. **Other U.S. locations:** Nationwide. **Subsidiaries include:** Bailey Banks & Biddle; Gordon's; Zales. **Listed on:** NASDAQ. **Stock exchange symbol:** ZALE. **Annual sales/revenues:** More than $100 million. **Number of employees at this location:** 1,000. **Number of employees nationwide:** 10,000.

Note: Because addresses and telephone numbers of smaller companies can change rapidly, we recommend you call each company to verify the information below before inquiring about job opportunities. Mass mailings are not recommended.

Additional small employers:

AUTO DEALERS

Arrow Ford Inc.
PO Box 5166, Abilene TX 79608-5166. 915/692-9500.

Autobahn Europlaza
3000 White Settlement Rd, Fort Worth TX 76107-1338. 817/336-0885.

Bledsoe Dodge Inc.
PO Box 967, Arlington TX 76004-0967. 972/595-5400.

Churchill Acura
PO Box 123049, Fort Worth TX 76121-3049. 817/244-9600.

Classic BMW
PO Box 515264, Dallas TX 75251-5264. 972/918-1100.

Classic Chevrolet Inc.
PO Box 1717, Grapevine TX
76099-1717. 817/421-1200.

Crest Infiniti Inc.
2501 N Central Expy, Plano TX
75075-2503. 972/578-7511.

Davis Oldsmobile
PO Box 1587, Arlington TX
76004-1587. 817/461-1000.

Discount Motors
PO Box 490, Arlington TX
76004-0490. 817/461-2222.

Don Davis Toyota
1661 Wet N Wild Way,
Arlington TX 76011-9007.
817/469-7711.

Don Snell Buick Inc.
11400 N Central Expy, Dallas
TX 75243-6609. 214/363-7251.

Eagle Isuzu
6200 Lemmon Ave, Dallas TX
75209-5718. 214/357-8899.

Ewing Buick Pontiac GMC
4464 W Plano Pkwy, Plano TX
75093-5623. 972/964-7400.

Five Star Ford
6618 NE Loop 820, Fort Worth
TX 76180-7844. 817/498-8838.

Frank Kent Cadillac
PO Box 121219, Fort Worth TX
76121-1219. 817/763-5000.

Frank Parra Autoplex
1000 E Airport Fwy, Irving TX
75062-4813. 972/721-4300.

Freeman Oldsmobile-Mazda-Hyundai
1800 E Airport Fwy, Irving TX
75062-4827. 972/438-2121.

Freeman Pontiac-Mazda
701 NE Loop 820, Hurst TX
76053-4604. 817/589-7956.

Frontier Automotive Inc.
PO Box 64540, Lubbock TX
79464-4540. 806/798-4500.

Gene Messer Ford
6000 19th St, Lubbock TX
79407-1616. 806/793-2727.

George Grubbs Enterprises Inc.
PO Box 845, Bedford TX
76095-0845. 817/268-6333.

Grand Prairie Ford Inc.
1102 W Pioneer Pkwy, Grand
Prairie TX 75051-4788.
972/641-1334.

Hall Mazda
1300 S Clack St, Abilene TX
79605-4606. 915/695-8811.

Herb Easley Motors Inc.
1125 Central Fwy, Wichita Falls
TX 76306-5944. 940/723-6631.

Hilcher Hyundai
PO Box 170659, Arlington TX
76003-0639. 817/467-3673.

Hillard Auto Park
PO Box 331599, Fort Worth TX
76163-1599. 817/370-5000.

Hudiburg Chevrolet
7769 Grapevine Hwy, Fort
Worth TX 76180-7101.
817/498-2400.

Huffine's Chevrolet-Subaru-Geo
PO Box 338, Lewisville TX
75067-0338. 972/221-8686.

Huffine's Chrysler-Plymouth-Jeep
PO Box 869270, Plano TX
75086. 972/867-5000.

Huffine's Dodge
PO Box 807, Lewisville TX
75067-0807. 972/434-2288.

Jerry's Chevrolet-Buick Inc.
PO Box 839, Weatherford TX
76086-0839. 817/594-8784.

John Eagle Sport City Toyota
12650 Lyndon B. Johnson,
Dallas TX 75228-8014.
972/681-3000.

King Chevrolet Company
PO Box 870, Tyler TX 75710-0870. 903/595-4531.

Leadership Ford Inc.
10510 N Central Expy, Dallas
TX 75231-2202. 214/361-8100.

Lee Jarmon Ford Inc.
PO Box 110098, Carrollton TX
75011-0098. 972/242-6415.

Mac Churchill Auto Group
3435 W Loop 820 S, Fort
Worth TX 76116-6646.
817/244-1111.

McDavid Honda
PO Box 165347, Irving TX
75016-5347. 972/790-6000.

Nashville Peterbilt Inc.
PO Box 560228, Dallas TX
75356-0228. 972/445-7505.

Patterson Auto Center
PO Box 5168, Wichita Falls TX
76307-5168. 940/766-0293.

Payton-Wright Ford Sales Inc.
440 W Highway 114,
Grapevine TX 76051-4015.
817/481-3531.

Pegues-Hurst Motor Company
PO Box 3686, Longview TX
75606-3686. 903/758-6211.

Performance Dodge
PO Box 1186, Atlanta TX
75551-1186. 903/796-2848.

Plains Chevrolet Inc.
2100-2200 I 40 E, Amarillo TX
79103. 806/374-4611.

Plano Lincoln-Mercury
3333 W Plano Pkwy, Plano TX
75075-8010. 972/964-5000.

Pollard Friendly Ford
PO Box 1978, Lubbock TX
79408-1978. 806/797-3441.

Reliable Chevrolet Inc.
PO Box 831240, Richardson TX
75083-1240. 972/952-1500.

Riley Lute Motors Inc.
PO Box 2557, Richardson TX
75080. 972/238-1700.

Ron Roberts Ford Inc.
PO Box 9289, Wichita Falls TX
76308-9289. 940/767-7711.

Rusty Wallace Honda-Volkswagen
12277 Shiloh Rd, Dallas TX
75228-1519. 214/348-7500.

Samuels Chevrolet-Geo
PO Box 7978, Waco TX 76714-7978. 254/772-8850.

Scoggin Dickey Chevrolet-Buick
PO Box 64910, Lubbock TX
79464-4910. 806/798-4000.

Sewell Lexus
6421 Lemmon Ave, Dallas TX
75209-5721. 214/352-8100.

Sewell Village Cadillac Co.
4707 LBJ Fwy, Dallas TX
75244-5909. 972/386-9000.

Shamrock Chevrolet
PO Box 65210, Lubbock TX
79464-5210. 806/747-3211.

Southwest International Trucks
PO Box 560685, Dallas TX
75356-0685. 214/638-4685.

Texas Motors Ford
2020 S Cherry Ln, Fort Worth
TX 76108-3602. 817/246-4921.

Town East Ford Sales Inc.
18411 LBJ Fwy, Mesquite TX
75150-4128. 972/270-6441.

Toyota of Richardson
1221 N Central Expy,
Richardson TX 75080-4606.
972/238-4400.

Trophy Nissan
5031 N Galloway Ave,
Mesquite TX 75150-1557.
972/613-2200.

Van Chevrolet Co. Inc.
PO Box 113149, Carrollton TX
75011-3149. 972/389-6700.

Vandergriff Chevrolet-Geo
PO Box 180189, Arlington TX
76096-0189. 817/784-2661.

Village Ford of Lewisville
1144 N Stemmons Fwy,
Lewisville TX 75067-2503.
972/221-2900.

Westgate Chevrolet Inc.
PO Box 50850, Amarillo TX
79159-0850. 806/356-5600.

Westway Ford
801 W Airport Fwy, Irving TX
75062-6314. 972/659-0333.

Wood Auto Park Inc.
PO Box 50779, Denton TX
76206-0779. 940/591-9663.

Young Chevrolet Inc.
9301 ERL Thornton Fwy, Dallas
TX 75228-6169. 214/328-9111.

CATALOG AND MAIL-ORDER HOUSES

ASD Systems Inc.
3737 Grader St, Ste 110,
Garland TX 75041-6180.
214/348-7200.

ASD Systems Inc.
10812 Alder Cir, Dallas TX
75238-1347. 214/348-3600.

Neiman Marcus Direct
5950 Colwell Blvd, Irving TX
75039-3121. 972/969-3100.

RX America Fort Worth
5450 N Riverside Dr, Fort
Worth TX 76137-2436.
817/850-5000.

Teleservice Resources Inc.
300 E Carpenter Fwy, Irving TX
75062-2727. 972/719-2800.

COMPUTER AND SOFTWARE STORES

IDX Systems Corporation
4901 LBJ Fwy, Ste 400, Dallas
TX 75244-6125. 972/458-1060.

Inacom Corp.
6321 Campus Circle Dr E,
Irving TX 75063-2712. 972/550-4671.

Micro Center
13929 N Central Expy, Dallas
TX 75243-1007. 972/664-8502.

CONSUMER ELECTRONICS STORES

Best Buy
3915 W Airport Fwy, Irving TX
75062-5900. 972/258-0001.

Best Buy
2333 N Central Expy, Plano TX
75075-2534. 972/578-8000.

Best Buy
1330 N Town East Blvd,
Mesquite TX 75150-4159.
972/270-9793.

Best Buy
9600 N Central Expy, Dallas TX
75231-5004. 214/696-2089.

Best Buy
1730 Pleasant Pl, Arlington TX
76015-4500. 817/467-3155.

Best Buy
7600 NE Loop 820, Fort Worth
TX 76180-8343. 817/788-2213.

Best Buy
6241 Slide Rd, Lubbock TX
79414-4611. 806/795-8090.

CONSUMER SUPPLY STORES

Lowes Home Improvement Center
4134 Ridgemont Dr, Abilene
TX 79606-2734. 915/692-2727.

DEPARTMENT STORES

Bud's Discount City
1200 W Main St, Mabank TX
75147-8020. 903/887-4180.

Dillard's
4501 N Beach St, Fort Worth
TX 76137-3218. 817/831-5111.

Dillard's
3901 Irving Mall, Irving TX
75062-5166. 972/258-4968.

Dillard's
2401 S Stemmons Fwy,
Lewisville TX 75067-8794.
972/315-3333.

Dillard's
841 N Central Expy, Plano TX
75075-8809. 972/423-6902.

Dillard's
4800 Texoma Pkwy, Ste 400,
Sherman TX 75090-2085.
903/868-1065.

Dillard's
3301 N Town East Blvd,
Mesquite TX 75150-3449.
972/681-9231.

Dillard's
100 Northpark Ctr, Dallas TX
75225-2222. 214/373-7000.

Dillard's
3560 W Camp Wisdom Rd,
Dallas TX 75237-2506.
972/298-4229.

Dillard's
33 Central Mall I30, Texarkana
TX 75503-2422. 903/838-6591.

Dillard's
3500 McCann Rd, Longview TX
75605-4406. 903/758-4436.

Dillard's
4601 S Broadway Ave, Tyler TX
75703-1330. 903/561-1221.

Dillard's
3821 S Cooper St, Arlington TX
76015-4122. 817/465-0718.

Dillard's
1700 Green Oaks Rd, Fort
Worth TX 76116-1701.
817/731-4711.

Dillard's
4850 Overton Ridge Blvd, Fort
Worth TX 76132-1932.
817/294-1449.

Dillard's
2201 S Interstate 35 E, Denton
TX 76205-8192. 940/566-6210.

Dillard's
3111 Midwestern Pkwy,
Wichita Falls TX 76308-2823.
940/692-9310.

Dillard's
3001 S 31st St, Temple TX
76502-1926. 254/778-1854.

Dillard's
2100 S W S Young Dr, Killeen
TX 76543-5352. 254/699-6116.

Dillard's
6001 W Waco Dr, Ste 200,
Waco TX 76710-6301.
254/776-3560.

Dillard's
7701 I-40 E, Ste 300, Amarillo
TX 79118-6915. 806/358-7771.

Dillard's
4310 Buffalo Gap Rd, Abilene
TX 79606-2724. 915/695-2200.

Foley's
2401 S Stemmons Fwy,
Lewisville TX 75067-8794.
972/385-6533.

Foley's
801 N Central Expy, Plano TX
75075-8809. 972/422-8910.

Foley's
4000 Town East Mall, Mesquite
TX 75150-4121. 972/681-6919.

Retail/251

Foley's
13138 Montfort Dr, Dallas TX 75240-5113. 972/385-6806.

Foley's
4700 S Broadway Ave, Tyler TX 75703-1308. 903/534-6990.

Foley's
2901 E Division St, Arlington TX 76011-6710. 817/640-5910.

Foley's
3841 S Cooper St, Arlington TX 76015-4122. 817/472-4639.

Foley's
4650 S Hulen St, Fort Worth TX 76132-1402. 817/294-6996.

Foley's
7650 Grapevine Hwy, Fort Worth TX 76180-8306. 817/284-6910.

Foley's
3111 S 31st St, Temple TX 76502. 254/770-3700.

JCPenney
2700 W Plano Pkwy, Plano TX 75075-8205. 972/881-6000.

JCPenney
3701 Irving Mall, Irving TX 75062-5157. 972/252-7541.

JCPenney
2401 S Stemmons Fwy, Lewisville TX 75067-8794. 972/315-3900.

JCPenney
821 N Central Expy, Plano TX 75075-8809. 972/578-8666.

JCPenney
6000 Town East Mall, Mesquite TX 75150-4132. 972/279-4100.

JCPenney
2400 Richmond Rd, Ste 61, Texarkana TX 75503-2461. 903/832-1561.

JCPenney
3550 McCann Rd, Longview TX 75605-4420. 903/758-4441.

JCPenney
4401 S Broadway Ave, Tyler TX 75703-1304. 903/561-3333.

JCPenney
3000 Grapevine Mills Pkwy, Grapevine TX 76051-2008. 972/874-1514.

JCPenney
1900 Green Oaks Rd, Fort Worth TX 76116-1703. 817/731-6371.

JCPenney
2201 S Interstate 35 E, Denton TX 76205-8196. 940/566-6086.

JCPenney
3111 Midwestern Pkwy, Wichita Falls TX 76308-2823. 940/692-9630.

JCPenney
2100 SW Young Dr, Killeen TX 76543-5352. 254/699-1919.

JCPenney
6001 W Waco Dr, Ste 300, Waco TX 76710-6302. 254/776-1250.

JCPenney
7701 I-40 E, Ste 600, Amarillo TX 79118-6915. 806/355-7241.

JCPenney
4310 Buffalo Gap Rd, Abilene TX 79606-2724. 915/695-2292.

Kmart
111 Central Expy S, Allen TX 75013-2784. 972/747-0004.

Kmart
5701 Broadway Blvd, Garland TX 75043-5819. 972/240-1626.

Kmart
3500 W Airport Fwy, Irving TX 75062-5922. 972/986-4000.

Kmart
800 W 15th St, Plano TX 75075-8825. 972/423-0600.

Kmart
845 N Beckley Ave, Desoto TX 75115-4806. 972/223-1070.

Kmart
712 S Walton Walker Blvd, Dallas TX 75211-4224. 214/330-9103.

Kmart
4520 W 7th St, Texarkana TX 75501-6354. 903/832-1588.

Kmart
1100 McCann Rd, Longview TX 75601-4541. 903/758-8266.

Kmart
2540 E Pioneer Pkwy, Arlington TX 76010-8786. 817/860-2177.

Kmart
1405 W Pipeline Rd, Hurst TX 76053-4628. 817/284-1491.

Kmart
1701 S Cherry Ln, Fort Worth TX 76108-3601. 817/246-4941.

Kmart
2300 W University Dr, Denton TX 76201-1650. 940/383-2602.

Kmart
3712 Call Field Rd, Wichita Falls TX 76308-2724. 940/691-0522.

Kmart
3809 S General Bruce Dr, Temple TX 76502-1017. 254/773-0156.

Kmart
1101 S Fort Hood St, Killeen TX 76541-7451. 254/526-9541.

Kmart
2747 Duniven Cir, Amarillo TX 79109-1620. 806/355-8142.

Kmart
3050 N Josey Ln, Carrollton TX 75007-5310. 972/492-0661.

Kmart
4220 N 1st St, Abilene TX 79603-6720. 915/673-5191.

Kohl's
Cedar Hill Ctr, Cedar Hill TX 75104. 972/299-9001.

Kohl's
The Crossing, Fort Worth TX 76180. 817/498-1808.

Macy's
13375 Noel Rd, Dallas TX 75240-5061. 972/851-5185.

Marshall Field's
13550 Dallas Pkwy, Dallas TX 75240-6609. 972/851-1515.

Mervyn's
103 W Loop 281, Longview TX 75605-4653. 903/663-4890.

Mervyn's
3881 S Cooper St, Arlington TX 76015-4122. 817/468-8888.

Mervyn's
2625 Old Denton Rd, Carrollton TX 75007-5125. 972/446-8833.

Mervyn's
1500 E Plano Pkwy, Plano TX 75074-8122. 972/422-1925.

Mervyn's
6002 Slide Rd, Lubbock TX 79414-4310. 806/793-1800.

Montgomery Ward & Company, Inc.
603 S Plano Rd, Richardson TX 75081-4512. 972/680-7421.

Montgomery Ward & Company, Inc.
500 E Pike Rd, Mesquite TX 75149. 214/320-6944.

Montgomery Ward & Company, Inc.
3662 W Camp Wisdom Rd, Dallas TX 75237-2500. 972/296-6372.

Montgomery Ward & Company, Inc.
10 Oaklawn Vlg, Texarkana TX 75501-4158. 903/838-6571.

Montgomery Ward & Company, Inc.
6000 Northeast Mall, Hurst TX 76053. 817/284-4700.

Montgomery Ward & Company, Inc.
4900 S Hulen St, Fort Worth TX 76132-1408. 817/294-9930.

Montgomery Ward & Company, Inc.
PO Box 8175, Waco TX 76714-8175. 254/776-1050.

Montgomery Ward & Company, Inc.
29 N Western St, Amarillo TX 79106-7866. 806/354-3400.

Montgomery Ward & Company, Inc.
5015 Boston Ave, Lubbock TX 79413-4413. 806/795-8221.

Montgomery Ward & Company, Inc.
4601 S 1st St, Abilene TX 79605-1463. 915/692-1260.

Sears Roebuck & Co.
2605 Preston Rd, Frisco TX 75034-9434. 972/458-3444.

Sears Roebuck & Co.
2501 Irving Mall, Irving TX 75062-5161. 972/570-8400.

Sears Roebuck & Co.
851 N Central Expressway, Plano TX 75075-8816. 972/422-8484.

Sears Roebuck & Co.
201 S Plano Rd, Richardson TX 75081-4504. 972/470-5500.

Sears Roebuck & Co.
4800 Exec Pkwy, Ste 800, Sherman TX 75090. 903/870-2261.

Sears Roebuck & Co.
3000 N Town East Blvd, Mesquite TX 75150-3950. 972/686-3601.

Sears Roebuck & Co.
3450 W Camp Wisdom Rd, Dallas TX 75237-2504. 972/780-4500.

Sears Roebuck & Co.
13131 Preston Road, Dallas TX 75240-5290. 972/458-3500.

Sears Roebuck & Co.
3060 Clarksville Street Paris TX 75460-7914. 903/737-2100.

Sears Roebuck & Co.
1 Central Mall, Texarkana TX 75503-2420. 903/832-2511.

Sears Roebuck & Co.
3510 McCann Road, Longview TX 75605-4420. 903/757-1680.

Sears Roebuck & Co.
4701 S Broadway Ave, Tyler TX 75703-1309. 903/534-2334.

Sears Roebuck & Co.
2921 E Division Street, Arlington TX 76011-6710. 817/649-4300.

Sears Roebuck & Co.
1101 Melbourne Rd, Hurst TX 76053-6205. 817/595-5200.

Sears Roebuck & Co.
110 Seminary Dr, Fort Worth TX 76115. 817/927-3400.

Sears Roebuck & Co.
1800 Green Oaks Rd, Fort Worth TX 76116-1702. 817/735-6895.

Sears Roebuck & Co.
2201 S Interstate 35 E, Denton TX 76205-8192. 940/566-8901.

Sears Roebuck & Co.
3111 Midwestern Pkwy, Wichita Falls TX 76308-2823. 940/689-7000.

Sears Roebuck & Co.
6001 W Waco Dr, Ste 100, Waco TX 76710-6301. 254/776-5224.

Sears Roebuck & Co.
7701 I-40 E, Ste 400, Amarillo TX 79118-6915. 806/354-7700.

Sears Roebuck & Co.
2400 S Stemmons Fwy, Lewisville TX 75067-8777. 972/315-4200.

Sears Roebuck & Co.
6002 Slide Rd, Lubbock TX 79414-4310. 806/796-4333.

Sears Roebuck & Co.
4310 Buffalo Gap Rd, Abilene TX 79606-2724. 915/691-7700.

Target
2620 N Josey Ln, Carrollton TX 75007-5516. 972/245-7526.

Target
850 Steger Towne Rd, Rockwall TX 75032-5658. 972/772-0894.

Target
1122 W Centerville Rd, Garland TX 75041-5903. 972/279-6711.

Target
3212 N Jupiter Rd, Garland TX 75044-6580. 972/530-1177.

Target
2325 S Stemmons Fwy, Lewisville TX 75067-2311. 972/315-0134.

Target
1720 W University Dr, McKinney TX 75069-3217. 972/542-0391.

Target
120 W Parker Rd, Plano TX 75075-2331. 972/424-9575.

Target
1625 N Town East Blvd, Mesquite TX 75150-4105. 972/681-9071.

Target
2417 N Haskell Ave, Dallas TX 75204-3707. 214/826-0331.

Target
940 Marsh Ln, Dallas TX 75220. 214/357-3980.

Target
4343 Gannon Ln, Dallas TX 75237-2901. 972/709-0031.

Target
13131 Montfort Dr, Dallas TX 75240-5112. 972/239-8161.

Target
2315 Richmond Rd, Texarkana TX 75503-2447. 903/838-6555.

Target
305 W Loop 281, Longview TX 75605-4426. 903/663-4921.

Target
1400 W Arbrook Blvd, Arlington TX 76015-4103. 817/465-5502.

Target
1101 Ira E. Woods Ave, Grapevine TX 76051-4020. 817/488-1800.

Target
1400 Precinct Line Rd, Hurst TX 76053-3828. 817/282-2533.

Target
2600 S Cherry Ln, Fort Worth TX 76116-3920. 817/244-9350.

Target
4317 Kemp Blvd, Wichita Falls
TX 76308-3717. 940/691-3310.

Target
3333 W Airport Fwy, Irving TX
75062-5921. 972/252-9888.

Target
2500 E Central Texas Expy,
Killeen TX 76543-5300.
254/526-8010.

Target
601 W State Highway 6, Waco
TX 76710-5575. 254/776-8790.

Target
8201 I-40 W, Amarillo TX
79121-1104. 806/358-4030.

Target
7302 University Ave, Lubbock
TX 79423-1423. 806/745-7579.

Target
3710 Ridgemont Dr, Abilene
TX 79606-2726. 915/695-4470.

Wal-Mart
6001 N Central Expy, Plano TX
75023-4702. 972/422-3000.

Wal-Mart
3178 Lavon Dr, Garland TX
75040-2900. 972/496-2711.

Wal-Mart
2140 N Jupiter Rd, Garland TX
75044-7702. 936/495-0550.

Wal-Mart
2615 W Pioneer Pkwy, Grand
Prairie TX 75051-3536.
972/660-4200.

Wal-Mart
801 W Main St, Lewisville TX
75067-3556. 972/436-9597.

Wal-Mart
1670 W University Dr,
McKinney TX 75069-3444.
972/542-2619.

Wal-Mart
1901 Preston Rd, Plano TX
75093-5102. 972/931-9846.

Wal-Mart
3500 W 7th Ave, Corsicana TX
75110-4869. 903/872-6691.

Wal-Mart
201 S Interstate 45, Ennis TX
75119. 972/875-9671.

Wal-Mart
200 US Highway 80 E,
Mesquite TX 75149-1656.
972/289-5478.

Wal-Mart
1900 W Moore Ave, Terrell TX
75160-2346. 972/563-7638.

Wal-Mart
13307 Midway Rd, Dallas TX
75244-5121. 972/980-2195.

Wal-Mart
2021 Highway 121 N, Bonham
TX 75418-2340. 903/583-9591.

Wal-Mart
2004 Live Oak St, Commerce
TX 75428-2437. 903/886-3108.

Wal-Mart
3855 Lamar Ave, Paris TX
75462-5210. 903/785-7168.

Wal-Mart
1750 S Broadway St, Sulphur
Springs TX 75482-4902.
903/439-3144.

Wal-Mart
4000 New Boston Rd,
Texarkana TX 75501-2819.
903/838-4007.

Wal-Mart
401 E North St 8, New Boston
TX 75570-3028. 903/628-5557.

Wal-Mart
1905 W Loop 281, Longview
TX 75604-2502. 903/297-1121.

Wal-Mart
2309 US Highway 79 S,
Henderson TX 75654-4448.
903/657-9528.

Wal-Mart
1811 US Highway 259 N,
Kilgore TX 75662-5529.
903/983-1494.

Wal-Mart
1701 E End Blvd N, Marshall TX
75670-0713. 903/938-0072.

Wal-Mart
6801 S Broadway Ave, Tyler TX
75703-4733. 903/581-4296.

Wal-Mart
1311 S Jackson St, Jacksonville
TX 75766-3050. 903/589-3434.

Wal-Mart
135 NE Loop 564, Mineola TX
75773-2913. 903/569-0180.

Wal-Mart
2223 S Loop 256, Palestine TX
75801-4701. 903/729-4441.

Wal-Mart
Loop 304 & US 287, Crockett
TX 75835. 936/544-5121.

Wal-Mart
4101 Highway 121, Bedford TX
76021-3033. 817/571-7928.

Wal-Mart
951 SW Wilshire Blvd,
Burleson TX 76028-5749.
817/447-2307.

Wal-Mart
1616 W Henderson St,
Cleburne TX 76031-3423.
817/645-1575.

Wal-Mart
930 N Walnut Creek Dr,
Mansfield TX 76063-1596.
817/473-1189.

Wal-Mart
3620 Highway 180 W, Mineral
Wells TX 76067-8236.
940/325-7808.

Wal-Mart
200 N Kimball Ave, Southlake
TX 76092-6676. 817/421-4770.

Wal-Mart
1401 S Cherry Ln, Fort Worth
TX 76108-3622. 817/246-6666.

Wal-Mart
6750 Mandy Ln, Fort Worth TX
76112-8619. 817/496-8700.

Wal-Mart
6360 Lake Worth Blvd, Fort
Worth TX 76135-3604.
817/237-0400.

Wal-Mart
1515 S Loop 288, Denton TX
76205-4729. 940/484-1717.

Wal-Mart
1000 Park Ave, Bowie TX
76230. 940/872-1166.

Wal-Mart
800 S US Hwy 81, Decatur TX
76234. 940/627-3028.

Wal-Mart
804 E Highway 82, Gainesville
TX 76240-2719. 940/668-6898.

Wal-Mart
3705 Kell Blvd, Wichita Falls
TX 76308-1604. 940/692-0771.

Wal-Mart
106 S Red River Expy,
Burkburnett TX 76354-3725.
940/569-2248.

Wal-Mart
303 N Northwest Loop 323,
Tyler TX 75702-8729. 903/597-2888.

Wal-Mart
2765 W Washington St,
Stephenville TX 76401-3782.
254/968-6002.

Wal-Mart
3732 W Walker St,
Breckenridge TX 76424-3917.
254/559-6570.

Wal-Mart
1547 4th St, Graham TX 76450-2920. 940/549-7714.

Wal-Mart
1923 N Wood St, Gilmer TX 75644-3577. 903/797-6501.

Wal-Mart
409 Plum St, Lampasas TX 76550-3361. 512/556-8217.

Wal-Mart
201 US Highway 59 Loop, Atlanta TX 75551-2011. 903/796-7916.

Wal-Mart
Hwy 79 W, Rockdale TX 76567. 512/446-5851.

Wal-Mart
401 Coke Ave, Hillsboro TX 76645-2671. 254/582-2523.

Wal-Mart
1007 E Milam St, Mexia TX 76667-2528. 254/562-3831.

Wal-Mart
15211 N 35th St, Waco TX 76707-1705. 254/867-8084.

Wal-Mart
4320 Franklin Ave, Waco TX 76710-6906. 254/751-0464.

Wal-Mart
12300 Lake June Rd, Mesquite TX 75180-1636. 972/286-8600.

Wal-Mart
1404 W Wilson St, Borger TX 79007-4420. 806/247-7257.

Wal-Mart
2309 N 3rd Ave, Canyon TX 79015-3104. 806/655-1175.

Wal-Mart
SW Dums Ave & 14th St, Dumas TX 79029. 806/935-9075.

Wal-Mart
800 S Cockrell Hill Rd, Duncanville TX 75137-2622. 972/709-1400.

Wal-Mart
2225 N Hobart St, Pampa TX 79065-3417. 806/665-0727.

Wal-Mart
1001 N Interstate 27, Plainview TX 79072-3904. 806/293-4278.

Wal-Mart
401 N East St 82, Sherman TX 75090-6007. 903/813-4825.

Wal-Mart
4610 Coulter Rd, Amarillo TX 79119-6403. 806/354-9300.

Wal-Mart
2211 Avenue F NW, Childress TX 79201-2221. 940/937-6166.

Wal-Mart
400 Clubview Dr, Levelland TX 79336-6306. 806/894-2993.

Wal-Mart
4515 College Ave, Snyder TX 79549-6012. 915/573-1967.

Wal-Mart
PO Box 871, Stamford TX 79553-0871. 915/773-2775.

Wal-Mart
465 N Judge Ely Blvd, Abilene TX 79601-5553. 915/677-5584.

Wal-Mart
1213 E Trinity Mills Rd, Carrollton TX 75006-1446. 972/466-2228.

DRUG STORES

Eckerd Drugs
5715 Interstate 20 W, Arlington TX 76017-1142. 817/483-4995.

GROCERY AND CONVENIENCE STORES

Albertson's
2150 N Josey Ln, Ste 400, Carrollton TX 75006-2993. 972/446-8226.

Albertson's
200 W Crawford St, Denison TX 75020-4604. 903/463-6076.

Albertson's
131 W Spring Creek Pkwy, Plano TX 75023-4609. 972/517-8104.

Albertson's
6921 Independence Pkwy, Plano TX 75023-1406. 972/618-1268.

Albertson's
6951 Preston Rd, Frisco TX 75034-5817. 972/377-3877.

Albertson's
822 E Centerville Rd, Garland TX 75041-3619. 972/271-3607.

Albertson's
5710 Broadway Blvd, Garland TX 75043-5818. 972/240-7339.

Albertson's
4126 S Carrier Pkwy, Grand Prairie TX 75052-3214. 972/642-2692.

Albertson's
535 W Airport Fwy, Irving TX 75062-6307. 972/257-3884.

Albertson's
7730 N MacArthur Blvd, Irving TX 75063-7514. 972/556-0026.

Albertson's
1087 W Main St, Lewisville TX 75067-3517. 972/420-1969.

Albertson's
3100 Custer Rd, Plano TX 75075-2060. 972/985-1456.

Albertson's
1341 W Campbell Rd, Richardson TX 75080-2815. 972/437-2896.

Albertson's
111 N Plano Rd, Richardson TX 75081-3827. 972/234-3337.

Albertson's
100 E Taylor St, Sherman TX 75092-2830. 903/868-9686.

Albertson's
1300 W Belt Line Rd, Desoto TX 75115-3628. 972/223-1998.

Albertson's
901 N Polk St, Desoto TX 75115-4013. 972/224-3544.

Albertson's
2828 Motley Dr, Mesquite TX 75150-3425. 972/270-2406.

Albertson's
2106 N Galloway Ave, Mesquite TX 75150-5730. 972/289-1647.

Albertson's
6464 E Mockingbird Ln, Dallas TX 75214-2406. 214/827-4870.

Albertson's
320 Casa Linda Plz, Dallas TX 75218-3414. 214/319-8220.

Albertson's
4008 S Polk St, Dallas TX 75224-4925. 214/371-1357.

Albertson's
4101 W Wheatland Rd, Dallas TX 75237-3312. 972/780-8991.

Albertson's
7007 Arapaho Rd, Dallas TX 75248-4158. 972/387-8996.

Albertson's
4625 Frankford Rd, Dallas TX 75287-7108. 972/732-6291.

Albertson's
2121 N Collins St, Arlington TX 76011-2878. 817/548-1414.

Albertson's
1050 W Arkansas Ln, Arlington TX 76013-6308. 817/277-8126.

Albertson's
301 SW Plaza Shopping Center, Arlington TX 76016. 817/478-4291.

Albertson's
9779 Forest Ln, Dallas TX 75243-5701. 972/234-0903.

Albertson's
5950 S Cooper St, Arlington TX 76017-4456. 817/557-0185.

Albertson's
2455 SE Green Oaks Blvd, Arlington TX 76018-1970. 817/419-9083.

Albertson's
1300 Airport Fwy, Bedford TX 76022-6700. 817/354-0622.

Albertson's
10020 Marsh Ln, Dallas TX 75229-6006. 214/350-6663.

Albertson's
833 NE Alsbury Blvd, Burleson TX 76028-2659. 817/447-9106.

Albertson's
4000 Glade Rd, Colleyville TX 76034-5901. 817/354-0505.

Albertson's
4801 Colleyville Blvd, Colleyville TX 76034-3936. 817/428-8011.

Albertson's
2100 W Northwest Hwy, Grapevine TX 76051-7808. 817/488-8037.

Albertson's
1495 Precinct Line Rd, Hurst TX 76053-3866. 817/284-5066.

Albertson's
989 N Walnut Creek Dr, Mansfield TX 76063-1503. 817/453-0442.

Albertson's
2201 W Southlake Blvd, Southlake TX 76092-6700. 817/421-0880.

Albertson's
1500 S Belt Line Rd, Mesquite TX 75149-5943. 972/285-0226.

Albertson's
4650 SW Loop 820, Fort Worth TX 76109-4429. 817/738-5293.

Albertson's
850 E Loop 820, Fort Worth TX 76112-1796. 817/451-0306.

Albertson's
3525 Sycamore School Rd, Fort Worth TX 76133-7805. 817/346-6497.

Albertson's
2165 Buckingham Rd, Richardson TX 75081-5477. 972/680-1711.

Albertson's
4400 Western Center Blvd, Fort Worth TX 76137-2044. 817/232-2180.

Albertson's
2720 Southwest Pkwy, Wichita Falls TX 76308-3704. 940/691-0420.

Albertson's
920 Steger Towne Rd, Rockwall TX 75032-5659. 972/722-1189.

Brookshire Brothers
3500 Hwy 66, Rowlett TX 75088. 972/475-0466.

Brookshire Brothers
PO Box 938, Mabank TX 75147-0938. 903/887-0126.

Brookshire Brothers
900 N Highway 175, Seagoville TX 75159-1776. 972/287-4753.

Brookshire Brothers
2505 Judson Rd, Longview TX 75605-4643. 903/758-3581.

Brookshire Brothers
100 Rice Rd, Tyler TX 75703-3761. 903/561-6247.

Brookshire Brothers
20100 State Highway 155 S, Flint TX 75762-9569. 903/825-7302.

Brookshire Brothers
210 E Cherokee St, Jacksonville TX 75766-4810. 903/586-9333.

Brookshire Brothers
PO Box 880, Lindale TX 75771-0880. 903/882-3167.

Brookshire Brothers
1003 N Main St, Rusk TX 75785-1027. 903/683-4212.

Brookshire Brothers
109 N Greenville Ave, Allen TX 75002-2235. 972/727-9106.

Brookshire Brothers
501 W Main St, Van TX 75790-2891. 903/963-8334.

Carnival Stores
1706 W Irving Blvd, Irving TX 75061-7137. 972/254-4220.

HEB Food Store
201 S 15th St, Corsicana TX 75110-5138. 903/874-4778.

HEB Food Store
600 W Henderson St, Cleburne TX 76031-4830. 817/641-6203.

HEB Food Store
2150 W Washington St, Stephenville TX 76401-3928. 254/965-7063.

HEB Food Store
3002 S 31st St, Temple TX 76502-1802. 254/778-4820.

HEB Food Store
525 N Main St, Belton TX 76513-3071. 254/939-0856.

HEB Food Store
901 S Fort Hood St, Killeen TX 76541-7434. 254/526-9674.

HEB Food Store
2300 E Waco Dr, Waco TX 76705-3206. 254/799-0253.

HEB Food Store
1345 Barrow St, Abilene TX 79605-5171. 915/690-5000.

IGA Foodliner
1202 S Fm 51, Decatur TX 76234-2412. 940/627-6438.

Kroger
3044 Old Denton Rd, Carrollton TX 75007-5016. 972/242-2787.

Kroger
2515 E Rosemeade Pkwy, Carrollton TX 75007-2036. 972/306-6601.

Kroger
7100 Independence Pkwy, Plano TX 75025-5703. 972/491-2594.

Kroger
532 W Interstate 30, Garland TX 75043-5700. 972/226-2681.

Kroger
515 S MacArthur Blvd, Irving TX 75060-2730. 972/259-8023.

Kroger
405 Interstate 30, Rockwall TX 75087-5406. 972/771-8021.

Kroger
1820 N Loy Lake Rd, Sherman TX 75090-0203. 903/893-6788.

Kroger
2400 Preston Rd, Plano TX 75093-2321. 972/867-8808.

Kroger
200 W Camp Wisdom Rd, Duncanville TX 75116-3329. 972/298-9962.

Kroger
525 N Galloway Ave, Mesquite TX 75149-3405. 972/288-5477.

Kroger
11925 Elam Rd, Mesquite TX 75180-2820. 972/557-1272.

Kroger
1610 S Westmoreland Rd, Dallas TX 75211-5767. 214/330-0366.

Kroger
1515 S Buckner Blvd, Dallas TX 75217-1706. 214/398-6631.

Kroger
752 Wynnewood Village, Dallas TX 75224-1831. 214/941-8311.

Kroger
2524 W Ledbetter Dr, Dallas TX 75233-4018. 214/333-3542.

Kroger
1310 Clarksville St, Paris TX 75460-6033. 903/785-5591.

Kroger
701 W Marshall Ave, Longview TX 75601-6218. 903/758-1726.

Kroger
325 E Spring St, Palestine TX 75801-2941. 903/729-5108.

Kroger
301 S Bowen Rd, Arlington TX 76013-1255. 817/277-5289.

Kroger
2580 E Arkansas Ln, Arlington TX 76014-1706. 817/861-2255.

Kroger
5701 W Pleasant Ridge Rd, Arlington TX 76016-4424. 817/483-0666.

Kroger
5330 S Cooper St, Arlington TX 76017-5938. 817/472-9491.

Kroger
1617 W Henderson St, Cleburne TX 76031-3422. 817/641-0771.

Kroger
235 E Fm 1382, Cedar Hill TX 75104-2147. 972/291-7333.

Kroger
1420 E Highway 377, Granbury TX 76048-2646. 817/573-8887.

Kroger
1740 Highway 157 N, Mansfield TX 76063-3921. 817/473-0264.

Kroger
102 College Park Dr, Weatherford TX 76086-6212. 817/599-9405.

Kroger
2515 E Rosemeade Pkwy, Carrollton TX 75007-2036. 972/306-7005.

Kroger
6246 Rufe Snow Dr, Fort Worth TX 76148-3315. 817/281-9433.

Minyard
4906 N Jupiter Rd, Garland TX 75044-5464. 972/530-0198.

Minyard
2200 W Shady Grove Rd, Irving TX 75060-5056. 972/790-5020.

Minyard
1280 W Main St, Lewisville TX 75067-3420. 972/221-5585.

Minyard
2240 Justin Rd, Lewisville TX 75077-7165. 972/317-5662.

Minyard
112 W Belt Line Rd, Cedar Hill TX 75104-2011. 972/291-0191.

Minyard
125 Hwy 175 & Hl, Seagoville TX 75159. 972/287-5488.

Minyard
1800 N Henderson Ave, Dallas TX 75206-7525. 214/826-8470.

Minyard
2128 Fort Worth Ave, Dallas TX 75211-1811. 214/941-0400.

Minyard
2118 Abrams Rd, Dallas TX 75214-3918. 214/823-6770.

Minyard
1212 N Beach St, Fort Worth TX 76111-6027. 817/429-9332.

Minyard
2610 Pioneer St, Fort Worth TX 76119-4631. 817/265-4863.

Sack N Save
106 Walnut Creek Shopping, Garland TX 75042. 972/276-7189.

Sack N Save
1220 N Town East Blvd, Mesquite TX 75150-7605. 972/279-5552.

Sack N Save
3563 Alton Rd, Fort Worth TX 76109-2834. 817/429-2571.

Super One
3265 Broadway Blvd, Garland TX 75043-1530. 972/271-2225.

Super One
2133 N Belt Line Rd, Mesquite TX 75150-5818. 972/289-8979.

Super One
2610 Richmond Road, Texarkana TX 75503-2327. 903/832-2258.

Super One
3000 W Northwest Loop 323, Tyler TX 75702-1336. 903/595-4693.

Thriftway
PO Box 700, Plainview TX 79073-0700. 806/293-8579.

Tom Thumb
2810 E Trinity Mills Rd, Carrollton TX 75006-2545. 972/416-1605.

Tom Thumb
4112 N Josey Ln, Carrollton TX 75007-1509. 972/394-4127.

Tom Thumb
820 South MacArthur, Coppell TX 75019. 972/393-0411.

Tom Thumb
3945 Legacy Dr, Plano TX 75023-8325. 972/491-2200.

Tom Thumb
745 Cross Timbers Rd, Flower Mound TX 75028-1365. 972/539-6828.

Tom Thumb
4010 N MacArthur Blvd, Irving TX 75038-6413. 972/717-9727.

Tom Thumb
1445 Beckingham, Garland TX 75042. 972/495-5870.

Tom Thumb
3535 N Belt Line Rd, Irving TX 75062-7804. 972/257-3420.

Tom Thumb
3001 Hardin Blvd, McKinney TX 75070-7736. 972/547-7100.

Tom Thumb
2200 14th St, Plano TX 75074-6454. 972/423-4105.

Tom Thumb
1380 W Campbell Rd, Richardson TX 75080-2814. 972/680-6010.

Tom Thumb
4836 W Park Blvd, Plano TX 75093-2330. 972/964-8190.

Tom Thumb
633 W Wheatland Rd, Duncanville TX 75116-4517. 972/780-0792.

Tom Thumb
6333 E Mockingbird Ln, Dallas TX 75214-2692. 214/824-1265.

Tom Thumb
6770 Abrams Rd, Dallas TX 75231-7115. 214/340-1119.

Tom Thumb
10455 N Central Expy, Dallas TX 75231-2213. 214/369-9694.

Tom Thumb
8698 Skillman St, Dallas TX 75243-8265. 214/340-1266.

Tom Thumb
925 Northwest Hwy, Garland TX 75041-5827. 972/271-0582.

Tom Thumb
2611 W Park Row Dr, Arlington TX 76013-2257. 817/792-2047.

Tom Thumb
5425 S Cooper St, Arlington TX 76017-6149. 817/419-2460.

Tom Thumb
302 S Park Blvd, Grapevine TX 76051-7835. 817/481-5669.

Tom Thumb
600 Grapevine Hwy, Hurst TX 76054-2758. 817/498-8480.

Tom Thumb
6377 Camp Bowie Blvd, Fort Worth TX 76116-5423. 817/654-0256.

Tom Thumb
206 N Grand Ave, Gainesville TX 76240-4320. 940/665-3801.

United Supermarket
311 S Avenue D, Burkburnett TX 76354-3541. 940/569-2541.

United Supermarket
1414 W Wilson St, Borger TX 79007-4420. 806/273-3185.

United Supermarket
3501 Olton Rd, Plainview TX 79072-6605. 806/293-4402.

United Supermarket
5807 W 45th Ave, Ste 100, Amarillo TX 79109-5257. 806/353-9700.

United Supermarket
1401 Tahoka Rd, Brownfield TX 79316-4828. 806/637-2321.

United Supermarket
106 N University Ave, Lubbock TX 79415-2812. 806/762-5656.

United Supermarket
2703 82nd St, Lubbock TX 79423-1429. 806/745-4443.

Whole Foods Market Southwest
2201 Preston Rd, Plano TX 75093-2307. 972/612-6729.

Winn-Dixie
1423 N Belt Line Rd, Irving TX 75061-1517. 972/986-4034.

Winn-Dixie
1450 W Pleasant Run Rd, Lancaster TX 75146-1392. 972/227-8584.

Winn-Dixie
1050 N Westmoreland Rd, Dallas TX 75211-2400. 214/339-7294.

Winn-Dixie
800 N Kilgore St, Kilgore TX 75662-5836. 903/984-6393.

Winn-Dixie
620 E End Blvd S, Marshall TX 75670-5614. 903/935-1721.

Winn-Dixie
219 S Palestine St, Athens TX 75751-2507. 903/675-5311.

Winn-Dixie
5434 I20 W, Aledo TX 76008. 817/441-5980.

Winn-Dixie
1300 E Pioneer Pkwy, Arlington TX 76010-6411. 817/548-1150.

Winn-Dixie
1701 W Randol Mill Rd, Arlington TX 76012-3037. 817/460-8551.

Winn-Dixie
5781 SW Green Oaks Blvd, Arlington TX 76017-1202. 817/478-3531.

Winn-Dixie
511 N Stewart St, Azle TX 76020-3237. 817/444-1147.

Winn-Dixie
648 SW Wilshire Blvd, Burleson TX 76028-5851. 817/295-6551.

Winn-Dixie
320 E Main St, Crowley TX 76036-2611. 817/297-3854.

Winn-Dixie
305 W Euless Blvd, Euless TX 76040-4578. 817/283-8561.

Winn-Dixie
143 E Harwood Rd, Hurst TX 76054-3005. 817/281-1683.

Winn-Dixie
1101 N Walnut Creek Dr, Mansfield TX 76063-2501. 817/473-2797.

Winn-Dixie
194 Garrett Morris Pkw, Mineral Wells TX 76067-9038. 940/328-1083.

Winn-Dixie
500 E Highway 199, Springtown TX 76082-2744. 817/220-1177.

Winn-Dixie
3320 Mansfield Hwy, Fort Worth TX 76119-6026. 817/536-9002.

Winn-Dixie
1824 S Jackson St, Jacksonville TX 75766-5800. 903/586-6135.

Winn-Dixie
6601 Watauga Rd, Fort Worth TX 76148-3330. 817/485-3660.

Winn-Dixie
10325 Lake June Rd, Dallas TX 75217-5312. 972/289-6189.

Winn-Dixie
3164 5th St, Wichita Falls TX 76301-1800. 940/723-2313.

Winn-Dixie
714 S Fort Hood St, Killeen TX 76541-7431. 254/526-3434.

Winn-Dixie
501 E Broadway St, Sweetwater TX 79556-4623. 915/235-8426.

Winn-Dixie
2525 W I20, Grand Prairie TX 75052. 972/988-1335.

Winn-Dixie
3801 Jacksboro Hwy, Wichita Falls TX 76302-2107. 940/761-1117.

MISC. FOOD STORES

Whole Foods Market Southwest
60 Dal Rich Village, Richardson TX 75080-5714. 972/699-8075.

Whole Foods Market Southwest
2218 Lower Greenville Ave, Dallas TX 75206. 214/824-1744.

MISC. GENERAL MERCHANDISE STORES

Sam's Club
4150 Belt Line Rd, Addison TX 75001-4354. 972/934-9274.

Sam's Club
751 W Main St, Lewisville TX 75067-3513. 972/436-8616.

Sam's Club
5555 S Buckner Blvd, Dallas TX 75228-6171. 214/320-2824.

Sam's Club
8282 Park Ln, Dallas TX 75231-6023. 214/373-3058.

Sam's Club
2900 W Wheatland Road, Dallas TX 75237-3535. 972/283-1704.

Sam's Club
12000 McCree Rd, Dallas TX
75238-3275. 214/342-9810.

Sam's Club
3310 N 4th St, Longview TX
75605-7954. 903/663-5588.

Sam's Club
4915 S Cooper St, Arlington TX
76017-5930. 817/557-2011.

Sam's Club
7500 Baker Boulevard, Fort
Worth TX 76118-5902.
817/589-1357.

Sam's Club
3801 Kell Blvd, Wichita Falls
TX 76308-1605. 940/691-0463.

Sam's Club
3333 S Highway 75, Sherman
TX 75090-9377. 903/813-0444.

Sam's Club
2301 East Waco Drive,
Bellmead TX 76705-3207.
254/799-2408.

Sam's Club
2201 Ross Osage Dr, Amarillo
TX 79102. 806/374-6651.

Sam's Club
4304 W Loop 289, Lubbock TX
79407-3730. 806/793-7184.

Sam's Club
4150 Belt Line Rd, Addison TX
75001-4354. 972/934-9243.

Sam's Club
5301 S 1st St, Abilene TX
79605-1336. 915/691-5480.

RETAIL BAKERIES

Mrs. Baird's Bakery
PO Box 937, Fort Worth TX
76101-0937. 817/568-3650.

SPORTING GOODS STORES

Academy Sport and Outdoors
110 W Arbrook Blvd, Arlington
TX 76014-3101. 817/472-9700.

Garland Tennis Center
PO Box 472251, Garland TX
75047-2251. 972/205-2778.

For more information on career opportunities in retail:

Associations

INTERNATIONAL COUNCIL OF SHOPPING CENTERS
665 Fifth Avenue, New York NY 10022. 212/421-8181. World Wide Web address: http://www.icsc.org. Offers conventions, research, education, a variety of publications, and awards programs.

NATIONAL ASSOCIATION OF RESALE & THRIFT SHOPS
P.O. Box 80707, St. Claire Shores MI 48080-0707. Toll-free phone: 800/544-0751. Fax: 810/294-6776. E-mail address: Webmaster@NARTS.org.

NATIONAL AUTOMOTIVE DEALERS ASSOCIATION
8400 Westpark Drive, McLean VA 22102. 703/821-7000. World Wide Web address: http://www.nada.com.

NATIONAL INDEPENDENT AUTOMOTIVE DEALERS ASSOCIATION
2521 Brown Boulevard, Arlington TX 76006. 817/640-3838. World Wide Web address: http://www.niada.com.

NATIONAL RETAIL FEDERATION
325 Seventh Street NW, Suite 1000, Washington DC 20004. 202/783-7971. World Wide Web address: http://www.nrf.com. Provides information services, industry outlooks, and a variety of educational opportunities and publications.

Directories

AUTOMOTIVE NEWS MARKET DATA BOOK
Crain Communications, 1400 Woodbridge Avenue, Detroit MI 48207-3187. 313/446-6000.

Online Services

THE INTERNET FASHION EXCHANGE
World Wide Web address: http://www.fashionexch.com. An excellent site for those industry professionals interested in apparel and retail. The extensive search engine allows you to search by job title, location, salary, product line, industry, and whether you want a permanent, temporary, or freelance position. The Internet Fashion Exchange also offers career services such as recruiting, and outplacement firms that place fashion and retail professionals.

RETAIL JOBNET
World Wide Web address: http://www.retailjobnet.com. This site is geared toward recruiting professionals and jobseekers in the retail industry.

STONE, CLAY, GLASS, AND CONCRETE PRODUCTS

You can expect to find the following types of companies in this chapter:
Cement, Tile, Sand, and Gravel • Crushed and Broken Stone
Glass and Glass Products • Mineral Products

Some helpful information: Bricklayers, stone masons, and tilesetters earn approximately $20,000 - $25,000 annually. Glaziers earn around $25,000 - $30,000.

AMERICAN FLAT GLASS DISTRIBUTORS, INC. (AFGD)
1201 Highway 67 East, Alvarado TX 76009. 817/477-1144. **Toll-free phone:** 800/777-5171. **Fax:** 817/783-7123. **Contact:** Mr. Carl Frey, Branch Manager. **World Wide Web address:** http://www.afgd.com. **Description:** Specializes in architectural insulated glass units and custom tempering. AFGD manufactures a complete line of insulated glass units for commercial and residential applications. The product line includes clear, tint, and reflective glass; wire glass; and equipment for the handling, storage, and transportation of glass. There are more than 20 AFGD locations throughout the United States. **Common positions include:** Blue-Collar Worker Supervisor; Branch Manager; Clerical Supervisor; Credit Manager; Customer Service Representative; Industrial Engineer; Industrial Production Manager; Management Trainee; Manufacturer's/Wholesaler's Sales Rep.; Mechanical Engineer; Metallurgical Engineer; Operations/Production Manager; Production Manager. **Educational backgrounds include:** Business Administration; Engineering; Finance; Marketing; Sales. **Benefits:** 401(k); Disability Coverage; Life Insurance; Medical Insurance; Profit Sharing; Savings Plan; Tuition Assistance. **Corporate headquarters location:** Atlanta GA. **Subsidiaries include:** AFGD Canada. **Parent company:** AFG Industries, Inc. **Listed on:** Privately held.

AMERICAN FLAT GLASS DISTRIBUTORS, INC. (AFGD)
2148 Royal Lane, Dallas TX 75229. 972/241-0943. **Fax:** 972/241-7803. **Contact:** Mr. Allan Vasquez, Branch Manager. **World Wide Web address:** http://www.afgd.com. **Description:** Specializes in architectural insulated glass units and custom tempering. AFGD manufactures a complete line of insulated glass units for commercial and residential applications. The product line includes clear, tint, and reflective glass; wire glass; and equipment for the handling, storage, and transportation of glass. There are more than 20 AFGD locations throughout the United States. **Common positions include:** Blue-Collar Worker Supervisor; Branch Manager; Clerical Supervisor; Credit Manager; Customer Service Representative; Industrial Engineer; Industrial Production Manager; Management Trainee; Manufacturer's/Wholesaler's Sales Rep.; Mechanical Engineer; Metallurgical Engineer; Operations/Production Manager; Production Manager. **Educational backgrounds include:** Business Administration; Engineering; Finance; Marketing; Sales. **Benefits:** 401(k); Disability Coverage; Life Insurance; Medical Insurance; Profit Sharing; Savings Plan; Tuition Assistance. **Corporate headquarters location:** Atlanta GA. **Subsidiaries include:** AFGD Canada. **Parent company:** AFG Industries, Inc. **Listed on:** Privately held.

DAL-TILE INTERNATIONAL
P.O. Box 170130, Dallas TX 75217. 214/398-1411. **Fax:** 214/309-4192. **Contact:** Steve Smith, Director of Human Resources. **World Wide Web address:** http://www.daltile.com. **Description:** One of the world's largest manufacturers of ceramic tile. Founded in 1947. **Common positions include:** Accountant/Auditor; Credit Manager; Systems Analyst. **Educational backgrounds include:** Accounting; Business Administration; Computer Science; Finance; Marketing. **Benefits:** 401(k); Employee Discounts; Life Insurance; Medical Insurance; Profit Sharing. **Corporate headquarters location:** This Location. **Listed on:** New York Stock Exchange. **Number of employees at this location:** 1,600. **Number of employees worldwide:** 7,700.

ELK CORPORATION
202 Cedar Road, Ennis TX 75119. 972/875-9611. **Fax:** 972/872-2392. **Contact:** Human Resources. **World Wide Web address:** http://www.elkcorp.com. **Description:** Manufactures residential roofing products and fiberglass mats. Founded in 1955. **Common positions include:** Accountant/Auditor; Blue-Collar Worker Supervisor; Chemical Engineer; Clerical Supervisor; Designer; Electrical/Electronics Engineer; Human Resources Manager; Manufacturer's/Wholesaler's Sales Rep.; Mechanical Engineer. **Educational backgrounds include:** Accounting;

Engineering; Marketing. **Benefits:** 401(k); Disability Coverage; Life Insurance; Medical Insurance; Profit Sharing; Savings Plan; Tuition Assistance. **Corporate headquarters location:** Dallas TX. **Other U.S. locations:** Tuscaloosa AL; Shafter CA. **Parent company:** Elcor Corporation. **Listed on:** New York Stock Exchange.

GUARDIAN INDUSTRIES CORPORATION
3801 South Highway 287, Corsicana TX 75110. 903/872-4871. **Fax:** 903/872-4263. **Contact:** Employee Relations Manager. **World Wide Web address:** http://www.guardian.com. **Description:** Manufactures fabricated and float glass primarily for the construction and automotive industries. **Common positions include:** Accountant/Auditor; Blue-Collar Worker Supervisor; Ceramics Engineer; Chemical Engineer; Computer Programmer; Credit Manager; Electrical/Electronics Engineer; Electrician; Human Resources Manager; Industrial Production Manager; Management Trainee; Mechanical Engineer; Operations/Production Manager; Purchasing Agent/Manager; Systems Analyst. **Educational backgrounds include:** Accounting; Business Administration; Chemistry; Engineering. **Benefits:** 401(k); Dental Insurance; Disability Coverage; Employee Discounts; Life Insurance; Medical Insurance; Pension Plan; Profit Sharing; Savings Plan; Tuition Assistance. **Corporate headquarters location:** Auburn Hills MI. **Other U.S. locations:** Nationwide. **Number of employees at this location:** 330. **Number of employees nationwide:** 10,000.

HANSON CONCRETE PRODUCTS, INC.
P.O. Box 569470, Dallas TX 75356-9470. 972/262-1571. **Contact:** Personnel Manager. **Description:** Produces concrete pressure pipe and pipe fittings.

LONE STAR INDUSTRIES
1801 Lone Star Drive, Dallas TX 75212. 972/386-0400. **Contact:** Personnel Department. **Description:** Manufactures and distributes cement, ready-mix concrete, and construction products.

MUR-TEX FIBERGLASS
P.O. Box 31240, Amarillo TX 79120. 806/373-7418. **Contact:** Human Resources. **Description:** Manufactures fiberglass tanks for industrial usage. **Corporate headquarters location:** This Location.

OLDCASTLE GLASS GROUP
2805 Dallas Parkway, Suite 450, Plano TX 75093. 972/747-3800. **Fax:** 972/747-3838. **Contact:** Human Resources Manager. **Description:** A leading manufacturer of glass products. The company's product line includes laminated glass, insulating glass units, heat-treated glass, silk-screened and decorative glass, and structural glass wall systems. **Corporate headquarters location:** This Location. **Parent company:** CRH plc

OWENS-CORNING FIBERGLAS CORPORATION
P.O. Box 8000, Amarillo TX 79114-8000. 806/622-1582. **Physical address:** 1701 Hollywood Road, Amarillo TX. **Contact:** Human Resources. **World Wide Web address:** http://www.owenscorning.com. **Description:** Manufactures and sells thermal and acoustical insulation products including insulation for appliances, glass fiber roofing shingles, roof insulation, and industrial asphalt. Other products include windows, glass fiber textile yarns, wet process chopped strands and specialty mats, and polyester resins. **Subsidiaries include:** Barbcorp, Inc.; Dansk-Svensk Glasfiber AS; Eric Co.; European Owens-Corning Fiberglas SA; IPM Inc.; Kitsons Insulations Products Ltd.; Owens-Corning AS; Owens-Corning Building Products; Owens-Corning FSC, Inc.; Owens-Corning Finance.

STRUCTURAL OF TEXAS INC.
P.O. Box 560568, Dallas TX 75356-0568. 214/638-8933. **Contact:** Personnel Department. **Description:** Manufactures and distributes concrete products.

TXI, INC.
1341 West Mockingbird Lane, Dallas TX 75247-6913. 972/647-6700. **Contact:** Human Resources. **World Wide Web address:** http://www.txi.com. **Description:** A leading supplier of cement and structural steel, primarily to the construction industry. **Common positions include:** Accountant/Auditor; Civil Engineer; Environmental Engineer; Financial Analyst; Human Resources Manager; Mining Engineer; Systems Analyst. **Educational backgrounds include:** Accounting; Business Administration; Engineering; Finance; Marketing. **Benefits:** 401(k); Dental Insurance; Disability Coverage; Life Insurance; Medical Insurance; Tuition Assistance. **Special programs:** Internships. **Corporate headquarters location:** This Location. **Subsidiaries include:**

Riverside Cement Company. **Listed on:** New York Stock Exchange. **Stock exchange symbol:** TXI. **Number of employees at this location:** 380. **Number of employees nationwide:** 1,800.

VETROTEX CERTAINTEED CORPORATION
4515 Allendale Road, Wichita Falls TX 76310. 940/691-0020. **Contact:** Human Resources. **Description:** Manufactures fiberglass products.

Note: Because addresses and telephone numbers of smaller companies can change rapidly, we recommend you call each company to verify the information below before inquiring about job opportunities. Mass mailings are not recommended.

Additional small employers:

CEMENT

CSA Concrete Inc.
5430 Redfield St, Dallas TX 75235-7308. 214/634-2990.

Lone Star Industries Inc.
PO Box 1639, Sweetwater TX 79556-1639. 915/288-4221.

North Texas Cement Company
PO Box 520, Midlothian TX 76065-0500. 972/723-2301.

EARTH AND MINERALS

Poco Graphite Inc.
1601 S State St, Decatur TX 76234-2742. 940/627-2121.

GLASS AND GLASS PRODUCTS

Ball-Foster Glass Container
2400 N Interstate Highway, Waxahachie TX 75165-5240. 972/937-3430.

D&S Glass Fabricators
PO Box 59209, Dallas TX 75229-1209. 972/484-8892.

Owens-Brockway Glass Container
5200 Beverly Dr, Waco TX 76711-1033. 254/754-9502.

MINERAL WOOL

American Rockwool Inc.
PO Box C, Nolanville TX 76559-0483. 254/698-2233.

Owens-Corning Fiberglas Corp.
PO Box 837, Waxahachie TX 75168-0837. 972/937-1340.

TILE

Acme Brick
Rural Route 1, Box AB1, Millsap TX 76066-9801. 940/682-4211.

Acme Brick
PO Box 425, Fort Worth TX 76101-0425. 817/332-4101.

Acme Brick
220 Daniels St, Denton TX 76205-7601. 940/387-5804.

Henderson Brick Company
PO Box 2110, Henderson TX 75653-2110. 903/657-3505.

Huntington Tile
PO Box 7292, Fort Worth TX 76111-0292. 817/838-2323.

Interceramic
PO Box 472479, Garland TX 75047-2479. 214/503-5500.

Monarch Ceramic Tile
359 Clay Rd, Mesquite TX 75182-9710. 972/226-0110.

Texas Clay Industries
PO Box 469, Malakoff TX 75148-0469. 903/489-1331.

For more information on career opportunities in stone, clay, glass, and concrete products:

Associations

NATIONAL GLASS ASSOCIATION
8200 Greensboro Drive, Suite 302, McLean VA 22102. 703/442-4890. World Wide Web address: http://www.glass.org.

Magazines

GLASS MAGAZINE
National Glass Association, 8200 Greensboro Drive, Suite 302, McLean VA 22102. 703/442-4890. World Wide Web address: http://www.glass.org.

ROCK PRODUCTS
PRIMEDIA Intertec, 29 North Wacker Drive, Chicago IL 60606. 312/726-2805.

TRANSPORTATION/TRAVEL

You can expect to find the following types of companies in this chapter:
Air, Railroad, and Water Transportation Services • Courier Services • Local and Interurban Passenger Transit • Ship Building and Repair • Transportation Equipment Travel Agencies • Trucking • Warehousing and Storage

Some helpful information: Commercial truckers earn an average of $20,000 - $30,000 per year. Water transportation workers earn about $25,000 - $30,000. Travel agents with 10 or more years of experience earn around $30,000 - $35,000 annually.

AMR CORPORATION
AMERICAN AIRLINES
P.O. Box 619616, Mail Drop 5106, DFW Airport TX 75261-9616. 817/963-1234. **Contact:** Human Resources Department. **World Wide Web address:** http://www.americanair.com. **Description:** An airline holding company. AMR Corporation's fleet consists of approximately 665 aircraft. AMR Corporation's operations fall within three major lines of business: the Air Transportation Group, the SABRE Group, and the AMR Management Services Group. The Air Transportation Group consists primarily of American Airlines, Inc.'s Passenger and Cargo Division and AMR Eagle, Inc., a subsidiary of AMR Corporation. **NOTE:** For positions other than flight attendants or pilots, request an application from American Airlines, Inc., P.O. Box 619040, Mail Drop 4146, DFW Airport TX 75261-9040. Send a self-addressed, 9-by-12 inch envelope with postage. **Common positions include:** Accountant/Auditor; Customer Service Representative; Electrical/Electronics Engineer; Marketing Specialist; Sales Representative. **Educational backgrounds include:** Aviation. **Corporate headquarters location:** This Location. **Subsidiaries include:** American Airlines provides service to 106 domestic cities and 66 cities worldwide. Domestic hubs are located in Dallas-Fort Worth, Chicago, Nashville, San Juan, Raleigh-Durham, and Miami. SABRE Group conducts computer reservation operations and provides electronic data processing, information management, and computer services to clients in several industries. American Eagle is an airline that serves 170 cities in the U.S., Bahamas, and Caribbean. AMR Management Services, which leases aircraft, offers financial services, conducts training operations, and provides ground and cabin services. **Listed on:** New York Stock Exchange. **Number of employees at this location:** 27,000. **Number of employees nationwide:** 116,300.

ABILENE AERO INC.
2850 Airport Boulevard, Abilene TX 79602. 915/677-2601. **Fax:** 915/671-8018. **Contact:** Mr. Joe Crawford, General Manager. **World Wide Web address:** http://www.abileneaero.com. **Description:** Operates a small airport offering flight instruction, charter and pilot service, aircraft fueling, parts, and maintenance. Abilene Aero Inc. is a fixed-base operator. Founded in 1968. **Common positions include:** Accountant; Aircraft Mechanic/Engine Specialist; Customer Service Representative; General Manager; Sales Manager; Secretary. **Benefits:** 401(k); Medical Insurance; Profit Sharing. **Corporate headquarters location:** This Location. **Subsidiaries include:** Lubbock Aero, Lubbock TX. **Annual sales/revenues:** $5 - $10 million. **Number of employees at this location:** 35.

ALFORD REFRIGERATED WAREHOUSES
318 Cadiz Street, Dallas TX 75207. 214/426-5151. **Fax:** 214/426-0245. **Contact:** Personnel. **Description:** A warehousing company engaged in the storage of frozen, cold, and dry food bought in grocery stores.

AMERICAN TRANSFER AND STORAGE
dba MAYFLOWER TRANSIT, INC.
4204 Lindberg Drive, Addison TX 75001. 972/490-4444. **Fax:** 972/233-3921. **Contact:** Human Resources. **World Wide Web address:** http://www.americantransfer.com. **Description:** Offers a full-range of moving and storage services for both commercial and individual customers.

ASSOCIATED GLOBAL SYSTEMS
755 Port America Place, Suite 345, Grapevine TX 76051. 817/481-8302. **Contact:** Human Resources. **World Wide Web address:** http://www.agsystems.com. **Description:** An air transportation company providing domestic, international, and same day delivery services.

Transportation/Travel/263

BALDWIN DISTRIBUTION SERVICES
7702 Broadway, Amarillo TX 79108. 806/383-7650. **Contact:** Human Resources. **World Wide Web address:** http://www.baldwin-dist.com. **Description:** Provides long-haul trucking services. Baldwin Distribution Services operates in 48 U.S. states, Canada, and Mexico. **Common positions include:** Truck Driver. **Benefits:** Disability Coverage; Life Insurance; Medical Insurance; Savings Plan.

BENCHMARK FOODS
2901 South Cravens Road, Fort Worth TX 76119-1857. 817/451-5599. **Contact:** Human Resources. **Description:** Transports food to penitentiaries.

BILBO TRANSPORTS INC.
2722 Singleton Boulevard, Dallas TX 75212. 214/637-1910. **Contact:** Human Resources. **Description:** A trucking company.

BOWDEN TRAVEL SERVICE
CLEBURNE TRAVEL
410 West Chambers, Cleburne TX 76031. 817/641-3477. **Contact:** Human Resources. **Description:** A travel agency. **Company slogan:** Let us take the ravel out of your travel. **Common positions include:** Sales Executive; Transportation/Traffic Specialist. **Annual sales/revenues:** Less than $5 million.

BUDGET RENT A CAR
P.O. Box 111520, Carrollton TX 75011. 972/404-7600. **Physical address:** 3350 Boyington Drive, Carrollton TX 75006. **Contact:** Human Resources. **World Wide Web address:** http://www.budgetrentacar.com. **Description:** A car and truck rental service.

BURLINGTON NORTHERN AND SANTA FE RAILWAY COMPANY
2650 Lou Menk Drive, Fort Worth TX 76131. 817/333-2000. **Contact:** Human Resources. **World Wide Web address:** http://www.bnsf.com. **Description:** A railroad transportation company operating on more than 33,000 miles of track. The company is one of the largest haulers of grain and low-sulfur coal in North America. **Corporate headquarters location:** This Location. **Listed on:** New York Stock Exchange. **Annual sales/revenues:** More than $100 million.

CENTRAL FREIGHT LINES, INC.
P.O. Box 540277, Dallas TX 75354-0277. 972/579-4111. **Contact:** Human Resources. **World Wide Web address:** http://www.centralfreight.com. **Description:** One of the largest regional motor carriers in the United States operating through 77 terminals.

CITY MACHINE & WELDING INC.
9701 Interchange 552, Amarillo TX 79124-2333. 806/358-7293. **Contact:** Personnel. **World Wide Web address:** http://www.cmwelding.com. **Description:** Manufactures transport trailers and performs welding services.

COMDATA CORPORATION
6000 Western Place, Suite 900, Fort Worth TX 76107. 817/731-8721. **Contact:** Human Resources. **World Wide Web address:** http://www.comdata.com. **Description:** Provides transaction processing and information services to the transportation, gaming, and retail industries. Comdata links more than 20,000 telecommunication ports of entry, processing over 100 million transactions per year. Services for the transportation industry increase productivity and control for trucking companies and truckstops. Products encompass fuel purchase, cash advance, driver settlement, money transfer, load matching, route planning, legalization permitting, fuel tax reporting, and management reporting. Comdata's consumer services include money transfer for emergencies or leisure activities. The company helps gaming organizations adapt to new technologies such as smart cards, linked progressive slot machines, and player tracking systems. Retail services include a check acceptance network to shorten customer checkout time and reduce losses from returned checks. **Parent company:** Ceridian Corporation.

CON-WAY TRUCKLOAD SERVICES, INC.
2322 Gravel Drive, Fort Worth TX 76118. 817/284-7800. **Contact:** Jerry Casey, Director of Personnel. **Description:** Con-Way Truckload Services provides expanded services for over-the-road truckload transportation. As a full-service, multimodal truckload logistics company, its capabilities include expedited regional and transcontinental highway operations with drivers and company-owned trucks and trailers. CWT also retains the flexibility to offer its domestic

intermodal operations. This service, marketed as the Con-Quest Premium Truckload Service, utilizes CWT's national long-haul alliances to provide time-definite, intermodal truckload transportation. In addition, the company continues to offer basic intermodal marketing services, local and interstate container drayage, and international LCL shipping with its GlobalRate program. **Common positions include:** Accountant/Auditor; Brokerage Clerk; Clerical Supervisor; Customer Service Representative; Operations/Production Manager; Services Sales Representative. **Educational backgrounds include:** Accounting; Business Administration; Marketing. **Benefits:** 401(k); Dental Insurance; Disability Coverage; Life Insurance; Medical Insurance; Pension Plan; Profit Sharing; Savings Plan; Tuition Assistance. **Corporate headquarters location:** This Location. **Parent company:** Con-Way Transportation Services. **Listed on:** New York Stock Exchange. **Number of employees at this location:** 140. **Number of employees nationwide:** 300.

CONCORDIA INTERNATIONAL FORWARDING CORPORATION
753 Port America Place, Suite 101, Grapevine TX 76051. 817/481-4560. **Contact:** Human Resources. **Description:** Transports freight and cargo.

DALLAS AREA RAPID TRANSIT (DART)
P.O. Box 660163, Dallas TX 75266-7240. 214/749-3259. **Fax:** 214/749-3636. **Recorded jobline:** 214/749-3690. **Contact:** Human Resources. **World Wide Web address:** http://www.dart.org. **Description:** A nonprofit, rapid transit system serving the Dallas metropolitan area. **Common positions include:** Administrative Assistant; Driver; Electrical/Electronics Engineer; Electrician. **Benefits:** 401(k); Dental Insurance; Disability Coverage; Life Insurance; Medical Insurance; Public Transit Available; Tuition Assistance. **Special programs:** Internships.

DALLAS-FORT WORTH INTERNATIONAL AIRPORT
P.O. Drawer 619428, DFW Airport TX 75261-9428. 972/574-6032. **Recorded jobline:** 972/574-8024. **Contact:** Human Resources/Employment Office. **World Wide Web address:** http://www.dfwairport.com. **Description:** An international airport with flights worldwide on 25 commercial airlines and several charter airlines.

DELTA AIR LINES, INC.
P.O. Box 610348, Dallas TX 75261-0348. 214/630-3200. **Contact:** Personnel. **World Wide Web address:** http://www.delta-air.com. **Description:** One of the largest airlines in the United States. The company provides scheduled air transportation for passengers, freight, and mail out on an extensive route that covers most of the country and extends to 32 foreign nations. The route covers 153 domestic cities in 43 states, the District of Columbia, Puerto Rico, the U.S. Virgin Islands, and 57 cities abroad. Major domestic hubs of Delta include Atlanta, Dallas-Fort Worth, Salt Lake City, and Cincinnati with minor hubs in Los Angeles and Orlando. Delta has over 550 aircraft in its fleet. Founded in 1929. **NOTE:** All hiring is done through Delta Air Lines, Inc., Employment Office, P.O. Box 20530, Hartsfield International Airport, Atlanta GA 30320. 404/715-2600. **Corporate headquarters location:** Atlanta GA.

DUNCAN-ALEXANDER
1010 East Dallas Road, Grapevine TX 76051. 817/329-6130. **Contact:** Human Resources. **Description:** Transports freight and cargo.

DYNAMEX INC.
1801 Royal Lane, Suite 400, Dallas TX 75229-3131. 214/637-4000. **Contact:** Human Resources. **Description:** Offers customized warehousing and local outsourcing delivery services for companies with no trucks or delivery vehicles. Founded in 1985.

FFE TRANSPORTATION SERVICES, INC.
P.O. Box 655888, Dallas TX 75265-5888. 214/630-8090. **Contact:** Personnel. **World Wide Web address:** http://www.ffeinc.com. **Description:** Provides trucking and transportation services nationwide.

FM INDUSTRIES, INC.
8600 Will Rogers Boulevard, Fort Worth TX 76140. 817/293-4220. **Contact:** Personnel Manager. **Description:** Produces hydraulic cushioning systems for railroad freight cars.

FEDERAL EXPRESS CORPORATION
1220 Riverbend, Dallas TX 75247. 214/634-3250. **Toll-free phone:** 800/GO-FEDEX. **Contact:** Recruiting. **World Wide Web address:** http://www.fedex.com. **Description:** Offers delivery services in the United States and 187 other countries. The company's fleet consists of

approximately 462 aircraft and over 30,000 delivery vehicles. The company also operates a business logistics service. Hubs and major sorting centers are located in Alaska, Illinois, Indiana, California, New Jersey, and Tennessee. **Corporate headquarters location:** Memphis TN. **Other U.S. locations:** Nationwide. **International locations:** Worldwide. **Number of employees worldwide:** 70,500.

FORT WORTH JET CENTER
4201 North Main Street, Fort Worth TX 76106. 817/625-2366. **Contact:** Human Resources. **Description:** Refuels private corporate aircraft.

FRITZ COMPANIES
660 Fritz Drive, Coppell TX 75019. 972/471-7171. **Contact:** Human Resources Department. **World Wide Web address:** http://www.fritz.com. **Description:** A freight transportation company.

GOLDEN CAB
3131 Halifax, Dallas TX 75247. 214/630-8151. **Contact:** Human Resources. **Description:** A taxi service.

GREYHOUND LINES INC.
P.O. Box 660606, Dallas TX 75266-0606. 972/789-7000. **Contact:** Manager of Human Resources. **World Wide Web address:** http://www.greyhound.com. **Description:** One of the country's largest private transportation networks. Greyhound conducts regular route, package express, charter, and food service operations. The fleet consists of over 1,600 buses that travel to more than 2,600 destinations. **Listed on:** American Stock Exchange.

J.B. HUNT TRANSPORT SERVICES, INC.
5701 West Kiest Boulevard, Dallas TX 75236. 214/333-9768. **Contact:** Human Resources. **World Wide Web address:** http://www.jbhunt.com. **Description:** A major freight transportation company. **Corporate headquarters location:** Lowell AR.

INTERNATIONAL TOTAL SERVICES
8413 Sterling Street, Suite A, Irving TX 75063. 972/621-0255. **Contact:** Human Resources. **Description:** Engaged in aircraft cleaning services.

INTERSTATE TRAILERS, INC.
1102 Interstate 20 West, Arlington TX 76017. 817/465-5441. **Contact:** Human Resources. **Description:** Supplies transportation equipment.

KITTY HAWK, INC.
1535 West 20th Street, P.O. Box 612787, DFW Airport TX 75261. 972/456-2498. **Contact:** Human Resources. **World Wide Web address:** http://www.kha.com. **Description:** Provides charter management and cargo services.

LUMINATOR
1200 East Plano Parkway, Plano TX 75074. 972/424-6511. **Contact:** Denise Boyd, Human Resources Manager. **World Wide Web address:** http://www.luminatorusa.com. **Description:** Manufactures aircraft parts, bus products, and rail products. Luminator aircraft products include batteries, lamps, search lights, interiors, and crew stations. Bus products include flip-out signs and voice systems. Rail products include various types of lighting, flip dot sign systems, electronic maps, voice systems, and air diffusers. **Corporate headquarters location:** This Location. **Parent company:** Mark IV Industries.

MARTINAIRE INC.
2550 Midway Road, Suite 190, Carrollton TX 75006. 214/358-5858. **Contact:** Human Resources. **World Wide Web address:** http://www.martinaire.com. **Description:** An air cargo carrier operating a fleet of 28 aircraft.

MESQUITE METRO AIRPORT
1130 Airport Boulevard, Suite 100, Mesquite TX 75181. 972/222-8536. **Contact:** Human Resources. **Description:** An airport.

NIPPON EXPRESS USA INC.
8065 Tristar Drive, Irving TX 75063. 972/621-1911. **Contact:** Human Resources. **Description:** Engaged in the transportation of freight and cargo.

NORTH TEXAS AIRCRAFT SERVICES
4480 Glenn Curtiss Drive, Addison TX 75001. 972/713-6163. **Contact:** Human Resources. **Description:** Offers air transportation services.

OGDEN AVIATION SERVICES
1625 West 18th Street, DFW Airport, Dallas TX 75261. 972/586-0031. **Contact:** Human Resources. **Description:** Provides ground handling and transportation services. **Corporate headquarters location:** New York NY. **Parent company:** Ogden Services Corporation.

SINGAPORE AIRLINES
8500 North Stemmons Freeway, Suite 1060, Dallas TX 75247. 214/631-6613. **Contact:** Human Resources. **World Wide Web address:** http://www.singaporeair.com. **Description:** An international airline providing passenger and cargo transportation to 90 cities in 40 countries.

SKY HELICOPTERS
2559 South Jupiter Road, Garland TX 75041-6011. 214/349-7000. **Contact:** Human Resources. **World Wide Web address:** http://www.skyhelicopters.com. **Description:** Engaged in helicopter transportation for both public and private use.

SOUTHWEST AIRLINES COMPANY
P.O. Box 36644, Dallas TX 75235-1644. 214/792-4213. **Fax:** 214/792-7015. **Contact:** SWA People Department. **World Wide Web address:** http://www.southwest.com. **Description:** One of the U.S.'s only major short-haul, low-fare, high-frequency, point-to-point carriers. Southwest Airlines flies to more than 50 cities in the U.S. offers over 2,500 flights daily. **Common positions include:** Accountant/Auditor; Administrator; Aircraft Mechanic/Engine Specialist; Computer Programmer; Customer Service Representative; Flight Attendant; Human Resources Manager; Marketing Manager; Public Relations Specialist; Receptionist; Sales Representative; Secretary; Systems Analyst. **Educational backgrounds include:** Accounting; Computer Science; Liberal Arts; Marketing. **Benefits:** 401(k); Dental Insurance; Disability Coverage; Employee Discounts; Life Insurance; Medical Insurance; Profit Sharing; Savings Plan. **Special programs:** Internships. **Corporate headquarters location:** This Location. **Other U.S. locations:** Nationwide. **Listed on:** New York Stock Exchange. **Number of employees at this location:** 3,600. **Number of employees worldwide:** 29,000.

STANLEY REFRIGERATED EXPRESS
P.O. Box 35209, Dallas TX 75325. 214/631-8420. **Contact:** Human Resources. **Description:** A trucking company that hauls produce.

SUPERIOR AVIATION SERVICES INC.
P.O. Box 780364, Dallas TX 75378. 214/350-2749. **Contact:** Human Resources. **Description:** Offers air transportation services.

THAI AIRWAYS INTERNATIONAL LTD.
8700 North Stemmons Freeway, Suite 133, Dallas TX 75247. 214/631-8424. **Contact:** Human Resources. **World Wide Web address:** http://www.thaiair.com. **Description:** One of Asia's leading airlines, offering flights to 72 cities in 37 countries.

TRINITY INDUSTRIES, INC.
P.O. Box 568887, Dallas TX 75356-8887. 214/631-4420. **Contact:** Human Resources Department. **World Wide Web address:** http://www.trin.net. **Description:** Manufactures an assortment of railroad and construction equipment and replacement parts. Trinity Industries also offers related services for the transportation, construction, aerospace, commercial, and industrial markets. Products include railcars, gas processing systems, petroleum transportation systems, guard rails, bridge girders and beams, airport boarding bridges, barges, tug boats, military marine vessels, and precision welding products. Trinity Industries also makes concrete and aggregates and produces metal components for the petrochemical, industrial, processing, and power markets. **Common positions include:** Accountant/Auditor; Data Entry Clerk. **Educational backgrounds include:** Accounting; Business Administration; Computer Science; Engineering. **Benefits:** Daycare Assistance; Disability Coverage; Employee Discounts; Life Insurance; Medical Insurance; Pension Plan; Profit Sharing; Savings Plan; Tuition Assistance. **Corporate headquarters location:** This Location. **Listed on:** New York Stock Exchange.

TRINITY INDUSTRIES, INC.
Route 13, Box 175, Longview TX 75602. 903/758-0761. **Contact:** Human Resources. **World Wide Web address:** http://www.trin.net. **Description:** This location builds tank cars. Overall, the company manufactures an assortment of railroad and construction equipment and

replacement parts. Trinity Industries also offers related services for the transportation, construction, aerospace, commercial, and industrial markets. Products include railcars, gas processing systems, petroleum transportation systems, guard rails, bridge girders and beams, airport boarding bridges, barges, tug boats, military marine vessels, and precision welding products. Trinity Industries also manufactures concrete and aggregates and produces metal components for the petrochemical, industrial, processing, and power markets. **Corporate headquarters location:** Dallas TX. **Listed on:** New York Stock Exchange.

TRINITY INDUSTRIES, INC.
P.O. Box 7596, Fort Worth TX 76111. 817/625-4161. **Contact:** Human Resources. **World Wide Web address:** http://www.trin.net. **Description:** This location builds rail cars. Overall, the company manufactures an assortment of railroad and construction equipment and replacement parts. Trinity Industries also offers related services for the transportation, construction, aerospace, commercial, and industrial markets. Products include railcars, gas processing systems, petroleum transportation systems, guard rails, bridge girders and beams, airport boarding bridges, barges, tug boats, military marine vessels, and precision welding products. Trinity Industries also manufactures concrete and aggregates and produces metal components for the petrochemical, industrial, processing, and power markets. **Corporate headquarters location:** Dallas TX. **Listed on:** New York Stock Exchange.

UNITED PARCEL SERVICE (UPS)
P.O. Box 2047, Grapevine TX 76099-2047. 972/456-4928. **Recorded jobline:** 888/877-0924. **Contact:** Human Resources. **World Wide Web address:** http://www.ups.com. **Description:** This location houses regional administrative offices. Overall, United Parcel Service is a parcel pickup and delivery service organization that provides service to all 50 states and to more than 185 countries and territories worldwide. The company delivers approximately 12 million packages daily. **NOTE:** The jobline lists mainly part-time positions. People in search of full-time positions should fax resumes to the attention of Tom Mullen at 214/353-6565. **Common positions include:** Data Entry Clerk. **Educational backgrounds include:** Computer Science. **Benefits:** Dental Insurance; Disability Coverage; Life Insurance; Medical Insurance; Pension Plan; Profit Sharing; Savings Plan; Tuition Assistance.

VIRTUOSO
500 Main Street, Suite 400, Fort Worth TX 76102. 817/870-0300. **Fax:** 817/877-3076. **Contact:** Human Resources. **World Wide Web address:** http://www.virtuoso.com. **Description:** A travel consortium specializing in leisure travel.

Note: Because addresses and telephone numbers of smaller companies can change rapidly, we recommend you call each company to verify the information below before inquiring about job opportunities. Mass mailings are not recommended.

Additional small employers:

AIR TRANSPORTATION AND SERVICES

Ameristar Jet Charter Inc.
PO Box 700548, Dallas TX 75370-0548. 972/248-2478.

AOG Inc.
PO Box 540423, Dallas TX 75354-0423. 214/350-5334.

Continental Airlines Inc.
PO Box 612429, Dallas TX 75261-2429. 972/263-0523.

Department of Public Safety
PO Box 610687, Dallas TX 75261-0687. 972/574-4454.

DHL Worldwide Express
1440 N Union Bower Rd, Irving TX 75061-5832. 972/445-0644.

Eagle One Aviation
4601 N Main St, Fort Worth TX 76106-2417. 817/626-0700.

Express One International Inc.
3890 W Northwest Hwy, Dallas TX 75220-8108. 214/902-2500.

Federal Express Corporation
2825 W Kingsley Rd, Garland TX 75041-2409. 972/840-0515.

Federal Express Corporation
PO Box 61205, Dallas TX 75261. 972/456-4440.

Federal Express Corporation
109 N Chandler Dr, Fort Worth TX 76111-3941. 817/831-2383.

Laidlaw Transit
418 Metro Park Dr, McKinney TX 75069-1827. 972/547-4499.

Richardson Bus Line
900 S Greenville Ave, Richardson TX 75081. 972/301-3586.

MAINTENANCE FACILITIES FOR MOTOR FREIGHT TRANSPORTATION

CF Motor Freight
3925 Singleton Blvd, Dallas TX 75212-3504. 214/637-5119.

Roadway Express
200 N Belt Line Rd, Irving TX 75061-6306. 972/790-3611.

MISC. TRANSPORTATION SERVICES

Dallas Freightliner
PO Box 560505, Dallas TX 75356-0505. 214/819-2500.

Progress Rail Services Corp.
PO Box 706, Waskom TX
75692-0706. 903/687-3388.

PACKING AND CRATING

Adamco Inc.
PO Box 5646, Arlington TX
76005-5646. 817/640-6430.

NCM
PO Box 165447, Irving TX
75016-5447. 972/550-0433.

PASSENGER TRANSPORTATION ARRANGEMENT SERVICES

American Express Travel Related Services
3110 Skyway Cir S, Irving TX
75038-4207. 972/257-6000.

American Express Travel Related Services
PO Box 63001, Dallas TX
75207. 214/749-4078.

Cendant Corporation
PO Box 1288, Arlington TX
76004-1288. 817/652-8000.

Sammons Travel
10726 Plano Rd, Dallas TX
75238-1318. 214/360-5050.

Southwest Airlines Co.
401 E Safari Pkwy, Grand
Prairie TX 75050-2342.
972/263-1717.

Trans Global Vacation
2100 N Highway 360, Grand
Prairie TX 75050-1009.
972/641-7875.

World Travel Partners LP
5420 LBJ Fwy, Ste 470, Dallas
TX 75240. 972/702-1000.

RAILROAD EQUIPMENT

Gunderson Southwest Inc.
101 Park St, Cleburne TX
76031-4038. 817/556-9191.

RAILROAD TRANSPORTATION

Burlington Northern and Santa Fe Railway
PO Box 30, Teague TX 75860-0030. 254/739-2291.

Burlington Northern and Santa Fe Railway
14100 John Day Rd, Haslet TX
76052-2521. 817/224-7008.

Burlington Northern and Santa Fe Railway
4028 Deen Rd, Fort Worth TX
76106-4111. 817/740-7225.

Burlington Northern and Santa Fe Railway
3001 Lou Menk Dr, Bldg A,
Fort Worth TX 76131-2800.
817/234-7478.

Burlington Northern and Santa Fe Railway
1901 S Johnson St, Amarillo TX
79102-3161. 806/379-3365.

Quality Terminal Services LLC
2400 Westport Pkwy W, Haslet
TX 76052. 817/224-7166.

Union Pacific Railroad Co.
905 E Pacific Ave, Longview TX
75602-1447. 903/238-2957.

Union Pacific Railroad Co.
PO Drawer 4427, Waco TX
76705. 817/878-4540.

Union Pacific Railroad Co.
200 Chicago St, Dalhart TX
79022. 806/249-4200.

TRUCKING

A1 Freeman Relocation Systems
2242 Manana Dr, Dallas TX
75220-7100. 972/263-2068.

ABF Freight System
4242 Irving Blvd, Dallas TX
75247-5820. 214/688-0458.

Active Transportation Company
2521 N Interstate 35, Denton
TX 76207-2027. 940/382-2541.

American Freightways Inc.
3100 S Belt Line Rd, Irving TX
75060-7100. 972/262-8911.

Armstrong Relocation Services
1405 Crescent Dr, Carrollton
TX 75006-3606. 972/242-0511.

Arnold Transportation Services
1840 NW Loop 286, Paris TX
75460-1780. 903/785-0326.

Atlantic Relocation Services
PO Box 344224, Dallas TX
75234. 972/263-4400.

Bancroft and Sons Transportation
2105 Oakwood Dr, Grand
Prairie TX 75050-1723.
972/790-3777.

Bekins Moving Systems
1232 Crowley Dr, Ste B,
Carrollton TX 75006-1353.
972/245-6799.

Boer Transportation
3485 Roy Orr Blvd, Grand
Prairie TX 75050-4210.
972/513-1302.

Bradford Trucking
PO Box 129, Cactus TX 79013-0129. 806/966-5164.

Caliber System Co.
4901 Martin St, Fort Worth TX
76119-5232. 817/561-3008.

Carter & Sons Freightways Inc.
1325 W Belt Line Rd, Carrollton
TX 75006-6916. 972/245-5402.

Central Freight Lines Inc.
PO Box 2638, Waco TX 76702-2638. 254/772-2120.

Chaney Trucking
PO Box 1665, Roanoke TX
76262-1665. 817/430-0923.

Con-Way Southern Express Inc.
4901 David Strickland Rd, Fort
Worth TX 76119-5209.
817/478-0129.

Con-Way Southern Express Inc.
14500 Trinity Blvd, Fort Worth
TX 76155-2542. 817/358-3840.

Con-Way Transportation Services
PO Box 982013, Fort Worth TX
76182-8013. 817/514-1300.

Continental Express Inc.
2578 Stae Hwy, Rockwall TX
75032. 972/722-3264.

CTC Distribution Services
3345 Miller Park N, Garland TX
75042-7764. 972/494-4442.

DeBoer Inc.
4115 Gazola St, Texarkana TX
75501-7131. 903/832-7581.

Driving Force Inc.
3131 N Stemmons Fwy, Dallas
TX 75247-6112. 214/637-0242.

Eastway
803 Port America Pl, Grapevine
TX 76051-7645. 214/654-3500.

Ennis Transportation Co. Inc.
PO Drawer 798, Ennis TX
75120-0798. 972/878-5801.

Federal Express Corporation
PO Box 612025, Irving TX
75014. 972/456-4400.

Federal Express Corporation
PO Box 610669, Dallas TX
75261-0669. 972/615-9936.

Great Western Express
PO Box 4529, Fort Worth TX
76164-0529. 817/336-2733.

Gulf Coast Transport Inc.
PO Box 851307, Mesquite TX
75185-1307. 972/226-3536.

Hawk Transport Inc.
2110 S Peachtree Rd, Mesquite TX 75180-1230. 972/285-8936.

Jack Cooper Transport Co.
PO Box 829, Arlington TX 76004-0829. 817/649-0821.

James Helwig & Son Inc.
PO Box 1390, Rockwall TX 75087-1390. 972/771-0927.

MDR Cartage Inc.
12784 State Highway 31 W, Tyler TX 75709-5141. 903/595-0740.

Mega Freight Lines Inc.
1002 Fountain Pkwy, Grand Prairie TX 75050-1511. 972/988-8088.

Middleton Transportation Co.
PO Box 4529, Fort Worth TX 76164-0529. 817/336-2900.

Move Solutions Inc.
1473 Terre Colony Ct, Dallas TX 75212-6220. 214/630-3607.

MS Carriers Inc.
310 Hwy 80 E, Dallas TX 75236. 972/266-1554.

Old Dominion Freight Line Inc.
2805 Mican Dr, Dallas TX 75212-4602. 214/951-7766.

Overnite Transportation Co.
2600 E Pioneer Dr, Irving TX 75061-8922. 972/721-9958.

Robert Heath Trucking Inc.
PO Box 2501, Lubbock TX 79408-2501. 806/747-1651.

Schneider National Carriers
3020 E Highway 80, Mesquite TX 75149-1207. 972/882-1329.

Skyway Freight System
2020 McDaniel Dr, Ste 110, Carrollton TX 75006-8348. 972/263-0020.

Southeastern Freight Lines
1415 S Loop 12, Irving TX 75060-6321. 972/579-9955.

Southwest Freight Distributors
8189 S Central Expy, Dallas TX 75241-7820. 214/371-1901.

Steere Tank Lines
3411 Summerhill Rd, Texarkana TX 75503-3559. 903/794-1423.

Stevens Transport Inc.
PO Box 279010, Dallas TX 75227-9610. 972/289-1611.

Transport Corp of America
3345 Miller Park N, Garland TX 75042-7764. 972/494-7344.

Trism Inc.
304 Reynolds Ln, Sherman TX 75092-6839. 800/879-4285.

USF Bestway Inc.
11430 Newkirk St, Dallas TX 75229-2028. 972/247-2426.

Western-Commerical Transportation
PO Box 270, Fort Worth TX 76101-0270. 817/335-4821.

Willis Shaw Express Inc.
2425 S University Parks D, Waco TX 76706-6427. 254/753-6331.

Wingtip Couriers Inc.
2700 N Haskell Ave, Dallas TX 75204-2907. 972/222-0222.

Yellow Freight System Inc.
4500 Irving Blvd, Dallas TX 75247-5704. 214/631-7400.

WAREHOUSING AND STORAGE

AMC
1475 Post N Paddock St, Grand Prairie TX 75050-1233. 972/988-0333.

Cross Dock
2230 N Highway 360, Grand Prairie TX 75050-1017. 972/602-0993.

DART
2121 Regency Dr, Irving TX 75062-4912. 972/554-6629.

DSC Logistics
1102 W Freeway St, Grand Prairie TX 75051-1439. 817/961-7509.

EMSI Shipping Supply
3003 LBJ Fwy, Ste 100, Dallas TX 75234-7755. 214/689-3600.

Exel Logistics Inc.
13601 Independence Pkw, Fort Worth TX 76178-4001. 817/608-2000.

Harper Group Inc.
PO Box 619023, Dallas TX 75261-9023. 972/456-0730.

Nortel Networks Inc.
PO Box 833858, Richardson TX 75083-3858. 972/684-8101.

Owen Oil Tools Inc.
PO Box 40666, Fort Worth TX 76140-0666. 817/551-0540.

United States Cold Storage
3300 E Park Row Dr, Arlington TX 76010-4001. 817/633-3070.

We Pack Warehousing & Distribution
2510 S Church St, Paris TX 75460-7659. 903/737-0522.

WATER TRANSPORTATION OF FREIGHT

Maersk Sea-Land Inc.
PO Box 803447, Dallas TX 75380-3447. 972/716-4900.

WHOLESALE OF TRANSPORTATION EQUIPMENT AND SUPPLIES

Aviall Inc.
PO Box 549015, Dallas TX 75354-9015. 972/406-6500.

New York Air Brake
36 Fair Green Dr, Roanoke TX 76262-5629. 817/491-4774.

Victor Equipment Company
PO Box 1007, Denton TX 76202-1007. 940/566-2000.

For more information on career opportunities in transportation and travel industries:

Associations

AIR TRANSPORT ASSOCIATION OF AMERICA
1301 Pennsylvania Avenue NW, Suite 1100, Washington DC 20004. 202/626-4000. World Wide Web address: http://www.air-transport.org. A trade association for the major U.S. airlines.

AIRLINE PILOTS ASSOCIATION INTERNATIONAL
535 Herndon Parkway, Herndon VA 20170. 703/481-4440.

AMERICAN BUREAU OF SHIPPING
2 World Trade Center, 106th Floor, New York NY 10048. 212/839-5000. World Wide Web address: http://www.abs-group.com.

AMERICAN SOCIETY OF TRAVEL AGENTS
1101 King Street, Suite 200, Alexandria VA 22314. 703/739-2782. World Wide Web address: http://www.astanet.com.

AMERICAN TRUCKING ASSOCIATIONS, INC.
2200 Mill Road, Alexandria VA 22314-4677. 703/838-1700. World Wide Web address:

http://www.truckline.org. A national federation of the trucking industry representing all types of trucking companies. ATA is affiliated with 50 independent state trucking associations and 14 national conferences. The association also publishes *Transport Topics*, a weekly trade newspaper.

ASSOCIATION OF AMERICAN RAILROADS
50 F Street NW, Washington DC 20001. 202/639-2100. World Wide Web address: http://www.aar.com.

INSTITUTE OF TRANSPORTATION ENGINEERS
525 School Street SW, Suite 410, Washington DC 20024. 202/554-8050. World Wide Web address: http://www.ite.org. Scientific and educational association, providing for professional development of members and others.

MARINE TECHNOLOGY SOCIETY
1828 L Street NW, Suite 906, Washington DC 20036. 202/775-5966. World Wide Web address: http://www.mtsociety.org.

NATIONAL MOTOR FREIGHT TRAFFIC ASSOCIATION
2200 Mill Road, Alexandria VA 22314-4654. 703/838-1810. World Wide Web address: http://www.erols.com/nmfta/index.htm. Works towards the improvement and advancement of the interests and welfare of motor common carriers.

Books

FLIGHT PLAN TO THE FLIGHT DECK: STRATEGIES FOR A PILOT CAREER
Cage Consulting, Inc., 13275 East Fremont Place, Suite 315, Englewood CO 80112-3917. Toll-free phone: 888/899-CAGE. Fax: 303/799-1998. World Wide Web address: http://www.cageconsulting.com.

WELCOME ABOARD! YOUR CAREER AS A FLIGHT ATTENDANT
Cage Consulting, Inc., 13275 East Fremont Place, Suite 315, Englewood CO 80112-3917. Toll-free phone: 888/899-CAGE. Fax: 303/799-1998. World Wide Web address: http://www.cageconsulting.com.

Directories

MOODY'S TRANSPORTATION MANUAL
Financial Information Services, 60 Madison Avenue, 6th Floor, New York NY 10010. Toll-free phone: 800/342-5647.

NATIONAL TANK TRUCK CARRIER DIRECTORY
National Tank Truck Carriers, 2200 Mill Road, Alexandria VA 22314. 703/838-1700.

Magazines

AMERICAN SHIPPER
Howard Publications, P.O. Box 4728, Jacksonville FL 32201. 904/355-2601. Monthly.

FLEET OWNER
PRIMEDIA Intertec, 11 Riverbend Drive South, P.O. Box 4211, Stamford CT 06907-0211.

HEAVY DUTY TRUCKING
Newport Communications, P.O. Box W, Newport Beach CA 92658. 949/261-1636.

ITE JOURNAL
Institute of Transportation Engineers, 525 School Street SW, Suite 410, Washington DC 20024-2797. 202/554-8050. World Wide Web address: http://www.ite.org. One year subscription (12 issues): $60.00.

MARINE DIGEST AND TRANSPORTATION NEWS
Marine Publishing, Inc., 1710 South Norman Street, Seattle WA 98144. 206/709-1840.

SHIPPING DIGEST
51 Madison Avenue, New York NY 10010. 212/837-7029.

TRAFFIC WORLD MAGAZINE
1230 National Press Building, Washington DC 20045-2200. 202/783-1101.

TRANSPORT TOPICS
American Trucking Associations, Inc., 2200 Mill Road, Alexandria VA 22314. 703/838-1778. World Wide Web address: http://www.ttnews.com.

Newsletters

AIR JOBS DIGEST
World Air Data, Department 700, P.O. Box 42360, Washington DC 20015. This monthly resource provides current job openings in aerospace, space, and aviation industries. Subscription rates: $96.00 annually, $69.00 for six months, and $49.00 for three months.

Online Services

THE AIRLINE EMPLOYMENT ASSISTANCE CORPS.
World Wide Web address: http://www.avjobs.com. Site for aviation jobseekers providing worldwide classified ads, resume assistance, publications, and over 350 links to aviation-related Websites and news groups. Certain resources are members-only access.

COOLWORKS
World Wide Web address: http://www.coolworks.com. This Website provides links to 22,000 job openings on cruise ships, at national parks, summer camps, ski areas, river areas, ranches, fishing areas, and resorts. This site also includes information on volunteer openings.

INTERNATIONAL SEAFARERS EXCHANGE
World Wide Web address: http://www.jobxchange.com. Over 300 listings on cruise ships or in other maritime positions that can be searched by location, title, skills, or salary.

TRAVEL PROFESSIONALS FORUM
Go: Travpro. To join this CompuServe forum, you will need to send an e-mail to the sysop for permission.

For information about the JobBank List Service visit www.adamsjobbank.com

Utilities: Electri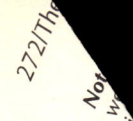

UTILITIES: ELECTRIC/GAS/W

You can expect to find the following types of compani
Gas, Electric, and Fuel Companies; Other Energy-Produ
Public Utility Holding Companies • Water Utilities

Some helpful information: Water and wastewater treatment plant operators and supervisors earn an average of $25,000 - $30,000 per year. Electrical power plant operators average about $35,000 - $40,000.

AMERICAN ELECTRIC POWER (AEP))
P.O. Box 660164, Dallas TX 75266-0164. 214/777-1000. **Contact:** Human Resources. **World Wide Web address:** http://www.aep.com. **Description:** An electric utility company serving approximately 4.8 million customers in the U.S. and over 4 million customers outside the U.S. **Corporate headquarters location:** Columbus OH.

B-K ELECTRIC COOPERATIVE, INC.
P.O. Box 672, Seymour TX 76380-2138. 940/888-3441. **Contact:** Human Resources Department. **Description:** An electric utility cooperative.

SOUTHWESTERN PUBLIC SERVICE COMPANY
P.O. Box 1261, Amarillo TX 79170-0001. 806/378-2121. **Contact:** Doris Brasille, Manager of Employee Services. **Description:** Provides electric service to the Amarillo area. **Corporate headquarters location:** This Location. **Other U.S. locations:** KS; NM; OK.

TEXAS UTILITIES COMPANIES
1601 Bryan Street, Dallas TX 75201-3411. 214/812-4600. **Fax:** 214/812-8419. **Recorded jobline:** 214/812-8633. **Contact:** Staffing and Placement Manager. **World Wide Web address:** http://www.txu.com. **Description:** A large, investor-owned, electric utility providing electric service to 2 million customers in north, central, and western Texas. **Common positions include:** Accountant/Auditor; Administrative Manager; Architect; Branch Manager; Budget Analyst; Buyer; Chemist; Civil Engineer; Claim Representative; Clerical Supervisor; Computer Programmer; Construction Contractor; Cost Estimator; Customer Service Representative; Designer; Draftsperson; Economist; Electrical/Electronics Engineer; Electrician; Financial Analyst; General Manager; Human Resources Manager; Mechanical Engineer; Mining Engineer; Nuclear Engineer; Public Relations Specialist; Purchasing Agent/Manager; Quality Control Supervisor; Software Engineer; Structural Engineer; Systems Analyst. **Educational backgrounds include:** Accounting; Business Administration; Computer Science; Engineering. **Benefits:** 401(k); Dental Insurance; Disability Coverage; Life Insurance; Medical Insurance; Pension Plan; Savings Plan; Tuition Assistance. **Special programs:** Internships. **Corporate headquarters location:** This Location. **Subsidiaries include:** BRI; Chaco; TU Electric; TU Fuel Company; TU Mini; TU Services. **Parent company:** TXU Corporation. **Listed on:** New York Stock Exchange. **Stock exchange symbol:** TXU. **Annual sales/revenues:** More than $100 million. **Number of employees at this location:** 2,000. **Number of employees nationwide:** 10,000.

TEXAS-NEW MEXICO POWER COMPANY
P.O. Box 2943, Fort Worth TX 76113. 817/731-0099. **Contact:** Melissa Davis, Human Resources Manager. **World Wide Web address:** http://www.tnpe.com. **Description:** A public utility engaged in the purchase, transmission, distribution, and sale of electrical power in Texas and New Mexico. **Common positions include:** Accountant/Auditor; Computer Programmer; Customer Service Representative; Electrical/Electronics Engineer; Systems Analyst. **Educational backgrounds include:** Accounting; Business Administration; Computer Science; Engineering. **Benefits:** Disability Coverage; Life Insurance; Medical Insurance; Pension Plan; Savings Plan; Tuition Assistance. **Corporate headquarters location:** This Location. **Parent company:** TNP Enterprises Inc. **Listed on:** New York Stock Exchange.

WEST TEXAS UTILITIES COMPANY
P.O. Box 841, Abilene TX 79604. 915/674-7000. **Contact:** Human Resources. **World Wide Web address:** http://www.aep.com. **Description:** An electric utility company. **Parent company:** American Electric Power (AEP).

Dallas Fort-Worth JobBank

Because addresses and telephone numbers of smaller companies can change rapidly, recommend you call each company to verify the information below before inquiring about job opportunities. Mass mailings are not recommended.

Additional small employers:

ELECTRIC SERVICES

Brazos Electric
PO Box 2585, Waco TX 76702-2585. 254/750-6500.

Garland Power and Light
PO Box 469002, Garland TX 75046-9002. 972/205-2650.

Industrial Generating Company
PO Box 800, Fairfield TX 75840-0800. 903/389-2625.

Southwestern Public Service
PO Box 631, Lubbock TX 79408-0631. 806/765-2800.

Texas New Mexico Power
PO Box 433, Clifton TX 76634-0433. 254/675-3512.

Texas Utilities Electric
200 W Carpenter Fwy, Irving TX 75039-2003. 972/791-2888.

Texas Utilities Electric
PO Box 1002, Glen Rose TX 76043-1002. 254/897-8500.

Texas Utilities Electric
3500 El Campo Ave, Fort Worth TX 76107-4581. 817/735-3937.

Tolk Station Power Plant
PO Box 429, Sudan TX 79371-0429. 806/965-2194.

GAS AND/OR WATER SUPPLY

Dallas Water Utilities
1500 Marilla St, Dallas TX 75201-6300. 214/670-3144.

North Texas Municipal Water District
PO Box 2408, Wylie TX 75098-2408. 972/442-5405.

Texarkana Water Utilities
PO Box 2008, Texarkana TX 75504-2008. 903/798-3800.

GAS UTILITY SERVICES

Aurora Natural Gas
3102 Maple Ave, Ste 600, Dallas TX 75201-1236. 214/880-0494.

Energas Company
PO Box 1121, Lubbock TX 79408-1121. 806/798-4451.

For more information on career opportunities in the utilities industry:

Associations

AMERICAN PUBLIC GAS ASSOCIATION
11094-D Lee Highway, Suite 102, Fairfax VA 22030. 703/352-3890. World Wide Web address: http://www.apga.org. Publishes a bi-weekly newsletter.

AMERICAN PUBLIC POWER ASSOCIATION (APPA)
2301 M Street NW, Suite 300, Washington DC 20037-1484. 202/467-2900. World Wide Web address: http://www.appanet.org. Represents publicly-owned utilities. Provides many services including government relations, educational programs, and industry-related information publications.

AMERICAN WATER WORKS ASSOCIATION
6666 West Quincy Avenue, Denver CO 80235. 303/794-7711. World Wide Web address: http://www.awwa.org.

NATIONAL RURAL ELECTRIC COOPERATIVE ASSOCIATION
4301 Wilson Boulevard, Arlington VA 22203. 703/907-5500. World Wide Web address: http://www.nreca.org.

Directories

MOODY'S PUBLIC UTILITY MANUAL
Financial Information Services, 60 Madison Avenue, 6th Floor, New York NY 10010. Toll-free phone: 800/342-5647. World Wide Web address: http://www.fisonline.com. Annually available at libraries.

Magazines

PUBLIC POWER
American Public Power Association, 2301 M Street NW, Suite 300, Washington DC 20037-1484. 202/467-2900. World Wide Web address: http://www.appanet/org.

For information about the JobBank List Service visit www.adamsjobbank.com

MISCELLANEOUS WHOLESALING

You can expect to find the following types of companies in this chapter:
Exporters and Importers • General Wholesale Distribution Companies

Some helpful information: *Wholesale sales representatives' salaries vary by type of firm, product, and amount of selling experience. On average, skilled sales representatives earn $35,000 annually. Top salespersons can earn $70,000 and up.*

ABATIX CORPORATION
8311 Eastpoint Drive, Suite 400, Dallas TX 75227. 214/381-1146. **Contact:** Human Resources. **World Wide Web address:** http://www.abatix.com. **Description:** A supplier of industrial safety supplies, construction tools, general safety products such as protective clothing and eyewear, and clean-up equipment. **Common positions include:** Sales Representative. **Corporate headquarters location:** This Location. **Other U.S. locations:** Phoenix AZ; Denver CO; Las Vegas NV; Houston TX; Seattle WA. **Listed on:** NASDAQ. **Stock exchange symbol:** ABIX.

BRIGGS-WEAVER-VINSON COMPANIES, INC.
3010 LBJ Freeway, Suite 800, Dallas TX 75234. 972/919-5770. **Toll-free phone:** 800/914-8443. **Fax:** 972/919-5781. **Contact:** Don R. Gathright, Vice President of Human Resources. **Description:** A distributor of industrial, marine, and oil field tubing and instrumentation to related industries throughout the Southwest. **Common positions include:** Manufacturer's/Wholesaler's Sales Rep. **Educational backgrounds include:** Business Administration; Marketing. **Benefits:** Dental Insurance; Disability Coverage; Employee Discounts; Life Insurance; Medical Insurance; Pension Plan; Profit Sharing; Tuition Assistance. **Corporate headquarters location:** This Location. **Parent company:** Sammons Corporation. **Listed on:** Privately held. **Annual sales/revenues:** More than $100 million.

CELEBRITY, INC.
P.O. Box 6666, Tyler TX 75711. 903/561-3981. **Contact:** Human Resources. **World Wide Web address:** http://www.celebrity-inc.com. **Description:** A supplier of artificial flowers, foliage, flowering bushes, and other decorative accessories to craft stores and other specialty retailers and to wholesale florists.

GOLDTHWAITE'S OF TEXAS INC.
1401 Foch Street, Fort Worth TX 76107. 817/332-1521. **Contact:** Human Resources. **Description:** A wholesale distributor of mowing and irrigation equipment for the maintenance of landscaped areas and turf. **Common positions include:** General Manager; Material Control Specialist. **Educational backgrounds include:** Marketing. **Benefits:** Dental Insurance; Disability Coverage; Employee Discounts; Life Insurance; Medical Insurance; Pension Plan; Profit Sharing; Savings Plan. **Corporate headquarters location:** This Location.

HI-LINE
2121 Valley View Lane, Dallas TX 75234. 972/247-6200. **Contact:** Cindy Grieser, Human Resources Manager. **E-mail address:** employment@hi-line.com. **World Wide Web address:** http://www.hi-line.com. **Description:** A distributor of fasteners including nuts, bolts, screws, and rivets; terminals including solder splice connectors, mechanical lugs, and ferrules; cable lugs; battery terminals; insulating materials including shrink tubing, grommets, and specialty tape; wiring accessories; drill bits; and various other industrial products. Founded in 1959. **Common positions include:** Manufacturer's/Wholesaler's Sales Rep. **Educational backgrounds include:** High School Diploma/GED. **Benefits:** Disability Coverage; Life Insurance; Medical Insurance; Pension Plan; Profit Sharing; Savings Plan; Tuition Assistance. **Corporate headquarters location:** This Location. **Number of employees at this location:** 65.

For more information on career opportunities in the wholesaling industry:

Associations

NATIONAL ASSOCIATION OF WHOLESALERS
1725 K Street NW, Suite 300, Washington DC 20006. 202/872-0885.

For information about the JobBank List Service visit www.adamsjobbank.com

EMPLOYMENT SERVICES

Many people turn to temporary agencies, permanent employment agencies, or executive recruiters to assist them in their respective job searches. At their best, these resources can be a valuable friend – it's comforting to know that someone is putting his or her wealth of experience and contacts to work for you. At their worst, however, they are more of a friend to the employer, or to more experienced recruits, than to you personally, and it is best not to rely on them exclusively.

That said, there are several types of employment services for jobseekers to check out as part of their job search efforts:

TEMPORARY EMPLOYMENT AGENCIES

Temporary or "temp" agencies can be a viable option. Often these agencies specialize in clerical and support work, but it's becoming increasingly common to find temporary assignments in other areas like accounting or computer programming. Working on temporary assignments will provide you with additional income during your job search and will add experience to your resume. It may also provide valuable business contacts or lead to permanent job opportunities.

Temporary agencies are listed in your local telephone directory and in *The JobBank Guide to Employment Services* (Adams Media Corporation), found in your local public library. Send a resume and cover letter to the agency, and call to schedule an interview. Be prepared to take a number of tests at the interview.

PERMANENT EMPLOYMENT AGENCIES

Permanent employment agencies are commissioned by employers to find qualified candidates for job openings. The catch is that their main responsibility is to meet the employer's needs – not necessarily to find a suitable job for the candidate.

This is not to say that permanent employment agencies should be ruled out altogether. There are permanent employment agencies specializing in specific industries that can be useful for experienced professionals. However, permanent employment agencies are not always a good choice for entry-level jobseekers. Some will try to steer inexperienced candidates in an unwanted direction or offer little more than clerical placements to experienced applicants. Others charge a fee for their services – a condition that jobseekers should always ask about up front.

Some permanent employment agencies dispute the criticisms mentioned above. As one recruiter puts it, "Our responsibilities are to the applicant and the employer equally, because without one, we'll lose the other." She also maintains that entry-level people are desirable, saying that "as they grow, we grow, too, so we aim to move them up the ranks."

In short, as that recruiter states, "All services are not the same." If you decide to register with an agency, your best bet is to find one that is recommended by a friend or associate. Barring that, names of agencies across the country can be found in *The Adams Executive Recruiters Almanac* (Adams Media Corporation) or *The JobBank Guide to Employment Services* (Adams Media Corporation). Or you can contact:

National Association of Personnel Services (NAPS)
3133 Mount Vernon Avenue
Alexandria VA 22305
703/684-0180

Be aware that there are an increasing number of bogus employment service firms, often advertising in newspapers and magazines. These "services" promise even inexperienced jobseekers top salaries in exciting careers — all for a sizable fee. Others use expensive 900 numbers that jobseekers are encouraged to call. Unfortunately, most people find out too late that the jobs they have been promised do not exist.

As a general rule, most legitimate permanent employment agencies will never guarantee a job and will not seek payment until after the candidate has been placed. Even so, every agency you are interested in should be checked out with the local chapter of the Better Business Bureau (BBB). Find out if the agency is licensed and has been in business for a reasonable amount of time.

If everything checks out, call the firm to find out if it specializes in your area of expertise and how it will go about marketing your qualifications. After you have selected a few agencies (three to five is best), send each one a resume with a cover letter. Make a follow-up phone call a week or two later, and try to schedule an interview. Once again, be prepared to take a battery of tests at the interview.

Above all, do not expect too much. Only a small portion of all professional, managerial, and executive jobs are listed with these agencies. Use them as an addition to your job search campaign, not a centerpiece.

EXECUTIVE SEARCH FIRMS

Also known as "headhunters," these firms consist of recruiters who are paid by client companies that hire them to fill a specific position. Executive search firms seek out and carefully screen (and weed out) candidates for high-salaried technical, executive, and managerial positions and are paid by the employer. The prospective employee is generally not charged a fee. Unlike permanent employment agencies, they often approach viable candidates directly, rather than waiting for candidates to approach them. Some prefer to deal with already employed candidates. Whether you are employed or not, do not contact an executive search firm if you aren't ready to look for a job. If a recruiter tries to place you right away and finds out you are not really looking yet, it is unlikely they will spend much time with you in the future.

Many search firms specialize in particular industries, while generalist firms typically provide placements in a wide range of industries. Look for firms that specialize in your field of interest or expertise, as well as generalist firms that conduct searches in a variety of fields. While you should concentrate on firms in your geographic area, you do not have to limit yourself to these as many firms operate nationally or internationally.

There are two basic types of executive search firms — retainer-based and contingency-based. Note, however, that some firms conduct searches of both types. Essentially, retainer firms are hired by a client company for a search and paid a fee by the client company regardless of whether or not a placement is made. Conversely, contingency firms receive payment from the client company only when their candidate is hired. Fees are typically based on the position's first-year salary. The range is usually between 20 and 35 percent, and retainer firm fees tend to be at the higher end of that scale, according to Ivan Samuels, President of Abbott's of Boston, an executive search firm that conducts both types of searches.

Generally, companies use retainer firms to fill senior-level positions, with salaries over $60,000. In most cases, a company will hire only one retainer firm to fill a given position, and part of the process is a thorough, on-site visit by the search firm to the client company so that the recruiter may check out the operation. These search firms are recommended for a highly experienced professional seeking a job in his or her current field. Confidentiality is more secure with these firms, since a recruiter may only use your file in consideration for one job at a time, and most retainer firms will not freely circulate your resume without permission. This is particularly important to a jobseeker who is currently employed and insists on absolute discretion. If that's the case, however, make sure you do not contact a retainer firm used by your current employer.

Contingency firms make placements that cover a broader salary range, so these firms are more ideal for someone seeking a junior or mid-level position. Unlike retainer firms, contingency firms may be competing with other firms to fill a particular opening. As a result, these firms can be quicker and more responsive to your job search. In addition, a contingency firm will distribute your resume more widely. Some firms require your permission before sending your resume to any given company, while others ask that you trust their discretion. You should inquire about this with your recruiter at the outset, and choose according to your needs.

That said, once you've chosen the specific recruiter or recruiters that you will contact, keep in mind that recruiters are working for the companies that hire them, not for you, the jobseeker. Attempting to fill a position – especially amongst fierce competition with other firms – means your best interests may not be the recruiter's only priority. For this reason, you should contact as many search firms as possible in order to increase your chances of finding your ideal position.

A phone call is your first step, during which you should speak with a recruiter and exchange all relevant information. Ask lots of questions to determine the firm's credibility, whether they operate on a retainer or contingency basis (or both), and any and all questions you have regarding the firm's procedures. Offer the recruiter information about your employment history, as well as what type of work you are seeking. Make sure you sound enthusiastic, but not pushy. The recruiter will ask that you send a resume and cover letter as soon as possible.

Occasionally, the recruiter will arrange to meet with you, but most often this will not occur until he or she has received your resume and has found a potential match. James E. Slate, President of F-O-R-T-U-N-E Personnel Consultants in Topsfield, Massachusetts, advises that you generally not expect an abundance of personal attention at the beginning of the relationship with your recruiter, particularly with a large firm that works nationally and does most of its work over the phone. You should, however, use your recruiter's inside knowledge to your best advantage. Some recruiters will help coach you before an interview and many are open about giving you all the facts they know about a client company.

Not all executive search firms are licensed, so make sure those you plan to deal with have solid reputations and don't hesitate to check with the Better Business Bureau. Also keep in mind that it is common for recruiters to search for positions in other states. For example, recruiters in Boston sometimes look for candidates to fill positions in New York City, and the reverse is true as well. Names of search firms nationwide can be found in *The Adams Executive Recruiters Almanac* or *The JobBank Guide to Employment Services*, or by contacting:

Association of Executive Search Consultants (AESC)
500 Fifth Avenue, Suite 930, New York NY 10110. 212/398-9556.

Top Echelon, Inc.
World Wide Web address: http://www.topechelon.com.
A cooperative placement networking service of recruiting firms.

CONTRACT SERVICES FIRMS

Firms that place individuals on a contract basis commonly receive job orders from client companies that can last anywhere from a month to over a year. The function of these firms differs from that of a temporary agency in that the candidate has specific, marketable skills they wish to put to work, and the contract recruiter interviews the candidate extensively. Most often, contract services firms specialize in placing technical professionals, though some do specialize in other fields, including clerical and office support. The use of these firms is increasing in popularity, as jobseekers with technical skills recognize the benefit of utilizing and demonstrating their talents at a sampling of different companies, and establishing contacts along the way that could lead to a permanent position, if desired. Most contract services firms do not charge a fee to the candidate.

For more information on contract services, contact:

C.E. Publications, Inc.
Contract Employment Weekly Magazine
P.O. Box 3006, Bothell WA 98041-3006. 425/806-5200.
World Wide Web address: http://www.ceweekly.com.

RESUME/CAREER COUNSELING/OUTPLACEMENT SERVICES

These firms are very diverse in the services they provide. Many nonprofit organizations – colleges, universities, private associations – offer free or very inexpensive counseling services. For-profit career/outplacement counseling services, on the other hand, can charge a broad range of fees, depending on what services they provide. Services offered include career counseling, outplacement, resume development/writing, interview preparation, assessment testing, and various workshops. Upon contacting one of these firms, you should ask about the specific services that firm provides. Some firms provide career counseling only, teaching you how to conduct your own job search, while others also provide outplacement services. The difference here is that those which provide outplacement will conduct a job search for you, in addition to the counseling services. Firms like these are sometimes referred to as "marketing firms."

According to a representative at Career Ventures Counseling Services in Salem, Massachusetts, fees for career counseling average about $85 per hour. Counseling firms located in major cities tend to be more expensive. Furthermore, outplacement fees can range from $170 to over $7,000! As results are not guaranteed, you may want to check on a firm's reputation through the local Better Business Bureau.

For more information on resume services, contact:

Professional Association of Resume Writers
3637 Fourth Street, Suite 330, St. Petersburg FL 33704.
Attention: Mr. Frank Fox, Executive Director. 800/822-7279.
World Wide Web address: http://www.parw.com.

CAREER FAIRS

Career fairs are another great, often overlooked job-hunting resource. These organized gatherings of representatives and hiring managers from various companies afford you the opportunity to introduce yourself and often interview on-the-spot. Since putting a face and personality to a resume is a crucial part of decision-making in the hiring process, going to a career fair is a proactive way to make a good impression and get your foot in the door. Here you are given the chance to exhibit your skills, enthusiasm, and experience to many companies all in one day at one location, some of which have specific openings to fill. In addition, this can save you time and money that would have been spent sending out multiple resumes by mail or waiting for advertised openings. You should be sure to dress just as you would for a formal interview and have lots of resumes on-hand to pass out to potential employers.

Many career fairs are industry-specific. For instance, you can find fairs that specialize in high-tech, sales and marketing, or health care fields. Others are simply labeled "professional," and consist of representatives from a wide variety of industries. Information on upcoming career fairs is often advertised in newspapers, and can also be obtained online through job-hunting Websites as well as Websites solely dedicated to providing career fair information. Some sponsors hold career fairs nationwide and year-round – such as Kaplan Career Services – and have information listed on their Website including dates, times, locations, and which companies will attend.

For more information on career fairs, contact:

Kaplan Career Services
The Lendman Group
1081 19th Street, Suite 100, Virginia Beach VA 23451-5100.
800/288-2890. Fax: 757/437-2256.
World Wide Web address: http://www.lendman.com.

American Job Fairs
266A Duffy Avenue, Hicksville NY 11801.
800/77-EXPOS. Fax: 516/681-8040.
World Wide Web address: http://www.americanjobfairs.com.

Note: On the following pages, you will find employment services for this JobBank book's coverage area. Because contact names and addresses can change regularly, we recommend that you call each company to verify the information before inquiring about opportunities.

TEMPORARY EMPLOYMENT AGENCIES

ABC TEMPS INC.
3109 Carlisle Street, Suite 208, Dallas TX 75204. 214/754-7052. **Fax:** 214/954-1525. **Contact:** Regional Manager. **Description:** A temporary agency. **Specializes in the areas of:** Accounting/Auditing; Manufacturing; Personnel/Labor Relations; Secretarial. **Positions commonly filled include:** Blue-Collar Worker Supervisor; Credit Manager; Customer Service Representative; Human Resources Specialist; Typist/Word Processor. **Benefits available to temporary workers:** Credit Union; Paid Holidays; Vacation Days. **Corporate headquarters location:** This Location. **Other U.S. locations:** Fort Worth TX. **Average salary range of placements:** Less than $20,000. **Number of placements per year:** 200 - 499.

ACCLAIM SERVICES, INC.
5445 La Sierra, Suite 317, Dallas TX 75231. 214/750-1818. **Fax:** 214/750-4403. **Contact:** Manager. **Description:** A temporary agency. **Specializes in the areas of:** Network Administration; Software Development; Technical Writing. **Positions commonly filled include:** Management Analyst/Consultant; Software Engineer; Systems Analyst; Technical Writer/Editor; Telecommunications Manager. **Average salary range of placements:** More than $50,000. **Number of placements per year:** 50 - 99.

ACSYS STAFFING
12655 North Central Expressway, Suite 310, Dallas TX 75243. 972/991-3330. **Contact:** Mimi Dykes, Area Manager. **Description:** A temporary agency that also provides some temp-to-perm placements. **Specializes in the areas of:** Accounting; Banking; Computer Science/Software; Engineering; Finance; Insurance; Sales; Scientific; Secretarial; Technical. **Other U.S. locations:** Nationwide.

AQUENT PARTNERS
Heritage Square Tower One, LBJ Freeway, Suite 870, Dallas TX 75244-6013. 972/503-8877. **Toll-free phone:** 877/PARTNER. **Fax:** 972/503-8878. **Contact:** Paul Donaghy, Manager. **E-mail address:** pdonaghy@aquent.com. **World Wide Web address:** http://www.aquentpartners.com. **Description:** A temporary agency that also provides some temp-to-perm, permanent, and contract placements. **Specializes in the areas of:** Administration; Art/Design; Computer Science/Software; Marketing. **Positions commonly filled include:** Computer Animator; Computer Engineer; Computer Operator; Computer Programmer; Computer Support Technician; Computer Technician; Content Developer; Database Administrator; Database Manager; Desktop Publishing Specialist; Editor; Editorial Assistant; Graphic Artist; Graphic Designer; Internet Services Manager; Managing Editor; MIS Specialist; Multimedia Designer; Network/Systems Administrator; Production Manager; Project Manager; Software Engineer; SQL Programmer; Systems Analyst; Systems Manager; Technical Writer/Editor; Webmaster. **Benefits available to temporary workers:** 401(k); Dental Insurance; Disability Coverage; Medical Insurance. **CEO:** John Chuang.

ATTORNEY RESOURCE, INC.
750 North St. Paul, Suite 540, Dallas TX 75201. 214/922-8050. **Toll-free phone:** 800/324-4828. **Fax:** 214/871-3041. **Contact:** Jennifer Colby, Manager. **E-mail address:** info@attorneyresource.com. **World Wide Web address:** http://www.attorneyresource.com. **Description:** A temporary agency that also provides permanent placements. **Specializes in the areas of:** Administration; Legal; Secretarial. **Positions commonly filled include:** Attorney; Legal Secretary; Paralegal. **Benefits available to temporary workers:** Paid Holidays; Referral Bonus Plan; Vacation Days. **Corporate headquarters location:** This Location. **Other U.S. locations:** Tulsa OK; Austin TX; Fort Worth TX. **Number of placements per year:** 100 - 199.

BDE TEMPORARIES
5601 Bridge Street, Suite 405, Fort Worth TX 76112. 817/446-1898. **Fax:** 817/446-1899. **Contact:** Donnie Harley-Hayes, Owner. **Description:** A temporary agency that also provides some permanent and contract placements. Founded in 1992. **Positions commonly filled**

include: Accountant/Auditor; Administrative Manager; Advertising Clerk; Aerospace Engineer; Civil Engineer; Clerical Supervisor; Computer Programmer; Customer Service Representative; Design Engineer; Designer; Draftsperson; Financial Analyst; Human Resources Specialist; Mechanical Engineer; Paralegal; Social Worker; Software Engineer; Structural Engineer; Systems Analyst; Technical Writer/Editor. **Benefits available to temporary workers:** Paid Holidays; Vacation Days. **Corporate headquarters location:** This Location. **Other area locations:** Dallas TX. **Average salary range of placements:** $20,000 - $29,999. **Number of placements per year:** 50 - 99.

BURNETT'S STAFFING, INC.
2710 Avenue E East, Arlington TX 76011. 817/649-7000. **Contact:** Paul W. Burnett, President. **E-mail address:** n.arlington@burnetts.com. **World Wide Web address:** http://www.burnetts.com. **Description:** A temporary agency that also provides temp-to-perm and permanent placements. **Specializes in the areas of:** Administration; MIS/EDP; Secretarial. **Positions commonly filled include:** Accountant/Auditor; Administrative Assistant; Administrative Manager; Advertising Clerk; Bookkeeper; Claim Representative; Clerical Supervisor; Computer Operator; Controller; Credit Manager; Customer Service Representative; Data Entry Clerk; Human Resources Manager; Marketing Specialist; Receptionist; Secretary; Typist/Word Processor; Webmaster. **Benefits available to temporary workers:** Medical Insurance; Paid Holidays; Profit Sharing; Vacation Days. **Average salary range of placements:** $20,000 - $60,000.

BURNETT'S STAFFING, INC.
1431 Greenway, Suite 145, Irving TX 75038. 972/580-3333. **Fax:** 972/580-7711. **Contact:** Manager. **E-mail address:** las.colinas@burnetts.com. **World Wide Web address:** http://www.burnetts.com. **Description:** A temporary agency that also provides some temp-to-perm and permanent placements. **Specializes in the areas of:** Administration; Clerical; Secretarial. **Corporate headquarters location:** Arlington TX.

CO-COUNSEL
600 North Pearl Street, Suite 430, Dallas TX 75201. 214/720-3763. **Fax:** 214/720-0555. **Contact:** Staffing Coordinator. **Description:** A temporary agency. **Specializes in the areas of:** Legal. **Positions commonly filled include:** Attorney; Paralegal. **Average salary range of placements:** $30,000 - $50,000.

CONSULTIS
10300 North Central Expressway, Suite 125, Dallas TX 75231. 214/691-8111. **Contact:** Kim Kent, Resource Coordinator. **Description:** A temporary agency. **Specializes in the areas of:** Computer Science/Software; Data Processing; Information Technology; Personnel/Labor Relations; Technical. **Positions commonly filled include:** Computer Operator; Computer Programmer; Internet Services Manager; Library Technician; MIS Specialist; Multimedia Designer; Software Engineer; Systems Analyst; Technical Writer/Editor; Telecommunications Manager. **Average salary range of placements:** $30,000 - $50,000. **Number of placements per year:** 200 - 499.

DEPENDABLE DENTAL STAFFING
18601 LBJ Freeway, Suite 707, Mesquite TX 75150-5600. 972/681-9490. **Fax:** 972/681-9657. **Contact:** Karen Houston, Vice President. **Description:** A temporary agency. **Specializes in the areas of:** Health/Medical. **Positions commonly filled include:** Dental Assistant/Dental Hygienist; Dentist. **Other U.S. locations:** Arlington TX. **Average salary range of placements:** $30,000 - $50,000. **Number of placements per year:** 200 - 499.

DIVIDEND STAFFING SERVICES
2107 Kemp Boulevard, Wichita Falls TX 76309. 940/723-0150. **Toll-free phone:** 800/687-1275. **Fax:** 940/766-1680. **Contact:** Bill Palin, President. **E-mail address:** dividend@dividend-staffing.com. **World Wide Web address:** http://www.dividend-staffing.com. **Description:** A temporary agency that also offers temp-to-perm and contract placements. Client company pays fee. **Specializes in the areas of:** Accounting; Administration; Computer Science/Software; Engineering; Finance; General Management; Health/Medical; Industrial; Light Industrial; Marketing; MIS/EDP; Sales; Scientific; Secretarial; Technical. **Positions commonly filled include:** Account Manager; Account Representative; Accountant; Administrative Assistant; Administrative Manager; Applications Engineer; Architect; AS400 Programmer Analyst; Assistant Manager; Auditor; Bank Officer/Manager; Blue-Collar Worker Supervisor; Branch Manager; Budget Analyst; Buyer; Chemical Engineer; Chemist; Chief Financial Officer; Civil Engineer; Clerical Supervisor; Clinical Lab Technician; Computer Engineer; Computer Operator; Computer Programmer; Computer Support Technician; Computer Technician;

Construction Contractor; Controller; Cost Estimator; Credit Manager; Customer Service Representative; Database Administrator; Database Manager; Draftsperson; Ecologist; Education Administrator; Electrical/Electronics Engineer; Electrician; Environmental Engineer; Finance Director; Financial Analyst; Fund Manager; Graphic Artist; Graphic Designer; Human Resources Manager; Industrial Engineer; Industrial Production Manager; Management Trainee; Manufacturing Engineer; Marketing Manager; Mechanical Engineer; Medical Records Technician; Metallurgical Engineer; MIS Specialist; Multimedia Designer; Network/Systems Administrator; Occupational Therapist; Paralegal; Physical Therapist; Physician; Production Manager; Project Manager; Purchasing Agent/Manager; Quality Assurance Engineer; Quality Control Supervisor; Registered Nurse; Sales Engineer; Sales Manager; Sales Representative; Secretary; Social Worker; Software Engineer; Statistician; Systems Analyst; Systems Manager; Technical Writer/Editor; Transportation/Traffic Specialist; Typist/Word Processor; Underwriter/Assistant Underwriter. **Benefits available to temporary workers:** Cafeteria Plan. **Corporate headquarters location:** This Location. **Other U.S. locations:** Dallas TX. **Average salary range of placements:** $20,000 - $29,999. **Number of placements per year:** 200 - 499.

DRIVING FORCE, INC.
2030 Las Vegas Trail, Fort Worth TX 76108. 817/246-7113. **Contact:** G. Wayne Brown, Sr., President. **Description:** A temporary agency. **Specializes in the areas of:** Transportation. **Positions commonly filled include:** Driver. **Benefits available to temporary workers:** Credit Union; Dental Insurance; Life Insurance; Medical Insurance. **Other U.S. locations:** Abilene TX; Austin TX; Dallas TX; Houston TX; San Antonio TX. **Average salary range of placements:** $30,000 - $50,000. **Number of placements per year:** 1 - 49.

ESPRIT TEMPORARY SERVICES
P.O. Box 35443, Dallas TX 75235. 214/631-3832. **Fax:** 214/638-2908. **Contact:** Recruiter. **Description:** A temporary agency. **Specializes in the areas of:** Administration; Customer Service; General Labor; Secretarial. **Positions commonly filled include:** Administrative Assistant; Administrative Manager; Blue-Collar Worker Supervisor; Computer Operator; Electrician; Human Resources Manager; Industrial Production Manager; Paralegal; Typist/Word Processor. **Benefits available to temporary workers:** Dental Insurance; Medical Insurance; Vacation Days. **Average salary range of placements:** $30,000 - $50,000. **Number of placements per year:** 200 - 499.

FIRSTWORD STAFFING SERVICES
10000 North Central Expressway, Suite 118, Dallas TX 75231. 214/360-0020. **Fax:** 214/360-9206. **Contact:** JoLynne Pratt, Recruiting. **Description:** A temporary agency. **Specializes in the areas of:** Computer Science/Software; Personnel/Labor Relations; Secretarial; Technical. **Positions commonly filled include:** Claim Representative; Clerical Supervisor; Computer Programmer; Cost Estimator; Customer Service Representative; Electronics Technician; Paralegal; Typist/Word Processor. **Benefits available to temporary workers:** Dental Insurance; Medical Insurance; Paid Holidays; Referral Bonus Plan; Vacation Days. **Corporate headquarters location:** Charlotte NC. **Average salary range of placements:** $20,000 - $29,999.

HIREKNOWLEDGE
13500 Midway Road, Suite 205, Dallas TX 75244. 972/385-9269. **Toll-free phone:** 800/937-3622. **Fax:** 972/385-1750. **Contact:** Recruiter. **World Wide Web address:** http://www.hireknowledge.com. **Description:** A temporary agency that also offers some permanent placements. Client company pays fee. **Specializes in the areas of:** Advertising; Art/Design; Computer Science/Software; Internet Development; Internet Marketing; MIS/EDP; Printing; Publishing. **Positions commonly filled include:** Applications Engineer; AS400 Programmer Analyst; Computer Animator; Computer Engineer; Computer Graphics Specialist; Computer Operator; Computer Programmer; Computer Scientist; Computer Support Technician; Computer Technician; Content Developer; Database Administrator; Database Manager; Editor; Editorial Assistant; Graphic Artist; Graphic Designer; Internet Services Manager; Managing Editor; MIS Specialist; Multimedia Designer; Network/Systems Administrator; Software Engineer; Systems Analyst; Systems Manager; Technical Writer/Editor; Webmaster. **Benefits available to temporary workers:** 401(k); Direct Deposit; Health Benefits; Vacation Pay. **Corporate headquarters location:** Providence RI. **Other U.S. locations:** Nationwide. **Average salary range of placements:** $30,000 - $49,999. **Number of placements per year:** 200 - 499.

IMPRIMIS STAFFING SOLUTIONS
5550 LBJ Freeway, Suite 100, Dallas TX 75240. 972/419-1631. **Fax:** 972/419-1970. **Contact:** Recruiter. **World Wide Web address:** http://www.imprimis-group.com. **Description:** A temporary agency that also offers some permanent placements. **Specializes in the areas of:**

Accounting/Auditing; Administration; Clerical; Computer Science/Software; Finance; Insurance; Legal; Nonprofit; Personnel/Labor Relations; Secretarial. **Positions commonly filled include:** Accountant/Auditor; Administrative Assistant; Auditor; Clerical Supervisor; Computer Operator; Customer Service Representative; Graphic Artist; Human Resources Specialist; MIS Specialist; Sales Representative; Software Engineer; Typist/Word Processor. **Benefits available to temporary workers:** 401(k); Medical Insurance; Paid Holidays; Vacation Days. **Other U.S. locations:** Fort Worth TX. **Average salary range of placements:** $20,000 - $29,999. **Number of placements per year:** 1000+.

INSURANCE TEMPORARY SERVICES, INC.
2777 Stemmons Freeway, Suite 946, Dallas TX 75207. 214/638-7777. **Fax:** 214/634-8500. **Contact:** Susie Lowry, President. **Description:** A temporary agency. **Specializes in the areas of:** Insurance. **Positions commonly filled include:** Adjuster; Claim Representative; Customer Service Representative; Typist/Word Processor.

KELLY SCIENTIFIC RESOURCES
18601 LBJ Freeway, Suite 140, Mesquite TX 75150-5629. 972/279-3265. **Contact:** Branch Manager. **World Wide Web address:** http://www.kellyscientific.com. **Description:** A temporary agency for scientific professionals. **Specializes in the areas of:** Biomedical; Biotechnology; Chemicals; Environmental; Food; Petrochemical; Pharmaceuticals.

KELLY SERVICES, INC.
1800 Teague Drive, Suite 100, Sherman TX 75090. 903/893-7777. **Contact:** Branch Manager. **Description:** A temporary agency. **Specializes in the areas of:** Accounting/Auditing; Banking; Clerical; Computer Hardware/Software; Engineering; Finance; Health/Medical; Legal; Manufacturing; Secretarial; Technical; Transportation. **Other U.S. locations:** Nationwide.

KELLY SERVICES, INC.
1616 South Kentucky, Building D, Suite 110, Amarillo TX 79102. 806/355-9696. **Fax:** 806/359-0308. **Contact:** Branch Manager. **Description:** A temporary agency. Founded in 1946. **Specializes in the areas of:** Accounting/Auditing; Administration; Finance; Insurance; Secretarial. **Positions commonly filled include:** Administrative Assistant; Marketing Specialist; Secretary; Typist/Word Processor. **Benefits available to temporary workers:** Medical Insurance; Paid Holidays; Vacation Days. **Other U.S. locations:** Nationwide. **Average salary range of placements:** $20,000 - $29,999. **Number of placements per year:** 500 - 999.

MANPOWER TEMPORARY SERVICES
12225 Greenville Avenue, Suite 495, Dallas TX 75243. 972/699-9337. **Contact:** Manager. **World Wide Web address:** http://www.manpower.com. **Description:** A temporary agency that also provides some permanent placements. **Specializes in the areas of:** Data Processing; Light Industrial; Office Support; Technical; Travel. **Benefits available to temporary workers:** Life Insurance; Medical Insurance; Paid Holidays; Referral Bonus Plan; Stock Purchase; Training; Vacation Days. **Number of placements per year:** 1000+.

NORRELL SERVICES
5605 North MacArthur Boulevard, Suite 200, Irving TX 75038. 972/263-5045. **Fax:** 972/432-9359. **Contact:** Recruiter. **Description:** A temporary agency. **Specializes in the areas of:** Secretarial. **Positions commonly filled include:** Customer Service Representative; Typist/Word Processor.

PRO STAFF PERSONNEL SERVICES
14755 Preston Road, Suite 120, Dallas TX 75240. 972/239-8800. **Toll-free phone:** 800/938-9675. **Fax:** 972/239-4600. **Contact:** Katherine Tolsch, Branch Manager. **World Wide Web address:** http://www.prostaff.com. **Description:** A temporary agency that also provides some permanent placements. **Specializes in the areas of:** Accounting/Auditing; Advertising; Computer Science/Software; Engineering; Finance; Light Industrial; Manufacturing; Sales; Secretarial; Technical. **Positions commonly filled include:** Accountant/Auditor; Administrative Manager; Advertising Clerk; Bank Officer/Manager; Blue-Collar Worker Supervisor; Branch Manager; Brokerage Clerk; Budget Analyst; Claim Representative; Clerical Supervisor; Computer Programmer; Cost Estimator; Design Engineer; Electrical/Electronics Engineer; Financial Analyst; General Manager; Human Resources Specialist; Industrial Engineer; Industrial Production Manager; Management Analyst/Consultant; Management Trainee; Manufacturer's/Wholesaler's Sales Rep.; Market Research Analyst; Mechanical Engineer; MIS Specialist; Operations/Production Manager; Purchasing Agent/Manager; Quality Control Supervisor; Services Sales Representative; Software Engineer; Systems Analyst; Technical Writer/Editor; Typist/Word Processor; Underwriter/Assistant Underwriter. **Benefits available to**

temporary workers: 401(k); Medical Insurance; Paid Holidays; Vacation Days. **Corporate headquarters location:** Minneapolis MN. **Other U.S. locations:** Nationwide. **Average salary range of placements:** $20,000 - $29,999. **Number of placements per year:** 1000+.

PRO STAFF PERSONNEL SERVICES
122 West John Carpenter Freeway, Suite 515, Irving TX 75039. 972/650-1500. **Fax:** 972/650-0857. **Recorded jobline:** 972/712-6528. **Contact:** Manager. **World Wide Web address:** http://www.prostaff.com. **Description:** A temporary agency. **Specializes in the areas of:** Accounting/Auditing; Administration; Art/Design; Secretarial; Technical. **Positions commonly filled include:** Customer Service Representative; Light Industrial Worker; Receptionist; Typist/Word Processor. **Benefits available to temporary workers:** 401(k); Medical Insurance. **Corporate headquarters location:** Minneapolis MN. **Average salary range of placements:** Less than $20,000. **Number of placements per year:** 1000+.

RESPIRATORY STAFFING SPECIALISTS INC.
310 East Interstate 30, Suite 310, Garland TX 75043. 972/226-5421. **Toll-free phone:** 800/758-3275. **Fax:** 972/226-0323. **Contact:** Carla DeWitt, President. **Description:** A temporary agency. **Specializes in the areas of:** Health/Medical. **Positions commonly filled include:** Respiratory Therapist. **Average salary range of placements:** $20,000 - $29,999. **Number of placements per year:** 1 - 49.

RESTAURANT SERVERS, INC.
P.O. Box 32, Colleyville TX 76034-0032. 214/350-1166. **Fax:** 214/350-0454. **Contact:** Manager. **Description:** A temporary agency that also provides contract services in event management. **Specializes in the areas of:** Food. **Positions commonly filled include:** Blue-Collar Worker Supervisor; Education Administrator; Management Trainee; Registered Nurse; Restaurant/Food Service Manager. **Average salary range of placements:** Less than $20,000. **Number of placements per year:** 200 - 499.

SOS STAFFING SERVICE
1111 Airport Freeway, Suite 215, Irving TX 75062. 972/870-9662. **Contact:** Manager. **Description:** A temporary agency that also provides some permanent placements. **Specializes in the areas of:** Administration; Industrial; Manufacturing; Personnel/Labor Relations; Secretarial. **Positions commonly filled include:** Accountant/Auditor; Automotive Mechanic; Blue-Collar Worker Supervisor; Buyer; Claim Representative; Clerical Supervisor; Computer Programmer; Cost Estimator; Credit Manager; Customer Service Representative; Design Engineer; Draftsperson; Hotel Manager; Human Service Worker; Landscape Architect; Mechanical Engineer; Operations/Production Manager; Purchasing Agent/Manager; Restaurant/Food Service Manager; Telecommunications Manager; Travel Agent; Typist/Word Processor. **Benefits available to temporary workers:** Paid Holidays; Vacation Days. **Number of placements per year:** 100 - 199.

ANNE SADOVSKY & COMPANY
7557 Rambler Road, Suite 1454, Dallas TX 75231. 214/692-9300. **Fax:** 214/692-9823. **Contact:** Manager. **Description:** A temporary agency. **Specializes in the areas of:** Housing; Sales. **Average salary range of placements:** $20,000 - $29,999. **Number of placements per year:** 1000+.

SPECIAL COUNSEL
AMICUS LEGAL STAFFING INC.
1412 Main Street, Suite 205, Dallas TX 75202. 214/698-0200. **Contact:** Manager. **Description:** A temporary agency that also provides some permanent placements and executive services. **Specializes in the areas of:** Legal.

TRC STAFFING SERVICES INC.
1300 Summit Avenue, Suite 634, Fort Worth TX 76102. 817/335-1550. **Contact:** Operations Manager. **E-mail address:** trc@onramp.net. **Description:** A temporary agency that also provides some temp-to-perm placements. **Specializes in the areas of:** Clerical; Industrial; Manufacturing; Secretarial; Technical. **Positions commonly filled include:** Accountant/Auditor; Buyer; Chemist; Claim Representative; Computer Programmer; Customer Service Representative; Paralegal; Systems Analyst; Technical Writer/Editor. **Benefits available to temporary workers:** Medical Insurance; Paid Holidays; Vacation Days. **Corporate headquarters location:** Atlanta GA.

TODAYS LEGAL STAFFING
700 North Pearl Street, Suite 350, Dallas TX 75201. 214/754-0700. **Toll-free phone:** 800/693-1514. **Contact:** Tom Gardner, Group Manager. **World Wide Web address:**

http://www.todays.com. **Description:** A temporary agency that also provides some permanent placements. **Specializes in the areas of:** Legal; Secretarial. **Positions commonly filled include:** Attorney; Paralegal; Typist/Word Processor. **Other U.S. locations:** Nationwide. **Average salary range of placements:** $30,000 - $50,000. **Number of placements per year:** 200 - 499.

TODAYS OFFICE STAFFING
8445 Freeport Parkway, Suite 310, Irving TX 75063. 972/915-0555. **Fax:** 972/915-0551. **Contact:** Operations Manager. **World Wide Web address:** http://www.todays.com. **Description:** A temporary agency. **Specializes in the areas of:** Secretarial. **Positions commonly filled include:** Administrative Manager; Advertising Clerk; Branch Manager; Claim Representative; Clerical Supervisor; Customer Service Representative. **Corporate headquarters location:** Dallas TX. **Other U.S. locations:** Nationwide. **Average salary range of placements:** $20,000 - $29,999. **Number of placements per year:** 1000+.

TODAYS OFFICE STAFFING
4100 Alpha Road, Suite 215, Dallas TX 75244-4332. 972/788-4435. **Fax:** 972/233-6388. **Contact:** Operations Manager. **World Wide Web address:** http://www.todays.com. **Description:** A temporary agency. **Specializes in the areas of:** Accounting/Auditing; Computer Science/Software; Legal; Personnel/Labor Relations; Sales. **Positions commonly filled include:** Clerical Supervisor; Financial Analyst; Human Resources Specialist; Human Service Worker. **Benefits available to temporary workers:** Paid Holidays; Vacation Days. **Corporate headquarters location:** Dallas TX. **Other U.S. locations:** Nationwide. **Number of placements per year:** 1000+.

TODAYS STAFFING
18111 Preston Road, Suite 700, Dallas TX 75252. 972/380-9380. **Fax:** 972/713-4196. **Contact:** Carol Crane, Payroll Administrator. **World Wide Web address:** http://www.todays.com. **Description:** A temporary agency. **Specializes in the areas of:** Accounting/Auditing; Banking; Legal; Secretarial. **Positions commonly filled include:** Accountant/Auditor; Administrative Manager; Advertising Clerk; Attorney; Brokerage Clerk; Claim Representative; Computer Programmer; Customer Service Representative; Paralegal; Typist/Word Processor. **Benefits available to temporary workers:** 401(k); Paid Holidays; Vacation Days. **Corporate headquarters location:** This Location. **Other U.S. locations:** Nationwide. **Average salary range of placements:** Less than $20,000. **Number of placements per year:** 1000+.

VOLT SERVICES GROUP OF DALLAS
9330 LBJ Freeway, Suite 1060, Dallas TX 75243-9946. 972/690-8358. **Contact:** Office Manager. **Description:** A temporary agency. **Specializes in the areas of:** Clerical; Computer Hardware/Software; Engineering; Manufacturing; Personnel/Labor Relations; Technical.

WESTAFF
323 East Las Colinas Boulevard, Irving TX 75039-5556. 972/831-8833. **Fax:** 972/831-8856. **Contact:** Staffing Coordinator. **Description:** A temporary agency. **Specializes in the areas of:** Industrial; Personnel/Labor Relations; Sales; Secretarial; Technical. **Positions commonly filled include:** Blue-Collar Worker Supervisor; Customer Service Representative; Human Resources Specialist; Management Trainee; Services Sales Representative. **Benefits available to temporary workers:** 401(k); Medical Insurance; Paid Holidays; Vacation Days. **Corporate headquarters location:** Walnut Creek CA. **Other U.S. locations:** Nationwide. **Number of placements per year:** 1000+.

PERMANENT EMPLOYMENT AGENCIES

ABILENE EMPLOYMENT SERVICE
1290 South Willis Street, Suite 111, Abilene TX 79605. 915/698-0451. **Fax:** 915/690-1242. **Contact:** Vi Ballard, Owner. **Description:** A permanent employment agency. **Specializes in the areas of:** Accounting/Auditing; Banking; Computer Science/Software; General Management; Health/Medical; Insurance; Legal; Manufacturing; Retail; Secretarial; Transportation. **Positions commonly filled include:** Accountant/Auditor; Administrative Manager; Advertising Clerk; Aircraft Mechanic/Engine Specialist; Automotive Mechanic; Bank Officer/Manager; Blue-Collar Worker Supervisor; Branch Manager; Buyer; Clerical Supervisor; Computer Programmer; Cost Estimator; Counselor; Customer Service Representative; Electrician; General Manager; Human Service Worker; Landscape Architect; Medical Records Technician; Operations/Production

Manager; Physical Therapist; Property and Real Estate Manager; Quality Control Supervisor; Real Estate Agent; Restaurant/Food Service Manager; Securities Sales Representative; Software Engineer; Systems Analyst; Travel Agent; Typist/Word Processor. **Average salary range of placements:** $20,000 - $29,999. **Number of placements per year:** 1 - 49.

ACCOUNTING ACTION PERSONNEL
3010 LBJ Freeway, Suite 710, Dallas TX 75234. 972/241-1543. **Contact:** Cheryl Bieke, Office Manager. **E-mail address:** acaction@airmail.net. **World Wide Web address:** http://www.gtesupersite.com/acctgaction. **Description:** A permanent employment agency that also provides some temporary placements. **Specializes in the areas of:** Accounting/Auditing; Administration; Finance. **Positions commonly filled include:** Accountant/Auditor; Administrative Assistant; Bookkeeper; Clerk; Credit Manager; Data Entry Clerk; Receptionist; Secretary; Typist/Word Processor.

AUSTIN MEDICAL PERSONNEL
3330 Matlock Road, Suite 210, Arlington TX 76015. 817/335-2433. **Fax:** 817/459-0761. **Contact:** Paula Zimmer, Owner. **E-mail address:** paula@austinmedical.net. **Description:** A permanent employment agency. **Specializes in the areas of:** Health/Medical.

AWARE AFFILIATES PERSONNEL SERVICE
1209 Lake Street, Fort Worth TX 76147. 817/870-2591. **Fax:** 817/870-2595. **Contact:** Mike Keeton, President. **Description:** A permanent employment agency. **Specializes in the areas of:** Accounting/Auditing; Administration; Advertising; Finance; General Management; Health/Medical; Insurance; Legal; Manufacturing; Nonprofit; Personnel/Labor Relations; Publishing; Retail; Sales; Secretarial; Technical; Transportation. **Positions commonly filled include:** Accountant/Auditor; Adjuster; Administrative Manager; Advertising Clerk; Blue-Collar Worker Supervisor; Branch Manager; Claim Representative; Clerical Supervisor; Computer Programmer; Cost Estimator; Counselor; Credit Manager; Customer Service Representative; Editor; Financial Analyst; General Manager; Health Services Manager; Hotel Manager; Human Resources Specialist; Insurance Agent/Broker; Library Technician; Management Trainee; Manufacturer's/Wholesaler's Sales Rep.; Operations/Production Manager; Paralegal; Property and Real Estate Manager; Purchasing Agent/Manager; Quality Control Supervisor; Securities Sales Representative; Services Sales Representative; Transportation/Traffic Specialist; Travel Agent; Typist/Word Processor; Underwriter/Assistant Underwriter. **Average salary range of placements:** $30,000 - $49,999. **Number of placements per year:** 200 - 499.

BABICH & ASSOCIATES, INC.
6030 East Mockingbird Lane, Dallas TX 75206. 214/823-9999. **Contact:** Anthony Beshara, President. **Description:** A permanent employment agency. **Specializes in the areas of:** Accounting/Auditing; Administration; Clerical; Computer Hardware/Software; Engineering; Finance; Manufacturing; Sales; Technical. **Positions commonly filled include:** Accountant/Auditor; Administrative Assistant; Agricultural Engineer; Bookkeeper; Ceramics Engineer; Civil Engineer; Computer Programmer; Customer Service Representative; Data Entry Clerk; EDP Specialist; Electrical/Electronics Engineer; Financial Analyst; General Manager; Human Resources Manager; Industrial Engineer; Mechanical Engineer; Medical Secretary; Metallurgical Engineer; Receptionist; Secretary; Systems Analyst; Typist/Word Processor. **Number of placements per year:** 500 - 999.

BABICH & ASSOCIATES, INC.
One Summit Avenue, Suite 602, Fort Worth TX 76102. 817/336-7261. **Contact:** Anthony Beshara, President. **Description:** A permanent employment agency. **Specializes in the areas of:** Accounting/Auditing; Administration; Clerical; Computer Hardware/Software; Engineering; Manufacturing; Sales; Technical. **Positions commonly filled include:** Accountant/Auditor; Administrative Assistant; Agricultural Engineer; Bookkeeper; Ceramics Engineer; Civil Engineer; Computer Programmer; Customer Service Representative; Data Entry Clerk; EDP Specialist; Electrical/Electronics Engineer; Financial Analyst; General Manager; Human Resources Manager; Industrial Engineer; Mechanical Engineer; Medical Secretary; Metallurgical Engineer; Receptionist; Sales Representative; Secretary; Stenographer; Systems Analyst; Typist/Word Processor. **Number of placements per year:** 500 - 999.

BRAINPOWER PERSONNEL AGENCY
4210 50th Street, Suite A, Lubbock TX 79413-3810. 806/795-0644. **Fax:** 806/795-0645. **Contact:** Phil Crenshaw, CPC/Owner. **Description:** A permanent employment agency. **Specializes in the areas of:** Accounting/Auditing; Administration; Computer Science/Software; Data Processing; Engineering; Finance; Health/Medical; Sales; Secretarial. **Positions commonly filled include:** Accountant/Auditor; Computer Programmer; Customer Service Representative;

Electrical/Electronics Engineer; MIS Specialist; Social Worker; Software Engineer. **Average salary range of placements:** $20,000 - $29,999. **Number of placements per year:** 1 - 49.

COLVIN RESOURCES GROUP
4141 Blue Lake Circle, Suite 140, Dallas TX 75244-5132. 972/788-5114. **Fax:** 972/490-5015. **Contact:** Sheila Bridges, Senior Account Executive. **Description:** A permanent employment agency that also provides temporary placements. **Specializes in the areas of:** Accounting/Auditing; Architecture/Construction; Banking; Finance; General Management; Health/Medical; Personnel/Labor Relations; Secretarial. **Positions commonly filled include:** Accountant/Auditor; Budget Analyst; Credit Manager; Financial Analyst; Human Resources Specialist; Property and Real Estate Manager; Typist/Word Processor. **Average salary range of placements:** $30,000 - $50,000. **Number of placements per year:** 200 - 499.

DALLAS EMPLOYMENT SERVICES, INC.
750 North St. Paul Street, Suite 1180, Dallas TX 75201-3230. 214/954-0700. **Toll-free phone:** 800/954-1666. **Fax:** 214/754-0148. **Contact:** Manager. **E-mail address:** des@des-inc.com. **World Wide Web address:** http://www.des-inc.com. **Description:** A permanent employment agency that also offers temporary placements. **Specializes in the areas of:** Accounting; Administration; Banking; Fashion; Finance; General Management; Health/Medical; Industrial; Insurance; Legal; Marketing; Personnel/Labor Relations; Publishing; Retail; Sales; Secretarial. **Positions commonly filled include:** Accountant; Administrative Assistant; Administrative Manager; Advertising Clerk; Assistant Manager; Budget Analyst; Claim Representative; Clerical Supervisor; Customer Service Representative; Financial Analyst; General Manager; Graphic Artist; Human Resources Manager; Management Trainee; Market Research Analyst; Marketing Specialist; Operations Manager; Paralegal; Production Manager; Public Relations Specialist; Sales Representative; Secretary; Typist/Word Processor; Underwriter/Assistant Underwriter. **Corporate headquarters location:** This Location. **Average salary range of placements:** $20,000 - $50,000. **Number of placements per year:** 200 - 499.

DATAPRO PERSONNEL CONSULTANTS
13355 Noel Road, Suite 2001, Dallas TX 75240. 972/661-8600. **Fax:** 972/661-1309. **Contact:** Jack Kallison, Owner. **Description:** A permanent employment agency. **Specializes in the areas of:** Computer Programming; Computer Science/Software. **Positions commonly filled include:** Computer Programmer; EDP Specialist; Project Manager; Software Engineer; Systems Analyst; Technical Writer/Editor.

EVINS PERSONNEL CONSULTANTS
209 South Leggett, Abilene TX 79605. 915/677-9153. **Contact:** Manager. **Description:** A permanent employment agency that also provides some temporary placements. **Corporate headquarters location:** This Location. **Other area locations:** Austin TX; Killeen TX; San Angelo TX; Tyler TX.

EVINS PERSONNEL CONSULTANTS OF KILLEEN, INC.
206 West Avenue B, Killeen TX 76541. 254/526-4161. **Fax:** 254/634-6913. **Contact:** Michelle G. Sweeney, Owner. **Description:** A permanent employment agency that also provides some temporary and contract services. **Specializes in the areas of:** Banking; General Management; Legal; Personnel/Labor Relations; Retail; Secretarial. **Positions commonly filled include:** Accountant; Administrative Assistant; Administrative Manager; Auditor; Bank Officer/Manager; Certified Nurses Aide; Clerical Supervisor; Computer Operator; Credit Manager; Dietician/Nutritionist; Editorial Assistant; Education Administrator; General Manager; Graphic Designer; Human Resources Manager; Licensed Practical Nurse; Management Trainee; Paralegal; Pharmacist; Physician; Registered Nurse; Sales Executive; Sales Manager; Secretary; Systems Analyst; Technical Writer/Editor. **Benefits available to temporary workers:** Paid Holidays; Sick Days. **Other area locations:** Abilene TX; Austin TX; San Angelo TX; Tyler TX. **Average salary range of placements:** $20,000 - $29,999. **Number of placements per year:** 1 - 49.

EXPRESS PERSONNEL SERVICES
P.O. Box 8136, Waco TX 76714-8136. 254/776-3300. **Toll-free phone:** 800/997-7377. **Fax:** 254/776-4822. **Contact:** Jerry Scofield, Owner. **World Wide Web address:** http://www.express-waco.com. **Description:** A permanent employment agency that also provides some temporary placements. Founded in 1983. **Specializes in the areas of:** Accounting/Auditing; Administration; Architecture/Construction; Banking; Clerical; Computer Hardware/Software; Engineering; Finance; Food; Health/Medical; Insurance; Legal; Manufacturing; Physician Executive; Sales; Secretarial. **Other U.S. locations:** Nationwide.

EXPRESS PERSONNEL SERVICES
3701 South Cooper Street, Suite 250, Arlington TX 76015. 817/468-9118. **Fax:** 817/468-9211. **Contact:** Gary Gibson, Manager. **World Wide Web address:** http://www.expresspersonnel.com. **Description:** A permanent employment agency that also provides some temporary and temp-to-perm placements. **Specializes in the areas of:** Accounting/Auditing; Banking; Computer Science/Software; Finance; General Management; Health/Medical; Industrial; Insurance; Personnel/Labor Relations; Publishing; Sales; Secretarial. **Positions commonly filled include:** Accountant/Auditor; Administrative Manager; Advertising Clerk; Bank Officer/Manager; Blue-Collar Worker Supervisor; Branch Manager; Clerical Supervisor; Cost Estimator; Customer Service Representative; General Manager; Human Resources Specialist; Industrial Production Manager; Management Trainee; Paralegal; Public Relations Specialist; Quality Control Supervisor; Technical Writer/Editor; Typist/Word Processor. **Benefits available to temporary workers:** Medical Insurance; Paid Holidays; Vacation Days. **Other U.S. locations:** Nationwide. **Average salary range of placements:** $30,000 - $50,000. **Number of placements per year:** 1 - 49.

FINANCIAL PROFESSIONALS
4100 Spring Valley Road, Suite 307, Dallas TX 75244. 972/991-8999. **Toll-free phone:** 800/856-5599. **Fax:** 972/702-0776. **Contact:** Vice President of Operations. **World Wide Web address:** http://www.fpstaff.net. **Description:** A permanent employment agency that also provides temporary placements. **Specializes in the areas of:** Banking; Finance. **Positions commonly filled include:** Accountant; Administrative Assistant; Auditor; Bank Officer/Manager; Branch Manager; Chief Financial Officer; Controller; Credit Manager; Customer Service Representative; Finance Director; Financial Analyst; Human Resources Manager; Operations Manager. **Benefits available to temporary workers:** Medical Insurance; Paid Holidays; Vacation Days. **Corporate headquarters location:** This Location. **Other area locations:** Fort Worth TX; Houston TX. **Average salary range of placements:** $20,000 - $29,999. **Number of placements per year:** 1 - 49.

LRJ STAFFING SERVICES
2010 Southwest HK Dodgen Loop, Suite 102, Temple TX 76504. 254/742-1981. **Toll-free phone:** 800/581-1850. **Fax:** 254/774-9675. **Contact:** David Kyle, Branch Manager. **Description:** A permanent employment agency. **Specializes in the areas of:** Computer Science/Software; Engineering; Industrial; Light Industrial; Manufacturing; Personnel/Labor Relations; Publishing; Technical. **Positions commonly filled include:** Blue-Collar Worker Supervisor; Computer Programmer; Customer Service Representative; Industrial Engineer; Industrial Production Manager; Services Sales Representative; Systems Analyst; Typist/Word Processor. **Benefits available to temporary workers:** Paid Holidays; Sick Days. **Corporate headquarters location:** Austin TX. **Other U.S. locations:** Dallas TX; San Antonio TX. **Average salary range of placements:** $20,000 - $29,999. **Number of placements per year:** 50 - 99.

MARQUESS & ASSOCIATES
15441 Knoll Trail Drive, Lockbox 1, Suite 280, Dallas TX 75248. 972/490-5288. **Fax:** 972/490-5004. **Contact:** Terri Marquess, Owner. **Description:** A permanent employment agency. **Specializes in the areas of:** Retail; Sales; Secretarial; Technical. **Positions commonly filled include:** Accountant/Auditor; Administrative Manager; Advertising Clerk; Buyer; Clerical Supervisor; Computer Programmer; Credit Manager; Customer Service Representative; Electrical/Electronics Engineer; Financial Analyst; General Manager; Human Service Worker; Industrial Engineer; Management Trainee; Mechanical Engineer; MIS Specialist; Services Sales Representative; Software Engineer; Systems Analyst; Technical Writer/Editor; Telecommunications Manager.

MEDTEX STAFFING
8140 Walnut Hill Lane, Suite 610, Dallas TX 75231. 214/368-1456. **Contact:** Office Manager. **Description:** A permanent employment agency. **Specializes in the areas of:** Health/Medical. **Positions commonly filled include:** Nurse.

OFICINA DE EMPLEOS, INC.
5415 Maple Avenue, Suite 112A, Dallas TX 75235-7429. 214/634-0500. **Fax:** 214/634-1001. **Contact:** Robert Wingfield, Jr., Owner. **Description:** A permanent employment agency that places documented workers, in the construction and landscaping industries. **Specializes in the areas of:** General Labor. **Number of placements per year:** 500 - 999.

PARKER WORTHINGTON
The Madison Building, 15851 Dallas Parkway, Suite 500, Addison TX 75001. 972/980-1744. **Contact:** Susan W. Parker, President. **Description:** A permanent employment agency.

PERSONNEL ONE, INC.
5400 LBJ Freeway, Suite 120, Dallas TX 75240. 972/982-8500. **Fax:** 972/982-8505. **Contact:** Branch Manager. **Description:** A permanent employment agency that also provides temporary placements. Client company pays fee. **Specializes in the areas of:** Administration; Computer Science/Software; Personnel/Labor Relations; Secretarial. **Positions commonly filled include:** Administrative Manager; Clerical Supervisor; Customer Service Representative; Data Entry Clerk; Mail Distributor; Receptionist; Secretary. **Benefits available to temporary workers:** 401(k); Medical Insurance; Paid Holidays; Vacation Days. **Corporate headquarters location:** Irving TX. **Other U.S. locations:** FL. **Average salary range of placements:** $20,000 - $29,999. **Number of placements per year:** 50 - 99.

PERSONNEL ONE, INC.
344 West Campbell Road, Richardson TX 75080. 972/234-2000. **Fax:** 972/234-2120. **Contact:** Jan Simpson, Operations Manager. **Description:** A permanent employment agency that also provides temporary placements. Client company pays fee. **Specializes in the areas of:** Administration; Computer Science/Software; Personnel/Labor Relations; Secretarial. **Positions commonly filled include:** Administrative Assistant; Clerk; Customer Service Representative; Data Entry Clerk; Mail Distributor; Receptionist; Secretary. **Benefits available to temporary workers:** 401(k); Medical Insurance; Paid Holidays; Vacation Days. **Corporate headquarters location:** Irving TX. **Other U.S. locations:** FL. **Average salary range of placements:** $20,000 - $29,999. **Number of placements per year:** 50 - 99.

PERSONNEL ONE, INC.
1200 East Copeland, Suite 102, Arlington TX 76015. 817/265-5401. **Fax:** 817/543-1716. **Contact:** Branch Manager. **Description:** A permanent employment agency that also provides temporary placements. Client company pays fee. **Specializes in the areas of:** Administration; Computer Science/Software; Secretarial. **Positions commonly filled include:** Administrative Assistant; Clerical Supervisor; Customer Service Representative; Data Entry Clerk; Mail Distributor; Receptionist; Secretary. **Benefits available to temporary workers:** 401(k); Medical Insurance; Paid Holidays; Vacation Days. **Corporate headquarters location:** Irving TX. **Other U.S. locations:** FL. **Average salary range of placements:** $20,000 - $29,999. **Number of placements per year:** 50 - 99.

PERSONNEL ONE, INC.
7515 Greenville Avenue, Suite 800, Dallas TX 75231. 214/361-6000. **Fax:** 214/890-0648. **Contact:** Branch Manager. **Description:** A permanent employment agency that also provides temporary placements. Client company pays fee. **Specializes in the areas of:** Administration; Computer Science/Software; Secretarial. **Positions commonly filled include:** Administrative Assistant; Clerical Supervisor; Customer Service Representative; Data Entry Clerk; Mail Distributor; Office Manager; Receptionist; Secretary. **Benefits available to temporary workers:** 401(k); Medical Insurance; Paid Holidays; Vacation Days. **Corporate headquarters location:** Irving TX. **Other U.S. locations:** FL. **Average salary range of placements:** $20,000 - $29,999. **Number of placements per year:** 50 - 99.

PERSONNEL ONE, INC.
TELESOURCE
7520 North MacArthur Boulevard, Suite 120, Irving TX 75063. 972/831-1999. **Fax:** 972/831-8668. **Contact:** Branch Manager. **Description:** A permanent employment agency that also provides temporary placements. Telesource (also at this location, 972/831-1115) is a temporary agency that also provides temp-to-perm placements. Client company pays fee. **Specializes in the areas of:** Administration; Computer Science/Software; Personnel/Labor Relations; Secretarial. **Positions commonly filled include:** Administrative Assistant; Clerk; Customer Service Representative; Data Entry Clerk; Mail Distributor; Receptionist; Secretary. **Benefits available to temporary workers:** 401(k); Medical Insurance; Paid Holidays; Vacation Days. **Corporate headquarters location:** This Location. **Other U.S. locations:** FL. **Average salary range of placements:** $20,000 - $29,999. **Number of placements per year:** 50 - 99.

PLACEMENTS UNLIMITED
932 North Valley Mills Drive, Waco TX 76710. 254/741-0526. **Fax:** 254/741-0529. **Contact:** Ginger Sharp, President. **Description:** A permanent employment agency. **Specializes in the areas of:** Banking; Industrial; Manufacturing; Secretarial. **Positions commonly filled include:** Accountant/Auditor; Aircraft Mechanic/Engine Specialist; Automotive Mechanic; Blue-Collar Worker Supervisor; Buyer; Clerical Supervisor; Customer Service Representative; MIS Specialist; Purchasing Agent/Manager; Technical Writer/Editor; Typist/Word Processor. **Average salary range of placements:** Less than $20,000. **Number of placements per year:** 100 - 199.

PROFESSIONS TODAY
2811 South Loop 289, Suite 20, Lubbock TX 79423. 806/745-8595. **Fax:** 806/748-0571. **Contact:** Genell Ward, Owner. **Description:** A permanent employment agency. **Specializes in the areas of:** Accounting/Auditing; Administration; Computer Hardware/Software; Engineering; General Management; Health/Medical; Industrial; Sales; Secretarial. **Positions commonly filled include:** Accountant/Auditor; Administrative Assistant; Bookkeeper; Clerk; Computer Programmer; Customer Service Representative; Data Entry Clerk; Legal Secretary; Marketing Specialist; Medical Secretary; Receptionist; Sales Representative; Secretary; Typist/Word Processor. **Number of placements per year:** 100 - 199.

REMEDY INTELLIGENT STAFFING
4225 Wingren Drive, Suite 115, Irving TX 75062. 972/650-2005. **Fax:** 972/650-1521. **Contact:** Manager. **Description:** A permanent employment agency. **Specializes in the areas of:** Secretarial. **Positions commonly filled include:** Accountant/Auditor; Clerical Supervisor; Customer Service Representative; Management Trainee. **Benefits available to temporary workers:** Medical Insurance; Paid Holidays. **Corporate headquarters location:** Aliso Viejo CA. **Other U.S. locations:** Nationwide. **Average salary range of placements:** $20,000 - $29,999. **Number of placements per year:** 100 - 199.

RESOURCE CONNECTION WORKFORCE CENTER
1400 Circle Drive, Suite 100, Fort Worth TX 76119. 817/531-5670. **Fax:** 817/531-6701. **Contact:** Sheila Perry, Program Coordinator. **Description:** A permanent employment agency that also provides career counseling services. **Specializes in the areas of:** Accounting; Administration; Computer Science; Education; Finance; Food; General Management; Health/Medical; Industrial; Manufacturing; Personnel; Retail; Sales; Secretarial; Transportation. **Positions commonly filled include:** Accountant; Administrative Manager; Automotive Mechanic; Biomedical Engineer; Blue-Collar Worker Supervisor; Budget Analyst; Claim Rep.; Clerical Supervisor; Clinical Lab Technician; Computer Programmer; Construction and Building Inspector; Counselor; Credit Manager; Customer Service Rep.; Dental Assistant/Dental Hygienist; Draftsperson; Education Administrator; EEG Technologist; EKG Technician; Electrical Engineer; Electrician; General Manager; Health Services Manager; Human Resources Specialist; Insurance Agent; Librarian; Medical Records Technician; MIS Specialist; Operations Manager; Property and Real Estate Manager; Purchasing Agent; Radiological Technologist; Restaurant/Food Service Manager; Securities Sales Rep.; Systems Analyst; Teacher/Professor; Travel Agent; Word Processor. **Average salary range of placements:** $20,000 - $29,999. **Number of placements per year:** 200 - 499.

SAY AHHH MEDICAL OFFICE SERVICES
909 West Magnolia Avenue, Suite 8, Fort Worth TX 76104. 817/927-2924. **Contact:** Manager. **Description:** A permanent employment agency that also offers some temporary placements. **Specializes in the areas of:** Health/Medical.

SNELLING PERSONNEL SERVICES
12801 North Central Expressway, Suite 600, Dallas TX 75243-1725. 972/701-8080. **Contact:** Owner. **Description:** A permanent employment agency that also provides executive searches. **Specializes in the areas of:** Accounting/Auditing; Engineering; Food; Health/Medical; Insurance; Legal; Manufacturing; Sales. **Other U.S. locations:** Nationwide. **Number of placements per year:** 200 - 499.

SNELLING PERSONNEL SERVICES
5151 Beltline Road, Suite 365, Dallas TX 75240. 972/934-9030. **Fax:** 972/934-3639. **Contact:** Sam D. Bingham, CPC/Owner. **Description:** A permanent employment agency that also provides some temporary placements and conducts executive searches on a contingency basis. **Specializes in the areas of:** Accounting/Auditing; Biology; Computer Science/Software; Engineering; Food; Industrial; Manufacturing; Sales; Secretarial; Technical. **Positions commonly filled include:** Accountant/Auditor; Chemical Engineer; Chemist; Computer Programmer; Credit Manager; Customer Service Representative; Electrical/Electronics Engineer; Environmental Engineer; Food Scientist/Technologist; Industrial Engineer; Industrial Production Manager; Mechanical Engineer; Metallurgical Engineer; Mining Engineer; Nuclear Engineer; Operations/Production Manager; Petroleum Engineer; Services Sales Representative; Software Engineer; Systems Analyst. **Other U.S. locations:** Nationwide. **Average salary range of placements:** $30,000 - $50,000. **Number of placements per year:** 100 - 199.

SNELLING PERSONNEL SERVICES
1925 East Beltline Road, Suite 403, Carrollton TX 75006. 972/242-8575. **Fax:** 972/242-7186. **Contact:** Manager. **Description:** A permanent employment agency. **Specializes in the areas of:**

Accounting/Auditing; Administration; General Management; Industrial; Legal; Personnel/Labor Relations; Sales; Secretarial. **Positions commonly filled include:** Accountant/Auditor; Administrative Assistant; Bookkeeper; Claim Representative; Clerk; Credit Manager; Customer Service Representative; Data Entry Clerk; Executive Assistant; Factory Worker; Legal Secretary; Light Industrial Worker; Marketing Specialist; Medical Secretary; Receptionist; Sales Representative; Secretary; Typist/Word Processor. **Other U.S. locations:** Nationwide. **Number of placements per year:** 50 - 99.

STAFFINGSOLUTIONS
702 West Loop 289, Suite 104, Lubbock TX 79416. 806/788-1500. **Fax:** 806/788-1510. **Contact:** Marka Roark, Branch Manager. **Description:** A permanent employment agency that also provides some temporary placements. Client company pays fee. **Specializes in the areas of:** Clerical; Light Industrial. **Positions commonly filled include:** Data Entry Clerk; Mail Distributor; Order Clerk; Receptionist; Secretary; Shipping and Receiving Clerk; Warehouse/Distribution Worker; Welder. **Benefits available to temporary workers:** 401(k); Medical Insurance; Paid Holidays; Vacation Days. **Corporate headquarters location:** Irving TX. **Other U.S. locations:** AL; AZ; CO; GA; KS; KY; MO; NC; NM; OK; SC; TN; UT; VA. **Average salary range of placements:** $20,000 - $29,999. **Number of placements per year:** 200 - 499.

STAFFINGSOLUTIONS
8585 North Stemmons Freeway, Suite 104S, Dallas TX 75147. 214/637-6300. **Fax:** 214/638-3333. **Contact:** Branda Nichols, Branch Manager. **Description:** A permanent employment agency that also provides temporary placements. Client company pays fee. **Specializes in the areas of:** Clerical; Light Industrial; Personnel/Labor Relations. **Positions commonly filled include:** Data Entry Clerk; Mail Distributor; Order Clerk; Receptionist; Secretary; Shipping and Receiving Clerk; Warehouse/Distribution Worker; Welder. **Benefits available to temporary workers:** 401(k); Medical Insurance; Paid Holidays; Vacation Days. **Corporate headquarters location:** Irving TX. **Other U.S. locations:** AL; AZ; CO; GA; KS; KY; MO; NC; NM; OK; SC; TN; UT; VA. **Average salary range of placements:** $20,000 - $29,999. **Number of placements per year:** 200 - 499.

STAFFINGSOLUTIONS/RESOURCEMFG
1200 East Copeland Road, Suite 102, Arlington TX 76011. 817/795-9595. **Fax:** 817/461-4776. **Contact:** Branch Manager. **Description:** A permanent employment agency that also provides temporary placements. Client company pays fee. **Specializes in the areas of:** Electronics. **Positions commonly filled include:** Machinist; Plant Manager; Quality Control Supervisor; Technician; Tool and Die Maker; Warehouse/Distribution Worker; Welder. **Benefits available to temporary workers:** 401(k); Medical Insurance; Paid Holidays; Vacation Days. **Corporate headquarters location:** Irving TX. **Other U.S. locations:** AZ; FL; GA; MO; NC; NM; SC; TN; VA. **Average salary range of placements:** $20,000 - $29,999. **Number of placements per year:** 200 - 499.

STAFFINGSOLUTIONS/RESOURCEMFG
1235 Northwest Highway, Garland TX 75041. 972/271-7303. **Fax:** 972/278-1340. **Contact:** Branch Manager. **Description:** StaffingSolutions/ReSourceMFG is a permanent employment agency that also provides temporary placements. Client company pays fee. **Specializes in the areas of:** Electronics; General Management; Personnel/Labor Relations. **Positions commonly filled include:** Machinist; Plant Manager; Quality Control Supervisor; Tool and Die Maker; Warehouse/Distribution Worker; Welder. **Benefits available to temporary workers:** 401(k); Medical Insurance; Paid Holidays; Vacation Days. **Corporate headquarters location:** Irving TX. **Other U.S. locations:** AZ; FL; GA; MO; NC; NM; SC; TN; VA. **Average salary range of placements:** $20,000 - $29,999. **Number of placements per year:** 200 - 499.

TSP PERSONNEL SERVICES, INC.
P.O. Box 266, Paris TX 75461. 903/785-0034. **Fax:** 903/784-0864. **Contact:** Kelley Ferguson, Owner/Manager. **Description:** A permanent employment agency that also provides temporary placements. **Specializes in the areas of:** Accounting/Auditing; Industrial; Light Industrial; Retail; Sales; Secretarial. **Positions commonly filled include:** Bank Officer/Manager; Clerical Supervisor; Electrician; Secretary. **Corporate headquarters location:** This Location. **Average salary range of placements:** $20,000 - $29,999. **Number of placements per year:** 200 - 499.

THOMAS OFFICE PERSONNEL SERVICE (TOPS)
3909 Flintridge Drive, Irving TX 75038. 972/252-2660. **Contact:** Margaret Thomas, Co-Founder. **E-mail address:** topsmom@aol.com. **Description:** A permanent employment agency. Founded in 1976. Client company pays fee. **Specializes in the areas of:** Accounting/Auditing; Administration; General Management; Insurance; Manufacturing; Personnel/Labor Relations;

Publishing; Secretarial. **Positions commonly filled include:** Accountant/Auditor; Branch Manager; Clerical Supervisor; Customer Service Representative; General Manager; Human Resources Specialist; Paralegal; Secretary; Typist/Word Processor. **Average salary range of placements:** $20,000 - $35,000. **Number of placements per year:** 1 - 49.

TRAVEL SEARCH NETWORK
12860 Hillcrest Road, Suite 112, Dallas TX 75230-1519. 972/458-1145. **Fax:** 972/490-4790. **Contact:** Gina Tedesco, Vice President of Operations. **Description:** A permanent employment agency that also provides temporary placements. **Specializes in the areas of:** Travel. **Positions commonly filled include:** Travel Agent. **Other U.S. locations:** Houston TX. **Average salary range of placements:** $30,000 - $50,000. **Number of placements per year:** 200 - 499.

TRAVELCARE UNLIMITED
2340 Trinity Mills, Suite 215, Carrollton TX 75006. 972/323-3388. **Fax:** 972/446-1920. **Contact:** Manager. **Description:** A permanent employment agency that also provides some temporary placements. **Specializes in the areas of:** Health/Medical. **Positions commonly filled include:** Occupational Therapist; Physical Therapist. **Benefits available to temporary workers:** 401(k); Dental Insurance; Life Insurance; Medical Insurance; Vision Plan. **Corporate headquarters location:** Albuquerque NM. **Average salary range of placements:** More than $50,000. **Number of placements per year:** 100 - 199.

VINSON AND ASSOCIATES
4100 McEwen, Suite 180, Dallas TX 75244. 972/980-8800. **Contact:** Fred Vinson, Manager. **Description:** A permanent employment agency that also provides temporary placements. **Specializes in the areas of:** Accounting/Auditing; Banking; Clerical; Finance; Insurance; Legal; Manufacturing; Sales.

EXECUTIVE SEARCH FIRMS

ACCOUNTANTS EXECUTIVE SEARCH
ACCOUNTANTS ON CALL
2828 Routh Street, Suite 690, Dallas TX 75201. 214/979-9001. **Fax:** 214/969-0046. **Contact:** Branch Manager. **Description:** An executive search firm operating on a contingency basis. Accountants On Call (also at this location) is a temporary agency. Founded in 1979. **Specializes in the areas of:** Accounting/Auditing; Finance. **Positions commonly filled include:** Accountant; Chief Financial Officer; Controller; Credit Manager; Finance Director; Financial Analyst. **Corporate headquarters location:** Saddle Brook NJ. **International locations:** Worldwide. **Average salary range of placements:** $30,000 - $50,000.

ACCOUNTANTS EXECUTIVE SEARCH
ACCOUNTANTS ON CALL
5550 LBJ Freeway, Suite 310, Dallas TX 75240. 972/980-4184. **Fax:** 972/980-2359. **Contact:** Branch Manager. **Description:** An executive search firm. Accountants On Call (also at this location) is a temporary agency. Founded in 1979. **Specializes in the areas of:** Accounting/Auditing; Finance. **Corporate headquarters location:** Saddle Brook NJ. **International locations:** Worldwide.

ACCOUNTANTS EXECUTIVE SEARCH
ACCOUNTANTS ON CALL
1612 Summit Avenue, Suite 420, Fort Worth TX 76102. 817/870-1800. **Fax:** 817/870-1890. **Contact:** Gary Guess, Branch Manager. **Description:** An executive search firm operating on a contingency basis. Accountants On Call (also at this location) is a temporary agency. Founded in 1979. **Specializes in the areas of:** Accounting/Auditing; Finance. **Positions commonly filled include:** Accountant/Auditor; Credit Manager; Financial Analyst. **Corporate headquarters location:** Saddle Brook NJ. **International locations:** Worldwide. **Number of placements per year:** 1000+.

ADVANCED SYSTEMS CONSULTING
12801 North Central Expressway, Suite 460, Dallas TX 75243. 972/726-9664. **Fax:** 972/726-9881. **Contact:** Manager. **E-mail address:** opportunities@asccareers.com. **World Wide Web address:** http://www.asccareers.com. **Description:** An executive search firm that also provides

contract and contract-to-hire services. **Specializes in the areas of:** Information Technology; Management. **Other area locations:** Austin TX.

AGRI-ASSOCIATES
131 Degan Street, Suite 203, Lewisville TX 75057. 972/221-7568. **Fax:** 972/221-1409. **Contact:** Lawrence W. Keeley, Owner/Manager. **Description:** An executive search firm. Founded in 1969. **Specializes in the areas of:** Accounting/Auditing; Administration; Advertising; Agriculture; Biology; Engineering; Finance; Food; General Management; Manufacturing; Personnel/Labor Relations; Sales. **Positions commonly filled include:** Accountant/Auditor; Administrative Manager; Agricultural Engineer; Bank Officer/Manager; Biochemist; Biological Scientist; Blue-Collar Worker Supervisor; Branch Manager; Budget Analyst; Buyer; Chemical Engineer; Chemist; Civil Engineer; Computer Programmer; Construction Contractor; Credit Manager; Customer Service Representative; Design Engineer; Editor; Environmental Engineer; Financial Analyst; Food Scientist/Technologist; Forester/Conservation Scientist; General Manager; Human Resources Specialist; Industrial Engineer; Landscape Architect; Licensed Practical Nurse; Management Trainee; Mechanical Engineer; MIS Specialist; Purchasing Agent/Manager; Quality Control Supervisor; Restaurant/Food Service Manager; Systems Analyst; Transportation/Traffic Specialist; Underwriter/Assistant Underwriter; Veterinarian. **Corporate headquarters location:** Kansas City KS. **Average salary range of placements:** $30,000 - $50,000. **Number of placements per year:** 1 - 49.

ALEXANDER & COMPANY
8308 Barber Oak Drive, Plano TX 75025. 214/495-8998. **Toll-free phone:** 877/495-8300. **Fax:** 214/495-8999. **Contact:** Penny Alexander, Principal. **E-mail address:** penny@dhc.net. **Description:** An executive search firm. **Specializes in the areas of:** Advertising; Computer Hardware/Software; Marketing; Multimedia; Public Relations. **Positions commonly filled include:** Internet Services Manager; Multimedia Designer; Public Relations Specialist; Strategic Relations Manager; Technical Writer/Editor. **Number of placements per year:** 1 - 49.

AUDIT PROFESSIONALS INTERNATIONAL
3312 Woodford Drive, Suite 400, Arlington TX 76013-1139. 817/277-0888. **Contact:** Keith Malcolm, CPA/Vice President. **Description:** An executive search firm that also provides contract services. Founded in 1987. **Specializes in the areas of:** Accounting/Auditing; Administration; Finance; Information Systems. **Positions commonly filled include:** Accountant/Auditor; Actuary; Internet Services Manager; Telecommunications Manager. **Average salary range of placements:** More than $50,000. **Number of placements per year:** 50 - 99.

KAYE BASSMAN INTERNATIONAL CORPORATION
18333 Preston Road, Suite 500, Dallas TX 75252. 972/931-5242. **Fax:** 972/931-9683. **Contact:** Manager. **World Wide Web address:** http://www.kbic.com. **Description:** An executive search firm. **Specializes in the areas of:** Health/Medical; Information Technology.

R. GAINES BATY ASSOCIATES, INC.
12750 Merritt Drive, Suite 990, Lockbox 199, Dallas TX 75251. 972/386-7900. **Fax:** 972/387-2224. **Contact:** R. Gaines Baty, President. **E-mail address:** rgba@rgba.com. **Description:** An executive search firm. **Specializes in the areas of:** Computer Science/Software; Finance; MIS/EDP. **Positions commonly filled include:** Accountant/Auditor; Management Analyst/Consultant; MIS Specialist; Systems Analyst; Telecommunications Manager. **Average salary range of placements:** More than $50,000. **Number of placements per year:** 1 - 49.

BEST/WORLD ASSOCIATES
505 West Abram Street, Arlington TX 76010. 817/861-0000. **Toll-free phone:** 800/749-2846. **Fax:** 817/459-2378. **Contact:** G. Tim Best, President. **E-mail address:** jobbank@bestworld.com. **World Wide Web address:** http://www.bestworld.com. **Description:** An executive search firm operating on a retainer basis. **Specializes in the areas of:** Banking; Computer Science/Software; Engineering; Finance; Food; Manufacturing; Personnel/Labor Relations; Sales. **Positions commonly filled include:** Accountant/Auditor; Chemical Engineer; Economist; Electrical/Electronics Engineer; Environmental Engineer; Financial Analyst; Food Scientist/Technologist; Human Resources Specialist; Management Analyst/Consultant; Market Research Analyst; Mechanical Engineer; MIS Specialist; Quality Control Supervisor; Software Engineer; Statistician; Systems Analyst. **Corporate headquarters location:** This Location. **Other U.S. locations:** Phoenix AZ; Houston TX. **Average salary range of placements:** More than $100,000. **Number of placements per year:** 50 - 99.

BILSON & HAZEL INTERNATIONAL
HAZEL STAFFING
5800 East Campus Circle, Suite 12A, Irving TX 75063. 972/753-1193. **Fax:** 972/753-0969. **Contact:** Frederick Sagoe, President. **Description:** An executive search firm that also offers temporary and contract services. Hazel Staffing (also at this location) provides temp-to-perm administrative staffing services. **Specializes in the areas of:** Computer Science/Software; Personnel/Labor Relations; Sales. **Positions commonly filled include:** Administrative Manager; Branch Manager; Claim Representative; Computer Programmer; Design Engineer; Electrical/Electronics Engineer; Human Resources Specialist; Manufacturer's/Wholesaler's Sales Rep.; Market Research Analyst; MIS Specialist; Software Engineer; Technical Writer/Editor; Telecommunications Manager. **Benefits available to temporary workers:** Dental Insurance; Medical Insurance. **Average salary range of placements:** More than $50,000. **Number of placements per year:** 50 - 99.

BIOSOURCE INTERNATIONAL
1878 Hilltop Drive, Suite 100, Lewisville TX 75077-2114. 972/317-7060. **Fax:** 972/317-0500. **Contact:** Ric J. Favors, Principal. **E-mail address:** mail@biosourceinternational.com. **World Wide Web address:** http://www.biosourceinternational.com. **Description:** An executive search firm. **Specializes in the areas of:** Biotechnology; Health/Medical; Pharmaceuticals; Scientific; Technical. **Positions commonly filled include:** Biochemist; Biological Scientist; Biomedical Engineer; Chemical Engineer; Chemist; Chief Executive Officer; Compliance Analyst; Computer Programmer; Electrical/Electronics Engineer; General Manager; Management Analyst/Consultant; Mechanical Engineer; MIS Specialist; Multimedia Designer; Physician; President; Production Manager; Quality Assurance Engineer; Quality Control Supervisor; Science Technologist; Software Engineer; Statistician; Systems Analyst; Technical Writer/Editor. **Corporate headquarters location:** This Location. **Other U.S. locations:** Carlsbad CA; Sarasota FL; Greensboro NC. **Average salary range of placements:** More than $50,000. **Number of placements per year:** 1 - 49.

THE HOWARD C. BLOOM CO.
INTERIM LEGAL PROFESSIONALS
5000 Quorum Drive, Suite 550, Dallas TX 75240. 972/385-6455. **Fax:** 972/385-1006. **Contact:** Howard Bloom, President. **Description:** An executive search firm. Interim Legal Professionals (also at this location) provides permanent placements. **Specializes in the areas of:** Legal. **Positions commonly filled include:** Attorney. **Number of placements per year:** 1 - 49.

BOLES & ASSOCIATES
1701 North Collins Boulevard, Suite 200, Richardson TX 75080. 972/480-0660. **Fax:** 972/480-9886. **Contact:** Terry C. Boles, Managing Partner. **E-mail address:** bolesassoc@aol.com. **Description:** An executive search firm operating on a retainer basis. Founded in 1989. **Specializes in the areas of:** Administration; Engineering; General Management; Human Resources; Sales. **Positions commonly filled include:** Telecommunications Manager. **Average salary range of placements:** More than $50,000. **Number of placements per year:** 1 - 49.

BORCHERT ASSOCIATES
17430 Campbell Road, Suite 111, Dallas TX 75252. 972/818-2801. **Toll-free phone:** 888/818-2801. **Fax:** 972/818-2777. **Contact:** Gregory Borchert, President. **E-mail address:** greg@glborchert.com. **World Wide Web address:** http://www.glborchert.com. **Description:** An executive search firm. Founded in 1987. **Specializes in the areas of:** Manufacturing; Metals.

BRIDGE PERSONNEL
6510 Abrams Road, Comerica Bank Building, Suite 540, Dallas TX 75231. 214/340-7055. **Contact:** Jim Peeler, CPA/Owner. **Description:** An executive search firm operating on both retainer and contingency bases. **Specializes in the areas of:** Accounting/Auditing; Administration; Computer Science/Software; Finance; Information Systems. **Positions commonly filled include:** Accountant/Auditor; Computer Programmer; Financial Analyst; Software Engineer; Systems Analyst; Telecommunications Manager.

BROOKLEA & ASSOCIATES, INC.
12200 Ford Road, Suite 108, Dallas TX 75234. 972/484-9400. **Contact:** Recruiter. **Description:** An executive search firm operating on a contingency basis. **Specializes in the areas of:** Accounting/Auditing; Architecture/Construction; Art/Design; Finance; Health/Medical; Sales; Secretarial. **Positions commonly filled include:** Accountant/Auditor; Architect; Draftsperson; Emergency Medical Technician; Health Services Manager; Landscape Architect; Licensed Practical Nurse; Medical Records Technician; Occupational Therapist; Physical Therapist; Physician; Recreational Therapist; Registered Nurse; Respiratory Therapist; Services

Sales Representative; Surgical Technician; Surveyor; Veterinarian. **Number of placements per year:** 100 - 199.

BUNDY-STEWART ASSOCIATES, INC.
13601 Preston Road, Suite 107W, Dallas TX 75240. 972/458-0626. **Fax:** 972/661-2670. **Contact:** Carolyn Stewart, Owner. **Description:** An executive search firm operating on a contingency basis. **Specializes in the areas of:** Accounting/Auditing; Administration; Computer Science/Software; Engineering; Industrial; Insurance; Manufacturing; Personnel/Labor Relations; Real Estate; Sales; Telecommunications. **Positions commonly filled include:** Accountant/Auditor; Aircraft Mechanic/Engine Specialist; Attorney; Buyer; Computer Programmer; Credit Manager; Customer Service Representative; Design Engineer; Draftsperson; Electrical/Electronics Engineer; Human Resources Specialist; Industrial Engineer; Industrial Production Manager; Market Research Analyst; Mechanical Engineer; MIS Specialist; Operations/Production Manager; Purchasing Agent/Manager; Quality Control Supervisor; Securities Sales Representative; Software Engineer; Systems Analyst; Telecommunications Manager.

CAP ASSOCIATES
15303 Dallas Parkway, Suite 230, Dallas TX 75248. 972/458-4700. **Toll-free phone:** 800/893-1550x2027. **Fax:** 972/458-4711. **Contact:** Recruiter. **E-mail address:** capassoc@ix.netcom.com. **World Wide Web address:** http://www.capassociates.com. **Description:** An executive search firm. **Specializes in the areas of:** Health/Medical; Information Technology.

CARPENTER & ASSOCIATES
11551 Forest Central Drive, Suite 305, Dallas TX 75243. 214/691-6585. **Fax:** 214/691-6838. **Contact:** Elsie Carpenter, President. **Description:** An executive search firm. **Specializes in the areas of:** Advertising; Fashion; Personnel/Labor Relations; Retail. **Positions commonly filled include:** Buyer; Retail Manager; Retail Merchandiser. **Number of placements per year:** 1 - 49.

COMPUTER PROFESSIONALS UNLIMITED
13612 Midway Road, Suite 333, Dallas TX 75244. 972/233-1773. **Fax:** 972/233-9619. **Contact:** V.J. Zapotocky, Owner/President. **E-mail address:** zipzap@onramp.net. **Description:** An executive search firm that also provides contract services. Founded in 1978. **Specializes in the areas of:** Computer Science/Software; Engineering; Information Technology. **Positions commonly filled include:** Computer Programmer; Electrical/Electronics Engineer; Internet Services Manager; MIS Specialist; Software Engineer; Systems Analyst; Technical Writer/Editor; Telecommunications Manager. **Average salary range of placements:** More than $50,000. **Number of placements per year:** 50 - 99.

CORPORATE SEARCH INC.
3028 Lubbock Avenue, Fort Worth TX 76109. 817/926-0320. **Toll-free phone:** 800/429-1763. **Fax:** 817/926-1610. **Contact:** John S. Gramentine, President. **Description:** An executive search firm. **Specializes in the areas of:** Computer Science/Software; Food; Personnel/Labor Relations; Retail; Sales. **Positions commonly filled include:** Branch Manager; General Manager; Human Resources Specialist; Management Trainee; Public Relations Specialist; Services Sales Representative; Software Engineer; Systems Analyst; Telecommunications Manager. **Average salary range of placements:** More than $50,000. **Number of placements per year:** 200 - 499.

CRAIG SEARCH
901 Waterfall Way, Suite 107, Richardson TX 75080. 972/644-3264. **Fax:** 972/644-4065. **Contact:** Edward C. Nemec, President. **Description:** An executive search firm. **Specializes in the areas of:** Food. **Positions commonly filled include:** Branch Manager; Buyer; General Manager. **Number of placements per year:** 50 - 99.

DDR, INC.
4925 Greenville Avenue, Suite 660, Dallas TX 75206-4014. 214/361-4608. **Contact:** Account Executive. **E-mail address:** ddrdal@gte.net. **Description:** An executive search firm. **Specializes in the areas of:** Technical. **Positions commonly filled include:** Computer Animator; Computer Operator; Computer Programmer; Database Manager; Financial Analyst; Hardware Engineer; Operations Manager; Project Manager; Software Engineer; Systems Analyst; Technical Writer/Editor. **Benefits available to temporary workers:** Dental Insurance; Life Insurance; Medical Insurance.

DFM & ASSOCIATES
14001 Dallas Parkway, Suite 1200, Dallas TX 75240. 972/934-6504. **Fax:** 972/934-6505. **Contact:** Denise M. Frost, President. **Description:** An executive search firm. **Specializes in the**

areas of: Legal. **Positions commonly filled include:** Attorney; Legal Secretary; Paralegal. **Number of placements per year:** 100 - 199.

DAMON & ASSOCIATES, INC.
333 West Campbell Road, Richardson TX 75080. 214/696-6990. **Fax:** 214/696-6993. **Contact:** Dick Damon, President. **Description:** An executive search firm. Founded in 1978. **Specializes in the areas of:** Sales. **Average salary range of placements:** $30,000 - $50,000. **Number of placements per year:** 50 - 99.

THE DANBROOK GROUP
4100 Spring Valley Road, Suite 700, Dallas TX 75244. 972/392-0057. **Contact:** Anne Kennedy, Senior Partner. **Description:** An executive search firm operating on a contingency basis. **Specializes in the areas of:** Accounting/Auditing; Banking; Finance; General Management; Insurance. **Positions commonly filled include:** Accountant/Auditor; Adjuster; Bookkeeper; Chief Financial Officer; Claim Representative; Credit Manager; Customer Service Representative; Finance Director; Financial Analyst; Insurance Agent/Broker; Sales Representative; Underwriter/Assistant Underwriter. **Average salary range of placements:** More than $50,000. **Number of placements per year:** 100 - 199.

C. MICHAEL DIXON ASSOCIATES, INC.
P.O. Box 293371, Lewisville TX 75029. 972/317-0608. **Fax:** 972/317-0349. **Contact:** Mike Dixon, President. **E-mail address:** cmdixon@flash.net. **Description:** An executive search firm. Founded in 1988. **Specializes in the areas of:** Chemicals; Engineering; Manufacturing; Petrochemical; Technical. **Positions commonly filled include:** Chemical Engineer; Electrical/Electronics Engineer; Industrial Engineer; Mechanical Engineer; Systems Analyst. **Average salary range of placements:** More than $50,000. **Number of placements per year:** 1 - 49.

DUNHILL PROFESSIONAL SEARCH
1301 South Bowen Road, Suite 370, Arlington TX 76013. 817/265-2291. **Fax:** 817/265-2294. **Contact:** Jon Molkentine, Director. **Description:** An executive search firm. **Specializes in the areas of:** Accounting/Auditing; Health/Medical. **Positions commonly filled include:** Accountant/Auditor; Human Resources Manager; Physical Therapist. **Number of placements per year:** 50 - 99.

E*ONLINE LEARNING RECRUITERS
14232 Marsh Lane, PMB 406, Addison TX 75001. 972/490-9171. **Contact:** Manager. **Description:** An executive search firm. **Specializes in the areas of:** Internet Development; Internet Marketing.

ENGINEERING MANAGEMENT STAFF RECRUITERS
12801 North Central Expressway, Suite 470, Dallas TX 75243. 972/239-6572. **Fax:** 972/239-6590. **Contact:** Scott Higby, Manager. **E-mail address:** opportunities@emsr.com. **World Wide Web address:** http://www.emsr.com. **Description:** An executive search firm. **Specializes in the areas of:** Engineering. **Other U.S. locations:** Raleigh NC.

EPPA, INC.
1953 Branch Hollow, Carrollton TX 75007. 972/394-9668. **Contact:** Manager. **E-mail address:** eppa@eppainc.com. **World Wide Web address:** http://www.eppainc.com. **Description:** An executive search firm. **NOTE:** This firm does not accept unsolicited resumes. Please only respond to advertised openings. **Specializes in the areas of:** Printing.

EXECUTIVE RESTAURANT SEARCH
2925 LBJ Freeway, Suite 253, Dallas TX 75234. 972/484-8600. **Contact:** Brian Blocker, Partner. **Description:** An executive search firm. Pinnacle Search Group (also at this location) is the agency's food sales division. **Specializes in the areas of:** Restaurant.

EXECUTIVE SEARCH INTERNATIONAL (ESI)
3033 West Parker Road, Suite 204, Plano TX 75023. 972/424-4714. **Fax:** 972/424-5314. **Contact:** Ed Nalley, Owner. **E-mail address:** mail@esihbc.com. **World Wide Web address:** http://www.esihbc.com. **Description:** An executive search firm operating on both retainer and contingency bases. Client company pays fee. **Specializes in the areas of:** Consumer Products; Food; Marketing; Sales. **Positions commonly filled include:** Account Manager; Market Research Analyst; Marketing Manager; Sales Executive; Sales Manager. **Corporate headquarters location:** This Location. **Average salary range of placements:** $50,000 - $100,000. **Number of placements per year:** 50 - 99.

H.P.R. HEALTH STAFF
1600 East Pioneer Parkway, Suite 340, Arlington TX 76010-6562. 817/261-3355. **Fax:** 817/543-3155. **Contact:** Vera E. Harris, CPC/Owner. **E-mail address:** vharris@iamerica.net. **Description:** An executive search firm operating on a contingency basis. **Specializes in the areas of:** Health/Medical. **Positions commonly filled include:** Chief Financial Officer; Clinical Lab Technician; Controller; Dental Assistant/Dental Hygienist; Dentist; Dietician/Nutritionist; EEG Technologist; EKG Technician; Environmental Engineer; Health Services Manager; Human Resources Manager; Licensed Practical Nurse; Medical Records Technician; Nuclear Medicine Technologist; Occupational Therapist; Pharmacist; Physical Therapist; Physician; Psychologist; Radiological Technologist; Registered Nurse; Respiratory Therapist; Speech-Language Pathologist; Surgical Technician. **Average salary range of placements:** $30,000 - $50,000.

HR SEARCH
12801 North Central Expressway, Suite 220, Dallas TX 75243. 972/458-8077. **Fax:** 972/458-0143. **Contact:** Manager. **E-mail address:** opportunities@hr-jobs.com. **World Wide Web address:** http://www.hr-jobs.com. **Description:** An executive search firm. HR Search is a division of MAGIC (Management Alliance Group of Independent Companies). **Specializes in the areas of:** Customer Service; Human Resources; Office Support.

HARAGAN ASSOCIATES
4925 Greenville Avenue, Suite 1105, Dallas TX 75206. 214/363-3634. **Contact:** Mr. Pat W. Haragan, Principal/Owner. **Description:** An executive search firm operating on a retainer basis. **Specializes in the areas of:** Biology; General Management; Health/Medical; Manufacturing; Sales; Technical. **Positions commonly filled include:** Biochemist; Biological Scientist; Biomedical Engineer; Chemist; Clinical Lab Technician; Food Scientist/Technologist; General Manager; Health Services Manager; Human Resources Specialist; Nuclear Medicine Technologist; Occupational Therapist; Pharmacist; Physical Therapist; Physician; Quality Control Supervisor; Registered Nurse; Veterinarian. **Average salary range of placements:** More than $50,000. **Number of placements per year:** 1 - 49.

HEALTH NETWORK USA
5902 Smoke Glass Trail, Dallas TX 75252. **Toll-free phone:** 800/872-0212. **Fax:** 972/818-9395. **Contact:** David J. Elliott, President. **E-mail address:** hninfo@hnusa.com. **Description:** An executive search firm. **Specializes in the areas of:** Health/Medical. **Positions commonly filled include:** Clinical Lab Technician; Dental Assistant/Dental Hygienist; Dental Lab Technician; Dentist; Dietician/Nutritionist; EEG Technologist; EKG Technician; Health Services Manager; Human Resources Manager; Licensed Practical Nurse; Medical Records Technician; Nuclear Medicine Technologist; Occupational Therapist; Pharmacist; Physical Therapist; Physician; Psychologist; Public Relations Specialist; Purchasing Agent/Manager; Radiological Technologist; Recreational Therapist; Registered Nurse; Respiratory Therapist; Social Worker; Speech-Language Pathologist; Surgical Technician. **Number of placements per year:** 50 - 99.

HUNTER & MICHAELS
7502 Greenville Avenue, Suite 500, Dallas TX 75231. 214/750-4666. **Fax:** 214/750-4476. **Contact:** President. **Description:** An executive search firm operating on both retainer and contingency bases. Client company pays fee. **Specializes in the areas of:** Marketing; Sales. **Positions commonly filled include:** Market Research Analyst; Marketing Manager; Sales Executive; Sales Manager. **Corporate headquarters location:** This Location. **Other U.S. locations:** Nationwide. **Average salary range of placements:** $50,000 - $100,000. **Number of placements per year:** 1 - 49.

INFORMATION SYSTEMS CONSULTING CORPORATION
North Central Plaza III, 12801 North Central Expressway, Suite 250, Dallas TX 75243-1712. 972/490-1881. **Toll-free phone:** 800/877-1881. **Fax:** 972/490-4429. **Contact:** Jim Henry, Recruiter. **E-mail address:** opportunities@iscc.com. **World Wide Web address:** http://www.iscc.com. **Description:** An executive search firm. **Specializes in the areas of:** Accounting; Computer Hardware/Software; Food; Telecommunications; Transportation. **Other U.S. locations:** Denver CO; Kansas City MO; Reston VA.

INSIDE TRACK
504 Hilltop Drive, Weatherford TX 76086-5724. 817/599-7094. **Fax:** 817/596-0807. **Contact:** Matthew DiLorenzo, Senior Technical Recruiter. **E-mail address:** trak1@airmail.net. **Description:** An executive search firm. Founded in 1989. **Specializes in the areas of:** Administration; Computer Science/Software; Engineering; High-Tech; Industrial; Manufacturing; Sales; Telecommunications. **Positions commonly filled include:** Computer Programmer; Design Engineer; Electrical/Electronics Engineer; General Manager; Marketing

Manager; Materials Engineer; Mechanical Engineer; MIS Specialist; Operations Manager; Quality Control Supervisor; Sales Manager; Software Engineer; Systems Analyst; Telecommunications Manager. **Average salary range of placements:** More than $50,000. **Number of placements per year:** 1 - 49.

INTERNATIONAL DATA SEARCH
12801 North Central Expressway, Suite 480, Dallas TX 75243. 972/661-5232. **Fax:** 972/991-1539. **Contact:** Manager. **E-mail address:** opportunities@idsjobs.com. **World Wide Web address:** http://www.idsjobs.com. **Description:** An executive search firm. **Specializes in the areas of:** Information Technology.

KENZER CORPORATION
3030 LBJ Freeway, Suite 1430, Dallas TX 75234. 972/620-7776. **Fax:** 972/243-7570. **Contact:** Dawn Jones, Vice President. **Description:** An executive search firm operating on a retainer basis. Founded in 1973. **Specializes in the areas of:** Fashion; Food; General Management; Retail; Sales. **Positions commonly filled include:** Accountant/Auditor; Branch Manager; Financial Analyst; Hotel Manager; Human Resources Specialist; Management Trainee; Manufacturer's/Wholesaler's Sales Rep.; Operations/Production Manager; Public Relations Specialist; Restaurant/Food Service Manager; Services Sales Representative. **Corporate headquarters location:** New York NY. **Average salary range of placements:** More than $50,000. **Number of placements per year:** 200 - 499.

KEY PEOPLE INC.
P.O. Box 24773, Fort Worth TX 76124-1773. 817/457-6108. **Contact:** Don (Petro) Petrusaitis, President. **Description:** An executive search firm operating on a contingency basis. **Specializes in the areas of:** Graphic Arts; Publishing. **Positions commonly filled include:** Administrative Manager; Blue-Collar Worker Supervisor; Buyer; Chemist; Clerical Supervisor; Computer Programmer; Customer Service Representative; Electrical/Electronics Engineer; General Manager; Human Resources Specialist; Industrial Engineer; Industrial Production Manager; Management Trainee; Mechanical Engineer; MIS Specialist; Operations/Production Manager; Quality Control Supervisor; Transportation/Traffic Specialist. **Average salary range of placements:** More than $50,000.

KFORCE.COM, INC.
5429 LBJ Freeway, Suite 275, Dallas TX 75240. 972/387-1600. **Contact:** Manager. **World Wide Web address:** http://www.kforce.com. **Description:** An executive search firm. **Specializes in the areas of:** Accounting/Auditing; Computer Hardware/Software; Engineering; Finance. **Corporate headquarters location:** Tampa FL.

KORN/FERRY INTERNATIONAL
500 North Akard Street, Suite 3232, Dallas TX 75201. 214/954-1834. **Fax:** 214/954-1849. **Contact:** Manager. **World Wide Web address:** http://www.kornferry.com. **Description:** An executive search firm that places upper-level managers. **Corporate headquarters location:** Los Angeles CA. **International locations:** Worldwide. **Average salary range of placements:** More than $50,000.

LUCAS FINANCIAL STAFFING
12655 North Central Expressway, Suite 730, Dallas TX 75243. 972/490-0011. **Fax:** 972/991-4144. **Contact:** Andrea Jennings, Regional Manager. **E-mail address:** lucaslfs@aol.com. **Description:** An executive search firm operating on both retainer and contingency bases. Lucas Financial Staffing also provides some contract placements. **Specializes in the areas of:** Accounting/Auditing; Finance. **Positions commonly filled include:** Accountant/Auditor; Budget Analyst; Chief Financial Officer; Controller; Credit Manager; EDP Specialist; Finance Director; Financial Analyst; Systems Analyst. **Benefits available to temporary workers:** 401(k); Medical Insurance; Vacation Days. **Corporate headquarters location:** Atlanta GA. **Average salary range of placements:** $30,000 - $50,000. **Number of placements per year:** 200 - 499.

MH EXECUTIVE SEARCH GROUP
P.O. Box 868068, Plano TX 75086. 972/578-1511. **Contact:** Recruiter. **E-mail address:** TXpkgjobs@mhgroup.com. **World Wide Web address:** http://www.mhgroup.com. **Description:** An executive search firm. **Specializes in the areas of:** Packaging. **Corporate headquarters location:** Palm Harbor FL. **Other U.S. locations:** Palm Harbor FL.

MANAGEMENT RECRUITERS INTERNATIONAL
15150 Preston Road, Suite 300, Dallas TX 75248. 972/991-4500. **Contact:** George Buntrock, Owner. **Description:** An executive search firm. **Specializes in the areas of:**

Accounting/Auditing; Administration; Computer Science/Software; Engineering; Food; General Management; Health/Medical; Paper; Retail; Technical. **Positions commonly filled include:** Ceramics Engineer; Chemical Engineer; Computer Programmer; Customer Service Representative; Electrical/Electronics Engineer; General Manager; Health Services Manager; Industrial Engineer; Industrial Production Manager; Materials Engineer; Mechanical Engineer; Metallurgical Engineer; Operations/Production Manager; Pharmacist; Physical Therapist; Purchasing Agent/Manager; Quality Control Supervisor; Registered Nurse; Software Engineer; Speech-Language Pathologist; Systems Analyst; Transportation/Traffic Specialist. **Corporate headquarters location:** Cleveland OH. **Other U.S. locations:** Nationwide. **Number of placements per year:** 1 - 49.

MANAGEMENT RECRUITERS INTERNATIONAL
1001 West Randol Mill Road, Arlington TX 76012. 817/469-6161. **Contact:** Bob Stoessel, Manager. **Description:** An executive search firm. **Specializes in the areas of:** Accounting/Auditing; Administration; Advertising; Architecture/Construction; Banking; Communications; Computer Hardware/Software; Design; Electrical; Engineering; Finance; Food; General Management; Health/Medical; Insurance; Legal; Manufacturing; Operations Management; Personnel/Labor Relations; Procurement; Publishing; Retail; Sales; Technical; Textiles; Transportation. **Corporate headquarters location:** Cleveland OH. **Other U.S. locations:** Nationwide.

MANAGEMENT RECRUITERS OF DALLAS
13101 Preston Road, Suite 560, Dallas TX 75240. 972/788-1515. **Fax:** 972/701-8242. **Contact:** Robert S. Lineback, General Manager. **Description:** An executive search firm operating on both retainer and contingency bases. **Specializes in the areas of:** Accounting/Auditing; Administration; Advertising; Architecture/Construction; Banking; Communications; Computer Hardware/Software; Design; Electrical; Engineering; Finance; Food; General Management; Health/Medical; Insurance; Legal; Manufacturing; Operations Management; Personnel/Labor Relations; Procurement; Publishing; Retail; Sales; Technical; Transportation. **Positions commonly filled include:** Accountant/Auditor; Actuary; Administrative Manager; Aerospace Engineer; Agricultural Engineer; Bank Officer/Manager; Biochemist; Biological Scientist; Biomedical Engineer; Branch Manager; Chemical Engineer; Chemist; Civil Engineer; Clinical Lab Technician; Computer Programmer; Design Engineer; Designer; Dietician/Nutritionist; EEG Technologist; EKG Technician; Electrical/Electronics Engineer; Emergency Medical Technician; Environmental Engineer; Financial Analyst; Food Scientist/Technologist; General Manager; Health Services Manager; Human Resources Specialist; Industrial Engineer; Licensed Practical Nurse; Management Analyst/Consultant; Management Trainee; Manufacturer's/Wholesaler's Sales Rep.; Mechanical Engineer; Medical Records Technician; Metallurgical Engineer; Mining Engineer; MIS Specialist; Multimedia Designer; Nuclear Engineer; Nuclear Medicine Technologist; Occupational Therapist; Operations/Production Manager; Petroleum Engineer; Pharmacist; Physical Therapist; Physician; Physicist; Purchasing Agent/Manager; Quality Control Supervisor; Radiological Technologist; Registered Nurse; Respiratory Therapist; Restaurant/Food Service Manager; Science Technologist; Securities Sales Representative; Services Sales Representative; Software Engineer; Structural Engineer; Surgical Technician; Systems Analyst; Telecommunications Manager; Transportation/Traffic Specialist; Underwriter/Assistant Underwriter. **Corporate headquarters location:** Cleveland OH. **Other U.S. locations:** Nationwide. **Average salary range of placements:** More than $50,000. **Number of placements per year:** 200 - 499.

MANAGEMENT RECRUITERS OF LBJ PARK/DALLAS
3003 LBJ Freeway, Suite 220E, Dallas TX 75234. 972/488-1133. **Fax:** 972/488-1099. **Contact:** Ray Vlasek, General Manager. **E-mail address:** mrdfw@airmail.net. **Description:** An executive search firm. Founded in 1960. **Specializes in the areas of:** Engineering; Manufacturing; Software Engineering; Telecommunications. **Positions commonly filled include:** Computer Programmer; Electrical/Electronics Engineer; Mechanical Engineer; MIS Specialist; Software Engineer. **Corporate headquarters location:** Cleveland OH. **Other U.S. locations:** Nationwide. **Number of placements per year:** 50 - 99.

MANAGEMENT RECRUITERS OF LEWISVILLE
1660 South Stemmons, Suite 460, Lewisville TX 75067. 972/434-9612. **Contact:** Manager. **Description:** An executive search firm. **Specializes in the areas of:** Plastics; Sales. **Corporate headquarters location:** Cleveland OH. **Other U.S. locations:** Nationwide.

McDUFFY-EDWARDS
3117 Medina Drive, Garland TX 75041. 972/864-1174. **Fax:** 972/864-8559. **Contact:** Tom Edwards, Partner. **E-mail address:** tomedwards@earthlink.net. **World Wide Web address:**

http://www.mcduffy-edwards.com. **Description:** An executive search firm that also provides consulting services and seminars. Founded in 1980. **Specializes in the areas of:** Computer Science/Software; Marketing; Sales; Scientific; Technical. **Positions commonly filled include:** Account Manager; Account Representative; Customer Service Representative; General Manager; Internet Services Manager; Management Analyst/Consultant; Market Research Analyst; Marketing Manager; Marketing Specialist; Operations Manager; Project Manager; Sales Engineer; Sales Executive; Sales Manager; Sales Representative; Software Engineer; Systems Analyst; Systems Manager; Telecommunications Manager; Vice President of Marketing and Sales. **Average salary range of placements:** More than $50,000. **Number of placements per year:** 50 - 99.

AUSTIN McGREGOR INTERNATIONAL
12005 Ford Road, Suite 540, Dallas TX 75234-7247. 972/488-0500. **Fax:** 972/488-0535. **Contact:** Chip McCreary, President. **E-mail address:** jobs@amidallas.com. **World Wide Web address:** http://www.amidallas.com. **Description:** An executive search firm operating on a retainer basis. Founded in 1987. **Specializes in the areas of:** Consumer Products; Industrial; Technical. **Other U.S. locations:** San Diego CA; St. Louis MO.

MEDIA EXECUTIVE SEARCH & PLACEMENT
1349 Regal Row, Dallas TX 75247. 214/630-9790. **Fax:** 214/630-9905. **Contact:** David Small, President/CEO. **E-mail address:** dsmall@mediaexecutive.com. **World Wide Web address:** http://www.mediaexecutive.com. **Description:** An executive search firm. **Specializes in the areas of:** Cable TV; Internet Marketing; Media Sales. **Positions commonly filled include:** General Manager; Marketing Manager.

MEDICAL SEARCH SOLUTIONS
15905 Bent Tree Forest Circle, Suite 1065, Dallas TX 75248. 972/490-3778. **Fax:** 972/934-2246. **Contact:** Penny Peters, CPC/Medical Recruiting Specialist. **Description:** An executive search firm. **Specializes in the areas of:** Health/Medical. **Positions commonly filled include:** Administrative Assistant; Administrative Manager; Assistant Manager; Clinical Lab Technician; Controller; Dietician/Nutritionist; EEG Technologist; EKG Technician; Emergency Medical Technician; Finance Director; Financial Analyst; Health Services Manager; Licensed Practical Nurse; Medical Assistant; Medical Records Technician; Nurse Practitioner; Occupational Therapist; Office Manager; Operations Manager; Pharmacist; Physical Therapist; Physician; Physician Assistant; Radiological Technologist; Recreational Therapist; Registered Nurse; Respiratory Therapist; Speech-Language Pathologist; Surgical Technician. **Average salary range of placements:** $30,000 - $50,000. **Number of placements per year:** 50 - 99.

NATIONAL SALES RECRUITERS, INC. (NSR)
P.O. Box 703816, Dallas TX 75370-3816. 972/436-3047. **Toll-free phone:** 800/469-6428. **Fax:** 972/221-6134. **Contact:** Rory Deal, Founder. **E-mail address:** rory@nsrjobs.com. **World Wide Web address:** http://www.nsrjobs.com. **Description:** An executive search firm. **Specializes in the areas of:** Marketing; Sales; Sales Management.

NOLL HUMAN RESOURCE SERVICES
5720 LBJ Freeway, Suite 610, Dallas TX 75240. 972/392-2900. **Toll-free phone:** 800/536-7600. **Fax:** 972/934-3600. **Contact:** Mr. Perry Smith, Dallas Division Manager. **World Wide Web address:** http://www.noll-inc.com. **Description:** An executive search firm operating on both retainer and contingency bases. **Specializes in the areas of:** Logistics; Sales; Transportation. **Positions commonly filled include:** Database Manager; Environmental Engineer; Industrial Engineer; Manufacturing Engineer; Marketing Manager; MIS Specialist; Physician; Registered Nurse; Sales Engineer; Sales Executive; Sales Manager; Sales Representative; Software Engineer; Systems Analyst; Systems Manager; Telecommunications Manager; Transportation/Traffic Specialist. **Corporate headquarters location:** Omaha NE. **Average salary range of placements:** More than $50,000. **Number of placements per year:** 50 - 99.

ODELL & ASSOCIATES INC.
12700 Park Central Place, Suite 1404, Dallas TX 75251. 972/458-7900. **Fax:** 972/233-1215. **Contact:** Executive Vice President. **Description:** An executive search firm. **Specializes in the areas of:** Accounting/Auditing; Data Processing; Engineering; Finance; Health/Medical; Legal. **Positions commonly filled include:** Accountant/Auditor; Actuary; Attorney; Computer Programmer; Financial Analyst; Medical Records Technician; Occupational Therapist; Registered Nurse; Respiratory Therapist; Systems Analyst. **Number of placements per year:** 100 - 199.

OPPORTUNITY UNLIMITED PERSONNEL CONSULTANTS
2720 West Mockingbird Lane, Dallas TX 75235. 214/357-9196. **Toll-free phone:** 800/969-0888. **Fax:** 214/357-0140. **Contact:** Ms. Jean Crawford, President. **E-mail address:** oui@opportunityunlimited.net. **Description:** An executive search firm operating on a contingency basis. Founded in 1959. **Specializes in the areas of:** Aerospace; Computer Science/Software; Data Processing; Engineering; Scientific; Technical; Telecommunications. **Positions commonly filled include:** Aerospace Engineer; Biomedical Engineer; Computer Programmer; Design Engineer; Electrical/Electronics Engineer; Mechanical Engineer; Multimedia Designer; Software Engineer; Systems Analyst; Telecommunications Manager. **Number of placements per year:** 200 - 499.

THE PAILIN GROUP PROFESSIONAL SEARCH CONSULTANTS
Center City Plaza, 1412 Main Street, Suite 601, Dallas TX 75202. 214/752-6100. **Fax:** 214/752-6101. **Contact:** David L. Pailin, Sr., Senior Partner. **World Wide Web address:** http://www.pailingroup.com. **Description:** An executive search firm operating on a retainer basis. Founded in 1989. **Specializes in the areas of:** Accounting/Auditing; Administration; Advertising; Banking; Computer Science/Software; Economics; Engineering; Environmental; Finance; Food; General Management; Health/Medical; Industrial; Insurance; Legal; Manufacturing; Nonprofit; Personnel/Labor Relations; Retail; Sales; Transportation. **Positions commonly filled include:** Accountant/Auditor; Administrative Manager; Aerospace Engineer; Architect; Attorney; Bank Officer/Manager; Budget Analyst; Ceramics Engineer; Civil Engineer; Computer Programmer; Construction Contractor; Cost Estimator; Credit Manager; Customer Service Representative; Design Engineer; Environmental Engineer; Financial Analyst; General Manager; Health Services Manager; Human Service Worker; Industrial Engineer; Materials Engineer; Mechanical Engineer; Metallurgical Engineer; Mining Engineer; MIS Specialist; Nuclear Engineer; Petroleum Engineer; Pharmacist; Physician; Quality Control Supervisor; Securities Sales Representative; Services Sales Representative; Software Engineer; Statistician; Systems Analyst; Technical Writer/Editor; Telecommunications Manager. **Corporate headquarters location:** This Location. **Other U.S. locations:** Philadelphia PA. **Average salary range of placements:** More than $50,000. **Number of placements per year:** 100 - 199.

PERI CORPORATION (PROFESSIONAL EXECUTIVE RECRUITERS)
1701 Gateway Boulevard, Suite 419, Richardson TX 75080. 972/235-3984. **Fax:** 972/437-2017. **Contact:** Ken Roberts, Manager. **E-mail address:** PERI@airmail.net. **Description:** An executive search firm operating on a contingency basis. Client company pays fee. **Specializes in the areas of:** Architecture/Construction; Engineering. **Positions commonly filled include:** Architect; Attorney; Chief Financial Officer; Civil Engineer; Construction Contractor; Electrical/Electronics Engineer; Environmental Engineer; Mechanical Engineer. **Corporate headquarters location:** This Location. **International locations:** Worldwide. **Average salary range of placements:** $50,000 - $100,000. **Number of placements per year:** 50 - 99.

PROFESSIONAL RECRUITING SOLUTIONS, INC.
2425 North Central Expressway, Suite 1000, Richardson TX 75080. 972/907-9100. **Toll-free phone:** 800/564-0293. **Fax:** 972/907-2550. **Contact:** Recruiter. **E-mail address:** mail@prsdallas.com. **World Wide Web address:** http://www.prsdallas.com. **Description:** An executive search firm operating on both retainer and contingency bases. PRS, Inc. also offers some contract placements and recruiting consulting services. **Specializes in the areas of:** High-Tech. **Other area locations:** Houston TX. **Other U.S. locations:** Detroit MI.

RAY & BERNDTSON, INC.
2200 Ross Avenue, Suite 4500 West, Dallas TX 75201. 214/969-7620. **Fax:** 214/754-0646. **Contact:** Manager. **World Wide Web address:** http://www.rayberndtson.com. **Description:** An executive search firm. **Positions commonly filled include:** Senior Management. **International locations:** Worldwide.

RAY & BERNDTSON, INC.
301 Commerce Street, Suite 2300, Fort Worth TX 76102. 817/334-0500. **Fax:** 817/334-0779. **Contact:** Manager. **World Wide Web address:** http://www.rayberndtson.com. **Description:** An executive search firm. **Positions commonly filled include:** Senior Management. **International locations:** Worldwide.

RECRUITING ASSOCIATES
P.O. Box 8473, Amarillo TX 79114. 806/353-9548. **Fax:** 806/353-9540. **Contact:** Mike Rokey, CPC/Owner/Manager. **E-mail address:** mikedr@arn.net. **Description:** An executive search firm operating on a contingency basis. Founded in 1978. **Specializes in the areas of:** Computer Science/Software; Engineering. **Positions commonly filled include:** Accountant/Auditor;

Applications Engineer; Computer Operator; Computer Programmer; Database Manager; Design Engineer; Electrical/Electronics Engineer; Mechanical Engineer; MIS Specialist; Software Engineer; Systems Analyst; Technical Writer/Editor. **Benefits available to temporary workers:** 401(k); Medical Insurance. **Average salary range of placements:** $30,000 - $50,000. **Number of placements per year:** 1 - 49.

RICCIONE & ASSOCIATES INC.
16415 Addison Road, Suite 404, Addison TX 75001. 972/380-6432. **Fax:** 972/407-0659. **Contact:** Nick Riccione, President. **E-mail address:** hitec@riccione.com. **World Wide Web address:** http://www.riccione.com. **Description:** An executive search firm operating on a contingency basis. The firm also provides some contract placements. **Specializes in the areas of:** Computer Science/Software; Engineering; High-Tech. **Positions commonly filled include:** Computer Programmer; Electrical/Electronics Engineer; Software Engineer; Systems Analyst; Telecommunications Manager. **Average salary range of placements:** More than $50,000. **Number of placements per year:** 50 - 99.

SALINAS & ASSOCIATES PERSONNEL SERVICE
1700 Commerce Street, Dallas TX 75201. 214/747-7878. **Contact:** Gerry Salinas, Owner/Recruiter. **Description:** An executive search firm operating on both retainer and contingency bases. Salinas & Associates also offers contract services and career/outplacement counseling. **Specializes in the areas of:** Accounting/Auditing; Advertising; Banking; Computer Hardware/Software; Fashion; Finance; Personnel/Labor Relations; Sales. **Positions commonly filled include:** Account Manager; Account Representative; Accountant; Administrative Assistant; Administrative Manager; Advertising Clerk; Advertising Executive; Auditor; Bank Officer/Manager; Budget Analyst; Buyer; Chemist; Claim Representative; Controller; Counselor; Credit Manager; Customer Service Representative; Database Manager; Human Resources Manager; Market Research Analyst; Marketing Manager; Marketing Specialist; Sales Engineer; Sales Executive; Sales Manager; Secretary. **Corporate headquarters location:** This Location. **Other U.S. locations:** Nationwide. **Average salary range of placements:** Less than $20,000. **Number of placements per year:** 50 - 99.

R.L. SCOTT ASSOCIATES
222 West Exchange Avenue, Suite 203, Fort Worth TX 76106. 817/877-3622. **Contact:** Randall Scott, President. **Description:** An executive search firm operating on both retainer and contingency bases. Founded in 1988. **Specializes in the areas of:** Health/Medical. **Positions commonly filled include:** Accountant/Auditor; Administrator; Chief Executive Officer; Chief Financial Officer; Controller; Counselor; Marketing Manager; Medical Records Technician; Recreational Therapist; Registered Nurse; Respiratory Therapist; Social Worker; Vice President of Finance; Vice President of Operations. **Corporate headquarters location:** This Location. **Average salary range of placements:** More than $50,000. **Number of placements per year:** 50 - 99.

SEARCH COM, INC.
12680 Hillcrest Road, Suite 101, Dallas TX 75230. 972/490-0300. **Contact:** Susan Abrahamson, President. **E-mail address:** susana1@airmail.net. **Description:** An executive search firm operating on a retainer basis. Founded in 1986. Client company pays fee. **Specializes in the areas of:** Advertising; Art/Design; Health/Medical; Internet Marketing; Publishing. **Positions commonly filled include:** Advertising Executive; Database Manager; Designer; Editor; Graphic Artist; Graphic Designer; Internet Services Manager; Managing Editor; Market Research Analyst; Marketing Manager; Marketing Specialist; Multimedia Designer; Public Relations Specialist; Technical Writer/Editor; Webmaster. **Average salary range of placements:** More than $50,000. **Number of placements per year:** 1 - 49.

SEARCH NETWORK INTERNATIONAL
12801 North Central Expressway, Suite 260, Dallas TX 75243. 972/934-3950. **Fax:** 972/934-3868. **Contact:** Manager. **E-mail address:** resumes@snint.com. **World Wide Web address:** http://www.snint.com. **Description:** An executive search firm operating on a contingency basis. Founded in 1976. **Specializes in the areas of:** Accounting/Auditing; Computer Science/Software; Engineering; Food; Industrial; Manufacturing. **Positions commonly filled include:** Accountant/Auditor; Aerospace Engineer; Architect; Biochemist; Biomedical Engineer; Buyer; Chemical Engineer; Chemist; Civil Engineer; Computer Programmer; Cost Estimator; Design Engineer; Designer; Draftsperson; Environmental Engineer; Financial Analyst; Food Scientist/Technologist; Geologist/Geophysicist; Industrial Engineer; Industrial Production Manager; Internet Services Manager; Mathematician; Mechanical Engineer; Metallurgical Engineer; Mining Engineer; MIS Specialist; Multimedia Designer; Operations/Production Manager; Petroleum Engineer; Public Relations Specialist; Purchasing Agent/Manager; Quality

Control Supervisor; Software Engineer; Statistician; Structural Engineer; Systems Analyst; Telecommunications Manager. **Number of placements per year:** 500 - 999.

SEARCHAMERICA INC.
5908 Meadowcreek Drive, Dallas TX 75248. 972/233-3302. **Fax:** 972/233-1518. **Contact:** Harvey Weiner, President. **E-mail address:** searchamerica@aol.com. **Description:** An executive search firm that also provides consulting services. Founded in 1974. **Specializes in the areas of:** Consulting; General Management; Hotel/Restaurant; Personnel/Labor Relations. **Average salary range of placements:** More than $50,000. **Number of placements per year:** 50 - 99.

SELECT STAFF
8200 Nashville Avenue, Suite C109, Lubbock TX 79423. 806/794-5511. **Fax:** 806/794-5869. **Contact:** Manager. **Description:** An executive search firm operating on a contingency basis. **Specializes in the areas of:** Accounting/Auditing; Administration; Food; General Management; Personnel/Labor Relations; Retail; Sales; Secretarial. **Positions commonly filled include:** Accountant/Auditor; Adjuster; Administrative Manager; Advertising Clerk; Architect; Attorney; Bank Officer/Manager; Blue-Collar Worker Supervisor; Branch Manager; Brokerage Clerk; Buyer; Chemical Engineer; Civil Engineer; Claim Representative; Clerical Supervisor; Counselor; Credit Manager; Customer Service Representative; Dental Assistant/Dental Hygienist; Draftsperson; Electrical/Electronics Engineer; Electrician; Environmental Engineer; General Manager; Health Services Manager; Hotel Manager; Human Resources Specialist; Human Service Worker; Industrial Engineer; Landscape Architect; Licensed Practical Nurse; Manufacturer's/Wholesaler's Sales Rep.; MIS Specialist; Operations/Production Manager; Paralegal; Pharmacist; Property and Real Estate Manager; Public Relations Specialist; Purchasing Agent/Manager; Quality Control Supervisor; Restaurant/Food Service Manager; Securities Sales Representative; Social Worker; Systems Analyst; Technical Writer/Editor; Telecommunications Manager; Transportation/Traffic Specialist; Underwriter/Assistant Underwriter. **Average salary range of placements:** $20,000 - $29,999. **Number of placements per year:** 500 - 999.

SHAW ASSOCIATES, INC.
1104 Commerce Drive, Richardson TX 75081-2307. 972/480-9400. **Fax:** 972/480-8700. **Contact:** Greg Shaw, Owner. **E-mail address:** greg@shawsassociates.com. **World Wide Web address:** http://www.shawassociates.com. **Description:** An executive search firm. Founded in 1995. **Specializes in the areas of:** Biotechnology; Medical Devices; Pharmaceuticals. **Corporate headquarters location:** This Location. **Other U.S. locations:** Hendersonville TN.

MARVIN L. SILCOTT & ASSOCIATES, INC.
5477 Glen Lakes Drive, Dallas TX 75231. 214/369-7802. **Fax:** 214/369-7875. **Contact:** Marvin L. Silcott, President. **Description:** An executive search firm operating on a retainer basis. Founded in 1973. **Specializes in the areas of:** Legal. **Positions commonly filled include:** Attorney. **Average salary range of placements:** More than $50,000. **Number of placements per year:** 50 - 99.

STAFF EXTENSION INTERNATIONAL (SEI)
13612 Midway, Suite 103, Dallas TX 75244. 972/991-4737. **Fax:** 972/991-5325. **Contact:** Jack R. Williams, President. **E-mail address:** dallas@staffext.com. **World Wide Web address:** http://www.staffext.com. **Description:** An executive search firm that also provides some temporary and contract placements. Founded in 1990. **Specializes in the areas of:** Accounting/Auditing; Administration; Computer Science/Software; Engineering; Finance; General Management; Human Resources; Manufacturing; Personnel/Labor Relations; Sales; Technical. **Corporate headquarters location:** This Location. **Other U.S. locations:** Houston TX. **Number of placements per year:** 50 - 99.

STEINFIELD & ASSOCIATES
2626 Cole Avenue, Suite 400, Dallas TX 75204. 214/220-0535. **Fax:** 214/665-9535. **Contact:** David Steinfield, President. **E-mail address:** steinfield@airmail.net. **Description:** An executive search firm. Founded in 1991. **Specializes in the areas of:** Accounting; Auditing; Finance; Human Resources. **Positions commonly filled include:** Accounting Supervisor; Auditor; Controller; Financial Manager; Human Resources Manager. **Average salary range of placements:** More than $50,000.

STRAIGHT SOURCE
100 North Central Expressway, Suite 1000, Richardson TX 75080. 972/437-2220. **Fax:** 972/437-2310. **Contact:** Recruiting Manager. **Description:** An executive search firm operating on a retainer basis. **Specializes in the areas of:** Computer Science/Software; Engineering;

General Management; Publishing; Sales; Technical. **Positions commonly filled include:** Branch Manager; Computer Programmer; General Manager; Software Engineer; Strategic Relations Manager; Systems Analyst. **Corporate headquarters location:** Dallas TX. **Average salary range of placements:** More than $50,000. **Number of placements per year:** 1 - 49.

TGA COMPANY
P.O. Box 331121, Fort Worth TX 76163. 817/370-0865. **Fax:** 817/292-6451. **Contact:** Tom Green, President. **Description:** An executive search firm. **Specializes in the areas of:** Accounting/Auditing; Computer Science/Software; Finance; Information Systems; Technical. **Positions commonly filled include:** Accountant/Auditor; Chief Financial Officer; Controller; Credit Manager; Financial Analyst; MIS Specialist; Software Engineer; Systems Analyst. **Average salary range of placements:** More than $50,000. **Number of placements per year:** 50 - 99.

TMP WORLDWIDE EXECUTIVE SEARCH
1601 Elm Street, Suite 4150, Dallas TX 75201. 214/754-0019. **Fax:** 214/754-0615. **Contact:** Judy Stubbs, Managing Partner. **World Wide Web address:** http://www.tmp.com. **Description:** An executive search firm. **Specializes in the areas of:** Biotechnology; Consumer Products; Finance; Health/Medical; Industrial; Pharmaceuticals; Technical. **Corporate headquarters location:** New York NY. **Other U.S. locations:** Nationwide.

THE TALON GROUP
16801 Addison Road, Suite 255, Addison TX 75001. 972/931-8223. **Fax:** 972/931-8063. **Contact:** Bob Piper, President. **E-mail address:** talongrp@gte.net. **Description:** An executive search firm operating on a retainer basis. **Specializes in the areas of:** Construction; Housing; Manufacturing; Real Estate. **Positions commonly filled include:** Architect; Chief Financial Officer; Civil Engineer; Construction Superintendent; Controller; Cost Estimator; General Manager; Marketing Manager; MIS Specialist; Operations Manager; Production Manager; Project Manager; Purchasing Agent/Manager; Sales Manager; Vice President. **Average salary range of placements:** More than $50,000. **Number of placements per year:** 50 - 99.

TECH-NET
14785 Preston Road, Dallas TX 75240-7876. 972/934-3000. **Contact:** Chris Cole, Owner. **Description:** An executive search firm. Founded in 1989. **Specializes in the areas of:** Computer Science/Software; Engineering; Sales; Technical. **Positions commonly filled include:** Aerospace Engineer; Design Engineer; Electrical/Electronics Engineer; Mechanical Engineer; MIS Specialist; Software Engineer; Technical Representative. **Average salary range of placements:** More than $50,000. **Number of placements per year:** 1 - 49.

TECHNICAL STAFFING SOLUTIONS
16775 Addison Road, Suite 240, Addison TX 75001. 972/248-0700. **Fax:** 972/248-1175. **Contact:** Don Fink, Office Manager. **E-mail address:** staff@technicalstaffing.com. **World Wide Web address:** http://www.technicalstaffing.com. **Description:** An executive search firm that also provides some contract services. Founded in 1989. **Specializes in the areas of:** Chemicals; Computer Science/Software; Engineering. **Positions commonly filled include:** Applications Engineer; AS400 Programmer Analyst; Chemical Engineer; Chemist; Computer Programmer; Content Developer; Database Administrator; Database Manager; Design Engineer; Environmental Engineer; Internet Services Manager; Mechanical Engineer; Metallurgical Engineer; Multimedia Designer; Network/Systems Administrator; Software Engineer; SQL Programmer; Systems Analyst; Systems Manager; Webmaster. **Corporate headquarters location:** This Location. **Other U.S. locations:** Nationwide. **Average salary range of placements:** $50,000 - $100,000. **Number of placements per year:** 100 - 199.

THERAPISTS UNLIMITED
2340 East Trinity Mills Road, Suite 215, Carrollton TX 75006. 972/418-1800. **Contact:** Recruiter. **Description:** An executive search firm that also provides temporary and contract placements. **Specializes in the areas of:** Health/Medical. **Positions commonly filled include:** Physical Therapist; Speech-Language Pathologist. **Average salary range of placements:** More than $50,000. **Number of placements per year:** 50 - 99.

TOTAL PERSONNEL INC.
P.O. Box 28975, Dallas TX 75228. 214/327-1165. **Contact:** Sherry Phillips, President. **Description:** An executive search firm operating on both retainer and contingency bases. Client company pays fee. **Specializes in the areas of:** Computer Science/Software; MIS/EDP. **Positions commonly filled include:** Applications Engineer; Architect; AS400 Programmer Analyst; Computer Animator; Computer Engineer; Computer Programmer; Content Developer; Database Administrator; Database Manager; Internet Services Manager; MIS Specialist;

Network/Systems Administrator; Software Engineer; SQL Programmer; Systems Analyst; Systems Manager; Webmaster. **Corporate headquarters location:** This Location. **Average salary range of placements:** $50,000 - $100,000. **Number of placements per year:** 1 - 49.

WARDRUP ASSOCIATES
2508 Springpark Way, Suite 300, Richardson TX 75082. 972/437-9333. **Fax:** 972/437-1208. **Contact:** Recruiter. **World Wide Web address:** http://www.wardrup.com. **Description:** An executive search firm. **Specializes in the areas of:** Communications; Computer Hardware/Software; Electronics; High-Tech; Information Technology.

WITT/KIEFFER, FORD, HADELMAN & LLOYD
2 Lincoln Center, 5420 LBJ Freeway, Suite 460, Dallas TX 75240. 972/490-1370. **Fax:** 972/490-3472. **Contact:** Manager. **World Wide Web address:** http://www.wittkieffer.com. **Description:** An executive search firm. **Specializes in the areas of:** Health/Medical. **Other U.S. locations:** Nationwide.

BRUCE G. WOODS EXECUTIVE SEARCH
25 Highland Park Village, Suite 100-171, Dallas TX 75205. 214/522-9888. **Contact:** Bruce Woods, Owner. **World Wide Web address:** http://www.contractexecutives.com/brucegwoods.html. **Description:** A global executive search firm. Founded in 1977. **Specializes in the areas of:** Cable TV; Consulting; Finance; Health/Medical; Manufacturing; Real Estate; Telecommunications; Wireless Communications.

THE WRIGHT GROUP
9217 Frenchman's Way, Dallas TX 75220. 214/351-1115. **Contact:** Jay J. Wright, President. **Description:** An executive search firm. Founded in 1985. **Specializes in the areas of:** Advertising; Marketing. **Positions commonly filled include:** Market Research Analyst; Marketing Specialist. **Number of placements per year:** 1 - 49.

R.S. WYATT ASSOCIATES, INC.
P.O. Box 92786, Southlake TX 76092. 817/421-8726. **Fax:** 817/421-1374. **Contact:** Robert S. Wyatt, Ph.D., Principal. **E-mail address:** rswassoc@aol.com. **Description:** An executive search firm operating on a retainer basis. The company also provides consulting services. **Specializes in the areas of:** Consulting; General Management; Personnel/Labor Relations; Retail. **Positions commonly filled include:** Accountant/Auditor; Branch Manager; Buyer; Computer Programmer; Credit Manager; Customer Service Representative; Design Engineer; General Manager; Human Resources Specialist; Industrial Engineer; Management Analyst/Consultant; Public Relations Specialist; Software Engineer; Systems Analyst; Transportation/Traffic Specialist. **Average salary range of placements:** More than $50,000. **Number of placements per year:** 1 - 49.

CONTRACT SERVICES FIRMS

B&M ASSOCIATES, INC.
AIR & SPACE DIVISION
2925 LBJ Freeway, Suite 278, Dallas TX 75234. 972/241-8408. **Toll-free phone:** 800/745-9675. **Fax:** 972/241-4363. **Contact:** Division Manager. **World Wide Web address:** http://www.bmanet.com. **Description:** A contract services firm. **Specializes in the areas of:** Aerospace; Computer Science/Software; Engineering; Industrial; Personnel/Labor Relations; Scientific; Technical. **Positions commonly filled include:** Applications Engineer; Biochemist; Buyer; Civil Engineer; Computer Operator; Computer Programmer; Design Engineer; Draftsperson; Electrician; Environmental Engineer; Graphic Artist; Graphic Designer; Internet Services Manager; Manufacturing Engineer; Mechanical Engineer; Metallurgical Engineer; MIS Specialist; Multimedia Designer; Operations Manager; Project Manager; Purchasing Agent/Manager; Quality Control Supervisor; Software Engineer; Systems Analyst; Systems Manager; Technical Writer/Editor; Telecommunications Manager; Webmaster. **Benefits available to temporary workers:** 401(k); Medical Insurance; Paid Holidays; Vacation Days. **Corporate headquarters location:** Boston MA. **Other U.S. locations:** San Diego CA; Santa Ana CA; Manchester NH; Vienna VA. **Average salary range of placements:** More than $50,000.

BELCAN TECHNICAL SERVICES
3333 Earhart Drive, Suite 120, Carrollton TX 75006. 972/239-0405. **Contact:** Michelle Williams, Team Leader. **World Wide Web address:** http://www.belcan.com. **Description:** A

contract services firm. **Specializes in the areas of:** Administration; Engineering. **Positions commonly filled include:** Aerospace Engineer; Applications Engineer; Buyer; Chemical Engineer; Civil Engineer; Computer Animator; Computer Operator; Computer Programmer; Cost Estimator; Database Manager; Design Engineer; Designer; Draftsperson; Electrical/Electronics Engineer; Environmental Engineer; Graphic Artist; Graphic Designer; Human Resources Specialist; Industrial Engineer; Mechanical Engineer; MIS Specialist; Multimedia Designer; Project Manager; Quality Control Supervisor; Software Engineer; Structural Engineer; Systems Analyst; Systems Manager; Technical Writer/Editor; Telecommunications Manager. **Benefits available to temporary workers:** 401(k); Medical Insurance; Paid Holidays; Vacation Days. **Corporate headquarters location:** Cincinnati OH. **Other U.S. locations:** Nationwide. **Average salary range of placements:** More than $50,000. **Number of placements per year:** 200 - 499.

BUTLER INTERNATIONAL
914 Royal Lane, Irving TX 75063. 817/355-9655. **Contact:** Manager. **Description:** A contract services firm. **Specializes in the areas of:** Aerospace; Computer Science/Software; Engineering; Food; Industrial; Manufacturing; Personnel/Labor Relations; Technical. **Positions commonly filled include:** Aircraft Mechanic/Engine Specialist; Budget Analyst; Buyer; Chemical Engineer; Chemist; Civil Engineer; Clinical Lab Technician; Computer Programmer; Cost Estimator; Customer Service Representative; Design Engineer; Designer; Draftsperson; Editor; Electrician; Environmental Engineer; Industrial Engineer; Mechanical Engineer; MIS Specialist; Petroleum Engineer; Software Engineer; Structural Engineer; Systems Analyst; Technical Writer/Editor; Telecommunications Manager. **Benefits available to temporary workers:** Paid Holidays; Vacation Days. **Corporate headquarters location:** Montvale NJ.

CONTRACT DESIGN PERSONNEL
2225 East Randol Mill Road, Suite 223, Arlington TX 76011. 817/640-6119. **Fax:** 817/640-6256. **Contact:** Stan Baker, Director of Recruiting Operations. **Description:** A contract services firm. **Specializes in the areas of:** Engineering; High-Tech; Multimedia; Technical. **Positions commonly filled include:** Aerospace Engineer; Architect; Chemical Engineer; Civil Engineer; Computer Programmer; Design Engineer; Designer; Draftsperson; Electrical/Electronics Engineer; Environmental Engineer; Industrial Engineer; Mechanical Engineer; Metallurgical Engineer; Mining Engineer; Multimedia Designer; Nuclear Engineer; Petroleum Engineer; Software Engineer; Structural Engineer; Systems Analyst; Technical Writer/Editor. **Benefits available to temporary workers:** Paid Holidays. **Number of placements per year:** 100 - 199.

DESIGN QUEST INC.
P.O. Box 6555, Tyler TX 75711. 903/561-6241. **Fax:** 903/534-9170. **Contact:** Louie Adams, Recruiter. **Description:** A contract services firm. **Specializes in the areas of:** Engineering; Personnel/Labor Relations. **Positions commonly filled include:** Chemical Engineer; Civil Engineer; Design Engineer; Designer; Draftsperson; Electrical/Electronics Engineer; Industrial Engineer; Mechanical Engineer; Petroleum Engineer; Structural Engineer. **Average salary range of placements:** More than $50,000. **Number of placements per year:** 100 - 199.

HALL KINION
1600 North Carolina Boulevard, Suite 2300, Richardson TX 75080. **Toll-free phone:** 888/989-4254. **Fax:** 972/783-2740. **Contact:** Manager. **E-mail address:** daresume@hallkinion.com. **World Wide Web address:** http://www.hallkinion.com. **Description:** A contract services firm that also provides some permanent placements. **Specializes in the areas of:** Computer Hardware/Software; Information Systems; Information Technology; Internet Development; Network Administration; Systems Administration; Systems Design; Technical Writing.

TECHNICAL CAREERS
12750 Merit Drive, Suite 1430, Park Central VII, Lockbox 56, Dallas TX 75251. 972/991-9424. **Fax:** 972/851-0651. **Contact:** Cary Tobolka, President. **E-mail address:** tobolka@technicalcareers.com. **World Wide Web address:** http://www.technicalcareers.com. **Description:** A contract services firm. Founded in 1978. **Specializes in the areas of:** Computer Science/Software; Engineering; Industrial; Manufacturing; Personnel/Labor Relations; Technical. **Positions commonly filled include:** Aerospace Engineer; Agricultural Engineer; Chemical Engineer; Civil Engineer; Computer Programmer; Design Engineer; Designer; Electrical/Electronics Engineer; Environmental Engineer; Human Resources Specialist; Industrial Engineer; Industrial Production Manager; Internet Services Manager; Management Analyst/Consultant; Manufacturer's/Wholesaler's Sales Rep.; Mechanical Engineer; Metallurgical Engineer; MIS Specialist; Multimedia Designer; Nuclear Engineer; Purchasing Agent/Manager; Quality Control Supervisor; Science Technologist; Software Engineer; Structural Engineer; Systems Analyst; Telecommunications Manager. **Benefits available to**

temporary workers: Dental Insurance; Life Insurance; Medical Insurance; Retirement Plan. **Corporate headquarters location:** This Location. **Other area locations:** Addison TX. **Other U.S. locations:** San Diego CA. **Average salary range of placements:** More than $50,000. **Number of placements per year:** 100 - 199.

VOLT SERVICES GROUP
275 West Campbell Road, Suite 211, Richardson TX 75080. 972/669-0458. **Toll-free phone:** 800/531-7426. **Fax:** 972/669-9749. **Contact:** Katherine Lockwood, Regional Manager. **E-mail address:** lockwood@gte.net. **Description:** A contract services firm. **Specializes in the areas of:** Computer Science/Software; Engineering; Technical. **Positions commonly filled include:** Administrative Manager; Aerospace Engineer; Aircraft Mechanic/Engine Specialist; Biochemist; Biomedical Engineer; Budget Analyst; Buyer; Chemical Engineer; Chemist; Civil Engineer; Computer Programmer; Design Engineer; Designer; Draftsperson; Electrical/Electronics Engineer; Electrician; Environmental Engineer; Human Resources Specialist; Industrial Engineer; Industrial Production Manager; Software Engineer; Statistician; Strategic Relations Manager; Systems Analyst; Technical Writer/Editor; Telecommunicatiosns Manager. **Corporate headquarters location:** New York NY. **Other U.S. locations:** Nationwide. **Average salary range of placements:** $30,000 - $50,000. **Number of placements per year:** 500 - 999.

H.L. YOH COMPANY
13601 Preston Road, Suite 1020E, Dallas TX 75240. 972/239-9875. **Contact:** Manager. **Description:** A contract services firm. **Specializes in the areas of:** Architecture/Construction; Computer Hardware/Software; Engineering; Manufacturing; Technical.

RESUME/CAREER COUNSELING SERVICES

ALLEN & ASSOCIATES
4099 McEwen, Suite 150, Dallas TX 75244. 972/385-7112. **Toll-free phone:** 800/562-7214. **Fax:** 972/788-2131. **Contact:** Manager. **World Wide Web address:** http://www.allenandassociates.com. **Description:** A career/outplacement counseling firm. **Corporate headquarters location:** Maitland FL. **Other U.S. locations:** Nationwide.

FAIRCHILD BARKLEY & ASSOCIATES
15770 Dallas Parkway, Suite 1000, Dallas TX 75248. 972/387-4800. **Fax:** 972/386-5210. **Contact:** R.J. Porter, President. **Description:** A career/outplacement counseling firm. **Positions commonly filled include:** Accountant/Auditor; Administrative Manager; Aerospace Engineer; Agricultural Engineer; Architect; Bank Officer/Manager; Biochemist; Biomedical Engineer; Branch Manager; Budget Analyst; Chemical Engineer; Civil Engineer; Claim Representative; Clerical Supervisor; Computer Programmer; Cost Estimator; Credit Manager; Customer Service Representative; Design Engineer; Economist; Environmental Engineer; Industrial Engineer; Management Analyst/Consultant; MIS Specialist; Operations/Production Manager; Petroleum Engineer; Public Relations Specialist; Restaurant/Food Service Manager; Services Sales Representative; Structural Engineer; Systems Analyst; Telecommunications Manager. **Average salary range of placements:** More than $50,000. **Number of placements per year:** 100 - 199.

INDEX OF PRIMARY EMPLOYERS

A

AC MOLDING COMPOUND • 98
ACS, INC. • 91
ACS TECHNOLOGY SOLUTIONS • 112
ADS ENVIRONMENTAL SERVICES INC. • 145
AMR CORPORATION • 262
ABATIX CORPORATION • 273
ABBOTT DIAGNOSTICS • 89
ABCO INDUSTRIES INC. • 217
ABILENE AERO INC. • 262
ABILENE CHRISTIAN UNIVERSITY • 124
ABILENE REGIONAL MENTAL HEALTH &
    MENTAL RETARDATION CENTER • 95
ABILENE, CITY OF • 167
ACE AMERICA'S CASH EXPRESS INC. • 91
ACKELS & ACKELS LLP • 209
ACKERMAN MCQUEEN, INC. • 57
ACTION COMPANY • 212
ADLETA & POSTON, REALTORS • 241
AEGIS COMMUNICATIONS GROUP • 57
AIR SYSTEMS COMPONENTS • 147, 217
ALCATEL USA • 105
ALCATEL USA INC. • 105
ALFORD REFRIGERATED WAREHOUSES • 262
ALL SAINTS EPISCOPAL HOSPITAL • 173
ALLERGAN, INC. • 89
ALLIED DIGITAL TECHNOLOGIES CORP. • 79
AMARILLO COLLEGE • 124
AMARILLO GLOBE TIMES • 234
AMARILLO NATIONAL BANK • 86
AMERICAN BANK NOTE COMPANY • 234
AMERICAN ELECTRIC POWER (AEP) • 271
AMERICAN EXCELSIOR COMPANY • 98
AMERICAN FLAT GLASS DISTRIB. • 259
AMERICAN HEART ASSOCIATION (AHA) • 95
AMERICAN PERMANENT WARE CO. • 212
AMERICAN PRODUCTS COMPANY • 156
AMERICAN RECREATION PRODUCTS • 212
AMERICAN TRANSFER AND STORAGE • 262
AMERICAN WAY • 234
AMERICREDIT CORPORATION • 151
AMERIMAX BUILDING PRODUCTS • 147
AMTECH CORPORATION • 138
ANALYSTS INTERNATIONAL CORP. • 112
ARTHUR ANDERSEN • 52
ANDERSEN CONSULTING • 112
ANDERSON INDUSTRIES, INC. • 68
ANDREW CORPORATION • 105
APAC TEXAS, INC. • 68
APPLIED EARTH SCIENCES • 145
ARROW ELECTRONICS • 138
ARROW INDUSTRIES • 212
THE ART INSTITUTE OF DALLAS • 124
ASSOCIATED AIRCRAFT SUPPLY • 61
ASSOCIATED GLOBAL SYSTEMS • 262
ASSOCIATES FIRST CAPITAL GROUP • 151
ATLAS MATCH CORPORATION (AMC) • 212
ATMOS ENERGY CORPORATION • 224
ATTEBURY GRAIN INC. • 156
JOHN ATWOOD LAW OFFICE • 209
AUGUST HEALTH CARE • 173
AUSTIN COMMERCIAL INC. • 68
AUTOMATIC DATA PROCESSING (ADP) • 91
AVNET, INC. • 138
AVO INTERNATIONAL • 138

B

B-K ELECTRIC COOPERATIVE, INC. • 271
BFX HOSPITALITY GROUP, INC. • 195
BMS ENTERPRISES INC. • 91
BP AMOCO • 224
BABBAGE'S ETC. • 243
BAILEY AND WILLIAMS • 209
BAKER BOTTS LLP • 209
BALDWIN DISTRIBUTION SERVICES • 263
BANCTEC, INC. • 112
BANK ONE SECURITIES • 151
BANK ONE TEXAS • 86
BANKERS DIGEST • 234
W.O. BANKSTON LINCOLN MERCURY • 243
BAPTIST ST. ANTHONY HEALTH SYST. • 173
BARON & BUDD, P.C. • 209
BATES CONTAINER INC. • 231
BAYLOR MEDICAL CTR. AT GARLAND • 173
BAYLOR MEDICAL CENTER IRVING • 173
BAYLOR SENIOR HEALTH CENTER • 174
BAYLOR UNIVERSITY • 124
BAYLOR UNIVERSITY MEDICAL CTR. • 174
BAYLOR/RICHARDSON MEDICAL CTR. • 173
BEAR, STEARNS & COMPANY, INC. • 151
JOHN F. BEASLEY CONSTRUCTION • 68
BELL HELICOPTER TEXTRON • 61
A.H. BELO CORPORATION • 105, 234
BENCHMARK FOODS • 263
BERNARD HODES ADVERTISING • 58
BERRY BROWN ADVERTISING • 57
BEST MAID • 156
BESTWAY RENTAL, INC. • 243
BFGOODRICH AEROSPACE • 61
BICKEL & BREWER • 209
BIG SKY RANCH • 95
BILBO TRANSPORTS INC. • 263
BLACK-EYED PEA RESTAURANT U.S.A. • 195
BLOCKBUSTER ENTERTAINMENT GRP. • 243
BLUE CROSS BLUE SHIELD OF TEXAS • 204
BLUE RIDGE PAPER PRODUCTS • 231
BOEING-IRVING • 61
BOISE CASCADE CORPORATION • 231
THE BOMBAY COMPANY, INC. • 243
BONHAM MANUFACTURING • 65
BOOTH, INC. • 217
BOOZ-ALLEN & HAMILTON, INC. • 52
BOWDEN TRAVEL SERVICE • 263
BOY SCOUTS OF AMERICA • 95
BRIDGESTONE/FIRESTONE, INC. • 243
BRIGGS-WEAVER-VINSON COMPANIES • 273
BRINKER INTERNATIONAL INC. • 195
THE BRINKMANN CORPORATION • 217
L.D. BRINKMAN/HOLLYTEX • 65
BROOKHAVEN COLLEGE • 124
BUDGET RENT A CAR • 263
BUELL DOOR COMPANY • 68
BUNGE FOODS GROUP • 156
BURK ADVERTISING & MARKETING • 57
BURLINGTON NORTHERN AND SANTA FE
    RAILWAY COMPANY • 263
BWAY CORPORATION • 147

C

C&C BAKERY INC. • 156
CEC ENTERTAINMENT INC. • 195
CNA COMMERCIAL INSURANCE • 204
CACTUS FEEDERS INC. • 156
CALTEX PETROLEUM CORPORATION • 224
CALYX SOFTWARE • 113
CAMPBELL SOUP COMPANY • 156
CANTEY & HANGER, LLP • 209
CAPROCK MANUFACTURING, INC. • 98
CARGILL INC. • 157

CARLSON RESTAURANTS • 195
CARLTON MANUFACTURING • 212
CARRINGTON LABORATORIES • 89
CARROLL COMPANY • 98
CAVALIER HOMES, INC. • 68
CELEBRITY, INC. • 273
CENTEX CONSTRUCTION COMPANY • 68
CENTEX CORPORATION • 69, 151
CENTEX WASTE MANAGEMENT, INC. • 145
CENTRAL FREIGHT LINES INC. • 263
CENTRAL TEXAS VETERANS HEALTHCARE SYSTEM • 174
CENTURY 21 REAL ESTATE CORP. • 241
CERNER CORPORATION • 113
CHAPARRAL STEEL COMPANY • 147
CHASE BANK OF TEXAS • 86
CHEMICAL LIME COMPANY • 98
CHESHIER AND FULLER, L.L.P. • 52
CHILDREN'S MEDICAL CTR OF DALLAS • 174
W.R. CHILDRESS OIL COMPANY • 224
CHRISTUS ST. JOSEPH'S HEALTH SYST. • 174
CHUBB GRP. OF INSURANCE COS. • 204
CHUCK E. CHEESE • 195
CISCO JUNIOR COLLEGE • 124
CITY FINANCIAL • 152
CITY MACHINE & WELDING INC. • 263
CITY OF DALLAS SHERIFF'S DEPT. • 168
COCA-COLA BOTTLING COMPANY • 157
CODA ENERGY INC. • 224
COLDWELL BANKER • 241
COLESCE COUTURE INTERNATIONAL • 65
COLLIN COUNTY COMMUNITY COLLEGE DISTRICT • 124
COLLMER SEMICONDUCTOR, INC. • 138
COLUMBIA/HCA • 175
COMDATA • 263
COMPAQ COMPUTER CORPORATION • 113
COMPUCOM SYSTEMS, INC. • 113
COMPUSA INC. • 244
COMPUTALOG • 224
COMPUTER ASSOCIATES INTNL. • 113, 114
COMPUTER HORIZONS CORP. • 114
COMPUTER SCIENCES CORP. • 114
CONAGRA BEEF COMPANY • 157
CONCORDIA INTNL. FORWARDING • 264
CONTINENTAL CABINETS • 69
CONTINENTAL CREDIT CORP. • 152
CONTINENTAL ELECTRONICS CORP. • 105
CONVEYORS, INC. • 217
CON-WAY TRUCKLOAD SERVICES • 263
COOK CHILDREN'S MEDICAL CENTER • 175
CORNING CABLE SYSTEMS • 106
CORSICANA DAILY SUN • 234
CREDIT CHOICE • 152
CRENSHAW DUPREE & MILAM • 209
W. PAT CROW FORGINGS • 61
CRUM & FORSTER INSURANCE • 204
CRYOVAC • 99
CULINAIRE INTERNATIONAL, INC. • 196
CULLUM CONSTRUCTION COMPANY • 69
CYRO INDUSTRIES • 99
CYTEC FIBERITE INC. • 99

D

DDB NEEDHAM • 57
D.F.W. COMMUNICATIONS • 106
DMR CONSULTING GROUP, INC. • 114
DAIMLERCHRYSLER CORPORATION • 83
DAIN RAUSCHER • 152
DAL-TILE INTERNATIONAL • 259
DALFORT AVIATION • 61
DALLAS AREA RAPID TRANSIT (DART) • 264
DALLAS BAPTIST UNIVERSITY • 125
DALLAS BUSINESS JOURNAL • 235

DALLAS CHRISTIAN COLLEGE • 125
DALLAS, CITY OF • 167
DALLAS CITY PACKING INC. • 157
DALLAS COUNTY COMM. COLLEGE DIST. • 125
DALLAS COWBOYS • 79
DALLAS MUSEUM OF ART • 79
DALLAS MUSEUM OF NATURAL HIST. • 79
DALLAS POLICE DEPARTMENT • 167
DALLAS PUBLIC SCHOOLS • 125
DALLAS PUB. WORKS & TRANS. DEPT. • 167
DALLAS SEMICONDUCTOR • 138
DALLAS WOODCRAFT • 212
DALLAS-FORT WORTH INTNL. AIRPORT • 264
DALLAS-FORT WORTH MEDICAL CTR. • 175
DARLING INTERNATIONAL INC. • 157
DART CONTAINER CORPORATION • 212
DATAMATIC.COM, LTD. • 139
DAVE & BUSTER'S, INC. • 79, 196
DAY CARE ASSOC./FORT WORTH AND TARRANT • 95
DE LONG SPORTSWEAR • 65
DE SOTO ANIMAL HOSPITAL • 175
DECIBEL PRODUCTS INC. • 106
DECISION ANALYST, INC. • 57
DELOITTE & TOUCHE • 52, 53
DELTA AIR LINES, INC. • 264
DESIGN SOURCE • 212
DEVRY INSTITUTE OF TECHNOLOGY • 125
DIAMOND SHAMROCK, INC. • 152, 224
DISCTRONICS • 79
DR. PEPPER/7-UP COMPANY • 157
DOCTORS HOSPITAL • 175
THE DOZIER COMPANY • 58
DUNCAN DISPOSAL • 145
DUNCAN-ALEXANDER • 264
DUNLAP COMPANY • 244
THE DWYER GROUP INC. • 92
DYNAMEX INC. • 264

E

EDS • 114
E.O.A.C. • 95
EAGLE-PICHER INDUSTRIES, INC. • 217
EARL'S APPAREL INC. • 65
EARTHGRAINS COMPANY • 158
EAST TEXAS MEDICAL CENTER • 175
EASTFIELD COLLEGE • 125
A.G. EDWARDS & SONS • 152
EL CENTRO COLLEGE • 125
EL CHICO RESTAURANTS, INC. • 196
ELCOR CORPORATION • 69
ELK CORPORATION • 69, 259
EMBASSY SUITES HOTEL • 196
ENNIS BUSINESS FORMS • 235
ENSCO INTERNATIONAL INC. • 225
ENTEX INFORMATION SERVICES • 114
ERICSSON INC. • 106
ERNST & YOUNG • 53
EVANS PONTIAC GMC • 244
EXECUTRAIN OF TEXAS • 115
EXXONMOBIL CORPORATION • 225

F

FAS TECHNOLOGIES • 139
FFE TRANSPORTATION SERVICES, INC. • 264
F.F.P./NU-WAY OIL COMPANY, INC. • 244
FM GLOBAL • 69
FM INDUSTRIES, INC. • 264
FARROW AND FARROW CPAS • 53
FEDERAL EXPRESS CORPORATION • 264
FEDERAL RESERVE BANK OF DALLAS • 86
FERGUSON MFG. AND EQUIPMENT • 217
FIDELITY INVESTMENTS • 152

Index/311

FINA OIL & CHEMICAL COMPANY • 99, 225
THE FINANCE COMPANY • 152
FIRST CASH, INC. • 244
FIRST COMPANY, INC. • 213
FIRST NATIONAL BANK OF ABILENE • 86
FIRST SOUTHWEST COMPANY • 153
FIRST UNION SECURITIES INC. • 153
FISHER CONTROLS INTERNATIONAL • 217
FLEMING COMPANY • 158
FLIGHTSAFETY INTERNATIONAL, INC. • 125
FLOWERS BAKING COMPANY • 158
FLOWSERVE CORPORATION • 217
FORD MOTOR CREDIT COMPANY • 153
FORNEY CORPORATION • 218
FORT WORTH JET CENTER • 265
FOSSIL, INC. • 213
FOUR SEASONS RESORT AND CLUB • 196
FOXTRONICS INC. • 61
FOXWORTH-GALBRAITH • 244
FRIENDLY CHEVROLET COMPANY • 244
FRIONA INDUSTRIES • 158
FRITO-LAY, INC. • 158
FRITZ COMPANIES • 265
FUJITSU NETWORK COMMS. • 106
FURR'S/BISHOP'S CAFETERIAS • 196

G

GAF MATERIALS CORPORATION • 69, 99
GE CAPITAL IT SOLUTIONS • 115
GNB TECHNOLOGIES INC. • 83, 218
GTE CORPORATION • 106
GTE DIRECTORIES • 235
GTE SOUTHWEST INC. • 106
GARLAND COMMUNITY HOSPITAL • 175
GAS EQUIPMENT COMPANY (GEC) • 225
GEER TANK TRUCKS INC. • 225
GENERAL ALUMINUM CORPORATION • 70
GENERAL CABLE COMPANY • 107
GENERAL CINEMA CORPORATION • 79
GENERALCOLOGNE RE • 204
GEO-MARINE, INC. • 145
GILES INSURANCE AGENCY • 204
THE GLADNEY CENTER • 95
GOLDEN CAB • 265
GOLDTHWAITE'S OF TEXAS INC. • 273
GOODWILL INDUSTRIES • 96
GRANT THORNTON LLP • 53
GREAT WESTERN DIRECTORIES • 235
GREYHOUND LINES INC. • 265
GRUBB & ELLIS • 241
GUARDIAN INDUSTRIES CORP. • 260
GULFSTREAM AEROSPACE CORP. • 62

H

H&R BLOCK • 53
HNTB CORPORATION • 70
HAGGAR CLOTHING COMPANY • 65
HALLIBURTON • 70
M.A. HANNA COLOR • 99
HANSON CONCRETE PRODUCTS, INC. • 260
HARBISON-FISCHER MFG. COMPANY • 225
HARDIN-SIMMONS UNIVERSITY • 126
HARMONY FAMILY SERVICES • 96
HARRINGTON CANCER CENTER • 176
HARRIS METHODIST FT. WORTH HOSP. • 176
HARVEY HOTEL/DFW AIRPORT • 196
HATCO • 65
HEALTHSOUTH MEDICAL CENTER • 176
HELI-DYNE SYSTEMS INC. • 62
HENDERSON MEMORIAL HOSPITAL • 176
HENDRICK HEALTH SYSTEM • 177
HENNINGSON, DURHAM & RICHARDSON, INC. • 70

G.H. HENSLEY INDUSTRIES, INC. • 148
HEWLETT-PACKARD COMPANY • 115
HI-LINE • 273
HILITE INDUSTRIES, INC. • 83
HOBART CORPORATION • 218
HOLLY CORPORATION • 226
HOLLY SUGAR CORPORATION • 159
HONEYWELL MICROSWITCH • 139
HORMEL FOODS CORPORATION • 159
D.R. HORTON, INC. • 70
HOWE-BAKER ENGINEERS, INC. • 70
HOWELL INSTRUMENTS, INC. • 139
HUCK INTERNATIONAL INC. • 218
HUGULEY MEMORIAL MEDICAL CTR. • 177
HUNT OIL COMPANY • 226
J.B. HUNT TRANSPORT SERVICES, INC. • 265
HYATT REGENCY DALLAS • 196
HYCO TEXAS • 218

I

I-CONCEPTS • 115
IBM CORPORATION • 115
IBP INC. • 159
ICS COMPUTER SYSTEMS CORP. • 115
IHS HOSPITAL AT DALLAS • 177
IRI INTERNATIONAL COMPANY • 226
I.T. PARTNERS, INC. • 116
THE IMAGE BANK, INC. • 235
INDEPENDENT BANKSHARES, INC. • 86
INDUSTRIAL MOLDING CORP. • 100
INGERSOLL-RAND COMPANY • 218
INSITUFORM TEXARK, INC. • 71
INSPIRE INSURANCE SOLUTIONS • 205
INTERCRAFT-BURNES COMPANY • 213
INTERNATIONAL AVIATION COMPS. • 62
INTERNATIONAL HOME FOODS INC. • 159
INTERNATIONAL PAPER COMPANY • 231
INTERNATIONAL TOTAL SERVICES • 265
INTERPHASE CORPORATION • 116
INTERSTATE TRAILERS, INC. • 265
INTERVOICE, INC. • 116
ITAC SYSTEMS, INC. • 116

J

JLN, INC. • 65
JRA INFORMATION SERVICES, INC. • 116
JRC HALLIBURTON ENERGY SVCS. • 226
JACK IN THE BOX • 197
JAMAK FABRICATION, INC. • 100
JCPENNEY COMPANY, INC. • 244, 245
JEFFERIES & COMPANY, INC. • 153
JOHN DEERE COMPANY • 218
JOHN PETER SMITH HEALTH NETWK. • 181
JOHNSON & JOHNSON MEDICAL • 177
JOHNSON CONTROLS, INC. • 218
JONES BLAIR COMPANY • 100
JORDAN HEALTH SERVICES • 177
JOSTENS, INC. • 213
JUMPKING INC. • 213
JUSTIN BOOT COMPANY • 65

K

KFDA-TV • 107
KLBK-TV • 107
KPMG • 54
KRLD/TEXAS STATE NETWORKS • 107
KVII-TV • 107
KVIL-AM/FM 103.7 • 107
KXXV-TV • 107
KANEB SERVICES, INC. • 116, 226
KELLY-SPRINGFIELD TIRE COMPANY • 100
KEVCO • 219
KEYSTONE CONSOLIDATED INDS. • 148

KIMBERLY-CLARK CORPORATION • 213
KINGS LIQUOR INC. • 159
KITTY HAWK, INC. • 265
KOCH-GLITSCH, INC. • 148
KRAFT FOODS, INC. • 159
KROGER • 245

L

LTC MEDICAL LABORATORIES, INC. • 89
LA GLORIA OIL AND GAS COMPANY • 227
LABORATORY CORP. OF AMERICA • 89
LASTING PRODUCTS • 214
LAUREN ENGS. & CONSTRUCTORS • 71
LAWYERS TITLE INSURANCE CORP. • 205
LEGAL DIRECTORIES PUBLISHING • 235
LENNOX INTERNATIONAL, INC. • 71
LEON'S TEXAS CUISINE • 160
LEVOLOR HOME FASHIONS • 214
LEWIS & LAMBERT METAL • 148
LINCOLN PROPERTY COMPANY • 241
LINX DATA TERMINALS, INC. • 117
LIPTON FOODS • 160
LITTON ELECTRO-OPTICAL SYSTEMS • 139
LOCKHEED MARTIN • 62
THE LOFLAND COMPANY • 148
LONE STAR INDUSTRIES • 260
LONE STAR STEEL COMPANY • 148
LONGVIEW REGIONAL MEDICAL CTR. • 177
LORD & TAYLOR • 245
BRUCE LOWRIE CHEVROLET • 245
LUBBOCK AVALANCHE-JOURNAL • 235
LUBBOCK METHODIST HOSPITAL • 178
LUBRICATION ENGINEERS INC. • 100
LUCENT TECHNOLOGIES INC. • 108
LUMINANT WORLDWIDE CORP. • 117
LUMINATOR • 62, 265

M

THE M/A/R/C GROUP • 58
MBNA INFORMATION SERVICES • 92
MADIX INC. • 219
MAGUIRE OIL COMPANY • 227
MALIBU ENT. WORLDWIDE • 80
MARATHON POWER TECHNOLOGIES • 63
MARCONI COMMUNICATIONS • 108
MARRIOTT SOUTH CENTRAL REG. OFFICE • 197
MARTIN SPROCKET & GEAR INC. • 219
MARTINAIRE INC. • 265
MARY KAY, INC. • 214
MASSEY CADILLAC • 245
MAXUS ENERGY CORPORATION • 227
McFARLAN REAL ESTATE • 241
McGRAW-HILL EDUCATIONAL & PROF.
    PUBLISHING GROUP • 235
McKINNEY INDEPENDENT SCHOOL DIST. • 126
McMURRY UNIVERSITY • 126
MEAD PAPER • 231
MEALS ON WHEELS • 96
MEDICAL CENTER OF PLANO • 178
MEDICAL CITY DALLAS HOSPITAL • 178
MERCER MANAGEMENT CONSULTING • 54
MERIDIAN OIL INC. • 227
MERLIN SOFTWARE SERVICES, INC. • 117
MERRILL LYNCH • 153
MESQUITE COMMUNITY HOSPITAL • 178
MESQUITE METRO AIRPORT • 265
METHODIST MEDICAL CENTER • 178
METROMEDIA RESTAURANT GROUP • 197
MICHAEL'S STORES, INC. • 245
MICRO COMPUTER SYSTEMS, INC. • 117
MICROGRAFX, INC. • 117
MICROPAC INDUSTRIES INC. • 140
MIDWESTERN STATE UNIVERSITY • 126

MILGO SOLUTIONS INC. • 117
MILLER BREWING COMPANY • 160
MILLER FREEMAN INC. • 235
MILLIPORE CORPORATION • 219
MINUTE MAID COMPANY • 160
MINYARD FOOD STORES, INC. • 245
MIRACLE HOME HEALTH CARE • 178
FRED MISKO, JR., P.C. • 209
MOHAWK LABORATORIES • 100
MONTGOMERY WARD & COMPANY • 245
MORGAN • 71
MORRISON SUPPLY COMPANY, INC. • 71
MOTEL 6 • 197
MOTHERAL PRINTING COMPANY • 235
MOTOROLA, INC. • 108
MRS. BAIRD'S BAKERIES • 160
MUR-TEX FIBERGLASS • 260
MYND CORPORATION • 117

N

NCH CORPORATION • 100, 219
NCR CORPORATION • 117
NEC AMERICA INC. • 108
NASH MANUFACTURING COMPANY • 214
NATIONAL BANNER COMPANY • 214
NATIONAL FOUNDATION LIFE INS. • 205
NATIONAL SEMICONDUCTOR CORP. • 140
THE NEIMAN MARCUS GROUP, INC. • 246
NESTFAMILY.COM, INC. • 80
NETWORK ASSOCIATES, INC. • 118
NICHOLS FORD • 246
NIPPON EXPRESS USA INC. • 265
NOKIA MOBILE PHONES INC. • 108
NORTH CENTRAL DISTRIBUTORS INC. • 160
NORTH LAKE COLLEGE • 126
NORTH TEXAS AIRCRAFT SERVICES • 266
NORTHWEST TX HEALTHCARE SYST. • 178
NORTON DRILLING COMPANY • 227
NORWEST BANK • 87
NOVAKOV DAVIS • 209
NURSEFINDERS • 179
NURSES TODAY INCORPORATED • 179

O

OCCIDENTAL CHEMICAL CORP. • 101
OFFICES OF NORMAN A. ZABLE, P.C. • 210
OGDEN AVIATION SERVICES • 266
O'HAIR SHUTTERS • 71
OLDCASTLE GLASS GROUP • 260
OMEGA OPTICAL COMPANY, INC. • 179
OMNI HOTELS • 197
OMNI RICHARDSON HOTEL • 198
183 ANIMAL HOSPITAL • 179
OPENCONNECT SYSTEMS INC. • 118
OPTEK TECHNOLOGY INC. • 140
ORTHOFIX INC. • 179
ORYX ENERGY COMPANY • 227
OVERHEAD DOOR CORP. OF TEXAS • 71
OWENS COUNTRY SAUSAGE INC. • 160
OWENS-CORNING FIBERGLAS CORP. • 260

P

PVI INDUSTRIES INC. • 220
PADGETT PRINTING CORPORATION • 236
PAGENET • 108
PAINEWEBBER INC. • 153
PALO PINTO GENERAL HOSPITAL • 179
PAMPA MEDICAL CENTER • 180
PANCHO'S MEXICAN BUFFET, INC. • 198
PANHANDLE COMMUNITY SERVICES • 96
PARK PLACE MID-CITIES • 246
PARK PLACE MOTORCARS • 246
PARKER HANNIFIN CORPORATION • 220

PARKLAND HEALTH & HOSPITAL SYST • 180
PATTERSON DRILLING COMPANY • 227
PEARLE VISION, INC. • 180, 246
PEPSI-COLA COMPANY • 160
PERRY EQUIPMENT CORPORATION • 220
PER-SE TECHNOLOGIES, INC. • 118
PETERBILT MOTORS COMPANY • 83
PHILLIPS COAL COMPANY • 228
PIER 1 IMPORTS • 246
PILGRIM'S PRIDE CORPORATION • 160, 161
PILLOWTEX CORPORATION • 65
PINDLER & PINDLER INC. • 66
PINKERTON SECURITY COMPANY • 92
PIONEER NATURAL RESOURCES • 228
PIONEER OIL COMPANY • 247
PIZZA INN INC. • 198
PLAINS COTTON COOP. ASSN. • 161
PLANO, CITY OF • 168
PLANTATION FOODS INC. • 161
PLAZA MEDICAL CENTER • 180
POLICY MANAGEMENT SYSTEMS • 118
POLITICAL RESEARCH, INC. • 236
POLY-AMERICA INC. • 101
PRATT & WHITNEY • 63
PRECISION AVIATION • 63
PRICEWATERHOUSECOOPERS • 54
PRIMEDIA WORKPLACE LEARNING • 80
PRIMROSE OIL COMPANY • 228
PROFORMA WATSONRISE BUS. SYST. • 58
PRO-LINE CORPORATION • 214
PROVIDENCE HEALTH CENTER • 180
PUBLICIS • 58

Q, R

Q THE SPORTS CLUB • 80
QUALITY CABINETS • 72
THE QUAKER OATS COMPANY • 161
QUEBECOR DALLAS • 236
QUEST DIAGNOSTICS INCORPORATED • 90
QUEST MEDICAL, INC. • 180
RF MONOLITHICS, INC. • 108
RHD MEMORIAL MEDICAL CENTER • 181
RIA • 92
RVSI ACUITY CIMATRIX • 118
THE RADIOSHACK CORPORATION • 247
RAYTHEON SYSTEMS COMPANY • 118, 140
REDI PACKAGING, INC. • 231
REGAL INTERNATIONAL INC. • 101
RENT-A-CENTER • 247
REPUBLIC BEVERAGE COMPANY • 161
REPUBLIC SUPPLY COMPANY • 228
REPUBLIC UNDERWRITERS INS. CO. • 205
REXEL INC. • 140
RIBELIN SALES INC. • 101
THE RICHARDS GROUP • 58
RICHLAND COLLEGE • 126
ROBERTSON UNIT • 168
ROBINSON NUGENT DALLAS, INC. • 141
ROCHESTER GAUGES, INC. • 141
ROCKWELL COLLINS • 63
RODRIGUEZ FESTIVE FOODS • 161
ROYAL OPTICAL U.S. VISION • 181
RUBBERMAID, INC. • 214
RUSSELL-NEWMAN MFG. CO. • 66

S

S2 SYSTEMS, INC. • 119
SCS/FRIGETTE CORPORATION • 83
SEI INVESTMENTS COMPANY • 153
SGS-THOMSON MICROELECTRONICS • 141
SAFETY-KLEEN CORPORATION • 145
ST. PAUL MEDICAL CENTER • 181
SAKS FIFTH AVENUE • 247

SAMSILL CORPORATION • 214
SANTA FE INTERNATIONAL CORP. • 228
SCHEPPS DAIRY INC. • 161
SCHUTZMAN COMPANY • 236
SCOTT GROUP • 66
SEED RESOURCE, INC. • 161
GUY SHADDOCK AND COMPANY • 220
THE SHERWIN-WILLIAMS COMPANY • 101
SHOPPER'S GUIDE • 236
THE SHOPPING NEWS • 236
SHOWCASE CHEVROLET • 247
SIDRAN INC. • 66
SIEMENS ELECTROCOM L.P. • 141
SIMEUS FOODS INTERNATIONAL • 162
SINGAPORE AIRLINES • 266
SKEETER PRODUCTS INC. • 214
SKY HELICOPTERS • 266
SKYLINE INDUSTRIES, INC. • 63
SMURFIT-STONE CONTAINER CORP. • 231
SOFTWARE SPECTRUM INC. • 119
SOURCE MEDIA, INC. • 119
SOUTH PLAINS COLLEGE • 126
SOUTHERN METHODIST UNIVERSITY • 127
SOUTHLAND CORPORATION • 247
SOUTHWEST AIRLINES COMPANY • 266
SOUTHWEST COCA-COLA BOTTLING • 162
SOUTHWEST SECURITIES GROUP, INC. • 153
SOUTHWESTERN ADVENTIST UNIV. • 127
SOUTHWESTERN BAPTIST THEO. SEM. • 127
SOUTHWESTERN LIFE INSURANCE • 205
SOUTHWESTERN PETROLEUM CORP. • 228
SOUTHWESTERN PUBLIC SERVICE CO. • 271
SPECTRO INC. • 63
SPORTS SUPPLY GROUP, INC. • 247
STANLEY MECHANICS TOOLS • 214
STANLEY REFRIGERATED EXPRESS • 266
STAR-TELEGRAM • 236
STATE FARM MUTUAL INS. COMPANY • 205
STEAKLY CHEVROLET-GEO-SUBARU • 247
STEELCASE INC. • 220
STERN REED ASSOCIATES • 181
STERN TYLER • 181
STEVENS INTERNATIONAL • 220
STRIPLING & COX • 247
STRUCTURAL OF TEXAS INC. • 260
STYROCHEM INTERNATIONAL • 101
SUIZA FOODS • 162
SULLINS & ASSOCIATES, INC. • 198
SUPERIOR AVIATION SERVICES INC. • 266
SUPREME BEEF PROCESSORS • 162
SUSQUEHANNA RADIO CORP. • 108
R.E. SWEENEY COMPANY INC. • 72
SWEETHEART CUP COMPANY, INC. • 214

T

TD INDUSTRIES, INC. • 72
TXI, INC. • 260
TANDY BRANDS ACCESSORIES, INC. • 66
TANDY WIRE AND CABLE COMPANY • 119
TANDYCRAFTS, INC. • 214
TARLETON STATE UNIVERSITY • 127
TARRANT COUNTY JUNIOR COLLEGE • 127
TAYLOR PUBLISHING COMPANY • 236
TECCOR ELECTRONICS INC. • 141
TELEDYNE BROWN ENGINEERING • 141
TEMPO/INFINITI LIGHTING • 215
TEMTEX INDUSTRIES INC. • 215
TENET HEALTHCARE CORPORATION • 181
TEXAS A&M UNIVERSITY/COMMERCE • 127
TEXAS CHRISTIAN UNIVERSITY • 127
TEXAS DEPT. OF TRANSPORTATION • 168
TEXAS EASTMAN • 102
TEXAS HEALTH RESOURCES • 181
TEXAS INSTRUMENTS, INC. (TI) • 142

TEXAS MEDICAL & SURGICAL ASSOC. • 182
TEXAS RECREATION CORPORATION • 215
TEXAS REFINERY CORPORATION • 102
TEXAS STADIUM • 80
TEXAS STEEL COMPANY • 148
TEXAS TECH UNIVERSITY • 128
TEXAS UTILITIES COMPANIES • 271
TEXAS VETERINARY MED. DIAG. LAB. • 90
TEXAS WESLEYAN UNIVERSITY • 128
TEXAS WOMAN'S UNIVERSITY (TWU) • 128
TEXAS-NEW MEXICO POWER CO. • 271
TEXOMA MEDICAL CENTER (TMC) • 182
THAI AIRWAYS INTERNATIONAL LTD. • 266
THERMALLOY INC. • 142
THINKSPARK • 119
THIRD COAST TECHNOLOGIES (TCT) • 220
THOMAS S. BYRNE INC. • 68
THOMPSON & KNIGHT LLP • 210
THORNTON STEEL COMPANY INC. • 148
TOM THUMB FOOD & PHARMACY • 248
TOWN EAST REALTORS • 241
TOWN NORTH YMCA • 96
TOYOTA OF DALLAS INC. • 248
TRADESTAR INVESTMENTS • 154
TRAMMELL CROW COMPANY • 241
THE TRANE COMPANY • 221
TRAULSEN & COMPANY, INC. • 221
TRAVELERS PROPERTY CASUALTY CO. • 205
TRAVELHOST • 237
TRI-CITY HOSPITAL • 182
TRIANGLE PACIFIC CORPORATION • 232
TRINITY INDUSTRIES, INC. • 221, 266, 267
TRITON ENERGY CORPORATION • 228
TROY AIKMAN AUTO MALL • 248
2021 INTERACTIVE • 120
TYLER PIPE INDUSTRIES, INC. • 221
TYSON FOODS INC. • 162

U

UMR COMMUNICATIONS • 237
U.S. ENVMNTL. PROTECTION AGY. • 168
U.S. FOODSERVICE • 162, 163
ULTRAK INC. • 142
UNICO CARPET COMPANY • 66
UNION PACIFIC RESOURCES • 228
UNITED AMERICAN INSURANCE CO. • 205
UNITED INSURANCE COMPANIES INC. • 205
UNITED PARCEL SERVICE (UPS) • 267
UNITED REG. HEALTHCARE SYSTEMS • 182
UNITED STATES BRASS CORPORATION • 72
UNITED STATES DATA CORP • 120
UNITED WAY OF METRO. DALLAS • 96
UNIVERSITY MEDICAL CENTER • 182
UNIVERSITY OF NORTH TEXAS • 128
UNIVERSITY OF TEXAS • 128, 129
UNIVERSITY OF TEXAS HEALTH CTR. • 183

UNIVERSITY OF TEXAS SOUTHWESTERN
 MEDICAL CENTER AT DALLAS • 183
UNIVEX INTERNATIONAL • 215
UNIVIEW TECHNOLOGIES • 120

V

VA MEDICAL CENTER • 183
VA NORTH TEXAS HEALTHCARE SYST. • 183
VF WORKWEAR • 66
VANDERVOORT DAIRY • 163
VANGARD TECHNOLOGY • 120
VECTA • 221
VENCOR HOSPITAL OF DALLAS • 184
VERNON WICHITA FALLS STATE HOSP. • 184
VERTEX COMMUNICATIONS CORP. • 109
VETROTEX CERTAINTEED CORP. • 251
VIRGINIA KMP CORPORATION • 102, 221
VIRTUOSO • 267
VISITING NURSE ASSOCIATION • 184
THE VISTAWALL GROUP • 72
VULCRAFT • 148

W

WACO TRIBUNE-HERALD • 237
WACO, CITY OF • 168
WADLEY REGIONAL MEDICAL CENTER • 184
WALLS INDUSTRIES, INC. • 66
WARRANTECH CORPORATION • 93
WARREN ELECTRIC • 142
WAUSAU INSURANCE COMPANIES • 206
WELLMARK INTERNATIONAL • 102
WEST TEXAS UTILITIES COMPANY • 271
WICHITA RIVER OIL • 229
WILLAMETTE INDUSTRIES, INC. • 232
WILLIAMSON PRINTING CORP. • 237
WILLIAMSON-DICKIE MFG. COMPANY • 66
WING INDUSTRIES INC. • 72
WINSTEAD SECHREST & MINICK P.C. • 210
WITHERSPOON ADV. & P.R. • 58
HOWARD B. WOLF INC. • 66
WORLD FINANCE • 154
WORLDCOM INC. • 109, 120
WYATT'S CAFETERIAS INC. • 198
WYNDHAM ANATOLE HOTEL • 198
WYNNE/JACKSON, INC. • 242

X, Y, Z

XEROX CORPORATION • 221
YMCA OF METRO. FORT WORTH • 96
H.B. ZACHRY COMPANY • 72
ZALE CORPORATION • 248
ZALE LIPSHY UNIVERSITY HOSPITAL • 184
ZIMMERMAN SIGN COMPANY • 142

JobBank List Service
Custom-Designed For Your Job Search

Generated by the same editors who bring you the nationally renowned *JobBank* series, the electronic *JobBank List Service* is a compilation of company information that is important to you. Our huge database is updated year-round to ensure that our data is as accurate as possible. Our company information is available to you by e-mail or on disk in ASCII delimited text format.

Whether you're looking for a small company to work for, or a large corporation to do business with, *JobBank List Service* can help! *JobBank List Service* is not mass-produced for the general public; it is built for *you* through a personal consultation with a member of the *JobBank* staff.

While other services offer their company information on pre-generated disk or CD-ROM, we construct the data explicitly to match your criteria. Your *JobBank* consultant will work with you to find the company information that applies to your specific job search needs. Criteria for companies or employment agencies can be specified geographically, by industry, by occupation, or any variation or combination you can imagine... you decide.

With the most current information on companies in more than thirty industries, job-seekers, recruiters, and businesses alike will find the *JobBank List Service* the perfect solution to their personal and professional needs. Industries covered include:

- Accounting and Management Consulting
- Advertising, Marketing, and Public Relations
- Aerospace
- Apparel, Fashion & Textiles
- Architecture, Construction, and Engineering
- Arts, Entertainment, Sports, & Recreation
- Automotive
- Banking/Savings and Loans
- Biotechnology, Pharmaceuticals & Scientific R&D
- Charities and Social Services
- Chemicals/Rubber & Plastics
- Communications: Telecommunications & Broadcasting
- Computer Hardware, Software, and Services
- Educational Services
- Electronic/Industrial Electrical Equipment
- Environmental & Waste Management Services
- Fabricated/Primary Metals & Products
- Financial Services
- Food & Beverages/Agriculture
- Government
- Health Care: Services, Equipment & Products
- Hotels & Restaurants
- Insurance
- Manufacturing
- Mining/Gas/Petroleum/Energy Related
- Paper & Wood Products
- Printing and Publishing
- Real Estate
- Retail
- Stone, Glass, Clay, and Concrete Products
- Transportation
- Utilities
- Miscellaneous Wholesaling

and many others

- NO MINIMUM ORDER — NO ORDER IS TOO SMALL!
- THOUSANDS OF PRIVATE & PUBLIC COMPANIES IN ALL 50 STATES & DC
- THOUSANDS OF EMPLOYMENT SERVICES
- EACH LISTING INCLUDES THE SAME TYPE OF DETAILED CONTACT & BUSINESS INFORMATION OFFERED IN THE *JOBBANK* BOOK SERIES
- STANDING ORDER DISCOUNTS ARE AVAILABLE

Contact a *JobBank* staff member now for your individual consultation and pricing information.
E-mail: jobbank@adamsonline.com
Phone: 800/872-5627 (in MA: 781/767-8100)
Fax: 781/767-2055

Other Adams Media Books

The Adams Jobs Almanac, 8th Edition

Updated annually, *The Adams Jobs Almanac* includes names and addresses of over 7,000 U.S. employers; information on which positions each company commonly fills; industry forecasts; geographical cross-references; employment prospects in all 50 states; and advice on preparing resumes and cover letters and standing out at interviews. 5½" x 8½", 952 pages, paperback, $16.95.
ISBN: 1-58062-443-X, ISSN: 1072-592X

The JobBank Series

There are 30 *JobBank* books, each providing extensive, up-to-date employment information on hundreds of the largest employers in each job market. The #1 best-selling series of employment directories, the *JobBank* series has been recommended as an excellent place to begin your job search by the *New York Times*, the *Los Angeles Times*, the *Boston Globe*, and the *Chicago Tribune*. *JobBank* books have been used by millions of people to find jobs. Titles available:

The Atlanta JobBank ♦ *The Austin/San Antonio JobBank* ♦ *The Boston JobBank* ♦ *The Carolina JobBank* ♦ *The Chicago JobBank* ♦ *The Connecticut JobBank* ♦ *The Dallas-Fort Worth JobBank* ♦ *The Denver JobBank* ♦ *The Detroit JobBank* ♦ *The Florida JobBank* ♦ *The Houston JobBank* ♦ *The Indiana JobBank* ♦ *The Las Vegas JobBank* ♦ *The Los Angeles JobBank* ♦ *The Minneapolis-St. Paul JobBank* ♦ *The Missouri JobBank* ♦ *The New Jersey JobBank* ♦ *The Metropolitan New York JobBank* ♦ *The Ohio JobBank* ♦ *The Greater Philadelphia JobBank* ♦ *The Phoenix JobBank* ♦ *The Pittsburgh JobBank* ♦ *The Portland JobBank* ♦ *The San Francisco Bay Area JobBank* ♦ *The Seattle JobBank* ♦ *The Tennessee JobBank* ♦ *The Virginia JobBank* ♦ *The Metropolitan Washington DC JobBank* ♦ *The JobBank Guide to Computer & High-Tech Companies* ♦ *The JobBank Guide to Health Care Companies*

EACH JOBBANK BOOK IS 6" X 9¼", OVER 300 PAGES, PAPERBACK, $16.95.
For ISBNs and ISSNs, please visit http://www.careercity.com/booksoftware/jobbank.asp

JobBank List Service: If you are interested in variations of this information in electronic format for sales or job search mailings, please call 800-872-5627, or e-mail us at jobbank@adamsonline.com.

Available wherever books are sold.
**For more information, or to order, call 800-872-5627
or visit www.adamsmedia.com**
Adams Media Corporation, 260 Center Street, Holbrook, MA 02343

Visit our exciting job and career site at http://www.careercity.com

Other Adams Media Books

The Adams Internet Job Search Almanac 2001-2002

Uncover thousands of jobs in minutes using your own computer! This comprehensive guide features hundreds of online resources available through commercial online services, the World Wide Web, newsgroups, and more. *The Adams Internet Job Search Almanac 2001-2002* also includes a selection of company joblines, advice on posting an electronic resume, and strategies for researching companies on the Internet. The book also features information on a variety of job-hunting software. 5½" x 8½", 320 pages, paperback, $10.95. ISBN: 1-58062-426-X, ISSN: 1099-016X

The Adams Executive Recruiters Almanac, 2nd Edition

The Adams Executive Recruiters Almanac contains comprehensive, up-to-date information on 7,300 executive search firms, permanent employment agencies, contract services firms, temporary agencies, and career/outplacement counseling firms nationwide. Recruiter profiles include names, addresses, phone and fax numbers, agency descriptions, information on each recruiter's areas of specialization, positions commonly filled, and benefits provided. Indexed by specialization and alphabetically. 5½" x 8½", 768 pages, paperback, $17.95. ISBN: 1-58062-332-8, ISSN: 1099-0216

The Adams Job Interview Almanac

The Adams Job Interview Almanac includes answers and discussions for over 1,800 interview questions. There are 100 complete job interviews for all fields, industries, and career levels. Also included is valuable information on handling stress interviews, strategies for second and third interviews, and negotiating job offers to get what you want. 5½" x 8½", 840 pages, paperback, $12.95. ISBN: 1-55850-612-8

Available wherever books are sold.
**For more information, or to order, call 800-872-5627
or visit www.adamsmedia.com**
Adams Media Corporation, 260 Center Street, Holbrook, MA 02343

Visit our exciting job and career site at http://www.careercity.com

Other Adams Media Books

The Adams Cover Letter Almanac

The Adams Cover Letter Almanac is the most detailed cover letter resource in print, containing 600 cover letters used by real people to win real jobs. It features complete information on all types of letters, including networking, "cold," broadcast, and follow-up. In addition to advice on how to avoid fatal cover letter mistakes, the book includes strategies for people changing careers, relocating, recovering from layoff, and more. 5½" x 8½", 736 pages, paperback, $12.95. ISBN: 1-55850-497-4

The Adams Resume Almanac

This almanac features detailed information on resume development and layout, a review of the pros and cons of various formats, an exhaustive look at the strategies that will definitely get a resume noticed, and 600 sample resumes in dozens of career categories. *The Adams Resume Almanac* is the most comprehensive, thoroughly researched resume guide ever published. 5½" x 8½", 768 pages, paperback, $12.95. ISBN: 1-55850-358-7

Available wherever books are sold.
For more information, or to order, call 800-872-5627 or visit www.adamsmedia.com
Adams Media Corporation, 260 Center Street, Holbrook, MA 02343

Visit our exciting job and career site at http://www.careercity.com

Other Adams Media Books

The Everything Get-A-Job Book
by Steven Graber
Managing Editor of the JobBank Series

The Everything Get-A-Job Book gives you the competitive edge, with a fun and non-intimidating approach to looking for your first job or just plain trying to find a better job. Jammed with tons of tips, strategies, and advice from the trenches, this comprehensive book will be indispensible to anyone hoping to land a great job. Find out how to:

- Find companies that are hiring without picking up the want ads
- Uncover valuable networking opportunities
- Search in-depth for job openings on the Internet
- Extensive information on writing cover letters and resumes—including what not to do
- Prepare for evil interview questions
- Dealing with head hunters and employment services
- Strategies to land multiple job offers
- Negotiate the best salary, bonus, and benefits package
- And much, much more!

Trade paperback, 1-58062-223-2, $12.95
8" x 9¼", 304 pages

Also Available:

The Everything Cover Letter Book
Trade paperback,
1-58062-311-5, $12.95
8" x 9¼", 336 pages

The Everything Resume Book
Trade paperback,
1-58062-312-3, $12.95
8" x 9¼", 336 pages

Available wherever books are sold.

**For more information, or to order, call 800-872-5627
or visit www.adamsmedia.com**
Adams Media Corporation, 260 Center Street, Holbrook, MA 02343

Visit our exciting job and career site at http://www.careercity.com

From the publishers of this book

CareerCity.com

Search *4 million* job openings at all the leading career sites with just one click!

Find all the great job openings without having to spend hours surfing from one career site to the next.

Now, with just one click you can simultaneously search all of the leading career sites . . . at CareerCity.com!

You can also have jobs come to you! Enter your job search criteria once and we automatically notify you of any new relevant job listings.

Plus! The most complete career center on the Web including . . .

- Descriptions and hot links to 27,000 U.S. companies
- Comprehensive salary surveys in all fields
- Expert advice on starting a job search, interviews, resumes and much more

You'll find more jobs at CareerCity.com!

Post your resume at CareerCity and have the job offers come to you!

It's fast, free, and easy to post your resume at CareerCity—and you'll get noticed by hundreds of leading employers in all fields.